# Alexander Montgomerie

*Poetry, Politics, and Cultural Change in*
*Jacobean Scotland*

MEDIEVAL AND RENAISSANCE
TEXTS AND STUDIES

VOLUME 298

# ALEXANDER MONTGOMERIE

*Poetry, Politics, and Cultural Change in Jacobean Scotland*

*By*

RODERICK J. LYALL

Arizona Center for Medieval and Renaissance Studies
Tempe, Arizona
2005

Library of Congress Cataloging-in-Publication Data

Lyall, R. J.
    Alexander Montgomerie : poetry, politics, and cultural change in Jacobean Scotland
/ Roderick J. Lyall.
      p. cm. -- (Medieval and Renaissance texts and studies ; v. 298)
    Summary: "A detailed investigation of Alexander Montgomerie's (c. 1550-1598)
biography with a careful reading of his verse. Situates Montgomerie's poetry within a
bipolar model of later sixteenth-century British culture, against the background of the
European development of Mannerist aesthetics and the early Baroque"--Provided by
publisher.
    Includes bibliographical references (p.  ) and index.
    ISBN-13: 978-0-86698-342-6 (alk. paper)
    ISBN-10: 0-86698-342-2 (alk. paper)
 1. Montgomerie, Alexander, 1545?-1598. 2. Politics and literature--Scotland--His-
tory--16th century. 3. Mannerism (Literature)--History and criticism. 4. Scotland--
Intellectual life--16th century. 5. Baroque literature--History and criticism. 6. Poets,
Scottish--To 1700--Biography. 7. Scotland--In literature. I. Title. II. Series:  Medieval
& Renaissance Texts & Studies (Series) ; v. 298.

    PR2315.M7Z76 2005
    821'.3--dc22

                                            2005027821

**About the Front Cover:**
Giuseppe Arcimboldo's *The Jurist* (1566)
Photo Credit : Erich Lessing / Art Resource, NY

∞
This book is made to last.
It is set in Adobe Caslon Pro,
smyth-sewn and printed on acid-free paper
to library specifications.
Printed in the United States of America

*For John Durkan*

# Contents

*Preface*                                                                                  *ix*

*Texts and Abbreviations*                                                     *xiii*

Chapter One

Introduction                                                                              1

Chapter Two

Arms, Man, and Song: The Making of a Makar                   33

Chapter Three

"The Prince of poets in our land": Montgomerie at
Court, 1580–1586                                                                   63

Chapter Four

"Bellona's Captain": In the Netherlands, 1586–1588        119

Chapter Five

Proving the Poet's Patience: Montgomerie's Final
Decade, 1588–1598                                                              145

Chapter Six

"The Court some qualities requires": Satire and Conviviality
in Montgomerie's Poetry                                                     195

Chapter Seven

"Under Venus wings": Montgomerie as Love Poet           227

Chapter Eight

"Teich me thy treuth": Montgomerie's Devotional Verse   281

Chapter Nine

"The lang guid nicht"                                                           333

*Bibliography*                                                                         351

*Index*                                                                                  373

# PREFACE

The writing of this book began in Leipzig, was largely carried out in Boston, and — after too long a delay — was completed in Amsterdam. I am grateful to the Deutsche Akademische Austauschdienst, to the University of Glasgow and to Boston College for making possible two invaluable periods of study leave, and to the Vrije Universiteit Amsterdam for inadvertently occasioning a long process of revision and rethinking which has, I hope, made it a better book than it might otherwise have been. A return to teaching English texts after nineteen years in the world's only Department of Scottish Literature has enriched my sense of both the distinctiveness of Older Scots culture and its complex relations with developments south of the Border, and I have tried to incorporate the results of this shifting vision (without too much damage to the original conception) into the book's final version.

A more particular set of debts is owed to many scholars whose own research, and whose comments on draft versions of sections of this work, have contributed to its emergence. Chief among these are David Parkinson, whose edition of Montgomerie's poems for the Scottish Text Society provides an invaluable basis for future investigation, and Sally Mapstone and Theo Bögels, who read virtually the whole manuscript and offered incisive commentary upon it. Dr. Mapstone's own pursuit of fugitive material in the Scottish records is frequently reflected in my footnotes; her valuable suggestions for improvements to the text, like those of Dr. Bögels, are in general quietly incorporated into my argument. Professor Parkinson greatly assisted the preparation of this book by allowing me to see and use successive drafts of his edition as it approached publication, and by commenting on a very early version of the first two chapters. Other scholars, notably Simon Adams, Michael Lynch, Hector MacQueen, and Henk van Nierop, read and provided helpful comments on parts of the manuscript. A further group, including Priscilla Bawcutt, Bob Cummings, Julian Goodare, Theo van Heijnsbergen, Tom James, Christine Jimack, Jamie Reid-Baxter, Richard Todd, and Louise Yeoman, contributed to the development of my thinking through their willingness to discuss problems and ideas, generously sharing insights and asking pertinent questions. I am grateful to Willem Frijhoff for assistance with the map which appears in Chapter 4 and to Sebastiaan Yerweij for hunting a fugitive reference at the proof stage. Parts of the material published here formed the basis of papers read to the Renaissance seminars at the Universities of Oxford and Cambridge and to the Atelier d'études écossaises of the Congrès de la Société des Anglicistes de l'Enseignement Supérieur, University of Perpignan, May 1993, and I am grateful to those audiences for their attention and the subsequent discussions. I also owe a debt of gratitude to the anonymous readers who advised the publishers, both for their positive reaction to the manuscript and for their thoughtful and constructive commentary, which has (I hope) led to improvements at a number of points, and to Dr. Leslie MacCoull, whose copy-editing extended beyond meticulous attention to questions of style and consistency and whose knowledge of biblical and patristic materials has enhanced the argument at a number of points. Roy Rukkila's cheerful e-mails formed a virtual transatlantic bridge which made long-distance publishing a more enjoyable experience than it might otherwise have been. My students, too, in Glasgow, Amsterdam, and elsewhere, have helped to sharpen the argument; a special role has been played by Katrien Daemen-de Gelder, whose study of the cultural implications of the canon of early modern Scottish literature developed in parallel with this book. Inge de Lange helped me with the first sixteenth-century Dutch texts I had to confront, when the language was a much greater mystery to me than it is now. The greatest debt of all is to John Durkan, without whose teasing encouragement and ready provision of information from his unparalleled knowledge of sixteenth-century Scottish sources this project might never have been begun and certainly would not have been finished. It is to him that the results are dedicated.

Some parts of the text which follows have previously appeared in print in another form. I am grateful to the editors and publishers of these journals for allowing me to draw on this work. Part of Chapter 3 first appeared in "Formalist historicism and Older Scots poetry," *Études écossaises* 1 (1991): 39–48, while an early version of Chapter 4 was published as "Alexander Montgomerie in the Netherlands, 1586–89," in *Glasgow Review* 1 (1993): 53–66. A section of Chapter 5 has appeared as "Alexander Montgomerie, Anti-Calvinist Propagandist?," *Notes and Queries* n.s. 49 (2002), 201–15. Parts of Chapters 7 and 8 derive from "Montgomerie and Marot: A Sixteenth-Century Translator at Work," published in *Études écossaises* 2 (1993): 79–94, and "Montgomerie and the Moment of Mannerism," *SLJ* 26/2 (Winter 1999): 41–58 is a compressed version of some aspects of the overall argument of the book.

Among the works which have appeared while this book was in press, the most significant is unquestionably Sarah Dunnigan's *Eros and Poetry at the Courts of Mary, Queen of Scots and James VI* (Basingstoke and New York: Palgrave Macmillan, 2002). Minor revisions of the text could not have done justice to Dunnigan's arguments, and her book is accordingly not taken into account in what follows.

# A Note on Dating

There were two calendars in use in later sixteenth-century Western Europe: the Julian (or "Old Style") system which had prevailed during the Middle Ages, and the Gregorian ("New Style") calendar first proclaimed by Pope Gregory XIII in a bull of 24 February 1582. The latter was intended to bring the calendar back into line with the solar date, a discrepancy which had risen to some ten days. Some governments followed the papal instruction; others retained the traditional dating. In the Netherlands the Duke of Anjou, briefly *stadhouder*, decreed that the Gregorian calendar would be introduced from 1 January 1583, which would immediately follow 21 December 1582; this instruction was followed by the most important institutions, including the States General, the Council of State, and the States of Holland and Zeeland, but not by all (see *Correspondentie van Leycester*, ed. H. Brugmans, 3 vols. [Utrecht: Historisch Genootschap, 1931], 1: xx–xxi); Leicester's administration used the Julian system. Since Scotland and England also retained the Old Style calendar (until the eighteenth century), I have converted all dates into this form, with the result that some dates in Chapter 4 differ slightly from those given in the earlier version of that material published in the *Glasgow Review*. Any cases which are likely to cause confusion are commented upon in the footnotes.

# Texts and Abbreviations

| | |
|---|---|
| Acta | *Acta Facultatis Artium Universitatis Sanctiandree*, 1413–1588, ed. Annie I. Dunlop, 2 vols. (Edinburgh: SHS, 1964) |
| AGR | Archives Générals du Royaume |
| AGS | Archivio General de Simancas |
| *APS* | *The Acts of the Parliaments of Scotland*, ed. T. Thomson and C. Innes, 12 vols. (Edinburgh: Record Commission, 1814–1875) |
| ARA | Algemeen Rijksarchief, The Hague |
| BL | British Library, London |
| *Booke of the Universall Kirk* | *The Booke of the Universall Kirk, Acts and Proceedings of the General Assemblies of the Kirk of Scotland, 1560–1618*, 3 vols. and Appendix (Edinburgh: Bannatyne and Maitland Clubs, 1839–1845) |
| *Bowes Corr.* | *The Correspondence of Robert Bowes of Aske, esq.*, ed. Joseph Stevenson (London: Camden Society, 1842) |
| Calderwood, *History* | David Calderwood, *History of the Kirk of Scotland*, ed. Thomas Thomson, 8 vols. (Edinburgh: Wodrow Club, 1839–1845) |
| CCSL | Corpus Christianorum, Series Latina |
| *CMC* | *Contaduría Mayor de Cuentas* |
| Constable, *Poems*, ed. Grundy | Henry Constable, *Poems*, ed. Joan Grundy (Liverpool: Liverpool University Press, 1960) |
| *Correspondentie van Leycester* | *Correspondentie van Robert Dudley Graaf van Leycester en andere documenten betreffende zijn gouvernement-generaal in de Nederlanden, 1585–1588*, ed. H. Brugmans, 3 vols. (Utrecht: Historisch Genootschap, 1931) |
| *CSP For.* | *Calendar of State Papers, Foreign, Elizabeth*, ed. J. Stevenson et al., 23 vols. (London : Public Record Office, 1863–1950) |
| *CSP Scot.* | *Calendar of State Papers relating to Scotland and Mary, Queen of Scots, 1547–1603*, ed. J. Bain et al., 13 vols. (Edinburgh: Scottish Record Office, 1898–1969) |

| | |
|---|---|
| *CSP Span.* | *Calendar of State Papers, Spanish*, ed. G. Bergenroth et al., 13 vols. (London: Public Record Office, 1862–1954) |
| *DOST* | *A Dictionary of the Older Scottish Tongue from the Twelfth Century to the End of the Seventeenth*, ed. W.A. Craigie et al., 12 vols. (Chicago/London [Oxford]: University of Chicago Press/ Oxford University Press, 1931–2002) |
| *ELH* | *ELH, A Journal of English Literary History* |
| *ELR* | *English Literary Renaissance* |
| EUL | Edinburgh University Library |
| Fraser, *Chiefs of Colquhoun* | Sir William Fraser, *The Chiefs of Colquhoun and their Country*, 2 vols (Edinburgh: Constable, 1869) |
| Fraser, *Douglas Book* | Sir William Fraser, *The Douglas Book*, 4 vols. (Edinburgh, privately printed, 1885) |
| Fraser, *Eglinton* | William Fraser, *Memorials of the Montgomeries, Earls of Eglinton*, 2 vols. (Edinburgh, privately printed, 1859) |
| GA | Gemeente Archief |
| *Gray Papers* | *Letters and Papers relating to Patrick, Master of Gray*, ed. Thomas Thomson (Edinburgh: Bannatyne Club, 1835) |
| *Historie of James the Sext* | *The Historie and Life of King James the Sext*, ed. Thomas Thomson (Edinburgh: Bannatyne Club, 1825) |
| HMC | Historical Manuscripts Commission |
| *HMC Ancaster* | *Report of the Manuscripts of the Earl of Ancaster*, ed. S.C. Lomax (Dublin: HMC, 1907) |
| *HMC Salisbury* | *Calendar of the Manuscripts of the Marquis of Salisbury*, ed. S.R. Bird et al., 24 vols. (London: HMC, 1883–1976) |
| *JAAC* | *Journal of Aesthetics and Art Criticism* |
| Jack, *Montgomerie* | R.D.S. Jack, *Alexander Montgomerie* (Edinburgh: Scottish Academic Press, 1985) |
| James VI, *Poems*, ed. Craigie | James VI of Scotland, *Poems*, ed. James Craigie, 2 vols. (Edinburgh: STS, 1955–1958) |
| *JEGP* | *Journal of English and Germanic Philology* |
| *JWCI* | *Journal of the Warburg and Courtauld Institutes* |
| Kervyn de Letterhove, *Relations politiques* | Kervyn de Letterhove, *Relations politiques des Pays-Bas et de l'Angleterre*, 11 vols. (Brussels: Commission Royale d'Histoire, 1882–1900) |
| *LASP For.* | *Lists and Analyses of State Papers, Foreign Series*, ed. R.B. Wernham (London: Public Record Office, 1964– ) |

| | |
|---|---|
| *Les Filigranes* | C.M. Briquet, *Les Filigranes*, ed. Allan Stevenson, 4 vols. (Amsterdam: Paper Publications Society, 1968) |
| *Lettres de Marie Stuart*, ed. Labanoff | *Lettres, Instructions et Memoires de Marie Stuart, reine d'Écosse*, ed. Alexandre Labanoff, 7 vols. (London, 1844) |
| Lindsay, *Works*, ed. Hamer | Sir David Lindsay, *Works*, ed. Douglas Hamer, 4 vols. (Edinburgh: STS, 1931–1936) |
| Marot, *Œuvres complètes*, ed. Mayer | Clément Marot, *Œuvres complètes*, ed. C.A. Mayer, 6 vols. (London: Athlone Press, 1958–1970) |
| *MLR* | *Modern Language Review* |
| Montgomerie, *Poems*, ed. Cranstoun | Alexander Montgomerie, *Poems*, ed. James Cranstoun (Edinburgh: STS, 1887) |
| Montgomerie, *Poems*, ed. Parkinson | Alexander Montgomerie, *Poems*, ed. David Parkinson, 2 vols. (Edinburgh: STS, 2000) |
| Montgomerie, *Poems*, ed. Stevenson | Alexander Montgomerie, *Poems*, Supplementary volume, ed. George Stevenson (Edinburgh: STS, 1910) |
| Moysie, *Memoirs* | David Moysie, *Memoirs of the Affairs of Scotland, 1577–1603*, ed. J. Dennistoun (Glasgow: Maitland Club, 1830) |
| *N&Q* | *Notes and Queries* |
| NAS | National Archives of Scotland, Edinburgh (formerly Scottish Record Office) |
| NLS | National Library of Scotland, Edinburgh |
| *OED* | *The Oxford English Dictionary*, 2nd ed., eds. J.A. Simpson and E.S.C. Weiner, 20 vols. (Oxford : Oxford University Press, 1989) |
| PRO | Public Record Office |
| *Reign of James VI* | *The Reign of James VI*, ed. Julian Goodare and Michael Lynch (East Linton: Tuckwell Press, 2000) |
| *Res. SG* | *Resolutiën der Staten Generaal van 1576 tot 1609*, ed. N. Japikse and H.P. Rijperman, 14 vols. (The Hague: Rijks Geschiedkundige Publicatiën, 1915–1970) |
| *Res. Staten van Holland* | *Resolutiën van de Heeren Staten van Holland en Westvriesland 1524–1795*, 249 vols. (The Hague, c. 1750–1798) |
| *RMS* | *Registrum Magni Sigilli Regum Scotorum (Register of the Great Seal of Scotland)*, ed. J.M. Thomson et al., 11 vols. (Edinburgh : Scottish Record Office, 1882–1914) |

| | |
|---|---|
| Ronsard, *Œuvres complètes,* ed. Laumonier | Pierre de Ronsard, *Œuvres complètes*, ed. P Laumonier et al., 20 vols. (Paris: STFM, 1914–1975) |
| *RPC* | *Register of the Privy Council of Scotland*, ed. J.H. Burton et al., 38 vols. (Edinburgh: Scottish Record Office, 1877–1898) |
| *RSS* | *Registrum Secreti Sigilli Regum Scotorum*, ed. M. Livingston et al. (Edinburgh: Scottish Record Office, 1948– ) |
| *Scots Brigade,* ed. Ferguson | *Papers illustrating the History of the Scots Brigade in the Service of the United Netherlands, 1572–1782*, ed. James Ferguson, 3 vols. (Edinburgh: SHS, 1899–1901) |
| *Scots Peerage* | *The Scots Peerage*, ed. Sir J. Balfour Paul, 9 vols. (Edinburgh: Scottish Genealogy Society, 1904–1914) |
| Scott, *Poems,* ed. Cranstoun | Alexander Scott, *Poems*, ed. James Cranstoun (Edinburgh: STS, 1896) |
| Shire, *Song, Dance and Poetry* | Helena Mennie Shire, *Song, Dance and Poetry of the Court of Scotland under King James VI* (Cambridge: Cambridge University Press, 1969) |
| *SHR* | *Scottish Historical Review* |
| SHS | Scottish History Society |
| Sidney, *Poems,* ed. Ringler | Sir Philip Sidney, *Poems*, ed. William A. Ringler Jr. (Oxford: Clarendon Press, 1962) |
| *SLJ* | *Scottish Literary Journal* |
| SRS | Scottish Record Society |
| *SSL* | *Studies in Scottish Literature* |
| StAU | University of St. Andrews |
| STFM | Société Française des Textes Modernes |
| STS | Scottish Text Society |
| Tilley, *Dictionary of Proverbs* | Morris Palmer Tilley, *A Dictionary of the Proverbs in England in the Sixteenth and Seventeenth Centuries* (Ann Arbor, MI: University of Michigan Press, 1950) |
| *Treas. Accts* | *Accounts of the (Lord High) Treasurer of Scotland*, ed. T. Dickson et al., 13 vols. (Edinburgh: Scottish Record Office, 1878–1908) |
| Watt, Fasti | D.E.R. Watt, ed., Fasti Ecclesiæ Scoticanæ Medii Aevi ad annum 1638 (Edinburgh: SRS, 1969) |

# CHAPTER ONE

# INTRODUCTION

On 4 July 1611, as part of a much larger struggle between Patrick Stewart, earl of Orkney, and opponents of his regime in the islands, Francis Mudie of Brekness was the subject of a complaint before the Scottish Privy Council. Between August and October 1609, it was alleged, Mudie had gone around Orkney insulting and threatening the Earl, claiming

> that he sould help to forfalt the said Erll, and hoipit to sie his airmes riven at the Croce, that he micht dicht his ers thairwith; and thairwithall callit the said Erll ane retrospitiane, whome God hes speuit furth of his mouth; with mony ma detestable and uncomelie speitches not worthy to be spokin of.[1]

Mudie was obviously no mean flyter, and other reports before the Privy Council contain evidence of his capacity for effective abuse of the Earl and his agents. But what is particularly interesting about this episode is the fact that he appears to be quoting. His description of the Earl as "ane retrospitiane, whome God hes speuit furth of his mouth" appears to be a direct allusion to a line by the poet Alexander Montgomerie, who had died in 1598. In a versified attack on his former lawyer, John Sharp, written during a bitter lawsuit in 1592–1593, Montgomerie had described his target as

> A treuthles tongue that turnes with eviry tyde,
> A double deillar with dissait indeu'd,
> A leuker bak vhare he wes bund to byde,
> A retrospicien vhom the Lord outspeud . . . . .[2]

"Retrospicien" is an extremely rare word, and Montgomerie's use of it is the earliest to be recorded. As we shall see later, it evidently derives from Luke 9:62, where Christ employs the metaphor of "looking back" (*spiciens retro* in the Vulgate text) for those renegades who shall be denied access to the kingdom of Heaven. While it is possible that the biblical phrase had some colloquial currency, the combination of this unusual item with the idea of vomiting out (as in Revelation

---

[1] *RPC*, 9:209.

[2] Montgomerie, *Poems*, ed. Parkinson, 1:113. Unless otherwise indicated, all quotations from Montgomerie's works are based on this edition.

3:16) seems so specific that Mudie's alleged words must surely derive from Montgomerie's poem. It should, however, be noted that the Privy Council found that the Earl's lawyers had failed to prove their claim, and it is possible that some or all of the charge against Mudie was invented. In that event, the allusion to Montgomerie's poem might have come from the Earl's Edinburgh lawyers, who included Thomas Hamilton and James King, both of whom were part of the network around James VI's court.[3] Either way, this rather obscure case indicates that one of the poet's less well-known sonnets (it now survives in only a single copy) was current a decade after his death, and that it is possible that a manuscript including poems by him had found its way to Orkney.[4]

There is little direct evidence of the manuscript circulation of Scottish Jacobean verse in the seventeenth century, and certainly nothing to compare with the scribal traditions of Sidney and Donne which have recently been investigated by H.R. Woudhuysen and others.[5] Our knowledge of Montgomerie's lyric poetry is almost wholly dependent on one manuscript, now preserved in Edinburgh University Library (MS. De.3.70), and relatively little is known about the circumstances of its compilation: we shall have occasion to return to this question later in this chapter. This witness apart, there are a few isolated poems in sixteenth- and seventeenth-century Scottish anthologies, and, significantly, a few more in seventeenth-century song-books;[6] from these latter sources it is possible to determine that some at least of Montgomerie's songs remained in currency during the century after his death. His longer works, *The Cherrie and the Slae* and his *Flyting* with Patrick Hume of

---

[3] King, indeed, had represented Montgomerie during the long legal dispute which dominated the poet's life in the first half of the 1590s; see below, 162–74.

[4] For further evidence of the continuing currency of Montgomerie's poetry in the seventeenth century, see below, 333–35.

[5] On the dissemination of Sidney's verse, see H.R. Woudhuysen, *Sir Philip Sidney and the Circulation of Manuscripts 1558–1640* (Oxford: Clarendon Press, 1996); for the wider seventeenth-century context, cf. Harold Love, *Scribal Publication in Seventeenth-Century England* (Oxford: Clarendon Press, 1993), and Arthur F. Marotti, *Manuscript, Print, and the English Renaissance Lyric* (Ithaca: Cornell University Press, 1995). Woudhuysen pays incidental attention to the Scottish situation, but does not attempt any general assessment of it.

[6] The sixteenth- and early seventeenth-century anthologies which contain one or more attributions to Montgomerie (or poems elsewhere attributed to him) are: Edinburgh, NLS MS. Adv. 1.1.6 (the Bannatyne manuscript); Magdalen College, Cambridge, MS. Pepys 1408 (the Maitland Quarto manuscript); Edinburgh UL MS. Laing III.447; and Cambridge UL MS. Kk.5.30 (the Murray of Tibbermure manuscript). The seventeenth-century song-books which include settings for lyrics by Montgomerie are those by David Melvill (1604), Alexander Forbes of Tolquhon (1611), William Mure of Rowallan (c. 1615), the Quintus Part of Thomas Wode's part-book (c. 1620), Robert Edwards (c. 1630–1635), William Stirling (1639), Lady Margaret Wemyss (1644), and Robert Taitt (1676).

Polwarth, received wider distribution, each going through several printed editions in the second quarter of the seventeenth century. Yet it is not improbable that the manuscript tradition was livelier than the surviving evidence might suggest, and Francis Mudie's apparent echo of Montgomerie's sonnet against John Sharp is a valuable clue. While it is easy for us to see Montgomerie's career as marking a definitive end of the Older Scots poetic tradition, therefore, there are grounds for suspecting that there was a greater degree of cultural continuity between the Scottish reign of James VI before his accession to the English throne in 1603 and the following generations in Scotland than is usually admitted, and that Montgomerie himself is a more significant figure than he has usually been held to be.

In what follows, I shall be setting out a threefold claim: that Alexander Montgomerie's poetic corpus represents a more original, substantial, and complex achievement than has generally been recognised, justifying a place for him not only within the canon of Older Scots writing, but as a distinctive voice within British poetry on the eve of the Union of the Crowns;[7] that his significance cannot be fully understood in isolation from the context of contemporary verse, not only in Scotland and England, but also on the Continent, in France above all, perhaps also in Spain, the Netherlands, and elsewhere; and finally that this European dimension is so important precisely because Montgomerie, like many of his contemporaries, must be located on one of the great cultural faultlines which occur at intervals throughout Western history.

The eclipse of Montgomerie's reputation is to a great degree part of a much larger process, the dominance of a *grand récit* which narrates the terminal decline of Older Scots poetic tradition in the later sixteenth century.[8] Five years after

---

[7] This use of "British" as a collective term for the Scottish and English cultural systems as they co-existed and interacted in the sixteenth century should not be taken to imply a premature unity: as Roger A. Mason has demonstrated (see *Kingship and the Commonweal: Political Thought in Renaissance and Reformation Scotland* [East Linton: Tuckwell, 1998], esp. 36–77, 242–68), the term was both current and politically loaded, but it unquestionably points the way towards a Union of the Crowns and a consequent cultural unification. The sense of a common culture even predates John Major's *Historia Majoris Britanniae* (1521): in the first years of the century William Dunbar was able to celebrate Chaucer as "rose of rethoris all . . . / That raise in Britane evir," the illuminator of "oure Inglisch," but James VI's insistence that Scots and English are different languages reflects a more complex reality. Given the Protestant agenda of many of the proponents of "British"-ness, the Catholic Montgomerie might himself have had particular difficulties with the term. See also the various essays in *British Identities and English Renaissance Literature*, ed. D.J. Baker and W. Maley (Cambridge: Cambridge University Press, 2002).

[8] For discussion of the wider implications of this process, see R.J. Lyall, "'A New-Maid Channoun'? Redefining the Canonical in Older Scots Literature," *SSL* 26 (1991): 1–18; and cf. K.A.L. Daemen-de Gelder, "Recitations of Nationhood: The Making of Scottish Literature and the Early Modern Canon" (Ph.D. diss., Vrije Universiteit Amsterdam, 2001).

Montgomerie's death, James VI of Scotland achieved his long-awaited inheritance of the English throne, with far-reaching and in many respects disastrous consequences for indigenous Scots culture. Already in 1603, ambitious poets like William Alexander of Menstrie and Alexander Craig of Rosecraig were publishing their work in English rather than in Scots, and the focus for much literary activity by Scots would henceforth be the court in London.[9] But the literary hegemony of England did not emerge unannounced with the exodus of careerist Scottish literati to Westminster in 1603, or even with the self-conscious anticipation of these events which characterised Scotland in the last years of Elizabeth's reign: arguably, it had its roots at least as far back as the first half of the fifteenth century, when James I of Scotland celebrated his impending release from eighteen years of captivity in and around the English court with his *Kingis Quair*, an allegorical poem thoroughly infused with the rhetorical fashions and literary expressions of Chaucer, Gower, and their successors.[10] Other Scottish poets would follow James, with much less success, in attempting to create an "Anglo-Scots" style; but the true and lasting effect of the *Kingis Quair* was perhaps to encourage within the mainstream Scots tradition a much greater generic and stylistic diversity than had previously been present.

After the flourishing of the Older Scots poetic heritage which grew out of this interaction of indigenous and imported literary styles, a movement which reached its apogee in the later fifteenth and early sixteenth centuries in the work of Robert Henryson, William Dunbar, and Gavin Douglas, the developing crisis of the Reformation in Scotland brought with it political, social, and cultural change. The resulting literary strains are apparent both in the later works of Sir David Lindsay, the leading court poet of the reign of James V (1513–1542), whose career extends into the minority of Mary, Queen of Scots, and in some of the lyrics of Alexander Scott.[11] Two parallel phenomena now combined to undermine the autonomy of Scots: the growing influence of the English Bible (since the Scottish Reformers seem never to have undertaken a vernacular translation of their own), and the emergence of a Protestant aesthetic which placed a high value on a "plain" diction largely composed of a lexis common to English and Scots.[12] This style was not

---

[9] On the immediate impact of James's accession for Scottish literature, see Morna Fleming, "The Impact of the Union of the Crowns on Scottish Lyric Poetry 1584–1619" (Ph.D. diss., University of Glasgow, 1997).

[10] See Gregory Kratzmann, *Anglo-Scottish Literary Relations 1430–1550* (Cambridge: Cambridge University Press, 1980), 33–62.

[11] Cf. in particular, "Ane New Yeir Gift to the Quene Mary" and "May is the moneth maist amene", in *Poems*, ed. Cranstoun, 1–8, 23–25.

[12] The function of the mid-sixteenth-century plain style in Scots has not been properly investigated. On parallel developments in England, see Douglas L. Peterson, *The English Lyric from Wyatt to Donne*, 2nd ed. (East Lansing, MI: Colleagues Press, 1990);

invented by the Reformers; it had its foundations in the moral and didactic verse of the later Middle Ages, and was frequently employed with great rhetorical skill by Dunbar. For it is important to recognise that the plain style does not dispense with rhetoric: it rather relies upon a rhetoric of its own, of compression rather than elaboration, of direct statement rather than metaphor, of *syncope* rather than *pleonasmus*. In Scotland, one of its effects was to encourage, between 1550 and 1580, a poetics in which the distinctiveness of Older Scots was sometimes attenuated almost to the point of disappearance, whatever gains might be achieved in lucidity and rhetorical sparseness:

> Fane wald I leif in concord and in peace,
> Without diuisioun, rancour or debait;
> Bot now, allace, in everie land and place
> The fyre of haitred kyndlit is so hait
> That cheritie doith ring in none estait,
> Thocht all concur to hurt the innocent:
> Quhat mervell is thocht I murne and lament?[13]

There is, therefore, some element of truth in a historical account which stresses the gradual decline of the Scots poetic tradition in the course of the sixteenth century; but it is important to recognise that, like most *grands récits*, this does not tell the whole story. Lyricists like Alexander Scott and polemicists like Robert Sempill are significant artists in their own terms, and their work is deserving of greater critical attention than it has so far received.[14]

Nor should we underestimate the achievement of James VI's court circle. The exact nature of the literary community which surrounded the king during the period of almost a quarter of a century between his formal assumption of the reins of government in 1579 and his accession to the English throne in 1603 is difficult to define: the prevailing view since the publication of Helena Mennie Shire's *Song, Dance and Poetry of the Court of Scotland under King James VI* in 1969 has been that there was a fairly highly organised group, perhaps known to its members as "the

---

J.V. Cunningham, "Lyric Style in the 1590s," in idem, *Collected Essays* (Chicago: Swallow Press, 1976), 311–24; and John N. King, *English Reformation Literature: The Tudor Origins of the Protestant Tradition* (Princeton: Princeton University Press, 1982).

[13] Alexander Arbuthnot, "A General Lament", ll. 29–35, in *The Maitland Folio Manuscript*, ed. W.A. Craigie, 2 vols (Edinburgh: STS, 1919–1927), 1:50.

[14] The case for Scott is powerfully made by John MacQueen in *Ballattis of Luve* (Edinburgh: Edinburgh University Press, 1970), and by Theo van Heijnsbergen, "The Love Lyrics of Alexander Scott," *SSL* 26 (1991): 366–79; for an important re-evaluation of Sempill, see Gregory Kratzmann, "Political Satire and the Reformation," *SSL* 26 (1991): 423–37, and Sandra Bell, "Poetry and Politics in the Scottish Renaissance" (Ph.D. diss., Queen's University, Kingston, Ontario, 1995), 29–55.

Castalian band", who participated in a collective "writing game", at least during
the mid-1580s, and that Montgomerie was at its centre until shortly before his de-
parture for the Continent in June 1586.[15] It is probably true, as Priscilla Bawcutt
has recently argued, that Shire's thesis greatly exaggerates the level of organisation
involved in all this, and it may even be that the term "Castalian" never assumed
for James and his circle the significance attached to it by modern scholars.[16] In
this respect, perhaps, the appropriate analogy is not with the *Pléiade* in France,
which did have a recognised identity and membership, but with the much more
shadowy phenomenon of the "Areopagus", that rather loose literary circle which
seems to have enjoyed a brief existence in London in the summer and autumn of
1579 under the leadership of Sir Philip Sidney and Edward Dyer: the hypostati-
zation of James's circle as "the Castalian band" bears a clear resemblance to schol-
arly interpretations of Spenser's and Gabriel Harvey's passing references to the
"ἄρειον πάγον" of Sidney and Dyer as evidence of a formally-structured literary
society.[17] In both cases, however, there is some substance behind the rather fanci-
ful construction: Sidney and Dyer, along with Spenser and Fulke Greville, clearly
*did* debate literary issues (and perhaps read one another's work) in the course of
1579, and in the same way there evidently *was* a community of poets and musi-
cians gathered around James VI in the early 1580s, who seem to have shared a
common objective and, to some degree at least, a common aesthetic. Given the
self-consciously classical style which they affected, it does not seem out of place
to pick up James's own use of the term (appropriately enough, in an epitaph for
Montgomerie) and to refer to the group and its poetics as "Castalian", provided
that we remember that no direct inferences can be made about the form of social
organisation that the term implies, and that its use by James may be no more than
a form of elegant compliment.[18]

---

[15] Shire, *Song, Dance and Poetry*, esp. 79–100.

[16] Priscilla Bawcutt, "James VI's Castalian Band: A Modern Myth," *SHR* 80 (2001):
251–59.

[17] For some of the more extreme early accounts of the Areopagus, see Jefferson B.
Fletcher, "Areopagus and Pléiade," *JEGP* 2 (1898): 429–53, and Howard Meynadier, "The
Areopagus of Sidney and Spenser," *MLR* 4 (1908–1909): 289–301. A more moderate view
is that of James E. Phillips, "Daniel Rogers: A Neo-Latin Link between the Pléiade and
Sidney's 'Areopagus'," in idem and Don Cameron Allen, *Neo-Latin Poetry of the Sixteenth
and Seventeenth Centuries* (Los Angeles: William Andrews Clark Memorial Library, 1965),
5–28.

[18] Bawcutt has justly pointed out that the "Castalian band" invoked by James more
probably refers to the Muses than to his own court circle, which had in any case largely dissi-
pated by 1598. True as this is, it does not dispel the sense of the circle's existence in the early
1580s, or of the appropriateness of the term "Castalian" in referring to its poetic values.

That Montgomerie was at the heart of this enterprise also seems to be beyond question. It was Montgomerie whom James addressed — probably in 1583 or 1584 — as "the maister poete", and it was Montgomerie who himself invoked the concept of a poetic "band" in his sonnets to the court musician and occasional poet Robert Hudson.[19] How long the king's initiative lasted is as difficult to determine as the degree of structure it acquired; what does seem clear is that his objective of a renewed Scottish poetics, adapted to a new cultural milieu, which he set out in his "Reulis and Cautelis to be obseruit and eschewit in Scottis poesie" (1584), was closely linked to the position of Alexander Montgomerie at the heart of the undertaking, perhaps its true originator, certainly its outstanding practitioner. To a greater degree than that of his fellow-courtiers John Stewart of Baldynneis or William Fowler, his poetry reflects all the tensions which were inevitably at work in such a literary environment: the anxieties of the professional courtier whose poetry was a form of self-advertisement; the rival claims of the Scots tradition and the contemporary literatures of England and the Continent; the constraining bonds of conventional language and imagery.[20] Montgomerie's own ambitions would be frustrated even as the "Castalian" project collapsed in the face of the king's imminent accession to the English throne, but through the tensions of the 1580s and the defeats of the 1590s emerges an original and skilful artist, who establishes through a variety of poses the authenticity of his own poetic voice.

The failure of modern criticism to give Montgomerie his due is, in fact, the consequence of *two* master-narratives, for he and his Scottish contemporaries are inevitably read, not only against the achievements of Henryson and Dunbar, but also against the extraordinary richness of Elizabethan literature in England. The standard account of the sixteenth century in Scotland, with the aureate court culture of James IV steadily declining through ossification, religious discord, and creeping Anglicisation, is a mirror image of an England in which the barbarities and metrical uncertainties of the generation of Barclay, Skelton, and Hawes gave way first to the "Drab" poetry of the mid-century and then, after 1580, to that great burst of "Golden" Elizabethan splendour, the pinnacles of which are Sidney, Spenser, and Shakespeare. C.S. Lewis's dichotomy, containing fundamental and obvious elements of truth, continues to haunt the English critical tradition, whatever modern scholarship may have done to encourage a revaluation of the line from Wyatt to Donne or to suggest that English Renaissance literature is more anxiously dynamic,

---

[19] For discussion of these poems in their respective contexts, see below, 101–2, 212–20.

[20] For Sandra Bell ("Poetry and Politics," 56–108, 148–73), James consciously used poetry as an instrument of statecraft, while Montgomerie, perhaps because of his Catholicism, remained equivocal about the king's view of monarchy. While I do not always agree with her readings of specific poems, her overall approach is stimulating, and broadly in line with that adopted here.

more politically aware and internally dialogic, than the master narrative of the Golden Age would have us believe.

By relocating Renaissance texts within a specific social context, in which conflict is endemic and the most fundamental issues have to do with authority and subversion, "New Historicist" critics like Stephen Greenblatt, Louis Montrose, and Jonathan Goldberg have transformed our understanding of the ways in which life is mediated through — and in some respects constructed by — art in later sixteenth-century England.[21] Not all their rereadings are equally persuasive, perhaps, but the central contention, that the Renaissance should be seen as a period in which "one can see acted out a clash of paradigms and ideologies, a playfulness with signifying systems, a self-reflexivity, and a self-consciousness about the tenuous solidity of human identity,"[22] has properly challenged both the formalism of much mid-twentieth-century criticism and older varieties of historical reading which regarded the mediation of history through literature as essentially unproblematic. For the New Historicists, the literature of the Elizabethan and Jacobean periods enacts the tensions within the court and the wider society, sharpened by the personal ambitions of the courtier-poets themselves. For Greenblatt, moreover, the pressures such texts articulate are not confined to the immediate political context: their anxieties are more fundamental, arising

---

[21] Some key New Historicist texts are Stephen Greenblatt, *Renaissance Self-Fashioning: From More to Shakespeare* (Chicago: University of Chicago Press, 1980), *Shakespearean Negotiations: The Circulation of Social Energy in Renaissance England* (Oxford: Clarendon Press, 1988), and *Learning to Curse: Essays in Early Modern Culture* (New York and London: Routledge, 1990); Louis A. Montrose, "Renaissance Literary Studies and the Subject of History," *ELR* 16 (1986): 5–12, "The Elizabethan Subject and the Spenserian Text," in *Literary Theory/Renaissance Texts*, ed. Patricia Parker and David Quint (Baltimore: Johns Hopkins University Press, 1986), 303–40, and *The Purpose of Playing: Shakespeare and the Cultural Politics of the Elizabethan Theatre* (Chicago: University of Chicago Press, 1996); and Jonathan Goldberg, *James I and the Politics of Literature: Jonson, Shakespeare, Donne and their Contemporaries* (Baltimore and London: Johns Hopkins University Press, 1983). There are important reviews of the approach by Jonathan Goldberg, "The Politics of Renaissance Literature: A Review Essay," *ELH* 49 (1982): 514–42, and Jean Howard, "The New Historicism in Renaissance Studies," *ELR* 16 (1986): 13–43; and valuable collections of essays in *The New Historicism*, ed. H. Aram Veeser (London: Routledge, 1989), and *The New Historicism Reader*, ed. H. Aram Veeser (London: Routledge, 1994). The position of "New Historicism" within the historicist tradition is intelligently discussed in Paul Hamilton, *Historicism* (London and New York: Routledge, 1996); for more extended recent overviews, see John Brannigan, *New Historicism and Cultural Materialism* (Basingstoke: Macmillan, 1998) and, from the original source itself, Catherina Gallagher and Stephen Greenblatt, *Practicing New Historicism* (Chicago and London: University of Chicago Press, 2000).

[22] Howard, "New Historicism," 16.

from an awareness in Renaissance artists of their own existential contingency. Sixteenth-century man, in Greenblatt's view, must "live one's life as a character thrust into a play, constantly renewing oneself extemporaneously and forever aware of one's own unreality."[23] Literature, then, is a way of constructing one's identity, of resisting the fragmentation of self which ultimately stems from the destruction of medieval certainties about human nature, however fallen that nature may have been believed to be.

Seen against this redrawn background, the achievement of Alexander Montgomerie is more intelligible. It is scarcely possible to locate his verse directly within the English tradition, for its rhetorical norms are still set within an Older Scots system which has a different history; it was with good cause that James VI remarked in his "Reulis and Cautelis", by way of justifying a treatise on Scots poetics, that of modern rhetoricians

> there hes neuer ane of thame written of it [*i.e.* "poesie"] in our language. For albeit sindrie hes written of it in English, quhilk is lykest to our language, yit we differ from thame in sindrie reulis of Poesie, as ye will find be experience.[24]

Many of the differences James was thinking of were, no doubt, trivial, but the stylistic systems of the two nations retained enough distinguishing features to mislead an unwary reader who fails to take account of them. With his marked use of alliteration, fondness for proverbial idioms, and sudden stylistic shifts, Montgomerie might easily be taken, as Lewis appears in part to have taken him, as a representative of Scottish "Drabness", as the equivalent of those mid-century poets whose work is found in *Tottel's Miscellany*. But the expectations of Montgomerie's original audience were not those which confronted Turberville or Gascoigne or, for that matter, Spenser and Sidney, and we must approach his work with a clear awareness of this fact.

There is, moreover, a chronological aspect to this question: Montgomerie's formative years were almost certainly the 1560s and 1570s, and some of his finest work was composed in the first heyday of James's "Castalian" circle, between 1580 and 1586. To set it in a British (or more strictly, Anglo-Scottish) context, then, we must acknowledge that much of his verse was contemporary with the *emergence* of the generation of Spenser and Sidney. Although Montgomerie's date of birth is uncertain, it is probable that he was born at about the same time as both of them.[25] By

---

[23] Greenblatt, *Renaissance Self-Fashioning*, 31.

[24] James VI, *Poems*, ed. Craigie, 1:67.

[25] Spenser was born in 1552, Sidney in 1554. For the likelihood that Montgomerie, too, was born in the early 1550s, see below, 37–38.

1580, it is true, Spenser's *Shepheardes Calender* had appeared and Sidney had produced the first version of the *Arcadia*, although the latter circulated only in manuscript. In 1579, as we have seen, Sidney, Dyer, and others were debating literary (and other) topics, at the very outset of their own cultural enterprise.[26] By the first half of the 1580s, the period of Montgomerie's greatest ascendancy at the Scottish court, Spenser was composing parts of *The Faerie Queene* and circulating them in manuscript, while Sidney was rewriting the *Arcadia* and at work upon *Astrophil and Stella*, which was probably complete by the end of 1582. Marlowe and Greene were still students in Cambridge for most of this period; Shakespeare was presumably still living in Stratford. The established literary reputations of the day were more those of George Gascoigne (who had died in 1577, and whose *Hundred Sundrie Flowers* and *Poesies* had been published in 1575 and 1576 respectively) and of John Lyly, whose *Euphues* appeared in 1578, followed by *Euphues and his England* in 1580.[27]

It is, perhaps, significant that the part of the Sidney corpus which bears the strongest resemblance to the work of Montgomerie is the miscellaneous group of texts printed in 1598 as *Certain Sonnets*. This collection of thirty-two poems — translations, formal sonnets, and stanzaic lyrics (many of the latter written for existing Italian, Spanish, English, and Dutch melodies) — was in William A. Ringler's view substantially complete by 1581, and thus antedates the compostion of *Astrophil and Stella*.[28] The authorial status of the collection, at least in the form in which it was printed from 1598 onwards, is not self-evident: the widespread occurrence of various items in contemporary miscellanies suggests the absence of a fixed, coherent structure, and it may be that the circulation of manuscript texts reflects a number of stages in Sidney's own construction of a sequence. Or it may be that the ordering is essentially scribal and editorial, as is probably the case with the principal witness to the Montgomerie corpus.[29] But however it came to assume its present shape, the group known as *Certain Sonnets* comprises the same mixture of carefully-turned Petrarchist sonnets and elegant songs that we find

---

[26] For a first-hand view of Sidney's relations with Dyer and Greville from his return to England in June 1577, see Daniel Rogers's Elegy XIII (dated 14 January 1579), printed in Jan van Dorsten, "Poets, Patrons and Professors" (Ph.D. diss., Rijksuniversiteit Leiden, 1962), 175–79.

[27] On Gascoigne, see C.T. Prouty, *George Gascoigne, Elizabethan Courtier, Soldier, and Poet* (New York: Columbia University Press, 1942); for Lyly, G.K. Hunter, *John Lyly: The Humanist as Courtier* (London: Routledge, 1962); and more generally, William O. Harris, "Early Elizabethan Sonnets in Sequence," *SP* 68 (1971): 451–69.

[28] Sidney, *Poems*, ed. Ringler, 423–24.

[29] On the circulation of various versions of *Certain Sonnets*, see Germaine Warkentin, "Sidney's *Certain Sonnets*: Speculations on the Evolution of the Text," *The Library* ser. 6, 2 (1980): 430–34, and Woudhuysen, *Sidney and the Circulation of Manuscripts*, esp. 210–12, 270–98, 403–5.

in the Montgomerie corpus. What is absent here is the larger literary ambition which characterises the *Arcadia* and *Astrophil and Stella*, not to mention Spenser's major works. Like the miscellaneous courtly poems of Dyer, Edward de Vere, earl of Oxford, and other pioneers of the Elizabethan Renaissance, these verses represent the state of lyric art around 1580, and therefore an appropriate point of comparison with the first phase of the "Castalian" initiative, and with the work of Montgomerie in particular.[30] The great Elizabethan age was only just beginning as James and his court set about their literary enterprise; that the latter was short-lived, doomed by history, and possibly misconceived in the first place, to be eclipsed by the developments in England over the next two decades, should not be allowed to obscure the real achievements, the uneasy originality, of its most important poet.

It is, in any case, a fundamental misreading of the circumstances of Scottish culture in the later sixteenth century to relate this Scottish Jacobean poetry primarily to English parallels. English poetry was, certainly, in circulation in James's Scotland; but its influence was only one among many.[31] Throughout the Older Scots period, the cultural links between Scotland and the Continent had been strong, stronger in many respects than those between Scotland and its uncomfortable neighbour. Although some of the traditional lines of communication had been disrupted by the Reformation, moreover, the patterns of association had been complicated rather than destroyed. Scots had studied and taught in the new or reformed Protestant universities in Germany and elsewhere since they began to emerge at the end of the 1520s, but others continued to visit Paris, Louvain, and the other Catholic institutions;[32] communities of Scottish emigrés were established in Paris and Rome, and an active network of underground contacts with Catholic families in Scotland provided material for English and Spanish espionage alike. Furthermore, the cultural associations formed by the marriage of Mary of Lorraine to James V and of their daughter Mary to Francis II of France continued to exert an influence, not least through the agency of the Guise family, after the

---

[30] For a valuable survey of this first phase of the Elizabethan Renaissance, see Steven W. May, *The Elizabethan Courtier-Poets, The Poems and their Contexts* (Columbia, MO: University of Missouri Press, 1991).

[31] The influence of contemporary English writing in Jacobean Scotland has not been properly investigated. For the ownership of a copy of Sidney's *Astrophil and Stella* (now EUL MS. De.5.96) by the poet William Fowler, see Woudhuysen, *Sidney and the Circulation of Manuscripts*, 357–62; James VI certainly seems to have seen Book V of Spenser's *Faerie Queene* soon after it appeared in 1596, and it is possible that Montgomerie, too, knew Spenser's work (see below, 305).

[32] On Scots in French universities in the later sixteenth century, see John Durkan, "The French Connection in the Sixteenth and Early Seventeenth Centuries," in *Scotland and Europe 1200–1850*, ed. T.C. Smout (Edinburgh: John Donald, 1986), 19–44.

deaths of Mary of Lorraine and of Francis II within a few months of each other in 1560.[33] Continental learning had a profound effect upon the upbringing of James VI, whose tutor George Buchanan, appointed in 1570 before the king was four years old, had taught in Paris, Bordeaux, and Coimbra and was recognised as one of the foremost European scholars of his day, in touch with an extraordinarily wide network of learned correspondents.[34] The influence of Buchanan, among others, is apparent in the contents of the king's library up to 1583, which includes many of the works published by contemporary Continental printers, including literary texts — by Dante, Petrarch, Montemayor, Marot, Ronsard, and du Bartas, among others — in Italian, Spanish, and French.[35]

It is not surprising, therefore, that the poetry produced at James's court in the 1580s and 1590s should reflect contemporary European taste. There was a keen interest in the work of Guillaume de Salluste du Bartas (1544–1590), for example: James's own *Essayes of a Prentise* (1584) contained a translation of the *Uranie*, while Thomas Hudson published in the same year his version of du Bartas' *Judit*. Du Bartas would soon return the compliment by translating the king's *Lepanto* into French; in the early 1590s, a later recruit to James's circle, the Flemish humanist Adriaan Damman, would prepare a Latin version of the first part of du Bartas' *La Sepmaine*.[36] John Stewart of Baldynneis took up the work of du Bartas' contemporary Philippe Desportes (1547–1606), turning his French abbreviation of Ariosto's great romance into Scots as *Roland Furious* and translating at least one of the French poet's own sonnets.[37] For William Fowler, Italian sources were more important: in the course of the 1580s, he produced Scots versions of Petrarch's *Trionfi* and Machiavelli's *Il Principe*, and some of his sonnets reflect the influence of

---

[33] Cf. Dana Bentley-Cranch and Rosalind K. Marshall, "Iconography and Literature in the Service of Diplomacy: The Franco-Scottish Alliance, James V and Scotland's Two French Queens, Madeleine of France and Mary of Guise," in *Stewart Style 1513– 1542: Essays on the Court of James V*, ed. Janet Hadley Williams (East Linton: Tuckwell Press, 1996), 273–88.

[34] For the definitive study of Buchanan's life and scholarly associations, see I.D. McFarlane, *Buchanan* (London: Duckworth, 1981); there is a useful summary account of the educational basis of James's upbringing in David Harris Willson, *King James VI and I* (London: Jonathan Cape, 1956), 19–27.

[35] The contemporary catalogue of this important (and now largely untraced) collection is printed, with a valuable commentary, by George F. Warner, "The Library of James VI," in *Miscellany of the Scottish History Society* (Edinburgh: Scottish History Society, 1893), 1: ix–lxxv.

[36] The Latin version is preserved in NLS, MS. Adv. 19.2.10. Damman's career, including his years at the Scottish court, is currently the subject of a study by K.A.L. Daemen-de Gelder.

[37] See G.A. Dunlop, "John Stewart of Baldynneis, the Scottish Desportes," *SHR* 12 (1915): 303–10.

Luigi Tansillo and other sixteenth-century Italian poets. Montgomerie, too, based some of his verse on French models, but his most direct sources tend on the whole to belong to an older generation than those favoured by the other "Castalians". Yet there is a puzzle here: while his most specific borrowings are from Clément Marot (1469–1544) and Pierre de Ronsard (1524–1585), much of his amatory verse is evidently influenced in a more general way by a range of French poets of the 1570s and 1580s, whose work he apparently knew although he did not choose to translate it. The complexity of Montgomerie's relations with contemporary French culture is a subject to which we shall frequently have cause to return in what follows.

By coupling this recognition of the importance of Continental cultural models for James's "Castalian" circle with the sharper political awareness which derives from a New Historicist approach, we can begin to place later sixteenth-century Scottish — and, by extension, English — literature into a wider European context. The tensions within English court culture which have been the focus of attention for New Historicist critics have themselves too often been seen in isolation, as if Tudor and early Stuart England were the only society in which poets were constrained by the demands of patronage and the play of power within aristocratic structures. The most influential of the New Historicists have, disappointingly, been almost as Anglocentric as any of their predecessors, and a good deal more so than much of the best earlier scholarship.[38] But the pressures exerted by assertive monarchies, exacerbated by the polarisation of religion, were apparent throughout Western Europe, and their aesthetic consequences can be detected in every culture from southern Italy to Scotland, from the Iberian peninsula to Bohemia, Dalmatia, and Lithuania. To fail to take account of the widespread nature of these cultural forces and of the parallels between what is happening in England (or, for that matter, Scotland) and contemporary developments in Continental Europe, is to risk sacrificing a full understanding of the nature of early modern culture on the altar of particularism.[39]

---

[38] Recent works which are centred on the literary relations between England and the Continent include Thomas M. Greene, *The Light in Troy: Imitation and Discovery in Renaissance Poetry* (New Haven and London: Yale Univerity Press, 1982); Thomas P. Roche, *Petrarch and the English Sonnet Sequences* (New York: AMS Press, 1989); Robin Kirkpatrick, *English and Italian Literature from Dante to Shakespeare: A Study of Sources, Analogy and Difference* (London: Longman, 1995); and Alistair Fox, *The English Renaissance: Identity and Representation in Elizabethan England* (Oxford: Blackwell, 1997). But the focus of these works is not, on the whole, that of the "New Historicist" school.

[39] For a bold recent attempt to see the overall pattern of the later Renaissance, see William J. Bouwsma, *The Waning of the Renaissance 1550–1640* (New Haven and London: Yale University Press, 2000). Bouwsma's terminology and methods are very different from those employed here, but the patterns he detects are very similar to the account in the following paragraphs.

This study of the œuvre of a single poet in a specific cultural context, therefore, assumes an overall model, the purpose of which is to attempt to see certain key aspects of sixteenth- and seventeenth-century culture whole; there remains a great deal of work to be done in refining the analytical techniques which are needed to make this approach comprehensive and to clarify the relationships between different artistic forms and different cultures, but it does provide us with a way of dealing with Scottish culture between about 1540 and 1700 which transcends the simplistic narrative of linguistic decline and intellectual betrayal. Central to this view are two terms originally drawn from the history of the visual arts: "Mannerist" and "Baroque" have stirred great passions among literary scholars, especially in the United Kingdom where a more particularist tradition has encouraged an endemic scepticism about the value of terms with comparatively sweeping and imprecise meanings. Each points, however, to a crucial aspect of the period we are dealing with, and recent scholarship has done much to establish the case for using them.[40]

We must be careful to specify the meanings these terms are here being given, since they are used differently in differing models of sixteenth- and seventeenth-century culture. For Wylie Sypher, Mannerism was the "missing term" between "High" Renaissance and Baroque, a distinct phase which is manifest in different cultures at different periods and which in England is represented by such literary figures as Donne, the later Shakespeare, and the Jacobean dramatists generally.[41] But not all scholars agree that "Mannerism" is properly a period term at all: for E.R. Curtius and some of his followers it is a recurrent, even a universal, tendency towards elaborate verbal artifice and formal eccentricity in reaction against the orderliness of "classical" art.[42] Such cyclical patterns may indeed be observable,

---

[40] For a comprehensive overview of the debate concerning the term "Mannerism", see James V. Mirollo, *Mannerism and Renaissance Poetry: Concept, Mode, Inner Design* (New Haven and London: Yale University Press, 1984), 20–71; a sceptical analysis of both this term and "Baroque" can be found in John M. Steadman, *Redefining a Period Style: "Renaissance", "Mannerist" and "Baroque"* (Pittsburgh: Duquesne University Press, 1990). A briefer account of my own approach is set out in "Montgomerie and the Moment of Mannerism," *SLJ* 26 (1999): 41–58, here 41–45; cf. idem, "James VI and the Sixteenth-Century Cultural Crisis," in *The Reign of James VI*, ed. Goodare and Lynch, 55–70, esp. 56–59.

[41] Wylie Sypher, *Four Stages of Renaissance Style: Transformations in Art and Literature 1400–1700* (New York: Doubleday Anchor, 1955), 100–79; cf. L.E. Semler, *The English Mannerist Poets and the Visual Arts* (Madison, WI and London: Fairleigh Dickinson University Press/ Associated University Presses, 1998), for whom Donne is apparently the first English Mannerist.

[42] E.R. Curtius, *European Literature and the Latin Middle Ages*, trans. Willard R. Trask (New York: Pantheon Books, 1953; repr. Princeton: Princeton University Press, 1973, repr. 1990), 273–301.

but there is also a specific sixteenth-century phenomenon to be accounted for, and there is a strong case for employing "Mannerist", a term with good sixteenth-century credentials, to refer to it. I am not myself persuaded that it is possible, even in Italy, to differentiate a Mannerist period. Rather, it seems more in keeping with the totality of the evidence to regard Mannerism as a stylistic option, or perhaps a series of related options, developed in the later Renaissance and then taken over, with modifications, by the artists of the Baroque period. I am, in this sense, inclined to accept both Hartmut Hatzfeld's definition of Mannerism as "un estilo de transición" from the later Renaissance to the Baroque and B.L. Spahr's dictum that "Mannerism is a style; Baroque is an era."[43] It is, however, less clear that Spahr is justified in further claiming that "Mannerism is the *maniera* of the Baroque," both because there are aspects of Baroque art which should be distinguished from the Mannerist line, and because that line had already been in existence for half a century when the earliest phase of the Baroque period can be identified. The model which fits most closely to my own approach is that of Harold B. Segal, for whom Mannerism is "a development in the arts coterminous with the dissolution of the Renaissance and the early formation of the Baroque."[44] This definition, to be sure, is merely a starting-point; but it enables us to distinguish some aspects of the literature of the period — and even some aspects of the work of individual writers — while recognising that other forms of discourse coexist with them.

Two apparently contradictory conceptions have competed throughout the debate about Mannerism: that which draws attention to "a tremor of malaise and distrust" (the phrase is Sypher's) which shook Europe during the later Renaissance, producing an art in which uncertainty and lack of balance are clearly inscribed;[45] and that which emphasises the stylishness of Mannerist art, taking as fundamental the contemporary sense of the term *maniera* itself. Only relatively recently have scholars succeeded in bringing these apparent opposites together, arguing that the stylish Mannerism described by John Shearman in his influential study[46] was in essence an escapist response which "seeks refuge into an aristocratic, hermetically sealed, introspective world of refinement, away from a troubled and disappointing external world."[47] The preoccupations with verbal artifice and with witty, "pointed"

---

[43] H. Hatzfeld, *Estudios sobre el Barroco* (Madrid: Gredos, 1964), 54 ; B.L. Spahr, "Baroque and Mannerism: Epoch and Style," *Collectanea Germanica* 1 (1967): 78–100, here 84.

[44] Harold B. Segal, *The Baroque Poem: A Comparative Survey* (New York: Dutton, 1974), 22.

[45] The classic statement of this view is that by Arnold Hauser, *Der Manierismus: Die Krise der Renaissance und der Ursprung der modernen Künsten* (Munich: Beck, 1964).

[46] John Shearman, *Mannerism* (London: Penguin, 1967).

[47] Aldo Scaglione, "Cinquecento Mannerism and the Uses of Petrarch," *Medieval and Renaissance Studies* 5 (1971): 122–55, here 127–28.

ratiocination both reflect, on this reading, a desire to transcend the conflicts of a divided, insecure society, either by abandoning the search for essential meaning in favour of an accumulation of elegant detail or by turning the profound spiritual, moral, and existential anxieties of the age into a series of intellectual quibbles. At a structural level, this aesthetic flight from conflict and doubt, which articulates the crisis as much by excluding it as by finding appropriate rhetorical forms for expressing it, leads to the elevation of detail over formal coherence, fragmenting texts where the humanist-influenced art of the earlier Renaissance tended to unify them. Composite forms such as the sonnet sequence and the *intermezzo* are clear expressions of this powerful preference for multiplicity, while genres like the romance were redefined to place their variety in the foreground, as Bernardo Tasso explains in the preface to his *L'Amadigi* (1542–1560).[48]

Once these formal patterns are recognised, it is possible to integrate into the model the rapid expansion of Petrarchism which is such a prominent feature of sixteenth-century poetry throughout Western Europe. For what the later Petrarchists took from their master was not the underlying spiritual argument which unified his *Canzoniere*, but rather the mosaic technique of the sequence and a large number of particular rhetorical and metaphoric details, most obviously the *contraposti* or antitheses which almost became synonymous with "Petrarchan" lyric. As Maria Rika Maniates has recently observed, "[a]lthough not all petrarchan poetry is manneristic, most mannerist verse . . . is petrarchistic,"[49] and the transmission across Europe of Italian Petrarchism is clear evidence of the international appeal of Mannerist style. It is scarcely possible to separate this process of cultural transmission from the institutional base of court society and patronage: it was in the movement of Italian artists to the court of Francis I that Mannerist techniques in the visual arts first reached France, for example, and — as Maniates has persuasively argued — the Petrarchist phenomenon was underpinned by the use of the sonnet as a lyric form for the performance of polyphonic court song.[50] In England and Scotland, as in France, Petrarchist verse was integrated into the aesthetic and social life of the court.

The development of Mannerist techniques in Italian poetry can be traced from about the same time as comparable changes can be discerned in the visual arts: indeed, it is striking that the characteristic pursuit of *difficoltà* which is one of the hallmarks of his version of Mannerism appears in the poetry of Michelangelo (in the sonnets he addressed to Tommaso de' Cavalieri from 1532 onwards) in the years shortly before he began work on the frescoes of the Last Judgement in the

---

[48] Quoted in Shearman, *Mannerism*, 139.

[49] Maria Rika Maniates, *Mannerism in Italian Music and Culture, 1530–1630* (Manchester: Manchester University Press, 1979), 66.

[50] Maniates, *Mannerism*, 63, and *passim*.

Sistine Chapel, perhaps the most unambiguous expression of a Mannerist aesthetic among his visual works. If these poems reflect Michelangelo's development of Mannerist techniques comparatively late in his poetic career, Italian writers of the following generations, such as Bernardo Tasso (1493–1569), Giovanni della Casa (1503–1556), Luigi Tansillo (1510–1568), and Giovanni Battista Guarini (1538–1612) enthusiastically developed a poetic style dominated by the *concetto*, by Petrarchist *contraposti*, and by fragmentation of literary form.[51] Nor were these developments long confined to Italy: the *Délie* (1540) of Maurice Scève marks the arrival in France of a Petrarchist poetic which would dominate the writing of amatory verse for the remainder of the century, while in Spain the italianising influence of Juan Boscán (c. 1490–1542) and Garcilaso de la Vega (1501–1536) would have a similarly pervasive effect.[52] With the Petrarchist translations and imitations of Sir Thomas Wyatt, it can even be argued that the beginnings of a Mannerist style are apparent in England contemporaneously with developments in Italy and elsewhere.[53]

North of the Alps, however, Mannerist styles encountered existing stylistic systems which differed in important respects from those prevailing in Italy and Spain. The schools of the *Grands Rhétoriqueurs* in France and the "aureate" tradition in Scotland and, to a lesser extent, in England constituted a late Gothic decorative style to which Mannerist techniques could readily be adapted, and the consequence is a degree of continuity which has obscured the importance of the new influences from Italy. While it may be an exaggeration to claim, as R.D.S. Jack has done, that "Mannerism in Scotland . . . had been the norm since Dunbar,"[54] there is

---

[51] On the Mannerist strand in Italian literature, see Ezio Raimondi, *Rinascimento Inquieto* (Palermo: U. Manfredi, 1965); Riccardo Scrivano, *Il manierismo nella letteratura del cinquecento* (Padua: Liviana, 1959), and *Cultura e Letteratura nel Cinquecento* (Rome: Atenei, 1966); *Problemi del Manierismo*, ed. Amedeo Quondam (Naples: Guida, 1975); and Scaglione, "Cinquecento Mannerism."

[52] The most extensive discussion of Mannerism in French poetry is still the introduction to the *anthologie raisonnée*, *La Poésie Française et le Maniérisme 1546–1610(?)*, ed. Marcel Raymond (London and Geneva: Droz, 1971), 5–47; cf. the useful critique by Richard Chaney, "The Problem of Mannerism in Sixteenth-Century French Literature," in *Miscellanea Musicologica: Adelaide Studies in Musicology* (Adelaide: Libraries Board of South Australia, 1980), 2:28–48.

[53] Wyatt is claimed as a Mannerist by Georg Weise, *Manierismo e Letteratura* (Florence: Olschki, 1976), 64–67. Weise draws attention to the presence in Wyatt's verse of "le peculiarità stilistiche tipiche della corrente anticlassica, concettosa e cerebrale della poesia cinquecentesca"; cf. Michael Adams, "Sir Thomas Wyatt and the Progress of Mannerism in Renaissance English Lyric" (Ph.D. diss., University of Michigan, 1988).

[54] R.D.S. Jack, "The Lyrics of Alexander Montgomerie," *RES* n.s. 20 (1969): 168–81, here 170.

a clear affinity between the elaborate rhetoric of Dunbar and Douglas and the more florid styles of such unequivocally Mannerist poets as Tansillo and Bernardo Tasso, and of followers like Philippe Desportes. The differences are, nevertheless, important, and are manifested not only in the adoption of new forms, and above all of the sonnet sequence, and in the development of new approaches to imagery which are most clearly articulated in the conceit,[55] but also in a redefinition of the persona of the poet himself, a more psychologically realised but essentially edgy creation, whose amatory, political, and religious anxieties, developed out of the medieval traditions of lyric verse, are now presented in sharper, less rhetorically poised relief.

Long held at bay by a Protestant poetics which distrusted rhetoric and preferred direct statement of established truth to the use of metaphoric language unless the latter was biblically authorised, Mannerism came late to Scotland. There are, however, strong reasons for regarding the literary movement initiated by James VI in the early 1580s as an essentially Mannerist phenomenon, and there are traces of an emerging Mannerist sensibility a little before this, perhaps in certain poems by Alexander Scott, less equivocally in the *Promine* with which Patrick Hume of Polwarth laid out his credentials as a courtier-poet in 1578.[56] In this series of developments the role of Montgomerie was clearly crucial, and his contribution to the emergence of a Scottish Mannerist poetics should therefore not be underestimated. In the elusiveness of his shifting poetic stance, in his subtle exploitation of subterranean meanings, in the anguished interiorism of much of his amatory verse, in his adaptations of Ronsard and his evident debt to later French "Neopetrarchists", in his fondness for such formal devices as heraldic rebuses, anagrams, and acrostics and such French rhyme-patterns as *rime battellée* and *rime enchainée*, Montgomerie reveals himself to be a true Mannerist. His is a more troubled Mannerism than that of Patrick Hume of Polwarth or, for that matter, of John Stewart of Baldynneis, whose presiding genius was Desportes; he is finally closer, we may conclude, to the disillusioned Joachim du Bellay, lamenting the venality of the Papal court.

The radical change which took place in the course of the century can, perhaps, best be demonstrated by comparing three amatory lyrics, the first written around 1500–1510 by William Dunbar, the second by Alexander Scott about the middle of the century, and the third by Montgomerie. Dunbar's "Sweit rois of vertew and of gentilnes" is one of his most concentrated and elegantly-constructed lyrics, in

---

[55] On Mannerist "metaphorism" and the *concetto*, see Hauser, *Manierismus*, 1:290–301.

[56] In Scott's case, apart from "Up, helsum hairt", which we shall examine below, the elaborate verbal play of lyrics like "Haif hairt in hairt" (*Poems*, ed. Cranstoun, 30) and of the Envoy to "Ane New Yeir Gift", and the elaborate, formal metaphorism of "Rycht as the glass" (43), are arguably Mannerist features; on Polwarth, see below, 66–70.

which parallelism and paradox are carefully deployed to define the lover's relation to a conventionally disdainful mistress:

> Sweit rois of vertew and of gentilnes,
> Delytsum lyllie of everie lustynes,
> Richest in bontie and in bewtie cleir               *goodness*
> And everie vertew that is held most deir,
> Except onlie that ye ar mercyles.

> In to your garthe this day I did persew.       *garden*
> Thair saw I flowris that fresche wer of hew,
> Baithe quhyte and rid, moist lusty wer to seyne,   *red*
> And halsum herbis upone stalkis grene,      *health-giving*
> Yit leif nor flour fynd could I nane of rew.

> I dout that Merche with his caild blastis keyne   *cold*
> Hes slane this gentill herbe that I of mene,    *of which I speak*
> Quhois petewous deithe dois to my hart sic pane  *pitiful*
> That I wald mak to plant his rute agane,
> So confortand his levis unto me bene.[57]

The poem begins, as John Speirs noted many years ago, with a deft reversal of epithets, for the lily might more naturally than the rose be associated with "vertew and gentilnes", while the rose seems in turn to be the more appropriate vehicle for "lustynes".[58] This paradoxical use of categories is easy to miss, however, in the prevailing rhetoric of praise: both rose and lily, the Lady possesses every virtue (which, at the level of the botanical conceit, certainly includes the medicinal sense of "healing power") except one. The reversal in the final line is repeated in the second stanza, the absence of "rew" reinforcing the sense of "mercyles", as "vertew" is picked up in l. 9 with the equally medicinal "halsum herbis" and as the rose and lily of the opening are echoed by the (admittedly conventional) "quhyte and rid" of l. 8. In one important respect, however, this stanza shifts the focus, for whereas the first refers only to the Lady, the second introduces the speaker as participant in his miniature narrative of the *locus amoenus*. He is present more forcefully in the third, where his grief at the demise of rue in the Lady's garden points, indirectly but unmistakably, to his unrequited love. Yet it is striking that this increasing note of sorrow does not disturb the poem's poised elegance; for all the language of deprivation and loss which enters the final stanza, it does not

---

[57] William Dunbar, *Poems*, ed. Priscilla Bawcutt, 2 vols. (Glasgow: Association for Scottish Literary Studies, 1998), 1:235.

[58] John Speirs, *The Scots Literary Tradition*, 2nd ed. (London: Faber, 1962), 58.

create a real sense of emotional crisis, and it is with a delicately coded appeal, in-
troducing the possibility of regeneration and relief, that the poem ends.

A poet of a later generation, Alexander Scott adopts a much less composed
stance in his "Up, helsum hairt":

Up, helsum hairt, thy rutis rais and lowp,                          *leap*
Exalt and clym within my breist in staige.
Art thou nocht wantoun, haill and in gud howp,
Fermit in grace and free of all thirlaige,                          *confirmed; servitude*
Bathing in blis and sett in hie curaige?
Braisit in joy, no falt may the affray,                             *firmly secured; frighten*
Having thy ladeis hart as heretaige
In blanche ferme for ane [ballat] every May.                       *nominal rent; song*
So neidis thou nocht now sussy, sytt nor sorrow,
Sen thou art sure of sollace evin and morrow.

Thou, Cupeid, rewardit me with thiss.
I am thy awin trew liege without tressone.
Thair levis no man in moir eis, welth and bliss.
I knaw no siching, sadnes nor yit soun,
Walking, thocht, langour, lamentatioun,                            *wakefulness*
Dolor, dispair, weiping nor jelosye.
My breist is void and purgit of pussoun.                           *poison*
I feel no pane; I haif no purgatorye,
Bot peirles, perfytt, paradisall plesour,
With mirry hairt and mirthfulnes but mesoure.

My lady, lord, thow gaif me for to hird,                           *look after*
Within my armes I nureiss on the nycht.                            *nurse, nourish*
Kissing, I say "My bab, my tendir bird,
Sweit maistres, lady luffe and lusty wicht,
Steir, rewll and gyder of my sensis richt."                        *helmsman*
My voice surmontis the sapheir cludis hie,
Thanking grit God of that tressour and micht.                      *treasure*
I coft hir deir, bot scho fer derrer me,                           *bought; more dearly*
Quhilk hasard honor, fame, in aventeur,
Committing clene hir corse to me in cure.                          *body*

In oxteris clois we kiss and cossis hairtis,                       *arms; exchange*
Brynt in desyre of amouris play and sport.
Meittand oure lustis, spreitles we twa depairtis.                  *dispirited*
Prolong with lasir, lord, I thee exort,                            *leisure*
Sic tyme that we may boith tak our confort,
First for to sleip, syne walk without espyis.                      *wake; spies*
I blame the cok, I plene the nicht is schort.

Away I went. My wache the cuschett cryis,              *go; watch; turtle-dove*
Wissing all luvaris leill to haif sic chance,          *wishing*
That thay may haif us in remembrance.[59]

While retaining the conventional language of sixteenth-century love poetry, Scott's poem is anti-Petrarchan in a number of important respects. Most obviously, this is a lyric about requited, and consummated, love: the second and third stanzas take us into the lovers' bedroom in a way which recalls — and may perhaps have been inspired by — Wyatt's "They fle from me". That the speaker is not the traditionally spurned and frustrated lover of *amour courtois* and of its Petrarchist variant is already apparent in the opening stanzas, where he catalogues the attributes of such a figure and asserts that they have nothing to do with *him*. *He*, he insists in a hyperbolic welter of alliteration, suffers none of the pains of love, he is, indeed, the happiest man alive.

Yet the poem's tone is not one of unequivocal celebration, and on closer reading we realise that even in the speaker's exhortation to his heart to "exalt and clym" there is an implied admission that he does not actually feel as contented as he claims he should. The reason is one which has its roots deep in the soil of courtly love, in the secrecy which is one of the essential features of medieval amatory lyric; but this is a secrecy which is driven not by some theoretical commitment to preservation of the Lady's sexual reputation but by the all-too-urgent social realities of courtly existence. This is already indicated by ll. 28–30, where the speaker, untypically, recognises that the stakes in this amatory game are much higher for the woman than they are for him, and acknowledges that this is so precisely because she has physically entrusted him with her body. And the point is reinforced in the final stanza, where the true cause of his dissatisfaction is revealed as the fleeting nature of the lovers' trysts, inspired largely by the fear that they will be seen. The precariousness of their situation is thus made fully explicit, and this explains the contradictory pulls of elation and uneasiness which run through the poem.

There is, moreover, a further level of ambivalence and of ambiguity in the last stanza. Abandoning the courtly language of praise with which he both describes his situation and represents himself addressing his lover, the speaker admits the reality of sexual passion in terms we are much more accustomed to find with pejorative moral connotations: "Brynt in desire of amouris play and sport, / Meittand our lustis". The context does not suggest that that moral framework is in play here; rather, Scott seems to be indicating that this is simply how it is. Yet he clearly runs a risk by allowing such language into his portrayal of the lovers' encounter.

---

[59] Scott, *Poems*, ed. Cranstoun, 44–45. Cranstoun reads "sallat" in l. 8, but Theo van Heijnsbergen points out to me that the Bannatyne MS. clearly reads "ballat", which strengthens the alliterative patterning of the stanza. I have slightly modified Cranstoun's punctuation at several points.

Perhaps this is why he concludes the line with a much more ambiguous statement: "Spreitles we twa depertis". At its weakest "spreitles" might simply mean "dispirited", reflecting the lovers' reluctance to separate, but it is tempting to push the meaning further, and to see a suggestion that they are "spreitles" because they leave their souls behind them, united by their passion, or even that each soul is now in the body of the other, as might be implied by "we kis and cossis hairtis". These ambiguities reinforce the doubleness of the speaker's plight, and it is certainly not resolved in the concluding couplet: does he hope that other lovers will remember him and his beloved because of the splendour of their passion, or because their desires can, in the end, only equivocally be satisfied?

In "Up, helsum hairt", Scott introduces anxieties into his amatory lyric which are subtler and more socially conditioned than is characteristic of the Petrarchist tradition; it is tempting to term this uneasy emotional balance within the formal elegance of the stanzaic lyric a version of Mannerism. The tone is unusual, perhaps even unparallelled, within the Scott corpus; but when we turn to Montgomerie we see that such a precarious balance is both more radically presented and much more widespread. "O pleasand plant" [42] illustrates the point very well:

| | |
|---|---|
| O pleasand plant passing in Pulchritude | *of surpassing beauty* |
| O lillie lude of all the Muses nyne | *loved* |
| I laik Ingyne to shau thy Celsitude. | *wit; heavenly qualities* |
| A tearie fluid dois blind thir ees of myne | |
| [                                    ] | |
| Thy eirs inclyne vnto my Cairfull cry | |
| Sen nane bot I hes for thy Person pyne | *pain* |
| Let me not tyn vhom thou intends to try. | *lose* |
| | |
| Tak tym in tym for tym will not remane | |
| Nor come agane if that it once be lost. | |
| Sen we ar voc'd, vhairfor suld we refrane | *spoken about (?)* |
| To suffer pain for ony bodies bost? | |
| My vexit ghost, quhilk rageing Love dois roste | *roast* |
| Is brint almost, thrugh heit of my desyr | *burned* |
| Then quench this fyre quhilk runneth ay the poste | *moves post-haste* |
| Out throu my cost, consuming bain and lyre. | *bone and flesh* |
| | |
| Nou if this heit descend into my Levir | |
| A fervent fevir sall soon my harte infect. | |
| Thairfor correct this humor nou or nevir | |
| Or we dissevir (Suppose we be suspect, | *part* |
| Go to, vhat rek?) and gar the bealing brek | *cause the boil to break* |
| For fra it lek I hald the danger done. | *leak* |
| Then speid you soon that we no tym neglect | |
| To tak effect in waning of the Mone. | |

Like Scott, Montgomerie's speaker focuses upon his own emotional situation from the outset — after a few perfunctory words of complimentary address — and quickly turns this into an explicit appeal for the lady's sexual co-operation. In this respect he is much more the conventional lover than the persona of "Up, helsum hairt", but the *carpe diem* motif with which the second stanza begins is more characteristic of Classical amatory verse than it is of the Petrarchist tradition.[60] And this leads to an outright rejection of the notion of secrecy: since we are already being talked about, the speaker argues, we may as well enjoy ourselves, paying no heed to what anyone says. As if to confirm his radicalism on this point, Montgomerie repeats his argument in the final stanza with an even stronger challenge to possible detractors: "Suppose we be suspect / Go to, vhat rek?" The latter part of the poem is, however, dominated by another concern, the intensity of the speaker's passion, conveyed through linked images of fire, burning, and disease. The hyperbolic language here is characteristic both of later Petrarchism and of much of Montgomerie's amatory verse, and the metaphors fit within well-established clusters of Petrarchist imagery. Yet the medical language is unusually graphic: not only does the speaker imagine the fever spreading through his body from the liver (the traditional seat of the passions) to his heart, but he likens a rupture in his relationship with the lady to the bursting of a boil, a degree of physicality which may stress the force of his passion but which does so in astonishingly unromantic terms.

In this sense, "O pleasand plant" conveys a real sense of emotional crisis, much stronger than the formality of Dunbar's complaint and more exaggerated than the uneasiness we found in Scott. Paradoxically, however, Montgomerie couches his alleged desperation in a favourite stanzaic form, marked by insistent use of internal rhyme, which requires considerable formal ingenuity. And this is a contradiction which is central to sixteenth-century Mannerism: as the emotional temperature rises, so does the level of *sprezzatura* with which the poet expresses the strength of his feelings. It does not seem that such devices are employed in spite of the powerful, uncontrolled emotions the text is seeking to convey; rather, it is *through* the display of linguistic virtuosity that the authenticity of the emotions is attested.

We can only guess at the breadth of Montgomerie's awareness of cultural developments on the Continent. Although he seems to have spent two periods at least outside Britain, the only country he can be demonstrated to have visited is the Netherlands, where he was engaged as a captain between 1586 and 1588. His licence to leave Scotland in the former year permitted him to travel in "the pairtis of France, Flanderis, Spane, and vthiris beyond sey," but there is no indication that he did so, and little time in which he might have. Of a previous sojourn in

---

[60] On this point, see Daniel L. Heiple, *Garcilaso de la Vega and the Italian Renaissance* (University Park, PA: Pennsylvania State University Press, 1994), 229–31.

the Netherlands we know even less, only that he claimed in 1586 to have fought there previously.[61] The expatriate Benedictine Thomas Duff, on the other hand, suggests that he had spent time at the court of Philip II of Spain, and it seems probable that, if this is true, it is likely to have been in the 1570s. There is, obviously, a great contrast between this situation and our knowledge of Philip Sidney's movements on the Continent in 1572–1575 and 1577: there are no extant letters recording Montgomerie's impressions or documenting his acquaintanceships, and no indication apart from Duff's somewhat enigmatic epitaph of the kind of circles in which he moved. The only foreign language Montgomerie can positively be shown to have known is French; he may, perhaps, have picked up a smattering of Dutch during his military service in the Netherlands, and he might conceivably have learned some Spanish if his visit to Spain was a reasonably long one. There are interesting parallels between the reception of Petrarchism in the Low Countries in the 1560s and 1570s, particularly through the work of Lucas d'Heere (1534–1584) and Jan van der Noot (1539–c.1600), and the situation in Scotland a decade later, but there is no evidence that Montgomerie was aware of these developments; van der Noot, it should be observed, characteristically presented his work in bilingual Dutch/French editions, but there is no reason to conclude that Montgomerie had read them.[62] The only clear channel for Montgomerie's Mannerism, then, is through France, and other cultural contacts must at present remain in the realm of fascinating possibilities. This apparently paradoxical situation is not, after all, so surprising, given the high prestige of French culture in the later sixteenth century.

Another note can, however, also be detected in Montgomerie's verse. By the time of his return to Scotland in 1588 a more radical cultural shift was beginning to become evident in several parts of Europe. By the 1590s, it would seem, there had been a qualitative change in poetic values, a kind of decisive leap. In Naples, the young Giambattista Marino was writing the first of his lyrics in a highly innovative style; in London, John Donne was producing the first of his *Songs and Sonets*; Jean de la Ceppède was working on his *Theorèmes* in Aix-en-Provence; in Cordoba, Góngora was developing that hyperbolic style which would become known as *góngorismo*. But Marino's first published collection did not appear until 1602;

---

[61] On these issues, see below, 46–49, 140–2.

[62] See Lucas d'Heere, *Den Hof en Boomgaerd der Poësien*, ed. W. Waterschoot (Zwolle: Tjeenk Willinck, 1969); Jan van der Noot, *Het Bosken en Het Theatre*, ed. W.A.P. Smit and W. Vermeer (Amsterdam and Antwerp: Wereldbibliotheek, 1953), and *De Poetische Werken*, ed. W. Waterschoot (Ghent: Koninklijke Academie voor Nederlandse Taal- en Letterkunde, 1975). It is significant that, like Montgomerie, both derive several of their poems from Marot; cf. W. Waterschoot, "Lucas d'Heere en *Den Hof en Boomgaerd der Poësien* (1565)," *Jaarboek "De Fonteine"* 14–15 (1964–1965): 47–119, here 98–105.

Donne's amatory poems remained in manuscript until 1633. The first twelve of La Ceppède's *Théorèmes* were published in 1594, but the first volume did not appear complete until 1613. Góngora's first published work, similarly, appeared in 1589, but the poems of the 1590s, in which his stylistic radicalism matured, were not to be printed until 1627. Whereas the development of Mannerism was essentially a process of diffusion, the new movement takes the form of a series of independent developments, each a distinctive response to local cultural conditions but sharing certain common features as well, rather than a chain reaction.

There is a strong case for regarding the emergence of Baroque sensibility — as these developments can conveniently be termed — as a genuine cultural revolution, transforming all the arts in a large number of societies within a very short time. In achieving this radical change, poets like Marino, Donne, La Ceppède, and Góngora incorporated many of the techniques and aesthetic values of Mannerism into new forms; their purposes may be fundamentally different, but the methods are often strikingly similar. If Mannerist art constitutes a disintegration of Renaissance unities and harmonies, an elevation of rhetorical detail over form and content alike, the Baroque seeks to achieve new kinds of integration, new forms of unity which are built upon Mannerist principles of multiplicity.[63] The tensions in sixteenth-century culture which Mannerist art sought to deal with did not dissipate as the century reached its end; on the contrary, with the emergence of scientific theories which challenged both religious doctrine and the very place of man at the centre of a divinely-designed cosmos, and with the horrors of civil war in the Netherlands and in France to which religious division could now be seen to have led, the crisis in European civilisation could be said to be growing more profound. This is not the place to attempt an extended account of the relationship between Baroque culture and the historical conditions in Europe around 1600; the theoretical difficulties inherent in such an enterprise should not be underestimated, and the literature in this controversial area is already vast.[64] But there is surely a case to be made for an integration of the analysis of Baroque literature with the New Historicist interpretation of Elizabethan and Jacobean writing, since both are seeking to explain, in their own terms, the same set of phenomena. Once again, it is important to give the New Historicist enterprise a European dimension.

The features of Baroque content and style which are evident in France, Spain, and Italy by the end of the sixteenth century can undoubtedly also be identified in English and Scottish literature, and not only in the poetry of Donne. It is, of

---

[63] Cf. Claude-Gilbert Dubois, *Le Maniérisme* (Paris: Presses Universitaires de France, 1979), 66–76; Fernand Hallyn, *Formes métaphoriques dans la poésie de l'âge baroque en France* (Geneva: Droz, 1975).

[64] See, for example, the bibliographical appendix in Steadman, *Redefining a Period Style*, 169–71.

course, true that, like Mannerism, the concept of the Baroque has not readily been incorporated into British critical discourse. The preference for the indigenous categories of "Metaphysical" and "Jacobean" has given a spurious sense of uniqueness to the transformation of poetry and drama, and in less obvious ways of prose, in England around 1600, in the same way that the European dimension of Elizabethan literature has been obscured by a reluctance on the part of critics to come to terms with the Mannerist phenomenon. But as comparatists like Praz, Wellek, Segal, and Warnke have argued, the importance of wit; the rethinking of metaphor and to some degree of poetic language itself; an increasingly revisionist approach towards the conventions of Petrarchism; a growing preoccupation with mutability, the impermanence of human affairs, and the oppressive nature of time; the emergence of new, more meditative forms of religious writing, all of which are characteristic of the Jacobean age in England, are all features of Baroque literature on the Continent, and an isolationist reading of Jacobean culture simply obscures the extent to which England, too, participated in these more general changes.[65] The same is true, at least to some degree, of Scotland: David Atkinson has made a convincing case for rereading William Drummond of Hawthornden (1585–1649), an early translator of Marino, as a Baroque figure,[66] and a similar argument could be mounted for other seventeenth-century writers such as Sir Robert Ayton, William Alexander, earl of Stirling, and Sir Thomas Urquhart of Cromarty.[67]

In all the cases indicated above, the first signs of the Baroque aesthetic revolution can be seen in a palpable discontent with the conventions and the language

---

[65] Mario Praz, *Studies in Seventeenth-Century Imagery*, 2 vols. (London: Warburg Institute, 1939); René Wellek, "The Concept of Baroque in Literary Scholarship," in *Concepts of Criticism* (New Haven and London: Yale University Press, 1963), 69–127; Segal, *The Baroque Poem*; Frank J. Warnke, *European Metaphysical Poetry* (New Haven: Yale University Press, 1961), and *Versions of Baroque* (New Haven and London: Yale University Press, 1972); Giancarlo Maiorino, *The Cornucopian Mind and the Baroque Unity of the Arts* (University Park, PA and London: Pennsylvania State University Press, 1990). Occasional attempts have been made to associate specific English poets with the Baroque: see, for example, Austin Warren, *Richard Crashaw: A Study in Baroque Sensibility* (London: Faber, 1939); Mario Praz, "The Flaming Heart: Richard Crashaw and the Baroque," in *The Flaming Heart* (Garden City, NY: Doubleday Anchor , 1958), 204–63 (originally published in Italian in *Secentismo e marinismo in Inghilterra* [Florence: La Voce, 1925]); Roy Daniells, *Milton, Mannerism and Baroque* (Toronto: University of Toronto Press, 1963); Murray Roston, *Milton and the Baroque* (London: Macmillan, 1980). For a more comprehensive view, see Giuliano Pellegrini, *Barocco inglese* (Messina: G. d'Anna, 1953), and *Dal manierismo al barocco: studi sul teatro inglese del XVII secolo* (Florence: Olschki, 1985).

[66] David Atkinson, "William Drummond as a Baroque Poet," *SSL* 26 (1991): 394–409.

[67] For a further discussion of the wider historical implications of this approach, see below, 344–47.

of Petrarchist discourse, a desire to renew the language of amatory verse, and to extend the power of this medium into religious lyric, through a more radical approach to poetic imagery. Very occasionally, we find in Montgomerie's poetry traces of these qualities. Such evidence of a desire to break away from the prevailing conventions can occur in a single image (as in "Quhy bene ye Musis all so long") or in the argumentative or dramatic structure of an entire poem ("The Secret Prais of Love"); it can be manifested in an amatory lyric ("Ressave this harte") or a religious one ("Come my childrene dere"). This last is an exceptional case, and it necessarily involves the difficult question of the relationship between the progress of the Counter-Reformation and the progress of the Baroque.[68] While it is undoubtedly true that Baroque style, in literature no less than in the visual arts and music, was not confined to Catholic cultures, the connection between post-Tridentine devotion and the emergence of Baroque religious poetry can scarcely be denied. It is possible to argue, as Alison Shell has recently done, for the existence of "an English Catholic Baroque," in which the poetry of the English Jesuit Robert Southwell (1561–1595) and the Catholic convert Henry Constable (1562–1613) plays a central part.[69] Each of these poets has his own distinctive voice, but the work of both repeatedly explores favourite Counter-Reformation themes, and their rhetorical techniques reflect both Baroque approaches to metaphor and the characteristic devotional strategies of post-Tridentine Catholicism. Even in the context of Reformed England, then, there is an evident connection between the appearance of Baroque literary forms and the reconstruction of Catholic devotional aesthetics.

---

[68] For a classic statement of the view that the two were largely coextensive, see Werner Weisbach, *Der Barock als Kunst der Gegenreformation* (Berlin: Cassirer, 1921); for a persuasive rebuttal, see Wellek, "The Concept of Baroque in Literary Scholarship." For an analysis of the Lutheran element in German Baroque, see Leonard Forster, "Deutsche und europäische Barockliteratur," *Daphnis* 6 (1977): 31–56; an extreme version of the case for Calvinist Baroque can be found in Herbert Cysarz, *Deutsche Barockdichtung* (Leipzig: H. Haessel, 1924).

[69] Robert Southwell, *Poems*, ed. James H. McDonald and Nancy Pollard Brown (Oxford: Clarendon Press, 1967); Constable, *Poems*, ed. Grundy, 183–92. On Southwell's poetry in its religious and cultural context, see Pierre Janelle, *Robert Southwell the Writer: A Study in Religious Inspiration* (New York: Sheed and Ward, 1935); Joseph D. Scallon S.J., *The Poetry of Robert Southwell S.J.* (Salzburg: Institut für Englische Sprache und Literatur, Universität Salzburg, 1975); and John R. Roberts and Lorraine Roberts, "'To weave a new webbe in their owne loome': Robert Southwell and Counter-Reformation Poetics," in *Sacred and Profane: Secular and Devotional Interplay in Early Modern British Literature*, ed. Helen Wilcox et al. (Amsterdam: VU University Press, 1996), 63–78; for a helpful comparison of the two men's work, see Constable, *Poems*, ed. Grundy, 77–83; and see now Alison Shell, *Catholicism, Controversy and the English Literary Imagination, 1558–1660* (Cambridge: Cambridge University Press, 1999).

Unlike his friend and fellow Catholic convert Henry Constable, Montgomerie seems to have chosen exile only at the very end of his life, if at all, and his religious poetry is, as we shall see in Chapter 8, much more equivocal doctrinally than Constable's "Spirituall Sonnettes". But "Come my childrene dere" is a remarkable hint of what his poetry might have become if he had succeeded in his reported desire to assume the Benedictine habit in Würzburg:[70]

> Whill I did behold the favor
>   Of his Countenance so fair,
> Whill I smellit the sweetest savor
>   Of his garments rich and rair,
>   "Oh" I said
>   "If I had
> To my Love yon Prince of glore
>   For my chose,
>   Wold I lose
> Others all I lov'd befor."
> (98: 21–30)

Taken together, these examples of a *baroquisant* tendency do not amount to more than half a dozen of Montgomerie's 130 or so extant poems, but they give some hint of the wider discontents which would transform Anglo-Scottish culture, no less than that of other European societies, in the years after James's accession to the English throne. Perhaps they are evidence of Montgomerie's participation in an end-of-century *Zeitgeist*, the full implications of which would only become apparent after 1600; perhaps they constitute his personal reaction to the particular circumstances in which he found himself. We shall return to the wider implications of this question at the conclusion of this study, when we are in a better position to assess not only the true force of the poet's oeuvre in and of itself, but also the significance of his career within the wider narrative of early modern Scottish literature.

As we noted at the beginning of this chapter, our knowledge of Montgomerie's verse is almost wholly dependent upon a single manuscript, once owned by a somewhat elusive Margaret Ker.[71] All that is known of it for certain is that it was in the hands of William Drummond of Hawthornden by 1627, when he gave it to Edinburgh University Library. There is no evidence that it was compiled

---

[70] For a full discussion of this poem, see below, 309–17.

[71] David Parkinson suggests in his STS edition (2:2–3) that it was Margaret Ker, daughter of Mark Ker of Newbattle and successively wife of James, Lord Hay of Yester and of Sir Andrew Ker, Master of Jedburgh, who owned the manuscript. This seems probable enough, since her family had connections with the dukes of Lennox, and the milieu in which she lived was therefore one in which access to Montgomerie's papers might easily have been possible.

by Montgomerie himself or during his lifetime, and although this possibility is tantalisingly held out by David Parkinson's dating limits of "c.1596–1600", his arguments for the earlier part of this chronological span do not seem convincing.[72] Assuming that his identification of the scribe is correct, it is not self-evident that she is more likely to have produced the manuscript before her marriage in 1598 than afterwards, or that in other respects "conditions would have grown more un-favourable for its production with every year" after 1596. As we shall see in due course, the final year of Montgomerie's life saw him convicted of involvement in a Catholic plot against the government, outlawed and apparently a fugitive. Yet even in such circumstances, the royal printer Robert Waldegrave published two editions of the poet's *Cherrie and the Slae*, claiming on the title-page of the second that Montgomerie himself had been involved in correcting the text. Perhaps the Ker MS., too, was written in 1597–1598, but R.D.S. Jack's suggestion that the scribe was working "shortly after Montgomerie's death . . . and almost certainly had access to his papers" seems to me to offer the most likely account of the manu-script's origins.[73] How soon after the poet's burial in August 1598 the manuscript was compiled must remain a matter for conjecture, but it does seem very probable that the collection is posthumous. Several important implications flow from this. First, the presence of at least two items which are not actually by Montgomerie at all, but are copied into the manuscript without any indication that they are another author's work, in one case incorporating a version of a sonnet by Henry Constable into a short sequence where the other two elements do appear to be Montgomerie's [77.II] can most easily be explained as an intervention by a scribe who was assem-bling the manuscript from a collection of loose papers, including copies of poems which Montgomerie had made from whatever source, or had acquired and pre-served among his own writings.[74] Conversely, it is not surprising that other collec-tions — specifically the Bannatyne and Maitland Quarto manuscripts — attribute to Montgomerie poems which are absent from Ker; the materials from which the Ker scribe compiled the manuscript may well have been incomplete, lacking some items of which the poet himself did not keep, or had lost, a copy.[75] It further follows

---

[72] *Poems*, ed. Parkinson, 2:1–6.

[73] Jack, *Montgomerie*, 35–39.

[74] The other clear instance of unacknowledged appropriation is the English poem "My fansie feeds vpon the sugred gall", which occurs on fol. 36v and which had been printed in Thomas Proctor's *Gorgious Gallery of Gallant Inventions* (1578). A possible third is "Away vane world" (fols. 81v–82r), which is elsewhere attributed to Elizabeth Melvill; for discussion of this question, see below, 300–1.

[75] This is especially understandable if we recall that there was a period of at least eighteen months, and possibly longer, when Montgomerie was away from Scotland, on military service in the Netherlands. The poems found in the Maitland Quarto MS., at any event, date from before his departure on this expedition, in the summer of 1586.

from this that a few genuine poems may lie unattributed in other extant collections, such as EUL MS. Laing III.447, in which two of Montgomerie's pieces from the Ker manuscript appear without attribution. But we should clearly be very cautious about making additions to the corpus on this basis, especially when the argument is as weak as George Stevenson's bald assertion that "[i]t is hard to believe that this and the following four sonnets could have been written by any other Scottish poet than Montgomerie."[76]

The theory that the organisation of the Ker manuscript is scribal also has important implications for our view of the ordering, including the arrangement of many of the sonnets in short sequences of between two and five poems. It is quite clear, as Jack demonstrates, that there is a conscious parallelism between the two main sections, the stanzaic lyrics and the sonnets: both begin with devotional poems, and then proceed through a number of more or less explicitly autobiographical pieces to an extended group of amatory poems. The first part then concludes with the two court entertainments, *The Navigatioun* and *A Cartell of the Thrie Ventrous Knichts* and a group of epitaphs for various figures in and around the court, while the second ends with three apologetic sonnets and a group associated with a number of personal friends. This patterned effect *may*, of course, have been reflected in the materials before the scribe began work on them, but we have no basis for assuming this. More significantly, we cannot be certain that all the sonnet sequences were structured in this way: as we noted above, the untitled group (fols. 71r–v) of three sonnets beginning "Bricht amorous ee vhare Love in ambush [lyes]" incorporates a poem by Constable as well as two translations from Ronsard, and it is more probable that this is a scribal construction than that Montgomerie himself appropriated his friend's work. How many other "sequences" might be scribal inventions can only be a matter for speculation; in most cases, the nature of the content or allusions within the sequence itself seem to confirm an authorial intention. The mere presence of an explanatory title is not, of course, any guarantee, since these, too, are likely to be scribal in some instances; it does seem, however, that in those cases where the scribe's statements can be calibrated against external evidence, his/her information was on the whole reliable, and I have tended to accept the manuscript's claims about the occasion of particular poems.

The most significant implication of the idea that our main witness is a scribal compilation, necessarily incomplete and in some sense edited, is that it raises a

---

[76] *Poems*, ed. Stevenson, 361; the poems in question are "My breist is maid the verray graif of woo", "I dreamit ane dreame, o that my dreame wer trew!" (sometimes attributed to Montgomerie by unwary anthologists), "Your outuard gesture, forme, and fassions fair", "I serve ane dame moir quheiter than the snaw" (subscribed I. Arnot in the manuscript), and "The royall palice of the heichest hewin". It is not clear on what basis Stevenson thought these five poems more likely to be Montgomerie's than the four which follow them.

fundamental problem for any attempt to achieve a clear view of Montgomerie's poetic achievement. We know that, pretty certainly, Montgomerie converted to Catholicism at some point in his career, probably before his presumed return to Scotland in 1578–1579, and that many of his associates and friends were fellow-recusants; near the end of his life, he was implicated in a Catholic conspiracy to assist a Spanish expedition to Ireland. Thomas Duff, moreover, states unambiguously that he wrote anti-Calvinist verse. Yet while there may be hints and nuances of Catholic views in the poems preserved in the Ker manuscript, there is nothing which can be called an unmistakable or overt doctrinal statement, whatever suggestions might be made to the contrary.[77] It is, therefore, possible that the version of Montgomerie which we are given by this collection is a carefully selective one, giving full expression to his doctrinal and political ambivalence but at no point presenting him in a light which unequivocally reveals his opposition to Calvinism. The poems, and especially the sonnets, certainly do not eschew controversy, and Montgomerie emerges at times as an exponent of devastating polemic, but his invective is wielded wholly in his own interest, and never employed in larger political causes. It is possible that we do have, in two sonnets attacking the ministers of Edinburgh which were written in October 1592, evidence of the missing reverse side of Montgomerie's output; but the Ker manuscript contains only his spirited denial of authorship [91].[78] We must always be aware that the Montgomerie we are reading may be the Montgomerie who was acceptable in Protestant Scotland.

There are, then, many theoretical problems, both general and particular, which combine to ensure that any account of Montgomerie's poetry in relation to its own times can only be provisional. One fundamental difficulty lies in the chronology: of the hundred-odd items in David Parkinson's recent edition of Montgomerie's verse, barely a quarter can with any confidence be assigned a date, even to the extent that they can be assigned to one or other of the two principal periods of the poet's literary career, 1580–1586 and 1589–1598. It may be tempting to locate the large number of amatory lyrics to the earlier of these periods, when Montgomerie's star as courtier-poet was in the ascendant, and his anti-curial satires to the 1590s, a time of growing disillusionment, but this would be to carry biographism a good deal further than the evidence warrants. These circumstances have led me to adopt a double approach in what follows. The discussion of the poet's life which forms the basis of Chapters Two to Five incorporates a good deal of new evidence, and seeks to locate both Montgomerie's career and those of his poems

---

[77] Jack, *Montgomerie*, 70, asserts that the religious lyrics "are clearly written from a Catholic viewpoint", while Parkinson, *Poems*, 2:3, speculates that it may have been the reflection of "Catholic sympathies" in the manuscript which led Margaret Ker to pass it on to Drummond. For a more qualified view of the poems' Catholicism, see below, 295–317.

[78] See below, 181–84.

which can be dated with some confidence in the context of the complex religious politics, both domestic and international, of the reign of James VI. This is a necessary process, for it has not been possible until now to develop a clear picture of the course of his life as a courtier-poet, or to see fully how his increasingly precarious situation is reflected in the multiple ambiguities and the silences which so frequently mark his writing. Such an analysis cannot yet be definitive: a satisfactory full-length study of the cultural implications of the king's doctrinal ambivalence is still a desideratum;[79] and the insights which can be obtained through the lens of Montgomerie's experience, especially on the basis of the few documents which have so far come to light, is only part of a much larger picture. By the same token, the generic and thematic framework of Chapters Six to Eight, with its underlying analysis of the tension among native, Mannerist, and occasionally early Baroque elements in Montgomerie's poetry, cannot aspire to do more than throw out some hints for a wider discussion of the connections between Scottish and English poetry and their Continental cognates in the last two decades of the sixteenth century. In these three chapters I discuss Montgomerie's poems concerning the court and friendship, his love poetry, and his religious verse, focusing principally on those pieces which cannot be assigned a date. This enterprise of situating Montgomerie's achievement within Scottish, British, and European poetry is an important one, and it is crucial that we should develop a methodology which transcends mere source-hunting, providing scholarship with the materials for a more sophisticated comparative understanding of the processes of cultural change at one of the major turning-points of European history.

---

[79] For an excellent concise overview, see Julian Goodare, "Scottish Politics in the Reign of James VI," in *Reign of James VI*, 32–54; cf. Maurice Lee Jr, *Government by Pen: Scotland under James VI and I* (Urbana, IL: University of Illinois Press, 1980), 3–26; and Mason, *Kingship and the Commonweal*, 187–214.

# Chapter Two

# Arms, Man, and Song:
# The Making of a Makar

Nothing definite is known of Montgomerie's life before 1580, and none of his surviving poems can with any certainty be dated earlier than that year. Admittedly circumstantial evidence, however, enabled George Stevenson to draw a number of convincing inferences nearly a century ago, and his conclusions form the basis of all subsequent attempts to understand the poet's fateful personal situation.[1] To the data Stevenson collected it is now possible to add a good deal more: R.D.S. Jack has drawn attention to several key documents; Fr. Mark Dilworth discovered in Würzburg University Library five early seventeenth-century Latin poems by Thomas Duff O.S.B., all commemorating Montgomerie's death and giving crucial information about his life; and recent research has shown that there is still more information to be unearthed in collections both in Scotland and on the Continent.[2] The purpose of this chapter is to draw these and other materials relating to Montgomerie's career before 1580 into a single biographical narrative; but it is more important that we should be in a position to use these bare facts to interpret the cultural significance of his final eighteen years, a period in which political, religious and personal affairs were interwoven with the poetic process to produce an art sometimes rarefied by convention, sometimes engrained with the harshness of immediate experience, sometimes looking back to a century of poetic achievement in Scots, sometimes reflecting the most current developments in European literature. In no other late sixteenth-century English or Scots poet, perhaps, are these contrasts more striking, or their consequences more tantalising.

Of the recently-discovered biographical evidence, Duff's Latin poems are certainly the most difficult to interpret. The facts they purport to offer are, as Dilworth acknowledges, veiled by the literary form; and we must inevitably ask

---

[1] Montgomerie, *Poems*, ed. Stevenson, 249–335.

[2] R.D.S. Jack, "Montgomerie and the Pirates", *SSL* 5 (1967–1968): 133–36; Mark Dilworth O.S.B., "New Light on Alexander Montgomerie", *The Bibliotheck* 4 (1965): 230–35; John Durkan, "The Date of Alexander Montgomerie's Death", *Innes Review* 34 (1983): 91–92; R.J. Lyall, "Montgomerie and the Netherlands, 1586–88", *Glasgow Review* 1 (1993): 52–66; and further material in Chapters Four and Five below.

how Duff could have come by his information. He was apparently already a graduate of the Jesuit University at Vilnius when he matriculated at Braunsberg in Prussia (now Braniewo in Poland) in 1610, and cannot therefore have been born much later than 1590; this is consistent with the fact that his father died in 1593.[3] Thomas was one of eleven sons, but since we do not know his position in the family (or, indeed, how many sisters he had) it is impossible to guess when he was born — it could, obviously, have been at any time between 1580 and around 1590, or possibly earlier still. If we put his date of birth near 1580, he would have been old enough to have known Montgomerie personally; otherwise we must infer that he derived his knowledge of the poet's career from a third party, in Scotland, or perhaps in one of the Continental centres he lived in, Vilnius, Braunsberg, or Würzburg. He certainly had access to the text of some of Montgomerie's poems, most probably a copy of *The Cherrie and the Slae*; since he translated "A godly Prayer" [4] and "Supreme Essence" [59] and produced a spiritualised version of "The Solsequium" [21], [4] we might assume that he owned John Wreittoun's edition, which also included these poems, were it not for the fact that his Latin translation of *The Cherrie and the Slae* itself was published in Würzburg in 1631. This is, perhaps, independent evidence for the existence of an earlier edition with the same or similar contents, perhaps the 1615 edition by Andrew Hart the existence of which is testified to by Allan Ramsay a century later.[5]

There seems to be a strong possibility that one or more members of the Bruce family played a part in the transmission of Duff's information about Montgomerie. When the former's Latin version of *The Cherrie and the Slae* appeared in 1631, it was dedicated to Captain Alexander Bruce of Kincavill, whose connection with the expatriate Benedictines in Germany is somewhat mysterious.[6] But two

---

[3] Dilworth, "New Light", 230; for a more detailed account of Duff and his Benedictine context, see idem, *The Scots in Franconia* (Edinburgh: Scottish Academic Press, 1974), esp. 50–51, 234–36.

[4] Würzburg UB, MS. M.ch.q.62, fols. 51r–52v, 55r–56r; cf. Mark Dilworth O.S.B., "The Latin Translator of *The Cherrie and the Slae*", SSL 5 (1967–68): 77–82.

[5] On the textual history of *The Cherrie and the Slae*, see below, 188–90.

[6] The eldest son of Sir John Bruce of Kincavill, who died in 1607, and grandson of Alexander Bruce of Stanehouse and Airth, Alexander Bruce of Kincavill was presumably born in the last years of the sixteenth century; he was certainly a university graduate, and can probably be identified with the man who completed the M.A. at Edinburgh in 1615 (*Catalogue of Graduates of the University of Edinburgh*, ed. David Laing [Edinburgh: Bannatyne Club, 1858], 29). He had at least six brothers and two sisters, including the ministers Robert Bruce (of Aberdour) and Walter Bruce (of Inverkeithing) (NAS, RS25/15, fols. 89r–90v; RS25/32, fols. 137v–138v); the former had Episcopalian leanings, but there is no hint of Catholicism in the immediate family. Alexander was recruiting for military service in Sweden at the beginning of September 1629 (*RPC*, 2nd ser., 3:288–89), but seems

members of the previous generation of the extended Bruce family were more closely linked to Montgomerie's milieu, and in one case was briefly associated with Würzburg as well. One of Montgomerie's friends, as we shall shortly see, was the Catholic activist Henry Keir, formerly secretary to Mary, Queen of Scots and a key link between Scottish Catholics and the ultra-Catholic faction of the Duke of Guise.[7] Keir's nephew William Bruce, a member of the Caithness family of the Bruces of Stanestill, studied at the Catholic college at Pont-à-Mousson from 1581 and is subsequently found at Cahors and Toulouse in or around 1586, eventually becoming professor of law at Würzburg, where he matriculated on 23 June 1590 and was supervising academic disputations in 1591.[8] William Bruce and Duff can scarcely have met in Würzburg (the former only remained there until 1594, later teaching at Zamość and eventually becoming the English representative in Danzig until his death some time after 1612), but their paths may well have crossed during Duff's student days in Poland; this conjunction of Montgomerie's translator and epitaphist with a prominent Catholic with a link to the poet's circle is in any case suggestive.

When William Bruce matriculated at Pont-à-Mousson, he was accompanied by a Robert Bruce, who subsequently became an even more active agent in the

---

clearly to have been in Scotland on 26 November 1631 (*RMS 1621–33*, no. 1856); it is thus uncertain how Duff's work came to be dedicated to him. He died before 14 March 1644 (NAS, RS25/32, fols. 185r–186r) and probably before 8 February (fols. 137v–138v).

[7] Born about 1525, Keir is found as a teacher in Paris in 1560, where he contributed verses to Charles Utenhove's *Epitaphium in Mortem Gallorum Regis Christianissimi ejus nomine Secundum*; by 1569 he was employed as a secretary in the retinue of the exiled Queen Mary (*Lettres de Marie Stuart*, ed. Labanoff, 2:302–3) and involved in various projects in the Catholic interest, with clear connections with the Duke of Guise. He accompanied Esmé Stuart (the future Duke of Lennox) to Scotland in 1579 and emerges as his closest associate, frequently appearing as a witness to documents involving Lennox and his adherents. He joined Lennox in exile in 1582, and was in Paris when the latter died; the following day he wrote seeking employment from Lord Cobham (PRO, SP78/9), but in fact returned to Scotland, where he consolidated his estates and was servant to the king (*RMS 1580–93*, no. 1976) and eventually to Esmé's son Ludovick (StAU Muniments SL110 L: E2.5–6; Laing Charters no. 1283; *RMS 1593–1608*, no. 400, etc.). He was still alive on 30 September 1607 (NAS, RS36/2, fols. 304v–305v). For a full account of his career, see R.J. Lyall, "'Thrie Truear Hairts': Alexander Montgomerie, Henry Constable, Henry Keir and Cultural Politics in Renaissance Britain", *Innes Review* 54 (2003): 186–215.

[8] *Records of the Scots Colleges* (Aberdeen: New Spalding Club, 1906), 1:1; *Matrikel der Universität Würzburg*, ed. Sebastian Merkle (Leipzig and Munich, 1922), 1:20; *De dolo malo, conclusiones iuridicae* (Würzburg: Heinrich von Aich, 1591) etc. The best account of Bruce's career is, unfortunately, still that by Stanisław Kot, *Polski słownik biograficzny* (Kraków: Polish Academy of Sciences, 1935– ), 2:3–4.

Catholic interest than Henry Keir.[9] The nephew of Robert Bruce of Binning, a prominent Edinburgh burgess, Bruce was servant to James Beaton, the exiled former archbishop of Glasgow, and spent much of his career travelling on the Continent, acting as messenger between prominent Scottish Catholics and their French and Spanish allies. There is no evidence to link him with Würzburg, but it is hard to believe that he was unacquainted with Keir and Montgomerie, and he is a possible channel for information passing to the next generation.[10] Duff certainly had access to the text of some of Montgomerie's poems and to information about the poet's life; we cannot tell whether he brought this material to Würzburg himself or derived it from an intermediary like one of the Bruces. What we certainly *can* say is that where we are able to verify the statements Duff makes about Montgomerie in his epitaphs, and most clearly in the case of the poet's death and its aftermath, he is strikingly accurate. Conversely, there is no point on which he can so far be demonstrated to be in error. I have accordingly assumed that Duff's information, however he acquired it, was essentially correct, and have made use of it in assembling the (frequently conjectural) account of the poet's life which forms the structural basis of this and the following three chapters. It is scarcely information which can be used uncritically, but the evidence we have at present supports the assumption that Duff should be taken seriously as a source.

The traditional account of Montgomerie's life takes as a starting point the attribution to him of several poems in the Bannatyne manuscript, which is dated 1568. If these pieces were written by Montgomerie in or before that year, the argument runs, he must have been born some time before 1550, and it is from this deduction that the generally-cited birth date of c. 1545 is derived. Unfortunately for this approach, however, there is no reason whatever to suppose that George Bannatyne had access to Montgomerie's work so early. As Denton Fox and William Ringler make clear in their facsimile edition of the manuscript, *all* the items attributed to Montgomerie appear to have been added on blank leaves after the main process of copying was completed.[11] This is certainly true of "*Peccavi, Pater, miserere mei*", the translations of Psalms 1 and 23, and "Lyik as the dum Solsequium", which are found on pp. 49–53 of the so-called Draft manuscript in company with a series of epigrams by William Alexander of Menstrie (1567–1649). But it seems to apply also to the two poems which occur in the main manuscript, both of which

---

[9] See T.G. Law, "Robert Bruce, Conspirator and Spy", in idem, *Collected Essays and Reviews*, ed. P. Hume Brown (Edinburgh: T. & A. Constable, 1904), 313–19.

[10] For a long self-exculpatory letter from Robert Bruce to James VI, written from Provin-en-Brie on 5 April 1601, see *CSP Scot.*, 13:1131–37.

[11] *The Bannatyne Manuscript (NLS Adv. MS. 1.1.6)*, ed. Denton Fox and William A. Ringler (London: Scolar Press, 1980), xv–xvi, xxxvi. There has been some debate about whether Bannatyne mainly compiled his manuscript in 1565 or 1568, but this has no bearing on the dating of the additional items, including the poems attributed to Montgomerie.

are copied into spaces at the end of quires: "Ane ansuer to ane Ingliss railar praysing his awin genealogy" among a group of anti-highlander poems on fol. 163r–v, and "Irkit I am with langsum luvis lair" on fol. 253r–v.[12] There is, furthermore, some question about the ascription of at least two of these items: the name "Montgomery" has been added to the last of them in a later hand, while "*Peccavi, Pater*" is actually ascribed by Bannatyne to "Robert Montgomery Poete". Since this latter poem is present in the principal manuscript of Alexander Montgomerie's verse and was routinely appended to seventeenth-century editions of his *Cherrie and the Slae*, Bannatyne's alternative Christian name seems quite likely to be a mistake, and on balance I am inclined to accept the authenticity of both;[13] but the fact is that all six poems could have been added to the manuscript at any time up to the compiler's death in c. 1607–1608. It is simply not possible to use their inclusion as a basis for the conclusion that Montgomerie was already active as a poet by 1568.[14]

It is clear enough that Alexander Montgomerie was the younger brother of Hugh Montgomerie of Hessilheid, and therefore the son of John Montgomerie, the fourth laird, who died in 1558.[15] Another brother, George, was described in a notarial instrument of 1560 as his parents' second son; since he was presumably then of legal age, it follows that he must have been born before 1540.[16] Alexander could in theory have been born at any date up to 1558, and there is no strong evidence — once the Bannatyne manuscript is withdrawn from the list of exhibits — to support the traditional date of c. 1545. Apart from his elder brothers Hugh and George, he also had at least two sisters, Agnes and Elizabeth, but we simply do not know whether they were older or younger than the poet, nor do we know whether there were further, unrecorded siblings. The issue is of some importance, since a more accurate dating of his birth would give a clearer idea of whether, for example, he was forty or twenty-five when he established himself at the court of James VI around 1580; but the plain fact is that we do not know.

---

[12] "Ane Answer to ane Helandmanis Invective" (fol. 163v) is *not* attributed to Montgomerie in the manuscript, and is therefore ignored in this discussion. David Parkinson has, however, included this text in his edition.

[13] Both these poems are also included by Parkinson in his edition. It is, of course, possible that Bannatyne's attribution is correct, and that "*Peccavi, Pater*" was the work of a Robert Montgomerie (most probably, then, the bishop-designate of Glasgow); its inclusion in the Ker MS. is, after all, not conclusive evidence, though it is significant.

[14] The nature of the Montgomerie additions was already recognised by James Cranstoun who, noting that these items were "apparently copied at a later date than the rest of the contents", concludes that the manuscript therefore "gives us no help in fixing their dates" (Montgomerie, *Poems*, ed. Cranstoun, 384). More recent scholars have, unfortunately, not always shared Cranstoun's perspicacity.

[15] *Poems*, ed. Stevenson, 256–58.

[16] *Poems*, ed. Stevenson, 257.

Perhaps "c.1550" would be the most neutral conjectural date in the present state of our knowledge, but it certainly does not tell us very much.

The Montgomeries of Hessilheid were undoubtedly a well-connected Ayr-shire family. Not only were they kin to the earls of Eglinton, the first laird of Hessilheid, the poet's great-great-grandfather, having been uncle to the first earl; but the aunt of this first laird married John Stewart, earl of Lennox, and was thus a lineal ancestor of Henry Stewart, Lord Darnley, the consort of Mary, Queen of Scots for eighteen months during the poet's youth, and of his son, King James VI himself. This (fairly remote) kinship obviously mattered to the poet, and per-haps to the king; it also probably played some part in the former's association with Esmé Stuart, duke of Lennox, and with his son Ludovick, whose patronage Montgomerie recognised in the closing years of his career.

According to Thomas Duff, the poet was brought up as a Protestant, con-verting to Catholicism only in adult life:

> Artibus ingenuis puer instituendis amara
>     Calvinistarum mente venena bibi.
> Ast ubi confirmata virum perfecerat ætas
>     In tenebris totos tæduit esse dies.

> [As a boy, when I should have been taught the liberal arts, I drank the bitter poison of the Calvinists. But when I reached a man's estate I tired of spend-ing all my days in darkness.][17]

If this is strictly true, the family must have been supporters of the Reformed faith *before* the constitutional crisis of 1559–1560; there is no conclusive evidence to support this inference, but it is no doubt significant that Hugh Montgomerie of Hessilheid was a member of the parliament which met in August 1560 to agree on the Confession of Faith of the new Kirk.[18] Two years later, when Knox alerted the people of Ayrshire to the threat of an attempt to restore the Catholic faith, the laird of Hessilheid was among those who signed a band at Ayr on 4 September 1562, swearing to defend the Kirk and "to mentain and assist the preatching of this holy evangell", and declaring that "whosoever shall hurt, molest, or truble ony of our body, shalbe reputed ennemye to the hoill."[19] It is more than probable that Hugh Montgomerie had become a Protestant some time before 1560, for the Ayrshire lairds had been involved in activity against the Catholic church for

---

[17] "New Light", 232. All references to Duff's Latin epitaphs are based on this source.

[18] *APS*, 2:526.

[19] John Knox, *Historie of the Reformation in Scotland*, in *Works*, ed. David Laing, 6 vols (Edinburgh: Wodrow Society, 1848–1864), 2:347–50. Another version of the text is given in Fraser, *Eglinton*, 2:193–4.

several decades: William Stewart, brother of Lord Ochiltree, was charged with iconoclasm as early as 1533, for example, and "divers gentlemen of Kyle" were among the hosts of George Wishart when he came to the west of Scotland to preach in 1545.[20] Ian Cowan observes, indeed, that in the years before the Reformation "Ayrshire . . . continued its open loyalty to the new opinions almost alone".[21] Nor did Hugh Montgomerie change his views in the aftermath of Reformation: he was a trusted correspondent of successive Regents, and he was one of the participants in the convention of the Kirk which met at Leith on 12 January 1572, bringing together "the regent Mar's commissioners and the leaders of the kirk" to resolve the vexed question of control of episcopal appointments.[22]

Closer to Alexander Montgomerie's later milieu was another member of the family, whose military title makes it all too easy to confuse him with the poet: Captain Robert Montgomerie. He it was, no doubt, who was mentioned as "a guid honest man" in the service of the Regent Morton in James Melvill's diary for 1576;[23] other evidence puts him firmly in the Morton household. He was already established there by 1 August 1573, when he is reported to be gathering information for the Regent about preparations for a Scottish expeditionary force to the Netherlands; a Protestant informer describes him as "ane gentilman of approvit treuth, gude creditt, and lang experience baith heir and in forein cuntreis".[24] On 2 August, Montgomerie himself wrote to the English ambassador Henry Killigrew, assuring him of his "symple gud will" and informing him that

> I am directit by my lordis Regentis grace to go towardes Flanderes to ye Prince of Orange till offer him ane thowsand horsmen or ma as he requyres for hes commoditie with twa thowsand futmen, to be liftit in yis cuntre till assist him in ye generall cause wnder my Lord of Cathcartis charge, he beand generall to ye haill & so intendes, God willing, to mak hastie expeditioun, yat after ye knawlege of ye Princes will to haue our men all reddy to marche & be imbarkit, as it will ples God to gewe ws prosperous woyaige.[25]

---

[20] Margaret H.B. Sanderson, *Ayrshire and the Reformation: People and Change, 1490–1600* (East Linton: Tuckwell, 1997), 48–68.

[21] Ian Cowan, *The Scottish Reformation* (London: Weidenfeld and Nicolson, 1982), 106.

[22] For various "cloiss writtingis" from Moray and Lennox to Montgomerie among others during the period of the civil war, see *Treas. Accts*, 12:178, 206 and *passim*; for an account of the Leith convention, see Calderwood, *History*, 2:172–96. The political background to this meeting is discussed by George R. Hewitt, *Scotland under Morton, 1572–80* (Edinburgh: John Donald, 1982), 103–4.

[23] *The Autobiography and Diary of Mr. James Melvill*, ed. Robert Pitcairn (London: Wodrow Society, 1842), 445.

[24] PRO, SP52/25, no. 81; this document is calendared in *CSPScot.*, 4:601.

[25] PRO, SP52/25, no. 83; *CSP Scot.*, 4:602.

He had reached the Prince's court in Delft by 13 September, when his arrival was reported by the English agent Thomas Morgan.[26] His success in his negotiations was evidently the object of some envy from English observers, if an eccentrically-spelled letter to Ralph Lane by the informant Richard Bingham is any guide:

> This league betwyxte the Prince and the Scotes growes vere great, and, to satisfye them, he spares not to make coler with ayne other nasyon wronge, spesyallye with us Engles. I doe fynde it heare spoken, My Lorde, but yet in very great secrete that ther is mosyon for maryage for the yonge Kynge of Scotland to the Prince his douther. She is, as I learne, a xij. or xiij. eayrs of age. He had here on his fyrest wyffe. The Scote that dealls here for thes caussis, is called Mountgomore, who the Prince douth use vere well, and, as itemes to me, over well for a Scote's imbasstyter.[27]

The idea of a marriage may have been a notion of Montgomerie's rather than a properly sanctioned piece of policy, or it may be a fantasy produced by English hypersensitivity at the favourable treatment of a Scottish envoy. At any event, it came to nothing; but Montgomerie returned to Scotland committed to increasing the contingent of his countrymen in the Netherlands. It was presumably he, on his way back from the Low Countries towards the end of the year, whose activities were reported on 22 December 1573 by Antonio de Guaras, the Spanish ambassador in London, to the Duke of Alva:

> Para alla ha partido de aqui un Escoces nombrado Mongonueri con cartas y recaudos de los de aquí para el dicho rigente de Escocia, en donde an leuentado mill y quinientos soldados Escoceses y va dicho Mongonueri para Olanda por capitan dellos, y no se puede entender si no que los angelotes heran para se proposito.

> [A Scot named Montgomerie has left here with letters and messages from those here to the said Regent of Scotland, where 1500 Scottish soldiers have been raised, and the said Montgomerie is going to Holland as their captain, and this is intelligible only if the English have proposed it.][28]

Still servitor to the Regent, Robert was granted a pension of £100 on 11 October 1575; he was already in receipt of payments from the Treasurer by October 1574, and occurs frequently between 1577 and 1579, sometimes as captain of the royal

---

[26] *CSP For.*, 10:417–18.

[27] Kervyn de Letterhove, *Relations politiques*, 6:825.

[28] AGS, Estado 827, no. 152.

guard.[29] His religio-political position is clear enough from James Melvill's story of the year 1576, alluded to above, according to which Montgomerie, "a guid honest man, the Regents domestic", punned tellingly on *prophet* and *profit* as a comment on the greed of Archbishop Patrick Adamson of St Andrews.[30] Tantalisingly, we also learn from a later confirmation that the Regent Morton, on 18 October 1578, gave Montgomerie a ship named the *Fle Boit* — for what reason, or what service, is not evident.[31] According to George F. Warner, editing the contemporary catalogue of King James VI's books, Robert Montgomerie was appointed one of twenty-five gentlemen pensioners "to attend on the kingis majestie at all tymes of his ryding and passing to the feildis"; by 1578, it would seem, he had given the King a copy of the *Mappemounde Papistique auec l'histoire de la description*, and perhaps of the *Institution des princes* "de Chelidonius Tigurinus en francoyo".[32] He appears, therefore, to have been a fairly close member of the royal household in the last months of the king's technical minority, and to have been a keen proponent of the Reformed faith.

There is, furthermore, good reason to believe that he was Alexander Montgomerie's half-brother. The poet's father certainly had an illegitimate son called Robert, for he was legitimated on 8 May 1550;[33] several subsequent documents give powerful support for the identification of this half-brother to the three legitimate Montgomerie sons with the captain in the Morton household. There is a fairly strong hint, for example, in the grant by John Blair of that Ilk, on 27 October 1580, of the wardship of certain lands belonging to the late David Blair of Adamstoun to John Mure of Rowallan and Captain Robert Montgomerie,[34] for John Blair's wife was sister to Marion Sempill, wife of Hugh Montgomerie of Hessilheid, while the latter's daughter Elizabeth later married the son of the laird of Rowallan. Some close kinship between Captain Robert and the Hessilheid family seems clear. And this conclusion is surely confirmed by the concession by Robert, on 4 March

---

[29] *RSS*, 7, no. 297; *Treas. Accts*, 13:35.

[30] This witticism is attributed to "Auld Captane Kirkburne" in Robert Sempill's *Legend of the Lyfe of the Bischop of Sanctandrois* (written c. 1584); see *Satirical Poems of the Time of the Reformation*, ed. James Cranstoun, 2 vols (STS, Edinburgh, 1891–1896), 1:346–90, here 358. Cranstoun (2:241) tries to link this figure with Alexander Montgomerie, but this seems improbable.

[31] *RSS*, 8, no. 471 (12 September 1581).

[32] Warner, "Library of James VI", 1, lix; Warner's source is perhaps David Laing, *Select Remains of the Ancient Popular Romance Poetry of Scotland*, ed. John Small (Edinburgh and London: Blackwood, 1885), 376, but Laing gives no location for the document (dated 17 May 1580) which he cites.

[33] *RMS 1546–80*, no. 458.

[34] SRO, RD1/18, fols. 141r–144r.

1581, to Hugh, laird of Hessilheid, of the superplus of the deanery of Glasgow, which he had been granted by the King on 19 January.[35] When Alexander Montgomerie arrived at the Scottish court around the end of 1579, then, he had a half-brother who was already part of the young King's household.

Through all this period there is no certain documentary reference to Alexander Montgomerie. If, as seems probable, he was born around 1550 or a little later — according to Timothy Pont, writing in 1603, his birthplace was Hazelhead Castle, "faumes . . . for ye birth of yat renomet poet, Alexander Montgomerie"[36] — he was still a child during the Reformation crisis of 1559–1560, and not yet of age when Queen Mary was deposed in 1567. We can only speculate about the kind of education he would have received: as a laird's younger son, he is likely to have attended a local grammar school, but there are few records relating to Scottish education outside the larger burghs in the sixteenth century.[37] The First Book of Discipline, accepted in 1561, laid down that "everie severall Churche [shall] have a Scholmaister appointed", and this provision of schools was a concern of the General Assembly of the Kirk from as early as 1562, although subsequent meetings (in 1565 and 1567) placed more emphasis on the need to ensure that the masters were examined and "found sound and abill in doctrine".[38] The nature and extent of ecclesiastical organisation in northern Ayrshire in the first years of the Reformation are poorly documented: William Kirkpatrick, monk of Kilwinning, whose family in Ayr included staunch Protestants, was minister of Kilwinning by 1567, and was also responsible for the parishes of Beith (in which Hessilheid was situated) and Dunlop in 1574, although by the latter year Beith had a reader in the person of Thomas Boyd.[39] Despite the best intentions of the Kirk, however, elementary education seems to have developed slowly, and as late as 1597 the Assembly was forced to admit that the rural situation was desperate. Nevertheless, as John Durkan has argued, the absence of records does not necessarily prove that no

[35] *RSS*, 8, nos. 123, 41.

[36] Timothy Pont, *Cuninghame Topographized, 1604–8*, ed. John Shedden Dobie (Glasgow: J. Tweed, 1876), 194.

[37] See John Durkan, "Education in the Century of the Reformation", in *Essays on the Scottish Reformation, 1513–1625*, ed. David McRoberts (Glasgow: J.S. Burns, 1962), 145–68; and idem, "Education: The Laying of Fresh Foundations", in *Humanism in Renaissance Scotland*, ed. John MacQueen (Edinburgh: Edinburgh University Press, 1990), 123–60.

[38] Knox, *Works*, ed. Laing, 2:208–12; *Booke of the Universall Kirk*, 1:17, 60, 108.

[39] *Register of Ministers*, 37; "Book of Assignations", *Wodrow Miscellany*, 384. Boyd was moved from Ardrossan to Beith at Beltane 1573, and was still active there in 1578 (*Register of Ministers*, 38, 85). Kilpatrick died shortly before 6 November 1588 (NAS, PS1/58, fo. 71r); for his career, see M.H.B. Sanderson, "Kilwinning at the Time of the Reformation, and its First Minister William Kilpatrick", *Collections of the Ayrshire Archaeological and Natural History Society* 10 (1972): 102–26.

institutions existed, and it is likely that a good deal of teaching took place, either through the initiative of individual ministers and readers, or with the support of lairds.[40] In this latter context, it is interesting that both Hessilheid and the nearby lands of Ladyland had their own schools by the first years of the seventeenth century; it is impossible to say how long these schools had existed, but their presence indicates an interest in education on the part of Montgomerie of Hessilheid and Barclay of Ladyland which *may* have begun much earlier.[41]

Assuming that the young Alexander would have received some degree of basic education, at Kilwinning, Beith, or conceivably even at home, we can form some impression of what it might have comprised. In addition to grammar and Latin, the First Book of Discipline had required that pupils should be instructed in Calvin's Catechism, and the description of his early education by James Melvill, who was a pupil of William Gray, minister of Logie in the mid–1560s, suggests that where teaching was provided the curriculum corresponded fairly closely to the framers' intentions:

> Ther we lerned to reid the Catechisme, prayers, and scripture, to rehers the catechisme and prayers par ceur, also nottes of Scripture efter the reiding therof . . . We lerned ther the Rudiments of the Latin grammair, with the vocables in Latin and Frenche, also divers speitches in Frenche, with the reiding and right pronunciation of that toung. We proceidit forder to the Etymologie of Lilius, and his Syntax, as also a lytle of the Syntax of Linacer; therwith was ioyned Hunters Nomenclatura, the Minora Colloquia of Erasmus, and sum of the Eclogs of Virgill and Epist. of Horace; also Cicero his epistles ad Terentiam. He laid a verie guid and profitable form of resoluing the authors, he teatched grammaticallie bathe according to the Etymologie and Syntax; bot as for me, the trewthe was, my ungyne and memorie war guid anneuche, bot my iudgment and understanding war as yit smored and dark, sa that the thing quhilk I gat was mair be rat ryme [*by rote*] nor knawlage.[42]

The emphasis on the reading of the Catechism and the Bible is scarcely surprising, and we may safely assume that any curriculum which would have been acceptable in the climate of the 1560s would have been structured in this way; we should not,

---

[40] Durkan, "Fresh Foundations", 129.

[41] Robert Landellis, "doctore [i.e. assistant master] in Hesilheid", occurs in two instruments by Margaret and Hugh Montgomerie, respectively daughter and son of Robert Montgomerie of Hessilheid, on 19 September 1604 (NAS, RS11/2, fols. 380r–383v); Robert Algeo was schoolmaster in Ladyland on 26 November 1600 (NAS, RS11/1, fol. 39r). I am grateful to John Durkan for the opportunity to consult his manuscript lists of Scottish schoolmasters.

[42] James Melvill, *Diary*, 14.

then, be surprised to find that Montgomerie's poetry draws on a sound knowledge of the Bible and expects no less of its readers. What is more striking, perhaps, is the presence of French alongside Latin in Gray's curriculum; he was not, perhaps, altogether typical in this respect, but it is possible that the foundations of Montgomerie's evident competence in that language were laid during his elementary education in Ayrshire.

Montgomerie presumably reached adulthood during the aftermath of the crisis of 1566–1567, when the supporters of Mary maintained an intermittent campaign of resistance against the regencies of Moray (1567–1570), Lennox (1570–1571), Mar (1571–1572) and Morton (1572–1580). His elder brother may have been a staunch Protestant, but the head of the wider family, Hugh, earl of Eglinton, remained loyal to the Marian cause until the middle of 1571, when he and a number of other magnates submitted to the King's party.[43] The young Montgomerie must surely have found himself embroiled in these powerfully competing claims, but there is no indication of his presence in the conflict. If the suggestion in Duff's account that Montgomerie was brought up a Protestant is to be believed, he no doubt conformed to the pro-government stance of his elder brother. His mother, on the other hand, may have remained sympathetic to the old faith: shortly before her death in August 1583, at any rate, she made Alexander, who had almost certainly converted to Catholicism by this time, her sole executor.[44] One of the witnesses was Thomas Boyd, "sumtyme redar at the Kirk of Bayth in Cunynghame".

The only hint we have of Alexander's role at this period is of necessity difficult to interpret. Around 1580–1581 he took part, as we shall see in due course, in a flyting or poetic duel, with a rival for the king's patronage, Patrick Hume of Polwarth.[45] Since hyperbolic abuse is the flyter's stock-in-trade, we must be cautious about granting any literal accuracy to the details of such contests; but it is striking that Polwarth twice links his antagonist with Argyll:

| | |
|---|---|
| On ruittis and ruinscheochis on the feild | *wild mustard* |
| With nolt thow nurischit neir a yeir | *cattle* |
| Quhill that thow past both puir and peild | *stripped* |
| Into Argyle sum guide to leir, | *to learn good manners* |
| As the last nicht ded weill appeir | |
| Quhill thow stuid fidging at the fyre | *fidgeting* |
| Fast fykand with thy hieland cheir, | *twitching; manner* |
| My flytting forcit the so to flyre. | *grimace* |
| (99 [IV], 57–64) | |

---

[43] *CSP Scot.*, 3:642–43.
[44] *Poems*, ed. Stevenson, 300–1.
[45] See below, 75–83.

Returning directlie agane to Argyle
Quhair last that I left him baith bairfute and bair,
Quhen richtlie I raknit thy race very vyld,                    *vile*
Discendit of a dewill as I did declair . . .
In Argyle with the gatis he yeid amange glennis             *goats; went*
Ay vsing the office thair of a beist
Quhill blistles wes banisit for handling the hennis         *joyless; banished*
Syne fordwart to Flanderis fast fleid or he ceist.           *fled*
    (99 [VIII], 5–8, 14–17)

The ridiculousness of the (traditional) claim that Montgomerie is "discendit of a dewill" might be taken to cast doubt on the evidential value of *any* flyting statement, and it is certainly the case that branding one's opponent as "Hieland" is a strategy at least as old as Dunbar's flyting with Walter Kennedy, who was like Montgomerie an Ayrshireman. But the point of such attacks is that they should bear some relation, however refracted, to the truth, and the truth, moreover, as it was known to the flyters' audience.[46] No doubt Polwarth did not expect his hearers to believe — or remember — that Montgomerie actually grazed on "ruittis and ruinscheochis" along with the cattle in the fields; but the image of poverty, coupled with time spent in the remoteness of Argyll, was presumably intended to strike a chord of familiarity. In that case, Polwarth must have had reason to believe that at least some of those at court in 1580–1581 would recall some association between Montgomerie and Argyll.

The suggestion that Alexander Montgomerie spent time in that part of Scotland before travelling to the Netherlands links him with another of his Montgomerie kin: Mr Robert Montgomerie, archdeacon of Argyll and successively minister of Cupar, Dunblane, and Stirling. Ten years later, when Alexander was a prominent poet at court, this controversial ecclesiastic would perhaps play a significant role in his fortunes;[47] there is no direct evidence that the poet's family connections in Argyll were involved in this earlier phase of his life, but it is certainly not impossible. Robert appears to have held the archdeaconry from 1554 until his resignation in 1601;[48] it may well be that his association with the diocese stemmed from his father, since there are grounds for suppposing that he was one of the three illegitimate sons

---

[46] Cf. Priscilla Bawcutt's observation, concerning the *Flyting of Dunbar and Kennedy*, that while "we can never be sure of the exact proportion of fact to humorous exaggeration . . . there must be some factual substratum": "The Art of Flyting", *SLJ* 10 (2) (December 1983): 5–21, here 21.

[47] For the suggestion that the grant to the poet of a pension out of the revenues of Glasgow Cathedral was connected to Robert Montgomerie's claim to the archbishopric, see below, 99.

[48] *RSS*, 4, no. 2429; Watt, *Fasti*, 36 (referring to *RSS*, 72, fol. 173r).

of Robert, bishop of Argyll, who died in 1533. All three were legitimated on 9 July 1543, but the bishop repeated the process on 18 February 1554, eight days before a Mr Robert Montgomerie was presented to the archdeaconry.[49] Later evidence proves that the minister did indeed have links with the archdeaconry of Argyll, and the timing of his presentation to the office strongly suggests that the second legitimation was an attempt to ensure (perhaps he could not prove the earlier act of legitimation) that there was no legal obstacle to his holding the office. Whatever the truth of this, there was a Montgomerie family connection with Argyll which may be related to the poet's reputed sojourn in the county early in his career.

We cannot be sure what reality underlies Polwarth's jibe about Alexander Montgomerie's presence in Argyll, but it is significantly followed by the suggestion that he travelled from there to Flanders, and it does indeed seem probable that he spent some part of the 1570s in the Netherlands. In 1586, as we shall see in due course,[50] he would claim to have previously "serued in the Low Contryes", and this involvement can scarcely have occurred between 1580 and 1586, when we are able to keep fairly constant track of his movements and activities. It follows that his period of service in the Dutch wars must have fallen between 1573, when the Scots first began to participate in that conflict, and the latter part of 1579, the time around which Montgomerie is most likely to have returned to Scotland. There is, indeed, a likelihood that he is the "Captain Mongomery" named on 1 August 1573, along with four other Scottish captains, as having responded to the recruiting efforts of Thomas Robinson, who was himself licensed by the Scottish Privy Council on 6 June to take three hundred men to the Netherlands and who was evidently engaged in raising further companies to augment his own.[51] Since Robert Montgomerie is mentioned separately in the same document, it follows that the Captain must be another individual with the same surname, and Alexander is clearly a strong candidate.

As early as June 1572, no doubt concerned about the effect of the armed bands operating at the end of the civil war on the famine conditions existing in Scotland, the Privy Council had given permission for troops to go to the Low Countries to support the rebels in their war against Spain. Contact had already been established between the States of Holland and at least one Scottish officer, Henry Balfour, who was given a passport to lead two hundred men to the Netherlands on 16 September 1572, and who was there in time to lead a relief force into the besieged city of Haarlem on 28 January 1573.[52] The beginning of the Scottish intervention

---

[49] Fraser, *Eglinton*, 2 :128; *RSS*, 4, no. 2402.

[50] See below, 119.

[51] For Robinson's licence, see *RPC*, 2:237; the letter (by Robert Cockburn) in which Montgomerie is named is calendared in *CSP Scot.*, 4:601.

[52] *Papers illustrating the history of the Scots Brigade in the service of the United Netherlands, 1572–1782*, 3 vols. (Edinburgh: SHS, 1899–1901), 1:3; this document is not recorded in

came as the rebellion in Holland and Zeeland under the leadership of the Prince of Orange was at its height, with much of Holland under Orangist control. The need for foreign mercenaries to augment the local troops in their resistance to the Spanish forces was, however, quite clear; and it evidently suited the Scottish government to have these potentially troublesome elements out of the way, as well as providing an opportunity for constructive support for the war against Spain and thus for a contribution to the security of Scotland itself.[53] Balfour and his men created a pattern, and they were followed, no doubt with government encouragement, by much larger numbers of troops in the following summer.

According to Killigrew, a Captain Edmonstoun was actively recruiting in Scotland for the Orangist cause in March 1573; he subsequently became ill, causing his departure for the Netherlands to be deferred, and he is presumably the captain of that name listed along with Montgomerie in Cockburn's letter of 1 August. Of the others named by Cockburn, Alexander Campbell and John Adamson had been licensed by the Council on 8 June and 16 July respectively; but there is no trace of licences for Montgomerie, or for the Captain Ogilvie who also appears in the list. Ogilvie is, however, one of ten or eleven Scottish officers mentioned in a Dutch pay-list for 1573–1574, which strikingly omits any reference to Montgomerie. While we cannot infer from this silence that the "Captain Mongomery" mentioned in August 1573 did not fulfil his apparent intention to embark for the Netherlands, it would seem that he did not join the Scots regiment commanded by Henry Balfour, which was paid for by the States of Holland and which formed the core of the Scottish contingent for most of the decade.[54]

---

*RPC.* On the conduct of this phase of the war, see Geoffrey Parker, *The Dutch Revolt* (London: Penguin, 1977), 126–68; for an account of the siege of Haarlem, see J.W. Wijn, *Het Beleg van Haarlem*, 2nd ed. (The Hague: Nijhoff, 1982).

[53] The licence to Thomas Robinson, for example, specified that he and his forces "sall na wayis serve with ony papistis aganis the Protestantis professouris of the Evangell of Jesus Chryst"; the Regent Morton wrote to Elizabeth of England on 21 January 1574 declaring that "principally I wishe of God that the Prince of Aurenge and people of the Low Cuntreis having sustenit sa lang and fearfull persequutioun, micht now in tyme be succoured and releivit, least thay being owerthrawin throw want of tymous ayd, the perell suld be nerar and greater to this haill Ile" (*CSP Scot.*, 4:638).

[54] Many Dutch records relating to Balfour's regiment are collected in *Scots Brigade*, ed. Ferguson, 1:36–46. Cf. Hugh Dunthorne, "Scots in the Wars of the Low Countries", in *Scotland and the Low Countries 1194–1994*, ed. Grant G. Simpson (East Linton: Tuckwell Press, 1996), 104–121. It is difficult to build up a coherent picture of the situation in the 1570s because most central Dutch records do not begin until after the Union of Utrecht in 1579; some material from the period immediately before this can be found in the archives of the Audience in the *Archives générale du royaume* in Brussels.

There are, certainly, strong grounds for supposing that the pay-list of 1573–1574 is incomplete as a record of Scottish forces in the Netherlands at this date. An anonymous report from Delft, written on 19 July 1573, notes the arrival of five hundred Scots (i.e. at least three or four companies), while a further four hundred had, according to Thomas Morgan, arrived in Zierikzee by 12 September. This latter group had immediately attacked "Barrow" (?Bergen-op-Zoom), but had failed because of lack of support from the Dutch. This party may well have joined the assault then being projected against Arnemuiden. The following day, Morgan reported that two hundred Scots had arrived in Zeeland, adding that a further seven companies were on their way.[55] If these groups are all different, we can presumably infer at least fifteen Scottish companies sailing to the Netherlands between July and September 1573, in addition to Balfour's men who had been in place since the beginning of the year. Yet the 1573–1574 pay-list gives the names of only ten or eleven captains.

The surviving accounts of the Dutch government for the 1570s are certainly fragmentary, and it is impossible to build up a comprehensive picture of the Scottish forces involved in the war at this early period. Perhaps some of the troops were paid for by the States of Zeeland, whose accounts for this period are unfortunately insufficiently detailed to enable us to identity particular companies, or by the authorities of other provinces. What is evident, however, is that not all the Scottish companies were integrated into Henry Balfour's regiment, and that some operated independently in different parts of the campaign. This is confirmed by scattered references in despatches from both sides in the war. The towns of Gorinchem and Zaltbommel, for example, which were holding out against the Spanish in August 1574, were reported by Philip II's representative in the Netherlands, Don Luis de Requesens, to be garrisoned with Scots; while when Oudewater was taken by the Spanish on 7 August 1575 it was in spite of "a brilliant defence" by four companies of French, Scottish, and Walloon forces, who were then all killed. Nearby Schoonhoven, captured a couple of weeks later, was similarly defended by, among others, Scottish troops, and forty Scots reportedly died in an attack on a fort between Oudewater and Gouda on 7 December.[56] Comparable allusions to Scots companies apparently operating independently of any larger Scottish force occur throughout the 1570s, leaving no doubt that the list of captains in Balfour's "Scottish Regiment" is by no means a comprehensive record of the Scottish participation in the war.

Any attempt to ascertain the possible cultural consequences of Montgomerie's inferred presence in the Netherlands during the 1570s is, of course, hampered by

---

[55] *CSP For. 1572–74*, 391, 417–18.

[56] *Correspondence de Philippe II sur les affaires des Pays-Bas*, ed. Prosper Gachard, 5 vols. (Brussels: Mucquardt, 1848–1879), 3:135, 352–58, 405.

the silence of the Dutch records. We have already seen that there are good reasons for supposing that the Scottish companies were, at least in some periods, dispersed among the garrisons of several towns; and even in the case of the main body of Balfour's regiment it is frequently unclear where they were at any given moment. Balfour himself was certainly at Haarlem when the town surrendered to the Spanish on 12 July 1573, but this was at any event probably before Montgomerie reached the Netherlands. In September 1574 the Scottish commander was apparently at Zaltbommel, for it was from there that the Spanish hoped to persuade him to travel to Rotterdam or Delft in order to capture or assassinate the Prince of Orange, one of the wilder schemes thrown up by the complex and frequently dubious loyalties of the foreign participants in the war.[57] In the same month, Captain John Pentland was ordered to take his company to garrison Delfshaven, while in October two unidentified companies were sent to Boskoop.[58] Between the fall of Haarlem and the Pacification of Ghent, signed on 8 November 1576, the only absolutely certain occurrence of the main Scottish force is towards the end of the siege of Zierikzee: on 5 June 1576, the English informant Robert Beale reported to William Cecil that Orange's forces there included two thousand Scots.[59]

It is not surprising, therefore, that there is nothing in the evidence on the Netherlandish side to confirm the departure of a Captain Montgomerie for the Netherlands in August 1573, or to indicate that the Montgomerie mentioned by Cockburn was Alexander, the future poet. The latter's own testimony in 1586, however, seems clear enough — especially since it is supported by the indirect evidence of Polwarth's remark and the later comments of Duff — to justify the inference that he was involved in the war for some part of the period between 1573 and 1579. He would certainly not have been the only poet to serve in the Netherlands at this time: the English forces included, at various points in the decade, George Gascoigne, Thomas Churchyard, and perhaps George Chapman, while in the Spanish army we find Francisco de Aldana, Francisco de Figueroa, and others. Unlike Montgomerie, Gascoigne found in his Dutch experiences material for his verse, producing for his patron Lord Grey of Wilton "Gascoigne's voyage into Holland":

> At laste the Dutche with butterbitten iawes
> (For so he was a Dutche, a deuill, a swadde,
> A foole, a drunkard, or a traytour tone)
> Gan aunswere thus: *Ghy zijt te vroegh* here come,
> *Tis niet goed tijt*: and staunding all alone,

---

[57] It had apparently been a condition for the release of Balfour when he was captured at Haarlem that he should carry out this assassination; v. *CSP Span.*, 2:484–85.

[58] Ferguson, *Scots Brigade*, 1:38.

[59] Kervyn de Letterhove, *Relations politiques*, 8:397.

Gan preache to vs, whiche fooles were all and som
To trust him soole, in whome there skill was none.[60]

First in a long line of English poets whose contempt for the Netherlands and the
Dutch would eventually be reinforced by political and commercial rivalry, Gas-
coigne gives little hint of the shared interests which supposedly underpinned the
involvement of England (and Scotland) in the Dutch resistance to Spain; but his
feelings were doubtless coloured by the bitter experiences he had suffered during
his abortive expedition of 1572–1574. But his jaundiced verses do indicate that he
had, in a comparatively short time, acquired at least a smattering of his despised
hosts' language, and this is obviously important if we attempt to assess the extent
to which any cultural contacts which arose from the presence of English and Scot-
tish companies in the Netherlands might have been based upon a mutual under-
standing of the vernacular.

As is so often the case when one tries to reconstruct the formative influences
upon Montgomerie's art, the evidence is sparse, even non-existent. It is true that
there are some structural parallels between the situation of vernacular Dutch po-
etry around 1565–1570 and the position in Scotland a decade or so later, with the
obvious difference that there was no single court in the Netherlands to provide
a natural focus for literary activity. A good deal of the intellectual and cultural
life of the Netherlands was in any case disrupted by the conditions of the revolt:
Lucas d'Heere, for example, was in exile in England between 1565 and 1577, for
some of that time in the company of his fellow-poet Jan van der Noot, so that
Montgomerie would have had little opportunity to meet the author of the *Hof en
Boomgaerd der Poësien* even if he had been so inclined. Nonetheless, his possible
presence in the Low Countries in the 1570s, and the more certain involvement of
another soldier-poet, James Halkerstoun, raises interesting questions about the
cultural relations between Scotland and the Netherlands at this period.[61] Jan van
Dorsten argued persuasively for the importance of the Anglo-Dutch connection
in the efflorescence of Elizabethan literary culture;[62] the possibility of a compa-
rable relationship in the case of Scotland remains largely unexplored. With the
possible exception of a Dutch phrase in one of Montgomerie's sonnets, moreover,
there is no evidence that he acquired even a smattering of the language during
his sojourns in the Netherlands.[63]

---

[60] George Gascoigne, *A Hundreth sundrie Flowres* (London: Richard Smith [1573]), 403.

[61] On Halkerstoun, see R.J. Lyall, "Alexander Montgomerie, Anti-Calvinist Propa-
gandist?", *N&Q* n.s. 49 (2002): 210–15.

[62] See Jan van Dorsten, "Poets, Patrons, and Professors", and idem, *The Anglo-Dutch
Renaissance*, ed. J. van den Berg and Alastair Hamilton (Leiden: E.J. Brill, 1988).

[63] The poem in question is "The Old Maister" [**95.IV**]; see below, 225–26.

Given the nature of the conflict in 1573–1576, it is most probable that Montgomerie, if he was indeed in the Netherlands at this period, would have spent much of his time garrisoning various Orangist towns, or attacking royalist ones, in southern Holland and Zeeland. According to the Würzburg epitaphs his military experience was not confined to the Low Countries, although it is difficult to judge what is meant by the vague term '*varias terras*' (I, 7). The following assertion is, however, much less imprecise:

> Sed fidei ignarum me docta Hyspania leges
> Vivendi vera cum pietate docet.
> Regis et exstabam pergratus in arce Philippi . . . . .

> [But, (when I was) ignorant of the laws of the faith, learned Spain taught me how to live in truth with piety. I was welcomed in the citadel of King Philip . . . . .]

If Duff's assertions are to be believed, Montgomerie was converted to Catholicism in Spain, and spent some time at the Spanish court. It is important to notice the '*docta*', which might merely be an epithet paying tribute to the scholarly traditions of Catholic Spain, but which could equally well suggest that it was in one of the centres of learning — Salamanca, for example, or Alcalá, or Valladolid — that Montgomerie was persuaded of the truth of Catholic doctrine. Investigations in the Spanish archives have not yielded any evidence in support of Duff's claims, but they seem too categorical to be mere invention; and the Spanish connection is just the sort of information we would expect William Bruce to have (if he was indeed Duff's informant).[64] They are, moreover, consistent with what we know about Philip II's policies: he took a keen interest in the propagation of the Catholic faith in England and Scotland (as his financial support of many Catholic dissidents reveals), and who could have been of greater value to his cause than a recently-converted, distant cousin of the Scottish king?

---

[64] Two visits to the Archivo General de Simancas have produced a good deal of information about Philip II's relations with Scotland and with individual Scots, but no trace of Montgomerie. Most significantly, his name is absent from the exhaustive lists of payments in the royal household for the period 1573–1578 (AGS, *Casa y Sitios Reales*, *legajos* 85–87, indexed in *legajos* 99–127). But the extant records of payments to foreign *entretenidos*, the king's pensionaries, do not begin until the late 1570s, when the alphabetical file for those whose Christian name begins with "A" (AGS, *CMC, 2a época, legajo* 119) includes six Scots, maintained at various dates between 1588 and 1598, but no mention of Montgomerie. It is possible that some document relating to the poet lies buried in the vast archives of the Spanish crown, but it will probably only emerge by chance.

If, as seems probable, Montgomerie was engaged in the Dutch wars in the mid-1570s, the Pacification of Ghent might well have provided him with a suitable occasion for leaving the Netherlands, and quite possibly for visiting the land of his former enemies. The level of political and military tension remained high through the winter of 1576–1577 and into the following summer, as the united Provinces prepared for renewed war against Spain: even before the conclusion of the Ghent agreement the States were considering the rehiring of Balfour's regiment, and he was given a new commission for sixteen companies at the beginning of December 1576; his regiment was reported to be encamped in Limburg at the end of the year.[65] After a period of intermittent skirmishing, Balfour himself seems to have decided to leave the Netherlands: he took his leave from the States-General on 7 June 1577, and the following month the Prince of Orange was reported to be ready to dismiss his English and Scottish forces in response to Spanish demands.[66] By 11 August, however, according to William Davison in Antwerp, Elizabeth had written to the Scottish Regent urging the return of "the bandes latelie dismissed from hence", while three weeks later the States were moving Balfour's fifteen companies to Gembloux, near Namur, where they would be able to confront the Spanish army under Don John of Austria.[67] Despite the continuing military preparations, however, the cessation of outright hostilities in November 1576 offers the best opportunity for comparatively easy movement between the Netherlands and Spain.

The Spain in which Montgomerie was reportedly converted was certainly the most powerful force on the Catholic side of the sixteenth-century Cold War. Philip's "citadel", if we interpret the term literally, was normally the Alcázar in Madrid, where the court was based and much government business was transacted; but by the mid-1570s the king spent as much time as he could at the astonishing palace-monastery he was building north of the capital, at San Lorenzo del Escorial.[68] If Duff is correct in his assertion that Montgomerie was welcomed at court, then it would almost certainly have been in one or both of these places

---

[65] *Res. SG.*, 1:22; Brussels, AGR, Audience, T109/960, fols. 193v–195r ; *CSP For. 1575–77*, 461.

[66] *Res. SG.*, 1:355; *CSPFor. 1577–78*, 30.

[67] Kervyn de Letterhove, Relations politiques, 9:452–53 ; *CSPFor. 1577–78*, 133–34. The States-General resolved to re-employ Balfour with ten companies on 30 August 1577 (*Res. SG.*, 1:376).

[68] Recent studies in English of the reign of Philip II are Geoffrey Parker, *Philip II* (London: Hutchinson, 1979), and *The Grand Strategy of Philip II* (New Haven and London: Yale University Press, 1998); and Henry Kamen, *Philip of Spain* (New Haven and London: Yale University Press, 1997); cf. the monumental study by Manuel Fernández Álvarez, *Felipe II y su Tiempo* (Madrid: Espasa-Calpe, 1998).

that the Scottish poet would have been received. It seems much more likely that he would have been honoured on diplomatic and political grounds than as a poet, not only because there is no evidence that he was already writing by this period, but also because there seems to have been little place for poetry at the austere court of Philip II. "Aficionado al retiro y a la soledad", in the words of one Spanish literary historian, the king was more favourably disposed towards religious meditation than Petrarchist poetry, and the life of the court did not normally include secular entertainment of the kind which was widely favoured in France and elsewhere.[69] It is true that the Library was given a central place in the design of the Escorial, and the collection being created there was indeed an impressive one; but its emphases were classical and religious, as was appropriate to its double function as the library of both monastery and palace.[70] There was little room at Philip II's court for anything as flippant as contemporary secular verse. It is, on the other hand, important to remember that music plays a crucial role in Montgomerie's subsequent œuvre; and the musical tradition of Philip's Spain, and even of his court, was a rich and vital one. Away from the court, the devotional verse of Luis de León and Juan de la Cruz and the amatory poetry of Fernando de Herrera, Francisco de Aldana, and others testify to a lively literary tradition, but it is unlikely that Montgomerie had any real knowledge of it.

Although any account of Montgomerie's movements in the 1570s must necessarily be based on guesswork, it would make sense if he had been converted to Catholicism by the beginning of 1578, since there is some reason to suspect that he was by then back in the Low Countries, and acting suspiciously. On 25 January, the former English ambassador in the Netherlands, Thomas Wilson, wrote to his successor William Davison:

> . . . I towlde Mon*sieur* de Famars latelie and willed h*ym* to signifie no lesse to the Pry*n*ce, that practises wer leide to corrupt the Scott*es*, and I named twoe m*en* especially, Capitayne Wyer, and Capitayne Montgomerie, who are suspected to bee on Don Jhons faction for the Scottish Queenes sake. Yow shal doe wel to enforme the Pry*n*ce hereof, that Coronel Bafour, maye by his Ex*cellen*cies meanes bee the rather warned to take heede and to looke about h*ym*, yf alreadie he bee not adu*er*tised.[71]

---

[69] Angel Valbuena Prat, *Historia de la Literatura Española*, 8th ed. (Barcelona: Gili, 1974), 597–98 ; cf. Gareth A. Davies, *A Poet at Court: Antonio Hurtado de Mendoza (1586–1644)* (Oxford: Dolphin, 1971), 87–94; and *La corte de Felipe II*, ed. José Martinez Millán (Madrid : Alianza Editorial, 1994).

[70] Cf. Miguel Bordonau, "La libreria y los libros de Coro del Real Monasterio de San Lorenzo del Escorial", *Bibliotecas y Museos* 71 (1963): 243–73.

[71] PRO, SP85/5, no. 28.

Even allowing for the English edginess about Catholic conspiracy, this is remarkably specific information. We cannot be certain, of course, that the Montgomerie believed to be a Catholic agent was Alexander; but it is likely enough in the circumstances. Wyer is a mysterious figure: he may perhaps be the same as a Captain Wijaert who was commanding a troop of a hundred lancers in February 1585, and who was either the same person as or was succeeded as captain by Alexander Wishart. Wishart, certainly, is stated in 1586 to have "servi longues années durant sous le commandement deson Altesse de prince d'Orange", and to have distinguished himself at the battle of the Couwensteinschedijk, outside Antwerp, in May 1585.[72] A confusion between "Wijaert/Wyer" and "Wishart" is certainly possible, but in any case nothing is known of Wishart's activities at this early period.

The suggestion of sympathy for Don John of Austria, the Spanish commander in the Netherlands, "for the Scottishe Queenes sake" is, in its political context, a highly pointed remark, for there had been persistent rumours of a projected marriage between them, perhaps supported by the Duke of Guise. The idea was not new: Mary commented that it had been mentioned to her "from divers places" as early as 8 February 1571, noting her belief that Philip II would welcome such a development, but both then and intermittently thereafter she indicated that she was not interested in such a match.[73] She informed her ambassador in Paris, James Beaton, the exiled Archbishop of Glasgow, on 20 January 1577 that the English were concerned about her (imaginary, she insisted) dealings with Don John, and she was right: four days later Wilson, who was then still in the Netherlands, expressed his fears that negotiations were taking place, and the same theme (though without the Guise twist) was explored at some length by the Prince of Orange in his instructions to Famars of 10 February.[74] Rumblings about the supposed scheme continue to occur in Wilson's despatches until his replacement by Davison at the beginning of August; on 25 April, indeed, in an audience with Don John himself, Wilson had challenged the Spanish governor with the rumours, receiving a spirited denial in which the latter had, in the ambassador's paraphrase, insisted that

> I woulde not have any bodie to be thus abused, nor to thynke me so voyde of judgement. For, although I bee yonge, yet I have some experience of the worlde, and hope to make my bargayne better than so.[75]

---

[72] On Wijaert/Wishart, see F.J.G. Ten Raa and F. de Bas, *Het Staatsche Leger 1568–1795*, 8 vols. (Breda: Koninklijke Militaire Academie, 1911–1921, cont. The Hague: Nijhoff, 1940–1964), 1:105, 201; cf. Ferguson, *Scots Brigade*, 1:48.

[73] *Lettres de Marie Stuart*, ed . Labanoff, 3:185 ; cf. 4:201–2 (4 August 1574), 378 (22 August 1577).

[74] Kervyn de Letterhove, *Relations politiques*, 9:158–60, 185–91.

[75] Kervyn de Letterhove, *Relations politiques*, 9:281–82.

Wilson, however, was not convinced, and a passing reference in a letter written by Philip II to Don John earlier in April indicates that his scepticism was justified.[76] A week later, Wilson was trying extraordinary measures to implicate Queen Mary and her alleged suitor, reporting to Walsingham that

> I am aboute a practise to get a Skot into Englande, eaven with letters from Don Jhon to the Scottishe Queene. I praye God this devise maye take place. Colonel Bafour hath promysed to worke this feate by one Henry Kesone, an old servante of the Scottishe Queene and one in favour with Don Jhon.[77]

There is no indication in the surviving records whether Wilson accomplished his project, which was in any event soon overtaken by a new source of concern: a proposed conference in Valenciennes, news of which reached the ambassador at the beginning of June, involving Don John, the Queen of Navarre, the Duke of Guise, other prominent French Catholics, and James Beaton. The latter, Wilson complained, "euir carieth myschief aboute hym and without fayle wil deale for his mystresse"; there was no doubt in his mind that the one purpose of the proposed meeting was "lainge a plotte for a mariage . . . yow know with whom".[78] Don John was indeed attempting in early June to set up such a meeting, having learned that the Queen of Navarre was intending to come to Spa, but she evidently abandoned the project and he wrote to Philip on 13 July to inform him that the meeting had not taken place.[79] But the situation was in any case deteriorating as the summer passed, with clear signs of a build up of the Spanish forces. When Davison arrived in the Netherlands at the beginning of August, he brought news of a request by Elizabeth to the Regent Morton that the Scottish forces which had returned home should be sent back again; not until November, in fact, were there positive reports of the arrival of Scots troops in Flanders, and by then the military position had taken a definite turn for the worse. Once the conflict resumed, Cecil placed the prospect of a marriage between Mary and Don John high on his list of arguments for an English intervention.

---

[76] *Correspondence de Philippe II*, ed. Gachard, 5:283.

[77] Kervyn de Letterhove, *Relations politiques*, 9:288. The identity of the proposed agent is mysterious: no Henry Kesson is recorded among Mary's adherents, but the name might conceivably be a pseudonym of Henry Keir, who was certainly "an old servante of the Scottishe Queene" and whose whereabouts in the mid- and late 1570s are largely unknown. He was later a friend of Montgomerie's, an associate of the dukes of Lennox, and an active proponent of the Guise cause. It is quite possible that he was here operating under a *nom de guerre*, and that he was playing some part as a double agent.

[78] Kervyn de Letterhove, *Relations politiques*, 9:328–33.

[79] *Correspondence de Philippe II*, ed. Gachard, 5:456.

There was, certainly, a good deal of evidence of a Scottish presence on the Spanish side. Towards the end of 1576, during the negotiations for a truce which were taking place at Marche-en-Famenne between Don John and the States, the English ambassador to the Spanish side, Edward Horsey, reported that "Hammelton . . . that slewe the Regent of Scotland" had been seen arriving.[80] This was James Hamilton of Bothwellhaugh, who had assassinated the Earl of Moray on 21 January 1570, had been proscribed in July 1572, and is named in a full list of traitors living abroad on 12 February 1574.[81] He and his brother David had been forfeited for supporting Mary in 1568, while another brother, John, sometime provost of Bothwell, was included along with John in the extensive lists of Hamiltons who were outlawed at the end of the civil war. John, who had supposedly conformed to Protestantism before his presentation to the vicarage of Bothwell in 1568, had almost immediately left the country; he was actively involved in Marian diplomacy on the Continent thereafter, and had fairly recently been joined in the Netherlands by James, who had in 1577 reportedly rejected a proposal that he should assassinate Admiral Coligny.

James had evidently been imprisoned in Brussels, but had escaped (apparently with help from Balfour and other Scots) and established himself in Don John's household, much to the concern of the English observers. Wilson wrote to Cecil on 14 January 1577 that Hamilton "hath receaued monye of hym to persuade the Scottes to revolte", and when Escovedo, the secretary of Philip II, was challenged about a supposed promise not to deal with Hamilton and his brother he replied that they were "creatos and pensionaries to the Kynge", and that they had received the written support of Mary.[82] By this time, however, one of the Hamiltons had apparently been seized by the States forces, along with a Spaniard named Dr. del Rio, and was sent to William of Orange, who imprisoned them both: Don John reported as much to Philip II on 2 February, and a similar account was given by Escovedo three weeks later.[83] They were evidently released soon afterwards, and apparently made their way to Spain, for on 15 September Davison noted that the Hamilton brothers and another Scot, Captain Jamie Shaw, had

---

[80] For the circumstances of the assassination of the Regent Moray, see Maurice Lee Jr, *James Stewart, Earl of Moray* (New York: Columbia University Press, 1953), 273–75; cf. *RPC*, 2:155, 334.

[81] *APS*, 3:47–54, 125–37 (the latter documents relate to the continuation of the proscription in the 1579 parliament); *RSS*, 6, no. 445.

[82] Kervyn de Letterhove, *Relations politiques*, 9 :144, 220. There is certainly a good deal of evidence in the Spanish archives of financial support for the Hamiltons from 1577 onwards (e.g. AGS, *CMC 2a época*, *legajo* 44, accounts of the *pagador* Martin de Unceta, 1577–1579; *Estado* 577, fol. 145, etc.).

[83] *Correspondence de Philippe II*, ed. Gachard, 5:178–9.

"come post out of Spayne to Namure . . . whose cominge, as I here, did bring His Alteze verie good contentment".[84] According to the English informant Edward Woodshaw, their arrival was part of a larger build up among the allies of the Spanish; writing from Brussels on 6 October, he noted that

> I knowe very well that dyvars of Her Majestis enemis do travell and come in post and otharwais, some throwe France, othars throwe Borgonia and Savoye, as well out of Spaine as from Rome douslye, both Spaniardes and Skotts, as for prinsipalst the ij. Brothers the Hameltons.[85]

Nor was this all: on 24 August 1577, as English anxiety about Spanish policy was growing, Davison reported to Walsingham that Lord Seton was in Mechelen, "bound, as he saith, towardes the Spaa for his health":

> The humour of the man may bewray some other cause of his transportation hither. For my self I know him so well as I cannot but deepely suspect him.[86]

As a former ambassador in Edinburgh, Davison knew the Scottish political situation well, and he had had ample opportunity to assess Seton's sympathy for the Catholic cause. His alarm grew when he discovered that Seton, who was in Liège early in September, was accompanied by David Clerk, "a trusty servante of the Scottish Quene and one that hath a yerly pension of 7 or 800 crownes (as I learne) out of her dowry in France"; and the suspicion that their true destination was Don John's household in Namur rather than Spa — it was, Davison noted, "unseasonable" for taking the waters — had been confirmed by 19 September, when he wrote to Leicester that Seton "I doubte not, hathe dayly intelligence with Don John".[87] No overt allegations are made, but Davison's language in these despatches indicates that he suspected an attempt to arrange a diversionary attack from Scotland, in order to prevent Elizabeth from committing her forces in the Netherlands; but it is also possible that subversion of the Scottish contingent there was at least part of Don John's reason for cultivating his Scottish sympathisers.

Such is the background, then, to Wilson's suspicions of 25 January 1578, that Montgomerie and Wyer were Spanish worms in the apple of Balfour's regiment. Before the message could reach Balfour through Davison and the Prince of Orange, however, and only four days after Wilson's letter was written, the Scots companies were badly mauled in the defeat of the States' forces at Gembloux: first reports suggested, wrongly as it turned out, that Balfour himself had been

---

[84] Kervyn de Letterhove, *Relations politiques*, 9:517.

[85] Kervyn de Letterhove, *Relations politiques*, 9:565–66.

[86] Kervyn de Letterhove, *Relations politiques*, 9:481.

[87] Kervyn de Letterhove, *Relations politiques*, 9:508, 517.

killed.[88] The Scots took heavy losses, and many of those who were not killed were captured by the Spanish, the survivors who escaped being posted in the days immediately after the battle either to Brussels, under Balfour's command, or to Mechelen. The prisoners were taken to Namur, where the Hispanophile Hamilton would again play a part in events. Davison wrote on 2 March that

> Th'elder Hamulton, who was lately taken and brought prisoner to Brussells, is, at the earnest labour of Balfour, released under pretext of redeming certein of his souldiers taken at the overthrow of the States, of whome diuers being at their first coming to Namure drowned, the rest taking oth never to serve against the King in this quarrell, are released and returned home into their country by way of France.[89]

Since the Captain Montgomerie who was believed by Wilson to be among Balfour's commanders does not appear in the Dutch records after Gembloux, it is more likely that he was among those who were captured and persuaded to depart than that he was one of the dozen or so Scottish captains who continued to operate in Flanders.[90] If this is a correct inference, then the detail about the returning forces passing through France is revealing; for there are good reasons for supposing that the poet did not reach Scotland until the end of 1579, at least eighteen months later, and that he arrived then in a context which suggests a French connection.

There was, certainly, a significant community of Scottish Catholic emigrés in Paris in the later 1570s. James Beaton, archbishop of Glasgow, had been there since the Reformation, and served as Mary's resident ambassador at the French court; more recently he had been joined by John Leslie, bishop of Ross, who had been forced to leave London in early 1575 after a period of imprisonment on charges of conspiracy in the Catholic interest. The nature and extent of the Scottish community which gathered round them has not yet been fully explored; but there are enough hints to suggest that it was well-connected. Mary's letters to Beaton often contain messages or references to her supporters in Paris, some of them, like Lord Seton and Lord Ogilvie, birds of passage, others clearly more established residents. The latter included George Douglas, Thomas Ker of Ferniehurst, Alexander Erskine, Master of Mar, Patrick Hepburn of Wauchton, and, by late 1579, Mary's former secretary Henry Keir, who was reported by the English agent Nicholas

---

[88] *CSP For. 1577–78*, 482–88.

[89] Kervyn de Letterhove, *Relations politiques*, 10:303.

[90] There is, of course, another possibility: that the Montgomerie in question was not the poet, and that he was killed in the battle itself or in its aftermath. Alternatively, the reference *could* be to Alexander's brother-in-law Adam of Braidstane, who was licensed to take a company to the Netherlands on 22 October 1577 (*RPC*, 2:730).

Errington to be living in the Paris residence of Esmé Stuart, sieur d'Aubigny.[91] Keir would serve both Esmé Stuart and his son Ludovick over the next quarter of a century, and he would have a leading part in the former's involvement in the Scottish court in the early 1580s, strongly supporting the Guisite project to win the young James VI over to Catholicism. Montgomerie would eventually number him among his closest friends, associating him with the English poet, convert, and Catholic activist Henry Constable in a moving testimony to the bonds between them.[92]

By the time he returned to Scotland, Alexander Montgomerie was ready to stake a successful claim to become a privileged member of the young king's immediate circle. The poet we shall now find plying his craft as "maister poete" is a skilled exponent of the musical lyric, the sonnet, and of such fashionable French forms as the *mascarade*; he is a translator and adapter of Clement Marot and (by 1582 at the latest) of Ronsard, a rhetorician capable of making sophisticated use of Ovid and Du Bellay, and — if not in the period of his greatest ascendancy, between 1580 and 1586, then later in his career — an experimenter with a poetic language which challenges and at times goes beyond the conventions of the Petrarchist forms which had dominated court poetry in France and elsewhere during the previous couple of generations. Shadowy as our present knowledge of his earlier years may be, it is surely probable that his travels on the Continent in the 1570s served Montgomerie as an apprenticeship for the role he would now assume.

It is, certainly, French poetry which most clearly suffuses Montgomerie's courtly verse, not only in those few cases in which we can identify a specific source, but in the forms and images he employs, the multiple public voices he adopts, the sheer technical virtuosity he so frequently displays. By the later 1570s, while the reputation of the ageing Ronsard remained very high, new voices had begun to emerge in France, fostered by the literary *salons* of the maréchale de Retz and the marquise de Villeroy.[93] Philippe Desportes, whose elaborate Mannerism would soon find Scots expression in the work of John Stewart of Baldynneis, had published his *Premieres Œuvres* in 1573; the earliest poems by Salluste du Bartas, James VI's favourite foreign poet, appeared the following year; and more minor figures like Amadis Jamyn and Nicolas Rapin equally enjoyed a certain currency in this fertile literary climate. Their "Neopetrarchist" poetry developed and in some respects radically revised the poetics of the *Pléiade*, and we shall find in due course that there are significant parallels between their predominant preoccupations and topoi and those employed by Montgomerie. Henry III himself was a notable patron of

---

[91] *CSP Scot.*, 5:356.

[92] See below, 177–80.

[93] See L. Clark Keating, *Studies on the Literary Salon in France, 1550–1615* (Cambridge, MA: Harvard University Press, 1941).

the arts, and much of the poetry of the decade engaged with the affairs and en-
tertainments of a court which contrasted sharply with the sobriety Montgomerie
would have encountered in Madrid and El Escorial.[94] We find as well, as we have
already noted, traces in the French poetry of this period of stylistic stirrings even
more radical than those which were yet apparent in Spain; in the work of poets as
different as Jodelle and Du Bartas we can detect the development of a new sensi-
bility, which would soon reach its full expression in Baroque art.

There was, moreover, a continuing awareness in France of the historic associ-
ation with Scotland: the Duke of Guise, Mary's first cousin, took an active inter-
est in Scottish affairs, and seems to have encouraged Esmé Stuart in his decision
to try his fortune at the Scottish court, while Ronsard himself, who had movingly
lamented the departure of the recently-widowed Mary in 1561, dedicated to her
one section of the 1578 edition of his *Œuvres*:

> Encores que la mer de bien loin nous separe,
> Si est-ce que l'esclair de vostre beau Soleil,
> De vostre œil qui n'a point aumonde de pareil,
> Jamais loin de mon cœur par letemps ne s'esgare.
> Royne, qui enfermez une Royne si rare,
> Adoucissez vostre ire, & changez de conseil :
> Le Soleil se levant & allant en sommeil
> Ne voit point en la terre un acte si barbare.
> Peuple, vous forlignez (auz armes nonchalant)
> De voy ayeux Renault, Lancelot & Rolant,
> Qui prenoient d'un grand cœur pour les Dames querelle,
> Les gardoient, les sauvoient où vous n'avez, François,
> Ny osé regarder ny toucher le harnois
> Pour oster de servage une Royne si belle.

[Although the sea puts a great distance between us, the light of your lovely
sun, your eye which has no equal in this world, never at any time strays far
from my heart.

Queen, who confines such a precious Queen, soften your anger and
change your mind: the sun rising and going to bed does not wish such a
barbarous action in this world.

People, sluggish in arms, you have declined from your predecessors,
Renaud, Lancelot and Roland, who always responded to the ladies' cause,
protected them and saved them, where you, O French, have not dared to

---

[94] On the tone of the French court at this period, see I.D. McFarlane, *A Literary
History of France: Renaissance France, 1470–1589* (London and New York: Macmillan,
1974), 364–423.

look at or touch military trappings to rescue such a beautiful Queen from servitude.][95]

The call to arms would, of course, go unanswered; far from being "aux armes nonchalant", Frenchmen on both sides of the great religious divide were too preoccupied with a murderous succession of civil wars to take up the cause of their former Queen, now absent from their kingdom for nearly twenty years. But Ronsard's sonnet testifies to more than an old man's sentimentality over the beautiful pupil of his youth; as long as she lived, Mary would provide a focus for those who desired a return to a Catholic Scotland and would perhaps generate a perilous ambivalence in some of those who, like Alexander Montgomerie, would find service with her son.

The patchy and admittedly conjectural account of Montgomerie's life before 1580 that we have been able to build up cannot do more than hint at the experiences which may have contributed to the formation of his art. If Duff is to be given any credence, we can be sure that the poet was brought up a Protestant and converted to Catholicism, probably in Spain. It is likely enough that his Spanish journey was in some way connected with a period of service in the Netherlands (for which we have both his own testimony and that of Patrick Hume of Polwarth), and that it brought out in him a dedication to the Marian cause which seems to have made him an object of English suspicion in early 1578. And it is entirely credible, given his subsequent association with the Lennox faction and with Henry Keir, that it was from Paris that he returned to Scotland towards the end of 1579. By that time, surely, he knew the work of Marot, Du Bellay, and Ronsard, and no doubt of other French poets. To what degree, if any, his literary experience also included the poetry of Spain and/or the Netherlands we can scarcely say; there is no direct evidence to support such a conjecture. But the poetry we shall be investigating in the following chapters demonstrates quite clearly that Alexander Montgomerie responded to the same literary forces that were motivating his contemporaries from Seville to Antwerp, making him a characteristically *European* poet of the closing decades of the sixteenth century.

---

[95] Ronsard, *Œuvres complètes*, ed. Laumonier, 17:378–79.

# Chapter Three

## "The Prince of Poets in our Land": Montgomerie at Court, 1580–1586

Esmé Stuart, sieur d'Aubigny, landed at Leith on 8 September 1579, accompanied, according to one contemporary account, by a household of twenty.[1] The arrival of this *ménage* caused a considerable stir: there was information that the purposes of the expedition were subversive, and the ministers of Edinburgh were alerted to the danger. English agents reported to their government that Aubigny and his servants were coming to draw the young king towards Catholicism, acting as agents of the Duke of Guise and the exiled Archbishop of Glasgow.[2] James himself was still at Stirling in early September, and it was there that he greeted his French cousin a few days after the latter's arrival in Scotland.

The timing of these events was of great significance. James was now beginning to assume personal authority over his kingdom, and on the point of taking up residence in his capital, Edinburgh. This was managed as one of the great rites of passage of the Renaissance kingdom: on 29–30 September he rode in great state from Stirling to Linlithgow and thence to Holyrood, greeted along the way by the burgesses of nearby towns and accompanied by a strong representation of the great families of southern Scotland.[3] After just over a fortnight's residence at Holyrood (during which time he imposed his authority by obliging the Edinburgh council to elect his nominee as Provost), James made his ceremonial entry into the burgh, to be met with *tableaux vivants* and other spectacles:

> [The West Port] presented to him the wisdome of Salomon deciding the plea between the two weomen who contended for the young childe, and the servant that presented the sword to the king, with the childe. After he had entered in at the port, Mr John Scharpe made an harang in Latine . . . At the old port of the Strait Bow hang a glorious globe, which opened artificially as the king came by, wherin was a young boy presenting the keys of the toun to his Majestie, all made of massive silver, and were presentlie receaved by one of the Lords of the Secreit Counsell. The musicians song the xx. Psalme,

---

[1] Moysie, *Memoirs*, 24.

[2] Bowes-Lyon Muniments (NRAS 885/9, no. 40) (14 September 1579); Bowes Corr., 16–17 (22 October 1579); *CSP Scot.*, 5:436–37 (23 May 1580).

[3] Calderwood, *History*, 3:457–58; Moysie, *Memoirs*, 25.

and others played upon the viols. When he came down to the Old Tolbuith, the fore-face wherof was covered with painted dailes, there he saw the crafts' standards and pinsells sett, and foure faire young maides representing the foure cardinall vertues, Justice, Temperance, Fortitude, and Prudence, or, as others report, Peace, Justice, Plentie, and Policie. Everie one of them had an oration to the king. The wheele of Fortune was burnt with powder. When he came doun over against the Great Kirk, Dame Religion desired his presence; so he lighted at the ladeis steppes, and went in to the Great Kirk. Mr James Lowsone made an exhortation upon Psalme II, ver.10, and exhorted the king and the subjects to doe their duetie, to enter in league and covenant with God, and concluded with thanksgiving. After sermon was sung the xx. Psalme. When he came to the Croce, there Bacchus satt on a puncheon, with his painted garment, and a flowre garland. He welcomed the king to his owne toun, and drank manie glasses, and cast them among the people. There were there runne three puncheons of wine. At the Salt Trone was described the genealogie of the Kings of Scotland: a number of trumpets sounded melodiouslie, and crying with a loude voice, "Weele fare to the king!" At the Neather Bow were represented the conjunction of the planets, as it was in the time of his nativitie, and Ptolomaeus describing his beautie and fortunes bestowed upon him by the influence of the starres.[4]

The six scenes described by Calderwood are not fortuitous: taken together, they establish a discourse of kingship, and of the relationship between the king and his capital city, which is as lucid as any of the great civic welcomes we find elsewhere in sixteenth-century Europe.[5] The Judgement of Solomon, of course, is a traditional vehicle for the embodiment of the royal virtues of wisdom and justice; there is no hint in Calderwood's or other contemporary accounts that the contending women were allegorised (as Kirk and Papacy, for example), and we may therefore perhaps assume that the scene was not given any topical signification. But the political message of the day was doubtless clear enough: even without the text of Sharp's "harang", the speeches of the Cardinal Virtues — which may, we should note, have had a more political twist — or Lawson's sermon, we can see that the conventional exhortation to rule justly and wisely was given a strong

---

[4] Calderwood, *History*, 3:458–9. Calderwood's account is largely based on that in *The Historie of King James the Sext*, generally ascribed to John Colvill, 178–79; cf. Moysie, *Memoirs*, 25.

[5] On the place of this event in the sixteenth-century Scottish tradition of royal welcome, see Douglas Gray, "The Royal Entry in Sixteenth-Century Scotland", in *The Rose and the Thistle: Essays on the Culture of Late Medieval and Renaissance Scotland*, ed. Sally Mapstone and Juliette Wood (East Linton: Tuckwell, 1998), 10–37, here 28–29; and Michael Lynch, "Court Ceremony and Ritual during the Personal Reign of James VI", in *Reign of James VI*, 71–92.

colouring of godliness. It was no doubt with great care that Lawson chose as his text Psalm 2:10 ("Be wise now therefore, o ye kings; be instructed, ye judges of the earth"); and the message was reinforced by the repeated singing of Psalm 20, "*Domine, in virtute tua lætabitur rex*" (which James himself would later translate as "The king, o Lord, reioysis in thy strenth"). Astrology and the traditional genealogical recital from the enthronement ceremony of the Scottish kings;[6] images of just kingship and of Bacchanalian plenty were brought together to embody an idealised version of James's relationship with his people.

The great entry of 17 October was an act of public ceremonial, in some ways a surrogate for the coronation which had taken place in the king's infancy, at a time of crisis, twelve years before. Other occasions derived their significance less from the enactment of the king's official function, and more from his role as the emerging prince, the source of patronage and a focus for an idealised representation of the court as the seat of civilised behaviour. It would appear that Alexander Montgomerie marked his arrival at court, whenever that occurred, with such a contribution to its entertainment, in the form of a *mascarade* and associated *cartel* of the kinds which were then well established at the court of the French kings.[7] The date of *The Navigatioun* [53], and of the *Cartel of the Thre Ventrous Knichts* [54] which appears to be linked with it, is uncertain: they are by common critical assent assigned to 1579, but there is no real evidence to associate them with the public ceremonial of September and October.[8] As I have recently pointed out,

---

[6] See R.J. Lyall, "The Medieval Scottish Coronation Service: Some Seventeenth-Century Evidence", *Innes Review* 28 (1977): 3–21.

[7] On the place of such entertainments at the court of Henry III, see Margaret M. McGowan, *L'Art du Ballet de Cour (1581–1643)* (Paris: Éditions du CNRS, 1963), 29–47; and, more generally, Pierre Champion, *Paris au Temps de Henri III* (Paris: Éditions C.-L., 1942), 106–26; and Frances A. Yates, *The French Academies of the Sixteenth Century* (London: Warburg Institute, 1947), 60–62, 236–74. The genre of the *mascarade*, which developed out of the Italian *mascherate* in the mid-sixteenth century, awaits full-scale investigation. There is a striking parallel to Montgomerie's text in Gascoigne's *Devise of a maske for Viscount Mountacute*, first published in *A Hundreth Sundrie Flowres* in 1573; here a twelve-year-old boy gives an account of his travels in the Mediterranean by way of introducing a group of eight "Venetians". According to the explanatory introduction, the costumes were made when Gascoigne was asked to invent a masque "convenient to render a good cause of the Venetians presence"! (*Hundreth Sundrie Flowres*, 382). The *cartel*, as Parkinson notes, was a fashionable French term for a dramatised prologue to chivalric feats of arms; for examples by Desportes (first published in 1573), see his *Cartels et Masquarades, Épitaphes*, ed. Victor E. Graham (Geneva: Droz, 1958), 34–39.

[8] For the claim that "'The Navigatioun' obviously belongs to the celebrations of 1579, either . . . in September or . . . in October", see Shire, *Song, Dance and Poetry*, 84; this view is essentially followed by Jack, *Montgomerie*, 17.

however, there are indications in the Treasurer's Accounts of a masque during the Christmas celebrations in 1579–1580: the household payments in late December included a total of £83 Scots "to his hienes violeris to be certane mask claithis", consisting of substantial lengths of red and yellow taffeta, smaller quantities of "touke of silver" and buckram, and six pairs of fencing swords and daggers.[9] The king certainly kept Christmas at Holyrood, the likely venue for Montgomerie's *mascarade*; and this would surely have been an appropriate occasion for an entertainment in which "the Turk, the More, and the Egyptien" — three men, at least, if not kings or magi, from the East — arrive to "do reverence" to the young king of Scots.[10] It may be, indeed, that the daringly hyperbolic Nativity allusion had a more specific occasion, and that the masque took place at the feast of the Epiphany, the traditional Twelfth Night of Christmas. If this hypothesis is correct it marks a significant conjunction, for "his hienes violeris" were the Hudson brothers, English musicians who first appeared at the Scottish court as early as 1565 and whose later careers would continue to intersect with that of Montgomerie — not always with happy results.[11] Mild, if inconclusive, textual support for a date in winter rather than autumn is offered by the narrator himself, who describes the final part of his supposedly recent voyage along the English coast:

> The vhilk to vs appeird very fair
> Thoght notwithstanding all wes ind and bair          *brought in*
> Yet fertill baith for bestiall and Corne             *livestock*
> Houbeit or than that all wes win and shorne          *before; bare*
>     (53: 242–245)

It is, then, not unlikely that the performance for which *The Navigatioun* was written took place at Christmas, and very possibly on 5 January 1580.

It is instructive to contrast Montgomerie's techniques of poetic ingratiation with those employed by his first major literary rival at James's court, Patrick Hume of Polwarth.[12] When James first took part in the courtly exercise of hunting, on 12 June 1579, the event seemed important enough as a token of the young king's

---

[9] *Treasurer Accts*, 13:301. The reference to six sets of weapons is particularly striking, in view of the tournament envisaged in *The Thre Ventrous Knichts*.

[10] The association of the three visitors with the Magi is made, without any reference to the dating issue, by Jack, *Montgomerie*, 21–22. For a possible later date for the poem (1581 or early 1582), see Lynch, "Court Ceremony and Ritual", 81.

[11] On the careers of Thomas, Robert, William, and James Hudson, see Shire, *Song, Dance and Poetry*, 71–75.

[12] The best account of Polwarth's life is that by Sally Mapstone, "Invective as Poetic: The Cultural Contexts of Polwarth and Montgomerie's *Flyting*", *SLJ* 26/2 (Winter 1999): 18–40, here 26–28.

progress towards adult rule for Polwarth, a favoured member of the household, to compose — and publish — a celebratory poem which incidentally provides the critical benchmark for the literary developments of the next five years. By contrast with the moral lyrics of Sir Richard Maitland of Lethington and the propagandist broadsides of Robert Sempill and others, the predominant poetic voices of the previous decade, *The Promine* is an elaborately courtly piece, more reminiscent of John Rolland's *Court of Venus* (published in 1575 but written before the Reformation) than of anything produced since Mary's abdication. In a real sense, Polwarth's poem marks not only a rather trivial occasion in the life of the court, but the reconstitution of the court itself as a cultural force after twelve years of regency.

*The Promine* is in many ways a curiously empty work, for all the density of its rhetorical display. In its tripartite structure, reminiscent of Lindsay's episodic poems, it makes explicit its author's pursuit of patronage:

> Schir, reid thairfoir, and mak me to rejois;       *rejoice*
> I hecht your Hienes, helping Goddis grace,       *promise*
> That I sall pen sum poetrie or prois            *prose*
> Mair profitabill, gif I get time and space . . .
>     ("Epistill", 25–28)[13]

"Time and space", of course, are money; and for Polwarth *The Promine* was evidently intended to negotiate the king's pecuniary support. It is relentless in its demonstration of Polwarth's poetic skill, in its celebration of James's prudence, wit and magnificence, and in its defiance of any critics and rivals:

> My bony bill, of barbour language brevit,       *composed*
> Gif thow be evill, thow will be wors reprevit    *criticised*
> Be witles, vaine, envyous ignorantis,
> Quhilk to speik evill, and do na gude thame hantis.   *are accustomed*
>     ("Envoy", 1–4)

Part of the function of these opening and closing sections, no doubt, is to demonstrate the range of styles at Polwarth's command, as well as to entertain the adolescent king with a carefully-modulated blend of mild flyting and rather less mild flattery. But it is courtier verse at its most determined: if, as Gary Waller suggests, poetry was "one of the means by which the courtier gained access to the monarch",[14] then here we find an unusually overt example of that process assuming a public

---

[13] *The Promine*, in Alexander Hume, *Poems*, ed. Alexander Lawson (STS, Edinburgh, 1902), 201; all quotations are from this edition.
[14] Gary Waller, *English Poetry of the Sixteenth Century* (London: Arnold, 1986), 17.

face. Polwarth worries away at the problem of poetic acceptance, anticipating
criticism and defying any detractors by suggesting (half-seriously, perhaps) that
to condemn his praise of the king is not merely to reveal lack of critical judge-
ment but in effect to commit a treasonable act:

> For sum will say thy febill eloquence
> Is evill cullourit, but intelligence;
> Sum will say this, sum utheris will say that,
> And pairt will speik in deid, and wait not quhat.    *know*
> Syne sum seditious craftie knaifis inding              *unworthy*
> Will say, perhaps, thow dois bot fleiche the King.    *flatter*
> ("Envoy", 7–12)

For the stylistic models for his central "Promine", Polwarth undoubtedly
looked back to Dunbar, Lindsay, and Scott. In his insistent use of alliteration,
Latinate poetic diction, complex syntax, and rhetorical figures like *anaphora* and
*amplificatio*, he establishes that he has fully absorbed their high-style manner;
what he largely fails to do is to turn these techniques to any larger purpose than
ingratiation. The essence of the poem's descriptive strategy is a form of pathetic
fallacy, by means of which the whole landscape and all its occupants are shown
celebrating the king's arrival among them. The individual features of this land-
scape are familiar enough, distinguished only by the degree of elaboration Pol-
warth lavishes upon them; three stanzas, for example, are devoted to the reverence
done to James by "fair Phebus, or utherwayis the Sone" (an explanation which no
doubt sets out to be educational and succeeds only in being bathetic). Such ex-
tended displays of rhetorical ingenuity conventionally serve, of course, to intro-
duce the allegorical action; here, by contrast, we find not the gods and goddesses
of *The Goldyn Targe* or *The Thrissill and the Rois*, but the figure of the king, moving
in a landscape which brings to its sub-allegorical space the kitschy excessiveness
of Walt Disney:

> Into the park did properlie appeir,
> Richt trimlie trottand into trowpis and twais,    *troops and pairs*
> The wilde quhite collourit ky and falow deir,      *cattle*
> With brawland bowkis, bendand ovir the brais,    *bucks*
> The flingand fownis, followand dune dais;          *leaping fauns; dun does*
> Sa curage causit beistis mak besines,
> His Majestie muifand to merines.                        *moving*
> ("Promine", 99–105)

There may well be a conscious connection between Polwarth's *Promine* and the
hunting poems fashionable in France, such as Amadis Jamyn's *Poeme de la Chasse*
(?1575), dedicated to Charles IX:

Si tost que le soleil de rayons attourné
A sur nostre horizons a clairté ramené
En ces beaux jours d'este : l'autre Soleil de France
S'eveille, et de son lict legerement s'élance,
S'habille, ceint l'espee, et tresdevotieux
Invoque a deuz genoux le Monarque de cieux . . .

[As soon as the sun, with his directed beams, has brought his clarity back to
our horizon in these beautiful summer days, France's other sun wakes, leaps
lightly from his bed, dresses, puts on his sword, and, kneeling, devoutly
prays to the Monarch of heaven . . .][15]

But Jamyn uses the opening description in a high classical style merely as an
introduction to a technical description of the hunt itself, while Polwarth stops
short after the king's arrival in the landscape and its welcome to him. He has,
moreover, assimilated the French genre to Scots descriptive convention: the evo-
cation of the scene is full of echoes of Dunbar such as "purpour springis aureat"
and "The ground ovirgiltand all with goldin glemis".

The topoi of natural description exploited by Dunbar in *The Goldyn Targe* are
in part remarkable for the degree to which they present the landscape in language
as stylised, formal, and ornate as the illustrations in a Book of Hours, an association
reinforced by the repeated metaphors (echoed by Polwarth here) of illumination and
gilding.[16] But Polwarth carries the fusion of nature and art a stage further:

| | |
|---|---|
| Than fair dame Flora glaiding gardings gay | *delighting* |
| Syilit with schaddow of the blumand bewis | *sealed; boughs* |
| Hir minglit mantill meiklie did display, | |
| Richt curiouslie ovirclethand all the clewis | *ravines* |
| With flouris of ane hundreth hevinlie hewis, | |
| Quhair besilie the bummand honie beis | *humming* |
| Tuik nurischement on Natures tapestreis. | |
| ("Promine", 78–84) | |

For Dunbar, the features of a natural landscape are materials to be woven into
a rich poetic fabric; Polwarth carries that process into the landscape itself, collapsing

---

[15] Amadis Jamyn, *Les œuvres poétiques*, ed. Samuel L. Carrington, 2 vols. (Geneva:
Droz, 1973–1978), 1:297.

[16] For an analysis of the development of Older Scots "aureate" style by Dunbar and
Gavin Douglas around the turn of the sixteenth century, see R.J. Lyall, "The Stylistic Re-
lationship between Dunbar and Douglas", in *William Dunbar: The 'Nobill Poyet'*, ed. Sally
Mapstone (East Linton: Tuckwell Press, 2001), 69–84.

the distinction between reality and its artistic imitation. The effect is achieved incidentally, as part of an entire process of hyperbolic images; but the blurring of the boundary between art and nature reveals that triumph of form over content which can properly be termed Mannerism.[17]

There are profound differences between the poetic stance of Polwarth in his *Promine* and Montgomerie's in *The Navigatioun*. There is no lack of flattering intent in the latter: from the opening invocation to the hyperbolic praise of the physical marvels of James's kingdom towards the end of the poem, Montgomerie does not miss an opportunity to pay court to the king, his genealogy and prospects, or the occasion. But whereas Polwarth's hyperbole is single-mindedly directed towards his royal subject, Montgomerie shrewdly works his flattery into a more complex and less obvious rhetorical strategy. Much of *The Navigatioun*, for example, consists of a barely-concealed geography lesson, a ploy perhaps borrowed from *The Dreme* of Sir David Lindsay, whose *Warkis* had been republished by Henry Charteris in 1568 and were doubtless known to both James and Montgomerie.[18] There is a quality of intimacy in the address of *The Navigatioun*, despite its ostensible formality, which is reminiscent of that adopted by Lindsay in his early poems for James V, and quite different from the statuesque rhetorical posturing of Polwarth.

This effect occurs even at the end of the formal opening passage, where Montgomerie begins by turning the traditional heraldic metaphor into a much more political allegory, soon to be given a more memorable expression by Shakespeare:[19]

| Haill bravest burgeoun brekking to the Rose, | *bud* |
| The deu of grace thy leivis mot vnclose, | *may* |
| The stalk of treuth mot grant the nurishing, | |
| The air of faith support thy florishing. | |
| Thy noble Counsell lyk trees about thy grace | |
| Mot plantit be, ilk ane into his place | |
| Quhais ruiting sure and toppis reaching he | *high* |
| Mot brek the storme befor it come to the. | |
| They of thy bluid mot grou about thy bordour | |

---

[17] The relation is, however, a complex one: as James V. Mirollo suggests (*Mannerism and Renaissance Poetry*, 70), "the mannerist work . . . may *seem* to move wholly within an aesthetic world and apparently is determined to remain faithful to the norm or model; however, its way of defending or justifying both is to prove the paradoxical point that, when totally absorbed in art, one discovers that he is not roaming freely in an attractively autonomous realm but traveling along a path that opens onto nature again".

[18] Sir David Lindsay, *Warkis* ([Edinburgh]: John Scot for Henry Charteris, 1568); there were three further editions in 1569, 1571, and 1574.

[19] Shakespeare, *Richard II*, 3.4.29–66, ed. Andrew Gurr (Cambridge: Cambridge University Press, 1984), 134–35.

> To hold the hedge into ane perfyt ordour
> As fragrant flouris of ane helthsome smell
> All venemous beistis from the to expell.
> The preachers treu mot ay thy Gardners be
> To clense thy root from weeds of heresie.
> Thy garden wall mak the neu Testament
> So sall thou grou without impediment.
> All lands about sall feir thy Excellence
> And come fra far to do thee reverence
> As I myself and all the rest ye se
> From Turkie, Egypt and from Arabie.
>     (53:1–20)

The deictic final comment, drawing attention to the three "guisers" in Eastern costume that it is apparently the speaker's function to introduce, brings in a homely and immediate note; but it is not the first change of tone accomplished by Montgomerie in this passage. The first line echoes, as clearly as Polwarth does but with much greater brevity, the heraldic tradition of Dunbar's *Thrissill and the Rois* and Alexander Scott's *New Yeir Gift* to James's mother soon after her return from France in 1561, where skilful reference is made to Mary's descent from the houses of Stewart, Tudor and Guise:

> Welcum, our lion with the fleur-de-lyce!
> Welcum, our thristill with the lorraine grein!    *laurel*
> Welcum, our rubent rose upon the ryce![20]    *red; branch*

But Montgomerie immediately turns his floral metaphor away from genealogical heraldry towards an *allegoria* which is carefully poised between political commonplace and the correct signals for the occasion. Whatever the private views of the poet and his associates might have been, this was clearly not a time to provoke trouble, and Montgomerie's language is either tactfully non-committal — "the stalk of truth" avoids suggesting *whose* truth; there is naturally no hint of the possible identity of any "venemous beistis" — or positively favourable to a Protestant interpretation. Thus, sandwiched between references to "preachers treu" and the New Testament, "weeds of heresie" surely implies Catholic doctrine rather than its opposite.

The subtle modulations of tone and evasions of doctrine in this opening reflect the fundamental difference of purpose — and perhaps of occasion — between *The Promine* and *The Navigatioun*. Polwarth's poem is located in a Never-Never-Land of allegorical convention; Montgomerie leads his audience from a Constantinople which is exotic but undoubtedly real to a Scotland which could scarcely be more immediate:

---

[20] Scott, *Poems*, ed. Cranstoun, 1.

Then we come sailing to the Porte of Leith.
To come right in we thoght it very eith                    *easy*
For other shippis ather sax or sevin
Had come befor ws thair in to the hevin.                   *harbour*
Becaus that we wer nevir thair afore
We tuke the Ludging nerest to the shore.
I haif bene far bot yit in all my lyfe
I neuer saw a mirrier hartsum wyfe.                        *cheerful*
"Be blyth," quod sho, "for ye sall se our King,
God blisse his Grace and mak him long to ring."           *reign*
Because she saw that it wes groune lait
Sho gart hir boyis come with vs all the gait              *caused; way*
Quho broght vs heir vnto your highnes yett                *gate*
Quharas the Court with torches all wes sett
To shau the way vnto your graces hall
That eftir supper we might sie the ball.
My fellouis comes nou. I mon mak auay.                    *must*
God blisse your Grace, I haif no more to say.
     (262–279)

The structure of these closing lines is no doubt determined by their dramatic context, leading neatly into the masque which is to follow. But while Montgomerie manages even here to introduce a further element of flattery, using his hostess to demonstrate the goodwill of the king's subjects, this note is lightly stressed, subordinated to the practical detail of the voyagers' arrival.

It may be, as we noted above, that the rhetoric of ingratiation is embedded in the very occasion itself, with James in the role of the infant Christ. But Montgomerie has other strategies as well with which to cultivate the king's favour. Thus, he interrupts his educational travelogue of the Mediterranean to "report" a conversation among the travellers when they reach Portugal, alluding to the traditional account of the origin of the Scots. Appropriately enough, it is the Egyptian who recalls that, according to this mythic narrative, Scota, the progenitrix of the Scots, was the daughter of Pharaoh, while the Turk (appropriating Turkish-occupied Greece) proudly adds that her husband, Gathelos, was a Greek. The point, of course, is that the travellers rival one another in claiming "Your grace wes cumming of thair Ancient blude" (211); and as the expedition proceeds from Portugal to Ireland, retracing the route of the Scots' ancestors, the debate continues.[21] This easy conversion

---

[21] On the origins and development of the Gathelus-Scota myth, see William Matthews, "The Egyptians in Scotland: The Political History of a Myth", *Viator* 1 (1970): 289–306; Marjorie Drexler, "Fluid Prejudice: Scottish Origin Myths in the Later Middle Ages", in *People, Politics and Community in the Later Middle Ages*, ed. Joel Rosenthal and Colin Richmond (Gloucester and New York: Sutton, 1987), 60–77; R. James Goldstein, *The*

of a political myth to the purposes of courtly discourse is typical of Montgomerie's methods: in the same way, a few lines later, he makes his companions respond to the sight of the White Cliffs of Dover by debating James's possible claim to the English throne, concluding that "Syndrie wes sibbe [*related*] bot ay your grace wes nar" (227–230). By such devices Montgomerie contrives to pander to the king's vanities without abandoning his narrative structure or the urbane, familiar idiom of his address, and to introduce potentially delicate subjects like the English succession (Mary, after all, was one of the rival contenders, still sequestered in an English prison) without sacrificing the lightness of tone appropriate to the occasion.

As we have already seen, the modulation of style and tone is one of the hallmarks of Montgomerie's poem, clear evidence that *The Navigatioun* is no apprentice work. There are, it is true, occasional passages of overt eulogy, but Montgomerie (unlike Polwarth) is careful to contain them, and to moderate them through the mediating voices of his "companions":

> "We shaip to saill neir the Septentrion          *intend; northern regions*
> Touards the North and helthsome regione
> Nou callit Scotland, as we haif hard report
> Of wandring fame vhilk fleeth ay athort          *abroad*
> Quhair presently beginneth for to ring
> So sapient a ying and godly King,          *young*
> A Salomon for right and judgement.
> In eviry langage he is Eloquent.
> All lands about do beir of him record.
> He is the chosen vessell of the Lord."
>      (73–82)

The minor rhetorical climax of this passage in the description of James in traditional Biblical language, echoing the political assertions of the royal entry into Edinburgh as well as its compliment to James's multilingualism, is effective precisely because it is placed in the foreground, marked by the contrast with the more down-to-earth narrative which precedes and follows it. The longest uninterrupted passages, indeed, are devoted to detailed accounts of the journey across the Mediterranean, full of geographical lore and vivid evocations of life on board ship:

> Vp uent our saillis tauntit to the huins.          *hoisted to the masthead*
> The Trumpets soundit tuentie mirrie tuins.
> Vp went our boyis to the Toppis abone

---

*Matter of Scotland: Historical Narrative in Medieval Scotland* (Lincoln, NE and London: University of Nebraska Press, 1993), 104–32; and Roger A. Mason, "Scotching the Brut: Politics, History and National Myth in 16th-Century Britain", in *Scotland and England 1286–1815*, ed. Roger A. Mason (Edinburgh: John Donald, 1987), 60–84.

And ou'r the bordour shook our Topsaill soon.
Some went before for to shaik out the blind.                    *spritsail*
Wp went our bonnets, our Missens vp behind.                    *extra pieces of sail*
Some to the gueit fattis for to bedeu the saillis.             *water casks; moisten*
Bothe foir and eft our Taikle drauis and haillis.
Our bottisman our geir perfytlie neits.                        *tidies*
Fair wes the wind and roum betuene tua sheits.
Maisters and Pilots cunning in that Arte
Went to the Compas for to prik the carte                       *chart*
For to persaiv the dangers vhair they lay.
We Passingers went to the chesse to play
For in that Airt we no thing vnderstude
Thairfor we did thame nather ill nor good.
    (95–110)

Despite this final plea of ignorance, Montgomerie is at pains here to display the richness of his maritime vocabulary.[22] It would be dangerous to draw too firm a conclusion about his actual experience of seafaring from this evidence, however, for the account falls within another well-established literary tradition. Here, for example, is part of a much longer passage in *The Complaynt of Scotland* (1550):

> And the maistir quhislit and cryit: "Tua men abufe to the foir ra, cut the raibandis and lat the foir sail fal; hail doune the steir burde lufe harde a burde; hail eftir the foir sail sheit, hail out the bollene!" Than the maistir quhislit ande cryit: "Tua men abufe to the main ra, cut the raibandis, and lat the mane sail and top sail fal; hail doune the lufe close aburde, hail eftir the mane sail scheit; hail out the main sail boulene!" Than ane of the marynalis began to hail and to cry, and al the marynalis ansuert of the samyn sound: "Hou, hou! Pulpela, pulpela! Boulena, boulena . . ."[23]

There are poetic parallels, too, for nautical terminology was also favoured by the poets of the Pléiade, though never perhaps in such relentless concentration as in Montgomerie's poem. Shorter catalogues occur, for example, in Ronsard's ode *A André Thevet* (1560), in Baïf's *Allegorie à Monsieur Brethe* (1573), and in Belleau's *Bergerie*:

> Puis ils viennent aux mains et à coups de canon
> Ils resrobe le mats, la poupe et le fanon,
> Raze voiles et bancs, bancades et antene,
> Apostis, et fougons iusques à la Carene . . .

---

[22] For an explanation of some of these terms, see David Parkinson, "Montgomerie's Language", in *Bryght Lanternis: Essays on the Language and Literature of Medieval and Renaissance Scotland*, ed. J. Derrick McClure and Michael R.G. Spiller (Aberdeen: Aberdeen University Press, 1989), 352–63, here 358–59.

[23] *The Complaynt of Scotland*, ed. A.M. Stewart (Edinburgh: STS, 1979), 32.

[Then they take the work in hand, and with cannon shots they strip the masts, the poop and the flags, remove sails and seats, benches and lateen-yard, rowlocks and the galley, down to the hull . . .][24]

In developing this line, then, Montgomerie was achieving a double purpose, ex-hibiting both his seafaring knowledge *and* his awareness of current literary fashion (and, no doubt, of Acts 27).

*The Navigatioun* is a fine rhetorical achievement, carefully pitched to impress the king without overwhelming him, to flatter him without seeming to do so, to comment in passing on serious issues of state without losing the essential lightness of touch which was required by the poem's festive occasion. Its levity is quietly pointed; its learning is lightly worn. By comparison, *The Cartell of the Thre Ventrous Knichts* is merely functional: its purpose is to introduce the jousting, and it does so without fuss or unnecessary rhetorical showmanship. *Syncope* is, indeed, an ex-plicit part of its strategy, as the speaker casts a passing glance at the nearly three hundred lines of *The Navigatioun* in his declaration that "we come not to that end / To wery you and wast the day in Verse" (54:14–15). The function of the *cartel* in French courtly practice was to introduce the joust, and Montgomerie's title is therefore thoroughly appropriate for the challenge which the three "errant Knichts" lay down. *The Navigatioun*, on the other hand, clearly makes its pitch for Montgomerie as court poet, and its subtlety contrasts strongly with the much more overt ingratiation of Polwarth's *Promine*.

The rivalry of the two poets would quickly become explicit, and the subject of court entertainment. Although the precise date of their *Flyting* [99] is uncertain, there is every reason to suppose that it followed on fairly quickly from *The Navi-gatioun*, and that it was connected in some way with Montgomerie's establish-ment as "maister poete". That, at any event, is how Montgomerie chose to present himself, and if Sally Mapstone is right to remind us that there is no real evidence to support Helena Shire's view that Polwarth was the resident court poet until Montgomerie ousted him by winning the poetic duel of the *Flyting*, it is neverthe-less true that James himself subsequently refers to the latter as his "maister poete", that Montgomerie is one of those who contributes liminary verses to the king's first published volume, and that Polwarth is at no point visible as a poet after the composition of the *Flyting*.[25] As well as the problem of dating, the textual situa-tion is slightly puzzling. There are, in essence, three versions of the sequence: that which survives in the printed tradition (the earliest extant edition is that printed by Andrew Hart in 1621, although it is possible that there were earlier editions which

---

[24] Rémy Belleau, *Œuvres poétiques*, ed. Charles Marty-Laveaux, 2 vols. (Paris: A. Lemerre, 1878), 2 :72.

[25] Mapstone, "Invective as Poetic", 20–21; for Shire's highly speculative reconstruc-tion of the episode, see *Song, Dance and Poetry*, 80.

are now lost); that preserved in the Tullibardine manuscript (Huntington Library MS. HM 105), supposedly owned by, and perhaps written for, Sir William Murray of Tullibardine, who died on 15 March 1583; and the version copied by John Rutherford (BL MS. Harley 7578), which largely agrees with the prints but which omits one stanza which they and Tullibardine include.[26] Rather than presenting the exchanges between the two poets in the order in which they seem to have been composed, the scribe of the Tullibardine MS. chose to copy Montgomerie's contributions first (fols. 2r–7r), followed by those of Polwarth (fols. 7r–15r). The effect of this, of course, is to place Montgomerie's work in the foreground, and to suggest that the elements of the *Flyting* function more as independent texts than as contributions to a shared, if competitive, exercise.

The witnesses differ in two other major structural respects: Tullibardine omits Montgomerie's opening contribution as the prints and Harley 7578 have it, but includes two stanzas in his long final poem (99.II: 66–91) and a stanza in one of Polwarth's pieces (IX: 73–80) which are not found in the printed version or in Rutherford's manuscript. As Mapstone observes, this evidence is somewhat contradictory, and it *may* perhaps suggest that one or both of the authors went on tinkering with the text for some time after the main flyting took place. It is difficult to determine what significance should be accorded to the manuscript's omission of Montgomerie's first piece; in Mapstone's words,

> this could simply have got lost from the MS's exemplar, or it could indicate that the MS. is an early copy of a work to which Montgomerie's first salvo was retrospectively added.[27]

There is, however, some indication that the former is the more likely, since both Tullibardine and the prints agree in making Polwarth's first contribution express his pleasure that Montgomerie has now "begun *in wreit* to flyt" [my italics], clearly suggesting that Polwarth had seen a written text. If this was not the poem omitted by Tullibardine, then the *Flyting* must once have had another opening, now lost. It seems more straightforward to assume that the prints reflect the original state of the text in this respect. The omission by the printed versions and Rutherford of II: 66–91 is in some respects more ambiguous. If the lines were included in the original version and omitted from Tullibardine or its exemplar, then this

---

[26] On the textual situation, and especially the position of the Tullibardine MS., see *Poems*, ed. Parkinson, 2:6–9, and Mapstone, "Invective as Poetic", 21–29; Mapstone concludes that "the 1621 printed edition would appear to derive from an exemplar containing elements of both the textual traditions that the Tullibardine and Harleian MSS. separately represent" (24).

[27] Mapstone, "Invective as Poetic", 23.

decision might be either authorial (and evidence of subsequent revision) or scribal; if they constitute an *addition* in the Tullibardine version, on the other hand, then since there is no reason to suppose that they are not Montgomerie's, they confirm that some degree of revision must have taken place. Since they are merely an extension of the catalogue of diseases which forms an important structural element of this poem, both views are equally credible: Montgomerie (or a scribe or printer) may have decided that the passage was too long, or the poet might have wished to prolong the joke.[28] The Polwarth stanza unique to Tullibardine is perhaps a more straightforward case. It is certainly obscure and fragmentary: the scribe omitted part of the first line, and it may be that Hart (or his exemplar, whether manuscript or print) chose to exclude a passage which was simply in the "too difficult" category.

These additional stanzas are not, in fact, the only evidence of significant differences between the principal witnesses. As Parkinson observes, hardly a line fails to provide a variant of greater or lesser moment, and there are numerous cases where whole lines, or several successive lines, are rewritten. Many of these variants are of the kind we would expect when comparing a Scottish manuscript of the 1580s with a text printed a generation later: there is a good deal of anglicisation in the work of Hart and his successors, combined with the elimination of "difficult" readings and of the more obviously obscene terms. This leaves, however, many points of difference which demand another explanation, and in at least some of these cases authorial revision seems a real possibility. Several good examples of this can be found in the Montgomerie poem in which Tullibardine provides the two additional stanzas, such as:

| | |
|---|---|
| "Vntrowit be thy tounge yit tratling all tymes, | *discredited; prattling* |
| Ay fals be thy fingeris bot laith to confes, | |
| All cuntreis quhair thow cwmes accuse the of crymes, | *comes* |
| Ay the langer that thow live thy luk be the les, | *luck* |
| Yit still be thow reivand bot rude of thy rymes . . ." | *raving* |
| (99:II: 118–122) | |

"Outrow'd be thy tongue, yet tratling all times.
Ay the langer that thou liues, thy lucke be the lesse.
All countries where thou comes accuse thee of crimes,
And false be thy fingers, bot leath to confesse,
Ay raving and rageing in rude rat rymes . . ."[29]

---

[28] Parkinson prefers the former explanation: "their omission . . . may be seen as scribal-editorial pruning of perceived excess" (*Poems*, 2:134).

[29] *The Flyting beuixt Montgomery and Polwart* (Edinburgh: Andrew Hart, 1621), 83r.

Even within this passage the evidence seems contradictory: the juxtaposition of tongue and fingers in Tullibardine is less immediate in Hart because of the inversion of the first and third lines, but on the other hand the printed version of the fifth line is more strongly alliterative. There are, in fact, many points at which Hart's version of a line accentuates the alliteration, although there are a few cases in which the reverse is true.[30] We certainly cannot rule out, therefore, Mapstone's suggestion that Tullibardine and the prints represent different states of a text which underwent some level of authorial revision over time; it is noteworthy, then, that the degree of variation is significantly greater in Montgomerie's parts of the *Flyting* than in Polwarth's.

Whatever the subsequent history of the text, it seems clear that the *Flyting* preserves the record of a series of poetic exchanges which originally took place over a fairly limited period of time. Just when that time was has been the subject of some debate: James's citation of part of the text of II in his "Reulis and Cautelis" suggests that it must have been before the autumn of 1584. From the assumption that Tullibardine was originally owned by Sir William Murray of Tullibardine, Stevenson concluded that "in all probability . . . this poetic encounter between Polwart and Montgomerie is to be dated from the year 1582";[31] Mapstone is less certain of this, however, and suggests that the manuscript *may* date from later in the 1580s.[32] Her research indicates pretty strongly that the sonnet which occurs on the first folio of the manuscript, which she tentatively attributes to Montgomerie himself, refers to both Sir William Murray and his wife Agnes Graham, but it does not necessarily follow from this that the volume was compiled during Sir William's lifetime.[33] Dating the Tullibardine manuscript, of course, can only provide us with a *terminus ad quem* for the *Flyting*, not a *terminus a quo*, so it offers

---

[30] A more radical form of inversion occurs at II: 209–234, where the order of two stanzas is reversed between the main witnesses; this case is complicated by Rutherford's omission of the second of these stanzas as printed by Hart. The most likely explanation of the latter fact is eye-skip (see *Poems*, ed. Stevenson, 162).

[31] *Poems*, ed. Stevenson, xxviii.

[32] Part of this argument hinges on the dating of the paper, but Parkinson rightly implies (*Poems*, 2:7) that the fact that the Pot watermark is closest to Briquet 12804, only occurring in a document of 1588 (*Les Filigranes*, no. 12804), does not necessarily mean that the paper on which Tullibardine was written could not have been produced earlier in the decade. In fact, there is evidence that this mark *was* in use at least a year earlier (N.P. Likhachev, *La signification paléographique des filigranes* [St Petersburg: V.C. Balaschiev, 1899], no. 4126); and the pot with the initials "PO" — probably referring to the papermaker Pierre Ollivier at Pont-Authou (*Les Filigranes*, 1:*34, *70) — is only one of a series of such marks in use from 1549 until the 1590s. It certainly cannot be invoked in support of a date for the manuscript later than 1583.

[33] Mapstone, "Invective as Poetic", 23–26.

little help with the fundamental problem. It does, on the other hand, seem unlikely that the exchange between the two rival poets could have taken place between 23 August 1582, when the king was seized by a Protestant faction led by William Ruthven, earl of Gowrie, and 7 July 1583, when he escaped from his captors. A date after this latter event is possible, but the most probable period for the *Flyting* to have taken place remains that between January 1580 and August 1582, shortly after Montgomerie's arrival in Edinburgh. And while it may be true that the court context is more complex than Montgomerie's later pleasure at the thought "Hou I chaist Polwart from the chimney nook" (72.III: 14) seems to suggest, it neverthe-less appears that the former's poetic fortunes flourished in the wake of, and perhaps as a consequence of, his literary battle with his rival. As a means of achieving po-etic pre-eminence at court, the *Flyting* is a mirror-image of *The Promine* and *The Navigatioun*: dispraise in place of panegyric, demolition of a rival substituted for flattery of a prospective patron.

Although there are analogous traditions of abusive writing in classical, medi-eval and Renaissance literature, the formal flyting or poetic duel seems clearly to have been a distinctively Scottish genre, its nearest analogues such Provençal forms as the *sirventes, tenso,* and *partimen.*[34] The earliest surviving example — and the only other complete one — is that between William Dunbar and Walter Ken-nedy, produced around 1500; it may be that Dunbar, like Montgomerie, used the occasion to establish his poetic credentials at court.[35] Not only is the contest it-self essentially Scottish, but the verse-forms employed, particularly by Sir David Lindsay in his exchange with James V and by Montgomerie and Polwarth, are markedly Scots as well, making heavy use of alliteration as a structural device. As has been noted by Bawcutt and Jack, poetic skill is itself an issue in the flyting form: the verse must demonstrate through its virtuosity its creator's superiority over his rival. *The Flyting betwixt Montgomery and Polwart* is in this sense the ul-timate achievement in the genre, for their command of form is much greater than that manifested by Dunbar and Kennedy nearly a century before.

This preoccupation with form is, as we shall see, one of the hallmarks of James's "Castalian" Renaissance, and is certainly not confined to flyting. The in-sistent use of internal rhyme initiated by Montgomerie and eventually capped by Polwarth has Scottish precedents, but it was also fashionable in contemporary

---

[34] S. Thiolier-Méjean, *Les poésies satiriques et morales des troubadours du XIIe à la fin du XIIIe siècle* (Paris : Nizet, 1978) ; M. Shapiro, "Tenson et partimen : la tenson fictive", in *Actes du 14ᵉ congrès internationale de linguistique et philologie romanes* (Naples: Macchiaroli / Amsterdam: Benjamins, 1981), 5:287–301.

[35] The date of Dunbar and Kennedy's flyting is uncertain, but it can scarcely be later than 1505; see Priscilla Bawcutt, *Dunbar the Makar* (Oxford: Clarendon Press, 1992), 225. Dunbar was granted a pension by James IV on 15 August 1500 (*RSS*, 1, no. 563).

French verse; here again we find, therefore, native and Continental practices coming together in Montgomerie's early work. The *style* of his opening onslaught on Polwarth is, however, unequivocally Scots:

> Beware what thou speiks, little foule earth Tade,          *toad*
> With thy Cannigate breiks, beware what thou speiks
> Or there salbe wat cheiks for the last that thou made,
> Beware what thou speiks, little foule earth Tade.
>          (99a: 5–8)

Although this appears to be the opening shot of the campaign, "the poetic equivalent of throwing down the gauntlet",[36] there is a clear suggestion in the reference to "the last that thou made" that Montgomerie has taken offence at something written by Polwarth. As always in dealing with flyting, we are immediately confronted by the problem of game and earnest: the contenders are taking part in a formalised and supposedly light-hearted entertainment, and yet their rhetoric often seems calculated to break through the opponent's defences and cause real pain. As with many modern sports, the boundary between rivalry and animosity is not a simple one, and the complexity of motivation is no doubt in direct proportion to the size of the stakes. We can hardly doubt that Montgomerie and Polwarth were, to some degree at any rate, "playing for keeps".

The dominant language and imagery employed by both poets is the traditional material of flyting: each associates his opponent with animals, with disease, with crime, violence and punishment, with sex and miscegenation, with filth and excrement, with the Satanic and the occult. But running through all this is the issue of poetic competence. Polwarth starts this line, rather rashly challenging Montgomerie's poetic skill:

> Thy raggit roundallis, reifand royt,                    *irregular; thieving fiddler*
> Sum schort, sum lang and out of lyne
> With skabrous collouris, fowsome floyt,                *metres; disgusting flautist*
> Proceiding from ane pynt of wyne
> Quhilk haultis for fault of feit lyk myne              *limp*
> Yit, fuuill, thow thocht na schame to wreit thame     *fool*
> At menis command that laik ingyne                     *wit*
> Quhilkis, doytit dyvouris, gart the dyt thame.
>          (99.III: 9–16)

There is a little evidence in Montgomerie's later work that the charge of alcoholic inspiration may not be altogether without foundation; but the suggestion

---

[36] Jack, *Montgomerie*, 28.

that he was not in control of the formal requirements of his verse could scarcely have been more inappropriately hurled at any poet. Montgomerie is quick to return the charge, referring contemptuously to Polwarth's "meitter mismaid" (99. I: 23).

Such dismissals of one another's writing were the flyters' stock-in-trade, but there is greater force, perhaps, in Montgomerie's accusation that

> Thy scrowis obscuir ar borrowit fra sum buik.     *scrolls*
> Fra Lyndsay thow tuik, thow art Chawceris cuik.
>     (99.I: 44–45)

Polwarth's debt to his Scots predecessors is, it is true, much greater than that of the more innovative Montgomerie, and the coupling of this jibe with the latter's declaration that "I sall debar the the kingis kitching nuik" (47) — which is, after all, as a symbol of domestic intimacy, the ultimate prize — suggests that beneath the surface of the rivalry there are conflicting views of poetry itself. It is, then, no accident that Polwarth criticises Montgomerie for his digressions and proverbial language:

> Thy pikkillit puir paremeonis but skill,     *proverbs*
> Pykit from Irisch Italianis, ar to blame,     *filched*
> Beggit from poetis brokingis for to blame.     *dishonest dealings*
> For laik of language I wat weill thow dois it . . .
>     (99.IX: 75–78)

The reference here is fairly obscure (obscure enough, as we have seen, for all versions of the *Flyting* except the Tullibardine MS. to omit this stanza), but if, as Stevenson suggests, "Irisch" is used in its generic sense of "contemptible", then the accusation may well be that Montgomerie draws excessively from foreign, and specifically Italian, verse.[37] It may not be literally true; but to the extent that Montgomerie is much more open to Continental influence than Polwarth, and that through him a more contemporary version of international culture enters the Scottish court, the jibe reflects a genuine, and decisive, cultural conflict.[38]

As Priscilla Bawcutt observes, "500 or so lines of name-calling would be extremely tedious",[39] and both poets demonstrate their poetic command by varying the rhetorical postures they adopt. This is clearest in Montgomerie's "Secund Invective" (99.II), a foray into burlesque narrative in the alliterative stanza, perhaps echoing the tale of *The Gyre-Carling* which may have been written by Sir

---

[37] *Poems*, ed. Stevenson, 353.

[38] Cf. Mapstone, "Invective as Poetic", 29–34.

[39] Bawcutt, "Art of Flyting", 17.

David Lindsay for James V.[40] It is in this section of the *Flyting*, moreover, that we are most aware of the true audience, the king whose favour the rival poets are pursuing. Montgomerie's attack stems from Polwarth's two preceding pieces, which deal with his opponent's "just genologie" (99.IV: 49) and with his supposed medical problems respectively. The result is a splendidly scabrous pseudo-narrative, as imaginative in its deployment of negative rhetoric as *The Navigatioun* is in its turning of indirect compliment. The account of Polwarth's conception, between an elf and an ape "on ane Alhallow evin", is a mere handle on which to hang an exuberant catalogue of diseases and symptoms, totalling well over a hundred, conferred on the unfortunate Polwarth by "the wirdsisteris" (99.II: 27):

> The frenesie, the fluikis, the fykis and the felt,
> The feveris, the totteris with the Spenyie fleis,
> The doyt and the dysmell indifferentlie delt,
> The pelodie, the plasie, the poikis lyk peis,
> The neising, the snytting with swaming to swelt,
> The wandevill, the wildfyre, the womeit, the weis,
> The mair, the migrum, the mureill, the melt,
> The warbillis, the wood worme that doggis of deid,
>    The phtiseik, the twithyaik, the tittis and the tirrillis,
>      The panefull poplasie, the pest,
>      The rottin roup, the auld rest,
>      With paines and parlasie opprest
>       And nippit with the nirrilis . . .
>      (53–65)[41]

The emphasis here shifts from the attack on Polwarth to the sheer copiousness of the list, an exhibition of alliterative virtuosity which demonstrates Montgomerie's rhetorical skill without actually detracting very much from his opponent.

In the wider context of the poem, however, there *is* a destructive subtext: the cursing of Polwarth, of which the list of ailments he is to suffer from forms part, both elevates his birth, in true flyting style, into a catastrophic event, and provides an "explanation" of his character in a passage we have already noted in another context:

> Vntrowit be thy tounge yit tratling all tymes,
> Ay fals be thy fingeris bot laith to confes,

---

[40] *The Bannatyne Manuscript*, ed. W. Tod Ritchie, 4 vols. (Edinburgh: STS, 1928–1934), 3:13–14; Lindsay himself recalls having told James stories of (among others) "the reid Etin, and the gyre carling" (*Dreme*, 45): *Works*, ed. Hamer, 1:5.

[41] For a gloss of this catalogue, see *Poems*, ed. Parkinson, 2:133–34.

> All cuntreis quhair thow cwmes accuse the of crymes,
> Ay the langer that thow live thy luk be the les . . .
>     (118–121)

The accusation of dishonesty is, of course, one of the standard ploys of the flyter, and Montgomerie is doing no more than return with interest the abusive charges levelled at him by Polwarth. But the deftness of his approach lies in the way in which these stock devices are integrated into the framing narrative, varying the rhetorical pattern of the exchange and "distancing" the abuse by putting it into the mouths of the Fates.

With his description of Polwarth's diabolical birth Montgomerie brings to a close his contribution to the *Flyting*. Polwarth, on the other hand, is far from finished, and he responds with a multiple outburst in which the nine line stanza of Gavin Douglas's *Palice of Honoure* is followed by a return to the alliterative stanza employed by Montgomerie, which is succeeded in turn by a burst of ballade stanzas. By this time, it would appear, his opponent's success with the king was beginning to irk Polwarth, if such an inference can properly be drawn from his allusion to the king's fireplace as a locus of privileged intimacy:

> Thy sentences of swit richt sweitlie smellis,          *soot*
> Thow sa neir the chymlay nuik that maid thame,
> Seik be the ingle amangis the oister schellis,          *fireplace*
> Dreidand my danger durst not weill debait thame.
>     (99.VIII: 13–16)

But Montgomerie had, indeed, won the day, and for all Polwarth's abusive virtuosity, nowhere more effectively displayed than in "Pollart Guid Nicht", the intricately-rhymed torrent of invective with which he concludes the contest, the latter seems to have been displaced. Apart from a single allusion in James's "Admonition to the maister poete" we hear no more of his poetic ambitions, and although he lived until 1609 he appears to have played no part in the subsequent development of the king's literary circle.[42]

Montgomerie's interests during this period were, evidently, not confined to poetry and court entertainment, and within a year of his return to Scotland he became involved in an enterprise which later caused him some difficulty, and which has led scholars to jump to some over-hasty conclusions. On 2 December 1580,

---

[42] This assumption has recently been challenged by Sally Mapstone ("Invective as Poetic", 21), who observes that the absence of poetic texts ascribed to Polwarth does not necessarily mean that he did not continue writing. As she concedes, however, there is no concrete evidence to support this conjecture.

with two other Scots, named Richard Ramsay and Andrew Martin, he bought for £300 sterling a barque called the "James Bonaventor of Southampton", the property of a merchant of that city, one Henry Giles. We know about this only because, nearly four years later, Giles was in Scotland pursuing the purchase-price, which seems never to have been paid; he was suitably armed, moreover, with "lettres of our admiraltie of Ingland, purchest or raisit" against the three debtors. On 12 October 1584, Giles and Montgomerie appear to have reached an agreement, for on that date the former, "for certane gratitudis and guid deidis done, and sovmes of money realie ressauit be me in novmerit money", discharged Montgomerie from his part of the debt, reserving the right to pursue Ramsay and Martin. This acquittance was registered by Giles, appearing personally before the Lords of Council, on 3 November; something evidently went wrong with the arrangement, however, for on 8 December Montgomerie had to sign a further document declaring himself content

> that the said allegeit acquittance and discharge be null and of nane availl in the selff, and the samin to haiff na strenth, force, nor effect, nather in jugment nor outwith in ony tyme cuming,

and acknowledging that Giles might properly pursue his debt before any judge as freely as if the revoked discharge had never been made. This renunciation was in turn registered by Montgomerie in person, on 30 December 1584.[43] There is no evidence that Giles ever received his money, but the case now disappears from the records.

A great deal has been read between the lines of these two legal transactions. Stevenson was the first to see papistry here, suspecting "from what is known of Montgomerie's career at a later date, that his dealings with Henrie Gelis were connected with political, and if so, pretty certainly with Catholic, intrigue."[44] Shire went further, claiming that

> [t]he legal records suggest that the acquiring of the vessel was connected with the Jesuit plan of that year for the overthrow of Protestantism both in Scotland and in England and the restoration to the throne of Mary, Queen of Scots.[45]

As Jack points out, however, there is nothing in the legal documents to support this conjecture; they speak merely of a commercial arrangement between an English merchant and three Scots, and the involvement of the English Admiralty by Giles

---

[43] The documents are printed by Stevenson, *Poems*, 302–5.
[44] *Poems*, ed. Stevenson, 265.
[45] Shire, *Song, Dance and Poetry*, 85.

makes the existence of a plot less rather than more likely, despite Shire's dark hints to the contrary.[46] Nor is there any inclination, as Shire supposed, that the sale in December 1580 was concluded in England; there is certainly no evidence in the Southampton port books for 1580–1581 of the *James Bonaventure*'s presence there at any time during the year.[47]

There is no doubt that there was a plan at this time for the Jesuit mission to England to be extended into Scotland, and that Philip II of Spain had his own schemes to invade first Ireland and then, through Scotland, England.[48] Robert Parsons and Edmund Campion had been in England since June 1580, but their brief was purely to concern themselves with the conversion of souls. Gradually, it would seem, their purposes, and especially those of Parsons, became more directly political, and closer to the larger objectives of the Spanish. But it was not until the middle of 1581 that Parsons sent his first missionary, the Welshman William Watts, into Scotland, following him up with the Scot William Holt in the course of the autumn. At about the same time, however, there would seem to have been another priest at work, an emissary from six unnamed Catholic lords in England to the Duke of Lennox, indicating that the English Catholics would suppport James's claim to the English throne should he convert to Catholicism.[49] Since this initiative did not take place until September 1581, however, and since Mendoza, the Spanish ambassador in London, specifically reported that he was "conveyed secretly across the border", it does not seem that it could in any way have been connected with the purchase of a ship by Montgomerie and his associates the previous December.

Henry Giles is a fairly well-documented figure in late sixteenth-century Southampton. He became a burgess of the town in 1577, two years after marrying Temperance Evans, whose grandfather was a Welsh butcher who settled there. It seems probable that Giles, too, was an immigrant.[50] The same year that he became a burgess, he was in trouble with the authorities, having apparently negotiated with "a pilot in a Scotche shippe" over the irregular purchase of "certane barrells of fyshe". On 15 February Giles denied having received the fish; the following day he told a rather different story, admitting to having received fifteen barrels.[51] He continues to occur at intervals in the Southampton records, but it has not been

---

[46] Jack, *Montgomerie*, 5; cf. Shire, *Song, Dance and Poetry*, 105.

[47] PRO, E190/815/9–11.

[48] For a detailed and carefully argued account of this episode, see T.G. Law, "English Jesuits and Scottish Intrigues, 1581–82", in *Collected Essays and Reviews*, 217–43.

[49] *CSP Span*, 3:171–72.

[50] Personal communication from Dr. T.B. James.

[51] *Books of Examinations and Depositions, 1570–1594*, ed. G.H. Hamilton and E.R. Aubrey (Southampton: Southampton Record Society, 1914), 28–30.

possible to locate any reference to him as a shipowner, or to the mysterious *James Bonaventure*.

It is more difficult to trace Montgomerie's partners in the enterprise, Andrew Martin and Richard Ramsay. An Andrew Martin, burgess of Crail, appears fairly frequently, often in cases of affray or other matters of dispute, in the last quarter of the century, and he might be regarded as a promising candidate.[52] Another individual of the same name, who held lands in Ingliston, on the other hand, is associated with Robert Montgomerie of Skelmorlie on 19 September 1589, and the family connection here might be significant.[53] Neither of these men can be shown to have engaged in either foreign trade or religious intrigue; but as a burgess of Crail the former can presumably be assumed to have taken part in mercantile activity. Richard Ramsay certainly *does* seem to have been something of a lawless spirit: in a list of claims against Scottish subjects, compiled in December 1587, he is stated to have despoiled Henry Giles of £500 on 4 July 1582, and Giles claims to have been made destitute pursuing his case.[54] It is striking to find Ramsay's name again linked with that of Giles in this way, but there is no hint that the two cases were directly related, and the sums at stake are different. This Richard can perhaps be identified with the son of Cuthbert Ramsay, burgess of Edinburgh, who occurs in February 1584;[55] if so, he, like Andrew Martin, had a background which suggests that, on balance, it is more likely that Montgomerie and his partners were engaged in some trading enterprise than that they were involved in a Jesuit plot. Given the extreme nervousness of the English government and the efficiency of its espionage network, it is improbable that such a political scheme should have left no trace in the surviving state papers, which are full of references during the Lennox ascendancy to the Catholic sympathies of those closest to the Scottish king. Whatever the deal was about, however, it seems to have gone sour, and the reality of Giles's pursuit of the three Scots through the courts is clear enough.[56]

Meanwhile, evidently, Montgomerie was pursuing his career at court. Following his flyting with Polwarth, he clearly formed part of the young king's familiar circle, which was dominated until August 1582 by Lennox and his supporters. The

---

[52] *RMS 1580–93*, no. 1197; *RPC*, 2:461; 3:616; 4:342, 351, 355, 418.

[53] *RPC*, 4:416.

[54] *CSP Scot.*, 9:516.

[55] *RSS*, 8, no. 1824.

[56] An interesting, and hitherto unnoticed, sequel to Giles's Scottish activities occurs in October 1585, in the midst of the crisis which led to the fall of Arran: a list of the "French faction" in Scotland, dated 30 October and preserved in the State Papers, is subscribed "This notte geven by Hareye Giles of Sirhanton" (*CSP Scot.*, 8:138–39). Giles *was*, then, involved in espionage, at least in a peripheral way, but it does not follow that this also applied to his business relations with Montgomerie.

nature of the poet's relationship with Lennox is, to some degree, a matter of conjecture; but we can find a revealing — if elusive — trace of his involvement with the court and its intrigues in the short sonnet-sequence entitled "A Ladyis Lamentatione" [75]. This dramatic piece is unique in the Montgomerie corpus, since it is written in the voice of a clearly-defined persona who is a disgraced noblewoman:

> For I wes matchit with my match and mair,
> No worldly woman neuir wes so weill.
> I wes accountit Countes but compare
> Quhill fickle fortun vhirld me from hir vheel . . .     *until*
>     (I: 9–12)

Three times she associates herself with Cresseid, clearly suggesting that her disgrace is the result of sexual infidelity; and the severity of her circumstances is reflected in her self-comparison with "the vgly oull", who according to popular belief was so loathed by other birds that it was unable to show itself in daylight.[57] It seems more than likely that this sequence, with its adoption of a definitely-delineated female voice, arises from some scandal which would have been known to Montgomerie's audience: why else would the giveaway reference to a "Countess" make its appearance?

This seems to me to be a more likely explanation that that tentatively suggested at one point by Jack: that the Lady may be a covert representation of Mary, Queen of Scots.[58] This argument was based in part on Cranstoun's erroneous extension of the sequence to six sonnets, for which there is no warrant in either the manuscript or the text of the poems themselves: the third and final sonnet states, unambiguously, "So with Peccavi Pater I conclude".[59] The reference to the rank of Countess, moreover, is quite explicit, and there is special pleading in the contention that Montgomerie

---

[57] For a Scottish version of this legend, see Richard Holland's *Buke of the Howlat*, written for the countess of Moray around 1450: *Longer Scottish Poems*, ed. Priscilla Bawcutt and Felicity Riddy (Edinburgh: Scottish Academic Press, 1987), 1:43–84.

[58] R.D.S. Jack, "The Theme of Fortune in the Verse of Alexander Montgomerie", *SLJ* 10/2 (December 1983): 25–44, here 37–38.

[59] Parkinson rightly prints this as a sequence of three sonnets. Cranstoun had made it a group of six (33–38), but Jack pointed out (*Montgomerie*, 86) that in the Ker MS. it comprises only three, thus ending "So with Peccavi Pater I conclude". Somewhat earlier, Jack had stated that the sequence was made up of *five* sonnets, but then quoted from the sixth in Cranstoun's arrangement; see "Theme of Fortune", 37. The echo of Luke 15:18 and 15:21 is repeated in "A godly Prayer" (see below, 299); it may be, as Parkinson suggests (*Poems*, 2:104), that there is an allusion here to the speaker as "the counterpart of the prodigal".

could not have made his allusion to the Queen overt, and therefore covered it up by giving his persona a line which conveyed nobility without making her "identity" clear. That the sequence is coded does seem probable; that it is the Queen rather than a participant in a contemporary scandal whose voice is simulated seems much more doubtful.

As it happens, two such scandals erupted almost simultaneously in early 1581, and it is likely that one or other of these formed the basis for Montgomerie's sequence. One involved Margaret Leslie, daughter of the earl of Rothes and wife of the earl of Angus, whom she married on Christmas Day 1575; on 25 February 1581, the English ambassador Thomas Randolph reported that Angus had suspected his wife of infidelity with the earl of Montrose, had attempted to catch the couple *in flagrante delicto* at his house in Dalkeith, and had apparently found her awaiting her lover. He had, moreover, obtained letters between the pair, dealing with a plot to get Angus out of the way by instigating his arrest. The king had been informed, Randolph added, and was "greatly offended" with Montrose.[60] It seems probable that this furore was connected with the imprisonment of Angus's uncle, the earl of Morton, who had been arrested on 31 December 1580: Angus was a focus for resistance to Lennox in his attack on Morton, and the affair involving the Countess must at least have been a distraction. The contemporary memorialist David Moysie, certainly, was suspicious: his note of the events of 25 February comments that "thir letters war thocht heirefter to be forged, as it appeared they wer indeid".[61] In the event, a relentless campaign against Angus was successful, and the earl was forced to flee to England at the beginning of June.[62]

The Countess, meanwhile, appears to have taken refuge with her father at Dysert; father and daughter acted together to protect her interests after her estranged husband's exile, successfully petitioning Parliament in November for the reservation of her dowry despite the earl's attainder.[63] The estrangement apparently continued after his return: in 1583 an English informant in Scotland, providing his employers with a detailed account of the circumstances and political allegiances of the Scottish nobility, observed of the earl of Angus that he was

> vnhappy in his mariage: his firste wyef was sister to therle of Marr, and dyed without issue; his laste, a woman touched in her honor with therle of Mountrois, and therfore abandoned of her husbande, is doughter to therle of Rothes.[64]

---

[60] *CSP Scot.*, 5:645–46.

[61] Moysie, *Memoirs*, 30.

[62] For an account of this complex political background, see George R. Hewitt, *Scotland under Morton, 1572–80* (Edinburgh: John Donald, 1982), 188–95.

[63] *APS*, 3:267–68.

[64] *Bannatyne Miscellany* (Edinburgh: Bannatyne Club, 1827), 1:63.

The Countess was still at Dysert on 23 December 1586, when she wrote to Sir David Wemyss of Wemyss, asking him for his support when she appeared before the Commissariot Court of Edinburgh on 28 December and assuring him that he would "haw na dishonor in respect of my inocensye".[65] She was, however, divorced by Angus early the following year, no doubt to clear the way for his third marriage, to the daughter of the earl of Glamis, on 29 July.[66]

A rather similar case involved the Countess of March, whose affair with Captain James Stewart became known a few weeks before Angus's confrontation with his wife, and shortly after Stewart was appointed tutor to the insane Earl of Arran. The basic facts are recorded by Calderwood, who notes that

> Captane James Stewart, after that he was made tutor to the Erle of Arran, he grew so familiar with the Countesse of Marche that he begott upon her a child. To cover this adulterous fact, a processe of divorcement was intended by her against her lawfull husband, the Erle of Marche, which was easilie obteanned, and so, the new made erle and she were joynned together in mariage. She was delivered of a man childe about this time.[67]

The divorce was granted on 19 May 1581, and the Countess married Stewart (who was actually not created Earl of Arran until 28 October) on 6 July. Their child was born on 8 January 1582.[68]

There were, then, two adulterous countesses in the first half of 1581, and Montgomerie's sequence might, on the fact of it, refer to either of them. Since both were the daughters of earls, moreover, the statement that "I wes matchit with my match *and mair*" [my italics] has a quite exact relevance in both cases: the earldoms of Angus and March, into which the women concerned had married, were arguably superior to those of Rothes and Atholl respectively. Margaret Leslie, countess of Angus, however, seems to have maintained her innocence and to have denied the authenticity of the apparently incriminating letters, and we have seen that she was sufficiently defiant to join her father in petitioning Parliament regarding her case. It may also be significant that Arran and his new wife were forced, after the birth of their child, to undergo a formal act of penance before the king, at Holyrood on 14 March 1582.[69] It is, therefore, not improbable that Montgomerie's

---

[65] Fraser, *Douglas Book*, 4:238.

[66] For the divorce, see NAS, RH6/2130.

[67] Calderwood, *History*, 3:593. Calderwood's main source was evidently *The Historie of King James the Sext*.

[68] *Edinburgh Commissariot Decreets*, 10, 19 May 1581; *Scots Peerage*, 5:355; 1:396, 445. For the suggestion that these poems may refer to Elizabeth Stewart, see Parkinson, *Poems*, 2:102–3.

[69] Calderwood, *History*, 3:595–96.

sequence contains an oblique reference to this event, by which time the scandal involving the Countess of Angus had perhaps begun to recede from the minds of the probable audience (and the Earl had been in exile for nine months). It is also notable that the poems concentrate entirely upon the woman's moral and spiritual condition, making no reference to the (presumably male) cause of her being "in a Cressede changed" — in the former Countess of March's case the influential Earl of Arran.

Whoever the sequence refers to, it is rhetorically striking in its adoption of a dramatised female voice. The ultimate model is Ovid's *Heroides*; but there were, equally, French and English precedents.[70] Clément Marot had imitated Ovid by writing occasional epistles in female character; Ronsard and Pontus de Tyard had composed elegies on elegantly lesbian themes, addressed by a female persona to another woman; and there is a closer analogue to Montgomerie's sequence in Desportes's "Plainte: Pour une Dame" (1573), although in this case — as in the principal English examples — it is Faith "mal reconnue", Love and Fortune against whom the lady complains:

> Et la Fortune encor sans raison mutinée,
> Rends, las ! Plus que ces deux ma vie infortunée :
> Car c'est par sa rigueur que je me vois priver
> Des fleurs de mon printemps par un fascheux hyver :
> Las ! C'est par sa rigueur que je languy captive,
> Et me voy jeune et belle enterrer toute vive.
>      (13–18)

> [And then Fortune, rebelling for no reason, destroys my unhappy life, alas, more than these two: for it is through her hostility that I see myself stripped of the flowers of my spring by a malevolent winter. Alas! it is through her hostility that I languish as a captive and see myself, young and beautiful as I am, buried alive.][71]

As in many English lyrics, the female speaker is here the innocent victim of male betrayal; as Kerrigan observes, even where the confessional element of penitential lyric is absorbed into the tradition of "female ventriloquism", "the most striking thing about plaintful women in Tudor poetry is their lack of 'defect'"[72] — although

---

[70] For English examples, see *Motives of Woe: Shakespeare and "Female Complaint"*, ed. John Kerrigan (Oxford: Clarendon Press, 1991), and Elizabeth D. Harvey, *Ventriloquized Voices: Feminist Theory and English Renaissance Texts* (London: Routledge, 1992). Neither of these works, however, places the English tradition within its wider European context.

[71] Philippe Desportes, *Diverse Amours*, ed. Graham, 128–29.

[72] Kerrigan, *Motives of Woe*, 27.

this is scarcely true of the Renaissance Cressede. In Montgomerie's sequence, however, the penitential dimension is clearly uppermost, and the speaker's guilt is quite explicit. The echoes of Henryson's *Testament of Cresseid* are far from casual, for Montgomerie's persona, like Henryson's heroine, begins by shifting the blame for her situation from herself to "fickle Fortun" and then comes to understand that — in the words of the *Testament* — "Nane bot myself as now I maun accuse".

Three female stereotypes are used to represent the stages of her progress: the virtuous Lucrece symbolises a time of innocence and prosperity; Cressede stands for her disgrace and misery; while Mary Magdalene is invoked in the sestet of the third and final sonnet to indicate that condition of redemption to which she now aspires. Cressede is central to this triad, being introduced in juxtaposition with Lucrece in the final line of the first sonnet and providing the key references in the second; it is clear from the Henrysonian context that it is the devastation she experiences which unites her with Montgomerie's persona. Both Lucrece and Mary Magdalene are potentially ambiguous figures, of course, linked to Cressede (and the Countess) through the associations of disorderly sexuality, but it is evident that it is the former's chastity and the latter's repentance which provide the underlying referential logic of the sequence.[73] The abruptness of the transition from complaint to appeal is due, no doubt, to the nature of the form, for Montgomerie is careful to maintain the tonal integrity of each of his sonnets, and there is no narrative element to provide a "justification" for the change in the lady's rhetorical position. Nevertheless, by making her abandon self-pity in favour of contrition, Montgomerie shows her assuming that moral awareness which is, according to both medieval and post-Reformation doctrine, necessary for true penance.[74]

The problem with this structure is to determine the extent to which the religious understanding of the third and final sonnet refutes the fatalistic perception of the first two. By relating the sequence to Montgomerie's other discussions of the role of Fortune, characteristically in his own life, Jack indicates that the hint of "one possible means of escaping from the deadly triumvirate of Fortune, love and death" is transitory, and that it is the fatalism which ultimately prevails.[75] Even when he realises that the penitential note is the final one in a sequence which is shorter than had previously been supposed, Jack does not fully recognise the implication, contenting himself with an unresolved distinction between Montgomerie's view in his own complaints and that of the dramatised Countess.[76]

---

[73] On the Renaissance debate about Lucrece, see Ian Donaldson, *The Rapes of Lucretia* (Oxford: Clarendon Press, 1982); and Stephanie H. Jed, *Chaste Thinking: the Rape of Lucretia and the Birth of Humanism* (Bloomington, IN: Indiana University Press, 1989).

[74] Cf. Frank Allen Patterson, *The Middle English Penitential Lyric* (New York: Columbia University Press, 1911), esp. 6–12.

[75] Jack, "Theme of Fortune", 39.

[76] Jack, *Montgomerie*, 102–3.

Yet the fact is that the logic of the sequence is diametrically opposed to the disgruntled recognition of Fortune's power which runs through Montgomerie's more autoreferential (and generally later) poetry.

As is so often the case, it is a mistake to isolate this inner debate within Montgomerie's own experience, without taking into account the wider cultural context within which it is located. The contest between fatalism and personal moral responsibility was, of course, as old as organised Christianity; and there is plenty of evidence that it did not diminish during the sixteenth century.[77] Against the strictures of theologians as diverse as Aquinas, Luther, and Calvin, it is clear that influential writers like Machiavelli and Montaigne asserted the power of Fortune, no matter what implications it might have for human freedom or the will of God. The Countess's opening questions, then — "Vhom suld I warie bot my wicked weard? / Vha span my thriftles thrauard fatall threed?" — would have been instantly recognisable as an articulation of this deterministic view; and it is crucial to the meaning of the sequence that this is a position which she finally abandons in favour of a more orthodox Christian piety. This, too, the repeated allusions to Henryson's *Testament* help to clarify: as Jack observes, "she thinks now not of pagan tragedy but of Christian redemption".[78] Unlike Henryson, Montgomerie makes this Christian dimension, through the evocation of Mary Magdalene and the biblical allusion of the final line, wholly explicit; he thereby takes the redemptive process further, at least in prospect, than Henryson does. But the texts are parallel in their qualified upward movement.

Aesthetically, Montgomerie manages to have it both ways, building the drama of his monologue out of the tragic rhetoric of the first two sonnets, while using the openness of the sonnet sequence to transcend this false if powerful consciousness with the penitential rhetoric of the third. It may be significant that, if the historical contextualisation proposed here is correct, the sequence represents comparatively early work, written when the poet had little reason to complain of the role of Fortune in his own career. There are dangers, certainly, in an approach which assumes that a poet's treatments of a single theme are likely to be wholly consistent over two decades of changing experience, to say nothing of the demands of generic convention or specific occasion. If these sonnets allude to particular events, ventriloquising a voice which would have been recognisable for at least some part of the original audience, then the transition from resentful complaint to true penitence

---

[77] For an excellent outline of this debate, see Jean Delumeau, *Le péché et la peur: la culpibilisation en Occident (XIIIe–XVIIIe siècles)* (Paris: Fayard, 1983), 601–10. For more specific discussion of the Calvinist view, see P. Jacobs, *Prädestination und Verantwortlichkeit bei Calvin* (Neukirchen: Buchhandlung des Erziehungsvereins, 1937); and J.S. Bray, *Theodore Beza's Doctrine of Predestination* (Nieuwkoop: De Graaf, 1975).

[78] Jack, *Montgomerie*, 103.

has a further meaning: it simulates, and perhaps advocates, a process of reconciliation, with a purpose which may well have been partially consolatory. It would scarcely be sensible, in such circumstances, to seek to align these poems with the bitterness of Montgomerie's own complaints of the 1590s.

The dating of this short sequence to 1581–1582, and more specifically to the latter year, gives these sonnets a further significance, for all three elements are in the *ababbcbccdcdee* form generally associated with the name of Spenser. But, as far as we can see, Spenser's earliest use of this rhyme-scheme was in the dedicatory sonnet to the Earl of Leicester which prefaces *Virgils Gnat*, not printed until 1591 but written "long since"; the first appearance of the "Spenserian" sonnet in print was in James VI's *Essayes of a Prentise* in 1584. The sonnets of "A Ladyis Lamentatione", then, are certainly among the earliest to employ this distinctive form, and they may constitute evidence that Montgomerie was closely involved in the invention of one of the most characteristic sonnet-types of the British Renaissance.[79]

If "A Ladyis Lamentatione" reveals Montgomerie covertly commenting upon the affairs of the court, the Ovidian strain is turned to a much more straightforwardly panegyric purpose in a group of poems celebrating the marriage, in May-June 1582, of his kinswoman Margaret, daughter of the Earl of Eglinton, to Robert, Lord Seton.[80] There is a clear contrast here between two alternative patterns of rhetoric: the expansiveness of the two stanzaic lyrics [**102–103**] is notably different from the compressed, anaphoric structure of the sonnet "O happy star" [**85**], which is translated from Ronsard's "Heureuse fut l'estoille fortunée". The lyrics' epithalamial character is indicated through the final appeal each makes to "the goddes Hemene", while elaborate Ovidian conceits are employed to emphasise the superior qualities of "maikles Margaret": Pygmalion would abandon Galatea in her favour, and all three goddesses would have withdrawn from the judgement of Paris had she been in the field. Such outrageous compliments are a natural feature of Mannerist discourse: the point is not that they should be taken seriously, but that they should be appreciated for their sheer excessiveness, through which both the lady's beauty and the poet's ingenuity are magnified.

The descriptive language employed by Montgomerie in these lyrics is predictable enough, drawing heavily on the high-style traditions of Scots verse:

> The myildest may, the mekest and modest,        *maid*
> The fairest flour, the freschest flourisching,

---

[79] In her discussion of the sonnet to Sir William Murray and his wife which precedes the Tullibardine manuscript, Sally Mapstone draws attention to the fact that this, too, is an early occurrence of the scheme ("Invective as Poetic", 25–26); as she suggests, this might plausibly be regarded as part of a case for Montgomerie's authorship of this sonnet.

[80] The marriage contract is dated 10 May 1582 (Fraser, *Eglinton*, 1:48).

The lamp of licht, of youth the lustiest,
The blythest bird, of bewtie maist bening,                     *benign*
Groundit with grace and godlie governing
As A per C, aboue all elevat,
To quhome comparit is na erthlie thing
Nor with the goddes so heichlie estimat.
    (102: 9–16)

This is the conventional language of love lyric, displaced from its directly amatory purpose by the epithalamial context.[81] Even the traditional concept of the lover's "service" is invoked: in 102 Montgomerie declares that "of my self ane seruand scho sall have / Vnto I die" (ll. 47–48), but in this other lyric the service is transferred from the lady to her prospective husband, and the poet declares that if she is granted a spouse worthy of her qualities "I sall serve him for hir saik" (103: 55). In this sense, perhaps, we may see these two very similar pieces as a matching pair, although in other respects they tend to duplicate a standard repertoire of courtly praise.

As epithalamia, they are by sixteenth-century criteria remarkably restrained. From the later fifteenth century, as Leonard Forster has demonstrated, there developed a lively tradition of marriage-poems, in which there is a recurrent emphasis, not only upon the personal qualities of the bride and groom, but also upon the physical events of the wedding-night.[82] "The epithalamium," Forster suggests, "celebrates a wedding under three aspects: as a religious event, a social or political event, and as an erotic event." Of these, clearly, only the second figures in Montgomerie's treatment of the occasion: his poems are celebrations of the personal attributes of his idealised kinswoman, and it is the marriage as dynastic event which emerges most clearly.

This is also to a large degree true of "O happy star", which is a skilful rendering of its French original, the version of Ronsard's "Heureuse fut l'estoille fortunée" which was first published in *Les Amours* in 1552 and which continued to appear in subsequent editions and in Ronsard's *Œuvres* until the sestet was substantially revised for the 1578 edition.[83] That it is the earlier version which Montgomerie has used is clear from his reference to "Inde and Egypts happynes" (l. 10), reflecting "le bon heir / L'Inde & l'Egypte" which Ronsard revised out of his second version. As

---

[81] On these poems, see the interesting discussion by Sarah M. Dunnigan, "Female Gifts: Rhetoric, Beauty and the Beloved in the Lyrics of Alexander Montgomerie", *SLJ* 26/2 (Winter 1999): 59–78, here 65–67.

[82] Leonard Forster, *The Icy Fire: Five Studies in European Petrarchism* (Cambridge: Cambridge University Press, 1969), 88–120.

[83] Ronsard, *Œuvres Complètes*, ed. Laumonier, 4:106–7. For a discussion of Montgomerie's use of the published text of Ronsard, see below, 241–43.

Helena Shire convincingly argued, moreover, Montgomerie probably intended the
Scots version to be sung, to the setting by Clément Jannequin which was assigned
to Ronsard's sonnet in the 1552 edition of *Les Amours*; in this respect, then, he can
be seen as responding to contemporary French (and Italian) practice.[84]

Both in French and Scots, the sonnet is remarkable in its concentration upon
the female body, and for the way in which it contrives to dissolve its ostensible
subject into a secondary object, between her mother, her husband, and her (pro-
spective) child. The octave begins with the star first gazed upon by the lady, but
then concentrates on the good fortune of her mother in bringing forth such a
prodigious daughter:

> Houreuse fut l'estoille fortunée,
> Qui d'un bon œil ma maistresse apperceut :
> Heureux le bers, & la main qui la sceut
> Emmailloter alors qu'elle fut née.
> Heureuse fut la mammelle emmannée,
> De qui lelaict premier elle receut,
> Et bienheureux le ventre, qui conceut
> Si grand beaulte de si grandz dons ornée.

> O happy star, at evning and at morne
> Vhais bright aspect my Maistres first outfand,                    *discovered*
> O happy credle and O happy hand                                   *cradle*
> Vhich rockit hir the hour that sho wes borne,
> O happy Pape, ye rather nectar horne
> First gaiv hir suck in siluer suedling band,
> O happy wombe consavit had beforne
> So brave a beutie, honour of our Land . . .

By developing the opening image, to make clear that the star in question is Venus,
Montgomerie might even be argued to have improved on his original; but in gen-
eral he stays close to the French. The implications, however, are modified by the
context: since the subject is no longer the Lady of a sonnet cycle but a particular
bride, the sense of familial continuity takes on a new resonance, and the maternal
attributes of hand, breast (enriched by the addition of "nectar horne"), and womb
become those of the bride's mother, the Countess of Eglinton. These physical de-
tails, in other words, are absorbed into Montgomerie's celebratory strategy. The
other differences are largely explicable in terms of the demands of his rhyme-scheme:
"in siluer suedling band" and "honour of our land", in particular, are added to set
up the rhyme, although the first makes the image of the wonderful infant more

---

[84] Shire, *Song, Dance and Poetry*, 150–56.

concrete and the latter phrase was presumably suggested by the beginning of the sestet in Ronsard's sonnet:

> Heureux les champs qui eurent cest honneur
> De la voir naistre . . .

The change of emphasis which Montgomerie achieves in his sestet is even more evidently the product of the different context within which he is working. Since for Ronsard the poem is part of an amatory sequence, there is a clear hint that the "celuy qui la fera / Et femme & mere" (ll. 13–14) will, he hopes, be his speaker. Montgomerie, on the other hand, is giving his version an implicitly epi-thalamial stance — a significance which is apparent more from the ascription, it is true, than from the detail of the poem itself — and the "happyer he" of l. 13 is by implication not the speaker but the husband-to-be, Lord Seton, echoing the "Happie is he that sall posseid / In marriage this Margaret" in one of the stanzaic lyrics. This, surely, is also the point of the introduction of a new l. 11 (a tactful ref-erence to the more explicitly sexual tradition of the Continental epithalamium):

> O happy bed vhairin sho sall be laid!

"O happy bed" is, it should be noted, one of the phrases which is emphasised by the patterns of repetition and prolongation of Jannequin's setting, all of which have been chosen by Montgomerie with evident concern for his theme: the others are "yit sho duells" (l. 9), "scho sall breid" (l. 12), "Bot happyer he" (l. 13) and "To mak both wyfe" (l. 14). As Shire observes, "The joyful iteration of these phrases is central to the celebratory nature of the wedding piece".[85] The preoccupation with the lady as the focus of others' sexual being, on the other hand, reinforced by the passive in "sho sall be laid", may strike us as strange, especially when the process of transformation from love poem to epithalamium makes the poet an onlooker rather than a participant. But again the social nature of the marriage-poem, understood in the context of the intrusiveness which was evidently an expected aspect of such works in the sixteenth century, provides an explanation: the notion of motherhood with which Ronsard's sonnet ends becomes in Montgomerie's altered context an anticipation of the dynastic outcome of the union of the houses of Seton and Eglinton achieved through this match.

All the poems we have examined so far, if the reading of "A Ladyis Lamenta-tione" proposed above is accepted, are in various respects occasional, illustrative of the ways in which Montgomerie was assimilated into the court during the Lennox ascendancy. The life of this cultured, but to the king's more Protestant magnates

---

[85] Shire, *Song, Dance and Poetry*, 152.

intolerably pro-Catholic, household was soon to be brusquely interrupted, however, for on 23 August 1582 James was seized by the Earl of Gowrie, the Master of Glamis, and other Protestant lords, and virtually imprisoned in Ruthven Castle. For nearly a year he was unable to act on his own initiative, and the court circle was decisively broken. The real target of the conspirators was, of course, Lennox and his faction; Robert Bowes reported to Walsingham on 22 September that, despite the urging of his friends (whose own interests presumably depended upon his presence) that he should remain in Scotland, Lennox was disposed to act on the king's advice that he should return to France.[86] Three weeks later, Bowes tells a revealing story: Walter Keir, the brother of Lennox's associate Henry, brought a message from Lennox to the king, which was conveyed to James by his page John Gibb,

> wheruppon the King pretended to go to the stole, called for John Gibbe to go with him, and being in secret, Gibbe told the King that Keyr had brought commendations from the Duke to him. But the King answered, that if the Duke and Keyr were wise, they would not thus sent to him to hurt themselves and endanger him; and hastily he went away without hearing any further at that time.[87]

Lennox made good his escape, dying in Paris the following June; the king escaped a few days after his former favourite's death, making his way to St Andrews on 27 June. Within a very short time, the principal members of the Lennox circle were once again the dominant figures at the court.

It was this trauma, perhaps, which enabled the fifteen-year-old king to find his poetic voice:

> Since thochtis ar frie, think quhat thow will,
> O trublet heart to ease thy payne                *troubled*
> Thoghtis vnreveillit can doe no ill
> Bot woirdis past out comes nocht agane
> Be cairfull ay for to invent
> The way to get thy awin intent.[88]

The version of this three-stanza poem in BL. MS. Addit. 24195, apparently written in the king's household around 1616 and evidently in some sense sanctioned by him, is entitled "the first verses that euer the King made", a claim which is consistent with the poem's inclusion in the Maitland Quarto manuscript (copied in 1586).

---

[86] *Bowes Corr.*, 189.

[87] *Bowes Corr.*, 205–6.

[88] James VI, *Poems*, ed. Craigie, 1:132.

But another early copy, preserved among fragments which probably once belonged to the lawyer Thomas Hamilton (1563–1637), eventually created Earl of Haddington, whose early associations were certainly more on the "Catholic" side than the Protestant one, gives a more specific context: "Thir maid in anno 1583, at ye duik of obiynnie his puting out of scotland".[89] Each of the three original stanzas, moreover, is also turned into an "Ansuer yairto":

> Since thoght is thraw to thy ill will                    *captive*
> O thrallit heart / gritt is thy payne
> Thoghtes vnreveillit may doe the ill
> Bot woirdis past cumes weill agane
> Be ever cairfull to invent
> To gett thy awin by Gods intent.[90]

If the original verses take on a new pregnancy in the political context claimed for them in the NAS manuscript, the "Answer" offers a poignant comment on the cautious lesson they provide. James may well have found it prudent to "let none know quhat thow does meane" (l. 8), but the long game he was playing spelled short-term disaster for Lennox and his adherents, and James — or whoever the author of the reply may have been — was perhaps entitled to feel that he had good cause for remarking that "God knawis all that thow dois meane".

No sooner had James made good his escape than the former members of his household began to be rewarded. Montgomerie had been in Edinburgh for at least part of the period of the king's captivity, for on 16 April 1583 we find him as a witness, along with his brother Hugh, in a transaction for Mr. William Roberton, a fellow-Catholic who was master of the grammar school in Edinburgh.[91] He now received the grant which reflected, in part at least, the extent to which he was in the king's favour, and which would ultimately lead to his bitter disillusionment: on 27 July 1583 he was granted an annual pension of 500 merks from the revenues

---

[89] NAS, RH13/38. I am grateful to Dr. Sally Mapstone for drawing my attention to this copy of the poem, and its significance.

[90] Another version of this "reply" is given by Calderwood in the manuscript of his *History* (B.L., MS. Addit. 4737, fol. 374v), and printed by Craigie, who regards its authenticity as "at best very doubtful" (James VI, *Poems*, 2:268). But the Hamilton copy indicates that it is of early date.

[91] NAS, RD 1/21, fol. 30r. I am grateful to John Durkan for drawing my attention to this document. It is possible that it was the poet who was the "Captane Montgomerie" who carried a message from the General Assembly of the Kirk of Scotland towards the end of April, warning the Assembly not to meddle with the affairs of the University of Glasgow (*Booke of the Universall Kirk*, 2:620) — but this might also have been his half-brother Robert.

of Glasgow cathedral, drawn from the lands of Dalbeath, Conflattis, Kenmuir, Daldowie Wester, Dalmarnock, and Shettleston and back-dated to the previous year.[92] This was not merely an individual act of patronage. It is almost certainly not a coincidence that Mr. Robert Montgomerie was at this time pursuing the archbishopric of Glasgow, a post for which he was seen as the nominee of the Duke of Lennox;[93] other members of the family, including Captain Robert Montgomerie (who was granted the superplus of the deanery of Glasgow on 19 January 1581), also obtained revenues from Glasgow Cathedral at about this time.[94] Family interests were pursued, in other words, with at least as much enthusiasm as they had been before the Reformation, reminding us of Alexander Scott's strictures against such practices twenty years before.[95] At first, no doubt, the poet was able to enjoy the benefits of this patronage, whatever its source: the king would later recall — no doubt at Montgomerie's prompting — that "he become in peceabill possessioun of vplifting and intrometting with his said pensioun fra ye tennentis",[96] and it was only later, during Montgomerie's absence in the Netherlands, that payment was interrupted. For the moment, at least, all was well.

The period from James's return to Edinburgh in June 1583 until Montgomerie's departure for the Netherlands in July 1586 would appear in many ways to have been the zenith of the "maister poete"'s fortunes. James may already have begun the project of cultural renewal which has sometimes been dubbed the "Castalian movement", although if both statements concerning "Sen thocht is frie" which we discussed above are true, his own poetic career did not begin until the winter of 1582–1583. Over the next two years he clearly wrote a good deal: *Ane Metaphoricall Invention of a Tragedie called Phoenix* is an explicit lament for the death of the beloved Lennox and was presumably composed (or at least finished) after May 1583, but we might perhaps see in the translations of the *Uranie* and other works by the impeccably Protestant Salluste du Bartas a suitable employment for the prisoner of Ruthven Castle.[97] Other poets, apart from Montgomerie and the brothers Hudson,

---

[92] *RSS*, 8, no. 1423 (from NAS, PS1/49, fol. 135v).

[93] *CSP Scot.*, 6:58–59 (Bowes to Cecil, 18 October 1581). The dispute over the provision of Robert Montgomerie, and the related complaints against him by the Presbytery of Stirling, dominated ecclesiastical affairs throughout 1582, and continued for several years thereafter.

[94] As indicated above (41–42), Captain Robert Montgomerie received his grant on 19 January (*RSS*, 8, no. 41), demitting it to John, son of Hugh Montgomerie of Hessilheid six weeks later (no. 123); Mr. William Montgomerie, who had received the superplus of Stewarton and Kilbride on 15 October 1580 (NAS, PS1/47, fol. 28r), was provided to the parsonage of Ayr on 20 June 1582 (*RSS*, 8, no. 870).

[95] *Poems*, ed. Cranstoun, 4–6.

[96] See Montgomerie, *Poems*, ed. Stevenson, 307.

were presumably now added to the king's circle: John Stewart of Baldynneis had already written New Year poems for James in 1582/3 and the following year, in the first instance while he was still a prisoner of the Ruthven raiders, whose coup is presumably also the subject of the verses "To his Majestie in Fascherie"; Alexander Hume, the brother of Polwarth, had attached himself to the court, where he subsequently admits to having squandered his time on "prophane sonnets and vaine ballats of loue", probably around 1583; while William Fowler had returned from London (where he had acted as an agent of the English government, infiltrating the pro-Marian circle there and even travelling with Lennox on part of his journey back to France) soon after James's escape from the Ruthven raiders, and apparently became part of the king's company in the course of the next few months.[98]

Perhaps, as Shire suggests, there was actually a "writing game" among the king and his companions, accompanied by role-playing and assumed names; as in Elizabeth's England, the language and techniques of ingratiation could certainly be transferred from the amatory context to a political one, but it is difficult to determine how far the business of nicknames went.[99] As we noted in Chapter 1, recent scholarship has tended towards scepticism about the contemporary currency

---

[97] For discussion of James's literary output at this period, see R.J. Lyall, "James VI and the Sixteenth-Century Cultural Crisis", in *Reign of James VI*, ed. Goodare and Lynch, 55–70, here 59–65. There is independent (if not disinterested) testimony to the rapid dissemination of the news that the Scottish king had developed literary aspirations: in September 1583 the young English poet Henry Constable, four years older than the king himself, visited Scotland as part of a mission by Walsingham, and addressed a sonnet to James "whome as yet he had not seene", in which he pays tribute to the king's writing and anticipates that he will in due course receive the "laurell garland". This poem certainly suggests that Constable knew something of James's earliest work; cf. Constable, *Poems*, ed. Grundy, 21, 140.

[98] On Stewart's biography, see Matthew P. McDiarmid, "John Stewart of Baldynneis", *SHR* 29 (1950): 52–63; the early poems addressed to James are printed in Stewart's *Poems*, ed. Thomas Crockett (Edinburgh: STS, 1913), 2:125–8. On Hume, see *Poems*, ed. Alexander Lawson (Edinburgh: STS, 1902), xii–lxvi; Hume states in his "Epistill to Maister Gilbert Mont-creiff" (ll. 135–141) that he had studied in Paris for four years and then worked as a lawyer in Scotland for three, after which he pursued a career at James's court. Since he completed his B.A. at St Andrews in 1574, he could not have entered this latter phase of his career before 1581; he did, in any case, have royal support by November 1584, when he was given a grant by James from the revenues of Dunfermline Abbey (Lawson, *Poems*, xxi). On Fowler, see *Works*, ed. Henry W. Meikle, James Craigie and John Purves, 3 vols. (Edinburgh: STS, 1912–1939), 3:ix–xl. A balanced critical overview of the group is given by R.D.S. Jack, "Poetry under King James VI", in *The History of Scottish Literature*, ed. idem (Aberdeen: Aberdeen University Press, 1988), 1:125–39.

[99] Shire, *Song, Dance and Poetry*, 87–91. But at least one of Shire's assumptions seems to have been wrong: there really *was* a poet called Robert Stevin, who was presumably the

of the "Castalian" label and the social organisation Shire sees underlying it. But at any event, the relationship between Montgomerie and the king was relaxed enough for the latter to tease his courtier with "An admonitioun to the maister poete", in which Montgomerie is chastised for his boastfulness and mocked for his evident chagrin at the defeat of his "broune" (that is, a brown horse) in a challenge race. This poem must, if our earlier conclusions about the origins of the king's poetic career are correct, date from between his escape from Ruthven in June 1583 and the autumn of 1584, since a stanza from it is quoted in James's "Reulis and Cautelis"; it *may* be connected with a reference to Montgomerie in the Treasurer's Accounts for March 1584:

> Item be his hienes precept to Alexander Montgomerie for ane horss resauit be his maiesties self As the precept producit vpoun compt beris
>
> £200[100]

In its self-conscious Classicism, alluding at length to the Virgilian narrative of the contest between Dares and Entellus (*Aeneid*, 5.380–484), in its playful reversal of the Aesopic roles of lion and mouse in the opening stanza, and in its references to the relationship between Montgomerie and other poets of the court, "Ane Admonitioun" illustrates very well the intimate, adolescent atmosphere of the king's circle. But it also reflects the more more serious rivalries to which James stood in a privileged position; the occasion for the king's poem, it is clear, was a squib from a fellow-courtier of Montgomerie's, perhaps either Robert Hudson or Robert Stevin,[101] while Hume of Polwarth was evidently still hoping to gain his revenge over the poet who had bested him in the *Flyting*:

> Nou for youre state sen thair is cause indeid,
> For all the poetis leaus you standand baire:
> Auld cruikid Robert makis of you the haire,      *hare*
> & elf-gett Polluart helpis the smithy smuik;      *elf-begotten; smoke*
> He countis you done & hopes but ony maire
> His time about to uinn the chimlay nuik.
>      (11–16)[102]

---

author of *Rob Stene's Dreme*, since a payment to "Robert Stevin poet" occurs in September 1582 (*Treas. Accts*, NAS, E21/63, fol. 75r) and elsewhere; see below, 156 n. 33.

[100] NAS, E22/6, fol. 157v.

[101] Hudson is perhaps the more probable: he was employed at court as a musician as early as 1565 (see Shire, *Song, Dance and Poetry*, 72), and is therefore likely to have been of an older generation. As noted above, Stevin was a poet at court in September 1582, but there is no evidence regarding his age or a possible physical disability.

[102] The text of James's "Admonitioun" is printed in his *Poems*, ed. Craigie, 2:120–29.

The allusions here to the language of the *Flyting* show James seeking common ground with Montgomerie against his adversaries, trying perhaps to win him back into the circle of literary friends. The mockery, then, is amicable, and without that edge which springs from the competition for the king's favour. In its own adolescent way, "Ane Admonitioun" displays that *magnanimitas* which was held to be one of the necessary attributes of kingship.

James had good reasons, of course, for wanting to hold Montgomerie within the court circle, for while his poem reveals the private world of the king's literary coterie, he certainly had more public ambitions. In the autumn of 1584 he published his *Essayes of a Prentise in the Divine Art of Poesie*: the printer Thomas Vautrollier was paid £225 in October "for the prenting of his maiesties buik", and it is conceivable that the "certane buikis deliuerit to his maiestie" the previous month were first copies of the volume.[103] The *Essayes* are, it is clear, a self-conscious projection by the seventeen-year-old king of a literary personality, one assured enough to lay down among his own verses "Some Reulis and Cautelis to be obseruit and eschewit in Scottis poesie". The inclusion of this programmatic work conveys very precisely the sense that this is to be a new beginning: after the conscientiously "plain" traditions of Protestant verse which had prevailed during his minority, James was signalling the revival, by his patronage and by his example, of a poetry worthy of a European court. As we noted above, something similar had occurred more spontaneously in England in the previous decade, as James may have been aware; but the transformation of Scottish verse would be a public, and published, manifestation of the king's superior talents.

As a rhetorical textbook, James's "Reulis and Cautelis" are scarcely groundbreaking. Modelled, at least in part, on Gascoigne's *Certayne notes of Instruction* (1575) and specifically invoking the authority of Du Bellay's *Deffence et Illustration de la Langue Françoyse* (1549), they provide some fairly rudimentary analysis of metrics, metaphor, and related matters; but they utterly lack the complexity and sophistication of a work such as George Puttenham's *Art of English Poesy* (1589).[104] The real importance of the treatise lies in its articulation of a determination to foster a new kind of poetry in Scots, clearly distinguished from English, "quhilk is lykest to our language". In its insistence upon the musical properties of poetry (summed up in James's principle of "Flowing, the verie twichestane quhairof is

---

[103] NAS, E22/6, fols. 211v, 203v. James Craigie believed that the publication date was December, basing his inference on a letter from the Earl of Arran to Cecil, written on 28 December, dispatched with a copy of "his hienes first pruif and prentissage in poesie"; see *Poems*, ed. Craigie, 1:xxv, lxix–lxv. But there is no implication in Arran's wording that the *Essayes* had only just appeared, and Craigie had not seen the references in the Treasurer's Accounts.

[104] See R.D.S. Jack, "James VI and Renaissance Poetic Theory", *English* 16 (1967): 208–11.

Musique"), in its careful attention to the relationship between content and form, and above all in its repeated praise of "Inuentioun, quhilk is ane of the cheif properteis of ane Poete", James constantly aligns himself with poetic values which are entirely consonant with those espoused at the courts of Italy and France, and currently being embraced in England, and implicitly rejects the literary functionalism of the Protestant aesthetics which had prevailed in Scotland for a generation. It represents, in cultural terms, a further rejection of the strict principles of his upbringing, and an endorsement of the richer traditions of Continental Europe.[105]

It would be wrong, however, to exaggerate the polarity between "Protestant" and "Catholic" aesthetics in late sixteenth-century Europe, or James's enthusiasm for the latter. One of the most powerful influences on *Essayes of a Prentise*, and on James's court circle generally, is that of the Protestant poet Salluste du Bartas, whose *Uranie* (1574) James had translated; the king would frequently revert to Du Bartas' works in subsequent years, while Thomas Hudson would soon publish his version of the same "devin and illuster poete"'s *Judit*. And the influence of the Pléiade, which pervades the "Castalian" enterprise, springs from that complex period of French literary history before the catastrophe of St. Bartholomew, when the division of society into mutually irreconcilable armed camps had not yet taken its final, deadly form. James's preference for Du Bartas, and for the Psalm paraphrases of Tremellius, reflect his broadly Protestant sympathies; but there is plenty of evidence in the *Essayes of a Prentise* of responsiveness to the Mannerist techniques which were so prevalent in contemporary French culture, even in the "difficile and prolixed Poems" of Du Bartas himself.[106]

Among the tributes to James's poetic genius which decorate the volume's opening pages, exemplifying the king's dictum that the sonnet is appropriate "for compendious praysing of any bukes, or the authouris thairof", is one by Montgomerie; the Ker MS. makes clear, however, that this was one of four composed "In Prais of the Kings Vranie" [67]. All four demonstrate the same panegyric style required of the successful courtier-poet, now much more blatant than in the witty, mediated compliments of *The Navigatioun*. James is a "second Psalmist", and is repeatedly associated with the sun, as Phoebus, Titan, and Apollo: extended comparisons reinforce this conceit in each of the four sonnets, running through them as a leitmotiv. The Petrarchan notion of the lady's beauty putting the sun, moon, and stars into the shade is here converted into a more literary hyperbole, by which Montgomerie and his fellow-admirers are downgraded in comparison with the king's rhetorical accomplishments. There is, however, an inherent contradiction here: the more ingenious Montgomerie's development of

---

[105] Cf. A. Walter Bernhart, "Castalian Poetics and the 'Verie Twichestane Musique'", in *Scottish Language and Literature, Medieval and Renaissance*, ed. Dietrich Strauss and Horst W. Drescher (Frankfurt/Main, Bern and New York: Verlag Peter Lang, 1986), 451–58.

[106] Lyall, "Cultural Crisis", 55–59.

the conceit, the more it subverts itself, demonstrating rather than denying his own poetic skill. The panegyrist and his subject are thus caught in a relationshp which is partly symbiotic, partly incompatible, and it is in the end difficult to say whether Montgomerie adds more lustre to James's achievement or to his own.

The elaborate rhetorical patterning which is characteristic of each sonnet individually extends to the sequence as a whole, for Montgomerie neatly links each of his four sonnets with those around it: the reference to James as "second Psalmist" connects, implicitly at least, with the allusion to "Titans harp" in the opening line of the second, which its itself echoed in the "goldin Titan" of the first line of the third. This third sonnet, with its insistent use of *interrogatio*, neatly switches the solar reference from Titan to Apollo, thus bringing the imagery of light and poetic inspiration together; the Apollo conceit becomes central to the fourth, while the closing apostrophe to James as "quintessenst of kings" (itself a remarkable coinage of a superlative adjective!) brings us around again to the comparison with David with which the sequence began. There is, moreover, in the sestet of this last poem of the group a deft covert allusion to James's allegorical *Phoenix*, his tribute to the departed Lennox: this topos of unique accomplishment is applied by Montgomerie to the king, as the king had applied it to his beloved courtier.

These complimentary sonnets exhibit, as their mode requires, the grand Mannerist style at its most sycophantically elaborate; and yet they are, as we have already noted, not without their internal tensions. The very intricacy of the eulogistic rhetoric even seems at one point to allow Montgomerie to disguise insult as panegyric. How else are we to understand the octave of the second sonnet of the sequence?

| | |
|---|---|
| Of Titans harp sith thou intones the strings | *since* |
| Of Ambrose and of Nectar so thou feeds | |
| Not only vther Poets thou outsprings | |
| Bot vhylis also thy very self excedes, | *sometimes* |
| Transporting thee as ravished vhen thou redes | |
| Thyn auin inventione, wondering at thy wit, | |
| Quhat mervell than thoght our fordullit hedes | *extremely stupid* |
| And blunter brainis be mare amais'd at it. | |
|    (67.II:1–8) | |

Carefully wrapped in the tribute to prodigious youth and the evocation of a marvelling audience, the glimpse of James "transported" by his own invention — this last word, we should remember, figures prominently in the king's "Reulis and Cautelis" — and "wondering" at his own wit is surely (at least partly) mocking, conveying precisely that sense of self-absorption which sometimes emerges from James's own youthful writings. Perhaps Montgomerie was relying on that very self-absorption to make the subterranean meaning invisible; or perhaps he was trading on his place as favoured poet within the royal circle. But the element of satirical representation seems unmistakable.

The eminence of Montgomerie's position among the king's emerging literary circle is attested by the fact that of the seven stanzas James cites in his "Reulis and Cautelis" to illustrate "the kyndis of versis", four are from works by his "maister poete". This demonstrates Montgomerie's reputation, but it also allows us to assign three more poems to 1584 or earlier. The fourth selection is not in this latter sense illuminating, for the example of *"Rouncefallis* or *Tumbling* verse" is a thirteen-line alliterative stanza from the *Flyting*; the king's taste is perhaps reflected in his choice of a whimsical rather than an uncompromisingly abusive passage. In the remaining cases, however, the evidence of the "Reulis and Cautelis" gives us a clearer picture of Montgomerie's verse of the early 1580s.

The appearance of the opening stanza of "To the Echo" [14], for example, illustrates both the degree to which Montgomerie participated in the current fashions in European verse, and the distinctiveness of the rhetorical craftsmanship with which he manipulated them. Few devices were more voguish in the later sixteenth century than the mimetic use of echoed syllables, alluding to the myth of Narcissus and the love-stricken Echo. Its origins lie in Ovid's account of the story (*Metamorphoses*, 3.379–392), but the distinctive placing of the echo at the end of a succession of lines appears in Angelo Poliziano's "Che fa' tu, Ecco" (*Rispetto* 36), published in his *Cosi volgare* in 1494 and subsequent editions of his works.[107] Thereafter, it was taken up by a succession of writers in many languages: Tebaldeo and Torquato Tasso, Johannes Secundus, Joachim du Bellay, Lope de Vega.[108] It also became intensely fashionable in England: Gascoigne employed the topos in the 'Princelie Pleasures' which entertained Elizabeth at Kenilworth in July 1575; John Grange's *Golden Aphroditis* (1577) contained no fewer than four examples; and Gascoigne's rather wooden attempt may, as Katherine Duncan-Jones has suggested, have inspired Sir Philip Sidney's pastoral dialogue between Philisides and Echo, the date of which is uncertain but which could be as early as 1575 (or as late as 1580, when it was incorporated in the Second Eclogues which formed part of the *Arcadia*).[109] So great was the vogue, indeed, that it ultimately acquired an

---

[107] Angelo Poliziano, *Rime*, ed. Daniela Delcorno Branca (Florence: Accademia Della Crusca, 1986), 307–8.

[108] On the popularity of the device, see Eldridge Colby, *The Echo-Device in Literature* (New York: New York Public Library, 1920); and Giovanni Pozzi, *Poesia per gioco. Prontuario di figure artificiose* (Bologna: Il Mulino, 1984), 94–102.

[109] George Gascoigne, *Complete Works*, ed. John W. Cunliffe, 2 vols. (Cambridge: Cambridge University Press, 1907–1910), 2:97–100; John Grange, *Golden Aphroditis* (London: Henry Bynneman, 1577), sig. I1r–v; Sir Philip Sidney, *Poems*, ed. William A. Ringler (Oxford: Clarendon Press, 1962), 62–64; Thomas Watson, *The Hekompathia, or Passionate Century of Love*, ed. S.K. Heninger Jr (Gainesville, FL: Scholars' Facsimiles and Reprints, 1964), 39. For the possible connection between Gascoigne and Sidney, see Katherine Duncan-Jones, *Sir Philip Sidney, Courtier Poet* (London: Hamish Hamilton, 1991), 98–99.

anthology to itself, the *Lusus imaginis iocosae* published by Theodor van der Does (Dousa) at Utrecht in 1638, which provides around thirty examples in Latin, Greek, Dutch, German, French, English, and Italian.[110]

It is not difficult to see why the device was so irresistible to sixteenth-century poets. Not only did it offer great opportunity for ingenious wordplay, but the highly-charged amatory context of the myth itself enabled the lover-poet to invest his own passion with the grief articulated by the disembodied voice. The "dialogue" thus created ironically counterpoints the lover's painful circumstances, using the disillusionment of the abandoned nymph to comment on his own suffering. Du Bellay's "Dialogue d'un Amoureux et d'Echo", published in his *Vers Lyriques* (1549), where ten of the poem's eighteen lines make use of the echoing device, relies heavily on bitter questions for its effect :

> Qu'estois-je avant qu'entrer en ce passaige? Saige.
> Et maintenant que sens-je en mon couraige ? Raige.
> Qu'est-ce qu'aimer, & s'en plaindre souvent ? Vent.
> Que suis-je donq', lors que mon cœur en fend ? Enfant.[111]

The parallel with Montgomerie's final stanza, the only one to employ the device, is close enough to suggest that the Scots poet may have known Du Bellay's "Dialogue" :

> Quhat lovers, Echo, maks sik querimony? Mony　　　*complaint*
> Quhat kind of fyre doth kindle thair Curage? Rage
> Quhat Medicine (O Echo, knouis thou ony?) Ony
> Is best to stay this Love of his Passage? Age
> Quhat merit thay that culd our sighs assuage? Wage
> Quhat wer we first in this our Love profane? Fane　　　*glad*
> Quhair is our Joy (O Echo tell agane)? Gane.
> 　(50–56)

The skill lies, of course, in the ironic relationship of rhyme-word and echo, a point Montgomerie foregrounds by using the unfamiliar, slightly pedantic "querimony" in his first line. "Curage / rage" is a precise enough parallel to suggest that he was aware of Du Bellay's poem; but whereas the French dialogue rather tails off with five further lines of complaint, Montgomerie concludes with the echo-device itself, picking up his refrain to end with the dramatic "Gane". It is the conclusion of a poet entirely in command of his materials.

---

[110] Theodor van der Does, ed., *Lusus imaginis iocosae, sive Echus* (Utrecht: Aegidius Romanus, 1638).

[111] Joachim du Bellay, *Œuvres poétiques*, ed. Henri Chamard, 6 vols. STFM (Paris : Hachette, 1908–1931), 3:148–49.

The poem to which this echoic stanza constitutes the climax is constructed around a systematic comparison of the lover's circumstances with those of the abandoned Echo. It demonstrates that many of Montgomerie's most characteristic techniques were already firmly established: the persistent use of anaphora, creating a compressed, aphoristic style, which is reinforced by a good deal of alliteration and a lexical range which includes both elevated latinisms and idiomatic Scots:

> Thy pairt to mine may justlie be compaird
> In mony poynts vhilk both we may repent.
> Thou hes no hope and I am clene dispaird.
> Thou tholis but caus, I suffer innocent.          *suffers*
> Thou does bewaill and I do still lament.
> Thou murns for nocht, I shed my teirs in vano.    *mourn*
> To the Echo and thou to me agane.
>      (8–14)

The emotional atmosphere of the poem is, of course, highly exaggerated: the lover's situation is defined only in the most general terms, and it differs from the traditional mainstream of amatory verse in that the persona has been betrayed by his beloved, rather than portraying himself as a faithful but unrequited lover. This lends the poem a sharper tone, reminiscent of some of Alexander Scott's lyrics; but it remains a genre-piece, skilled in its manipulation of standard materials but not particularly innovative in either form or content. It demonstrates the expertise with which Montgomerie deployed the materials of Mannerism, but it does not do a great deal more.

"Some Reulis and Cautelis" also provides evidence, however, that Montgomerie was by 1584 engaged in a much more substantial project, the only really extended poem he is known to have composed. *The Cherrie and the Slae* [**100–101**], of which James cites ll. 99–112 as an example of "all kyndis of cuttit and brokin verse, quhairof new formes are daylie inuentit according to the Poets pleasour", was to have an extraordinary publishing history, seemingly appearing in print only in the last year or so of Montgomerie's life, and then going through repeated editions in the course of the seventeenth and eighteenth centuries. It seems clear that, although he had begun this remarkable, if ultimately unconvincing, allegorical work by late 1584, he did not then complete it, leaving it unfinished until provoked to take it up again by the appearance in print in 1597 of the fragment he had written nearly fifteen years before. We cannot be sure that the whole of this first, incomplete version was composed by the time James quoted an early stanza in his "Reulis and Cautelis"; but on the whole it is likely that the entire 930 lines, or 66-and-a-bit fourteen-line stanzas, were written by the end of 1584.[112]

---

[112] For further discussion of *The Cherrie and the Slae* and its versions, see below, 188–91, 317–31.

It was at this period that several members of the royal circle were at work upon such large-scale projects, although most of them were (despite James's strictures against translation, in which "ye essay not your awin ingyne of *Inuentioun*") translations: the king himself with his *Uranie*, Thomas Hudson was scottishing another of Du Bartas' works as *The Historie of Judith*, Stewart of Baldynneis was producing his version of Ariosto's *Orlando Furioso*, partly through the medium of Desportes' French abridgement, while William Fowler was at work on *The Triumphes of Petrarke*. It is striking that Montgomerie alone chose to try his "awin ingyne of Inuentioun", although the ingenuity of the poem perhaps lies more in its bold metrical scheme than in the brilliance of its allegorical structure. The latter point, indeed, may in part explain the fact that *The Cherrie and the Slae* was left unfinished for more than a decade.

As Helena Shire has shown, the poem's metrical scheme was not "inuentit according to the Poets pleasour": Montgomerie chose to adopt a stanza which fitted a well-known dance tune, known as "The Nine Muses" in England and as "The Banks of Helicon" in Scotland.[113] It may be, indeed, as Shire argues, that the idea of applying this lyric form to a dream-vision was directly influenced by Thomas Howell's "Dreame", published in his *Devises: Delightful Discourses* (1581). But the stanza was already established in Scotland: when Sir Richard Maitland, some time between 1553 and 1568, composed his "Ballat of the Creatioun of the Warld" to this tune, he was providing a spiritualised version of the love-song "The Bankis of Helicon", which would subsequently be copied into his daughter's manuscript anthology.[114] Other poets used it in other contexts, and it was separately copied (sometimes as "The Bankis of Helicon") in music manuscripts from the 1570s onward, in one instance in a four-part setting by the experienced composer Andrew Blackhall (c. 1536–1609). It may be, indeed, as Shire suggests, that Blackhall's setting, recorded in Thomas Wood's part-books between 1575 and 1584 and in one case explicitly named "The Cherrie and the Slae", was made specifically for a performance of Montgomerie's poem.[115]

But this notion is not without its difficulties. There is a radical shift of genre, even from Howell's eight-stanza piece, written in two alternating stanza forms, to the extended allegorical narrative of *The Cherrie and the Slae*. The repetition of the intricate "Bankis of Helicon" tune through the 67 stanzas of Montgomerie's incomplete first version, still more of the 114 stanzas the poem would comprise in its eventual form, would have been challenging for both performers and audience; and while we must beware of imposing our own expectations of performance upon

---

[113] Shire, *Song, Dance and Poetry*, 165–73.

[114] For Maitland's poem, see *Bannatyne Manuscript*, ed. Tod Ritchie, 2:26–32; and *The Maitland Quarto Manuscript*, ed. W.A. Craigie (Edinburgh: STS, 1920), 152–59.

[115] Shire, *Song, Dance and Poetry*, 171.

sixteenth-century culture, there are few parallels for such a leviathan of court entertainment. Perhaps the fact that the poem was left incomplete also reflects the fact that its overgrown nature displaced it from its originally-intended mode of circulation, leaving Montgomerie with no means of bringing his work to its audience, and hence no reason for finishing it. Or perhaps he could not yet find a satisfying way of concluding an allegorical debate which lacks a powerful rhetorical momentum, and hence abandoned it at a point at which it might, in principle, go on for ever.

*The Cherrie and the Slae*, paradoxically, demonstrates through its manifest imperfections Montgomerie's mastery of *lyric* form. The sonnets and stanzaic lyrics we know him to have written by 1584 reveal the rhetorical skill with which he manipulates received materials within a restricted formal compass, and the wit with which he can give such conventional pieces an original twist. But in attempting to apply the local structures of lyric to an extended allegorical narrative he essays the impossible, an enterprise admirably — but no doubt unwittingly — expressed in the episode early in the poem in which the persona makes an Icarus-like flight with Cupid's wings. It is in Cupid's wings, ironically, that Montgomerie's flight is most assured; it is when he takes on a much more ambitious poetic scheme that he falls to the ground. Yet even in the incomplete version of the poem there are many fine passages, especially in the opening description of the spring landscape (where there are, of course, plenty of traditional materials for the poet to draw on) and in the self-mocking exchange with Cupid. The intricate stanza-form, of course, lends itself naturally to the joyful atmosphere of summer plenty which is the subject of the first hundred lines:

> The dew as diamondis did hing            *hang*
> Vpon the tender twistis and ying        *twigs; young*
> Ouir-twinkling all the treis
>     And ay quhair flowris flourischit faire
> Thair suddainly I saw repaire
> In swarmes the sownding beis.
>     Sum sweitly hes the hony socht
> Quhil they war cloggit soir,
>     Some willingly the waxe hes wrocht,
> To heip it vp in stoir,
>       So heiping with keiping
>         Into thair hyuis thay hyde it,         *hives*
>       Precyselie and wyselie
>         For winter thay prouyde it.
> (100: 57–70)

Montgomerie expertly deploys the tripartite structure of his measure to organ-
ise the stanza: the conventional imagery of jewel-like dew on morning foliage
culminates in the introduction of the swarm of bees (the principal subject of the
stanza) with the concluding rhyme; the intermediate quatrain is built around a
constrastive but finely balanced 'sum . . . some' construction, which flows easily
into the final section with its insistent feminine internal rhymes. It is instructive
to compare these lines with Polwarth's similar use of industrious bees in *The Pro-
mine*;[116] there is no blurring of art and nature in Montgomerie's landscape, and his
approach to natural description here is in this respect closer to Alexander Hume's
*Day Estivall* than it is to the work of the latter's brother. But the stronger rhetorical
influence is Dunbar's *Goldyn Targe*: Montgomerie avoids the heraldic artificiality
of the earlier poem, but numerous echoes hint at his recollection of it.[117]

In one important respect, however, Montgomerie does significantly combine
the natural and the human. The harmonious quality inherent in the *locus amoenus*
is conventional enough, but here the point is developed in a stanza which seems
to mimic the musicality of the poem itself:

> To heir thae startling stremis cleir
> Me thocht it musique to the eir
> Quhair deskant did abound
>     With Trible sweit and Tenor iust,
> And ay the Echo repercust
> Hir Diapason sound
>     Set with the Ci-fol-fa-uth cleife
> Thairby to knaw the note,
>     Thair soundt a michtie semibreif
> Out of the Elphis throte
>         Discreitlie, mair sweitlie
>             Nor craftie Amphion
>         Or musis that vsis
>             At fountaine Helicon.
>     (100: 85–98)

The musical terminology is less insistent than Henryson's two encyclopedic stanzas
in *Orpheus and Erudices*, but its function is comparable:[118] Montgomerie delicately
evokes, through his allusions to worldly music, that universal harmony which un-
derlies it and which articulates the divine order. But it is into this idyllic world
that Cupid appears, luring the persona into his ill-fated attempt to fly and to use

---

[116] See above, p. 69–70.

[117] *Poems*, ed. Stevenson, 342–43. Stevenson also notes echoes of other earlier Scots
poems, including *The Kingis Quair* and Gavin Douglas' *Palice of Honoure*.

[118] ll. 226–39: Henryson, *Works*, ed. Fox, 139–40.

the god's own bow. Again, *The Goldyn Targe* provides an intertext: as Dunbar's dreamer, fascinated by the splendour of the gods and goddesses, draws Venus's attention to his presence, so it is the curiosity of Montgomerie's persona which marks him as Cupid's "pray".

The stanza-form proves itself in what follows as well-adapted for an action scene as it is for description:

> Gif I had rypelie bene aduysit
> I had not rashlie enterprysit
> To soir with borrowit pennis　　　　　*soar; feathers*
> 　Nor yit haue saied the archer craft　　*attempted*
> Nor schot my self with sik a schaft
> As resoun quyte miskennis.　　　　　*denies*
> 　Fra wilfulnes gaue me my wound
> I had na force to flie
> 　Then came I granand to the ground.　　*groaning*
> "Freind, welcome hame," quod he.
> 　　"Quhair flew ye, quhome slew ye
> 　　　Or quha bringis hame the buiting?
> 　I sie now," quod he now,
> 　　"Ye haif bene at the schuting."
> (100: 183–196)

The argument is again neatly fitted to the formal patterning, but now with a bi-partite structure, the reflective comment of the first six lines balanced by the narrative progression of the rest. But Montgomerie does more than this, introducing the opposed pair "resoun" and "wilfulnes" which will reappear four hundred lines later as participants in the allegorical debate. Since Experience ("the Skuil-maister of fuillis") is invoked in the previous stanza, it seems evident that Montgomerie already has the lines of the ensuing moral argument in view. However effective this opening episode may be, it serves as no more than an *hors d'oeuvre* for the introduction of the Cherrie and the Slae at ll. 305–308 and the long discussion to which they give rise. By the time Montgomerie apparently abandoned work on his poem, the debate extended to almost six hundred lines, two-thirds of the whole — and when it was eventually completed, fifteen years later, this would be doubled. Here was the central aesthetic problem: deftly as Montgomerie managed individual stanzas, the sheer weight of the moral debate threatened to throw the whole work out of balance. In the priority of lyric form over narrative structure, and in the triumph of local effect over larger patterns of meaning, *The Cherrie and the Slae* is a characteristically Mannerist work; that it seems to have posed aesthetic problems for its author which he was, at least at that time, unable to solve and to which, I shall later argue, he was *never* able finally to provide a completely convincing solution, reflects the challenge which a quintessentially medieval genre like the dream vision presented to the later Renaissance. Even Spenser's much more ambitious and radically revisionist version of allegorical form in *The Faerie Queene* would remain unfinished: Spenser, clearly, was a more accomplished narrative artist than Montgomerie, and he had a greater understanding both of the demands and possibilities of allegory and of the meanings he wanted his poem to embody. He had the good sense, too, to plant his poem in the strong narrative soil of romance, while Montgomerie relies on the by now less fertile soil of the *psychomachia*. It was not, as far as we know, a mistake he made twice: his uncompleted experiment with the long poem was put to one side until it was discovered by the printer Robert Waldegrave nearly fifteen years later, and Montgomerie thereafter seems to have confined himself to the lyric forms of which he was truly the master.

Of Montgomerie's poems quoted by James, the most enigmatic is certainly "Before the Greeks durst enterpryse" [43], an elegant lyric of which the final stanza provides the king with his example of the "Common stanza . . . suitable for materis of love":

> Quhilk Ansueir maid thame not so glad
> That thus the Victors they suld be
> As evin the Ansuer that I had
> Did gritly ioy and comfort me
>   Quhen lo thus spak Apollo myne,
>   "All that thou seeks it sall be thyne."
>   (19–24)

James, then, read the poem as an amatory lyric, from which it would follow that "Apollo myne", the oracle whose favour the speaker celebrates in these closing lines, must be the Beloved. But there is a good deal more to the text than meets the eye, and it is equally unclear that love is its true subject and that the persona's pleasure at the apparent reassurance he has received is justified.

The poem is built, almost in the manner of a sonnet, around a central conceit: the persona's search for an unspecified favour is compared to the petition supposedly made by the Greeks to the Delphic oracle to know in advance the outcome of their proposed expedition against Troy. The first three stanzas of the lyric might be seen as equivalent to three sonnet quatrains, with the fourth and last, which expresses the tenor of the conceit, fulfilling in expanded form the function of a final couplet. In its elegant deployment of a classical anecdote, the song displays the self-consciously erudite manner of much "Castalian" poetry and of its French models. Whether directly or through some intermediary, Montgomerie appears to base his conceit upon the account in Guido della Colonna's *Historia Destructionis Troiae*:

At quiam postquam Achilles et Patroclus, Grecorum nuncii, pervenerunt, de intrando in templum Apollonis congrua hora captata cum consilio sacerdotum in ipso templo seruencium ipsi deo qui colebatur in ipso, templum ipsum deuoto corde humiliter intrauerunt. Et factis eorum oblacionibus in multorum donarum prodiga quantitate, petentibus ab eo de Grecorum negociis habere responsum, sic eis predictus Apollo submissa voce respondit: "Achilles, Achilles, reuertere ad Grecos tuos a quibus missus es, et dic eis quod pro certo futurum se salubriter ad Troyam ituros ibique prelia multa committere, sed infallibiliter erunt decimo anno uictores, Troyanam urbem dabunt funditus in ruinam, regem Priamum, eius consortem, eiusque filios morti tradent et omnes maiores eorum, illos tantum uiuere permittendo quos elegerit ipsorum Grecorum sola uoluntas." Quo ab Achille percepto et facto exinde ualde leto . . .

[After Achilles and Patroclus, the Greek messengers, had reached this island, they took the proper hour for entering the temple, at the advice of the priests in the temple who served the god who was worshipped in it, and they entered this temple humbly with devout heart. When they had made their offerings with a lavish amount of large gifts, and as the messengers of the Greeks were seeking to have an answer from him concerning the affairs of the Greeks, this Apollo replied to them thus in a low voice: "Achilles, Achilles, go back to the Greeks by whom you were sent, and tell them they will assuredly go in safety to Troy and carry on many battles there, but they will be victors without fail in the tenth year, and will completely ruin the city of Troy, and will deliver King Priam, his wife, their children, and all the nobility to death, and will permit only those to live whom the will of the Greeks chooses." When Achilles had understood this, he was made very happy by it . . .][119]

It seems probable that Montgomerie's reference to the devotions of "the wysest Grekis",

> Quha with the teiris vpon thair Cheeks
> And with the fyrie flammis of wod            *wood*
> And all such rites as wes the guyse
> They made that grit God sacrifyce,
> (9–12)

is inspired by Guido's description of the entry of Achilles and Patroclus "deuoto corde humiliter" and of their offerings "in multorum donorum quantitate"; and the complete destruction of Troy, indicated by Montgomerie's "Troy and Trojans

---

[119] Guido della Colonna, *Historia Destructionis Troiae*, ed. N.E. Griffin (Cambridge, MA: Harvard University Press, 1936), 97–98 ; the translation is by M.E. Meek (Bloomington and London: Indiana University Press, 1974), 94–95.

haiv they suld / To use them hailly as they wold" (ll. 17–18), is predicted in graphic detail in the Latin. Similarly, the joy of the Greek emissaries at the promise of victory, the mainspring of the Scots poem, is signalled by Guido's "Quo ab Achille percepto et facto exinde ualde leto . . ."

Like Dares and other historians of the Trojan war, however, Guido makes the oracle explicitly include the fact that the victory will come "decimo anno". This detail is one of the most fundamental elements of the story as it was passed down through the Middle Ages; John Barbour, for example, writing in 1375–1376, asks in the context of a list of treasonable acts

> Wes nocht all Troy with tresoune tane
> Quhen ten yeiris of the wer wes gane?
> Then slayn wes mony thowsand
> Of thaim withowt throw strenth of hand,
> As Dares in his buk he wrate
> And Dytes, that knew all thar state.[120]

In Montgomerie's presentation of the Greeks' joy at the prospect of victory, however, there is no hint of awareness that the triumph will be delayed. This omission is, moreover, extended to the speaker, whose pleasure at *his* oracle's promise of "all that thou seeks" clearly anticipates that the reward will come very soon. But the proclivity of the Delphic oracle for verbal ambiguity, puzzling or misleading its enquirers, was itself well known in later tradition, and although there is no earlier suggestion than Montgomerie's poem that the Greeks were misled about the war, a reference in the *Odyssey* (8. 72–82) indicates a highly ambiguous allusion to the eventual quarrel between Odysseus and Achilles.[121] To the audience of Montgomerie's song, then, the omission of the prospect of a ten-year war, and the narrator's apparent obliviousness to the implications of his oracle's promise in the context of the Delphic analogy, would surely have been significant.

But what are the *interpretative* implications of this gap between the narrator's understanding of his situation and the audience's background knowledge of the story upon which the conceit depends? If we permit this knowledge to impinge upon our reading, turning the words of the oracle into the kind of misleading truth so frequently associated with oracular pronouncements, the resultant irony undermines both "Apollo myne" and, because his joy is so obviously misplaced,

---

[120] John Barbour, *The Brus*, 1. 521–526, ed. Matthew P. McDiarmid and James A.C. Stevenson, 3 vols. (Edinburgh: STS, 1980–1985), 2:20.

[121] On the nature of this reference, see H.W. Parke and D.E.W. Wormell, *The Delphic Oracle* (Oxford: Blackwell, 1956), 1:313; for the later reputation of the oracle, see Joseph Fontenrose, *The Delphic Oracle: Its Responses and Operations* (Berkeley: University of California Press, 1978).

the poet's own persona. The poem turns from a celebration into a veiled complaint, or at least a challenge: how long, the poet (as distinct from his gullible persona) seems to be asking, will you make me wait for the fulfilment of your promise? What we make of this will depend to a great degree upon whether we take "Apollo myne" to be the Beloved, as James himself implies, or the king. Modern critics are divided: Jack sides with James, while Shire prefers a political reading. The text itself, we should observe, gives us no help: either reading is possible (as is a still more tantalising possibility, that James is addressed as both Beloved *and* prospective patron), and we may well suppose that this ambiguity is just what Montgomerie intended. The fact that James "misses" the possible direction of the irony towards himself is in turn capable of more than one interpretation, and it certainly does not prove that Montgomerie did not intend the challenge to be a Dunbar-like begging message to his prospective, but not over-generous, patron.[122] The delicately enigmatic balance of the poem surely makes this political subtext more rather than less likely: on this reading, Montgomerie is entering into an interpretative conspiracy with the audience with himself as victim, and the skill with which this self-ironising posture is established wins the sympathy of a listener who recognises the omission which the poetic persona "fails" to see. Such a ploy *might*, it is true, be adopted to earn the approval and co-operation of a mistress, but it is even more likely to impress a king who prides himself on his classicism. It would, moreover, be in keeping with this game for the object of the challenge to exercise his interpretative right to miss the point, and to do so publicly by insisting that it is directed towards something quite different.

Only two of Montgomerie's poems can with any confidence be assigned to the period between the publication of James's *Essayes of a Prentise* in the autumn of 1584 and Montgomerie's departure for the Netherlands in July 1586. Both link the poet with Sir Humphrey Colquhoun of Luss, a powerful laird in the west of Scotland, and the title assigned to one of them in the Ker MS. casts further interesting light on the relationship between Montgomerie and the king. "His Maistres Name" [82] is a typically Mannerist piece, an elegant puzzle-poem which scornfully challenges the reader to identify the speaker's beloved, whose initials l. 3 reveals to be "H.J." or "J.H.". Thanks to Pamela Giles and David Parkinson, we can now see that the lady in question was Jean Hamilton, who married the twenty-year-old Sir Humphrey Colquhoun in the winter of 1585–1586, and it therefore seems likely that this is one of several sonnets Montgomerie wrote on behalf of suitors in praise of their beloved.[123]

---

[122] The point would, of course, have had greater sharpness before July 1583, when the king granted the poet his pension.

[123] *Poems*, ed. Parkinson, 2:109–10; the marriage contract was completed on 29 December 1585, and specified that the marriage was to take place before 26 January 1586 (Fraser, *Chiefs of Colquhoun*, 1:145–46).

But it is also apparent that this sonnet is linked to another, "To his Majestie that he wrote not against vmquhill Maistres Jane Cuninghame" [93], in which Montgomerie is at pains to explain to the king that he is innocent of having sought to "detract the dead", or of having taken money to do so. The root of the suspicion may derive from a line in "His Maistres Name", for Jean Cunninghame was Sir Humphrey Colquhoun's late wife, who had died in 1584 after a marriage of about six months, and Montgomerie's dismissive remark to the incompetent reader of his riddle that "I count your Cunning is not worth a cute" (82: 11) would seem to have caused offence to the Cunninghame family. It is striking, however, that Montgomerie addresses his apology not to the Cunninghames, or indeed to Sir Humphrey, but to James, whose good opinion he is evidently very keen to retain.[124]

That there was a good deal of playfulness in the king's relations with his courtier-poets is clear enough: we have seen in the case of James's "Admonitioun to the maister poete" that he was capable of teasing his friends, and the ambiguities of Montgomerie's sonnets in praise of his translation of Du Bartas' *Uranie* suggest that the process could be mutual. During the ascendancy of Lennox's former associate and rival, the Earl of Arran, from August 1583 until 2 November 1585, the court was evidently a fertile centre of literary activity, and while we cannot assign any more of Montgomerie's poems to this period, it is likely that many of them were in fact now produced for the entertainment of James, Arran and their companions. But the rivalries of the poets were merely a pale reflection of the more serious hostilities which characterised the world of the politicians; and by the beginning of 1585 James had acquired a new favourite, Patrick, Master of Gray. Gray may have been regarded as a papist when he arrived at court in the company of the ten-year-old Ludovick, son of the late Duke of Lennox, in November 1584, but his true devotion was to self-advancement, and it was his contest with Arran which concluded with the overthrow of the latter in November 1585.[125] All this had both religious and political implications: Arran, who was at the very least anti-Presbyterian, was on the whole hostile to improved relations with England, while Gray, whatever his personal views, publicly supported the proposed "league" between Scotland and England which was being promoted by Maitland of Thirlestane and other members of the government.

---

[124] As Parkinson suggests (*Poems*, 2:119), there may be a connection between this poem and the eruption of bad blood between the Cunninghames and the Montgomeries: Hugh, earl of Eglinton was murdered by some of the former on 18 April 1586, a few weeks before Montgomerie's departure for the Netherlands (see *Historie of James the Sext*, 239; Fraser, *Eglinton*, 1:49–50).

[125] For a thorough discussion of the political climate at this period, see Maurice Lee Jr, *John Maitland of Thirlestane and the Foundation of the Stewart Despotism in Scotland* (Princeton: Princeton University Press, 1959), 44–76.

A Catholic whose career at court was deeply rooted in the influence of Lennox and Arran, Montgomerie can scarcely have viewed these developments with equanimity. Although James and his government continued to be resistant to the demands of the more extreme Protestants, the negotiations of 1585–1586 over the creation of a new understanding in the relations of Kirk and State equally showed that any hopes of the king's conversion to a pro-Catholic stance were fantasy; and the political demise of Arran may well have had adverse effects on the cultural climate at court. At any event, by the summer of 1586 Montgomerie had evidently resolved to return to the Continent, in the first instance as a captain in the Netherlands. There may have been other dimensions to his departure — he obtained a licence from the king, as we shall see, which permitted him to travel to "the pairtis of France, Flanderis, Spane and vtheris beyond sey" — but the phrasing may be formulaic, and it was to the Netherlands that he actually sailed. The "Castalian" moment had passed, and Montgomerie would never again enjoy that intimacy with the king which had provided the underlying basis of his writing since the beginning of 1580.

# Chapter Four

## "Bellona's Captain": In the Netherlands, 1586–1588

On 24 June 1586 a Scottish barque was seized by an English pinnace between Gravesend and Brielle (The Brill), one of the Dutch towns of which the English had assumed control as a condition of their support in the struggle against the Spanish. The governor of Brielle, Sir Thomas Cecil, was returning to the Netherlands on board the English ship; the skipper of her prize was Alexander Montgomerie. Also on board the Scottish ship were around a hundred and twenty soldiers and an illegal cargo of sea-coal and salt, all of which was taken by Cecil and his men. Montgomerie declared that he was "nere in credytt and place to the kyng of Skottland, one that hath serued in the Low Contryes"; and he was permitted to take letters of credit he was carrying to the Earl of Leicester, the English governor-general in the Netherlands (who was then at his headquarters in Utrecht), while his ship and his men were held hostage by Cecil.[1] Clearly Montgomerie was not "a takyng man" or pirate, as Cecil suspected, but one of the Scottish captains recruited by Patrick, Master of Gray, to take part in Leicester's campaign against the Spanish. He was, at any event, commissioned by Leicester three weeks after his capture, on 14 July, taking his captain's oath a further three weeks later, on 6 August.[2] He was apparently given a first payment for his company even before these formalities were completed, since a series of accounts for 1586–1587 record a payment of 600 guilders on 14 July.[3]

The political and military situation in the Netherlands was now very different from that which Montgomerie had probably last seen in the later 1570s. With the Spanish forces under Don John's successor, the Duke of Parma, making steady military gains, and a political vacuum created by the assassination of William, prince of Orange, in July 1584, the northern United Provinces agreed to accept

---

[1] PRO, SP84/8, fols. 289r–v; cf. *CSP For.*, 21.2:55–56. The existence of this document was first pointed out by R.D.S. Jack, "Montgomerie and the Pirates", *SSL* 5 (1967–1968): 133–36.

[2] The Hague, ARA, Raad van State, no. 1524, fols. 80r–81r. For the full text of this document, see R.J. Lyall, "Alexander Montgomerie and the Netherlands, 1586–89", *Glasgow Review* 1 (1993): 52–66, here 53–54; that article represents an earlier version of the present chapter.

[3] PRO, SP9/93, fol. 63r; cf. below, 130.

an offer of assistance from Elizabeth of England, who sent Robert Dudley, earl of Leicester, as her commander in the Low Countries. The Treaty of Nonsuch, specifying the terms of English aid to the Dutch, was signed on 20 August 1585, and the first contingent of the new expeditionary force was dispatched in September 1585, even before Leicester was appointed commander; by the end of the year he was in the Netherlands with an English force of forty-nine infantry companies and up to a thousand horsemen.[4] Of these forces, only a core was to be paid for by the English government; twenty-one of the first forty-nine companies, for example, were to be financed by the Dutch, and Leicester clearly intended to build up this part of his army as much as possible.

The idea of a significant increase in the continuing Scottish contingent was apparently under discussion even before Leicester's departure for the Netherlands. It had no doubt been one of the topics dealt with, and was perhaps the main topic, when a Dutch embassy visited Scotland in August 1585, just at the time the first troops of the new English force were making their way to the Netherlands.[5] On 13 December 1585, Patrick, Master of Gray, one of the Scottish king's most trusted courtiers, wrote to Secretary Walsingham offering to raise troops in Scotland for Leicester's expedition.[6] Gray's own enthusiasm was evidently fostered by the presence in the English force of Sir Philip Sidney, with whom he had struck up a friendship during his embassy to England in the latter part of 1584; and he was encouraged by Sidney himself, Leicester, and Walsingham. On 17 May 1586, Sidney wrote to Gray from the English camp at Nijmegen:

> My Lord is exceeding desirous to have your presence here; but, by reason there is not yet so full and established authority as there should, the moiens come in so slowly, as, in good faith, I know not whether I should wish the coming of so dear a friend or no.[7]

The warning was entirely justified, for financial difficulties would continue to dog the enterprise, and Gray was already concerned about the cost to himself of raising a force.

---

[4] For a compact summary of the arrangements for Leicester's expedition, see Simon Adams, "A Puritan Crusade? The Composition of the Earl of Leicester's Expedition to the Netherlands, 1585–1586", in *The Dutch in Crisis, 1585–1588: People and Politics in Leicester's Time* (Leiden: Sir Thomas Browne Institute, 1988), 7–34. The Leicester period is usefully surveyed by F.G. Oosterhoff, *Leicester and the Netherlands, 1586–1587* (Utrecht: HES, 1988), but Oosterhoff pays little regard to the Scottish presence in the States forces.

[5] NAS, E21/64, fol. 85r.

[6] *CSP Scot.*, 8:171. A report quickly reached Spain that Leicester's force would include Gray and six hundred Scots (*CSP Span.*, 3:553–57).

[7] *Gray Papers*, 78.

In the Netherlands, as Sidney signalled, severe financial problems were threatening to undermine the war effort. By early 1586, unpaid men were already beginning to desert and return to England.[8] The problem was not new, for some of the Scottish companies which had been in the Netherlands for years had already defected to the Spanish: Captain David Boyd, who was garrisoning Bruges, for example, joined the submission to Parma in May 1584, taking eight other captains with him.[9] In such cases, religious loyalties may have played their part, for some of the Scottish companies which abandoned the Dutch cause were certainly commanded by Catholics. But a vestigial Scottish presence remained even before the troops recruited by Gray began arriving: the command of the "Scots regiment" was given after Boyd's defection to Bartholomew Balfour, the half-brother of the Henry Balfour who had been colonel during the 1570s and who had been killed at Wassenaar in 1580, and at the end of August 1585 he was ordered to join the garrison at Bergen-op-Zoom with his seven companies, all that remained, apparently, of the twenty-five companies commanded by Henry Balfour and Sir William Stewart of Houston in 1579.[10] It was this reduced Scottish contingent that the companies now to be recruited by Gray would reinforce.

Little practical support was forthcoming, however, from either the English government or the Scottish. Mendoza, the Spanish ambassador in London, was reporting as early as April 1585 that James VI was resisting pressure from Elizabeth to join in an intervention in the Low Countries, and the king gave a spirited reaction in May of the following year when urged by Archibald Douglas to support the English expedition.[11] Elizabeth, meanwhile, had fallen out with Leicester, who was reported to be anxious to return to England; personal politics therefore aligned with the English reluctance to provide an advance payment in discouraging Gray from going ahead with his plan. Nevertheless, the first elements of the new force were, according to Archibald Douglas, in place by the end of April 1586, when he reported to his English employers that "the hoile capitanis and ane gud part of the soddartis ar such as hath servit of before in the Low Cuntrey"; and Gray declared to Douglas on 27 May that he was resolved to send fifteen hundred men "within fifteyn dayis".[12] The next day he wrote to

---

[8] Leicester reported "lewd and dangerous" mutinies at Utrecht on 29 March (*CSP For.*, 20:497); on 18 June he reported 300 defections out of 1100 men, most of whom were subsequently recaptured (*CSP For.*, 21.2:26).

[9] *Staatsche Leger*, 1:266. For the Spanish account of this episode (where Boyd is mentioned but not named), see *Correspondence de Philippe II*, Part II, ed. Joseph Lefèvre, 4 vols. (Brussels: Palais des académies, 1940–1960), 2:474–84.

[10] *Staatsche Leger*, 1: 267.

[11] *CSP Span.*, 3:536; *CSP Scot.*, 8:360–63.

[12] *CSP Scot.*, 8:399–400.

Walsingham stating that "sume already ar gone, uthers going, and within a tuentye dayes I hoype to haue at his lordship a fyftein hundrethe footmen"; the day after that, "Montgomery eldir" and "Montgomery younger" appeared in a list of 68 colonels, captains and other officers ready to sail to the Netherlands under his command.[13] In view of Alexander Montgomerie's arrival a month later, it seems very probable that he was one of the two men in question, though it is impossible to determine which one; the other is harder to identify, but the only other Montgomerie who can be found in the Low Countries in the following years is the poet's brother-in-law, Adam Montgomerie of Braidstane. He, certainly, had good reason to get out of Scotland: on 21 May he had failed to appear before the Privy Council to answer charges of piracy "some yeiris syne or thairby" which had been brought against him by Thomas Copran of Dublin, and was denounced as a rebel.[14] Whatever Alexander's motives may have been, escape from his legal difficulties would have loomed large in Adam's mind.

Negotiations regarding the Scottish contribution continued. There was a constant exchange of letters through June: Gray was backing away from his commitment on the 8th, but four days later it was reported to Randolph that he was willing to go if he received a direct invitation from Leicester, a line which Gray confirmed in a letter to the latter on 16 June.[15] By this time, it seems, a substantial force had been together for some weeks; the men were restive, and Gray himself, who had incurred considerable costs in raising them, scarcely less so. All this time, the English government, deeply immersed in negotiations for an alliance with Scotland, held back from encouraging Gray in his schemes. Douglas wrote to Walsingham on 23 June:

> Truly, Sir, the gentleman doth not a little marvayle, howe it hath fallen oute, that he was first animated to the said voyage, then discharged, after noe small losse of expenses bestowed, as well for his particular preparacion, as for the entertaynment of diuers that would have gone with him in companie . . .[16]

It was at this moment, apparently, that Montgomerie, like a small number of other captains, took ship for the Netherlands. Mendoza reported on 23 July that some three or four hundred Scots had done so; although it is difficult to say how many of this number were officers, the figure suggests around three companies.[17]

---

[13] *CSP Scot.*, 8:405, 410.
[14] *RPC*, 4:72.
[15] *CSP Scot.*, 8:444.
[16] *Gray Papers*, 98.
[17] *CSP Span.*, 3:595.

The difficult discussions, punctuated by haggling over money, dragged on into the autumn. Once the Anglo-Scottish agreement was concluded in July, Elizabeth wrote to James urging him to license Gray to depart; this was reported done by 1 August.[18] Recruitment now regained some momentum, but on 9 September Gray was in Dunfermline, still demanding that the English meet his substantial costs. The previous day he had written to Leicester:

> I never haid deyr to be vithe you til nov, vould God I ver, bot I sweir the fault is not in me.[19]

It is, however, despite this disclaimer, difficult to resist the conclusion that Gray had for some time been at best lukewarm about the project, and the final straw seems to have been the death of his friend Sidney; on 6 November he wrote to Douglas that this tragedy had caused him to decide positively not to go:

> And nou Sir I must confess the treuthe, he & I haid that freindschipe that moued me to desyr so mutche my voyag to the Lou Countreis. But nou I aschur yow I mynd not to go althocht I micht have great aduancement by it, & greater than euer I did see by it. Theirfor nou, Sir, since it has pleasit God to call one that man, I content my self to leiue at home.[20]

The arrival of Montgomerie at the beginning of July with his hundred and twenty men, therefore, came at a crucial moment in the proposed Scottish intervention in the Netherlands, and the English nervousness about his position is understandable. Nor was it confined to Cecil: while prepared to grant him a commission on the basis of his "vertus preudhomme, valeur dexterite experience et bonne diligence" (the epithets are, of course, formulaic), Leicester was evidently concerned about his reliability and that of another Scot, David Oliphant, who was commissioned the day before Montgomerie and who took his oath at the same time.[21] The previous day, 5 August, Leicester had written from Utrecht to his newly-established chamber of finance, expressing some disquiet about the dependability of the Scottish forces he was taking on:

> En oultre, que donnies commission a quelque commissaire d'aller passer monstre les Écossais estantz a Delff soubz les capitaines Montmory et David Olifour, a quoy il sera besoing d'user de bon soing affin que ladicte monstre

[18] *CSP Scot.*, 8:478.

[19] "Correspondence inedite de Robert Dudley, comte de Leycester et de François et Jean Hotman", ed. P.J. Blok, *Archives du Musée Teyler*, 2e ser., 12 (1910): 79–296, here 143.

[20] *HMC Salisbury*, 3:191.

[21] ARA, RS 1524, fol. 79r–v.

se face pertinamment et fidelement. Et sera necessaire qu'enchargiez ledict commissaire qu'il prenne le serment de chasque officier desdictes compaignies en particulier tant sur leur fidelite que de leur religion, et que ceulx, qui ne sont de la religion reformee, ne soyent passez ny acceptez en service, ains rejettez nonobstant que les capitaines y voulussent contredire et ce pour certaines raisons que nous en avons.

[We further wish you to give a commission to some authorised person to go and muster the Scots who are at Delft under Captains Montmory and David Olifour, with whom it will be necessary to use great caution to ensure that the said muster takes place competently and faithfully. It will be necessary to charge the said authorised person that he take the oath of each officer of the said companies, and in particular as much regarding their faithfulness as their religion; and that those who are not of the Reformed religion are not passed or accepted into service, but rejected even if the captains wish to challenge this; this for certain reasons we have concerning this matter.][22]

That Montgomerie and Oliphant were linked in Leicester's mind is here quite evident, as is his suspicion that the religious convictions of some of the Scots might make them unreliable allies. The doubt clearly extended to the captains themselves, and in Montgomerie's case we know that he had some justification: not only was he a Catholic convert, but there is a strong possibility that his loyalty had been in doubt during his previous period of service in the Netherlands.[23]

Leicester's suspicions, moreover, were not confined to the loyalties of these individuals. Responding to the increasing note of caution in Gray's letters, Leicester had written to Walsingham on 5 July:

Vppon the vewe of the master [of] Greys letter I fell into some doubt of some matters told me a good whyle since, though I beleeued it not, which was, that there was a plott laid to bringe manie Scotts over, by a device of some here, to make a bridle of our nacion to strengthen some other.[24]

It is true that Leicester, who was experiencing great difficulties with both Elizabeth and the Dutch, was understandably jumpy at this time, and that there was a fairly widespread tendency to smell plots on the slightest of evidence. But there was some basis, after all, to his concern: James VI *was* refusing to adopt an openly anti-Spanish stance, there *was* a fairly strong Catholic party in Scotland, and many in

---

[22] *Correspondentie van Leycester*, 1:207–8.

[23] See above, 53–57.

[24] *Correspondence of Robert Dudley Earl of Leicester*, ed. John Bruce (London: Camden Society, 1844), 348.

Areas under
Spanish occupation

FRIESLAND

OVER-ISSEL

Deventer

Zutphen

HOLLAND  Woerden  ECHT

Schoonhoven  UT  Utrecht

Doesburg

Oudewater

Arnhem

Wassenaar
Den Haag  Delft

Rhenen

Rotterdam

Gorinchem

Nijmegen

De
Briel

Wesel

Dordrecht

ZEELAND

Geertruidenberg

Gelder

Breda

Bergen op
Zoom

Antwerp

DIOCESE
OF
LIÈGE

MILITARY  SITUATION  IN THE  NETHERLANDS  c. 1588

the Netherlands *were* unhappy about the implications of the English intervention. The 'certaines raisons' that Leicester had for not trusting his new recruits therefore had their foundation in his more general fear that the Scottish troops now arriving in dribs and drabs were really the agents of some other power; he would surely have used a stronger form of words to Walsingham if he had suspected Spanish involvement, so the "some other" nation of the alleged plot was perhaps France. It was, after all, only three years since the Dutch had attempted to persuade Henry III to intervene, and Henry of Navarre (though he certainly had his own difficulties) was a potential leader of the Protestant cause.[25] Nor did Leicester trust Bartholomew Balfour, the Scottish commander already in the field; on 1 July he had written to Walsingham that

> I haue noe liking of Balford here, he is a bad fellow; and wholy at others direction and not mine; indeed and if the master of Greie come not, he will looke to be collonell-generall over them all, which I will no way consent to.[26]

None of this tells us much, of course, about Montgomerie's real reasons for arriving, with his ship's somewhat mysterious cargo of salt and sea-coal, in the Netherlands, nor about his relationship, if any, with David Oliphant. The latter is himself a somewhat shadowy figure: it is probably he who occurs along with the two Montgomeries among the Scots intending to accompany the Master of Gray in May. He must have arrived in the Netherlands earlier than Montgomerie, for on 19 June one of his men, William Thomson, was married to a local woman in Dordrecht.[27] Such matches did not, it would seem, necessarily take long to develop: Thomas Chilmor (Chalmer), in Montgomerie's own company, married Jaeneke Verhagen in Delft on 6 August, the same day that the two companies were sworn in. Like many of the other women who wed Scottish soldiers at this period, Verhagen was from the south, from Menen in Flanders, and it is no doubt significant that she was the widow of another Scot, Thomas Brunol.[28] The marriage of William Thomson in Dordrecht might reasonably be taken to imply that Oliphant's company had arrived some weeks before Montgomerie's, but Leicester's

---

[25] On the relationship between French politics and the Dutch wars, see Pieter Geyl, *The Revolt of the Netherlands, 1555–1609*, 2nd ed. (London: Benn, 1958), 195–96, 218–26; and Geoffrey Parker, *The Dutch Revolt*, 176, 225–27. Simon Adams has suggested to me that Denmark might be the foreign power in Leicester's mind; it is true that a marriage between James and a daughter of the Danish king had been under discussion for some time, having been proposed by Elizabeth of England as early as June 1585 (*CSP Scot.*, 7:678).

[26] *Correspondence of Leicester*, 347.

[27] J. Maclean, *De huwelijksintekeningen van Schotse militairen in Nederland, 1574–1655* (Zutphen: Walburg, 1976), 81.

[28] Maclean, *Schotse militairen*, 68.

instructions to his chamber of finance makes it clear that by 5 August the two Scottish companies were together at Delft, just south of The Hague.

Montgomerie and Oliphant, once their commissions were completed, were presumably assigned, along with a number of other newly-recruited Scottish units, to take part in Leicester's expedition into Gelderland. Some Scots, very probably these companies, were certainly involved in the capture of Doesburg on 2 September, Leicester having reported to Walsingham three days earlier that

> [w]e are hardlie handled by the States now for monie, yet are there Scotts arrived latelie xii[c] and as many more looked for.[29]

It was the army from this engagement, under Leicester's own command and including Sir Philip Sidney, which then proceeded to Deventer, moving on to commence a siege of Zutphen.[30] It was there, of course, that Sidney was mortally wounded on 23 September, dying on 17 October. By an extraordinary coincidence and the fortunes of war, the foremost poets of their generation in England and Scotland had happened together on a Dutch battlefield; we cannot definitely put them in the same camp until Zutphen, but it is highly likely that their companies had been part of the same force since Doesburg, and that they had been together at least from the time that Leicester led his army into Gelderland in the latter part of August. That Montgomerie and the other newly-arrived companies were at Zutphen is beyond question: on 26 September, three days after Sidney was wounded, a list of "Bandes present in the campe before Zutphen" includes nine companies of the "Scootes Regiment", the captains' names including "Holliphant" and Alexander Montgomerie.[31] This thorough (if mathematically uncertain) document gives the number of men in each company, divided into "holle", "sicke", and "hurte": Montgomerie's band now consisted of ninety-two men with no casualties. Two further such lists survive, for 4 and 5 October, and in both cases Montgomerie's company comprises seventy-nine fit men and twenty-one 'sycke'.[32]

---

[29] On the presence of the Scots at Doesburg, *CSP For.*, 21.2:150–52.

[30] See Pieter Christiaansz. Bor, *Oorsprongk, begin en vervolgh der Nederlandschen oorlogen, beroerten en borgerlyke oneenigheden* (Amsterdam: widow of Johannes van Someren et al., 1679–1684), 3:750.

[31] PRO, SP84/10, fols. 67r–68r. This list of nine companies tallies with a much briefer summary, undated but also belonging to September 1586, which attributes 1350 men to "Balfors Regiment, ix.companies" (fol. 94r).

[32] The list for 5 October appears in Bodleian MS. Tanner 78, fol. 161r. Although the list for 4 October (BL, MS. Harley 285, fol. 251r) is damaged at the bottom of the leaf where the Scots names ought to be, the numbers of men in each company are largely intact, and it is therefore clear that Montgomerie's company was in the same condition as on the following day.

By the time Montgomerie arrived in the Netherlands, Sidney was campaigning in Flanders, returning to Vlissingen in mid-August; the first opportunity for a meeting of the two poets would therefore have been in Gelderland at the end of the month. If the companies of Sir Philip Sidney and Alexander Montgomerie were together for several weeks in August and September 1586, it is probable that they had some opportunity to discuss literary matters. Cecil's letter of 26 June demonstrates Montgomerie's readiness to assert his position at the Scottish court, and it would be surprising if he had not drawn Leicester's attention to his reputation as James's "maister of our arte"; conversely, Sidney was undoubtedly aware of James's cultural milieu, and probably knew about the Scottish king's literary activities.[33] That Montgomerie and Sidney are likely to have had acquaintances in common is undeniable: we have seen, for example, that Sidney and the Master of Gray were friends, and in the narrow circle of the Scottish court it is unlikely that Montgomerie and Gray were unacquainted, even before the former's recruitment to the Dutch service. By the same token, Henry Constable, who first visited Edinburgh in 1583 and who addressed sonnets to the Princess of Orange in 1584 and to Lady Penelope Rich (Sidney's "Stella") later in the decade, is a possible link between the two men.[34] It is even conceivable that they had met during a visit by Montgomerie to London in the early 1580s. Sidney had certainly not left his literary interests behind; as Jan van Dorsten pointed out, the English expedition as a whole embraced chivalric and cultural ideals which Sidney represented more clearly than anyone, and 'it shows the campaigner's *vertu* to find so many men of culture in their leading ranks'.[35]

Any incipient relationship between the two men was, of course, cut short by the wound which Sidney received on 23 September; they were together in the field for no more than four weeks. As is so often the case with Montgomerie, the record is silent: there is no hint of the Scottish poet's presence in the evidence regarding Sidney's last days, and nothing among Montgomerie's extant corpus that

---

[33] On Sidney's relations with Scotland and with James, see Dominic Baker-Smith, "Sidney's Death and the Poets", in *Sir Philip Sidney: 1586 and the Creation of a Legend*, ed. Jan van Dorsten, Dominic Baker-Smith and Arthur F. Kinney (Leiden: Brill, 1986), 83–103, here 93–95. It seems very probable that the inclusion of "King James of Scotland" among the patrons of "Sweete Poesie" in Sidney's *Apologie for Poetry* (*Prose Works*, ed. Albert Feuillerat, 4 vols. [Cambridge: Cambridge University Press, 1912], 3:35) is an allusion to James's *Essayes of a Prentise*.

[34] On the possible association of Constable with Sidney, see H.R. Woudhuysen, *Sir Philip Sidney and the Circulation of Manuscripts, 1588–1640* (Oxford: Clarendon Press, 1996), 289–91; on the connections among Constable, Penelope Rich and Continental Protestant scholars, see van Dorsten, "Poets, Patrons, and Professors", 82–90; for Constable's relationship with Montgomerie, see below, 178–79, and Lyall, "'Thrie Truear Hairts'".

[35] Van Dorsten, "Poets, Patrons, and Professors", 107.

alludes to his life, work, or death. James VI and members of his circle (including the Master of Gray and Captain James Halkerstoun, the latter a veteran of the Dutch wars who was now back in Scotland) contributed verses, mostly in Latin, to the memorial volume published in Cambridge by Alexander Neville early in 1587, but Montgomerie, on active service somewhere in the Netherlands, was naturally not involved.[36] That he was unaware of, or unmoved by, Sidney's death seems very improbable; but it finds no echo in his extant work, and the possible implications of this remarkable chance conjunction for his future writing are equally unfathomable. There is, for that matter, nothing in any of his surviving verse that relates directly to his military career in the Netherlands, if we except 'The Poets Complante aganst the wnkyndnes of his Companions vhen he wes in prisone' [11], which seems more likely to relate to some episode in Scotland than to his undoubted imprisonment in Holland. Perhaps poetry was for Montgomerie inseparably linked with courtiership and his life in Scotland, and had no place in the life of a soldier; or perhaps any verse he did produce while abroad simply failed to find its way into the materials available to the scribe of the Ker manuscript. Whatever the reason, his experiences while in the States' service, including the death of Sidney, are nowhere visibly reflected in his surviving verse.

Soon after Sidney was wounded, it became apparent to Leicester that his attack on Zutphen was bound to fail. The Spanish defenders were having little difficulty in supplying their men, and the besiegers were unable to prevent provisions reaching the town.[37] Expected reinforcements of German troops failed to eventuate, and there began to be defections on the English side. By mid-October, Leicester was redirecting his forces to secure Deventer, Doesburg, and the Veluwe, and by the end of the month he had abandoned the siege, returning to Utrecht and leaving a token force in a fortification outside Zutphen. At the same time, further financial problems led to a scaling-down of the Dutch-funded part of the army: whereas there were fifty companies of English troops on the States' payroll on 21 May 1586 (in addition to the thirty-nine funded by the English government), this figure had been reduced to twenty-three by the time Leicester returned temporarily to England in November.[38] This reorganisation clearly also affected the Scottish forces which had expanded rapidly in the course of the summer: their greatest extent would appear to be recorded in a set of accounts for 1586–1587 which lists a total of thirty-five Scots companies, eleven in Balfour's regiment and a further twenty-four among the "Anglois, Irlandois et Ecossais estant a la charge du pais", among whom

---

[36] Alexander Neville, *Academiae Cantabrigiensis Lachrymae Tumulo Nobilissimi Equitis, D. Philippi Sidneij Sacratae* (London: John Windet, 1587), sig. K1–12; on Halkerstoun's career in the Netherlands, see Lyall, "Anti-Calvinist Propagandist?", 212.

[37] Bor, *Nederlandtschen oorlogen*, 3:751–52.

[38] Adams, "Puritan Crusade?", 13.

are seventeen captains who subsequently disappear completely from the record and whose forces must either have been absorbed into other units or returned home.[39] But with so many contending political agencies — Leicester's administration, the formal organs of central power in the Republic, the States of the individual provinces, and field commanders like Count Hohenlohe and Sir John Norris — there was little certainty in the military structure, and it is evident that some companies continued to serve although they were not officially on the books.

Montgomerie's men, it would seem, soon fell into that category. The 1586–1587 accounts show that he was paid on a regular basis between 14 July 1586 and 1 February 1587:

| | |
|---|---|
| 24ᵉ du Juillet 1586 — | fl. 600 |
| 23ᵉ d'Aoust 1586 — | fl. 500 |
| 10e de Septembre 1586 — | fl. 200 |
| Les mois de Juillet et Aoust par Lodenstein surquoy est suyuie ordonnance le 12ᵉ de decembre 1586 — | fl. 1151 |
| 11ᵉ 19ᵉ 28ᵉ de Septembre et 4ᵉ d'Octobre surquoy est ensuyuie ordonnance le 23 de decembre — | fl. 693 |
| Par ceulx de Delft surquoy est ordonnance de 10ᵉ de Januier 1587 — | fl. 385 - 6 - 7 |
| Par ceulx de la Briele surquoy est suyuie ordonnance au mesme jour — | fl. 24 - 3 - 0 |
| 16ᵉ de Januier — | fl. 60 |
| Par ceulx de Gorinchem surquoy ordonnance de 11ᵉ de feburier 1587 — | fl. 135 - 3 - 0 |
| | |
| Somme | fl. 3748 - 12 - 7[40] |

Part of this total may also be represented by the accounts up to 20 November 1586 preserved in the Dutch archives, which record a total payment to Montgomerie of fl. 1700 up to that date;[41] it is typical of the accounting methods involved that this figure does not correspond exactly to any group of payments reported to the English. In both cases, though, Montgomerie's company occurs alongside Oliphant's, among units which were apparently independent of Balfour's regiment — on this point, Leicester would appear to have had his own way.

[39] PRO, SP9/93. It is, perhaps, just possible that some of the Scots may have found employment on the Spanish side, but there is no evidence of this at this particular point of the conflict.

[40] PRO, SP9/93, fol. 63r (the dates in this document are, in accordance with the Dutch practice, according to the "new style", Gregorian calendar). The total appears, for some reason, to be nearly fl. 700 too high.

[41] *Scots Brigade*, ed. Ferguson, 1:51.

In December 1586, as part of the reorganisation of the States forces, a second Scottish regiment was established, with Archibald Paton taking over as colonel of five companies. Thomas Wilkes, the English lawyer who was a member of the Council of State, reported to Leicester on 6 December that he had urged this division of the Scottish force because of Balfour's promised support for Count Hohenlohe (who had through his pursuit of an independent line emerged as the *bête noire* of the English) in any action "in diminution of your lordship's authority", adding that he had implemented Leicester's earlier wish

> that one of the regiments shoulde be conferred on Mr Patton, whome I knowe to be at your lordship's devocion and well affected to our nation.[42]

Despite the inequality in the size of the regiments, Wilkes observed, "I have gotten the foure companies under Patton to be of the honestest captaines".[43] The result of this reduction was to ensure that the total Scottish contingent in English pay was no larger than 2150 men, only slightly in excess of the two thousand "appointed to be entertaind of that nation". No room was found for the companies of either Montgomerie or Oliphant in this reorganisation, and they must have remained among the independent units garrisoning towns or otherwise operating (at the expense, notionally at any rate, of the Dutch) under non-Scottish field commanders. Oliphant's company was present at least until June 1587, and we know that Montgomerie continued to serve for at least a further year from February of that year.

It is, in fact, possible to keep track of his company's movements for a few months after the failure at Zutphen. By 18 October, the day after Sidney's death from the wound he had received more than three weeks earlier, they were in the vicinity of Dordrecht, for on that date "Vanawius" (?Gavin) Kennedy, a soldier in Montgomerie's company, was admitted to the Heilige Sacramentsgasthuis in the town, which was now being employed as a military hospital.[44] Although the main register of the sick and wounded treated there does not survive, two separate indexes, in which the casualties are arranged under the names of their captains, leave no doubt that Montgomerie and his men were in or near Dordrecht in the

---

[42] *Correspondentie van Leycester*, 1:299. This assessment of Paton was spectacularly wrong, since he would soon betray Geldern to the Spanish (see below, 134); Archibald Douglas had warned Walsingham as early as 6 May 1586 of his unreliability, noting his "highe humour" and adding that he "inclines somewhat towardes mutiny" (*Gray Papers*, 97).

[43] A set of accounts dated 19 February 1587 assigns Paton five companies apart from his own: (William) Nisbet, (?William) Murray, (William) Renton, (John) Dallachy, and William Paton (ARA, SG 11094, fol. 139r); this corresponds with an undated list, incorrectly assigned to 1590 in the inventory, ARA, Oldenbarnevelt Papers, 2855.

[44] GA Dordrecht, 21/595.

last months of 1586: in one of them, covering the period October-December, in which each case is apparently identified by the number it was given in the register, a group of six cases (ranging between 24 and 38) occurring together under Montgomerie's name implies that several of the unit were ill or wounded at the time of their arrival from Zutphen. Given the date of Kennedy's admission, the move from Gelderland to the southern edge of Holland must have come at an early stage in the break-up of the siege; Leicester himself had moved to Deventer by 11 October, and it must have been soon after this that Montgomerie's company marched south, presumably to reinforce the line of what the Dutch now call the "great rivers" — the Maas and the Waal — against a possible Spanish attack from Brabant.

The importance of Dordrecht as a centre of military operations is not difficult to explain: situated on an island on the northern side of the River Waal, commanding the landward end of the Hollands Diep, it was a key point in the line of fortified towns which protected the southern edge of Holland against the northward advance of the Duke of Parma's forces. Fifteen kilometers south, Breda had been in Spanish hands since 1580; further east, 's-Hertogenbosch and Nijmegen were also occupied by the enemy. Much of Brabant was thus under Spanish occupation, while pressure along the second front in Gelderland meant that the heartland of the northern provinces was under attack both from the south and from the north-east. It is not surprising, then, if forces were rapidly switched, as some of the Scots clearly were in the autumn of 1586, from one sphere of operations to the other, or if great emphasis was placed upon the defence of Holland's vulnerable southern frontier. Montgomerie and his men were evidently still in the Dordrecht area towards the end of January 1587: another member of the company, William Tornes, was admitted to the Gasthuis on 26 December, while on 30 January a marriage proclamation was entered in the Dordrecht parish register for Thomas Sinclair, of Edinburgh, under Montgomerie's command, and Maricken Jansdochter of Gouda, widow of Jan Berck.[45] Someone evidently intervened to prevent the subsequent ceremony, however, for the *predikant* [*minister*] has added: "is dit houwelick opgehouden door een maecht" [*this marriage was held up by a young woman*]. Sinclair would be neither the first soldier nor the last to have made promises to more than one local woman. But the presence of the note presumably suggests that Montgomerie's company remained in the vicinity of Dordrecht for at least a few days after 30 January 1587. The records of the Heilige Sacramentsgasthuis for 1587, on the other hand, although they give information about at least eleven Scottish companies, make no mention of Montgomerie, and those who do appear are (with the striking exception of Oliphant's, one of whose

---

[45] GA Dordrecht, 11/16, fol. 73r; cf. Maclean, *Schotse militairen*, 81 (where the marginal note is not recorded).

men was treated in June 1587) all among those stated elsewhere to have been re-tained on the payroll of the States General.

The last payment recorded for Montgomerie in the 1586–1587 paylist, it may be recalled, is from 1 February, just at the time of Thomas Sinclair's proposed mar-riage. None of the accounts which cover the following year suggest that he and his men were still part of the army of the States. Both his company and Oliphant's are notably absent from a set of accounts prepared on 9 February 1587, for example, which records payments to Bartholomew Balfour and three other companies in Holland and to Paton and eight others in Gelderland and Overijssel.[46] A list of the Scottish forces, prepared in April 1587, similarly mentions Colonels Balfour and Paton and thirteen captains, including four of the nine who had been at Zutphen the previous September — but neither Montgomerie nor Oliphant.[47] Confirmation that this is not a mere oversight is provided by a paylist compiled in December 1587, which gives Balfour and eleven captains: Paton's regiment, which had defected to the Spanish side and handed over the town of Geldern on 4 July, is naturally missing, but Balfour's companies — now heavily depleted — are repeated almost exactly in the order of April, again without Montgomerie and Oliphant.[48] It is impossible to determine what happened to Oliphant's men after June 1587, but it is evident that Montgomerie remained in the Netherlands, presumably in some other part of the Dutch service.

Keeping track even of the officially recognised troops is far from simple, for despite the nominal organisation of many of the Scottish companies into two regi-ments, they were actually dispersed throughout the central and eastern parts of the Republic during 1587. At the beginning of the year, for example, James Traill and his men, theoretically part of Balfour's regiment, were in reality under the command of Sir John Norris in an attack on Wesel; while William Waddell was evidently somewhere near Dordrecht along with a number of other companies, including Montgomerie's. On 11 January, the companies of Waddell and of William Hay (who was then stationed in Rhenen) were ordered by Count Maurice van Nassau to move to Arnhem.[49] In a major reinforcement of the line north of the "great rivers" in early February, eight Scottish companies were sent by the States of Holland to garrison a number of towns from Rotterdam to Gorinchem; a month later, three of these units were actually in 's-Heerenberg, whence they were ordered

---

[46] ARA, SG 11094, fols. 129r–144v. A complete set of accounts for the period 1585–13 June 1588 (SG 12536, fols. 1–82) is also confined to Balfour's regiment of twelve com-panies, but this is presumably connected with the resolution of a long-running dispute between Balfour and the States.

[47] PRO, SP84/14, fols. 155r–158r.

[48] *Scots Brigade*, ed. Ferguson, 1:51.

[49] *Res. SG 1585–87*, 593; GA Dordrecht, 21/596; GA Arnhem, OA 296, fols. 82–83.

into Gelderland on 8 March.[50] Two of these were the companies of Archibald and William Paton, and it was the former who would a few months later surrender Geldern to the Spanish. Balfour, meanwhile, had been sent to garrison Zaltbommel with half his regiment; they withstood a determined siege until mid-August, but then they surrendered to the attackers and were reported to be moving towards Utrecht.[51] The overall picture created by this mosaic of details is of a fragmented force, deployed by the States-General and by individual provinces to deal with particular emergencies which occurred at various points along the long front lines through southern Holland and Gelderland. But none of the details which have emerged so far reveals the presence of Montgomerie's company.

Yet present they undoubtedly were. We find him next on 3 August 1587, petitioning the States of Holland "tot betalinge van syne Ruyteren" [*for payment of his horsemen*]; the States referred him to Leicester on the grounds that they themselves "geen kennisse hebben van de Commissie nochte deportement van den Suppliant alhier, nochte oock van zyne diensten ofte achterwesen" [*have no knowledge of the petitioner's commission or conduct here, nor of his services or the arrears*].[52] Montgomerie was evidently not alone: by 9 August, Hohenlohe had also written, seeking payment for five troops of cavalry and seven Scottish companies.[53] In both cases the States seem to have sought a middle course, offering to help find the necessary resources provided that Leicester in the first instance and Hohenlohe himself in the other were prepared to contribute; in Hohenlohe's case, the best they were willing to offer was a loan of 7,000–9,000 guilders. The minute concerning Montgomerie's claim is somewhat puzzling, since this is the only indication we have that he was commanding horsemen rather than infantry. Given the declared ignorance of the authorities in Holland concerning his activities, it is quite possible that this is a mistake. There is, however, an alternative explanation: if Montgomerie's foot-soldiers had been absorbed into other units or sent home following the reorganisation of 1586–87, had he "acquired" command of a cavalry unit between February and August 1587? If so, how? Whatever the nature of his command, the fact that Montgomerie petitioned the States of Holland indicates that his company had been active somewhere in that part of the Netherlands, and that he recognised that the debt was owed at provincial rather than national level. The States, on the other hand, seem (or at any rate, claimed) to have had no record

---

[50] *Res. Staten van Holland*, 48–49; *Res. SG 1585–87*, 621.

[51] *CSP For.*, 22.3:64, 264.

[52] *Res. Staten van Holland*, 214. For a lucid account of the complex governmental relations within the Dutch Republic at this period (and in particular between the federal States-General and the provincial States of Holland), see Jonathan I. Israel, *The Dutch Republic: Its Rise, Greatness, and Fall, 1477–1806* (Oxford: Clarendon Press, 1995), 276–306.

[53] Israel, *Dutch Republic*, 219.

of his employment; and the absence of his name from surviving lists lends some support to their protest. At any event, there appears to have been no immediate sequel to Montgomerie's unsuccessful petition. He must presumably have accepted the advice of the States to approach Leicester, as we shall see in a moment, but it took several months for his claim to lead to further action.

As Hohenlohe's petition of 9 August reveals, the problem of non-payment was a widespread one, and with large numbers of increasingly disaffected soldiers at large it could have disastrous consequences. As early as 4 February 1587, for example, the magistrate of Woerden wrote to the States of Holland complaining of the depredations of English, Scottish and other troopers and soldiers there and around Oudewater, who were looting and extorting money from local farmers "want . . . sy de selve mosten geven eten en drinken" [*because they had to provide food and drink for them*], and at the end of the month there were similar outrages in the vicinity of Schoonhoven. On 22 February the States decided to put rural Holland on a war footing, calling upon the population to arm themselves against such incursions.[54] No names are recorded, but it is evident that these must have been companies who had fallen outside the normal payment system and/or had been discharged but had failed to leave the country. It is unlikely that Montgomerie and his men were involved in these particular raids: they were, as we have seen, in or around Dordrecht, south-west of Schoonhoven, until the end of January, while the outrages reported in February in the line Woerden-Oudewater-Schoonhoven strongly suggest a party moving southwards, possibly heading towards the rivers from Utrecht or from further east. But the evidence of a military situation threatening to break down into chaos is clear enough.

As the strains within the anti-Spanish alliance became more evident, the hostility between the Dutch leaders, and especially Hohenlohe, and their English allies grew more overt; and the Scots, never really trusted by Leicester and in part disaffected by the execution of Queen Mary in February 1587, were more obviously a rogue element. Another factor may help to explain the difficult circumstance that Montgomerie and his men disappear from the Dutch accounts at this point but that he at least remained in the country and would subsequently claim to have continued in the service: on 25 January the States of Holland, acting in concert with the delegates of Zeeland, moved to take advantage of Leicester's absence and to regain political control by appointing Count Maurice of Nassau as Captain-General, requiring among other things that all serving officers take a new oath of "getrouwheid en gehoorzaamheid" [*loyalty and obedience*].[55] Whether or not this was his intention, the logic of the subsequent evidence is that Montgomerie managed to avoid making such a commitment.

---

[54] Bor, *Nederlandtschen oorlogen*, 2:904–6.
[55] Bor, *Nederlandtschen oorlogen*, 2:894.

Having failed to persuade the States of Holland to honour his claim, Montgomerie again disappears from the record for a few months, while financial haggling continued between Leicester's administration, the Council of State, and the provincial States, especially Holland. On 1 December, Bardesius and Teelincx, members of the Council of State, together with the Treasurer Joris de Bie, presented the States-General with a written memorandum which included a petition for payment from several of the senior commanders in the Veluwe and Overijssel, notably the brothers Hohensachsen, Count Nieuwenaar, and Arent van Groeneveld. To this powerful claim by key figures in the army is added, remarkably, that of "Capiteyn Mongommery Schot, bij zijn E*xcellencie* hoochlicke gerecomandeert" [*highly recommended by His Excellency*]; we presumably see here the fruits of the approach to Leicester which the States of Holland had suggested in August.[56] It is apparent that, at this stage at least, the Council of State was prepared to back Montgomerie's claim, but the States-general responded more cautiously, calling upon the Council's representatives to

> bericht doen van de pretensie van de capiteinen van de compaigniën, in't verscreven gescrifte vervat, mitsgaders wanneer hen de leste betalinge is gedan.

[make account of the claim of the captains of the said companies, contained in the said writings, together with the date when the last payment was made to them.][57]

The Council of State responded relatively quickly to this request for more information, writing on 24 December with an extract of the payments "Alexander Montgommeri Schots capitain" had received.[58] This was considered by the States-General five days later, when Jakob Valcke, pensionary of Goes and a member of the Council of State, presented the Council's views and was asked to report back from the States, who were, if the cryptic minute of the discussion is any guide, still not ready to make a decision.[59] The Council of State, by the time it was further consulted, had had second thoughts about backing Montgomerie's claim, for when Jan van der Beke, pensionary of Vlissingen, reported back to the States on 15 January concerning the discussions, he announced that the Council had declared

---

[56] ARA, SG 11094, fols. 602r–603r.

[57] *Res. SG 1585–87*, 738.

[58] ARA, SG 533/3120, fol. 5v. This unambiguous document removes any possibility that the captain in question was someone else of the same surname; the States of Holland had also given Montgomerie's name as Alexander on 3 August (see above).

[59] *Res. SG 1588–89*, 105.

dat zy sulcke ende dyergelycke affrekeningen ofte liquidatiën bevonden van te zer groote consequentie voir de provintiën ten respecte van andere oversten ende capitainen; dat zy mitsdien nyet geraden en vonden daerinne te treden; dan veeleer den heren Staten wel hadden willen adviseren, dat zy beter vonden, dat men denselven sal toevuegen voir eene recognitie eene redelycke somme van penningen, daermede deselve remonstrant uuyter herbergen verlost mach wordden, versuickende mitsdien die verscreven Van der Beke, dat d'heren Staten daerop willen resolveren.

[. . . that they had found such accounts or settlements to have too great consequences for the provinces with respect to other commanders and captains; that they therefore did not think it advisable to take the matter up; that they thus wished to advise the States that they found it better, in view of the claimant's good and faithful service, that the latter be given a reasonable sum of money as a recognisance, by means of which the said claimant may be liberated from the inns; the said Van der Beke further requesting that the States should agree to this.][60]

Montgomerie appears now to have been in serious financial difficulties, incarcerated in some form of house arrest in "the inns" (perhaps the winter lodgings of his company); but with so many captains demanding payment, the Dutch government was evidently reluctant to set a dangerous precedent by acknowledging the justice of his claim. At least the Council had been persuaded, by some means, of his "good and faithful service", and the recommendation that he be given an *ex gratia* payment was passed on by the States General to the States of Holland:

Na deliberatie is geresolvert, dat die heren Staten van Hollandt wordden versocht aen den verscreven suppliant, desenvolgende, te willen verstricken de somme van drye ofte vier hondert guldens, in mindernesse van heure quote in de ordinaris contributien van de provintien oft van de quote, die zy extraordinarie sullen gehouden zijn te dragen in de oude schulden, daerop de provintien alsnu wordden bescreven.

[After consideration it was agreed that the States of Holland be requested to give to the said supplicant, in view of these arguments, the sum of three or four hundred guilders, subtracting that from their share of the ordinary contributions of the provinces, or from the share that they are exceptionally liable for in respect of the old debts, about which letters are now to be sent to the provinces.]

---

[60] *Res. SG 1588–89*, 116–117.

Four hundred guilders was more than a year's pay for a captain, which had been set at one guilder per day in August 1586;[61] if, as seems more likely, the payment was intended to cover the whole company, then it was much more of a token sum. At any event, the decision taken on 15 January, which was after all only a recommendation to the States of Holland to whom Montgomerie had originally appealed four months earlier, was not immediately implemented, and remained part of ongoing negotiations over back pay: four days later, the minutes record that Henry Killigrew, an English member of the Council of State, and De Bie brought forward the claims of several cavalry companies, adding that they "hebben nochmaels gerecommandeert [*have once again recommended*] den capitain Mont-gommery".[62] Still no immediate action was taken, but the case was again before the States General on 24 January, when they agreed that "om verscheyden goede consideratien" [*for various good reasons*] he should be paid six or seven hundred guilders — perhaps the increase reflects the further delay since his claim was recognised nine days earlier — out of money originally designated for the payment of German cavalry which it had been decided to recruit a year before but which had failed to arrive. It was also agreed to give Montgomerie a "behoorlycke descharge" [*honourable discharge*], although the States noted that this was not a necessary consequence of the financial arrangement.[63] Here, therefore, it was intended that the matter should end. The following day the Council of State confirmed the payment of fl. 700 "hors des deniers estanz a Bremen consignez pour les reitres" [*out of the money at present in Bremen, intended for the cavalry*].[64]

The only note of discord in the discussion of 24 January was a refusal by the deputies of Holland to accept responsibility for the financial implications of the decision, but it was to the States of Holland that the matter now returned. On 2 February they accepted at least interim liability:

> De Staten van hollandt geheort hebbende t'Rapport vander saecke aengaende den noot ende achterwesen van capiteijn Mongommerij ende dat opde assig-natie hem verleent bij den van State ter somme van zeven hondert ponden van xl. groot omme daer van betaelt te worden uijt de penningen die van Bremen verwacht worden bij den Ontfanger Generael Philips Doublet de voorschrij-vene penningen op zijn Credyt gelicht zouden worden omme de vornoemden Montgommerij promptelijck uijt gereijct te worden / zoo verre bij gebreecke van de penningen die van Bremen alsvooren commen zullen, de middelen van die van Hollandt voor't remboursement der voorschrijvene penningen zouden moogen verbonden worden, Soe ist dat de Staten voornoemt, tot vorderinge

---

[61] *Scots Brigade*, ed. Ferguson, 1:96.

[62] *Res. SG 1588–89*, 121.

[63] ARA, SG 3120, fol. 51r.

[64] ARA, RS 6, fol. 239r.

van betaelinghe voornoemt belooft hebben ende beloeven bij desen dat bij gebreke van Remboursement van de voorschrijvene vij$^c$ £ uijt de penningen van Bremen commende, binnen drye Maenden t'selfde Remboursement gedaen zal worden uijt de gemeene middelen van den lande van Hollandt, die daer vooren zullen verbonden blijven.

[The States of Holland having heard the report of the continuing matter of the need and the arrears of Captain Montgomerie and of the allocation allowed him by the Council of State to the sum of 700 *livres de 40 gros*, to be paid out of the money expected from Bremen by the Receiver-General Philips Doublet, the foresaid money to be laid to his credit so that the fore-named Montgomerie may be promptly paid, to the extent that in the event of a lack of the money which will soon come from Bremen the resources of Holland should be committed for the reimbursement of the said money; it is so that the said States, in order to make progress with the foresaid payment have promised and promise by these presents that in the absence of a reimbursement of the foresaid £700 out of the money coming from Bremen the same reimbursement shall be made within three months out of the regular resources of the province of Holland, which shall remain liable for them.][65]

However reluctantly, then, the States of Holland seem to have recognised their ultimate responsibility for the acknowledged debt to Montgomerie, and to have agreed to cover it should the expected money not be forthcoming from Bremen. We must assume that Montgomerie had his money, and thereafter the record again falls silent. Difficult negotiations between the Dutch paymasters and their Scottish forces continued through the summer of 1588, fuelled in part by further defections to the Spanish side.[66] But Montgomerie is never mentioned among the petitioners, or in any other context, until he reappears in Scotland on 12 December 1588.

The period of his absence from Scotland, from June 1586 until December 1588, can, therefore, be divided into four separate phases. Between June 1586 and the end of January 1587 his movements can be followed in a reasonable degree of detail; a gap then ensues, from January to August 1587 (and presumably through to December), when he and his company — in whatever form it now took — appear to have been operating on the margins of the allied army, as part of a force such as Hohenlohe's or as a garrison in one of the less strategically-important towns; from December 1587 to February 1588 he was apparently under

---

[65] ARA, Staten van Holland, 344, fols. 143v–144r.

[66] The very full set of accounts for Balfour's regiment, completed on 13 June 1588 and signed by Balfour himself and each of his eleven captains (ARA, SG 12536, fols. 1–82) appears to be some kind of final accounting procedure. It is noteworthy that most of these officers were then given new commissions, several of them in June 1588 (cf. ARA, RS 1524).

some form of house arrest because of his inability to pay off his debts; and be-
tween February and December, presumably after he had received his £700 from
the States of Holland, his position and activities are again invisible. If the bal-
ance of probability is that he spent 1587 fighting for the Dutch cause, this last
interval is much more difficult to explain. Perhaps he returned to Scotland early
in the year and the absence of any evidence to that effect is mere chance; but it
is equally possible that he remained in the Netherlands for some time, or that he
visited one or more other countries on his way home.

In view of the political and military situation in 1588, the latter possibilities
raise some intriguing questions. Even before his final departure from the Neth-
erlands in December 1587, Leicester was aware of the implications of the fact
that Parma was preparing a huge fleet against England, and expressing concern
that the unreliability of the Scottish forces in the Low Countries might be mir-
rored by a much more serious treachery by their king. As early as 5 November, he
was warning Cecil about Parma's intentions in Scotland, adding that "that place
ys to be feared of all other, yf yt be not frendly disposed".[67] On 21 November he
was even more specific:

> Hit ys more than tyme, Hir Majesty has a good strong navye abrode; [Par-
> ma] prepares to shipp at the least x^m men and by all probabillytie for Scot-
> land; *for he hath workers of the king ther about him* [my italics], and the most
> secrett intelligence comes uppon that servyce.[68]

In the field, certainly, Scots were following Archibald Paton's example and join-
ing the Spanish cause. An English informer in Antwerp at this time reported
to Walsingham that the regiment of Sir William Stanley, an English Catholic
defector, was mostly composed of Irish and Scottish troops, while Paton was re-
ported to have six companies at his disposal on 15 April 1588.[69]

This movement was apparently encouraged by Colonel William Stewart, who
was stated by Sir William Russell, governor of Vlissingen, on 2 February 1588 to
be recruiting among the Scots for the Duke of Parma, and who (as a former Cap-
tain of the Royal Guard) must have been well known to Montgomerie.[70] Stewart's
role complicates the picture significantly. A former colonel of a regiment in the
Dutch service, he had a long-running dispute with the States over arrears which

---

[67] *Correspondentie van Leycester*, 3:285.

[68] *Correspondentie van Leycester*, 3:348.

[69] *CSP For.*, 21.3:430–1; 22:293. The record of Spanish payments to Paton between 6
August 1587 and 24 November 1589 is preserved in AGS, CMC, 2a época, legajo 119.

[70] *CSP For.*, 21.4:53–54; cf. T.G. Law, "Sir William Stewart of Houston", in *Collected
Essays and Studies*, 327–31 (but Law was apparently unaware of Stewart's 1586 licence).

were owed to him from that period, and it was partly in pursuit of this case that he obtained, on 21 May 1586, the king's licence to travel "to the pairtis of France, Flanderis and uthiris beyond sey, during the space of fyve yeiris". But his travelling-companion on this occasion was Hugh Barclay of Ladyland, certainly a Catholic agent as well as a friend of Montgomerie's, and whatever the "certane honorabill affaires committit to thair charge to the profitt and commoditie of the publict estait of this realme" may have been, they eventually took Stewart at least to the Netherlands; he was reported on 15 December to have arrived in Paris, having been "of layte" with the Prince of Parma.[71] One of Stewart's preoccupations was certainly the estate of his wife Erika, widow of the Graf von Manderscheidt, which had been confiscated after her departure from the Spanish-controlled Netherlands; as early as 15 August 1584 Guy de Fontenay, the French ambassador in Edinburgh, was writing to Mary, Queen of Scots on his behalf, asking her to write to Philip II

> un petit mot en sa recommendation, à ce qu'il plaise à la Majesté catholique faire rendre et restituer à sa femme les biens qui luy ont esté ostez au Pais Bas durant la guerre, promettant le dit Colonel en ce cas de demeurrer à jamais bon et fidel vassal dudit Roy d'Espagne, et que pour preuve de ce il mettroyt entre les mains du Prince de Parma toutes les compaignies qu'il avoyt au service des Estatz,

> [. . . a little word recommending him, that it might please His Catholic Majesty to cause to be given and restored to his wife the goods which were confiscated from her in the Low Countries during the war, and promising that the said Colonel would then remain for ever the good and faithful vassal of the said King of Spain, and that at proof of this he would place in the Prince of Parma's hands all the companies which he had in the service of the States][72]

adding that Stewart already had letters of support from Parma and from the Duke of Guise. Stewart himself had obtained further personal support from Frederick II of Denmark on his way back to the Netherlands in 1586. But his activities were certainly suspected of going beyond his own affairs: in August 1587 he was rumoured to be discussing with Parma the possibility of a Spanish marriage for

---

[71] For James's licence, see Montgomerie, *Poems*, ed. Stevenson, 273–74; for Stewart and Parma, *CSP Scot.*, 9:195. Stewart and Barclay were also charged with "ye advancement of vthiris his maiesteis honorabill intentions", and in view of their visit to Denmark immediately after leaving Scotland it would appear that this may have involved the proposed match between James and Elizabeth, the daughter of Frederick II.

[72] *HMC Salisbury*, 3:52.

James, and on 1 January 1588 he was declared to be "very busy and in good credit with the Prince".[73] By February 1588 he had evidently been on the Spanish side for some considerable time and was presumably in a strong position to win over disaffected Scottish employees of the States.

Whether Montgomerie was in touch with Stewart at this period must remain a matter of conjecture. As Stevenson first pointed out, there is a fascinating conjunction between James's licence of 21 May 1586 to Stewart and Barclay and that which was subsequently stated to have been given, at about the same time, to Montgomerie. The phrasing of the permission to travel to "France, Flanderis, and vythiris beyond sey" is doubtless formulaic, but then it is interesting that the Privy Seal letter of 21 March 1589, which partially rehearses the terms of Montgomerie's licence, adds "Spane" to the list. Whether he actually travelled to Spain during his absence from Scotland seems extremely doubtful, but what is clear is that the account he gave of his circumstances while abroad in order to obtain his letter bore little relation to the truth.[74] Why, then, should he have lied about his experiences abroad? As we shall see in the following chapter, his appeal to the Privy Council regarding his pension coincided with the uncovering of disturbing evidence about the links between Parma and the Catholic nobility in Scotland, and it is possible that Montgomerie's economical approach to the truth was intended to distract attention from at least some of his activities in the Netherlands. But further than this the evidence does not permit us to go.[75]

As far as we can tell, the surviving canon of Montgomerie's works contains no trace of the time he spent in the Netherlands. Thomas Duff made his subject boast

> Hostis eram gravis haereseon semperque perodi
> Falsa, Picarditas carmine Marte premens,

---

[73] *CSP Scot.*, 9:475–76, 533.

[74] See below, 147–48.

[75] It has in the past been suspected that the poet can be identified either with the Montgomery who was in prison in London between November 1588 and March 1589 or with the mysterious "Captain Montgomery" who was involved in negotiations between the garrison of Geertruidenberg and Parma in March 1589 (see A.F. Westcott, *New Poems of James I of England* [New York: Columbia University Press, 1911], xxxi; Jack, "Montgomerie and the Pirates", 134; *Shire, Song, Dance and Poetry*, 108–9). But the servant of Thomas Fowler who was imprisoned in London was named John Montgomery (*CSP Scot.*, 9:645–46; HMC Salisbury, 3:398); and it is clear that the messenger to Parma, who was travelling with letters of commendation from James, was actually Adam Montgomerie (of Braidstane), as Shire herself suspected (*HMC Ancaster*, 215–17). Alexander, it seems, was continuously in Scotland from 12 December 1588 at the latest.

[I was the stern enemy of heresy, always hating lies, and pursuing the Calvinists with martial song]

which *might* be taken to imply that Montgomerie wrote anti-Protestant verses while he was in the Low Countries. Just what "Picarditas" means in this context, however, is far from clear, and in any case no such works survive. As we noted above, there is no hint of an allusion to the death of Sidney in any of his extant verse. There appears, in short, to be a remarkable division between Montgomerie's literary output and the political crises outside Scotland in which he played an active, if minor, part. It is, however, important to remember that our knowledge of his work depends very heavily — indeed, almost exclusively — upon a single manuscript, which probably reflects a substantial element of editorial selection and scribal intervention.

It is difficult to believe that Montgomerie remained wholly unaffected by the two years or so he spent in the Low Countries in 1586–1588, by his contact with the Leicester circle and the experience of the war itself, quite apart from any involvement in international intrigue which may be figured by the strange gaps in the record and the discrepancies in the story he told after his return. But the increasingly embittered view expressed in some of his later poetry has more to do with his circumstances in Scotland after his return than with the grievances he evidently developed in his dealings with the Dutch, and while the recurrent vein of disillusionment we can observe in such pieces may have been informed in a general way by a belief that life had treated him unkindly, there is nothing in his extant corpus which relates directly to his service in the Netherlands. Its main effect, indeed, may have been negative. His absence of two years from James's court evidently created for Montgomerie a kind of displacement from which he seems never to have recovered; by 1589 the momentum of the literary movement which had begun early in the decade had been lost, and although James would publish his *Poeticall Exercises at Vacant Houres* in 1591, even that title suggests that poetry was now more a diversion from more pressing matters than a centre of the court's existence. In more personal terms, moreover, Montgomerie's absence had provided an opportunity for William Erskine, claimant to the archbishopric of Glasgow, to challenge his right to the pension he had been granted by the king, and he would find on his return that he would have to fight to regain possession of what he not unreasonably regarded as his by right.[76] In a number of senses the poet was no longer "worth his place", and he would quickly come to lament the marginalisation which seems to have followed upon his absence during these critical years.

---

[76] *Poems*, ed. Stevenson, 305–6.

# Chapter Five

## Proving the Poet's Patience: Montgomerie's Final Decade, 1588–1598

By 12 December 1588 at the latest Montgomerie was back in Scotland, for on that date he witnessed an instrument of sasine relating to the transfer of the lands of Eglinton, a transaction which was carried out on the lands themselves.[1] There is no immediate evidence that he resumed his association with the court: his family connections and the lands from which he doubtless hoped to derive his income were both in the west, and his occurrence in a Montgomerie context suggests that his first moves on returning to Scotland may have been to re-establish his family base before seeking to take up his career as courtier-poet.

The political situation at the court was very different on Montgomerie's return from that he had left in the summer of 1586. The invasion crisis of the summer of 1588, during which James maintained a policy of publicly supporting England while privately tolerating a pro-Spanish faction in case the Spanish should prevail, ended with the defeat and dispersal of the Great Armada in August; James celebrated with *Ane Meditatioun on 1 Chronicles 15:25–29*, concluding with a triumphal sonnet, translated into Latin by John Maitland, recording how "The natiounis bandit gainst the Lord of micht" but were defeated by the forces of Nature:

| | |
|---|---|
| The wynds begouth to toose them heir and thair; | *began; toss* |
| The seas begouth in foming waues to swell; | |
| The number that escapt, it fell them fair; | |
| The rest wer swallowed vp in golfis of Hell. | *gulfs* |
| Bot how wer all thir thingis miraculous done; | |
| God lewch at them out of his heuinlie throne.[2] | *laughed* |

Not everyone, however, shared these triumphalist sentiments, and soon after Montgomerie's return Scotland experienced another of the periodic scandals in which members of the Catholic faction were implicated. In January 1589, the earls of Huntly and Erroll and a number of other prominent Scottish Catholics had written to Parma in the Netherlands, commiserating with him on the defeat of the

---

[1] NAS, GD3/1/206. This document is in fact a transumpt of several related instruments, given by John Skene on behalf of the Lords of Council in 1614.

[2] James VI, *Poems*, ed. Craigie, 2:164.

Armada and assuring him of their continuing sympathy for the Spanish cause.[3] On 21 February, news reached Scotland that a Thomas Pringle, servant of Colonel William Sempill, who had been acting as an agent of the Catholic earls, had been intercepted by the English and interrogated, and details of the correspondence, and of the Jesuit plot which it revealed, were transmitted to James.[4] The king's behaviour in the weeks that followed seemed to many — and especially to the English agent Thomas Fowler — to reveal his ambivalence: Huntly was briefly imprisoned, then released, and on 13 March James met with both Huntly and Erroll while they were out hunting. Fowler witnessed this exchange, which lasted an hour and which culminated in the two earls riding to Dunfermline while James and the earl of Bothwell returned to Edinburgh. Huntly was dismissed as captain of the royal guard and James wrote privately to him disapproving of his conduct, but on 20 March the king himself protested Huntly's innocence to Fowler.[5] James seems to have gone to particular lengths to defend Huntly in public, but other members of the conspiracy were less fortunate: on 21 March, the Privy Council, meeting at Holyrood House, proclaimed Erroll a rebel and issued a summons for the arrest of David Graham of Fintry, who was also suspected.[6]

The same day that Erroll was put to the horn, James issued to "his gude servitour Alexander Montgomerie" a letter under the Privy Seal confirming the pension he had first granted in 1583. This is the first sign of the resumption of the dispute which had arisen soon after Montgomerie had left for the Netherlands in 1586 and which would now last for four more years, ending in Montgomerie's legal defeat and very considerable bitterness against his opponents and against the king himself. The letter restates the terms of the original grant, but then notes that during his absence abroad Montgomerie's "factouris and servitouris hes bene maist wranguslie stoppit, hinderit, and debarrit in the peceabill possessioun of his said pensioun, bot ony guid ordour or forme of justice, to his greit hurt, hinder, and preiudice, quhair as his guid service meritit rather augmentacioun nor diminisching of the said pensioun".[7] The source of this illegal intervention was presumably William Erskine, parson of Campsie and former claimant of the archbishopric

---

[3] PRO, SP77/5, fol. 2; cf. Calderwood, *History*, 5:8–35.

[4] *RPC*, 4:360, 820–21, 367. For this episode, its background and its aftermath, see Ruth Grant, "The Brig o' Dee Affair, the sixth earl of Huntly and the politics of the Counter-Reformation", in *The Reign of James VI*, ed. Goodare and Lynch, 93–109.

[5] *CSP Scot.*, 10:4–5; *Letters of King James VI and I*, ed. G.P.V. Akrigg (Berkeley: University of California Press, 1984), 89–91.

[6] *RPC*, 4:367. On 18 March, the English informant William Asheby remarked that "the King carrieth such a fond affection to Huntly as is incredible" (*CSP Scot.*, 10:9).

[7] Stevenson, *Poems*, 307 (from NAS, PS1/59, fols. 88r–89r; cf. E2/14, fol. 254r–v, the Comptroller's copy of the same text, most of which was presumably drafted by Montgomerie or his lawyers).

of Glasgow, whose earlier legal action against the poet we noted in the previous chapter.[8] The terms of the confirmation which the king now granted are quite unambiguous: not only was the pension to be specifically exempted from the envisaged restitution of James Beaton as archbishop of Glasgow, but Montgomerie was to receive back-payment of the sums owing to him since "the first termes payment of the crope and yeir of God jᵐ vᶜ fourescore sex yeiris". Montgomerie had, it would seem, been given everything he sought.

If the Privy Seal letter of March 1589 is unequivocal in its declaration of Montgomerie's entitlement to his pension, however, it is curiously misleading in at least one other respect. Montgomerie had received payment until 1586, it states, presumably on the basis of a brief provided by the poet or his lawyers,

> at the quhilk tyme, vpoun speciall and guid respectis moving our said souerane loird, his hienes gave and grantit to the said Capitane Alexander his maiesties licence to depairt and pas of this realme to the pairtis of France, Flanderis, Spane and vthiris beyond sey, for the space of fyve yeiris thaireftir . . . According to the quhilk, he depairtit of this realme to the pairtis of Flanderis, Spane and vthiris beyond sey, quheras he remanit continewallie sensyne deteynit and halden in prison and captiuitie, to the greit hurt and vexatioun of his persoun, attour the lose of his guidis.

There is an obvious ambiguity in the phrase "he remanit continewallie sensyne deteynit and halden in prison and captiuitie": even if we separate "remanit continewallie sensyne" from "deteynit and halden in prison and captiuitie", thereby removing the implication that he had been imprisoned for more than two years, it is striking that there is no mention here of honorable service in the Protestant cause in the Low Countries, the emphasis being laid instead upon the damaging consequences of Montgomerie's imprisonment in an unspecified foreign land.[9] There is no attempt, on the other hand, to disguise the fact that, at some point during his two-year absence, he apparently visited Spain. Given the conjunction of this renewed grant to a prominent Catholic with the political scandal involving Huntly and Erroll, the letter seems to be extraordinary both in what it says and in what it omits.

---

[8] Erskine was presented to the archbishopric by James VI in December 1585, on the deprivation of Robert Montgomerie. He was supposed to hold only the temporal rights of the office, with ecclesiastical authority residing with the presbytery, but this arrangement was rejected by the General Assembly in 1587 (Watt, *Fasti*, 151).

[9] It is, of course, apparently true that Montgomerie suffered some kind of incarceration in the Netherlands in the winter of 1587–1588 because of his financial difficulties with the Dutch authorities, but the document seems to suggest a stronger form of imprisonment than this.

What are we to make of this puzzling document? Was the tale of Montgomerie's imprisonment abroad — which may, of course, have had some basis in truth — a cover-story of some kind, intended to draw a veil over the real nature of his activities? If so, it is equally unclear whose interests were thus being protected. It may be that Montgomerie was misleading the king, hiding the true extent of his involvement in a Catholic network whose intrigues with the Spanish were already causing James considerable embarrassment — but then why declare so openly a recent visit to Spain? It is also possible, on the other hand, that James's "speciall and guid respectis" for approving Montgomerie's departure in the summer of 1586 included some covert aspect of his foreign policy, and that Montgomerie's activities abroad, whatever they were, were in some sense carried out on the king's behalf. This would, certainly, explain the very similar terms of James's licences to William Stewart of Houston and Hugh Barclay of Ladyland.[10]

It does not seem likely that Montgomerie was directly involved in the plotting of Huntly and Erroll with the Spanish, or with the rebellion which they subsequently mounted.[11] The northern earls assembled their forces in the north at the beginning of April, while the Earl of Bothwell, who had his own reasons for supporting them, did the same in the Borders. On 7 April, Thomas Fowler was able to report to Cecil that the king had been apprised of what was afoot and was gathering together the Protestant lords to take on the rebels.[12] The loyalist forces proceeded northwards to confront Huntly at Brig o'Dee, just south of Aberdeen, on 17 April, but the dissidents' forces broke up without a battle and James entered the city in triumph, remaining there until early May. Montgomerie, meanwhile, was safely established in the west: on 23 April he acted as witness to a precept of *clare constat* produced at Irvine in respect of the lands of Wrychthill and Drumdour in Kyle.[13] Whatever his sympathies may have been, then, it seems that he did not participate in this abortive uprising by the Catholic lords.

On 14 August, Montgomerie returned to the king with new arguments. The letter which was now produced, and registered in the names of the king, the Chancellor John Maitland, the Comptroller David Seton of Parbroath, and the Collector-General Robert Douglas, differed from that of 21 March in three important respects. First, it omitted any mention of Montgomerie's absence from Scotland or his supposed imprisonment. Second, it offered a greatly expanded version of the arguments relating to the archdiocese of Glasgow:

---

[10] See above, 141–42.

[11] Grant, "Brig o'Dee Affair", cogently argues that the rebels' true target was Chancellor Maitland rather than James himself, and that James emphasised the doctrinal aspect of the affair for his own political ends. But the Catholic element cannot be ignored, and Montgomerie must surely have been aware of it.

[12] *CSP Scot.*, 10:25–26.

[13] NAS, GD3/1/686.

And our said souerane Lord vnderstanding that the first gift of the foirsaid pensioun was grantit be his hienes to the said Alex*ander sede vacante* And the haill archiebischoprik than being in his Ma*ie*sties handis and at his gift as patrone thairof Throw deceis of vmq*uhi*ll Mr. James Boyde than last archiebischop of glasgw And the gift and dispositioun of the said benefice maid tharefter to Mr. Williame Erskin being a*n*nullit and taken away be restitutioun of the said James Beaton sumtime archiebischop of glasgw Quhilk restitutioun is now be act of secreit counsale maid null and ineffectuall Q*u*h*a*rthrow the said benefice will not onelie pertene to His Ma*ie*stie and be at his dispositioun Bot als be the act of parliament maid anent the a*n*nexatioun of the temperall land*is* of all benefices to the patrimonie of his hienes croun The landis abouew*r*ittin q*u*h*a*rof the victuallis is assignit and disponit for payment of the said pensioun pertenis to o*u*r souerane lord and his hienes declairit to have I*ntromi*ssio*un* th*a*h w*ith* And th*row* th*at oc*ca*si*ou*n* l*ie*s f*ull* a*nd* v*n*d*ou*btit richt to dispone the said pensioun Thairfore for the caussis abouew*r*ittin His Ma*ie*stie ordanis ane l*et*tre to be maid to the said Alex*ander* montgomerie Ratefiand approvand and confermand the l*et*tres of gift maid to the said Alex*ander* of the pensioin abouespe*c*ifiet l*et*tres of ratificatioun and new gift thairin pertenit and all and sundrie pointis passis claussis and articles.[14]

By contrast with the terse reference to the restoration of the deprived Archbishop James Beaton in the earlier letter, this much more developed analysis suggests that Montgomerie had received some expert advice in the intervening five months, and it anticipates, as we shall see, the case he would eventually make when the dispute came to court. But as with the account of Montgomerie's travels in the letter of 21 March, this argument is as remarkable for what it omits as what it contains: it is true that James Boyd, archbishop of Glasgow had died in possession on 21 June 1581 and that William Erskine was presented to the benefice on 21 December 1585, but these two statements tactfully elide the fact that when Montgomerie was granted his pension in 1583 the nominal archbishop was his kinsman Robert, who was provided by James around the beginning of October 1581 and not deprived until the last weeks of 1585.[15]

The reason for this crucial omission is, however, clear: if, Montgomerie claims (and James appears to accept), the archdiocese was vacant and its revenues in the king's hands in 1583 then the initial grant was legal, while Erskine lost *his* claim to the archbishopric with the proposed restoration of Beaton. Since this latter plan had now formally been abandoned by means of a Privy Council decision of 29 May 1589,[16] the revenues were again at the king's disposal, so that the confirmation which James now made would be as valid as that made six years earlier. The king

---

[14] NAS, E2/13, fols. 13v–14v, here 14r.
[15] Watt, *Fasti*, 150–51.
[16] *RPC*, 4:388–89.

seems at this point to have been prepared to go along with these contentions, and even to go a stage further:

> And forder oure Souerane Lord fayt*h*fullie promittis *in verbo principis* To ratefie and approue thir *prese*ntis in ye nixt parliament q*uha*rby ye said alex-*ande*r may peaceablie bruik Ioiss and vplift the said pensioun . . .

How much reliance might be placed on the word of a prince Montgomerie would in due course discover: Parliament would not meet again until April-June 1592, by which time both the legal battle and James's intentions would have moved on. While many personal cases were dealt with in that forum, Montgomerie's was not among them, and Erskine had developed a strategy of his own which would lead to the final collapse of the poet's hopes.

Dependent as he was at this period on the king's goodwill, there is a surprising absence in Montgomerie's extant verse of any reference to the other major event of 1589–1590, the king's marriage to Anne of Denmark. By the time of Montgomerie's return to Scotland, James had virtually abandoned any thought of a possible match with Catherine, the sister of Henry of Navarre, and had returned to the former notion of a marriage to a daughter of the Danish king. From the Catholic point of view, this latter option was certainly preferable: although Denmark had early espoused the Reformation cause, the Lutheranism which the Danes adopted placed them in the middle ground between the Catholic and Calvinist parties, and it is surely significant that the initial negotiations were conducted during 1588 by Colonel William Stewart, whose connections with the Catholic faction are, as we have already noted, clear.[17] After a formal wedding by proxy in August 1589, James himself travelled to Norway and Denmark in the winter of that year, remaining in Oslo for a month and in Copenhagen for three, leaving Scotland on 22 October 1589 and only returning on 1 May 1590.[18] As a leading court poet, Montgomerie might well have been expected to contribute to the celebration of this important dynastic event: James himself wrote several sonnets to the Queen at this time, including two complaining against "the contrary Wyndes that hindered the Queene to com to Scotland from Denmarke", and began a long poem on the occasion of his departure; the Edinburgh burgess John Burel offered celebratory verses; and Adriaan Damman, a humanist poet from Ghent who had, after two years teaching at Leiden, made his way to Scotland and established himself at the court, published to mark the marriage a volume

---

[17] It could not, of course, be anticipated that Henry of Navarre would revert to Catholicism in July 1593.

[18] For an account of the negotiations and James's travels, see Willson, *King James VI and I*, 85–95; and Lee, *Maitland of Thirlestane*, 193–214.

of Latin poems entitled *Schediasmata*.[19] The English poet Henry Constable, apparently on a visit to the Scottish court, produced a poem lamenting the king's absence from Scotland.[20] Yet from Montgomerie we have nothing, even though it seems very likely that he was about the court at this period.

If this silence is enigmatic, some of the poems which can probably be assigned to this period are scarcely less so. There are, certainly, complex nuances in his sonnet addressed to Patrick Galloway, which is presumably connected with the latter's appointment as the king's Minister in June 1589:

> Cry out, and he shall heir the from the Heuin,
> And wish the King his Court and counsell clenge     *cleanse*
> Or then the Lord will in his wrath revenge.
>     (63: 12–14)

That Montgomerie is here criticising the court seems beyond question; but the dedication of the poem to the Calvinist Galloway implies that he is adopting an ultra-Protestant rather than a Catholic position in doing so. This Sveykian gambit may not have fooled anyone who was aware of his true attitudes, but at the very least it denies the poet's enemies a line of attack while leaving no doubt that Montgomerie finds much to condemn in the Scotland to which he has returned:

> Quhat Justice sauld, vhat pilling of the pure,     *robbing*
> Quhat bluidy Murthers ar for gold forgivin!
> God is not sleipand thoght he tholde, be sure.     *tolerated*
>     (9–11)

The complaint against the remission of serious crimes, including murder, is a traditional one, and even the allusion to the "sleep of God" appears to be an echo of Henryson's *Morall Fabillis*, where the Scheip laments his miserable condition as a victim of injustice with the questions "O lord, quhy sleipis thow sa lang?" (1295) and "Allace, gude lord, quhy tholis thow it so?" (1313).[21] This may be Reformed Scotland, Montgomerie seems to be implying, but in reality little has changed.

Both similarities in language and the pairing of the two poems in the Ker manuscript indicate that there is a connection between the sonnet to Patrick Galloway and another addressed to James himself:

---

[19] James VI, *Poems*, ed. Craigie, 2:68–69; for Burel, see *Poems* (Edinburgh: Robert Waldegrave, [?1590]), sig. L1r–M3r, reprinted in James Watson, *A Choice Collection of Comic and Serious Scots Poems* (Edinburgh: James Watson, 1706–11), 2:1–15; Adriaan Damman, *Schediasmata* (Edinburgh: Robert Waldegrave, 1590).

[20] *Poems*, ed. Grundy, 143. Constable also wrote a sonnet commenting on one of the king's (ibid., 142); cf. Lyall, "'Thrie Truear Hairts'", 208–9.

[21] Henryson, *Poems*, ed. Fox, 53 (the allusion is to Psalm 44:23).

Shir, clenge your Cuntrie of thir cruell crymis,
Adultreis witchcraftis, incests, sakeles bluid.          *innocent*
Delay not, bot (as David did) betymis
Your Company of such men soon secluid.
Out with the wicked, garde you with the gude.
Of mercy and of Judgment sey to sing.                    *make sure*
Quhen ye suld stryke I wald ye vnderstude.
Quhen ye suld spair I wish ye were bening.               *benign*
Chuse godly Counsel, leirne to be a King.
Beir not thir burthenis longer on your bak.
Jumpe not with Justice for no kynd of thing,
To just Complantis gar gude attendance tak.
   Thir bluidy sarks cryis alwayis in your eiris.     *shirts*
   Prevent the plague which presently appeirs.
    [64]

Once again, much of the political argument here is familiar from the tradition of political advice which stretches back into the fifteenth century: the emphasis on the need for good counsel and for the even-handed administration of justice, in particular, recalls the advice offered in such works as "De regimine principum", *The Thre Prestis of Peblis*, and Dunbar's *Thrissill and the Rois*.[22] What is distinctive, however, is the apocalyptic tone, which may partly be a consequence of the compression inherent in the sonnet form but which also stems from the very language of "adultreis, witchcraftis, incests, sakeles bluid". The reference to "witchcraftis" is particularly striking, since the summer of 1590 would see the first signs of that spate of persecutions of alleged witches, the ideological justification for which James would eventually provide in his *Demonologie* (1597). But the events of 1590 did not arise in a vacuum, and there is some evidence of concern with witchcraft towards the end of the 1580s.[23]

---

[22] See R.J. Lyall, "Politics and Poetry in Fifteenth and Sixteenth Century Scotland", *SLJ* 3/2 (December 1976): 5–29; and Sally Mapstone, "The Advice to Princes Tradition in Scottish Literature, 1450–1500" (D.Phil. diss., University of Oxford, 1986). Dr Mapstone has pointed out to me that Montgomerie's l. 9 specifically echoes "De regimine principum" (ll. 71–72: *Maitland Folio MS.*, ed. Craigie, 1:115–25), a text originally composed in the reign of James II but fairly widely known in sixteenth-century Scotland.

[23] For the background to these events, see Christina Larner, *Witchcraft and Religion: The Politics of Popular Belief* (Oxford: Blackwell, 1984); and *A Source-book of Scottish Witchcraft*, ed. Christina Larner et al. (Glasgow: SSRC, 1977), 3. Although the first indications of an organised witchhunt can be seen in the immediate aftermath of James's voyage to Denmark (*CSP Scot.*, 10:348, 365), it is important to recognise that isolated cases had occurred before this: cf., for example, the case against Alesoun Peirsoun on 28 May 1588 (R. Pitcairn, *Ancient Criminal Trials in Scotland* [Edinburgh: Bannatyne Club, 1833], 1:161–65), and that against Lady Fowlis in 1589–1590. For an overview of witchcraft cases before

There is no mistaking, either, the minatory tone which Montgomerie adopts in the exhortation to "leirne to be a king". We might almost be inclined to assign such terse advice to an early period of their relationship, but there is no need to do so: James was, after all, still only twenty-two in 1589, and the newly-returned poet may well have felt that he did not need to mince his words. The role of dispenser of political advice, in any case, was in some respects a privileged one, and it may be no coincidence that Montgomerie seems to echo Henryson once again in his declaration that "Thir bluidy sark cryis alwayis in your eiris". The allusion here is a complex one, but it is unlikely to have eluded James. Within the structure of the sonnet, the "bluidy sarks", like the "burthenis" of l. 10, refer back anaphorically to the catalogue of crimes in l. 2; but beyond the boundaries of the text the connection is probably with a poem by Robert Henryson, in which the "bludy sark" bequeathed by a dying knight (Christ) to the lady he has rescued (the human soul) is allegorically interpreted as a sign of the Crucifixion.[24] The reference may, indeed, extend beyond this, to fifteenth-century events to which "The Bludy Sark" may itself allude, and more generally to the social practice by which a blood-stained shirt might be exhibited as evidence of the commission of a violent crime.

Since the story of the rebellion of "the Bludy Sark" is told by Buchanan in his *De Rerum Scoticarum Historia* (1583) and — intriguingly, given Montgomerie's views — by John Leslie, bishop of Ross in his *De origine, morum, et rebus gestis Scotorum* (published in Rome in 1578), it is hardly credible that James was unaware of it: in 1489, the year after the death of James III at Sauchieburn in a rebellion led by his son, the lords opposed to the new regime (those in the north according to Buchanan, those in the west according to Leslie) themselves rebelled, raising their forces by riding around the country with a blood-stained shirt they claimed was the dead king's.[25] Although James IV was able to put this incipient rebellion down with little difficulty, the lesson seems clear: unjust actions can give rise to resistance. If Montgomerie's sonnet to James is indeed connected to that addressed to Galloway, it is very likely to have been written in 1589, exactly a hundred years after the abortive rising of "the Bludy Sark"; and the echo of the

---

1590, see now P.G. Maxwell-Stuart, *Satan's Conspiracy: Magic and Witchcraft in Sixteenth-Century Scotland* (East Linton: Tuckwell Press, 2001), where the Peirsoun case is discussed at 98–107, and Julian Goodare, *The Scottish Witch-Hunt in Context* (Manchester: Manchester University Press, 2002).

[24] Henryson, *Poems*, ed. Fox, 158–62.

[25] Buchanan, *Rerum Scoticarum Historia* (Edinburgh: Alexander Arbuthnet, 1582), fol. 144r; John Leslie, *De origine moribus, et rebus gestis Scotorum libri decem* (Rome: Casa del Popolo Romano, 1578), 330–31. For concise modern accounts, see Ranald Nicholson, *Scotland: The Later Middle Ages* (Edinburgh: Oliver and Boyd, 1974), 536–39; and Norman Macdougall, *James IV* (Edinburgh: John Donald, 1989), 62–76.

rebellion against an arguably patricidal monarch is, moreover, aimed at a king whose own mother had been executed with his connivance just two years before. The threat is densely veiled, but the language of Montgomerie's sonnet leaves little doubt: "the plague that presently appeirs" (as well as perhaps indicating a new outbreak of the "pest") may refer to injustice itself, but it might also be interpreted as the menace of rebellion, perhaps even the rebellion of Huntly, Erroll, Bothwell and their allies in April 1589. Himself a supporter of the Catholic cause but — he would have the king believe — a staunch if critical loyalist, Montgomerie is in a powerful position to offer such a caution. On balance, then, there seems to be good reason for assigning the sonnet to James to 1589, while acknowledging the possibility that it actually belongs to the following year.

Stylistically, both these sonnets reveal Montgomerie's command of a blunt, vigorous plain style, in which alliteration and such rhetorical devices as intermittent anaphora are deployed to make practical political points. A more conventionally eulogistic manner is apparent in the sonnet addressed to the Chancellor John Maitland [66]: since Maitland was appointed to this office in May 1587, while Montgomerie was in the Netherlands, this piece must presumably have been composed between the poet's return to Scotland and its subject's death on 3 October 1595, and almost certainly before the dismissal of Maitland from the court — though not from the chancellorship — at the end of March 1592.[26] The most likely occasion for its composition, especially in view of its closing reference to Maitland's adoption of a coat-of-arms, is his elevation to the peerage at the coronation of Anne of Denmark in May 1590, when, in the words of Maitland's biographer, he "stood at the pinnacle of political and personal success".[27]

Montgomerie must have been well acquainted with the chancellor, whose political career at James's court began during the ascendancy of Esmé Stuart in 1580–1582. But Maitland, despite his early attachment to the Marian cause, had developed into a firm supporter of a closer relationship with England, and was an equally staunch opponent of Huntly and the Catholic faction. He was, arguably, the true target of the 1589 rebellion, and urged a stronger line against the rebels than James was willing to adopt. We might, then, find it surprising that Montgomerie should eulogise him with such apparent enthusiasm. Given Maitland's proximity to the king, on the other hand, we might detect in Montgomerie's declaration that "A Cunning King a Cunning Chanceller chuisis" (l. 8) a form of ingratiation aimed at James rather than at the Chancellor. It is, moreover, striking that Montgomerie's sonnet not only emulates one by the king himself, in which

---

[26] Parkinson (*Poems*, 2:13, 88–89) infers from this poem that Montgomerie may have returned to Scotland as early as July 1587; for evidence that he was still in the Netherlands between December 1587 and 2 February 1588, see above, 136–39.

[27] Lee, *Maitland of Thirlestane*, 216.

he focusses wholly upon Maitland's contribution as translator of some of James's Scots verses into Latin, but also picks up its closing conceit:

> For what in barbarous leide I blocke and frames     *language*
> Thou learnedlie in Mineru's tongue proclames.[28]

James's literary, and somewhat self-reflexive, compliment is extended by Montgomerie into a more comprehensive tribute to Maitland's accomplishments. The formality of the panegyric is marked by the elaborate patterning of the opening lines:

> Of Mars, Minerva, Mercure and the Musis
> The Curage, Cunning, Eloquence and vain
> Maks maikles Maitland mirrour to Remane     *unequalled*
> As instrument vhilk these for honour vsis,
> Quhais fourfald force with furie him infusis
> In battells, Counsels, Orisones and brain.

Minerva, it will be noted, is here associated with wise counsel rather than with learned poetic language; it is Mercury and the Muses that are invoked in praise of Maitland's rhetorical and poetic skills.[29] But the most perplexing dimension of the eulogy is the repeated reference to military prowess: while Maitland had been among the Marian defenders of Edinburgh castle during the civil war of the early 1570s, and had taken part in some of the raid which the "Castilians" mounted against their enemies, it is scarcely likely that Maitland, who had firmly put his Marian origins behind him, would welcome being reminded of that long-past defeat. His only more recent military activity appears to have been a minor role as a supporter of the king in his foray against Lord Maxwell in 1588, although this skirmish can hardly be called a major campaign — and it was carried out against a Catholic activist who might, one would think, have been one of Montgomerie's natural associates.[30] Is it then possible that Montgomerie is once again leaving room within his panegyric for a counter-meaning, one which permits a sharp and sceptical reader to detect hints of a less than wholly admirable aspect of the subject's character? The praise here might be so formal that its divergence from the literal truth is neither here nor there, but the references to Mars, to "Curage" and

---

[28] James VI, *Poems*, ed. Craigie, 2:107.

[29] For a comparable representation of Mercury as rhetorician, see Henryson's *Testament of Cresseid*, esp. ll. 239–245: *Poems*, ed. Fox, 118.

[30] Keith Brown, "The Making of a *Politique*: The Counter Reformation and the Regional Politics of John, Eighth Lord Maxwell", *SHR* 66 (1987): 152–75, here 166–67. During the crisis of March-April 1589, Maitland had raised a force of 100 horsemen as a bodyguard for the king (cf. *CSP Scot.*, 9:704; 10:4), but there is no sign of his taking part in the actual "raids".

to "battells", each time heading the list of Maitland's qualities and achievements, are so insistent as to suggest that Montgomerie means what he says, though not perhaps in the way we assume on first reading.[31] Any doubts we may still have about this are surely dispelled by that "furie" in l. 6: the word was not, certainly, unequivocally negative in the sixteenth century, but the sense of wild, even imprudent, impetuosity clearly undermines Montgomerie's seeming encomium.

A curious commentary on this triangular relationship among Maitland, Montgomerie, and the king is provided by *Rob Stene's Dream*, an attack on the Chancellor which was most probably composed in late 1591 or early 1592.[32] Helena Shire believed that the true author of this piece was Montgomerie, using "Rob Stene" as a *nom de guerre* in a courtly game; but this view has been convincingly rejected by David Reid, the poem's most recent editor.[33] The *Dream* nevertheless casts some interesting light on Montgomerie's position at this period, for the poet's speaker, declaring himself inadequate to address the mighty theme of the king's recent voyage to Norway to collect his bride, announces that he is

| | |
|---|---|
| Howping to heir with in schort quhyle | |
| Montgumry, with his ornat style | |
| And cunning, quhilk nane can rehers, | *imitate* |
| Your wit and vallour, put in vers. | |
| For quhy, your poyet laureat | |
| Your giftis sowld only registrat. | |
| Montgumry, quhome the sacred nymphis | |
| In Helecon, with hallowit lymphis, | *streams* |
| And in Pernase the musis chyld, | |
| Pallas, the pedagog preclair, | *supreme teacher* |

---

[31] There is an interesting parallel to Montgomerie's praise of Maitland in a poem by Daniel Rogers in praise of Janus Dousa, printed in the latter's *Poemata* (Leiden: [Andries Verschout], 1576), sig. *v, where Dousa is contended over by Mars and Apollo (cf. van Dorsten, "Poets, Patrons, and Professors", 34–35).

[32] *Rob Stene's Dream*, ed. David Reid (Stirling: University of Stirling Bibliographical Society, 1989); for the dating, see 10–12.

[33] Shire, *Song, Dance and Poetry*, 110; *Dream*, ed. Reid, 25–35. Reid's candidate for the authorship was Robert Sempill, but he was unaware of references to "Robert Stevin poet" in the Treasurer's Accounts for September 1582 and elsewhere (see above, 101, n. 99). For a suggested identification of the courtier with Mr. Robert Stevin, schoolmaster of Edinburgh, see George Neilson, "Rob Stene: A Court Satirist under James VI", *SHR* 2 (1905): 253–59; and cf. now Amy Lynne Juhala, "The Household and Court of James VI of Scotland, 1567–1603" (Ph.D. diss., University of Edinburgh, 2000), 179–80. Juhala canvasses the possibility that "Stevin" was a pseudonym of Montgomerie's, but acknowledges that the continuation of the payments during the latter's absence in the Netherlands makes this improbable — or, indeed, impossible.

For the this subject did prepair.
Quha bot Apelles with owt sklandir          *slander*
Sowld paynt a nobill Alexander?
    (568–581)[34]

As we have already noted, there is no evidence that Montgomerie rose to Stevin's challenge, but the view of him as James's "poyet laureat" is a clear indication that he was still seen by at least one contemporary as a central figure at court. So, perhaps, he still saw himself, and his poems at this period can best be understood in this light.

If Montgomerie's attitude towards Maitland of Thirlestane remains ambiguous, other poems of the early 1590s show him less equivocally as a journeyman-poet of the court, producing epitaphs for Robert, Lord Boyd (d. 3 January 1590), the brothers John and Patrick Shaw (who were killed resisting an attack on the king by Bothwell and his supporters in December 1591), Sir Robert Drummond of Carnock, Master of Works (d. 1592), and Robert Scott, former director of Chancery (d. 20 March 1593). These are for the most part undistinguished pieces, offering ritualised praise in terms which tell us little about either their subject or Montgomerie's poetic skills. The most interesting is that devoted to the Shaw brothers [57], where the political circumstances provide a greater opportunity for poetic invention. Again there is a connection between Montgomerie's poem and one written by the king himself: James had already made his tribute to John Shaw, as Montgomerie's remark that "His sacred self your trumpet bravely blauis" (l. 12) acknowledges.[35] But by comparison with the king's rather bland sonnet, Montgomerie's is closer to the idiom of the apocalyptic sonnets to Galloway and the king than to his more conventional epitaphs:

If ethnik ald by superstitious stylis          *pagan*
(Quhilk poyson yit of Paganisme appeirs)
Wer stellified to rule the rolling spheirs
(As Pagnisme Poets and profane compylis,
Quhais senceles sences Satan so ou'rsylis          *covers up*
By Oracles illuding all thair eirs          *deceiving*
In double speches ansuers sik as speirs          *ask*
Quhilk godles gods the graceles Grekes begylis)
Then more praisuorthie Pelicans of Shawis
Quhais saikles bluid wes for your souerane shed          *innocent*
    (1–10)

The wordplay is typical of the Mannerist Montgomerie; but its function here is to intensify the feeling of the poem rather than merely impressing the reader with the poet's wit. The intricacy is not merely based upon such obvious paradoxes as

---

[34] *Dream*, ed. Reid, 76.
[35] James VI, *Poems*, ed. Craigie, 2:106.

"senceles sences" and "godles gods", but runs through the syntax and diction of the octave, with its parentheses and the series of Latinate words (*ethnik — superstitious — stellified — illuding*) which run counter to the anti-classical argument Montgomerie develops. Against the usual Jacobean praise of classical poetics, he here adopts a position which can only be regarded as puritan, distancing himself from the "poyson" of pagan belief in his eulogy of the Shaw brothers and describing them instead in terms which are implicitly Christian, even christological. The pelican, after all, portrayed as wounding her own breast in order to feed her young with her blood, was associated iconographically with the sacrifice of Christ, and this mythic image is clearly the basis of ll. 9–10. It is tempting, moreover, to see in the attack on the duplicity of oracles a recollection of "Before the Greeks durst enterpryse", in which the "double speches" of the speaker's Apollo might conceivably be attributed to the king himself.[36] Yet, despite his disavowal of paganism, Montgomerie reverts to a comparison between the Shaws and the brothers Castor and Pollux, whose proverbial devotion to one another had ensured them, according to Roman legend, a shared "stellification".

Of Montgomerie's other epitaphs, only that for Sir Robert Drummond of Carnock [56] goes beyond a mere recitation of fact or formal compliment. As Master of Works between 1579 and 1583 — the earliest period of Montgomerie's prosperity at court — Drummond had held responsibility for all the royal building projects, and he developed plans for the reconstruction of Stirling Castle.[37] He was replaced six months after the fall of the Ruthven regime, however, perhaps as part of a purge of supporters of the Earl of Mar, and had lived in virtual retirement for nine years until his death at the age of seventy-four. Upon his memory Montgomerie lavishes an intricate example of *rime batellée*:

> All knoues this treu, vho noble Carnok kneu.
> This Realme may reu that he is gone to grave.
> All buildings brave bids Drommond nou adeu
> Quhais lyf furthsheu he lude thame by the laiv.
> (5–8)

The use of such fashionably Mannerist devices here suggests that Montgomerie took more trouble with Drummond's eulogy than with those for Robert Scot and Lord Boyd; there may, of course, have been personal reasons for this, especially since Drummond had been out of office for so long at the time of his death. Perhaps what we are seeing, then, is the acknowledgement of the subject's craftsmanship through the lavishing of comparable skills by the poet. Montgomerie makes

---

[36] See above, 115.

[37] Aonghus Mackechnie, "James VI's Architects and their Architecture", in *Reign of James VI*, ed. Goodare and Lynch, 154–69, here 159–61.

the conventional observation that Drummond's gifts were merely lent to him by God, but we are put in no doubt of the legacy of "buildings brave" which have been left to Scotland as a result of his career. While lacking the bitter passion of the sonnet to the Shaw brothers, that for Drummond reveals the poet at his most stylishly elegant, fitting the presumable elegance of the subject's designs.

Elegance is also the keynote of a sonnet the political purpose of which is more immediately apparent: that addressed to the Duchess of Lennox [74]. The association between Montgomerie and the first Duke has already been noted, and we shall see below that he was also dependent upon Ludovick, Esmé's son, who was born in 1574 and who arrived in Scotland within a few months of his father's death in 1583. In April 1591 the sixteen-year-old Duke married the daughter of the Earl of Gowrie, incurring the displeasure of James, who had attempted to prevent the match. That it was this Duchess (the first of Lennox's three wives) to whom Montgomerie's sonnet is addressed seems clear from the title in the Ker manuscript, "To Mistress Lily Ruthuen Duches of Lennox"; although genealogists and historians have insisted that her name was Sophia, Jamie Reid-Baxter has recently suggested that Montgomerie was correct, and that she was indeed named Lilias, or Lily.[38] Since she is reported on 29 May 1592 to have recently died,[39] moreover, the sonnet must have been written before that date, and can perhaps be associated with Lennox's wooing of her in early 1591. Its complimentary strategy is fairly straightforward, celebrating the lily "as the first of flours" and imagining the homage of other flowers to her beauty. In its direct citation of this praise (ll. 6–14) it is reminiscent of the conclusion of Dunbar's *The Thrissill and the Rois*, where Margaret Tudor is hailed in very similar terms. Even here, however, we must consider the possibility of covert significances: the lily was, of course, traditionally associated with the Virgin, and in the Catholic milieu of the Lennox household the language of praise which Montgomerie deploys here may have had residual resonances of which Lilias Ruthven's Protestant relations would have strongly disapproved.

Two other sonnets, those "To M.D., for Skelmurley" [84], apparently belong to this period. The poet's kinsman, Robert Montgomerie of Skelmorlie, married Margaret Douglas in November 1593, and this pair of sonnets presumably antedated that event, providing an interesting parallel to the group of poems for the marriage of Margaret Montgomerie and Robert Seton in 1582.[40] They again

---

[38] Jamie Reid-Baxter, "Politics, Passion and Poetry in the Circle of James VI", in *A Palace in the Wild: Essays on Vernacular Culture and Humanism in Late-Medieval and Renaissance Scotland*, ed. L.A.J.R. Houwen, A.A. Macdonald, and S.L. Mapstone (Leuven: Peeters, 2000), 199–248, here 244–45.

[39] *CSP Scot.*, 10:677–78.

[40] NAS, GD3/2/13/9; on these poems, see Dunnigan, "Female Gifts", 67–69.

show Montgomerie playing the Mannerist, turning the Douglas arms into a Petrarchist conceit with his reference to the lover's "bluidy hart", and intricately punning on the lady's name. There is, however, a crucial ambiguity: is the lamenting persona Skelmorlie himself, with the poet ventriloquising his lovesickness in hopes of winning the lady over for his kinsman (as Dunnigan believes), or is Montgomerie "declaring" his own sorrow at his failure to win her, as some kind of elaborate compliment to his cousin's good fortune? Both the tone of the poems and the "For" of the title in the Ker manuscript support the former reading, and this might then be taken to imply an occasion nearer the start of the wooing than the marriage itself.

The first of the pair bears a striking resemblance to another of Montgomerie's love sonnets, "Suete Nichtingale, in holene grene that hants" [86.I], and may even be a rewriting of it.[41] It relies for its effect on intense alliteration, and on a highly-charged evocation of the lover's misery which is reinforced by the symmetrical rhyme-scheme in each quatrain, generating the couplets *hants/wants, chants/grants*, and *exyld/begyld*. As Dunnigan notes, the sonnet is full of dissonances, not least the underlying Ovidian conceit of the transformed Philomela lamenting her rape and mutilation. Both sonnets are recognisably part of a sixteenth-century tradition of nightingale poems, ultimately descending from Petrarch, but there is a particularly striking parallel with Montgomerie's strategy here in one of Sir Philip Sidney's *Certain Sonnets*, "The Nightingale, as soone as Aprill bringeth".[42] Like Montgomerie's, Sidney's speaker actually invokes the rape of Philomela explicitly while insisting that his own situation is worse, even claiming that "she hath no other cause of anguish / But Thereus' love, on her by strong hand wrokne" (ll. 13–14). Montgomerie does not go quite so far, placing himself as Philomene's "mirthles match" (l. 9). Even by the standards of Petrarchist hyperbole, the equation of this distress with the speaker's love-longing seems excessive, and the focus on the nightingale and the speaker, both bewailing their own misery, has the curious effect of marginalising the poem's nominal subject, who is introduced only in the heraldic conceit of the final line. This cannot be said of the second sonnet, in which Margaret Douglas is given a central place through the metaphors of the pearl (*margareta*) and the dove; this poem is much more composed, both in its emotional tone and in the care with which its punning conceits provide the argumentative structure. But if the beloved occupies the centre ground here, it is through her representation as a commodity: the speaker explicitly wishes that

---

[41] See below, 237–78. Since the sequence "To The For Me", which opens with "Suete Nichtingale", is undatable, the priority of one version over the other cannot be established; the picture is complicated by the influence of Ronsard's "Rossignol mon mignon qui part cette saulaye".

[42] *Poems*, ed. Ringler, 137; I am grateful to Dr. Sally Mapstone for pointing out to me the significance of this parallel.

the jewel could be bought (Dunnigan justly notes the impersonal *it* of l. 5), and dreams of placing "the turtle Dou" an "ane costly Cage of cleirest cristall GLAS" (ll. 10–12). The techniques of Petrarchism deployed in this sonnet both mask and reveal the economic realities of sixteenth-century marriage, and the cultural tensions which recur so frequently in Montgomerie's poetry are clearly reflected even when he seems to be ventriloquising.

During the period that he was producing these court- and family-oriented pieces, the former reflecting his continuing engagement with the royal household though in more equivocal terms than he had employed during his heyday in the early 1580s, the latter similarly carrying a greater ideological freight than, for example, the poems addressed to Margaret Montgomerie in 1582, Montgomerie was attempting to secure the pension which James had confirmed in March and August 1589. It had been apparent to the king by May of that year that the restoration of Beaton was a lost cause, at least in the short term: the effort to rehabilitate him could not get around the problem of conformity, for the Act of Ratification of 1587 had specifically included in its exculpatory embrace only those who were willing to accept the Reformed Kirk, and this Beaton would clearly never do. The political balance which had recommended this byzantine initiative in 1587 had undergone a series of radical shifts by 1590: the king had married an impeccably Protestant princess; both the defeat of the Armada and the discovery of Catholic conspiracy within his own kingdom had made a policy which sought overt reconciliation with the Catholic faction less attractive; and James was enjoying much better relations with the Assembly and ministers.[43] Soon after Parliament declared that the 1587 Act no longer applied to Beaton, in June 1592, James had in any case switched to another course: in a ploy which recalls the worst excesses of pre-Reformation commendatorship, he granted the temporalities of the archdiocese of Glasgow to Ludovick Stewart, duke of Lennox.[44]

In his festering dispute with William Erskine, who was still claiming the archbishopric and apparently drawing the income which Montgomerie insisted was his, the poet had prudently taken the precaution of getting Lennox to confirm his pension. This was apparently not difficult: as early as 5 August 1591, declaring that "we haif now vndoutit rycht to the said bischoprik", Lennox duly obliged (though with the pension reduced from five hundred merks per year to four hundred), "for guid and thankfull seruice done and to be done be the said Capitane Alexander to ws, and to gif him occasioun to continew therin". Three months later, Lennox had his grant recorded in the Register of Deeds.[45] As Stevenson points out,

---

[43] On James's relations with the Kirk at this period, see Lee, *Maitland of Thirlestane*, 222–23.

[44] *APS*, 4:19–20 (21 July 1593).

[45] NAS, RD1/40, fols. 40r–41v; the text is printed by Stevenson, *Poems*, 308–11.

the list of witnesses to this act of ratification gives a valuable indication of the wider political context: it includes such notable adherents of the Catholic party as the Earl of Huntly, Lord Claude Hamilton, and Robert, Lord Seton. All were, furthermore, present to sign the registered version of the document on 2 November.

While these transactions may testify to the close relations between Montgomerie and the Lennox faction, they were mere by-play in the struggle between the poet and William Erskine. Only if Lennox were able to substantiate his claim to the temporalities of the archdiocese would his grant be of any significance, and Erskine was determined to ensure that this would not happen. He had, at some time before November 1592, begun an action in the Commissary Court of Edinburgh, challenging Montgomerie to produce both the king's original grant of 7 July 1583 and any subsequent letters of ratification issued after Erskine's provision to the archbishopric in 1585, apparently so that they could be "retreittit, rescindit, cassit and annullit". Although the Edinburgh Commissary Court was a higher court with a legitimate claim to review cases from all over Scotland,[46] Montgomerie believed he knew why Erskine, a scion of the house of Mar, was following this course: three of the judges of the Court were, he claimed in an action before the Lords of Session, "ordiner procuratouris, favouraris and dependaris of the hous of Mar", while one of them, Mr. John Prestoun, was actually Erskine's own procurator in the present case. Montgomerie had, it should be noted, succeeded in invoking royal authority in support of his objection, for the Lords of Session considered, in dealing with the problem on 10 November 1592, "our souerane lordis lettres, purchest at the instance of Capitane Alexander Montgomery".[47]

Reasonable as his claims of improper interest might seem to have been, and despite the king's involvement on his side, Montgomerie's appeal to the Lords of Session was only minimally successful. John Prestoun insisted that he had never intended to adjudicate on the matter, since he was acting for Erskine, and on the assurance of the other commissaries that they had not "gevin ony partiall counsall" to any of the parties, the Lords remitted the dispute back to the Commissary Court; to add insult to injury, they awarded costs against Montgomerie. Although the king's letter, clearly written by Montgomerie or his lawyers, rehearses many of his arguments in support of his claim to the pension, rebutting Erskine's counter-arguments and detailing the evidence of partiality against the commissaries, there is no indication that the Lords of Session addressed the substantive issues in the case, or that they gave much consideration to Montgomerie's claim that the commissaries' conduct of the proceedings so far, in particular their ruling

---

[46] For a statement of Commissary Court procedures, originally laid down in March 1564, see Sir James Balfour of Pittendreich, *Practicks*, ed. Peter G.B. MacNeill, 2 vols. (Edinburgh: Stair Society, 1962–1963), 2:655–77.

[47] *Poems*, ed. Stevenson, 311–16.

out some of his strongest arguments, revealed their sympathy for Erskine's cause. The poet's lawyers, John Sharp and Alexander King, may or may not have done justice to his case (he, unlike the commissaries, was not present), but there is no doubt that the decision went against him, the Lords effectively washing their hands of the affair.

After further delays, due to some degree to evasiveness on Montgomerie's part, the substantive hearing took place before the Commissary Court on 13 July 1593. To Erskine's tripartite argument — that the king had no power to make a grant from the revenues of a vacant diocese, that any such grant was in any case annulled by the terms of Erskine's provision as archbishop, and that the king's subsequent ratification could have no force since the initial grant itself was invalid — Montgomerie's procurator, James King (the son of Alexander, who had represented the poet before the Lords of Session), put forward a long and complex answer, enumerating no fewer than thirty-four heads under which Erskine's case should fail. For all its forensic intricacy, the argument depends upon a straightforward assertion, that James Beaton and not Erskine was the lawful archbishop of Glasgow. Several layers of casuistry were employed to support this contention, from the assertion that the 1587 Act did indeed accomplish his restoration, through a suggestion that whatever the effect of the legislation may have been the king had restored Beaton by appointing him as his ambassador to France, to the astonishing claim that Beaton had actually never ceased to be archbishop — and that both Erskine and his predecessor James Boyd had therefore been intruded. This latter argument was partly technical, relating to the distinction between forfeiture (presumably for the crime of treason) and punishment for "baratrie", the lesser offence of trafficking in ecclesiastical offices; but its implications were deeply political, as Montgomerie and his procurator must have realised. It challenges, indeed, the whole rationale for the post-Reformation reorganisation of the Kirk: Erskine could not be lawfully bishop if, as Montgomerie claimed, *his predecessor* was not, since "thair was ane vthir persoun standing laufullie prowydit, quha is yitt on lyiff, and his prowisioun neuer tane away, and as to the possessioun it is rather *intrusio in beneficio vnientis*".[48]

The rationale for this legal strategy was no doubt to challenge the opposition on the most fundamental grounds possible: at the very least, Montgomerie and King must have hoped, the insistence that Erskine's case required the demonstration of the validity of the forfeiture of Beaton would require a delay while the documentary evidence was located. But its implication was that the Catholic hierarchy was, legally speaking, still in possession; and if that were true, the whole basis of the Reformation settlement would be at risk. Tactical considerations and political principles thus coincided in suggesting this line of approach, but it was a

---

[48] *Poems*, ed. Stevenson, 317–24, here 324.

high-risk strategy, since it could hardly be expected that the Commissary Court, itself a Protestant institution, would accept an argument with such radical implications for the Reformed Kirk. It was presumably this element of interest which led Montgomerie and King to anticipate defeat and to give notice of an appeal, "protesting in caice your lordships do in the contrair for reductioun of the proces, nullitie therof, remeid of law, tyme and place".

Their argument, however, was almost as notable for its silences as for the fundamental attack it made on Erskine's claims. Montgomerie's weakest ground, perhaps, related to the validity of the initial grant of his pension: in the words of Erskine's claim,

> Oure said souerane lord, hawand than onlie the rycht of patronage of the said archbischoprie, in respect of the place and seate therof being vacand in his hienes handis, and sua during that tyme had na power to geiwe ony pensiounis furth of the samyn, nor diminische the patrimonie therof in preiudice of the archibischope to be electit.[49]

There is a tacit recognition of the strength of this argument in the silence of Montgomerie's case upon the point; but the assertion that Beaton had never properly been deposed actually compounded the difficulty, since it is hard to see what right the king had to grant pensions out of the revenues of the archdiocese if its lawful possessor were in exile in France. Nor could Montgomerie reply with the one answer which might have met the point: that the archdiocese was not vacant in 1583 because it was in the hands of his own kinsman, Robert Montgomerie. For the attempt to give the latter the see had long since been abandoned, and no one would give any credence to such a claim, which would in any case be incompatible with the argument that Beaton was still legally in possession. For practical purposes, Montgomerie's hopes rested upon Beaton or nobody; but the plain truth was that this argument could have no prospect of success before the Commissary Court.

Erskine's victory was indeed comprehensive. The Court found that Beaton had been properly deprived and had never been reinstated because he had not accepted the Confession of Faith; that the king's appointment of him as ambassador was irrelevant; that Erskine had been lawfully provided to the archdiocese by virtue of Boyd's death (the unfortunate episode of Robert Montgomerie was again ignored); that only one pensioner's rights had been protected in that provision; and that the king had in any case no business making grants from the temporalities of a vacant bishopric. The commissaries therefore declared that they "reducis, retreittis, cassis and annullis the said pretendit lettre of pensioun, with the said

---

[49] *Poems*, ed. Stevenson, 318.

ratificatioun and new gift of the samyn" for the period since Erskine's provision in 1586, a clear challenge to an abuse of royal power as well as total defeat for the poet. Montgomerie had, of course, the right of appeal to the Lords of Session, but there is no evidence that he exercised it, and it would appear that with this devastating judgement the battle was effectively over.

At some point before the end of the dispute, it would seem, Montgomerie spent some time in prison; this can be inferred from an incidental reference in one of the sonnets he addressed to James in the later stages of the case.[50] But we also have a poem which was apparently composed during his imprisonment, titled in the Ker manuscript "The poets complante against the wnkyndnes of his companions vhen he wes in prisone" [11]. There is little in this text which enables us to determine the circumstances, and we cannot be certain that it was at Erskine's behest that the poet found himself imprisoned; it has been suggested, indeed, that it was in the Netherlands, after his capture by the English, that this occasion took place — this would be at least partly consistent with the terms of the regrant of March 1589. This now seems highly unlikely, although it is just possible that the period of incarceration to which the poem refers was the result of the financial difficulties which evidently beset Montgomerie during his service for the States in the winter of 1587–1588. It is more probable, however, in view of the link he makes in his sonnet to the king between his imprisonment and his pension, and the language of the "Complante" itself, that this further disaster took place in Scotland, at some point between 1589 and 1593. It is even possible that it had wider implications, and that it was connected in some way with the Catholic intrigues of 1589 or of 1592–1593.

That said, the terms of the "Complante" are altogether personal, focusing almost obsessively on the miseries of the poet's condition.[51] The stanza form is less intricate than many of Montgomerie's songs, combining two simple quatrain structures to produce the pattern $a^4b^3a^4b^3c^4c^4c^4b^3$. This formal simplicity is consistent with the rhetorical posture, which relies almost entirely on direct, unmetaphorical statement, presenting the poet's lamentable condition in literal terms:

> All day I wot not vhat to do
>   I loth to sie the licht
> At evin then I am trublit to,
>   So noysum is the nicht.                    *unpleasant*
> Quhen Natur most requyrs to rest

---

[50] "To recompence my prisoning and pane", 68.III: 11, *Poems*, ed. Parkinson, 1:108.

[51] We should, however, note Arthur F. Marotti's observation that "such [prison] poems carried with them a strong sense of political oppositionalism, for religious or philosophical reflection could serve as an oblique attack on the current regime" (*Manuscript, Print, and the English Renaissance Lyric*, 6).

With pansing so I am opprest                              *thinking*
(So mony things my mynd molest)
   My sleiping is both slicht.
    (25–32)

The portrait of a sobbing, swooning prisoner — reminiscent of the dream in *The Kingis Quair* — may appear hyperbolic, more in keeping with the traditional miseries of a lover than with a serious exposition of the poet's personal circumstances; and the form of a stanzaic lyric seems to trivialise the experience in ways which are not apparent in Montgomerie's complaints in sonnet form. Only occasionally does he escape from the hazards of hyperbole. One such moment comes, significantly, when he presents himself as denying the anguish to which the poem is devoted:

Quhen men or wemen visitis me
   My dolour I disguyse
By outuard sight that nane may sie
   Quhair inward langour lyis.
    (17–20)

What, we may then ask, is the purpose of the song? To whom is it addressed, if not to those from whom the poet claims to hide his pain? The final stanza, with its minatory echoes of Matthew 7:12, apostrophises "Belouit brethren all", but this phrase is itself capable of a variety of interpretations: a common sixteenth-century acceptation would give it a quasi-religious nuance, appropriate to the Gospel context, and this might or might not be understood to refer to Montgomerie's co-religionists. Or, bearing in mind his use of "brother" elsewhere to specify his fellow-poets of the court, we might see the appeal for reciprocal goodwill as being addressed to the literary "brotherhood". Either way, the final lines might reasonably be taken to convey a certain *frisson*:

Your feet ar not so sicker sett                          *securely*
   Bot fortun ye may fall.
    (55–56)

Montgomerie actually prepares for this conclusion in the only reference in the poem which even hints at the context of his imprisonment:

Remembring me vhair I haif bene
   Baith lykit and belov't
And nou sensyne vhat I haif sene
   My mynd may be commov't.                         *vexed*
    (33–36)

The contrast between former prosperity and present misery is, of course, a commonplace of the Fortune tradition since Boethius; but it fits the circumstances of the poet's life uncomfortably well, and it is a theme to which he constantly returns in his later work. Its function here, as elsewhere, is to hint at a situation which some at least of his readers will recognise, and by implication perhaps, to challenge the king whose former affection is the real subtext of the lines. But by contrast with the much more powerful language, direct argument and specific allusion of the pension sonnets, the mixture here of dramatised emotion and conventional wisdom does little to further Montgomerie's cause.

The pressures of his legal process against and defeat by Erskine drew from Montgomerie three short sonnet-sequences and one single sonnet, which undoubtedly contain some of the most remarkable writing he ever produced. There is little here of the rhetoric of ingratiation which colours so much of his other verse, and the polemic does not display the formal qualities of exaggeration associated with the set-pieces of the *Flyting* with Polwarth. Montgomerie flytes here, but the abuse has a different tone from that which he and Polwarth had exchanged for the entertainment of the court. This is real bitterness, and there is a poignant sense that now, at last, Montgomerie is writing for himself. At times, indeed, it is scarcely possible to see an ulterior motive in the sonnets: those directed against Erskine's lawyers and his own former advocate in particular seem simply to articulate the poet's rage, disappointment and frustration, without any clear intention of affecting the outcome of events.

The sequence of four sonnets "To the Lords of Session" [69] was presumably written during the Lords' consideration of the question of jurisdiction, probably in the latter part of 1592. These poems do seem directed towards the progress of the case. Their tone is dark, and becomes darker as the sequence continues: the last is unambiguously hostile, and it is possible that the four pieces were written over some fairly extended period of time. The last, we shall see, corresponds quite strikingly to the terms of public criticism of the Session in 1592. At the outset, Montgomerie lays down a challenge:

> Quhare bene ye brave and pregnant sprits becum?
> Quik vive inventionis ar ye worne auay?          *lively*
> I am assuird by simpathie that sum
> Wald nevir wish that Cunning suld decay.
>     (69.I:1–4)

The characterisation of the nation's senior judges as "brave and pregnant sprits" is at first sight encouraging, even ingratiating, but it quickly becomes clear that Montgomerie uses the phrase only to undermine it through his contrast between the Lords' former intelligence and their present apparent lack of "cunning". The thinly veiled criticism of the system, while it is evidently motivated by Montgomerie's personal interest, was not unjustified: the convention of estates of June

1590 and the Parliament of June 1592 both sought to improve the operation of the Lords of Session, but with only limited success.[52] On the latter occasion, it was resolved that any vacancy should be filled by "ane man fearing God, off gude literature, practique, jugement and understanding of the lawes", and that such nominees should be examined by the king and the Lords themselves. All judges should be at least twenty-five years old, and their salary should be a thousand merks of annual rent or "20 chalderis of wictuall". Both the suitability of the appointees and their financial circumstances, therefore, were matters of concern: it had been a long-standing problem that underpaid judges were open to bribery, and this undoubtedly compounded the issue of personal suitability. Between these two parliamentary enactments, the king himself had offered a pithy analysis of the relationship between the administration of "justice" and family and factional allegiance:

> . . . all men set themselves more for freendes then for justice and obedience to the lawe . . . . . let a man commyt the most filthie crymes that can be, yet his freendes take his parte, and first keepe him from apprehencion, and after by feade or favour, by false assiss or some waie or other, they fynd moyne of his escape from punishmente.[53]

The "weeds of Vertue" that Montgomerie attributes to his judges, then, were rather ideal than real.

Despite his disillusionment, Montgomerie at first remains guarded in his attack on judicial incompetence. The first two sonnets, in particular, partly argue his case:

> Than mak the Poet Pensioner I pray
> And byde be justice as ye haif begun.
>            (I: 7–8)

> Mak Bishop Beaton vhat they lyk to be,
> He must perforce be ather quik or deid.         *either*
> If he be deid, the mater maks for me.
> If he be quik then they can cum no speid.
>    (II: 5–8)

The insistence on the relevance of Beaton's claims to the outcome of the case was, as we have seen, both central to Montgomerie's argument and a lost cause: its presence in the middle of the second sonnet indicates that these poems were

---

[52] *APS*, 3:569. On the legal background, see R.K. Hannay, *The College of Justice: Essays on the Institution and Development of the Court of Session* (Edinburgh: Hodge, 1933; repr. Edinburgh: Stair Society, 1990), 110–20.

[53] *CSP Scot.*, 10:523–24.

indeed intended to contribute in some way to his pursuit of the case. But legal and non-legal arguments are interwoven in a manner which suggests that Montgomerie was not entirely clear in his own mind what he was up to. The first sonnet of the sequence, for example, ends with a curious, but authentically self-promoting, invocation of his poetic accomplishments:

> Hald evin the weyis, the Victory is wun,
> As I confyde in King and solid Sharpe
>     Quhom I culd len a lift, your Lordships knauis,     *lend*
>     War they in Love as I am in the Lauis.

"King" here is, of course, not *the* king, but Alexander King, who appeared with John Sharp on Montgomerie's behalf on 10 November 1592; no doubt his position was not wholly arbitrary, for he is described in one contemporary account as "a malicious Papist", and he had returned to Scotland, espousing anti-English views, during the ascendancy of Lennox and Arran.[54] While he was a natural choice for Montgomerie to make, therefore, he can scarcely have been the most politically acceptable of representatives.

The notion that the poet is in a position to serve through his literary gifts those to whom he is well disposed returns, now perhaps with a slightly menacing subtext, at the end of the third sonnet:

> Sa to do Justice, I you all conjure,
> As ye will merit ather hell or hevin.
>     Deserve not de- (before your Lordships) —fames
>     For I may able eternize your Names.     *perhaps*
>     (III: 11–14)

The promise to "eternise" the poet's subject is a Petrarchist commonplace, more usually extended to a lady than to members of the judiciary; but it is coupled here with the complex, punning penultimate line, where "fame" and "defame" hover uncertainly around the parenthesis, as if the poet is unsure whether he will more appropriately praise or excoriate his subjects. He has placed himself, indeed, in a position previously allocated in this pivotal sonnet to God:

> He vnderstands your offices and your airts.
> He knauis vhat is committit to your Cure.
> He recompencis as ye play your pairts.
> Once, soon or syne, your Lordships must be sure     *late*
> For he respects no Princes more then pure.     *the poor*
>     (III: 5–9)

---

[54] Calderwood, *History*, 4:414.

If God has the power to judge the judges in a truly eternal context, the poem's claim to the power of "eternising" worldly reputations is, in temporal terms, God-like, a secular mirroring of the divine prerogative of judgement. Whereas in the couplet of the opening sonnet it is the voice of the surrogate wooer which is invoked, here the poet has become the voice of God Himself.

If the appropriate verdict on their Lordships remains in question in the third sonnet, it is clearly resolved in the last:

> Your Colblak Conscience all the Cuntrey knauis.
> Hou can ye live except ye sell your vote?
> Thoght ye deny, thair is aneu to note          *enough*
> How ye for Justice jouglarie hes vsit          *jugglery, trickery*
> Suppose ye say ye jump not in a jote.          *you don't deceive at all*
>     (IV: 3–7)

The note of resilient, qualified hope which ran through the three previous poems is now inaudible: all that we can hear is the bitterness of defeat and the outrage of perceived injustice. Montgomerie's generalisation of his attack is, no doubt, partly tactical: he is not only representing his own interests, but is complaining against a bench which has brought ruin to "mony hundreth" (l. 10). But however self-serving this attempt to widen the complaint may be, it is not without a certain legitimacy, given the acknowledged inadequacies of the system. The venality of the judiciary was not a problem that was readily solved, and attempts at reform would continue well into the seventeenth century.

Montgomerie's rhetorical strategy in these two final sonnets is to reverse the process of judgement, emphasising that the Lords of Session must in due course submit to a higher court, presided over by "Plotcok" (that is, Satan). His animosity is now quite overt, the vengefulness undisguised. But there is also a curious note of reminiscent intimacy in the opening of the last:

> My Lords, late lads, nou leidars of our Lauis,
> Except your gouns some hes not worth a grote.

Perhaps there is a suggestion in the sharply-alliterative first line of the judges' comparative youthfulness: certainly the use of "lads" implies that it is not so long since their Lordships were little different from Montgomerie himself, possibly even companions in youthful exploits. The 1592 Act had, as we saw above, attempted to deal with these abuses; the allegations made or implied in these lines therefore reflect quite precisely contemporary concern about the competence and integrity of the Lords, as well as Montgomerie's personal grievances.

The next sonnet in the Ker manuscript's arrangement of the group, that addressed "To his Aduersars Lauyers" [70], is more difficult to date precisely, and might in theory come at any point between the opening of legal hostilities and the conclusion of the case in 1593. From the harshness of its tone, however, we may fairly safely conclude that it, too, refers to the closing phase of the struggle, perhaps between the decision of the Lords of Session in late 1592 and that of the Commissary Court in July 1593. Its keynote is bravado, its dominant mode ingenious play with the names of the lawyers on both sides of the case:

> Presume not Prestone, Stirling is no strenth
> Suppose ye come to cleik auay my King.
> Beleiv me baith, ye sall be lost at lenth.
> Assure your selfis and think nane other thing.
> Byde ye the brash vhill I my battrie bring,     *assault*
> For all your CRAIG vharin ye so confyde
> Experience will play you sik a spring,
> Sall pluk your pennis and pacifie your pryde.     *feathers*
>     (1–8)

"Prestone" is, of course, John Prestoun, who represented Erskine in November 1592 — and who himself was to become a Lord of Session in the spring of 1596.[55] "Stirling" is James Stirling, Erskine's advocate in July 1593, while "Craig" is probably, as Cranstoun suggested, the prominent jurist Thomas Craig, author of *Jus Feudale*.[56] The primary sense of "King" is likewise an allusion to either (and more probably) Alexander King or his son James, while the "Sharpe" who occurs in the final line of the sonnet is John Sharp. But the *conceit* woven out of these names is a tellingly military one: Montgomerie refers as well to the historic role of Stirling Castle as a strategic fortress, and conceives of himself as a beseiging commander, attacking his enemies on their "craig" of the Castle Rock. He is armed, he declares, with a "Cannoun royal" (l. 12) which will destroy their defences and ensure their defeat: a clear reference to the poet's confidence, not only that James will intervene on his behalf, but that the intervention will be decisive. There is, moreover, a revealing and complex pun on the supposedly-intended "cleiking away" of the speaker's "King": while the lawyer's name is implied by the overall pattern of the sonnet's discourse, we cannot ignore — and the contemporary audience could scarcely have ignored—the further insinuation that it is really Montgomerie's relationship with James which is his enemies' true target.[57] The blustering of this sonnet, uncomfortably close to the stereotype of the *miles*

---

[55] Hannay, *College of Justice*, 119.

[56] *Poems*, ed. Cranstoun, 337.

[57] Perhaps there is also a buried reference to a game of chess in the idea of the "cleiking away" of the King, since in that context this would bring about the speaker's immediate defeat.

*gloriosus*, is partially redeemed by the wit with which Montgomerie combines his play on names with his military metaphor; but in the light of the outcome of the real contest, the bravado is inevitably inverted into pathos.

This is particularly the case since the confidence which the final line declares in the expertise of John Sharp — "Sho suits so SHARPE ye dou not byde a brattill" — evidently did not survive very long thereafter. Sharp's name is absent from the account of the final hearing, and Montgomerie reveals the reason in a pair of sonnets [71] which are merciless in their condemnation of his former lawyer's failings, however imprecise they are about the circumstances. The first is the more ingeniously indirect, anaphorically constructed around a series of calculatedly riddling "If . . . then" constructions:

> If he be sure vho sweirs and sayis he sall
> Then certainly I wot weill vho wer sure.
> If he be firme vho neuer feirs to fall
> I doubt not then vhose dayis suld lang indure.
> (9–12)

From this, the most lucid of the sonnet's three quatrains, we can infer that, in Montgomerie's view at least, there was a connection between Sharp's apparent withdrawal from the case and his ambition; perhaps, we may wonder, pressure had been brought to bear by those who had an interest, in view of the wider political implications of Montgomerie's argument, in seeing the poet lose. There is a further puzzle in the final couplet:

> *Sed quæritur*, vhat Lau he leivis at least?
> He wald not preich, he can not be a preist.

"He wald not preich" is perhaps an ironic allusion to Sharp's unwillingness to speak on Montgomerie's behalf; but there are hints here of a larger issue as well. If, as seems probable, the poet's lawyer was the same Mr. John Sharp who had spoken in Latin at the king's entry into Edinburgh in 1579, then events appear to have completed a circle in a most striking way: having "harangued" the king at the outset of his personal reign, Sharp now fails to manifest truth and justice when the leading poet of that reign faces (as he evidently sees it) persecution and disgrace.[58]

---

[58] John Sharp, who can perhaps be identified with the man of that name who graduated M.A. from St Andrews in 1557 (*Acta*, 408), occurs as an advocate and burgess of Edinburgh as early as 7 September 1569 (*RMS 1546–80*, no. 1883). He was depute keeper of the Privy Seal in 1576 (no. 2539), and occurs, significantly in view of his participation in, and withdrawal from, Montgomerie's case, as *advocatus coram concilii et sessionis regis* on 20 December 1591(*RMS 1580–93*, no. 1980). On his career, see Margaret Sanderson, *Mary Stewart's People: Life in Mary Stewart's Scotland* (Edinburgh: James Thin, 1987), 22–33.

The hopes associated with d'Aubigny's arrival in Scotland in the autumn of 1579 have been frustrated; the Catholic party has failed to achieve the power it aspired to, and Montgomerie's situation is in some sense a product of that failure.

If the first element of the pair is remarkable for its structured indirection, the second (despite its own claim to be a "riddill") is rhetorically much more straightforward:

| | |
|---|---|
| A Baxters bird, a bluiter beggar borne | *baker's boy; filthy* |
| Ane ill heud hursone lyk a barkit hyde, | *ugly; tanned hide* |
| A saulles suinger seuintie tymes mensuorne, | *forsworn* |
| A peltrie pultron poyson'd vp with pryde, | *despicable coward* |
| A treuthles tongue that turnes with eviry tyde, | |
| A double deillar with dissait indeu'd, | |
| A luiker bak vhaire he wes bund to byde, | *sworn* |
| A retrospicien vhom the Lord outspeud, | |
| A brybour baird that mekle baill hes breud, | *vagabond poet* |
| Ane Hypocrit, ane ydill Atheist als, | |
| A skurvie skybell for to be esheu'd | *wretch* |
| A faithles, feckles, fingerles and fals | *unregenerate* |
| A turk that tint Tranent for the Tolbuith: | *lost* |
| Quha reids this riddill he is sharpe forsuith. | |

Many of the techniques of flyting are recognisable here: the relentless listing; the images of bestiality, disease, physical ugliness, and poison; the charge of being an infidel; all reinforced by consistently-maintained alliteration. But these expansive modes are now contained by the discipline of the sonnet, and the result is invective of powerful intensity. It does not, it is true, give any clear idea of the nature of Montgomerie's grievance, beyond suggesting that Sharp had broken his word; but the point is made with a powerful echo of the Bible. By repeating "luiker bak" in the Latinate "retrospicien" — perhaps Montgomerie's own coinage, since its use here antedates the earliest occurrence elsewhere — the poet recalls the Vulgate text of Luke 9:62:

Ait ad illum Iesus: Nemo mittens manum suam ad aratrum et respiciens retro aptus est regno Dei.

The previous line, by the same token, echoes the sixteenth-century English translation, of which the Geneva version is typical:

. . . No man that putteth his hand to the plough, and looketh backe, is apt to the kingdome of God.

Between them, then, ll. 7–8 evoke both the English and Latin versions of Jesus's dictum: but it is the latter line which clinches the allusion with its concluding "vhom the Lord outspeud" (Revelation 3:16). We should not, obviously, take too seriously the charge of "atheism", which tended to be levelled at any sixteenth-century figure who was seen to put political considerations over dogmatic loyalties; but by deploying the New Testament in this way Montgomerie effectively attacks his enemies on their own favourite ground.

The sequence of four sonnets addressed to the King [68] naturally called for a more subtle manipulation of rhetoric. These are the most difficult to date precisely: on the one hand, the despair which they articulate might suggest that they were composed at a point in the struggle at which Montgomerie had abandoned any hope of a decisive intervention by James on his behalf. The letter sent to the Lords of Session in November 1592 in the king's name was only formally from James himself; the document was, indeed, "purchest at the instance of" Montgomerie, and cannot therefore be interpreted as meaningful royal support. And it may, conversely, be significant that this sequence in the Ker manuscript precedes the other sonnets associated with the pension case: while there is a growing note of finality in its closing stages, culminating in the farewells of the final sonnet, this may be a rhetorical posture rather than a serious indication that the dispute was now over. We cannot, then, assume with any certainty that this group was completed after July 1593, and the tone of the first three might argue that they, at least, were written earlier. If, as we shall suggest below, the allusion to "Constable" in IV:3 refers to Henry Constable, the English courtier-poet, then the most likely occasion would be during one of the latter's visits to Scotland in the autumn of 1589 or early 1590; from late 1591 onward Constable was on the Continent, a Catholic exile, and he is not known to have visited Scotland again until 1599.

The sequence, like that addressed to the Lords of Session, begins with apparent optimism, and gradually becomes bleaker as the argument develops. But here the appeal is cloaked in Montgomerie's most intricate verbal play, a series of quibbles which break the rhythmical flow of the sonnet and suggest a mind which is both determined to avoid any misunderstanding and severely troubled by misfortune:

> Help, PRINCE, to vhom, on vhom not, I complene
> Bot on, not to, fals fortun ay my fo
> Quha but, not by a resone reft me fro        *without; stole*
> Quha did, not does, yit suld my self sustene.
>     (I: 1–4)

Even within this first quatrain, Montgomerie subtly modulates his appeal, yet it would be difficult to imagine a more anti-"Castalian" opening, violating almost every principle James had enunciated in his "Reulis and Cautelis". Exploiting the ambiguity of the relative pronouns, the poet shifts within four lines from appeal to challenge, since the "Quha" of l. 4 more probably refers to the king than to Fortune. The casuistical oppositions of prepositions *seem* to affirm that Montgomerie's quarrel is with Fortune and not with James, and yet we can scarcely doubt that it is the latter who "suld" ensure his loyal servant's welfare.

This sense that the complaint is not some abstract lament about misfortune but a carefully-structured political argument is confirmed by the rest of this opening sonnet:

> Of Crymis not cairs since I haif kept me clene
> I thole, not thanks thame Sir vho serv'd me so,          *suffer*
> Quha heght, not held to me and mony mo          *promised*
> To help, not hurt, bot hes not byding bene          *constant*
> Sen will not wit, to lait vhilk I lament,
> Of sight not service, shed me from your grace.          *separated*
> With, not without your warrand yit I went
> In wryt, not words, the papers ar in place.
>     Sen chance not change hes put me to this pane
>     Let richt, not reif my Pensioun bring agane.          *theft*

At a purely technical level, Montgomerie's rhetorical skill is attested by the multiple ways in which he varies his basic device of chiasmus, switching after the opening quatrain from opposed prepositions to more substantive words. These contrasts are again deployed to shift the responsibility for the poet's plight away from the king, but now to an undefined "they" who have betrayed him in unspecified ways.[59] As in his sequence to the Lords of Session, moreover, he widens his complaint by asserting that the betrayal does not only affect him, but "mony mo" as well. This suggests a larger political dimension (as we have seen Montgomerie's case to have had), and while the poem gives no explicit indication of what he means, it is likely that James, as addressee, was intended to understand the point.

Much of the latter part of the sonnet, indeed, is written in a thinly-disguised code. The departure of the poet from James's sight, the ultimate source of all the former's troubles but undertaken with the king's written warrant, must surely refer to Montgomerie's voyage to the Continent in 1586, which we know to have been licensed by the king. It was soon after he left Scotland, as we have seen, that his pension was legally challenged by Erskine. But what are we to make of the suggestion that, while he was no longer in James's presence, he continued to serve him: is this a merely formal declaration of continuing loyalty, or is there a hint here of something more specific? There is, clearly, an uncertainty about the king's position in Montgomerie's foreign projects between 1586 and 1589, an

---

[59] The attack on those who "hes not byding bene" should, perhaps, remind us of the second sonnet against John Sharp, which describes him as "a luiker bak vhare he wes bund to byde". Should this sonnet to the king then be dated after Sharp's apparent abandonment of his client?

uncertainty which the terms of the confirmation of his pension in the latter year do little to resolve. A suspicious mind might even find in the terse "the papers ar in place" rather more than an assertion that the poet can prove that his departure was with James's permission: is it possible that the documents in question gave some hint of the king's true purposes in 1586, the purposes which led him to license not only Montgomerie, but his fellow-Catholics Hugh Barclay of Ladyland and Colonel William Stewart of Houston?

Whether or not the opening sonnet of the sequence contains a subtle attempt at blackmail, Montgomerie shifts his rhetorical posture in the second from chiasmus to anaphora. The first two quatrains accumulate a long series of misfortunes, all of which are invoked to support the hypothesis that misery is the lot of poets, and that Montgomerie's circumstances therefore make him "of all that craft . . . chief". This wry echo of his earlier title implies a carefully-pitched balancing of modesty and hubris, which we repeatedly observe in Montgomerie's poetry in the ingratiating mode. The motif is continued into the sestet:

| | |
|---|---|
| With August Virgill wauntit his reuard | *lacked* |
| And Ovids lote als lukeles as the lave. | *rest* |
| Quhill Homer liv'd his hap wes wery hard | *fortune* |
| Yit vhen he died sevin Cities for him strave. | |
|     Thoght I am not lyk one of thame in Arte | |
|     I pingle thame all perfytlie in that parte. | *rival* |

Despite the disclaimer in the final couplet, the comparisons which precede it are obviously intended to associate Montgomerie, artistically as well as financially, with the masters of classical poetry; and by implication to associate James with those rulers, like the Emperor Augustus, whose failure to reward genius which had served them has made them notorious. But there is no hint of petition in this second sonnet, unlike the first; while dealing only descriptively with his present circumstances, Montgomerie seems resigned to misfortune, and the making of common cause with the unrecognised poets of the past prepares the way for the confrontation with a despairing future which dominates the rest of the sequence.

This further change in rhetorical posture is marked at first by defiance:

| | |
|---|---|
| If I must begge it sall be far fra hame. | |
| If I must want it is aganis my will. | |
| I haif a stomok thoght I hold me still | |
| To suffer smart, but not to suffer shame. | |
| In spyt of fortun I sall flie with fame. | |
| Sho may my Corps bot not my Curage kill. | |
| My hope is high houbeit my hap be ill | |
| And kittle aneugh and clau me on the kame. | *ticklish; claw me on the comb* |
|     (III: 1–8) | |

The reversion to the Fortune theme might look at first glance like another way of deflecting the blame away from James; but the argument of the sestet will make clear that this is far from Montgomerie's intention. The tone of the first two quatrains is one of dignified, qualified resignation: the poet may be unable to have any substantial influence over his fate, but he will accept it only on his own terms. The insistence on "shame" and "curage" is revealing, for Montgomerie leaves no doubt that he retains a keen sense of his own worth: it is the prospect of dishonour which he evidently finds intolerable, and the qualities he invokes are not now literary, as they were in the previous sonnet, but those of the courtly gentleman, whose "fame" is his most valuable possession.

By contrast with the generalised terms of the octave, Montgomerie turns in the sestet to a version of events which which is even more specific than that of the first poem of the sequence:

> Wes Bishop Beaton bot restord agane,
> To my ruin reserving all the rest
> To recompence my prisoning and pane,
> The worst is ill, if this be bot the best.
>     Is this the frute Sir of your first affectione,
>     My Pensioun perish vnder your protectione?
>     (9–14)

The challenge of the closing couplet represents the poet's last appeal to the king, a final attempt to play upon the relationship the two had enjoyed a decade earlier; and it may well refer back to the letters Montgomerie had obtained in the course of 1589. But he links this claim with the main legal ground of his case, Beaton's restoration, and with a cryptic allusion to "my prisoning". As we have already noted, the evidence of "The Poets Complante" confirms that he did indeed suffer a period of imprisonment, and most probably in Scotland. This sonnet implies, moreover, that these events were somehow related to the dispute with Erskine, although the indirectness of the reference again suggests the use of a code: James will understand the connection, no doubt, and Montgomerie evidently hopes that this will be enough to persuade him to intervene. But there is a note of despair in the final question as well: the request for support is implied rather than directly stated, and we do not gain the sense that the poet really expects his appeal to be successful.

In the final sonnet of the sequence, indeed, he decisively shifts the rhetorical address away from James altogether. After the opening "Adeu, my King", Montgomerie apostrophises a succession of other audiences, literal and abstract, and by l. 9 James has become a third-person presence rather than the second-person object of the address. The range and specificity of those to whom Montgomerie now bids farewell, while partly influenced by the demands of alliteration, is highly revealing:

Adeu, my King, Court, Country, and my kin,
Adeu suete Duke vhose father held me deir,
Adeu Companiones Constable and Keir
(Thrie treuar hairts I trou sall neuer tuin).                    *unite*
    (IV: 1–4)

The opening line is remarkable in its comprehensiveness as well as for the explicit
inclusion of the court which had for so long been the locus for Montgomerie's am-
bitions, the scene of his rhetorical triumphs, and the source — at least in part —
of his distress. But what follows turns our attention away from the formal and the
generic to a very particular environment, that of Ludovick, duke of Lennox, and
his circle. That Montgomerie chooses to invoke his relationship with Lennox's father,
Esmé Stuart, undoubtedly recalling the bitter nature of his eclipse and death, is a clear
declaration of factional loyalty; and this is reinforced by the address to Constable and
Keir. Henry Keir was not only a key member of Ludovick's household, but had
also been a long-standing supporter of Queen Mary and an associate of Esmé
Stuart in the Guise-inspired attempt to Catholicise the king.[60] For Montgomerie
to mention him in the present context must surely be calculated to leave no doubt
about the poet's own commitments, whatever ambiguities might remain about
James's attitudes.

The king's ambivalence is further implied by the inclusion of Henry Constable,
whose conversion to Catholicism in 1591 had been a *cause célèbre* in England. His
first visit to James's court had, as we noted above, been in September 1583, when he
was still a rising young Protestant gentleman under the patronage of Walsingham.
He was still a committed Protestant in 1588, when he published *A short view of a
large examination of Cardinall Allen his trayterous justification of Sir W. Stanley and
Yorck*, and although his *Examen pacifique de la Doctrine des Huguenots*, completed
after the assassination of Henry III of France and published in October 1589,
purports to be the work of a Catholic, it is evident that it is actually Protestant
in character.[61] In the same month that the *Examen pacifique* appeared, Constable
was back in Scotland, acting in concert with Jean Hotman on behalf of Penelope
Rich, her brother the Earl of Essex, and Arabella Stuart, all of whom were "con-
cerned to secure their own positions in the event of James's succession in . . . the
near future". It is evident from the detailed reports on this mission by the English
agent Thomas Fowler that he had several secret meetings with the king, leaving

---

[60] On Keir, see above, 58–59; and Lyall, "'Thrie Truear Hairts'", 192–96.

[61] On Constable's career generally, see *Poems*, ed. Grundy, 15–50. The *Short view*
survives only in manuscript extracts, in Dublin, Marsh's Library MS. Z3.5.21, fols. 93v–
110r. On the authorship of the *Examen pacifique*, see *Poems*, ed. Grundy, 31–32; cf. David
Rogers, "'The Catholic Moderator'", *Recusant History* 5 (1960): 224–35; John Bossy, "A
Propos of Henry Constable", *Recusant History* 6 (1961–1962): 228–37.

on 21 October, the day before James sailed to Denmark to bring home his bride.[62] And although there is no documentary substantiation, his sonnet "To the K. of Scots vpon occasion of his longe stay in Denmarke by reason of the coldnesse of the winter and freezing of the sea" implies that Constable was again in Scotland, awaiting the king's return, in the first months of 1590.[63] Eighteen months later, when he joined Essex's expedition to France in the late summer of 1591, he was on the point of declaring his conversion to Catholicism. That Montgomerie, in 1592–1593, should associate him with Lennox and Keir, therefore, strongly suggests that this Guise-ite environment played a part in his change in religious views, and that his conversion may have caused less surprise north of the Border than it did in England.

It is his companions that Montgomerie is now addressing, and he strikes a characteristically plangent note as he contrasts his present misery with his former prosperity:

> If byganes to revolve I suld begin
> My Tragedie wald cost you mony a teir
> To heir hou hardly I am handlit heir
> Considring once the honour I wes in.
> Shirs, ye haif sene me griter with his grace     *greater*
> And with your vnquhyle Maister to and myne     *former*
> Quha thoght the Poet somtyme worth his place
> Suppose ye sie they shot him out sensyne.     *later*
>     Sen wryt nor wax nor word is not a word
>     I must perforce ga seik my fathers suord.
>     (5–14)

We have encountered the reminiscent tone elsewhere in Montgomerie's later verse, but here he achieves a kind of resigned dignity which is often missing from his complaints. There is a subtle equilibrium between pride in his former eminence and subdued grievance; and the proverbial declaration of the final line (which means "I must become a wandering beggar" but has echoes too of Montgomerie's former military career)[64] forcefully captures the poet's despair. The effectiveness of the sonnet is greatly enhanced by a characteristic series of displacements: whereas the emotion in "The Poetes Complante" is hyperbolically expressed through the persona's sobbing, for example, the tears in "Adeu, my King" are significantly

---

[62] *HMC Salisbury*, 3:434–43. Hotman had arrived in Edinburgh by 7 October, and it is probable that Constable travelled with him.

[63] *Poems*, ed. Grundy, 143.

[64] Tilley, *Dictionary of Proverbs*, F98, glossed by James Kelly in 1721 as being applied to "idle Vagrants who go a travelling without any good or worthy Design".

those of the fictional sympathetic hearers, and the blame for the poet's maltreatment is carefully cloaked in ambiguity. The crucial question is who the "they" are in l. 12: it is theoretically conceivable that the antecedents are "his grace" (James) and "your vmquhyle Maister" (the first, or just possibly the second, Duke of Lennox), but it is more likely that there is no antecedent, and that "they" are Montgomerie's unnamed enemies. This grammatical space constitutes Montgomerie's neat if-the-cap-fits ploy, for the "wryt, nor wax, nor word" of l. 13 are surely intended to cause the king — the true addressee of this poem and of the whole sequence, whatever the rhetoric may be suggesting — to reflect on the promises he had signed, sealed, and failed to deliver.

Montgomerie's eleven sonnets on the theme of his legal battle for his pension constitute a rhetorical achievement without parallel, not only in Older Scots verse, but in early modern English as well. Perhaps the most personal poems of Sir Thomas Wyatt and Sir Walter Ralegh most nearly approximate this note of suffering and disillusionment, but even they tend to resort to commonplace or to Petrarchist conceit where Montgomerie makes use of contorted syntax, aphoristic proverbs, and coded personal allusions to argue with his addressees. On a European plane, only *Les Regretz* of Du Bellay (1558) capture the same tone, and they perhaps provide the closest analogue to Montgomerie, though they generally lack his tortured language and constantly allude to Petrarchist convention:

> J'ayme la liberté, & languis en service,
> Je n'ayme point la court, & me fault courtiser,
> Je n'ayme la feintise, & me fault deguiser,
> J'ayme simplicité, & n'apprens que malice . . .

> [I love liberty, and languish in service ; I don't like the court, and must play the courtier ; I don't like feigning, and must disguise myself; I love simplicity, and learn nothing but malice . . .][65]

Personal as Du Bellay's rhetoric is, the intensity of the emotional effect of Montgomerie's remarkable group of sonnets stems from the fact that they are more than merely expressive, that they are manifestly intended, for the most part at least, to have a specific outcome, that they constitute an attempt to influence the course of events. The insight which they give into the workings of the judicial and patronage systems in the early modern period has, it is true, a wider significance, but that is largely incidental; their primary function is to engage with the legal process as it unfolds, and thereby to persuade those to whom the poems are

---

[65] Joachim du Bellay, *Les Regrets et autres œuvres poëtiques*, ed. J. Jolliffe and M.A. Screech, 2nd ed. (Geneva: Droz, 1974), 107.

addressed to respond to the various challenges Montgomerie lays down. A comparison with the most directly autobiographical of Ralegh's verse illustrates how distinctive the voice of the poems we have been discussing really is:

> Twelve yeares intire I wasted in this warr
> twelve yeares of my most happy younger dayes,
> butt I in them, and they now wasted ar
> of all which past the sorrow only stayes,
> So wrate I once and my mishapp fortolde
> my minde still feelinge sorrowfull success
> yeven as before a storme the marbell colde
> douth by moyste teares tempestious tymes express.[66]

Ralegh's griefs, like Du Bellay's, are mediated by Petrarchist convention, the "Cynthia" to whom the poem is addressed being a thinly-veiled representation of Elizabeth I. Montgomerie, by contrast, speaks directly, if frequently in code, about his circumstances and his vestigial ambitions. The result is a poetry which, paradoxically, transcends its immediate rhetorical purposes, expressing the agonies of the Renaissance courtier more eloquently than less brutally personal verse can do.

The personal struggle between Montgomerie and Erskine was played out against a backdrop of political intrigue and counter-intrigue. Huntly and other Scottish lords were still in touch with Parma until his death in December 1592; Sir Robert Bowes continued to gather as much intelligence as he could, to report it to Cecil and Walsingham, and to conduct strenuous discussions with the king; and the Edinburgh ministers, scandalised as ever by the state of the court and alleging a conspiracy to repeat St. Bartholomew's Day in the Scottish capital, attacked James's favourites by name from the pulpit. In October 1592 there was a flurry of additional controversy in Edinburgh over a series of measures initiated by the Council and the Kirk: merchants were to be prevented from trading in Spain, ostensibly because of the impositions of the Inquisition; the traditional Monday market was to be moved to one or two other days to avoid prophanation of the Sabbath by persons travelling to Edinburgh the day before the market; and a levy was to be introduced to pay the stipends of the ministers of the eight parishes into which it had been decided the previous August to divide the city, and to build the necessary churches. On 24 October a pair of scurrilous sonnets were thrown into the pulpit of St. Giles' Church and into the house of John Cairns, one of the leading ministers. Bowes transmitted a copy of these offending texts to England, thereby ensuring their survival:

---

[66] Sir Walter Ralegh, "The 21th and last booke of the Ocean to Scinthia", ll. 120–127, *Poems: An Historical Edition*, ed. Michael Rudick, MRTS 209 (Tempe, AZ: Arizona Center for Medieval and Renaissance Studies, 1999), 52–55.

Will Watsons wordes or Bruces boist availl?
Can Carnis or Craige mak marchants to remaine?
Malcankers cryes a whitt shall not prevaill
Balfour may bark but all wilbe in vaine
Ye spewe your spytes on sic as sayles to Spaine
And leaues lyk lardes by bryberye of the poore          *live like lords*
Howbeit we beg providinge ye gett gaine
Ye of your stipends will not want ane stuir            *stuiver*
Ye crye for kirks for furnishinge of your cuir
Not taking tent howe men maye doe the tourne           *paying regard*
I fear your falles your dayes cannot endure
The best amange you wilbe laith to burne
     Ye curse but cause by warrand of the word
     We neid not feare the furye of your sworde.

What moves your myndes to mell with markett dayes.     *meddle*
What lawe alleidge you for sic foolish acts
Your gukket zeale procures ane great disprais          *foolish*
And heapes contempt and hatred on your backes
The common people craues your publick wrackes
Detests your tournes and dammis your devilish deids
The devill himself can forge na curster factes
Ye are but wolues cledd vpp in wethers weides.
Ye look lyk lambes yet in your bossome breids
A poison'd speech poore people that perverts
I hope to see your selues or elles your seids
Abandon'd all lyk vtlawes in deserts
     Ye scorne but Christ, your Countrye, kirk, and kinge,
     Prescryband points as Scribes in euerye thinge.[67]

Bowes gives no indication of the authorship of this pasquil, and nothing in the surviving record adds significantly to his account.[68] It is apparent that the sonnets must be the work of an opponent of the Calvinist faction who was in Edinburgh in October 1592 and who was a very considerable poet and polemicist. And the most likely candidate, who clearly had both motive and opportunity, is Alexander Montgomerie.[69]

---

[67] PRO, SP52/49/391. The text is printed, together with Bowes's letter transmitting it, in *CSP Scot.*, 10:800–2.

[68] Calderwood gives a brief account of the episode (*History*, 5:177), but provides no information additional to that in Bowes's correspondence.

[69] For a fuller discussion of the authorship question, on which the following paragraphs are largely based, see Lyall, "Anti-Calvinist Propagandist?".

There can be no doubt about the poems' rhetorical effectiveness. In the first of the two, the alliterative onslaught on a succession of Edinburgh ministers (William Watson, Robert Bruce, John Cairns, John Craig, and James Balfour), who between them represent the full force of the Calvinist party, focuses upon their language, deriding the inability of their formidable preaching skills to affect the behaviour of the laity. This defiance is coupled with the accusation of cupidity, contrasting the ministers' allegedly affluent lifestyle, now to be compounded by the financing of new churches, with the comparative poverty of their parishioners. The poet seems, moreover, to have coined an expressive new word to sum up his contempt for the preachers: "malcanker". Presumably formed on "canker", a spreading sore or ulcer, "malcanker" is a compound which parallels such words as "malcontent", a borrowing from French which appears in both English and Scots in the 1500s and which seems to have been something of a political vogue-word in the later sixteenth century.[70] "Malcanker" is, of course, much more graphic, the literal meaning of its second element suffusing the compound; and it therefore more effective as a term of political abuse, especially since "canker" was often specifically associated with infections of the mouth. It may be, indeed, that a particular link between canker and orality lies behind the coinage of the word and its use here: in 2 Timothy 2:17, Paul writes of false teachings that *sermo eorum ut cancer serpit* (translated in the Geneva Bible as "and their word shall fret as a canker"). I take "malcankers" here to be a possessive plural, so that l. 3 means: "the cries of malcankers shall not prevail in the slightest", interrupting the sequence of names with a generalisation which anticipates the collective "ye" of the rest of this sonnet and its companion. It seems an entirely legitimate inference that the poet wishes the reader to remember the biblical association of "canker" with "profane and vain babblings", and to link the Edinburgh ministers with the false teachers condemned by St. Paul as well as with the contemporary idea of political trouble-making.

The anonymous poet was certainly capable of such ironic biblical allusion. In the couplet of the second sonnet, following up the New Testament metaphor of the clergy as wolves in sheep's clothing, he accuses the ministers of contempt and of obsessive legalism:

> Ye scorne but Christ, your countrye, kirk, and Kinge,
> Prescryvand points as Scribes in euerye thinge.

---

[70] Interestingly, "malcontent" had a very specific significance in the Netherlands at this period, where it was used of the opponents of Spanish rule. Since both Montgomerie and the other leading candidate for the authorship, Captain James Halkerstoun, had fought in the Dutch wars, this may lurk somewhere in the subtext of the sonnet.

The biblical echoes of this final jibe are unmistakable: since the fourteenth century "scribe" had been the standard English translation of the Latin *scriba*, the Vulgate's term for the class of professional interpreters of the Law in post-Exilic Jewish society. It was the scribes, along with the Pharisees, who represented the spearhead of the Jewish opposition to Christ, and who are the subject of the latter's diatribe against the current state of religion, reported in Matthew 23:

> . . . because ye shut vp the kingdome of heauen before men: for yee yourselues goe not in, neither suffer yee them that would enter to come in . . . for ye make cleane the vtter side of the cup and of the platter, but within they are full of briberie and excesse. (Matt. 23:13, 25)

It is in this role of false and meddling lawmakers that the final couplet casts the upholders of Calvinist orthodoxy. By turning the authority of the New Testament back upon them, certainly in his final couplet and very probably through his coinage of the term "malcankers", our satirist daringly challenges his enemies on their own favourite ground. The device is, moreover, one we have already noted in Montgomerie's undeniably authentic polemical verse: most strikingly, in his use of "retrospicien" in the second of the sonnets against John Sharp.

   The style and diction of the two sonnets of 24 October 1592, indeed, closely resemble those of the more personal poems which Montgomerie was producing in 1592–1593. The rhetorical questioning with which both sonnets against the ministers begin is a frequent ploy in Montgomerie's complaints, while the tendency of both groups of poems to revert to a series of pithy one-line assertions creates a distinctive note of serial accusation. There are more specific echoes as well: the final couplet of the first of the anonymous sonnets has the same rhyme-pair as the first of the group "To his Majestie, for his Pensioun", while "Ye scorne but Christ, your Countrye, kirk, and kinge" looks rather like a reworking of "Adeu my King, Court, Country, and my kin". If the author of the pasquil of 24 October was not Montgomerie, it was someone who knew how to emulate his style with equal effectiveness. And if it was Montgomerie himself, then we can see him, in the midst of his dispute with Erskine, a month before his challenge to the jurisdiction of the Commissary Court of Edinburgh, deploying the same rhetorical skills with which he was pursuing his own cause in what he would have seen as the wider public interest. The absence of these poems from the Ker manuscript should not surprise us: were the anonymity of the two sonnets to be destroyed, the effect on Montgomerie's personal circumstances would presumably have been catastrophic, and it would therefore be entirely natural for him not to have retained a copy of such incriminating work.

   Whether or not Montgomerie wrote this pair of poems, they provide an explanation for a sonnet which appears among his work in the Ker manuscript, under the title "The Poets Apologie to the Kirk of Edinburgh" [91]. Here he scornfully dismisses an allegation that he has written something offensive to the church, rejecting

"Yon Couhorne vhereof ye me accuse" and insisting that *his* attack would be much more effective were he moved to make one:

> For if I open wp my Anger anes
> To plunge my pen into that stinking styx
> My toongue is lyk the Lyons vhair it liks,
> It brings the flesh lyk Bryrie fra the banes.          *briars*
>     I think it scorne besyd the skaith and sklander
>     To euin an Ape with aufull Alexander.          *compare*
>     (9–14)

This poem appears to give a strong indication that Montgomerie was suspected of having written the pasquil of 24 October 1592, and that he denied the charge; it does not, of course, prove that he did not do so, for such a denial is precisely what we would expect if he had indeed been the culprit. The suggestion that the sonnets are much less powerful (and less funny) than he would have written is, as we have seen, scarcely sustainable, but the combination of poetic hubris with a hint that his own anger is real enough even if he hasn't expressed it yet is characteristic of his literary persona. It is also tactically very effective, and would be even more so if he had actually been responsible for the original attack.

Montgomerie's short sequence to the king concludes with a rhetorical farewell, but there is no evidence that he now left Scotland, or that he made the proverb about seeking his father's sword literal by again taking up his military career. Nor are there many signs of continuing poetic activity. Only one new poem can confidently be assigned to the period after the judgement of July 1593: the encomiastic verses addressed to Robert, Lord Semple, evidently on his return from France [48]. The poem is undated, but it must surely have been written after Montgomerie's return to Scotland in 1588: Semple was still a minor in 1587 (although he was apparently in Parliament in 1584), and it is therefore unlikely that he performed the chivalric deeds with which the poem credits him before Montgomerie's departure to the Netherlands in 1586.[71] The most likely occasion for the poem's composition, indeed, is Semple's return to Scotland early in 1596, after an absence of almost nine months; he certainly spent much of this time in France, for he was in Paris — with Huntly and Bothwell — in July 1595, and wrote to the Earl of Essex from Rouen on 12 December.[72] If this is correct,

---

[71] For a summary of Semple's career, see *Scots Peerage*, 7:551–54. According to one contemporary account, he was sixteen in 1583, which is consistent with his still being a minor in 1587; other reports which give his age as thirty in 1589 and twenty-nine in 1592 are presumably in error.

[72] *CSP Span.*, 4:617; *HMC Salisbury*, 5:496. He was back in Scotland by 29 January 1596 (*CSP Scot.*, 12:137).

however, Montgomerie's partial reticence is striking, for Semple had visited the Spanish Netherlands on his departure from Scotland and his activities abroad had included communication with Philip II (apparently through the poet's friend Barclay of Ladyland).[73] The background to the episode, then, was the continuing series of Catholic intrigues with Spain, of which Montgomerie can scarcely have been unaware. But none of this, understandably, is even hinted at in the poem.

The "Welcome" is in one of Montgomerie's less complex stanza-patterns, made up of six trimeter lines rhymed *ababcc* and including a refrain. The praise it offers is conventional, almost perfunctory, and the opening seems almost insulting in its frank admission of a pecuniary interest:

> Aualk Montgomries Muse
>     And sey vhat thou can say,
> Thy long and just excuse
>     Maecenas taks auay
>     Quhais high heroique actis
>     His Name immortall maks.
>         (1–6)

The suggestion that the poet's inspiration has been justifiably absent for a considerable time offers strong support for a late dating of the piece, and incidentally explains the absence of other poems which give indications of having been composed after 1593: the "long and just excuse" is, presumably, the destruction of the poet's career through the loss of his pension. The overt allusion to financial inducements is, therefore, a coded complaint about his straitened circumstances; it is, significantly, now Semple and not the king who functions as his Maecenas. But this is not all. The penultimate stanza returns to this niggardly mode, suggesting that Montgomerie's decision to sing his subject's praises merely emulates the work of other poets:

> Sen poets maist profound
>     Thy praysis do proclame
> My trompet, to, sall sound
>     The famphar of thy fame                                     *fanfare*
>     Quod he vhom siknes wraks
>     And the Immortall maks.
>         (37–42)

---

[73] *CSP Dom. 1595–97*, 39; *LASP For.*, 6:261. For Ladyland's mission to Spain, see *CSP Span.*, 4:615; *LASP For.*, 6:253–54.

The hint here that Montgomerie is ailing is certainly gratuitous, an attempt to extract sympathy from an audience whose attention is ostensibly not on the poet at all but upon his noble subject; but it ties in with the allusion in the opening lines to the poet's long silence. The connection between poetic performance and financial reward is clear enough, and the underlying sense of alienation, though lightly touched upon, connects this piece of formal celebration with Montgomerie's more overtly personal poetry of the earlier 1590s. There is a further link in the nudging of the refrain: by l. 42, we should observe, it is no longer Semple's own qualities which render him "immortall" but the poet's praise, an echo of the offer/threat of "eternization" which Montgomerie had previously extended to the Lords of Session.

Only in the declaration that "Thy cuntrie, king *and Kin* [my italics] / Thy qualities decoird" (ll. 31–32), perhaps, can we detect any trace of genuine and committed praise for Semple, though even here Montgomerie manages to bring the argument back to himself. For the poet could claim kinship to his subject: the Semples and the Montgomeries had long been connected by marriage, and Lord Semple himself was married to the daughter of the Earl of Eglinton, while his aunts, Janet and Dorothy Semple, were the wives of Montgomerie's brother Hugh, the laird of Hessilheid, and of Robert Montgomerie of Skelmorlie respectively.[74] There is, then, a family interest reflected in this poetic praise of the chivalric achievements of Semple, and perhaps a family reason for the silent suppression of those aspects of his foreign activities which were politically sensitive. Montgomerie's own connections with Spain, and with Semple's Catholic associates such as Hugh Barclay of Ladyland, were themselves too compromising to allow him any indiscretion on that score.[75]

We know very little, this poem of early 1596 apart, concerning Montgomerie's activities between the summer of 1593 and the spring of 1597, although it seems probable that he had virtually abandoned his career as courtier-poet. Perhaps, as Helena Shire conjectured, he spent these years living in retirement, or exile, in the West. He was certainly in Ayrshire on 16 November 1595, when he was among the witnesses to a transaction at Ladyland involving David Barclay, feuar of Ladyland, and Grissell Montgomerie, his spouse.[76] The bride was the daughter of the poet's kinsman Patrick Montgomerie of Giffen, and the document provides important evidence of the family connection between the Montgomeries and the Barclays, both of them significant landowners in northern Ayrshire, as well as one of two surviving examples of the poet's signature.

---

[74] This Robert Montgomerie, sixth of Skelmorlie, was the father of the seventh laird, whose marriage to Margaret Douglas Montgomerie had celebrated in 1593.

[75] For an indication that it was though Ladyland that Semple was in touch with Philip II, see *CSP Span.*, 4:615.

[76] NAS, RH6/3374; cf. *Poems*, ed. Parkinson, 2:122.

Montgomerie's association with Hugh Barclay of Ladyland, coupled no doubt with his personal disaffection, brought him to the final crisis of his life. In October 1596, according to information communicated to Cecil by Sir Robert Bowes, a meeting took place in Nantes between the Spanish ambassador in France, Barclay of Ladyland, and Colonel James Halkerstoun, who had, it will be remembered, also fought in the Netherlands. The purpose was to plan an occupation of Ailsa Craig, the barren island off the Ayrshire coast,

> to set off and manteyne ane publique mass in this Island quhilk sould be patent to all distressed papy[s]te[s] quhairfra so euer they sall come, ane place of releife & refreshment to the Spanyart, or rather a porte to them at ther arryvall in Ireland, and ane store house to keipe furnishing & all thingis profytable to the vse of therle of Tyrone . . .[77]

What seems at first sight like a wildly futile endeavour can therefore be seen to have been quite carefully calculated in strategic and logistical terms: as the Spanish planned their support for Tyrone's rebellion, they attempted to secure, at little risk to themselves, a base in the lower Clyde estuary, and Ladyland and other Scottish Catholics were apparently willing to be employed in this way.[78]

It is not evident how Montgomerie became involved in this doomed initiative, but his family links with Ladyland, and possibly a former military association with Halkerstoun, provide sufficient explanation. Nor is it apparent that he was actually present on Ailsa at the beginning of June 1597, when Ladyland's party were confronted by Andrew Knox, minister of Paisley, a militant opponent of Catholic conspiracy in the west of Scotland and the discoverer of the "Spanish Blanks" five years before. The charge levelled against Montgomerie before the Privy Council on 14 July was that he "wes arte, parte, at the leist vpoun the counsale, divise, and foirknawledge with vmquhile Hew barclay of Ladyland", a wording which suggests that the authorities themselves may have been unsure how deeply he was implicated.[79] By not appearing to defend himself, however, Montgomerie seems to have declared his guilt — or so the Council determined, resolving that he should be denounced as a rebel. He continued to elude capture, and there is no evidence that he was apprehended by the government before his death in Edinburgh more than a year later.

There is, on the other hand, a strong indication that he spent some of the last year of his life revising and completing his major poem of fifteen years earlier, *The Cherrie and the Slae*. Some time in 1597, and presumably before Montgomerie became

---

[77] PRO, SP61/12; the text is given by Stevenson, *Poems*, 334–35.

[78] For the background to this campaign, see Cyril Falls, *Elizabeth's Irish Wars* (London: Methuen, 1950), 184–212; Wallace T. MacCaffrey, *Elizabeth I: War and Politics, 1588–1603* (Princeton: Princeton University Press, 1992), 385–417.

[79] *RPC*, 5:402.

implicated in the Ailsa Craig conspiracy, Robert Waldegrave published the unfinished version, in an edition which may well have been produced without the author's knowledge or consent. The timing seems strange: it is, of course, possible that Montgomerie was still regarded as a significant literary force at court, but we have seen that there is little evidence of new writing by him in this period and it is hard to see why Waldegrave should suddenly have printed a work which had been in existence for so long and which was in any case fragmentary, even breaking off in the middle of a stanza.

This first Waldegrave edition, moreover, was full of typographical errors, and was soon followed by a second, which claimed on its title page to be "Prented according to a Copie corrected be the Author himselfe". This tacit acknowledgement of the unsatisfactoriness of the earlier text is entirely justified; and many of the errors are indeed eliminated in the second edition. George Stevenson, however, challenged the veracity of Waldegrave's claim to have received his corrections from Montgomerie himself, noting that

> Waldegrave's second impression contains some errors which it is hard to believe would have been allowed to remain in any manuscript read by the author himself and intended for the press; and these are not of a kind to be charged to the printer.[80]

He does not state what these errors are, but it is hard to find the justification for his contention in the evidence of the editions themselves. Not all the "corrections" in the second edition, it is true, may seem to us to be improvements, but the number of categorical mistakes is quite small.[81]

One group, in particular, is highly suggestive: at several points, there is clear evidence of a confusion of <f> and long <s>. At l. 267, for example, where the first edition correctly reads

Bot yit, allace, bide it behuiffit,

the second prints 'behuissit'. Less unequivocal errors of the same kind can be found in ll. 77 (*muiffit/mussit*) and 665 (*haist/haif*). The explanation is obvious: the printer of *1597 II* has had difficulty distinguishing the two letter-forms in his copy-text, and has accordingly produced wrong or weaker readings; such confusions are, of course, more likely to occur where the exemplar is a manuscript, but they are also feasible where a printer is working quickly and carelessly from printed copy, especially where this text is marked with manuscript corrections. Nor is it necessary to

---

[80] *Poems*, ed. Stevenson, xvii.

[81] The total number of new errors is not larger than sixteen, including several straightforward examples of eye-skip, confusion over minims, transposed letters, and so on.

suppose that Montgomerie himself sanctioned or missed such mistakes. If the "copie" he saw and corrected was of *1597 I*, rather than a manuscript, then he may simply have delivered the revised text to Waldegrave, and then not seen it again until after it was published, with its own quota of errors. This is all the more credible if he was already a fugitive from justice during the printing of the second edition.

A more substantial difficulty with such a scenario is Stevenson's second argument: that it is hard to believe that Montgomerie would have participated in a further edition of his poem in its fragmentary state. There is no ready answer to this, except to remark that, strictly interpreted, Waldegrave's title page for *1597 II* does not actually state that Montgomerie had sanctioned a revised edition, or indeed that he had provided a corrected text; it merely states that the author had corrected a copy, and that this was now the basis of the new edition. This is consistent with the typographic nature of the editions, as we have seen, and it is even possible that an irritated poet sent his corrections to the printer; but we are surely not required to infer that it was the former's intention that this, too, should appear in print. He may, on the contrary, simply have been registering his displeasure, and the idea of a corrected version may well have been Waldegrave's own.

Whatever the nature of Montgomerie's involvement in Waldegrave's second 1597 edition, it seems that the sudden appearance in print of his long-abandoned allegory spurred him into taking the poem up again, modifying the opening, inserting ten additional stanzas, and adding a further thirty-eight stanzas to bring the action to a satisfactory conclusion. That, at least, is the implication of the supposed title page of the lost first edition of the complete version, which on the testimony of Allan Ramsay, editing *The Cherrie and the Slae* in 1724, was printed by Andrew Hart in 1615; this stated, it would seem, that the text was "Newly altered, perfyted, and divided into 114 Quatorziems, not long before the Author's death".[82] This is convincing enough: we now know (as Ramsay presumably did not) that there were at least eight months and probably more between the appearance of Waldegrave's second edition and the poet's death, and Montgomerie had good reason to put his *magnum opus* into a more satisfactory state. If this is an accurate picture of events, then the additions to *The Cherrie and the Slae* are certainly among Montgomerie's last works, and quite probably the last of all.

It would be pleasing if he had taken the opportunity to resolve some of the fundamental structural problems which were inherent in the first version, and which may have contributed to its abandonment. But this is not, I think, the case; and it is arguable that the weaknesses in Montgomerie's conception were so basic that they could not be corrected without complete reorganisation of the whole poem. In Shire's view, the new, completed version represents a radical revision, a "perfyting"

---

[82] Allan Ramsay, *The Evergreen* (Edinburgh: Thomas Ruddiman for Allan Ramsay, 1724), 2:98.

of that begun nearly fifteen years before, bringing to a lucid, if covert, conclusion the anti-Calvinist message which was already implicit in the earlier text.[83] This view stands or falls with the doctrinal interpretation Shire advances, to which we shall have occasion to return in a subsequent chapter.[84] But we can for the present observe that the completion of the tropological debate adds nothing new in *structural* terms, and that whatever changes Montgomerie makes to the natural description at the opening are of the order of nuance, rather than any fundamental rethinking of the poem's design. In this last work we can see the qualities of craftsmanship which characterise Montgomerie's poetry throughout his career; but there is surely no evidence of a radical change of view, aesthetically, politically, or doctrinally.

During this period as a fugitive, apparently, Montgomerie conceived the idea of fleeing to Germany, to join the Scottish Benedictine community in Würzburg, which had been established by the bishop of Würzburg in 1595.[85] That, at least, was the subsequent claim of Thomas Duff, who makes the poet's voice declare that

> Franconicam Herbipolim suasit mihi Nursius heros
> Quaerere, Scotigenas qua Benedictus alit,
> Tempore quo patriae pater Antistesque refecit
> Julius hospitibus reddita tecta pius.

> [The Nursian hero led me to seek Würzburg in Franconia, where Benedict nourished the Scots, at the time when Julius, bishop and father of his land, was restoring and rebuilding the monastery there.][86]

Duff's lines need not be taken, *pace* Fr. Dilworth, to indicate that Montgomerie had ever visited the Würzburg community, and the knowledge we now have of the circumstances of his death make it most unlikely that he did so. But Duff is quite categorical that he intended to make the journey, and that his aim was to become a monk:

> Nursius Artaunum vocitat Benedictus alumnum
> Montgomry insignem relligione virum.

> [Benedict of Nursia calls to Würzburg his disciple Montgomerie, a man famous for his religious devotion.]

---

[83] Shire, *Song, Dance and Poetry*, 130–7.

[84] See below, 318–30.

[85] On the history of this house, and the circumstances of its foundation, see Dilworth, *Scots in Franconia*, esp. 23–49.

[86] Dilworth, "New Light", 232.

It would, in many ways, have been a poignantly fitting end to a turbulent career, but Montgomerie was not to live to achieve his purpose.

Some time before 22 August 1598 Montgomerie died, presumably in or very near Edinburgh. He was, as far as we can tell, still an outlaw, and he was certainly a Papist. Nevertheless, it is clear that he was, with the consent of the baillies of the burgh of the Canongate (some of whom were also members of the Kirk Session), buried in their church, which at this date was still the former church of Holyrood Abbey, adjacent to the king's palace. On 22 August, the presbytery of Edinburgh called upon the baillies to present themselves the following week to explain why, in view of Montgomerie's Catholicism, they had permitted him to be buried in the church. Their defence, that "gif thai had knawin the said umquhill Alexander to hawe bene a papist he suld nocht hawe bene bureit in the kirk", seems to have cut little ice with the presbytery, and they were "scharplie rebukit for contravening the actis of the Generall Assemblie".[87] Given the proximity of the burgh to the royal court, one can see why there was some scepticism about the claim of ignorance; it was, it is true, fifteen years since the period of Montgomerie's greatest prominence, but it is hard to believe that his religious views were wholly unknown to the officers of the kirk and burgh.

The relationship between the kirk of the Canongate and Holyrood Palace suggests, moreover, that there may have been royal involvement in the poet's burial. Twenty years later, in distant Würzburg, Thomas Duff claimed that the citizens of Edinburgh petitioned the king himself to intervene on Montgomerie's behalf, and implied that it was James's pressure which caused the church authorities to relent from their initial opposition to a Catholic's body lying in their kirk. Of the funeral he says:

> Nobilitas favet, affines dant munera, cives
> Hortantur, studio Rex favet ipse pio.
> Nulla tamen rabidos Calvini jura catellos
> Flectunt, o scelerum monstra odiosa Deo !
> Donec regali comitatu satellite vatem
> Arma et vis tumulant, dum cecidere preces.

[The nobility supported it; his relations gave money; the citizens urged it; the king supported it with godly zeal. No sense of justice, however, moved the rabid Calvinist curs (O wicked portents, hateful to God!), until the poet was buried with an escort of armed men of the royal household, when all entreaties failed.]

---

[87] Durkan, "Date of Alexander Montgomerie's Death", 91.

We must make due allowances for poetic licence, propagandist intentions, and inaccuracies introduced by the lapse of time, but it is obvious that Duff's information about this episode was in general terms reliable. It seems very likely that, however much he may have failed his erstwhile favourite during his lifetime, James did indeed act to ensure that his mortal remains received suitable interment in what was virtually his own parish church. We do not know where exactly in Holyrood Abbey Montgomerie lies, but we can be reasonably certain that the king had a hand in the matter.

This victory won, James paid his final tribute to the "maister poete" whose career had been so inextricably involved with the past twenty years of his reign, whose literary tastes had no doubt done much to form his own, and whose doctrinal convictions had given him such a precarious position within the circle of the court:

> What drousie sleepe doth syle your eyes, allace,          *seal*
> Ye sacred brethren of Castalian band:
> And shall the prince of poets in our land
> Goe thus to graue vnmurned in anie cace?          *unmourned*
> No; whett your pens, ye imps of heauenlie grace,
> And toone me wp your sweete resounding strings
> And mounte him so on your immortall wings
> That euer he may liue in euerie place.
> Remember on Montgomeries flowand grace,
> His suggred stile, his weightie words diuine,
> And how he made the sacred sisters nine
> There montane quitte to followe on his trace.
> > Though to his buriall was refused the bell,
> > The bell of fame shall aye his praises knell.[88]

The poetic qualities claimed for Montgomerie by the king undoubtedly reflect his own priorities: if his claim to a "suggred stile" or even to "weightie words" is less obvious to us than it was to James, there is more than a formal recognition of Montgomerie's rhetorical mastery in these lines. And there can be few reservations about his "flowand grace", a phrase which has for James a clear technical significance: "flowing" is, after all, "the verie twichestane [of] Musique", the metrical regularity about which a great deal is said at the beginning of the king's "Reulis and Cautelis".[89]

But James's sonnet is not only concerned with Montgomerie's poetic skills. In the interplay between "the sacred Sisters nine" and "ye sacred brethren of Castalian band" there is an unmistakable note of reproof: as I argued at the outset of

---

[88] James VI, *Poems*, ed. Craigie, 2:107–8.
[89] *Poems*, ed. Craigie, 1:71–74.

this study, the "brethren" must surely be the "Castalian" poets of the king's own circle, whose eyes are now blinded and whose instruments are silent in the face of Montgomerie's death. The challenge, then, is to William Fowler, to John Stewart of Baldynneis, to Alexander Hume, to William Alexander of Menstrie, none of whom is known to have composed an elegy marking the event: only James, it would seem, was willing to lament the passing of the finest Scottish poet of his generation. The reasons for this are, of course, likely to have been in part political, for Montgomerie's religious persuasion must have contributed greatly to his literary eclipse in his last years, and he had, after all, died an outlaw, even if the king was magnanimous enough to overlook the fact. Yet there may have been a larger reason as well: with Elizabeth of England nearing the end of her reign, the eyes of many of the "sacred brethren" were focusing more on the glittering possibilities of a future in London than they were upon the "Castalian" experiment of fifteen years before. By the time of his death, Montgomerie represented an initiative the time for which had passed, and only James, the apparent initiator and Montgomerie's true disciple, whose future did not depend upon the vicissitudes of patronage, was willing to cast backward in commemorating what had been achieved. Montgomerie himself had taken a divergent literary path, and we have seen that from soon after his return to Scotland in 1589 the most powerful and effective of his poems employed a very different language from the "suggred stile" praised by the king. The conflict over his burial is emblematic of his alienation, and in the context of the *English* Jacobean age which Montgomerie did not live to see, and the cultural transformation which it brought to Scotland, the final line of James's epitaph acquires an unintentionally ironic note.

# CHAPTER SIX

## "THE COURT SOME QUALITIES REQUIRES": SATIRE AND CONVIVIALITY IN MONTGOMERIE'S POETRY

Throughout Montgomerie's career, from his return to Scotland, probably in 1579, until his death in 1598, it was the monarch and his court which exerted the most powerful influence, whether positively or — as they did, predominantly, in his final decade — negatively, upon his life and his art. In this, of course, he was not unusual: the same had been true of Dunbar, Lindsay and Scott in Scotland, and of many poets in England, France and Italy as well. But we have come to understand that there were qualitative changes in the ways in which sixteenth-century rulers exploited the dependence of artists upon their patronage, and in the view which sixteenth-century poets took of their own role. Nowhere is this more apparent than in England, where recent scholarship has stressed both the propagandist manipulation of poetry by Elizabeth I and the anxieties which are expressed by the courtier-poets through their verse.[1] The dynamics of the process were different in Scotland: the assimilation to the monarch of the traditional role of the courtly beloved was scarcely a strategy which was available to James VI, and the king's part in court culture was in any case conditioned by his own literary aspirations, which dominated the early phase of courtly production (say, from 1583 until the king's marriage in 1589) and which gave Montgomerie himself a special place as his poetic mentor.

To a much greater extent than in England, moreover, the Scottish court was the locus for a cultural struggle, the prize in which was the king's religious loyalties. In this conflict, Montgomerie's Catholic convictions must have placed him in a difficult position, one which is paradoxically apparent precisely in the *absence* of overtly doctrinal religious discourse in his extant poetry. We have already seen, indeed, that in some of his "official" poems, those in which he directly addresses the king or those around him, he is careful to use language which offers acceptably Protestant meanings, though these are never pursued into an extended exposition of political theory. Nowhere, at least in those works which are unequivocally his, do we find even a broad hint of Montgomerie's own Catholic views; even when,

---

[1] See above, 8–9.

towards the end of his career, he alludes to his affiliations with the Lennox house-
hold, he does so in purely personal terms. This reticence is, it is true, in conformity
with James's firm assertion that poets should steer clear of "materis of commoun
weill",[2] but it is also consistent with the broader goal of self-advancement which
clearly dominates Montgomerie's poetic priorities from his appearance at court at
the beginning of 1580 until the collapse of his financial hopes in 1593.

In the poems we have so far considered, those which can because of their content
be related (positively or negatively) to Montgomerie's career at court, techniques
of ingratiation and panegyric obviously predominate. Where he wishes to subvert the
rhetoric of praise or his own posture as eulogist or petitioner, he does so through
the subtle intrusion of ironic possibilities rather than through overt declaration:
only within the licensed confrontations of the *Flyting* and in the bitter poems of
the period of his legal struggle with Erskine have we encountered a full-blooded
articulation of alternative, negative meanings, and even here the criticism is some-
times wrapped within a protestation of loyalty or a declared belief that the system
will ultimately vindicate itself. Yet it is apparent that Montgomerie's relationship
with the court was neither straightforward nor an untroubled one, and there is a
strand within his work of poems which confront the experience of court politics
in much more explicitly antagonistic terms.

In pursuing such themes, of course, Montgomerie was on a well-trodden
path. The court as an institution, and the courtier as a social type, had long been
targets for satire. One of the most influential products of the twelfth-century
"Renaissance", the *Policraticus* of John of Salisbury (1159), is significantly sub-
titled *De nugis curialium*, and systematically attacks the hedonism, materialism,
and duplicity of the court and its inhabitants. Its themes were widely taken up in
sermons and in other didactic works, and there is a marked growth in such writ-
ings, both in Latin and in the vernaculars, after the turn of the fifteenth century.
In texts like Alain Chartier's *De vita curiali*, the *De curialium miseriis epistola*
(first published c. 1473) of Aeneas Silvius Piccolomini (later Pope Pius II), and
Pierre Michault's *Doctrinal de Court* (1466), we find an ever more disillusioned
view of the life of the courtier, and a recurring emphasis on the vanity and dis-
honesty which are held to be characteristic of it.[3]

In the sixteenth century, however, this tradition of "anti-aulic" satire under-
went marked changes. Partly because of the renewed influence of such classical
authors as Horace and Lucian, partly because of the success of more recent works
such as Piccolomini's *De curialium miseriis epistola*, Ulrich von Hutten's *Misaulus*

---

[2] James VI, *Poems*, ed. Craigie, 1:79.

[3] For a useful overview of the medieval tradition, see Pauline M. Smith, *The Anti-Courtier
Trend in Sixteenth-Century French Literature* (Geneva: Droz, 1966), 38–54; cf. G.R. Owst, *Lit-
erature and Pulpit in Medieval England*, 2nd ed. (Oxford: Blackwell, 1961), 579–84.

(1518), and above all of Antonio de Guevara's *Avisos de Privados y Doctrina de Cortesanos* and *Menosprecio de Corte y Alabanca de Aldea* (1539), and partly in reaction against Baldassare Castiglione's *Cortegiano* (1514), there was an upsurge in writing on the theme; but the qualitative differences from the works of the earlier period are as striking as the sheer quantity of work involved.[4] These differences reflect, too, the transformation of the royal servant into "a cultivated, full-time dilettante".[5] Castiglione's treatise, and in another sense Machiavelli's *Il Principe* (1513), articulate a philosophy of ingratiation in which personal accomplishment and calculated, self-serving deviousness are carefully balanced, confirming for many sixteenth-century readers those accusations which had been made against courtiers throughout the Middle Ages.

These developments are apparent in vernacular British literature, as elsewhere in Europe. It is possible to trace the themes of the *Policraticus* through such works as Hoccleve's *Regement of Princes* (1412); but here they are incidental to a larger political argument. Between 1490 and about 1540, however, there are four significant English expressions of the changing spirit: John Skelton's *Bowge of Courte* (1498) and *Magnyfycence* (?1515), Alexander Barclay's translation of Piccolomini in the first three of his *Egloges* (1513), and the first of Sir Thomas Wyatt's satires (probably either 1536 or 1541). Each has its own distinctive rhetorical posture: Skelton's is cast in the first case in the form of a dream-allegory, his complaints mediated through the experience of a persona who is unconventionally named Drede, in the second in that of a morality drama whose protagonist is beset by a group of courtiers whose names impersonate duplicity; Barclay employs the dialogue structure of pastoral to articulate a former courtier's disillusionment with the courtier's life; while Wyatt, more personally, casts his criticism in the form of a verse-epistle addressed to his fellow-courtier John Poyntz. Sharp as the condemnations of Skelton and Barclay may be, with Wyatt's satire we must surely be struck by a new kind of sensibility:

> My wit is nought, I cannot learne the way,
> And much the less of things that greater be,
> That asken help of colours of device
> To join the mean with each extremity:
> With the nearest virtue to cloak alway the vice,
> And as to purpose likewise it shall fall
> To press the virtue that it may not rise,

---

⁴ Smith, *Anti-Courtier Trend*, 57–97.

⁵ The phrase is Sydney Anglo's, in his essay on "The Courtier: The Renaissance and Changing Ideals", in *The Courts of Europe: Politics, Patronage and Royalty, 1400–1800*, ed. A.G. Dickens (London: Thames and Hudson, 1977), 33–53, here 36.

As drunkenness good fellowship to call,
The friendly foe with his double face
Say he is gentle, and courteous therewithal,
And say that favel hath a goodly grace
In eloquence, and cruelty to name
Zeal of justice and change in time and place,
And he that sufferth offence without blame
Call him pitiful, and him true and plain
That raileth reckless to every man's shame,
Say he is rude that cannot lie and feign,
The lecher a lover, and tyranny
To be the right of a prince's reign:
I cannot, I — no, no, it will not be![6]

This catalogue of the multiple hypocrisies required of the courtier is partly impassioned, no doubt, by Wyatt's recent experience of imprisonment; but his sharper awareness of the *personal*, psychological costs of life at court is manifested both through a more direct expression of his own position and through a language which breaks out of the conventional limits of complaint, creating a voice which is lucid, aphoristic and almost wholly unmetaphoric. Wyatt's methods here find no parallel in France for at least thirty years, but his model was probably Juvenal's third satire, either directly or by way of the tenth satire of Luigi Alamanni (1532–1533).[7]

At the same time that Skelton and Barclay were expressing conventional criticisms of courtiers and the court in a Tudor context, the Scot William Dunbar was giving a much more personal view of the problem. Dunbar is in many ways the consummate courtier-poet, and he was too deeply involved in the patronage system, it seems, to articulate any generalised critique. His frequent petitions to James IV, sometimes demanding, sometimes wheedling with affected modesty, seldom offer a broader analysis of the courtier's condition, and when he launches into a lively but ultimately fairly conventional catalogue of the king's less worthy adherents,

| | |
|---|---|
| Fenyeouris, fleichouris and flatteraris, | *dissemblers; hypocrites* |
| Cryaris, craikaris and clatteraris, | *clamourers; chatterers* |
| Soukaris, groukaris, gledaris, gunnaris, | *parasites* |
| Monsouris of France, gud clarat cunnaris, | *tasters* |
| Inopportoun askaris of Yrland kynd | |
| And meit revaris lyk out of mynd, | *stealers* |

---

[6] Sir Thomas Wyatt, "Satire I", ll. 57–76, in idem, *Collected Poems*, ed. Joost Daalder (Oxford: Oxford University Press, 1975), 102–3.

[7] *The Works of Henry Howard, Earl of Surrey and of Sir Thomas Wyatt the Elder*, ed. G.F. Nott (London: Longman , 1815–1816), 562; Wyatt, Collected Poems, ed. Kenneth Muir and Patricia Thomson (Liverpool: Liverpool University Press, 1969), 347–50.

> Scaffaris and scamleris in the nuke          *scroungers; spongers*
> And hall huntaris of draik and duik . . . ,[8]

it comes as part of a rhetorical strategy which carefully balances both the "profit-able" and the undeserving against Dunbar's own claims, enabling him to conclude that he does not mind the former being rewarded by the king but begrudges any patronage granted to the latter. We encounter a more generalised view of court life only in the moral lyrics, where the court becomes a mirror of the vanities of the world at large:

> Fredome, honour and nobilnes,
> Meid, manheid, mirth and gentilnes,
> Ar now in cowrt reput as vyce;
> And all for caus of cuvetice.[9]

The predominant mode in such pieces is complaint rather than satire; while it is true that in poems like "To the Merchantis of Edinburgh" and "Thir Ladyis fair that in the Court ar kend" Dunbar develops more specific criticisms of particular abuses, these usually relate to economic or legal issues rather than to the nature of the court itself.[10]

The court in which Dunbar pursued his career was still largely dominated by the great families of medieval Scotland, but the sixteenth century brought new pressures and a new courtier class there as elsewhere, and by the time that Montgomerie was seeking to establish himself there were tensions with which Dunbar had never had to deal. In a Protestant country like Scotland, the changes which affected the culture of the court were particularly profound. The laicisation of the administration which had in any case been taking place in the earlier sixteenth century was now completed: before the reign of Mary, the normal route into royal service was through clerkly orders, and as late as the regency of Mary of Guise the majority of officers of both the state and the household were at least in minor orders.[11] While there are fifteenth-century examples of laymen who rose to prominence in

---

[8] William Dunbar, *Poems*, ed. Priscilla Bawcutt, 2 vols. (Glasgow: ASLS, 1998), 1:223.

[9] Dunbar, *Poems*, ed. Bawcutt, 1:77.

[10] Dunbar's complex relationship with the court of James IV is intermittently discussed in the two most important critical studies of his work: Ian Simpson Ross, *William Dunbar* (Leiden: Brill, 1981), and Priscilla Bawcutt, *Dunbar the Makar* (Oxford: Clarendon Press, 1992). For a brief and stimulating alternative view, see Waller, *English Poetry of the Sixteenth Century*, 110–13.

[11] On the relative positions of the clergy and laity in late medieval Scotland, including the assertion that "the clerical monopoly of the higher reaches of learning remained virtually complete", see Mason, *Kingship and Commonweal*, 21–22, 104–38.

the royal household, even in certain cases being ennobled, there can be no doubt that this phenomenon was much more evident after 1500; and once the ecclesiastical route to royal patronage and influence was closed off, the prevailing climate of the court became more secular.

The fortunes of William and John Maitland, two of the most successful courtier-politicians of the second half of the century, clearly illustrate this development. Sons of the East Lothian laird Sir Richard Maitland of Lethington, both William (c. 1528–1573) and John (1543–1595) rose to prominence during the reign of Mary, and supported the Queen's cause after her deposition. Both attracted more than their share of obloquy, and William in particular became a butt of violent satirical abuse from such contemporary observers as Robert Sempill and George Buchanan.[12] But both were successful in their own terms, and John went on, after his brother's death, to become one of the most influential members of James VI's government, the subject, as we have seen, of eulogistic sonnets by both Montgomerie and the king himself.

It is particularly striking, therefore, that the one Scottish attempt at a positive account of the courtier's art was written by the Maitlands' father, and is titled in the later of the family's poetic anthologies "The Laird of Lethingtounis Counsale to his Sone beand in the Court".[13] This "Polonius-like poem of advice"[14] does not deny the dangers of life at court, nor does it seek to refute the accusations habitually made against courtiers; it rather sets out the principles on which one should endeavour to survive in such a hostile environment. By doing so, it implicitly concedes many of the arguments employed in the anti-aulic tradition:

> Be war quhamto thy counsale thow reveile;
> Sum may seim trew and yit dessemblit be.
> Be of thy promeis and conditioun leill;
> Waist nocht thy gude in prodigalitie.

---

[12] For Sempill's pasquil "The Bird in the Cage", see *Satirical Poems of the Time of the Reformation*, ed. James Cranstoun, 2 vols. (Edinburgh, STS, 1891–1896), 1:160–64; for Buchanan's *Chamaeleon*, see idem, *Vernacular Prose Works*, ed. P. Hume Brown (Edinburgh: STS, 1892), 37–53.

[13] On Maitland senior, see Alasdair A. MacDonald, "The Poetry of Sir Richard Maitland of Lethington", *Transactions of the East Lothian Antiquarian and Field Naturalists' Society* 13 (1972): 7–19, and, in a wider context, idem, "Early Modern Scottish Literature and the Parameters of Culture", in *The Rose and the Thistle: Essays on the Culture of Late Medieval and Renaissance Scotland*, ed. Sally Mapstone and Juliette Wood (East Linton: Tuckwell, 1998), 77–100, here 82–86; cf. Maurice Lee Jr., "Sir Richard Maitland of Lethington: A Christian Laird in the Age of Reformation", in *Action and Conviction in Early Modern Europe*, ed. T.K. Rabb and J.E. Seigel (Princeton: Princeton University Press, 1969), 117–32.

[14] Lee, *Maitland of Thirlestane*, 22.

> Nor put thyne honour in-to jeopardie.
> With folk diffamit nother gang nor ryde;
> With weilfull men to argoun is folie;     *argue*
> He reulis weill that weill in court can gyde.
>      (17–24)[15]

The tradition within which this poem stands is a long one: it goes back to the *Disticha de Moribus ad Filium* attributed to Cato and a common medieval school book, and its Scottish predecessors include *Ratis Raving*, *The Consail and Teiching at the Vys Man gaif his Sone*, and (Maitland's immediate model) Dunbar's "To dwell in court, my freind, gife that thow list".[16] Reverting to this tradition, the moral argument of Maitland's advice systematically contrasts the behaviour he advocates for his son with that he will find in others. He should avoid dishonesty, and immoderate gambling, and even excessive ambition:

> Preis nocht to be exaltit abone vther,
> For gif thow do thow sall be sair invyit.
>      (49–50)

Espousing these traditional values, Maitland sets up a model of conduct which is founded on loyalty and "suthfastnes"; unlike Castiglione's *cortegiano*, his ideal courtier is less interested in polished manners and self-advancement than in service to his God, his king, and his people. His sons may even have believed that they carried out his advice; but that is certainly not how they were perceived by their detractors, to whom the accusation of "Machiavel" came readily to hand.

Sir David Lindsay (c. 1486–1555), himself no mean exponent of the courtier's arts, understood this discrepancy in perception perfectly well: when his personifications of the courtier's duplicity, Flatterie, Falset, and Dissait, assume their clerical disguises in *The Thrie Estaitis* (1552), they adopt the names of Devotioun, Sapience, and Discretioun, each of which holds up an ironic mirror to the deceptiveness which is their stock-in-trade. (This unholy trinity is, interestingly, echoed by Maitland, who urges his son to "Flie feinyeing, flattering, falsheid and dissait".)[17] By the later sixteenth century, propagandists on all sides had found a justificatory label for the deployment of such rhetoric in the service of deceit: the discipline of "casuistry", viewed in one perspective, is no more than a device for

---

[15] Quotations are from *The Maitland Folio Manuscript*, ed. W.A. Craigie, 2 vols. (Edinburgh: STS, 1919–1927), 1:21–24.

[16] Cf. Dunbar, *Poems*, ed. Bawcutt, 1:264–65.

[17] The extent to which Lindsay reflects the older pattern of court life is demonstrated by the fact that all three vices adopt clerical disguises; Lindsay himself, as a layman, can be seen as an example of a more secular form of courtiership.

making respectable that "economy with the truth" which is the key to the pru-
dent courtier's success. In Gary Waller's words,

> [i]ndirection, dissimulation (what Puttenham terms *Beau semblant*), orna-
> ment, calculated ostentation, are all characteristics that are simultaneously
> those of the poet and the courtier.[18]

The twists and turns of Jacobean politics gave ample opportunity for the ex-
ercise of such skills. As a (very probably approving) observer of the "conversion"
of Lennox and Henry Keir to the Protestant faith in 1580, Montgomerie can
scarcely have failed to be aware of the wider ramifications of life at court; and we
have already seen how much of his verse is constructed around those techniques
of ingratiation which were indispensible to the successful courtier, in life as well
as in art. From the subtle manipulations of the masquer's voice in *The Naviga-
tioun*, through the sonnets in praise of the king's poetic skills, to such politically-
judged panegyrics as those addressed to Patrick Galloway and John Maitland of
Thirlestane in or after 1589, we can see Montgomerie crafting his verse to achieve
the greatest possible political advantage. Yet works like Du Bellay's *Les Regretz*
(1558) and Ronsard's *Bocage Royal* to Henry III of France (published as a col-
lection in 1584) demonstrate that it was possible to attack the abuses of the court
while still maintaining one's aspirations to succeed there;[19] and there is accord-
ingly no need to presume that the small number of overt and powerful condem-
nations of the court which Montgomerie produced must have been written after
the poet had himself abandoned hope of retaining or regaining the prominence he
evidently enjoyed between 1580 and 1586.

The relationship between widely-accepted criticisms of courtiership and the
frustration of personal ambition can be extremely complex, as the example of Ed-
mund Spenser illustrates. We can hardly doubt that the sharp analysis of duplicity
and ruthlessness at court in *Colin Clouts Come Home Again* (1595) is informed by
the poet's resentment of his treatment in London in 1590–1591, a point which is
actually made to his eponymous persona by the shepherd Thestylis and denied
by Colin Clout himself (ll. 676–687).[20] But the criticisms themselves are scarcely

---

[18] Waller, *English Poetry of the Sixteenth Century*, 16–17.

[19] On Du Bellay, see Henri Weber, *La Création Poétique au XVIe Siècle en France*
(Paris: Librairie Nizet, 1955), 416–62, and Yvonne Bellenger, "Du Bellay satirique dans
Les Regrets ?", in *Du Bellay: Actes du Colloque International d'Angers de 26 au 29 mai 1989*,
ed. Georges Cesbron, 2 vols. (Angers: Presses de l'Université d'Angers, 1990), 45–58 ; on
Ronsard, see Smith, *Anti-Courtier Trend*, 185–90.

[20] Edmund Spenser, *Shorter Poems*, ed. William A. Oram et al. (New Haven and
London: Yale University Press, 1989), 519–62. For relevant discussions of *Colin Clouts
Come Home Again*, see David W. Burchmore, "The Image of the Centre in *Colin Clouts*

new, or uniquely related to Spenser's own circumstances, and there is no real need to suppose that the very similar, if more extended, attack in *Mother Hubberds Tale* (1591) was the result of revision of a work which may have been begun a dozen years before its publication and which Spenser himself declared to have been written 'long sithens . . . in the raw conceipt of my youth'.[21] This may be partly political, an unsuccessful attempt to avoid the censor's wrath, but it is nevertheless true that the picture of courtly behaviour Spenser provides here precisely parallels those we find in sixteenth-century Italy and France, and in Wyatt and Lindsay:

> Yet the braue Courtier, in whose beauteous thought
> Regard of honour harbours more than ought,
> Doth loath such base condition, to backbite
> Anies good name for enuie or despite:
> He stands on tearmes of honourable minde,
> Ne will be carried with the common winde
> Of Courts inconstant mutabilitie,
> Ne after euerie tattling fable flie;
> But heares, and sees the follies of the rest,
> And thereof gathers for himselfe the best;
> He will not creepe, nor crouche with fained face,
> But walkes vpright with comely stedfast pace,
> And vnto all doth yeeld due curtesie;
> But not with kissed hand belowe the knee,
> As that same Apish crue is wont to doo . . .
>           (717–731)

What is distinctive here is not the nature of the attack, but the rhetorical framework of the beast-fable — partly, of course, a reversion to older, classical and medieval satiric forms[22] — and the terse precision with which Spenser marshals his case (as in the image, developing a standard criticism of courtiers' extreme fashions, of the Ape dressed *alla turchesa*). The plain vernacular style which Spenser deploys here is characteristic also of Montgomerie's anti-aulic satires; both men are, no doubt, conforming to traditional principles of generic decorum, but each is able to create a tone which conveys both personal engagement and an awareness of larger concerns. If their motivations are in part self-interested, they speak for others as well in their condemnation of a world of which they are inescapably part.

---

*Come Home Again"*, *RES* n.s. 28 (1977): 393–406; John D. Bernard, *Ceremonies of Innocence: Pastoralism in the Poetry of Edmund Spenser* (Cambridge: Cambridge University Press, 1989), 106–34.

[21] *Shorter Poems*, ed. Oram et al., 334.

[22] Cf. Annabel Patterson, *Fables of Power: Aesopian Writing and Political History* (Durham, NC: Duke University Press, 1991), 64–66.

Montgomerie's most direct, if subtly modulated, attack on the world of the court as an institution is the lyric entitled in the Ker manuscript "The Oppositione of the Court to Conscience" [8]. Its targets are traditional, but its language and its rhetorical methods reflect the poet's distinctive style, and his close personal involvement with his subject. The basic proposition, enunciated in the opening line and then repeated as a refrain, sets up a fundamental and illuminating dichotomy: "The Court and Conscience wallis not weill". In taking conscience as his touchstone, Montgomerie locates his argument within a central sixteenth-century debate, and the poem presents a modern reader with the difficult challenge of attempting to determine the extent to which its moral categories are constructed by the different views which were held by Catholic and Protestant, especially Calvinist, writers on the subject.

This is a topic which has increasingly interested scholars in the recent past, and attempts have been made by such writers as John S. Wilks to draw a clear distinction between Catholic and Protestant positions.[23] "Conscience", according to this view, had radically different significances in different theological camps. Its general sense might be accessible to readers of any religious persuasion; but the word would, in a theological context, have had a resonance for Montgomerie and his fellow-Catholics which was quite distinct from that which would have been apparent to Calvinists. This is a tempting argument, with rich potential for an exploration of the presence of a counter-text in Montgomerie's lyric, but it is not without its own problems.

First, we must consider the extent to which the technicalities of theological dispute are relevant to a lyric written by a layman for a non-specialist audience. "Conscience", as we have already noted, has a general sense, commonly employed in the sixteenth century by theologians and in ordinary discourse, which transcends doctrinal boundaries. We find repeated references in legal documents, for example, to conscience as a kind of normative index of moral responsibility, and this is how it appears to be used by John Knox when he challenges the Catholic opinions of James Tyrie:

> . . . when with better mynd, God gaue me to considder, that whosoeuer opponis not him self bouldly to blasphemy & manifest leis, differis lytill fra tratouris . . . to quyet therefore my owne conscience, I put hand to the pen as followeth.[24]

[23] John S. Wilks, *The Idea of Conscience in Renaissance Tragedy* (London and New York: Routledge, 1990), 9–43.

[24] Knox, *Works*, ed. Laing, 6:479; cf. James Tyrie S.J., *The Refutation of ane Ansuer made by Schir Johne Knox to ane letter, send be James Tyrie, to his vmquhyle brother* (Paris: Thomas Brumeau, 1573), sig. +3r.

There is no significant difference, surely, between Knox's understanding of the term here and that employed by Tyrie's fellow-Jesuit, William Allen, in a context which would certainly have been meaningful to Montgomerie, the wars in the Netherlands:

> Of al men in the world, the souldiar should most specialy attend to his conscience; and stand vpon good & sure groundes, for the justice of the quarel, he hath in hand, being hovverly more subiect to death, and danger then any other kind of men . . . Let no christian conscience, therefore, excuse, or flatter itselfe, in this case, vpon the Princes commandement or the Superiors authoritie, or vpon the danger of disobeying the Quenes lawes: no mortal creature hauing lawful power to command, nor any subiect bound, or permitted to obey, in matters directly against God.[25]

In practical moral terms, then, both specialist and non-specialist writers, both Catholic and Protestant, recognised a sense in which man's conscience was an indispensable tool in determining right actions (fairly closely equivalent to the core meaning of *ratio* in medieval thought), and any course of action which is "against conscience" ought not to be pursued. This was the basis, moreover, of the casuistical argument, the central tenet of which, shared by both Catholic and Protestant exponents, is the supremacy of the individual conscience which, in the words of Camille Wells Slights, "was less the still, small voice that disturbs the sleep of the sinful than the intellectual and practical activity of judging past actions and legislating future ones".[26] This is entirely compatible with the definition offered by Alexander Hume at the outset of his *Briefe Treatise of Conscience* (written in 1593 and published the following year):

> Conscience . . . is a perfite knawledge, or a suir perswasioun in the hairt of man, that his thochtis, wordis, or deidis, ar gude, or that they are euil.[27]

Beyond this shared understanding, however, it is evident that there *were* significant differences, and that the dispute over the role of conscience has its roots in the conflicting approaches to human nature which divided Catholics and Protestants (though of course each group was capable of recognising, if continuing to resist, the other's view). Although there were differences in nuance on both sides,

---

[25] William Allen S.J., *The Copie of a Letter Concerning the Yeelding Up of Daventrie* (Antwerp: Joachim Trognesius, 1587), 11. It does not affect the validity of my point that Allen is here justifying the betrayal of Deventer to the Spanish by Sir William Stanley!

[26] Camille Wells Slights, *The Casuistical Tradition in Shakespeare, Donne, Herbert and Milton* (Princeton: Princeton University Press, 1981), 10–11.

[27] Hume, *Poems*, ed. Lawson, 97–98.

post-Tridentine Catholicism generally continued to assert the view which had been predominant in the later Middle Ages: that, despite the fact that mankind is fallen, the operation of natural reason enables us to perceive the divine will and to act upon it. There is, according to the influential view of Thomas Aquinas, a natural disposition towards ethical behaviour (*synderesis*) which informs our attempts to apply the most basic of moral principles to particular circumstances, a process which is in fact the exercise of conscience. It is, of course, possible through the exercise of free will for the imperfect human conscience to err, leading us into sin; but there is no doubt in the minds of Aquinas and his successors that the general effect of this process is potentially positive, and that conscience is a powerful influence for good in human affairs.

From this opinion the Reformers, and especially the Calvinists, dissented strongly. Taking from the Neo-Augustinianism of the later scholastics a much more pessimistic view of human nature, first Luther and then Calvin argued that mankind is so deeply inured to sin that the human will, unaided by the direct and personal intervention of God's prevenient grace, is unable by its own efforts to choose a virtuous course. The resulting sense of moral anxiety, of an oppressive awareness of guilt, is very different from the idea of the conscience as a moral touchstone which derived from the Thomist tradition.[28] Again, this emphasis is clear in Hume's *Briefe Treatise*, where eight of the thirteen chapters are devoted to the 'troublit' or "woundit" conscience: "the whole course of a christians life," Hume observes,

> is but a continuall battell, a continuall falling by sin, and rising by repentance; And . . . the Lord will not suffer the Consciences of his servants to be long vnexercised.[29]

In appealing to conscience as the standard by which the conduct expected of a courtier must be judged, then, Montgomerie employs language which offers both a general, shared understanding and shades of meaning which may well have appealed differently to different members of his audience. Yet the principal focus of his argument is not upon the operation of conscience as an issue in moral theology, but rather upon the implications of such ethical discrimination, however it is understood, for the life of the prospective courtier. Montgomerie is in this regard much more pessimistic than Maitland: whereas the older poet had sought, following a long-established tradition, to articulate a line of conduct which might reconcile good conscience with the successful practice of the courtier's art, Montgomerie

---

[28] This issue inevitably assumes great significance with regard to Montgomerie's penitential lyrics, on which see below, 298–302.

[29] Hume, *Poems*, ed. Lawson, 134.

simply declares that this is impossible. The essential "qualities" of the courtier all centre on duplicity, that recurrent feature of anti-aulic satire.

Montgomerie's illustrations of these general principles focus first on the relationship between the courtier and the prince:

> First thou mon preis thy Prince to pleis
> (Thoght contrare Conscience he commands)
> With Mercuris mouth and Argo's eis
> And with Briarius hundreth hands
>> And seme vhatsoever he sayis to seill          *endorse*
>> So Court and Conscience wallis not weill.     *don't fit well together*
>> (13–18)

We can scarcely help recalling Allen's assertion that a prince's instruction against conscience is not lawful; but Montgomerie is less interested in theological niceties than in raw political realities, and in the real world of the courtier there is obviously no choice but to obey. In a poem which generally relies on direct, unmetaphorical statement, the series of Classical allusions is striking, and on the whole favourable in connotation: while Mercury's rhetorical skills often serve as a byword for duplicity, the watchfulness of Argos and the manifold dexterity of Briarius are images of heroic attainment rather than of any of the traditional vices of the courtier.[30] The stanza thus strikes a somewhat unexpected balance, emphasising the demands made on courtiers at least as much as it attacks them for their professional dishonesty. Montgomerie's rhetorical strategy is an artfully indirect one: rather than attack the actions of the courtier directly, he offers a "sympathetic" account of the ways in which he will be forced to contravene his conscience.

The same technique is applied to the courtier's relations with his fellows:

> Syn evirie minioun thou man mak          *must*
> To gar thame think that thou art thairs
> Houbeit thou be behind thair bak
> No furtherer of thair effairs
>> Bot mett thame moonshyn ay for Meill     *flour*
>> So Court and Conscience wallis not weill.
>> (19–24)

The duplicity which is such an omnipresent feature of the anti-aulic tradition is here presented almost matter-of-factly, not as the subject for outright condemnation, but as something which must be adopted by anyone who chooses to subordinate

---

[30] It is perhaps appropriate to recall here that Montgomerie associates John Maitland's rhetorical skills with the figure of Mercury in the sonnet dedicated to him; see above, 154–56.

his conscience to advancement at court. The aphoristic counsel, linked with the medieval fable of the wolf betrayed by the moon's reflection in water, found in both Caxton and Henryson and used proverbially at least as early as the fifteenth century,[31] is of course ironic; but the laconic assertion of the inevitability of such dishonesty contrasts strongly with the much more overtly satirical statements which are the norm elsewhere. Montgomerie achieves this in part by a reversal of the traditional roles: where we generally see the operation of flattery and back-biting from the point of view of the victim, here they are recommended from the perspective of the prospective practitioner. We should notice, too, the careful use of "minioun" to characterise other courtiers, by implication distinguishing "thou" from them: the term was almost wholly pejorative for Montgomerie and his contemporaries, clearly implying the parasitical, often sexually compromised position of the royal favourite.[32] But the "thou/they" rhetoric Montgomerie employs suggests that the addressee is not himself a minion; he is, on the contrary, one who will be forced to deceive such creatures in order ("legitimately") to advance his own fortunes.

This contemptuousness is carried into the final stanza, where the aspiring courtier is "advised" to "give glorifluikims" in the faces of those he is flattering: the phrase is calculatedly jocular, deviously suggesting that such tactics are almost justifiable against those who make their career at court. What we have here, in effect, is the use of an almost casuistical technique to "excuse" the courtier's duplicity, counterpointing the claims of conscience with the practical necessities of self-pro-motion. Two versions of casuistry, in other words, compete within the poem: a more serious claim that one should act in conformity with one's conscience, and the more cynical view of those actions one is called upon to perform if one sets one's conscience aside in the interest of success as a courtier. The insistency of the refrain ensures that the first prevails, but the second constantly threatens to assert itself through the pseudo-advice which the poet gives to his reader.

If the extent to which the speaker in "The Oppositione of the Court to Con-science" sympathises with the dilemmas of the courtier rather than condemning him outright is the central ambiguity of the poem, there is a comparable balance, this time of complaint and advice, in "Ane Inventione against Fortune" [9], a poem which the Ker manuscript significantly subtitles "conteining ane Admonitione to

---

[31] It is used by an unnamed correspondent to John Paston II in October 1468: *Paston Letters and Papers of the Fifteenth Century*, ed. Norman Davis, 3 vols. (Oxford: Clarendon Press, 1971– ), 2:389; cf. Tilley, *Dictionary of Proverbs*, 473 (M1128). The proverb may derive from the fable's presence in the *Disciplina clericalis* of Petrus Alfonsi, one of the most popular of medieval schoolbooks.

[32] Cf. Michael B. Young, *James VI and I and the History of Homosexuality* (Basing-stoke: Macmillan, 2000), 40–42, 60–62.

his freinds at Court". It is difficult not to be reminded of Lindsay's Papyngo, uttering her dying advice against trusting Fortune to "hir brether of courte",[33] but there is no mediating fiction here to deflect the vehemence of the rhetoric. Montgomerie begins, indeed, by insistently personalising his complaint, explicitly adopting as his muse Megara, who is not a Muse at all but one of the Furies, and calling upon her

> For to inspyre my spreit with thy despyte
> And with thy fervent furie me infuse
> Quhat Epithets or Arguments till vse
> With fals and feinyed fortun for to flyte.
> Both wey my words and waill my verse to wryte            *weigh; measure*
> That curst, inconstant Cative till accuse
> Quhais variance of all my wois I wyt.                     *woes; blame*
>     (3–9)

The bitterness of the tone here might imply a date for the poem fairly late in the poet's career, but there is no detail specific enough to enable us to be certain, and after this opening stanza of personal grievance Montgomerie temporarily abandons the first person in favour of a third-person description of Fortune's character, shifting at l. 55 to a second-person address — with an associated return to the first-person allusions — to the "freinds" who are signalled in the subtitle. We may suspect that the "men of merit" who are disregarded by Fortune include Montgomerie himself, but after the first stanza nothing in the language of the poem forces us to make this connection. The poet may be a victim, but he is merely one of many, and those whose present prosperity contrasts with his own circumstances are living on borrowed time.

The firm establishment of a personal subtext nevertheless contrasts with the more abstract complaints against Fortune which are characteristic of the tradition. The personal element, moreover, is reinforced by the intensity of the speaker's "admonitione", which seems to me to be characterised less by "the more gentle tones of rational persuasion"[34] than by a somewhat hectoring manner:

> Remember shirs that somtym ye war small
> And may be yit, I will not say ye sall
> For I confes that war a fut too far.
> Houbeit ye think my harrand something har           *snarling rather harsh*
> Quhen ye leist wein your baks may to the wall.      *imagine*
> Things byds not ay in ordour as they ar.
>     (58–63)

---

[33] Lindsay, *Works*, ed. Hamer, 1:66.
[34] Jack, "Theme of Fortune", 26.

As so often with Montgomerie, the language subtly combines meanings which are public and private: the unidentified fellow-courtiers who have risen from humble beginnings are evidently expected to recognise themselves through the general address, and to be cautioned, perhaps even intimidated, by the threat of Fortune's inevitable enemy. Beneath the pretence at comradely warning, one senses, there is a hint of grim satisfaction at the prospect that the speaker's own fate awaits those who now enjoy the prosperity he has lost. There may also be an echo or anticipation of the sonnets to the Lords of Session in the claim that "ladds vploips to lordships" (l. 33), although the phrase goes back to Lindsay's *Testament of the Papyngo*.[35] Montgomerie is, indeed, careful to situate his attack within a wider tradition: he invokes Boccaccio's *De casibus* (or Lydgate's translation of it) (ll. 41–42), and ends with the fall of Caesar:

| | |
|---|---|
| Had Cæsar sene the Cedul that wes sent | *document, letter* |
| Ye wat he had not with the wicked went | |
| Quha war concludit causles him to kill | |
| Bot in his bosome he put vp that bill | *document* |
| The vhilk at last, thoght lait, maid him repent. | |
| His vnadvertence only did him ill. | |
| | |
| Judge of your self by Julius my Joyes | *companions* |
| Quhais fenyeid freinds wer worse then open foes | |
| (67–74) | |

It suits Montgomerie's rhetorical purpose, of course, to assert Caesar's innocence, and to represent his assassination as "causles": the blame can then be squarely placed, not only upon Fortune, but also upon the duplicity of his "fenyeid freinds". The lesson is also to be learned, he adds, from the fate of "those / Quha war your auin Companyeons", a group of victims which presumably includes but is not confined to the speaker himself. The political history of James's reign is littered with fallen favourites, the earliest of whom, of course, was Montgomerie's erstwhile patron Esmé Stuart. No one, the logic of the argument insists, is powerful enough to stand against the might of Fortune.

While it comments less directly upon the vicissitudes of life at court, and raises no moral issues, "Hay nou the day dauis" [46] can in some respects be related to this line in Montgomerie's thought. Ostensibly optimistic, the poem — based on a much older song — opens with a joyful celebration of the dawn:

Hay nou the day dauis,
The jolie Cok crauis,

---

[35] *Poems*, ed. Parkinson, 2:32.

> Nou shrouds the shauis
>   Throu Natur anone,
> The thissell-cok cryis
> On Louers vha lyis,
> Nou skaillis the skyis,
>   The nicht is neir gone.
>     (1–8)

The landscape is full of natural details which recall both the *locus amoenus* setting of *The Cherrie and the Slae* and the more poised description of the hunting park in Polwarth's *Promine*:

> Nou hairts with hynds
> Conforme to thair kynds,
> Hie tossis thair tynds
>   On grund vhair they grone . . .
>     (17–20)

Despite the amatory associations evoked in the opening stanza and in subsequent references to Cupid and Venus, however, Montgomerie turns in his final three stanzas to another aspect of courtly life: the tournament. That such chivalric exercises were not extinct in Montgomerie's lifetime is well attested, and we have noted his praise of Lord Semple's prowess "in pastyme and alarmes"; these entertainments continued, indeed, into James's English reign. But they belonged to an obsolescent world of courtiership, a world which was crudely punctured by the bullet which pierced Sir Philip Sidney's thigh near Zutphen in 1586. The romantic chivalric values which motivated Sidney and which Spenser sought to turn to a patriotic literary purpose in *The Faerie Queene* could scarcely be maintained in a Europe more realistically portrayed in Breughel's *Dulle Griet*, that devastated (and devastating) landscape of total, unrelenting warfare. Montgomerie's celebration of courtly jousting speaks, therefore, to an age which was in many respects already past, and which would certainly not survive long after the poet's death. The poem itself hints at something of this, perhaps, in its recognition that a tournament is not only about chivalric pageantry:

> So hard ar thair hittis
> Some sueyis, some sittis
> And some perforce flittis
>   On grund vhill they grone,
> Syn grooms that gay is
> On blonks that bray-is
> With suords assayis,
>   The night is neir gone.
>     (49–56)

And with these lines the text breaks off, leaving us in the middle of the action. It may be that, as Helena Shire argued, "the piece is by its very nature an 'introit' and the rest is action",[36] but it is tempting to see in this abrupt ending a figuration of Montgomerie's own abortive career, and indeed a prefiguration of the end of the courtly world of Edinburgh five years later. Such grim realities are apparently belied by the insistently cheerful rhythm of the verse; nevertheless, the introduction of the motif of defeat and injury acts as a powerful counterpoint to the idealism of what has gone before.

Nowhere does Montgomerie strike a more subtle balance between ingratiation and complaint, between the deployment of rhetorical pyrotechnics and a direct representation of his personal circumstances, than in his sequence of five sonnets "To Robert Hudsone" [72]. The language of this sequence is much less dependent upon the traditional language of anti-aulic satire; and yet they constitute an implicit critique which is all the more powerful because it is so manifestly motivated by Montgomerie's own misery. Paradoxically, this personal topicality makes the group impossible to date accurately: they refer to a particular occasion, but they do so in terms which make few direct references to any external reality against which the poems can be calibrated. So Helena Shire assigns them to 1585–1586 or to "the later 1580s", while R.D.S. Jack associates them with the pension sequences of the early 1590s; John MacQueen proposes "in or about the year 1584".[37]

Two pieces of evidence might be taken to support a date earlier than 1584, and perhaps as early as 1582–1583. In his "Admonitioun to the Maister poet", which must, as we have seen, have been composed before late 1584, James VI ends with a sonnet which reinforces the underlying theme of Montgomerie's boastfulness:

> Proud Dares fall, for all his micht & menis,
> Culd nawayes teache you to be uarr of glorye;           *beware*
> Not yit ye uald not call to memorie
> Quhat grund ye gaue to Cristiane Lindsay by it,
> For nou sho sayis which makis us all full sorie.[38]

We shall see in a moment that Hudson's response to the sequence addressed to him — or rather, his lack of response — provoked Christian Lindsay into composing a highly critical sonnet of her own, which might well have made the king and his court "full sorie"; in which case the Hudson sonnets must antedate the writing of the "Admonitioun", suggesting a date fairly soon after James's escape

[36] Shire, *Song, Dance and Poetry*, 149.

[37] Shire, *Song, Dance and Poetry*, 106; Jack, *Montgomerie*, 100; John MacQueen, ed., *Ballattis of Luve* (Edinburgh: Edinburgh University Press, 1970), xliv–xlv.

[38] James VI, *Poems*, ed. Craigie, 2:129. For the dating of this poem, see above, 101–2.

from the Ruthven Raiders. On the other hand, the "Admonitioun" itself seems to be predicated in Montgomerie's continuing presence at court, whereas the Hudson sonnets clearly suggest that the poet has been excluded from the king's presence for some time. Nor is there any reason to suppose that Christian Lindsay could have intervened only once on Montgomerie's behalf, and that it is therefore to the extant sonnet that James is referring. Corroborative evidence is perhaps provided by the reference to "old Scot" in the first sonnet of the sequence: if, as seems very probable, this is an allusion to Alexander Scott, the outstanding court poet of the previous generation, and if his date of death has been correctly put between June 1582 and July 1583, then it follows that the Hudson sonnets must be earlier than the latter date.[39] This leads to a further difficulty: court life was, of course, seriously disrupted by the seizure of the king by the Ruthven Raiders on 23 August 1582, and it does not seem likely that the "Admonitioun" was written during the ten-and-a-half months of his captivity. Since Scott was apparently dead by 30 July 1583, three weeks after James's escape, it follows that the "Admonitioun" would have to have been written in or before August 1582 if it is directly linked to the Hudson sonnets. Yet "Sen thocht is fre" is reliably described in one manuscript as "the first verses that euer the King made" and in another is dated to 1583.[40] Montgomerie's Hudson sonnets may need on the basis of the reference to Scott to be dated 1582–1583, or even earlier; but then the circumstances to which they refer cannot be directly related to those which underlie the "Admonitioun", whatever James's allusion to Christian Lindsay may suggest to the contrary.

If an early dating of the Hudson sonnets is correct, it follows that the complaint is not related to the poet's pursuit of his pension, and must arise from some other source of estrangement between Montgomerie and the king. Such episodes do not, of course, find their way into the records, and we can therefore only speculate about the causes of Montgomerie's disgruntlement. Whatever the occasion, it is with the conditions of his exile from the court that Montgomerie begins, locating himself "vpaland" where his diet is Spartan and his health poor. There is no sense here of rustic repose, of the poet's being, as it were, "in Ayrshire and Christendom";[41] this is no idealised pastoral world, but harsh reality, remote from the pleasures of the court, however equivocal they may be. This opening sonnet is, indeed, a clear denial of that recurrent sixteenth-century tradition of anti-aulic discourse which derives from Horace's Epode II, contrasting the miseries of the court with the pleasures of a humble existence in the country. The line descends through Claudian to Ariosto and Alamanni, to Guevara and Luis de León, to Ronsard and Desportes,

---

[39] MacQueen, *Ballattis of Luve*, xliv.

[40] See above, 97–98.

[41] Wyatt's first satire concludes with the poet celebrating his absence from the court and his relative ease in "Kent and Christendom": *Collected Poems*, ed. Daalder, 104.

and everywhere we find the idealisation of a rural existence which is clearly enunciated (albeit within an ironic framework) in Horace's poem:

> non me Lucrina iuverint conchylia
>     magisve rhombus aut scari,
> si quos Eois intonata fluctibus
>     hiems ad hoc vertat mare ;
> non Afra avis descendat in ventrem meum,
>     non attagen Ionicus
> iucundior quam lecta de pinguissimis
>     oliva ramis arborum
> aut herba lapathi prata amantis et gravi
>     malvae salubres corpori
> vel agna festis caesa Terminalibus
>     vel haedus ereptus lupo.
>         (*Ep.* 2.49–60)

[Not Lucrine oysters would please me more, nor scar, nor turbot, should winter, thundering on the eastern waves, turn them to our coasts; not Afric fowl nor Ionian pheasant would make for me a repast more savoury than olives gathered from the richest branches of the trees, or the plant of the meadow-loving sorrel, and mallows wholesome to the ailing body, or than a lamb slain at the feast of Terminus, or a kid rescued from the wolf.][42]

Montgomerie, it seems, systematically repudiates these traditional benefits of the countryside. He complains about the food and drink, and about the misery of his condition, and the intensifying alliteration is insistent, linked with the harsh colloquialism of much of the language:

| | |
|---|---|
| This is no lyfe that I live vpaland | *in the country* |
| On rau rid herring reistit in the reik, | *cured in the smoke* |
| Syn I am subject somtyme to be seik | |
| And daylie deing of my auld diseis, | |
| Eit breid, ill aill and all things are ane eik. | *oat bread; the same* |
| This barme and blaidry buists up all my bees. | *froth; nonsense; marks* |
| Ye knau ill guyding genders mony gees | |
| And specially in Poets . . . | |
| (72.I: 3–10) | |

---

[42] *Horace, Odes and Epodes*, ed. and trans. C.E. Bennett, 7th ed., Loeb Classical Library (London and Cambridge, MA: Harvard University Press, 1946), 368–69.

The rhyme on *bees/gees* is an extraordinary stroke of ingenuity: the words mean "whims" and "fancies" respectively, but they might reasonably be taken also to refer to the *b*s and *g*s which are being engendered in these bitterly rustic lines. Montgomerie's physical and mental condition are equally poor (though his wit is evidently unaffected!); in Christian Lindsay's subsequent sonnet he is unambiguously stated to be "deing of the gravell" (i.e. kidney stones), which presumably explains the reference to "my auld diseis".

It is to Lindsay that Montgomerie indirectly appeals in the decidedly cryptic conclusion to this opening sonnet:

> . . . for Example
> Ye can pen out tua cuple ane ye pleis.                    *couple(t)*s
> Yourself and I, old Scot and Robert Semple,
>     Quhen we ar dead that all our dayis bot daths,     *squander*
>     Let Christian Lyndesay wryt our Epitaphis.

This is tantalising, and very difficult to interpret. Much of the ambiguity arises from l. 11: does "cuple" mean "two pairs" (the pairs of poets, presumably, which immediately follow), or "two couplets"? That "copill" could carry this literary sense is evident from *The Kingis Quair*; and it seems to fit with the rather specific use here of "pen out", with its suggestion of literary creativity.[43]

These final lines do, however, gather up the opening, ingratiating address to Hudson, with its insiders' reference to the "sillie smiddy smeik", a recurring "Castalian" metaphor for the scene of literary endeavour. It is, after all, as poets that Montgomerie and Hudson are bound together, and the image of the blacksmiths' forge both dignifies the role of poet by emphasising the notion of craftsmanship which is shared by the Latin *faber* and the Scots "makar", and gives it a mock-modest ring as a form of physical labour, pointed here by "sillie", with its connotations of poverty and simplicity. Just how insincere this imagery is, of course, is apparent from the structural contrast between the "smeik" of the forge and the "reik" in which the poet's homely diet has been prepared: there is no doubt that the second, more literal smoke is anathema to him precisely because it lacks the sophistication which is the true nature of the courtly locus for which the smithy stands, and which is manifested in the very wit by which the images are deployed. If the rusticity of his environment is reflected in the homely language of this opening sonnet, it is paradoxically denied by the skill with which the argument is managed.

As the point of the first, anti-Horatian sonnet is to establish the misery of Montgomerie's present circumstances, the second begins to focus our attention

---

[43] See M.R.G. Spiller, "The 'Copill' in The Kingis Quair", *SLJ* 4/1 (May 1977): 61–63.

on the world of the court from which he is separated. It does so through an elaborate use of *excusatio*, as Montgomerie disclaims any interest in "mightie maters". This is a neat rhetorical ploy, for it makes two points at once, emphasising the poet's modesty and denying any political commitment — and incidentally either echoing or anticipating the king's literary precepts in avoiding "wtyring [*uttering*] any thing of materis of commoun weill . . . because . . . they are to graue materis for a Poet to mell in".[44] Both poetic and documentary evidence suggest, of course, that this is not entirely true, but Montgomerie insists that it is in Cupid's court that his real fame is based. There is some ingenious play with the contrast between Cupid's court in l. 6 and that of James in l. 14, and Montgomerie proceeds to negate his appeal through *excusatio* by resorting to a Petrarchist claim to immortality:

> Quhair Musis yit some of my sonets sings,
> And shall do aluayis to the world[i]s end.
>    (II: 6–7)

Modesty and hubris run together in the sestet, turning on the carefully-calculated reversal of the "yit":

> Yit ye haif sene his Grace oft for me send
> Quhen he took plesure into Poesie.
>    (11–12)

Again there is a crucial ambiguity: dois "Quhen" have the force of "whenever", or does it mean "back in those times when", implying that the king has now abandoned poetry for other pursuits? Upon our answer will turn our sense of the nature of Montgomerie's grievance, merely personal in the first case, part of a wider complaint against a change of cultural climate at court in the second. But the text permits no definitive answer, and it is through these gaps of indeterminacy that Montgomerie increases the allusive force of his necessarily indirect criticism of the king for his apparent neglect.[45]

By the end of this second sonnet of the sequence, James is beginning to occupy the foreground, a position he retains throughout the third, in which Montgomerie exploits both the figure of the lizard's love of the human face[46] and a standard

---

[44] James VI, *Poems*, ed. Craigie, 1:79.

[45] This interpretation of these lines is, moreover, related to the issue of dating: the meaning "back in those times when" could scarcely have been intended in 1582–1583, when James's interest in poetry was apparently still gathering momentum. It would, however, fit quite well with the conditions of the 1590s.

[46] Montgomerie also employs this image in "Adeu O Desie of delyt" [44] ("Lyk as the lyssard does indeid / Leiv by the manis face", 7–8), as does James — if this poem really

Petrarchan rhetorical figure, the contrarieties of love and hate. After two sonnets where the structure is argumentative, Montgomerie now resorts to a conceit: the octave is constructed around the contrast of lizard and snake, physically similar and yet of different natures. By the final lines of the second quatrain, however, he is generalising from his conceit to a more allusive "some":

> Vhare some taks plesur, others tak despyte,
> One shap, one subject, wishis weill and ill.
>      (III: 7–8)

The allusiveness makes these lines difficult: logically, l. 8 should complete the idea that different natures respond differently to the same stimulus, and yet it seems to indicate the opposite, that a *single* entity is capable of both affection and enmity towards the same object. One way of resolving the problem would be to take the grammatical subject of "wishis" to be "some . . . others", with "one shap, one subject" as the grammatical object. But the uncertainty is continued into the opening lines of the sestet:

> Euen so will men (bot no man judge I will)
> Baith loue and loth and only bot ane thing.

Now it *does* seem that the contradictory responses are contained within a single, notional person, that the lizard and the snake do not represent distinct categories of courtiers. In some people, Montgomerie appears to be suggesting, the lizard and the snake coexist, so that you cannot rely upon their reactions or their conduct. *He*, by contrast, is consistently affectionate, his love of the king a dependable constant.

It does not seem that the complexity of the argument here is merely fortuitous; the difficulty of the argument reflects the nature of the problem, as Montgomerie indicates with his dismissive "I can not skan these things above my skill" (l. 9). As in the previous sonnet, where he represents himself as 'merely' a love poet, unconcerned with affairs of state, he adopts the "plain man" role, claiming that the intricacy of court politics are a mystery to him in his innocence. The poem ends with a "straightforward" reversion to his love of the king, but it is carefully coded to recall the occasion, and indeed the language, of the *Flyting*, by means of which Montgomerie had established his primacy within the favoured circle of court poets.

----

is by him — in his "Cheuiott hills" ("Lezardlike I feede vpon her face", 35: *Poems*, ed. Craigie, 2:71); on the authorship question, with the suggestion that this and other pieces apparently claimed by the king may have been (co-)authored by Sir Thomas Erskine of Gogar, see Curtis Perry, "Royal Authorship and Problems of Manuscript Attribution in the Poems of King James VI and I", *N&Q* n.s. 46 (1999): 243–46. I have, however, not been able to find the source of the idea that lizards love to gaze upon the human face.

While the link between the third and fourth sonnets is less obvious than the repetition of "his Grace" which unites the third with its predecessor, it is nevertheless an important element in the integration of the sequence. It is partly thematic (the lizard/snake conceit leads naturally into the Aesopic fable which follows) and partly atmospheric: the nostalgic recollection of the couplet of III paves the way for the "Remembers thou" and the autobiographical allusiveness of IV. The fable which Montgomerie adapts in this sonnet is widespread in the Aesopic tradition. It occurs as I.16 in the prose Romulus collection, under the title "Asinus Domino blandiens", as 17 in the 'Elegiac Romulus" sometimes (wrongly) attributed to "Gualterus Anglicus", and as I.17 in Caxton's English version of the Steinhöwel collection.[47] It is impossible to establish which version served as Montgomerie's source, if indeed he used a single model, but comparison of these widespread versions with his sonnet reveals some interesting points about the latter.

The most obvious differences stem from the traditional *moralitates* appended to the fable:

Prose Romulus:

Fabula hęc monet, ne quis indignus se ingerat ad hoc ut melioris officium faciat.

[Let no one unworthy undertake so much as to performed the office of a better.]

Elegiac Romulus:

Quod natura negat, nemo feliciter audet:
  Displicet imprudens, unde placiri putat.

[What nature denies, noone dares happily: The foolish man displeases where he hopes to please.]

Caxton:

And therefore none ought to entermete hym self for to doo a thynge / whiche as for hym impossyble is to be done / For the vnwyse displeaseth there / where as he supposeth to please.

---

[47] *Les Fabulistes latins depuis le siècle d'Auguste jusqu'à la fin du Moyen Age*, ed. Léopold Hervieux, 2nd ed., 5 vols. (Paris: Firmin-Didot, 1893–1899), 2:201–2, 323–24 ; *Caxton's Aesop*, ed. R.T. Lenaghan (Cambridge MA: Harvard University Press, 1967), 85–86.

The emphasis throughout is on the folly of the ass, and on the futility of its conduct. This is reinforced by references in the fable itself to the enviousness which motivates the ass (e.g. Prose Romulus: "melior sum catulo, meliori uita possum frui et maximum honorem habere", "I am better than the dog; I can enjoy a better life and have greater honour").

Montgomerie, however, casts himself in the role of the Ass. Even here he is having it both ways, as he did in his use of modesty and hubris in the previous sonnet: he is "a beist of blunter brane" (a phrase which seems to render with wonderful idiomatic force the sense of the Elegiac Romulus's "Asellus iners"), yet he breaks away from his sources to observe that

> To pleis hir Maister with the counterpane     *equivalent*
> Sho clambe on him with hir foull clubbit feet     *climbed*
> To play the Messan thoght sho wes not melt.     *lapdog; suitable*
> Sho meinit weill, I grant hir mynd wes guid . . .
>     (IV: 7–10)

This subtle self-exculpation is repeated in the couplet, which changes the whole application of the fable and deftly throws the blame back onto the anonymous "some", who are implicitly equated with the "they" (servants of the lord or master in the Aesopic tradition) who beat the ass. The sonnet form is ideally suited to the conciseness of the Aesopic fable, but Montgomerie has not merely translated skilfully: he has turned the fable around in applying it to his own circumstances, and the envious ass has become the tragic victim of others' envy.

Since the first line of the opening sonnet, Robert Hudson has been conspicuously absent from the sequence which is ostensibly addressed to him. Montgomerie, no doubt anticipating the effect of his final appeal to Hudson to "Shau to the King this poor Complant of myne", seems almost to have been addressing the king over Hudson's shoulder; now, however, he turns to his "best belouit brother" with a burst of flattery which both sets out to cultivate Hudson's sympathy and at the same time demonstrates what he is capable of in a high classical style, "a short hint," to borrow Henry Fielding's words, "of what we can do in the sublime". The change of register is marked not only by the increased classicism of the imagery, but also by the more obviously hypotactic syntax, the extensive periphrasis, and the elevated vocabulary. Although Hudson's stylistic superiority is the ostensible subject, it is Montgomerie's rhetorical skill to which this final sonnet ostentatiously draws attention.

The references to Pegasus' foot and the discovery of Hippocrene take us back to the origins of the "Castalian" school itself, and are doubtless calculated to strike the same nostalgic chord which is present in the third and fourth elements of the sequence. The claim to fraternity, equally, unites this last sonnet with the first. But the brotherhood which Montgomerie claims with Hudson in l. 3 is denied in l. 11, where the latter is addressed as "Thou *onlie* brother of the Sisters Nyne" [my italics]. If we pay any attention at all to the literal sense of these phrases, clearly, they cannot both be true, and it is the latter, the culmination of a sestet which compares Hudson with Homer and Petrarch, which takes rhetorical priority, introducing the concluding petition. Excessive as this panegyric may be, it has a clear purpose, and it fits neatly into the mosaic pattern of five highly individual sonnets, each of which makes its own distinctive contribution to the overall effect. Only in the very last line does Montgomerie reveal what we may well have suspected all along: that the true audience for the sequence is not Hudson but the king, to whose attention the poet hopes his 'brother' will bring this sophisticated piece of ingratiation.

The compiler of the Ker manuscript, however, is at some pains to let us know that Montgomerie's petition went unheeded, adding to the sequence a single sonnet by Christian Lindsay, whose literary skills Montgomerie had invoked in the final line of his opening poem.[48] Unmitigated by any need to cloak her message with ingratiating tactics, Lindsay's sonnet attacks Hudson, and through him the values of the court, in wholly unambiguous terms. A comparison of the much more direct voice of a poet who clearly does not see herself as part of the network with the deviousness of Montgomerie's rhetorical strategies, even where he appears to be straightforwardly condemning the courtier's way of life, emphasising the nature of the compromises the courtier-poet must make, even when he is thoroughly alienated:

> Oft haive I hard, bot ofter found it treu
> That Courteous kyndnes lasts bot for a vhyle.
> Fra once your turnes be sped, vhy then Adeu,
> Your promeist freindship passis in exyle.
> Bot Robene, faith ye did me not beguyll,
> I hopit ay of you as of the lave.                          *rest*
> If thou had wit thou wald haif mony a wyle
> To mak thy self be knaune for a knaive.
>     (72.[VI]: 1–8)

The contempt with which Lindsay dismisses Hudson, motivated by sympathetic friendship rather than by more personal considerations, is testimony both to her poetic skill and to her regard for Montgomerie, while her closing reference to the indifference of "the smeikie smeithis", picking up the language of the first sonnet

---

[48] The identity of Christian Lindsay remains something of a problem, and some scholars have been disinclined to credit her authorship of this sonnet. For the identification of Lindsay with the wife of William Murray, master of the king's carriage, see *Poems*, ed. Parkinson, 2:98; cf. Sarah M. Dunnigan, "Scottish Women Writers, c. 1560–c. 1650", in *A History of Women's Writing in Scotland*, ed. Douglas Gifford and Dorothy McMillan (Edinburgh: Edinburgh University Press, 1997), 15–43, here 15–17.

of his own sequence, makes a tellingly disillusioned comment on the fraternity which had assembled round the king.

But if the friendship of his fellow-courtiers was, as Lindsay declares, inherently false, Montgomerie evidently had other networks of amity. Two sonnets addressed to members of the Murray family, both apparently connected with the royal household, reflect in differing ways the same ambivalence which we have consistently found in Montgomerie's verse. Essentially private in tone, they are nevertheless marked by the pressures of the court and are notable for the way in which they hint at meanings which are no longer recoverable but which must have emerged clearly enough for the addressee and for some of their potential wider readership. One, addressed according to the Ker manuscript "From LONDON to William Murray", adopts a familiar rhetorical strategy, hinting through proverbial phraseology at meanings which are evidently intended to be intelligible to at least its most immediate audience:

> Bot ye sall find me byding lyk a bur
> Quhilk lichtlie will not leiv the grip it gettis
> And am right dortie to come ou'r the Dur     *fastidious*
> For thame that by my kyndnes no-thing settis
> Thus haif I bene as yit and sal be so,
> Kynd to my freind, bot fremmit to my fo.     *unfriendly*
>    (94:9–14)

The contrast in Montgomerie's declared attitudes must be understood in the context of his opening address to Murray as "belouit brother", a phrase which not only places the poem's addressee on the side of friendship but perhaps implies membership of the literary circle at court.[49] And yet there is a strong hint of an alternative meaning: that Murray would do well to hold on to the poet's amity, since he makes an implacable enemy. There is much in the poem which assumes privileged information: the significance of "the pece of lether from your spur" (l. 6) which Montgomerie has taken as a keepsake; the nature of the "service of the King" (l. 4) which has apparently brought the poet to London; even the basis of the relationship which has caused him to send Murray a "lytil pretie ring" (l. 2) with its accompanying verses, a possible suggestion of homoeroticism. Whether the tensions which the poem reflects are primarily personal or political must, in view of this characteristic allusiveness, remain uncertain; but we may notice, as Shire points out, that a William Murray in the royal household during the king's captivity in 1582–1583 was

---

[49] There is, however, no evidence that a William Murray was writing poetry at this period; Shire's association of him (*Song, Dance and Poetry*, 98) with the mysterious "M.W." who contributed a eulogistic sonnet to James's *Essayes of a Prentise* is surely fanciful.

apparently a supporter of the Gowrie faction and hence an opponent of Lennox.[50] The poem implies a relationship under serious challenge: whether that challenge comes from private disillusionment or political rivalry remains uncertain, but the note of threat in the couplet seems unmistakable.

The combination of a courtly milieu with an equivocal personal friendship seems also to inform the sonnet addressed "To Master J. Murray" [73]. Its theme is ambition, and Shire argues persuasively for an identification of the addressee with the poet John Murray, who died in 1616 and who was praised by Sir William Alexander as "Albiones sweetest swaine".[51] While the argument here is not overtly anti-aulic, Montgomerie's minatory tone once more hints at more than it states:

> Flie louer (PHŒNIX): feirs thou not to fyre
> Invironing the aluayis-upuard ayr
> Vhich thou must pas before that thou come thair
> Vharas thy Sprit so spurris the to aspyre,
> To wit, aboue the Planetis to impyre
> Behind the Compas of APOLLO's Chayr
> And tuinkling-round of burning rubies rare
> Quhair all the Gods thy duelling do desyre?
> Bot duilfull Doom of Destinies thee Dammis
> Before thy blissit byding be above
> The mortal from Immortall to remove
> To sacrifice thy self to Phœbus flammis.
>     I prophecye vhen so sall come to passe
>     We nevir sie such one come of thy Asse.

The choice of the phoenix conceit seems to echo the king's allegorical elegy for the fallen Lennox,[52] and it is logical to associate "Apollo's Chayr" with the throne. Murray's ambition, then, is intimately connected with his place at court, and Montgomerie's warning appears to imply that his willingness to accept self-immolation will bring him no reward. Though the point is not made explicit, the Aristotelian "aluayis upuard ayr" aptly conveys the world of courtly aspiration;[53] the failure of the phoenix — unlike Lennox in James's poem — to achieve regeneration presents a bleak vision of the courtier's fate. But Montgomerie has skilfully merged the

---

[50] Shire, *Song, Dance and Poetry*, 91.

[51] Shire, *Song, Dance and Poetry*, 181–86. Shire's speculative attribution to Murray of most of the anonymous poems in NLS MS. 2065, fols. 16–32 and fol. 35 is possible, but far from certain.

[52] See Lyall, "James VI and the Cultural Crisis", 60–62.

[53] There is an interesting parallel to this idea in John Stewart of Baldynneis's sonnet "Of Ambitious Men", where those who seek worldly advancement are compared with "dryest dust — vinddrift in drouthie day" (*Poems*, ed. Crockett, 1:155).

figure of the phoenix with two others which, as we shall see, are characteristic of contemporary French poetry: that of Icarus, and that of Phaethon.[54] The lover's sacrifice to "Phœbus flammis" inevitably evokes the image of the former's burned wings, while the latter is indirectly implied by the reference to "APOLLO's Chayr", with its secondary sense of "chariot". The auguries are all hostile: whether or not poetry is Murray's chosen means of advancement, the vagaries of his environment will, Montgomerie asserts, doom him to defeat.

In an important sense, these informal pieces offer an alternative social framework to that which characterises the court: the relationships are private, the language of the poems correspondingly intimate. They contrast, too, with the sonnets which were exchanged in Latin and the vernaculars between sixteenth-century poets in Italy, France, Spain, and elsewhere: the latter are, on the whole, formal in their address and largely concerned with elegant compliment, whereas their Scottish counterparts are much less elaborately literary.[55] The precise nature of the personal friendships and rivalries to which these sonnets refer may now be irrecoverable, especially since it is impossible to locate them within the known trajectory of Montgomerie's career. Perhaps they reflect tensions which were already apparent between 1580 and 1586, and belong in some way to the world of the Hudson sonnets or James's "Admonitioun". But it is equally possible that they are pieces from the final decade, when Montgomerie's anxieties were steadily turning to despair.

However we place them, the equivocal expression of friendship in these pieces finds a curious echo in the group of four sonnets composed in Ayrshire, probably in the last years of Montgomerie's life, and involving Montgomerie, Hugh Barclay of Ladyland, and Captain Ezechiel Montgomerie [95].[56] The only real basis for dating is an allusion in the fourth to the return of "suete Semple", which suggests that this poem — and perhaps the other three — is more or less contemporary with the verses addressed by Montgomerie to Lord Semple in 1596.[57] If we can on such grounds locate this exchange in the period between Semple's return to Scotland and the beginning of the Ailsa episode, several other aspects begin to fit into place. Opening his first sonnet with an apostrophe to Montgomerie as

---

[54] See below, 238–39.

[55] Du Bellay's *Regretz* are, once again, an exceptional case; but they are closer to the political themes of Montgomerie's Hudson sequence than to the private world of the poems to the Murrays and the Ayrshire exchanges.

[56] The textual evidence here is somewhat uncertain: the four poems are arranged together in the Ker MS. (fols. 78v–79v), and they have generally been regarded as a single group. Parkinson, however, detaches "The Old Master" from the others; its introductory couplet provides some justification for this, but it unquestionably belongs to the same social milieu as the other three.

[57] See above, 185–87.

"my best belouit brother of the craft"– a clear echo of the "Castalian" terminology with the revealing substitution of "craft" for "band" — Hugh Barclay of Ladyland outdoes his addressee's complaints, representing himself as even more unfortunate. Miserable as he is, however, his unhappiness is exacerbated by Montgomerie's lack of friendly concern:

> Bot maist of all, that hes my bailis bred                *sorrows*
> To heir hou ye on that syde of the Mure
> Birlis at the Wyne and blythlie gois to bed              *carouses*
> Foryetting me, Pure Pleuman, I am sure.
>     (95.I: 9–12)

This might almost be a rustic parody, with an added echo of Langland's *Piers Plowman*, of Montgomerie's appeal to Hudson, a reversal of his characterisation of himself as deprived of all civilised pleasures; in his final couplet Ladyland even evokes an image of Montgomerie "pouing [*pulling*] Bacchus luggis". Neglect of one's true friends, it would seem, is a vice which is not confined to court: secure on his side of "the Mure" (the local nature of the topographical reference is striking, an insiders' allusion to the bare upland landscapes along the Renfrewshire-Ayrshire border which are the setting for the whole group), Ladyland suggests, Montgomerie has no time for a friend less fortunate than himself. Just why Ladyland should be excluded from the circle is unclear; perhaps the codes of the exchange are involved in some way with the Catholic project which would culminate in his death in June 1597, but it is difficult to see how this might be the case.

The reaction Ladyland's sonnet called forth purports to come from Montgomerie's cousin Ezechiel, although it is evident that Ladyland believed that its author was Alexander himself. That is, certainly, credible enough: its flyting rhetoric of professional defiance seems to be a voice that we have heard before, and the quiet elision from "I" to "vs" in l. 11 may well give the game away. It is scarcely surprising that Ladyland replies by asserting that "Ye crak so crouse I ken because ye'r tuo" (III: 7), and, lest there be any ambiguity about the tone of the exchange, he ends his second contribution by urging that the outcome should be amicable:

> Grou I campstarie it may drau to ill                 *quarrelsome*
> Thairfore it's good in tyme that we wer shed.        *separated*
> My Bee's aloft and daggit full of skill.             *imagination; clogged*
> It getts corne drink sen Grissall toke the bed.
>     Come on good gossopis, let vs not discord.
>     With Johne and George ye must convoy my Lord.

The references to members of the common circle are no doubt significant, but difficult to pin down: they are initiated by "Ezechiel" Montgomerie's allusion to Peter Barclay in the final line of sonnet II, and Grissell, John, and George are, presumably, all Barclays or Montgomeries, or related to one or other family by marriage. A Grissell Montgomerie, as we have seen, was the wife of David Barclay, feuar of Ladyland, in 1595; the point of Hugh Barclay's remark appears to be that now she is seriously ill her brewing skills are no longer available to him.[58] The identity of John and George is impossible to determine, but Montgomerie's response suggests that "my Lord" is Semple; the burden of Ladyland's appeal for concord may therefore be that now, with the return of this leading Catholic expected, is not the time for religio-political allies to fall out.

Cryptic as Ladyland's second sonnet is, it is a model of clarity beside Montgomerie's closing contribution to the exchange, if that is indeed what it is:

> To my old Maister and his yong Disciple
> Tua Bairnis of Beath, by Natur taught to Tipple.
>
> The OLD Maister
>
> The LESBIAN lad that weirs the wodbind wreath
> With CERES and CYLENUS gled your ging.     *gladden your company*
> Be blyth KILBVRNIE with the bairns of BEATH
> And let LOCHWINNOCH lordie lead your ring.
> Be mirrie men, feir God and serve the King
> And care not by Dame Fortuns feid a flea.     *enmity*
> Syne "Welcome hame suete SEMPLE" sie ye sing
> "Gut ou'r and let the wind shute in the sea."
> I, RICHIE, JANE and GEORGE ar lyk to dee,
> Four crabit cripilis crackand in our crouch.     *talking; crutch*
> Sen I am trensh-man for the other thrie,     *spokesman*
> Let drunken PANCRAGE drink to me in Dutch
>     "Scol frie, al out, albeit that I suld brist.
>     Ih wachts, hale beir, fan hairts and nych[tsum] drist".

Amidst so many uncertainties, we will do well to establish whatever is immediately clear: the importance of the insiders' local references; the reductiveness of "gled your ging" after the pointed classicism of the opening; the defiance of Fortune and the appeal for political loyalty; the familiar demand for sympathy in the sestet.

---

[58] Parkinson (*Poems*, 2:122) prefers an alternative explanation, that this is a "mysogynist commonplace, strong ale said to be available to the men only when the mistress of the house has gone to bed". But to "take the bed" seems likely to imply more than merely retiring, and "corne drink" does not necessarily seem a positive description of the beverage in question.

Beyond this, we are bound to miss much of the resonance. Who, for example, are the "tua bairnis of Beath" to whom the poem is addressed? Helena Shire believed that the "yong disciple" was none other than John Murray, to whom Montgomerie had earlier dedicated another sonnet;[59] "the Old Maister", then, must be Montgomerie himself, to whom the poem would be addressed in some kind of curiously self-reflexive gambit. But the text, at least in the sestet, seems clearly to speak on behalf of the ageing poet, while "the bairns of Beath" are mentioned along with the lairds of Kilbirnie and Lochwinnoch in ll. 3–4. Both the master and his disciple, it would seem, are to be distinguished from the poet, who portrays himself as one of a company of carousers, defying mortality with what would later be called Dutch courage. The catalogue of the "crabit cripilis" may recall the "Yourself and I, old Scot and Robert Semple" of Montgomerie's Hudson sonnets; but the substitution of Christian names reflects both a contrasting informality and a coded intimacy which is *supposed* to make sense only to those who are part of the circle. The pidgin Dutch (if that is indeed what it is) of the couplet may well form part of the code, apparently Montgomerie's only surviving reference to his foreign exploits of the previous decades, giving an insight into a world for which the "trensh-man" is, tragically, drunkenly incoherent. It is a world to which, finally, Montgomerie denies us access.

In the dichotomy between the court and its rural alternative which emerges from Montgomerie's poetry we see clearly delineated all the ambivalence which beset those who would build their worldly fortunes upon literary self-creation in the later sixteenth century. Montgomerie can never quite escape the claims of court and king; from his earliest quest for royal support in *The Navigatioun* to the late poems which reveal him, old and ill, among his fellow-Catholics in Ayrshire, we can see him manipulating friendship, ties of blood and his poetic gifts in an arduous game of political self-promotion. Whatever the dangers and uncertainties of the court, he is inescapably a creature of it, and his rhetoric is ultimately the rhetoric of survival: he may join many of his contemporaries in condemning the duplicity which he is condemned to practise, but he practises it nevertheless, albeit with an elegance and wit which gives him a legacy denied to mere politicians like James Stewart, earl of Arran and Patrick, master of Gray. Even when he openly decries the unconscionable nature of the courtier's profession he does so in terms which invite sympathy for the courtier's inability to behave otherwise; even when he celebrates the virtues of good company away from the court, he implicitly invokes the world of the court in doing so. Not for him the simple oppositions of Horatian anti-aulic satire: he is deeply implicated in a world he cannot reject however harshly it may reject him. In the inner tensions of Montgomerie's poetry of the court we can see his personal tragedy once again inscribed.

---

[59] Shire, *Song, Dance and Poetry*, 181.

# CHAPTER SEVEN

# "UNDER VENUS WINGS":
# MONTGOMERIE AS LOVE POET

It is with some justice that Montgomerie insists to Robert Hudson that "I wantonly wryt vnder Venus wings": like any other sixteenth-century courtier-poet, he addressed the subject of love, in both sonnets and stanzaic lyrics, more often than he wrote on any other topic. Like other poets of his age, as well, he wrote with constant reference to the conventions which had developed out of Petrarch's *Canzoniere*, the body of rhetorical postures and conceits which dominated amatory writing everywhere in western Europe throughout the later Renaissance.[1] But the tradition was by the last quarter of the sixteenth century a varied and complex one, and Montgomerie was not an unthinking imitator; his direct sources may often be a little old-fashioned, but there is abundant evidence in his verse of the care with which he adapts his materials, and of the distance that he is capable of putting between his own work and the Petrarchism he inherited from his reading. Here, in unmistakable form, we encounter signs that the cultural assumptions which had dominated courtly verse for two or three generations were beginning to hold no longer; like Jodelle in France, Herrera in Spain, and Sidney and Greville in England, Montgomerie finds himself wrestling with the linguistic, aesthetic, and emotional limits imposed by Petrarchist convention, and if he never quite succeeds in breaking away from them, the impulse to find a new voice is quite evident in the most original of his songs and sonnets.

It is important not to underestimate the influence of the cultural milieu within which Montgomerie operated upon the character of his verse, and to recognise the complex dynamics of "Neo-petrarchism" which constituted a dominant strand in

---

[1] On the Petrarchist phenomenon, see Giorgio Santangelo, *Il petrarchismo del Bembo e di altri poeti del '500* (Rome: Istituto Editoriale della Cultura Europea, 1967); Luigi Baldacci, *Il petrarchismo italiano nel Cinquecento*, 2nd ed. (Padua: Liviana, 1974); Leonard Forster, *The Icy Fire: Five Studies in European Petrarchism* (Cambridge: Cambridge University Press, 1969); Stephen Minta, *Petrarch and Petrarchism: the English and French Traditions* (Manchester: Manchester University Press, 1980); Heather Dubrow, *Echoes of Desire: English Petrarchism and its Counterdiscourses* (Ithaca: Cornell University Press, 1995); Gordon Braden, *Petrarchan Love and the Continental Renaissance* (New Haven and London: Yale University Press, 1999); Joseph G. Fucilla, *Estudios sobre el Petrarquismo en España* (Madrid: Consejo Superior de Investigaciones Científicas, 1960).

the court poetry of the last quarter of the sixteenth century. Recent scholarship has laid much greater emphasis upon the function of the court as the locus for early Elizabethan poetry in England, and similar social forces can be identified in the French verse of the 1570s and 1580s. For Steven W. May, the great innovation in English poetry in the 1570s is the development by Edward de Vere, earl of Oxford and by Sir Edward Dyer of "extravagant rhetoric and passionate stances . . . more clearly intended for the entertainment of the queen and her courtiers", the creation of "a poetics which is to an important degree fictional".[2] In recreating a tradition of love poetry which had virtually disappeared in the face of a severely functional Protestant-humanist aesthetic, Oxford and Dyer, the latter soon joined by Sir Philip Sidney and Fulke Greville, unquestionably brought the English literary scene closer to that which existed in France, where the elaborate rhetoric of Philippe Desportes, finely tuned for the *salons* of the Maréchale de Retz and the Marquise de Villeroy as well as for the court of Henry III, represented a serious challenge to the older traditions of Ronsard and the Pléiade.[3]

In both England and France, the impulse towards a poetry of sheer entertainment, a diversion for a courtly society in which elegant expression and rhetorical sophistication outweigh more substantial concerns, would soon in different ways give place to a newfound integration of formal and thematic considerations. For Sidney and Greville, as May observes, "the task ahead was to combine lyric delight with sound moral instruction";[4] and the hedonistic Muse of Desportes, Amadis Jamyn, and their fellow-denizens of the French *salons* would soon be displaced by the more philosophical and theological poetry of Du Bartas, d'Aubigné, and Malherbe. It is a striking feature of the group of poets at the Scottish court that, on the whole, no such harmonisation of social, amatory and moral concerns seems to have been achieved. Two key figures, John Stewart of Baldynneis and Alexander Hume, went to the extent of explicitly repudiating their secular muse: Stewart claims to abandon the "scribling" of love poetry in favour of his extended religious work *Ane Schersing out of Trew Felicitie* (though the presentation manuscript of his work includes both the *Roland Furious* and the *Rapsodies of the Authors Youthfull Braine* before giving the last word to the religious allegory of the *Schersing*), while Hume actually destroyed his amatory verse altogether before publishing his *Hymnes, or Sacred Songes* in 1599. But these are acts of generic choice; we do not find in Scottish poetry before William Drummond of Hawthornden a consistently serious

---

[2] Steven W. May, *The Elizabethan Courtier Poets: the Poems and their Contexts* (Columbia, MO and London: University of Missouri Press, 1991), 57.

[3] L. Clark Keating, *Studies on the Literary Salon in France, 1550–1615* (Cambridge, MA : Harvard University Press, 1941), 81–124 ; Gisèle Mathieu-Castellani, *Les Thèmes amoureux dans la poésie française (1570–1600)* (Strasbourg: Klincksieck, 1975), 214–19.

[4] May, *Courtier Poets*, 68.

attempt, comparable with that of Sidney, Greville, and Spenser, to redefine in more substantial terms the limited scope of Neo-petrarchism.[5]

In Montgomerie's case, it is true, the situation is a little more complex. In the vast majority of his stanzaic lyrics and in many of his sonnets, he seems content to rework, skilfully but in a sense passively, the materials that lay most readily to his hand. He does not attempt to redefine or problematise the lover's situation as Sidney was doing in *Astrophil and Stella*; and while he borrows sonnets from Ronsard, he does not take up the possibility of a serious exploration of the different forms of love embodied in the French poet's *Amours*. It may be that a partial explanation of this comparative conservatism can be found in the nature of the court society for which he was writing: the importance of the musical element in his stanzaic lyrics (and perhaps, as we shall see, in the sonnets as well) is evidence of the function of these pieces as court entertainments, and it is generally true in sixteenth-century verse, as the cases of Wyatt and Scott illustrate very clearly, that the presence of music as a vehicle for the lyric can tempt the poet into a less adventurous approach towards his text.[6] Songs, in other words, tend on the whole to be more trite than poems where the words must stand on their own, and in this respect Montgomerie is manifestly unexceptional. We should pay particular attention, therefore, when he does seem, however hesitantly or eccentrically, to be straining against the limitations of his medium, and we shall conclude this chapter with some striking examples of such innovation. It may be, too, that *The Cherrie and the Slae* can properly be seen as an attempt to break the bounds of Neo-petrarchism, an issue to which we shall return in the following chapter.

As is the case with the work of many other sixteenth-century poets, Montgomerie's amatory verse generally comprises a sophisticated rewriting of pre-existing materials, either through the inflection of conventional rhetorical strategies amd conceits or through the translation and adaptation of specific texts. In this chapter, therefore, we shall begin with a discussion of a range of poems which seem to be indebted in general terms to the Petrarchist tradition, and then examine Montgomerie's translations and adaptations from three particular sources: Ronsard, Marot, and Ovid. We shall conclude by discussing a small number of

---

[5] See now two recent discussions of the king's own love-poetry: M.R. Fleming, "The *Amatoria* of James VI: Loving by the *Reulis*," in *Royal Subjects: Essays on the Writings of James VI and I*, ed. D. Fischlin and M. Fortier (Detroit: Wayne State University Press, 2002), 124–48, and Sarah M. Dunnigan, "Discovering Desire in the *Amatoria* of James VI", idem, 149–81.

[6] On the relationship between text and music in sixteenth-century lyric, see John Stevens, *Music and Poetry in the Early Tudor Court* (London: Methuen, 1961); Paula Johnson, *Form and Transformation in Music and Poetry of the English Renaissance* (New Haven and London: Yale University Press, 1972); and Winifred Maynard, *Elizabethan Lyric Poetry and its Music* (Oxford: Clarendon Press, 1996).

poems in which Montgomerie can be seen to be breaking away from the rhetori-
cal modes which had dominated the love poetry of the two previous generations
and moving towards a style which can be termed "Metaphysical", or perhaps even
"Baroque". By moving counter-chronologically in our analysis of the three authors
to whom Montgomerie owes the most particular debt, we can observe the poet
dealing with an increasing measure of cultural distance, while this triad of influ-
ences is framed by a consideration of those parts of his œuvre which respectively
follow traditions and fashions most closely and evince a desire to escape from the
limitations of convention.

It is helpful — and a fair reflection of the overall balance of his amatory verse —
to begin with those poems in which Montgomerie can be seen at his most un-
critically Petrarchist. There is, for example, the untitled sequence of three sonnets
[**76**] which follows "A Ladyis Lamentatione" in the Ker manuscript.[7] Although no
immediate source has been identified for any of these poems, each represents an
amalgam of typically Petrarchist devices: the *contraposti* of the first and second; the
images of fire, burning, illness, and death; the formal, anaphoric structures which
characterise all three. They share, with each other and with countless similar poems
in Italian, Spanish, French, and Dutch, that heightened discourse of emotional
anguish which runs through the Petrarchan tradition from Bembo onwards:

> I flie the flammis yit folouis on the fyre.
> I lyk my lote and yit my Luk is ill.                                          *fate*
> I yoldin am and yit am stryving still.                                   *have surrendered*
> I dreid Dispair yit hope he heght me hyre . . . . .          *promises me reward*
>    (76.I:5–8)

and which simulates the lover's pain without ever persuading us — or, perhaps,
seeking to — that it is more than a literary exercise. Such poems exemplify Sid-
ney's contemptuous allusion to those who "poore Petrarch's long deceased woes, /
With new-borne sighes and denisend wit do sing" (*Astrophil and Stella*, 15: 7–8),[8]
and if they were all the evidence we had of Montgomerie's amatory verse they
would scarcely justify lifting him out of the great mass of more or less anonymous

---

[7] These poems were wrongly included in the previous group by Cranstoun; this er-
ror was pointed out by Jack (*Montgomerie*, 86), and they are arranged as a separate item by
Parkinson. Although they are numbered as a sequence in the Ker MS., this is one instance
where there may be some doubt about whether the arrangement is authorial or scribal: as
in 77, the third sonnet has a different rhyme-scheme from the other two, and while the
thematic link is quite strong, each of the three could perfectly well stand on its own. Given
the group's proximity to 77, where the arguments for scribal intervention seem quite strong
(see below, 243–44), we may suspect that these were originally separate sonnets.

[8] Sidney, *Poems*, ed. Ringler, 172.

sonneteers of the Italian anthologies and their imitators elsewhere in Europe. They are indeed, as R.D.S. Jack observes, "neat but unremarkable restatements of a well-known literary vision of love".[9]

Nor is this evidence of a substantial debt to the characteristic posture, metaphorics, and poetic diction of the Petrarchist school confined to the most obviously Petrarchist of poetic forms. In some of his stanzaic lyrics, both in the complex verse-forms which he apparently derived from French music and in more straightforward, "native" stanza-patterns, he employs familiar materials:

> The more I drink, more I desyr.
> As I aspyre
> The fervent fyre
>     My cairfull Corps consume.
> Me to torment no tym ye tyre,
> Baith bane and lyre *bone and flesh*
> Throu Cupids yre
>     To dead but ony dome.
> I burne      I freize in yce also.
> I turne      For freindship to my fo.
>     (49: 11–20)

Sixteenth-century audiences appear to have had an inexhaustible taste for such sentiments, and Montgomerie was as willing as any other labourer at the "Castalian" forge to turn it into Tin Pan Alley. The characteristic intricacy of the internal rhymes reinforces the sense that it was the technical challenge of the form which fed both the poet's inspiration and the hearer's appreciation: hackneyed as the contrarieties and paradoxes, the overheated emotional rhetoric and the threats to die of love may be, such pieces are to some degree redeemed by their sheer virtuosity. It is here that the crucial importance of musical arrangement in Montgomerie's lyric verse is most obvious, and the craftsmanship of his compositions must, for the original audience, have compensated for the familiarity, and the formality, of the poses adopted. The very form of the part-song, after all, lends an inevitable element of artificiality, so that it is the elegance of the performance which is placed in the foreground rather than the authenticity of the emotional discourse. The multiplicity of voices and parts, moreover, can have the effect of distancing, even depersonalising, the expression of emotion.[10]

---

[9] Jack, *Montgomerie*, 87.

[10] An interesting example of this effect occurs in "Before the Greeks", where there is a clear separation of voices on the only occurrence of "I" in the entire poem (43: 21), neatly fragmenting the speaker's identity.

The greater the emphasis we place upon the dimension of court performance in seeking to come to terms with Montgomerie's love poetry, the less we are likely to see in the repeated protestations of devoted suffering the reflection of an actual relationship with a real woman. Jack's suggestion that "many of the verses were addressed to a lady at court, probably from a nobler family than Montgomerie's own" is not demonstrably false;[11] but the material he adduces as evidence, in references to the beloved's higher social position and to a threat from jealous observers, is so conventional that it is scarcely overwhelming. We cannot, of course, rule out the possibility that the songs and sonnets were addressed to a particular woman (or, indeed, to more than one woman at different points in the poet's career), but there is at least as much reason to see them as entertainments in which a variety of postures is adopted for an audience thoroughly versed in the niceties of Petrarchan convention. The sonnets he composed for others, for example, are as "authentic" in their emotional expression as many of the poems which apparently represent Montgomerie's own feelings; and there is no more basis for finding the "true" lover in "On Love and fortune I complene" [36] than in the sonnets addressed "To M.D. for Skelmurley" [84], where in the absence of the manuscript's superscription we might be tempted to attach autobiographical meaning to the speaker's declaration to the nightingale that "As thou art banished, so am I exyld".

"On Love and fortune I complene" is a deftly-constructed amalgam of familiar elements, many of which are shared not only by the Petrarchists but also by that wider medieval tradition of amatory lyric of which Petrarchism is a late variant. The battle imagery of the second and third stanzas, for example, is certainly found in Petrarch's "Amor che nel penser mio viva e regna" (*Canzoniere*, 140) and in many subsequent adaptations, but it runs through the poetry of courtly love and occurs, linked as here with the motif of captivity, in Dunbar's "Bewty and the Prisoneir" and forms the basis of such extended erotic/ethical allegories as *King Hart*.[12] Montgomerie neatly integrates the theme into the central conceit of the lyric, the catalogue of those responsible for the lover's misery: his eyes, his heart, Cupid, the Lady herself, and Fortune. An essential feature of the wider medieval tradition of *amour courtois* is the Lady's higher social position, the point with which Montgomerie concludes his poem:

> I wyt Dame fortun, not that sho                    *blame*
> Hes set you highest in degrie
> Bot rather that sho wald not do
> The lyk in all respects to me.

---

[11] Jack, "Theme of Fortune", 32.

[12] For *King Hart* see *Shorter Poems of Gavin Douglas*, ed. Priscilla J. Bawcutt (Edinburgh: STS, 1967), 141–70; as Bawcutt herself pointed out, there is no real basis for the attribution to Douglas.

> Had our Estates bene weill compaird
> I had not vterlie dispaird.
> (31–36)

Here Jack finds evidence of the autobiographical, but it is important to observe the *rhetorical* effect of this final stanza: in the pattern of blame which forms the lyric's rhetorical structure, Montgomerie moves from his own eyes and heart to the external forces which have contributed to his distress, and while he suggests at the outset that it is his own eyes that he blames "most of all" (l. 3), by the penultimate stanza he is loading his condemnation upon the beloved. This turns on a carefully-balanced opposition. Cupid, the speaker says, "band me bundman to the best":

> To wit vnto your womanheid,
> Quhilk worst I wyt of all my woes
> Quhais beutie (be it homicide?)
> I feir it most of all my foes,
> > Quhilk Natur set so far above
> > The rest vhill that it vanquisht Love.
> > (25–30)

The Lady, then, is both the best and the worst, a figure of unparalleled beauty but, in her inaccessibility, a potential killer. The conventional rhetoric here leads Montgomerie into a tactical difficulty, for the ultimate point of such lyrics is elegant compliment, not forensic accusation. His solution is to deflect the attack onto Fortune, whose disposition of social origins has created the distance between the speaker and his beloved which is perhaps the chief barrier to his success. This softening device has a twofold effect: it compliments the Lady on her high social status, and it provides her with an excuse — an entirely conventional excuse in the tradition of *amour courtois* — for her rejection of the lover's advances. It also reflects, incidentally and in a slightly curious sense, more favourably upon the lover himself; perhaps, he hints, he would be acceptable if only differences of birth did not make him unsuitable.

It is possible to see in this rhetorical gambit evidence of a larger phenomenon, the preoccupation with social hierarchy which is a natural feature of the court society for which Montgomerie was writing. We do not need, in this sense, to presuppose an actual object for the poem's amatory address: we should, perhaps, rather see it as mimicking, or modelling, anxieties and tensions which had become conventional precisely because they were endemic to the culture for which the texts were produced. The same might be said of the references to jealous outsiders which occur in Montgomerie's lyrics as in the work of many other court poets, and which are also cited by Jack as signs of a "real" relationship. Alexander

Scott, we should remember, expresses a longing to "walk [wake] without espyis",[13] and the theme of secrecy had been a feature of amatory verse since the twelfth century. Again, it reflects social reality, both in the sense that women's sexual reputations were, in medieval and Renaissance societies, virtually a kind of social commodity — "I coft [*bought*] hir deir," Scott revealingly declares, "bot scho fer derrer me" — and because in the confined space of the court sexuality was always the potential subject of scandal and political intrigue. The displacement of such dangerous activity into polite wooing-songs is a sign of its central importance, and the recurrence of the motif of secrecy and the hazards of discovery reflects the proximity of the fiction to the hidden realities of the courtier's existence.

To emphasise the conventional nature of much of Montgomerie's amatory verse is, however, not necessarily to deny the particularity of the choices he makes within the range of postures and rhetorical devices available within the tradition. The dominant motif of his love poetry, as it is ultimately in a great deal of his writing, is that of powerlessness in the face of hostile forces outside his control. While the theme of fated, unhappy love is in itself a commonplace of Neo-petrarchism, in Montgomerie it approaches the level of an obsession. This is reflected not only in the omnipresence of the figure of Fortune, as Jack has pointed out, but also in the repeated references to Cupid's archery, the most frequent single image in his love poems. This often occurs as merely an incidental feature in the poet's account of his distress, but it can also become the central, unifying conceit, as in "Quhen folish Phaeton" [38] or in "In throu the windoes of myn ees" [28]. In this latter case, the protagonist concedes that his defiance of Cupid has contributed to his present misery:

> "Now gesse", quod he, "if thou be glaid.
>     Nou laugh at Love.
>     That Pastym prove.
>  Am I ane Archer nou or nocht?"
>     His skorne and skaith                                              *harm*
>     I baid them baith
>  And got it sikker than I socht.                              *more surely*
>     (16–22)

The mocking tone, paralleled by the lover's aphoristic response, belies the Petrarchist excess of what follows. If there is an element of game in the challenge to Cupid, the emotional consequences are potentially disastrous:

> Fra hand I freiz'd in flamis of fyre                         *immediately*
> I brint agane also in yce.                                          *burned*

---

[13] "Up, helsum hairt", l. 36: Scott, *Poems*, ed. Cranstoun, 44–45 ; cf. above, 20–22.

My dolour wes my auin devyce.
Displesur wes my auin desyre.
All thir by Natur nou ar nyce.                    *misguided*
   Bot Natur nou
   (I wot not how)
Sho meins to metamorphose me
   In sik a shappe
   As hes no happe
To further weill nor yit to flie.
   (23–33)

The origins of the lover's misery, then, lie beyond his control, in the hands of Love and Nature. But the open conclusion of the poem leaves room for a remedy: if only the beloved will take pity on his condition, there is still hope that he can be saved. From vulnerability to the uncontrollable force of love he moves to dependence upon the response of the Lady: nowhere in such pieces do we gain the sense that the protagonist has any ability to determine his own fate.

This emphasis upon the sufferings of a lover whose condition is radically beyond his own control brings us back to a paradox we noted at the outset of this study: that while the specific borrowings which can be found in Montgomerie's poetry are predominantly from the work of poets of the two previous generations in France, Marot and Ronsard, in a more general sense his verse is informed by the most contemporary of fashions. Nowhere is this more apparent than in his modulation of Petrarchist convention. In her important study of French amatory poetry in the last third of the sixteenth century, Gisèle Mathieu-Castellani distinguishes between a "néo-pétrarquisme 'blanc'," characterised by Philippe Desportes, Jean Bertaut and Jacques Davy du Perron, and a "néo-pétrarquisme 'noir'," the leading exponents of which are Étienne Jodelle and Amadis Jamyn. Both are marked by a new psychologism, a preoccupation with the analysis of the interior experience of love rather than the exploration of the relationship between the lover and the beloved, and they mediate their expression through "la rhétorique et . . . la casuistique amoureuses". Where the language of Desportes and his followers remains animated by the polite world of the salons, however, that of Jodelle and Jamyn has a more tortured and violent character, breaking more conclusively with the emotional balance of Ronsard and bringing an autumnal note to the expression of love.[14] Not only can Montgomerie be seen to be combining elements of both these versions of Neo-petrarchism; he repeatedly uses themes and metaphors which are characteristic of them. Sometimes this is a matter of specifics (as in the case of imagery of overaspiring flight, which we shall shortly explore); more often it is a question of the ways in

---

[14] Mathieu-Castellani, *Thèmes amoureux*, 219–22.

which conventional motifs like martyrdom, illness, and poison are combined in a psycho-erotic matrix of helpless misery. This is more apparent, interestingly, in the stanzaic lyrics than in the sonnets, where the influence of Ronsard seems to exercise a restraining function.

It is not difficult to find illustrations of this mode of representation of the lover's condition in Montgomerie's lyrics. Many of its essential features come together in the opening stanzas of "A late regrate of Leirning to Love" [12]:

> I knou not nou vhat Countenance to keep
> For to expell a poysone that I prove.
> Alace, alace that evir I leirned to Love.
>
> A frentick fevir thrugh my flesh I feill,
> I feill a passione can not be exprest,
> I feill a byll within my bosum beill,                        *boil; swell*
> No Cataplasme can weill impesh that pest,                    *poultice; prevent;*
> I feill my self with seiknes so possesst.                    *plague*
> A madnes maks my mirth from me remove.
> Alace, alace that evir I learned to love.
>       (5–14)

The images of illness, poison, wounding and madness are all familiar enough in the Petrarchist tradition: what links Montgomerie with his French contemporaries is the insistence with which he concentrates (managed here through the anaphoric repetition of "I feill") upon the interior nature of the experience, virtually without reference to the exterior world in which the relationship with the object of his desire is actually situated. Only in the penultimate line does he entertain the possibility of obtaining "hir jelous glove", as a token of the Lady's responsiveness to his desire.

The fact that these themes are, on the whole, more fully developed in songs than in sonnets should serve to remind us that the medium in which Montgomerie explores such desperate emotions is, as we noted earlier, *performance*. It follows from this that the experience he portrays is in essence a reflection of the tastes he attributes to his audience, and that it is in the manipulation of Petrarchist amatory language, interacting with a music of which we sometimes have direct evidence, sometimes must infer, that the pleasure of his love poetry mainly resides.[15] Desportes, in Mathieu-Castellani's words, is not a love poet as such, but an "artisan du langage,

---

[15] Of Montgomerie's forty or so extant stanzaic love lyrics, only eight have known musical settings (if we exclude the sonnets which might have been set to music by Jannequin), but the patterning of stanzaic form suggests that many others were originally intended to be sung.

ouvrier des mots"; in Montgomerie's case, this craftsmanship is doubled by the skilful harmonisation of rhetorically effective language with a (perhaps generally pre-existing) musical text. Again, the obvious analogy is with the earliest phase of the Neo-petrarchist revival in England, and specifically with Sidney's *Certain Sonnets*, where the 1598 edition frequently indicates the Italian, Spanish, or English tune for which the words were written. In those cases where we have the music Montgomerie used, as in "In throe the windows of myn ees", "A late regrate of Leirning to Love" and "Evin dead, behold I breath", there is a remarkable contrast between its formal stateliness and the extreme emotions which the text portrays, and it must be assumed that this conjunction was an essential part of the aesthetic effect. Yet Montgomerie is also extremely skilled in his use of the music to underline a rhetorical point. In "Evin dead, behold I breath" [26], for example, the introduction of the third of each stanza's musical elemento coincidec each time with a turn in the argument, and in the opening stanza this reinforces a heightening of the emotional language:

> O cruell deidly feid,
> O Rigour but remorse!
> Since thair is no remeid
> Come Patience perforce.
>     (9–12)

To stress the significance of such motifs in Montgomerie's lyrics, however, is not to deny that his sonnets sometimes reflect similarly fashionable preoccupations. The clearest illustration of this can be found in the short sequence headed in the Ker manuscript "To The For Me" [86]. If this title is authorial, it might be taken to suggest that here, at least, Montgomerie is speaking for himself, not ventriloquising for another or engaging in mere Petrarchist entertainment. The conceits he employs are highly conventional (the comparison of the lover's situation with that of the nightingale; the motif of aspiring but unsuccessful flight; the *envoi* addressed to the text itself), and the language of "louing langour" thoroughly familiar. The nightingale theme, for example, is one of the most widespread of Petrarchist images, occurring in Petrarch's own "Quel rossignuol che sì soave piagne" (*Canzoniere*, 311) and "Vago augelletto, che cantando vai" (353), in Pietro Bembo's "Solingo augello, se piangendo vai" (*Rime*, Sonnet 41) and "O rosignuol, che 'n queste verdi fronde" (*Canzone*, 3), Ronsard's "Rossignol mon mignon, qui dans cette saulaye" (*Continuation des Amours*, 43), and in the work of numerous other members of the school. Shire suggests that Montgomerie's poem "is linked with" Ronsard's,[16] but while it may be the case that Ronsard's opening line, and specifically his explicit reference to the willow, may have influenced the

---

[16] Shire, *Song, Dance and Poetry*, 157–58.

Scots version, Montgomerie's application of the conceit has virtually nothing to do with the French text. Whereas Ronsard's argument turns in the sestet upon a *distinction* between the lover and the bird, the latter's mate responding to the poignancy of the song while the speaker's lady remains unmoved, Montgomerie develops a neat parallel, suggesting that as the nightingale continues to sing while the holly's "piercing pykis" wound her breast, so the speaker is "in gritest danger vhair I most delyte" (I: 10); this no doubt explains his decision to substitute the holly for Ronsard's more romantic willow. In a further twist, Montgomerie combines the Ovidian motif of the nightingale with the mythical phoenix in order to emphasise the uniqueness of his beloved. Here he seems to be responding to the most current of French fashions, for the phoenix is repeatedly employed by Desportes and his contemporaries.[17] For the French poets, however, the phoenix is more commonly associated with the lover than with the Lady, and Amadis Jamyn is relatively unusual in making the bird represent, at least in passing, the superlativeness of the beloved's beauty:

> Comme cet Univers de tout temps n'a porté
>     Qu'un seul rare Phœnix, qui mourant renouvelle:
>     Ainsi de tous costez la terre universelle
>     Ne porte que vous seule unique de beauté.[18]

[As this universe has at all times had only one singular phoenix, which renews itself in dying, so of all the quarters this world has only you, unique in your beauty.]

But in picking up this fashionable motif, Montgomerie reflects his proximity to French Mannerism of the 1570s. Nor is this the only time he employs the image: in "The cruell pane and grevous smarte" [35], he again concludes with an address to "freschest Phœnix, friend and fo". In this case it is the phoenix's double nature, rather than its uniqueness, which is the point of the comparison; nevertheless, it may be that there is some connection between the lyric and the sonnet-sequence.

If Montgomerie is manifestly in touch with one of the most contemporary French trends in his use of the phoenix image in his opening sonnet, he is even more clearly so in the second, where he builds the entire poem around the motif of the "grand vol audacieux". This is one of the most characteristic conceits in the poetry of the generation after Ronsard, and the figure of Icarus "with wanton

---

[17] For the uses of the phoenix theme by Isaac Habert, Amadis Jamyn, Bernier de la Brousse and others, see Mathieu-Castellani, *Thèmes amoureux*, 268–78.

[18] Amadis Jamyn, *Œuvres poétiques* (Paris: Guillaume Colletet, 1579), cited in Mathieu-Castellani, *Thèmes amoureux*, 276.

waxit wings" (II: 6) is at its centre.[19] Going back to Sannazaro's "Icaro cadde qui quest' onde il sanno" (*I Fiori*, 281), the motif is prominent in Desportes and in the work of his circle: Montgomerie adheres to the tradition by emphasising the vulnerability of Icarus's wings and the futile audacity of the whole enterprise. Yet his sonnet ends in defiance: although he admits the danger he is in, his speaker's heart "yit . . . in hoping hings" (the connotation of stasis in flight is an interesting twist!), and he assures himself that "If thou be brunt, it is with beuties bemes". As Mathieu-Castellani observes of a sonnet by Flaminio de Birague,

> La chute, alors, n'est plus la fin lamentable qui attend l'audacieux et le punit d'avoir osé, mais au contraire la preuve éclatante d'une victoire remportée sur soi-même.[20]

Montgomerie, indeed, has suppressed the notion of the fall entirely, leaving his protagonist suspended in mid-air, still hoping that all will be well. This sonnet contrasts in this respect with The *Cherrie and the Slae*, where the theme of over-ambitious flight is again used in an erotic context, this time with painful results.[21] The sense of a negotiation in progress is maintained into the final sonnet of this sequence, where the speaker relies upon his poetic art to "anatomeze my privie passionis plane" (III: 9), and thereby to win the lady's favour. Throughout the sequence, Montgomerie treads the fine line between irredeemable sorrow and persistent hope, concentrating consistently upon his speaker's emotional circum-stances but always working his way towards the final appeal to the Lady's mercy.

The title of this sequence in the Ker MS. is, of course, no guarantee that the poems were written in his own voice, or that they related to a specific moment in his life. We have noted elsewhere in this study cases of amatory ventriloquism, and there is at least one other which has not been noted before. "I wald se mare nor ony thing I sie" [78] is not, as Helena Shire argued, a coded reference to a shared Marian politics between the court musician James Lauder and Montgomerie,[22] but part of a related pair of texts which articulate the love of another James Lauder and an un-identified Isobel Young. As "I wald se mare" begins with an anagram of Lauder's name, so "I trou your Love by loving so vnsene" [79] has an opening anagram of Young's. Not only do both sonnets employ the fashionable French device of *vers enchaînée*, moreover, but the technique is carried over from one to the other:

---

[19] Mathieu-Castellani, *Thèmes amoureux*, 260–64, 292–307.

[20] Mathieu-Castellani, *Thèmes amoureux*, 303.

[21] See below, 319–20.

[22] Shire, *Song, Dance and Poetry*, 75–79; the association with the musician is accepted by Parkinson, *Poems*, 2:107. Apart from the connection with the Isobel Young sonnet demonstrated here, Shire's theory that "mare" is a reference to "*Ma[ria] Re[gina]*" is surely undermined by the fact that the metre requires that the word be read as a monosyllable.

> Assay I sall, hap ill or weill, I vou.                  *come good or bad luck*
> I vou to ventur, to triumph *I trou.*                   *take a chance*
> (78:13–14)

> *I trou* your Love by loving so vnsene
> Vnsene siklyk I languish for your Love
> (79:1–2)

The point is therefore unequivocal: this pair of sonnets celebrates the love of a separated couple named James Lauder and Isobel Young. The former can scarcely be the musician, who about 1570 married a woman called Jean Hay who evidently survived him, dying in 1614.[23] Lauder is a common enough name in Scotland, though it is possible that the subject of Montgomerie's poem was one of the musician's sons; Shire cites a letter of 1582 in which he acknowledges having seven children. The family had long been burgesses of Edinburgh, and since there was also a long-standing burgess family of Youngs in the burgh, it may be that this possible association provides a social context for Montgomerie's poems. What is certain is that "I wald se mare" is not a coded piece about Mary Queen of Scots.

Having established this point, we are free to concentrate on the amatory strategies of the two sonnets, and the ways in which Montgomerie represents the lovers' voices. Common to both is the starting-point of separation: "Lauder" regrets that he cannot see the object of his desire, while "Yong" replies by acknowledging that she is "vnsene". The gender roles, we may think, are entirely conventional, with the male eye seeing and the woman seen; yet it equally clear that "Yong" is, in a sense, as active a lover as he is ( "I languish for your Love"), and she goes on to emphasize their reciprocity:

> Your Love is comely, constant, chaste and clene
> And clene is myne, Experience sall prove
> (79: 3–4).

"Lauder" gives an account of his emotional condition which owes much to Petrarchist convention, the *vers enchaînée* creating a pattern of implied logical consequences, each repetition suggesting a further progression in the psychology of love. Parkinson notes the sestet's echoes of "the *Cherrie* theme of courage in spite of danger", and we may note that "Yong" matches this by invoking Experience, who plays a crucial role in the longer poem.[24] "Aspyre", too, the term employed

---

[23] Shire, *Song, Dance and Poetry*, 261–62; and cf. eadem, "Musical Servitors to Queen Mary Stuart", *Music and Letters* 40 (1959), 15–18.

[24] *Poems*, ed. Parkinson, 2:107; cf. below, 000–00.

by "Lauder" (78: 7–8) to convey his amatory ambitions, may evoke the persona's rash flight in *The Cherrie and the Slae*, a motif we have also noted in the second element of "To the for me". Yet there is no sense of irony here; "Lauder"'s aspirations are matched by his lady's, and in this sense the Petrarchist language of "I wald se mare" is lent a very un-Petrarchist context. "Yong" responds to her lover's declarations by asserting the power of Hymen, and leaves no doubt that she is ready to marry him at the earliest opportunity. Her final appeal, however, is not to a pagan deity but to the Christian God:

> Right beiring Rule, the righteous suld rejose,
> Rejose in God, and on his will repose.
>     (79: 13–14)

Petrarchist passion, then, is ultimately resolved into a modest piety: their love is so "meit", "Yong" insists, that there need be no suspicion that it will not be acceptable to God. The social circumstances which generated this touching pair of ventriloquized poems may not be apparent to us, but it is clear that Montgomerie takes the lovers' part in more senses than one.

The subtle manipulations of Petrarchist convention which we have noted in these poems are also apparent in Montgomerie's translations and adaptations from Ronsard, where Petrarchist conceits are manifestly mediated through a specific French original. As Hoffmann demonstrated a century ago, there are at least seven instances in which Montgomerie bases sonnets upon poems in Ronsard's *Amours*;[25] of these, the only one which can be dated is "O happie star", which was, as we have seen, composed for the marriage of Margaret Montgomerie in 1582. No other source for Montgomerie's amatory sonnets has as yet been identified, which makes the extent of this borrowing from Ronsard all the more remarkable. We can, in fact, be reasonably certain which of the many editions of *Les Amours* Montgomerie employed, at least as his principal source. Jack suggests that a study of Ronsard's many revisions of his work, coupled with the fact that (as he claims) the eight sonnets in question only appear together for the first time in the *Œuvres* of 1560, indicates quite strongly that the Scots poet had access either to that edition or to its successor of 1567.[26] To these two possibilities we should, in principle, add the 1557 edition, in which Ronsard's *Continuations des Amours* were brought together in uniform format with the *Amours* proper; as we shall see in a moment, there are textual grounds for excluding this edition as Montgomerie's source-text, but it should be recognised as the first collected version containing all the poems translated or adapted by Montgomerie.

---

[25] Oscar Hoffmann, "Studien zu Montgomerie", *Englische Studien* 20 (1895), 24–69, here 44–45.

[26] Jack, *Montgomerie*, 82–83.

If we assume that Montgomerie employed the same copy of Ronsard in making all eight Scots texts (which is certainly the most economical hypothesis, even if it is not self-evidently correct), then we can definitely exclude the 1567 *Œuvres* from further consideration, since between 1560 and 1567 Ronsard thoroughly revised the sestet of his opening poem, "Qui voudra voir", of which Montgomerie's "Vha vald behold" [87.IV] is a fairly close translation. Comparison of the three texts leaves no doubt which of the French versions Montgomerie used:

> Il cognoistra combien la raison peult
> > Contre son arc, quand une foys il veult
> > Que nostre cœur son esclave demeure:
> Et si voirra que je suis trop heureux
> > D'avoir au flanc l'aiguillon amoureux,
> > Plein de venin don't il fault que je meure.
> > (1560)

> Il coignoistra combien peult la raison
> > Contre son trait quand sa douce poison
> > Tourment un cœur que la jeunesse enchante,
> Et connoistra, que je suis trop heureux
> > D'estre en mourant nouveau Cygne amoureux,
> > Qui plus languist & plus doucement chante.
> > (1567)[27]

> Thair sall he sie vhat Resone then can do
> Against his bou, if once he mint bot to                    *strives*
> Compell our hairts in bondage basse to beir.
> Yit sall he se me happiest appeir
> That in my hairt the amorous heid does lie
> Vith poysond poynt, vhairof I glore to die.

Ronsard's replacement of the bow by an arrow in l. 10, his earlier mention of poison, and the image of the amorous swan are nowhere reflected in the Scots, while the ideas of bondage (l. 11) and of death (l. 14) are evidently based upon the earlier version. For this translation at least, Montgomerie must have made use of the 1560 edition or one of its predecessors. In "Ha! lytill dog" [83], on the other hand, based on Ronsard's "Ha, petit chien", the reference to Cassandra in l. 3 of the French, present in 1555 and 1557 but eliminated from 1560 onwards, is likewise

---

[27] Ronsard, *Œuvres complètes*, ed. Laumonier, 4:5–6. It should be noted that Ronsard revised this sestet again for the 1584 edition of his works; this version, where the sestet begins "Il cognoistra qu'Amour est sans raison" is even further away from Montgomerie (cf. Shire, *Song, Dance and Poetry*, 157).

absent from Montgomerie's Scots, which consistently follows the revised version. In other words, it is only in the 1560 *Œuvres*, of which (as Jack reminds us) James VI owned a copy, that "Qui voudra voir" and "Ha, petit chien" occur together in the forms in which Montgomerie used them; the conclusion that this was his principal source therefore seems irresistible.

Does it follow from this that we should reject Helena Shire's hypothesis that Montgomerie followed French practice in composing sonnet texts suitable for musical arrangement? The fact that he seems to have followed the printed text of 1560 rather than that of the first, 1552 edition of *Les Amours*, in which musical settings by Clément Jannequin and others were included, does not, of course, prove that he had not seen a copy of the latter, or that he did not have access to the music for "Qui voudra voir". Shire argues convincingly that the organisation of Montgomerie's translation of "O happie star" seems to fit Jannequin's music very cloooly; and the nature of the occasion for which the Scots sonnet was composed certainly encourages the idea of musical performance. Whether the same argument applies to other Scots versions is less clear: Shire does not go further than to claim that "Vha vald behold" "is *amoene* to the four-part setting" published in 1552, and to add that the inclusion of a translation of "Pardonne moy, Platon" (also attached to Jannequin's setting in the 1552 *Amours*) in the five-sonnet mini-sequence in which it appears "shows that a link existed in Montgomerie's mind" between his two originals, which are sonnets 1 and 60 in *Les Amours* but which occur next to one another in the Scots sequence.[28] This reflects unwonted caution on Shire's part, for the fact is that all five sonnets sing as well as "O happie star" to the Jannequin setting, lending credibility to the idea that the sequence may have been similarly intended for performance.

These five sonnets [87] do, in fact, provide an excellent example of the rhetorical sophistication Montgomerie brings to the composition of a short sequence of conventional love poems, and this is all the more evident if we allow the possibility of oral performance (with or without music) in a court setting. Montgomerie is in this respect, as in others, the heir of Alexander Scott, the poet-musician who flourished at the court of Mary and who apparently survived into the "Castalian" period. The first sonnet of this sequence, certainly, recalls the subtle strategy of Scott in "Luve preysis bot comparesone", where the poem's amatory subject is referred to only in the third person in a way which works most effectively if we imagine her to be among the original audience:

> Suld I presome this sedull schaw,                *document*
>     Or lat me langouris be lamentit?
> Na! I effrey, for feir and aw                          *terror*
>     Hir comlie heid be miscontentit.

---

[28] Shire, *Song, Dance and Poetry*, 156–57.

I dar nocht preiss hir to present it,
 For be scho wreth I will not wow it;     *angry; acknowledge*
Bot pleiss hir proudens to imprent it,
 Scho may persave sum Inglis throw it.
 (33–40)[29]

So with "Vhat subject, sacred sisters" (87.I): "hir grace", though mentioned, is only hinted at, a form of indirection which invites speculation among the hearers but leaves the identity of the beloved (if, indeed, she is more than a necessary fiction) tantalisingly unspecified. This suggests, perhaps, a courtly game which belies the passionately Petrarchan language to come, as the opening questions seem to imply a casting-around for a suitable subject:

Vhat subject, sacred Sisters, sall I sing?
Vhase praise, Apollo, sal my pen proclame?
Vhat Nymph, Minerva, sall thy novice name?

This sense of a poet playing with his audience is enhanced, moreover, by the self-quotation the sonnet contains, with apparent allusions to the songs "Melancholie, grit deput of Dispair" [34] ("Angels ees", l. 7) and, more distinctively, "The Solsequium" [21] ("on staitly stalk new sprouting", l. 5); in this latter case, the integral nature of the image in the lyric and its incidental quality here surely confirm that it is the sonnet which is engaged in quoting. All of this amounts, as so often in Montgomerie, to a form of rhetorical display, ironically negating the speaker's claim to be Minerva's "novice": the ostensible purpose may be a wooing game, but we may perhaps be forgiven for suspecting that, quite naturally for the courtier-poet, the self-advancement which is the subtext is literary rather than sexual.

The wit which informs such an enterprise is apparent, too, in the relationships among the elements of the sequence. A recurring motif here is archery: in the opening sonnet it is the persona's Muse who "mints" [*aims*] at the target of the Lady's beauty, but in the following poem, "Hir brouis tuo bouis", it is the speaker himself who is under fire. But Montgomerie here combines two familiar Petrarchan conceits into a single argument, moving in the second quatrain from the archery metaphor to that of a lawsuit. The precise nature of the transition is obscured by the omission of l. 5 in the Ker manuscript, but it is clear that the dominant structure of the sonnet is a list of attributes arranged in two allegorical scenes, in the first of which Cupid uses the Lady's brows as bows with which to pierce the lover's breast, while in the second the persona presents himself as a

---

[29] Scott, *Poems*, ed. Cranstoun, 27. It is possible that there is a pun in the last line, and that the lady's surname was "Inglis".

petitioner at his beloved's court, concluding in a pessimistic but somewhat enigmatic final line that "My pairties [*opponents*] are my javellour and my judge". Here, too, as in the first poem of the sequence, the opening gives us a false expectation of what is to follow:

> Hir brouis, tuo bouis of Ebane ever bent,                    *ebony*
> Hir Amorous ees the awfull Arrouis ar . . .

We might reasonably anticipate from these lines a poem in the tradition of *effictio*, or *blason*, cataloguing the Lady's beauties — the tradition parodied by Shakespeare in "My mistress' eyes are nothing like the sun" — but this expectation is twice defeated, first by the conversion of the imagery of her brows and eyes into the larger allegory of Cupid's archery, and then into the conceit of the lawsuit.

The two following sonnets enable us to observe the creative skill with which Montgomerie manages his adaptations of Ronsard. The third element in the sequence, a translation of "Pardonne moy, Platon", marks a rather surprising shift in the overall argument, despite Jack's sense that the imagery of the first two sonnets "naturally leads" into the philosophical debate with Plato. But while the address to Plato introduces an element of rhetorical disjunction, the emotional plane remains that of extravagant grief. As has been observed before, there is a sharp difference in Montgomerie's strategy between octave and sestet: the former is a very close translation of the French as it was printed in 1560, but in his final six lines the Scots poet transforms his original:

> Il est du vague, ou certes s'il n'en est,
>     D'un air pressé le comblement ne naist:
>     Plus tost le ciel, qui bening se dispose
> A recevoir l'effect de mes douleurs,
>     De toutes partz se comble de mes pleurs,
>     Et de mes vers qu'en mourant je compose.[30]

> [It is empty, or certainly if it is not then its fullness is made up of compressed air; or rather heaven, which is kindly prepared to receive the effect of my misery, is completely filled with my tears, and with the verses which, dying, I write.]

> Suppose the solids subtilis ay restraints
> (Vhich is the maist, my Maister, ye may mene),                    *hold*

---

[30] Ronsard, *Œuvres complètes*, ed. Laumonier, 4 : 62.

Thoght all war void yit culd they not contene          *empty*
The half, let be the haill of my Complaintis.
Vhair go they then, the Question wald I crave,
Except for ruth the hevins suld thame ressave?
     (87.III: 9–14)

While Montgomerie's version parallels Ronsard's in a general way, much of the detail is different. By adding his parenthetical l. 10, for example, Montgomerie creates a greater sense of unity, explicitly continuing his philosophical discussion with Plato. In the same way, l. 9 refers more precisely than the equivalent passage in Ronsard to *Timaeus* 52–57 and Platonic theories of the elements and the void, accentuating in the process the hyperbolic nature of the argument with "yit culd they [that is, the Platonic "solids"] not contene / The half, let be the haill" of the speaker's complaints. Montgomerie has, on the other hand, dropped Ronsard's very specific reference to his writing, and he opens up the sonnet's conclusion by asking a question rather than by making a positive statement. The effect of these changes, I think, is to focus more single-mindedly upon the speaker: the cosmological quibbling of Ronsard's sestet has been absorbed into a more rhetorical emphasis upon the vastness of the lover's unhappiness. In one respect, however, the rhetoric is more subdued: nothing in the Scots corresponds to Ronsard's "en mourant". The explanation of this may be structural, for the motif of the lover's impending death concludes the following sonnet, and Montgomerie may have decided not to repeat this idea in the couplets of two successive poems.

     In "Vha wald behold", as we have already noted, it is the earliest version of Ronsard's sonnet which forms Montgomerie's model, as he returns to the motif of archery which had run through the first two elements of the sequence. Here the transformations are subtle but consistent, as the Scots poet retains the principal structural features of the French, but once again shifts the balance of the rhetoric towards his own emotional condition:

Qui voudra voyr comme un Dieu me surmonte,
     Comme il m'assault, comme il se fait vainqueur,
     Comme il r'enflamme, & r'englace mon cuœur,
     Comme il reçoit un honneur de ma honte . . .[31]

Vha wald behold him vhom a god so grievis,
Vhom he assaild and danton'd with his dairt,          *subdued*
Of vhom he freizis and Inflams the hairt,
Vhais shame siclyk him gritest honour givis . . .
     (IV:1–4)

---

[31] Ronsard, *Œuvres complètes*, ed. Laumonier, 4:5.

The most obvious adjustment here is from Ronsard's "comme" to a series of relative pronouns, which are assigned the dominant anaphoric function in the quatrain, shifting the focus from Cupid to the speaker. We are thus invited to observe the object of the process rather than the process itself, and this emotional refocusing is reinforced by Montgomerie's use of more vivid verbs: "grievis" replaces "surmonte", and the parallel structure of l. 2 is abandoned in favour of the more graphic "assaild and danton'd". This pattern of intensification is then completed by the conversion of Ronsard's "honneur" into the superlative "gritest honour", making the conquest of the speaker Cupid's most powerful achievement. But Montgomerie is skilled enough to know when to leave well alone: the climax of Ronsard's octave comes at the beginning of l. 7, with "Me vienne voir", and the Scots version retains this effect with "Behold bot me". In translating the rest of the octave, however, Montgomerie again intensifies the effect of the French, this time through the use of alliteration:

> . . . il voirra ma douleur,
> Et la rigueur de l'Archer qui me donte.

> . . . Persaiv my painfull pairt
> And tharcher that but mercy me mischeivis.

The nuancing of the sestest is less radical, but here too Montgomerie makes subtle adjustments to the effect. The inversion of the opening phrase, for example, again places the emphasis on the condition of the speaker: "Il cognoistra" becomes "There sall he sie", with the stress on "There" referring the sestet back more insistently to the argument of the octave. Ronsard's metaphors, too, are strengthened through the continued use of alliteration ("bondage basse", l. 11; "in my hairt the Amorous heid", l. 13; "poyson'd poynt", l. 14), while the final phrase, building on the more powerful sense of closure which comes from the concluding couplet, again reinforces the speaker's emotional state: by contrast with "dont il faut que je meure", "vhairof I glore to die" takes up the idea of happiness we find in l. 12 (the Scots "happiest" again goes some way beyond Ronsard's "trop heureux"), reinforcing the Petrarchan paradox of the lover's willing acceptance of his fate. If Ronsard's speaker ends with a passive recognition of the inevitability of his condition, Montgomerie's compounds the hyperbole by embracing his death with enthusiasm.

This flourish anticipates the heightened rhetoric of the sequence's final sonnet, which chiefly comprises a catalogue of anaphorically-linked questions. Here the focus is much more directly upon the speaker's anguish, and the language is for the most part stereotypically Petrarchan. It is also connected structurally with the rest of the sequence: l. 4 returns to the motif of Cupid's archery, for example, while l. 6 ("Hou long sall weping blind my watrie ee?") echoes the conceit of tears in "Pardon me, Plato". Once again, the lover is presented as a helpless victim, yet the final three lines, in the extravagantly Mannerist figure of *vers rapportées*, suggest the possibility of a kind of resolution:

> Vp once and my Melancholie remove.
> Revenge, Revert, Revive, Revest, Reveall
> My hurt, My hairt, My hope, My hap, My heall.

Since inaction is one of the characteristics of the melancholic, the speaker's attempt to galvanise himself into action is quite specifically pointed, and if the exact nature of the intended course of action remains imprecise, the series of paired phrases at least points towards a successful conclusion. Throughout the sequence, the lover has swung between abject, hopeless misery and a barely perceived hope; in the final couplet it is the latter mood which prevails, concluding on a more positive note of elegantly poised expectation. If we are justified as seeing this as a performance piece, then this dissolution of the prevailing mood of psychological anguish ensures that the final effect of the sequence is not too dark, and is therefore appropriate for a court entertainment.

The Ronsard translations which the Ker manuscript does not present as elements in a mini-sequence reveal many of the same subtle adjustments we have observed in "Pardon me, Plato" and "Vha wald behold". "Had I a foe that hated me to dead" [89], for instance, remains close to its original, the 1560 text of "Si j'avois un hayneux qui me voulust le mort"; yet here too a few modifications have significant implications for the effect. This is clearly apparent in the octave:

> Si j'avois un hayneux qui me voulust la mort
> Pour me venger de luy je ne voudrois lui faire
> Que regarder les yeus de ma douce contraire,
> Qui si fiers contre moi me font si dur effort.
> Ceste punition, tant son regard est fort,
> Luy seroit peine extréme, & se voudroit deffaire:
> Ny le mesme plaisir ne lui scauroit plus plaire,
> Seulement au trespas seroit son reconfort.[32]

> Had I a foe that hated me to dead
> For my Revenge I wish him no more ill
> Bot to behold hir eyis vhilk ever still
> Ar feirce against me with so sueet a feid.      *feud*
> Hir looks belyve such horrour suld him breid    *immediately*
> His wish wold be his Cative Corps to kill.
> Euen plesurs self could not content his will
> Except the Death no thing culd him remeid.

---

[32] Ronsard, *Œuvres complètes*, ed. Laumonier, 4:171–72.

Montgomerie doubles the intensity of the opening line by converting Ronsard's "hayneux" into a verb and substituting "a foe" as the noun; this idea is then picked up in the reorganisation of ll. 3–4, where "ma douce contraire" is represented by "so sueet a feid", transferring the Petrarchist paradox from the Lady herself to her conduct towards the speaker and emphasising the notion of bitter enmity. Line 4 may also contain one of his very few genuine mistranslations, for "feirce" does not correspond to Ronsard's "fiers" (proud); on the other hand, Montgomerie may have chosen the alliteration (and assonance) of "feirce" and "feid", and may also have found the former word more appropriate to the tone of his sonnet. A more radical shift occurs in the first lines of the second quatrain: where Ronsard's language is somewhat abstract, even slightly euphemistic ("punition", "peine extréme", "se deffaire'), Montgomerie's is much more graphic ("such horrour", "his Cative Corps to kill"). This is his characteristic note, and its effect here is once again to make the pain of the lover's situation much more immediate.

In the sestet, the tonal shift is less radical, but Montgomerie nevertheless makes some significant changes. Most obviously, he extends the initial statement from two lines to three, and this may have to do with the structural demands of the rhyme-scheme. Ronsard's sestet is arranged *ccdede*, and the first couplet is syntactically separate from the rest:

> Le regard monstrueux de la Meduse antique
> Au prix de sien n'est rien que fable poëtique.

Montgomerie, on the other hand, adopts a more common Italian *ccdeed* pattern, and extends the idea with an additional explanatory clause:

> The vgly looks of old MEDUSA's eyis
> Compaird to hirs ar not bot Poets leyis          *lies*
> For hirs exceids them in a sharper sort.

This may seem weaker, but the expansion is compensated for by the double sense of "old Medusa" and by the greater sharpness of "Poets leyis" in comparison with Ronsard's "fable antique". In the concluding triplet, moreover, Montgomerie avoids the repetition of "Meduse", substituting "the Gorgon", and the extended enumeration of the transformations worked by Medusa upon her victims: in the process, he assimilates this idea to the well-established Petrarchist contrariety of fire and ice ("Bot she inflammis and freizis both at anis"). The final line of the Scots completes this increasing concentration with a pithily idiomatic expression:

> To spulzie hairt that Minion maks hir sport.     *despoil*

This is much stronger than Ronsard's "Et si en les tuant vous diriez qu'el' se joue": "spulzie" goes back to the feud imagery of the octave, while "Minion" is a complex word whose contemptuous connotations are here very close to the surface. The final effect, then, is of a steady intensification of the emotional quality of the French original.

In "Ha! lytill dog" [83], Montgomerie's rendition of the 1560 version of Ronsard's "Ha, petit chien", the same interplay of creative transformation is at work. Here Montgomerie seems to be at pains to avoid the repetitions which are a keynote of the French: the recurrence of "dommage" and "ennuis" as rhyme-words in ll. 9–10 and 13–14 has no parallel in the Scots, and the translator similarly omits the repetition of "chetif" (ll. 5 and 12) and "las!" (ll. 5 and 7). Other little touches, such as the more physical "thou crap" [crept] to describe the dog's proximity to his mistress in the opening line, the addition of "secreit" in l. 3, and the promotion of "Bot I" to emphasise the contrast between the dog's situation and that of the speaker at the beginning of the second quatrain, add to the effectiveness of the Scots version, but it is in the sestet that the most substantial modifications are to be found:

> Mon trop d'esprit qui cause mon dommage
> Ne comprendroit, comme il fait, mes ennuis
> Béche à la vigne, ou fagotte au bocage!
> Je ne serois chetif comme je suis,
> Le trop d'esprit ne me seroit dommage,
> Et ne pourrois comprendre mes ennuis.[33]

> Vhy haif I not, O God, als blunt a braine
> As he that daylie worbleth in the wyne                     *wallows*
> Or to mak faggots for his fuid is fane?
> Lyk as I do I suld not die and duyn.
> My pregnant spreit the hurter of my harte
> Lyk as it does suld not persave my smarte.

Taking a hint from Ronsard's "béche à la vigne, ou fagotte au bocage", highly colloquial by the standards of the Pléiade, Montgomerie here breaks into a diction we associate more with his personal complaints than with his amatory verse. The alliterative phrase "als blunt a braine", indeed, echoes one of his sonnets to Robert Hudson, and it is possible that the whole passage recalls the negative view of rustic fare we find in that sequence. "Worbleth in the wyne" is an effective transformation of the first part of Ronsard's line; it is possible that Montgomerie misunderstood "fagotte au bocage", since "[se] fagoter" [to dress like a scarecrow] is a comparatively rare word, but if so he produces an inspired mistranslation. Ignored by *OED* and *DOST*, his use of "faggots" antedates the earliest attestation (from Henry Mayhew)

---

[33] Ronsard, *Œuvres complètes*, ed. Laumonier, 7:156.

by 250 years, and captures graphically the courtier's contempt for such a crude rustic sausage. This interpolation of vivid colloquial language, violating the stylistic conventions of Petrarchist verse, again intensifies the articulation of the lover's misery, a process which is continued in the final three lines with more alliteration, the hysteron proteron of "die and duyn", and the balanced anaphora of "Lyk as I do . . . Lyk as it does". Once again, Montgomerie's translation subtly shifts the emphasis of his French original, sharpening the emotional expression while faithfully maintaining the structure of Ronsard's argument.

The two remaining translations from Ronsard present, as we noted at the outset of this study, an important textual problem, since they are grouped in the Ker manuscript with a sonnet which seems unquestionably to be by Henry Constable.[34] The safest course appears to be to assume that this sequence is a scribal creation, and that "Bricht Amorous Ee vhare Love in ambush lyes" [77.I] and "So suete a Kis yistrene fra thee I reft" [77.III] were originally separate poems. The former is a comparatively free rendition of Ronsard's "Œuil, qui portrait dedans les miens reposes"; Montgomerie's radical reorganisation of the structure ensures that the effect is quite different. In the French, the invocation of each of the four aspects of the Lady which will be gathered up in the final line ("Un œuil, un ris, une larme, une main") is given two lines of the octave. Montgomerie, who names five attributes ("Ane ee, a teir, a sigh, a voce, a hand"), compresses the initial reference to each into a single line, making room not for a more extended assertion of the lover's devotion in the same vein as Ronsard, but for another version of the legal conceit he employs in "Hir brouis tuo bouis":

> I challenge you, the causers of my smarte,
> As homiceids and murtherers of my harte
> In Resones Court to suffer ane assyse.
> Bot oh I fear, yea rather wot I weill,
> To be repledg't ye plainly will appeill          *redeemed*
> To Love vhom Resone never culd command.
> (77.III: 6–11)

The opposition of the courts of Reason and Love, with the Lady's attributes refusing the jurisdiction of the former, is a much more clearly focused application of legal terminology than we find in Ronsard, emphasising once again the irrational power of desire and picking up Montgomerie's introduction of the idea of ambush into the opening line. There is little hint here of the langorous emotion of Ronsard's sonnet, rather a concentrated expression of pain and regret which is characteristic of Montgomerie's Neo-petrarchist reinscription of Pléiade poetics.

---

[34] See above.

In translating Ronsard's "Hyer au soir que je pris maugré toy", Montgomerie was confronted with a more fundamental question, since the French original he employed comprised twenty lines rather than the usual fourteen.[35] His solution is, on the whole, to follow his model on a quatrain-by-quatrain basis for the first twelve lines, and then to compress Ronsard's final eight lines into his couplet; to say this, however, is to do less than justice to the subtle modifications to the sense and tone which he makes along the way. As we have noted in previous examples, this begins in the opening line, where Montgomerie moves the kiss itself into the first phrase, and then renders Ronsard's somewhat euphemistic "je pris maugré toy" with the much more forceful "fra the I reft".[36] This note is continued into the following line, where the sense of physical actuality and movement gives much greater eroticism to Montgomerie's "In bouing down thy body on the bed". But the Scots goes beyond the French in another respect as well: where Ronsard's lover loses first his soul and then his heart through the medium of the kiss, Montgomerie's speaker loses life, spirit, and heart, emphasising the point by observing that "So thou hes keepit Captive all the thrie" (III: 11). Here, again, Montgomerie is faithful to the spirit of his original, but his mastery of the technical possibilities of Scots verse ensures that his version is an effective recreation, the final sharpness of which is defined by the pithiness of the couplet, which contrasts with the relative diffuseness of Ronsard's last eight lines:

Except thy breath thare places had suppleit
Euen in thyn armes thair doutles had I deit.

In his translations of Ronsard, Montgomerie can be seen adapting the work of a near-contemporary to his own rhetorical requirements. Where he chooses models from a generation earlier, in the verse of Clément Marot, we can see even more clearly that he is never a passive conductor of the materials he is working with. In both "A bony No" [47], translated from Marot's epigram "De Ouy et Nenny", and in "The Elegie" [52], a Scots version of the French poet's Élégie III, we find Montgomerie modifying, and in some respects developing, his source in order to give the Scottish text a distinctive emphasis. In the case of "De Ouy et Nenny", Shire remarks upon the way in which "Montgomerie skilfully translated Marot's

---

[35] As Jack points out (*Montgomerie*, 83), the Scots version is based upon the twenty-line poem which first appeared in Ronsard's *Nouvelle Continuation des Amours* in 1556, and not the longer form first published in 1578, beginning "Harsoir, Marie, en prenant maugré toy", as Shire suggested (*Song, Dance and Poetry*, 157).

[36] The data collected by *DOST* suggests that the notion of spoliation is strongly present in the verb "to refe" in the sixteenth century; Montgomerie's is one of only two occurrences of the word in this (supposedly) weakened sense.

words to match the four-part music [of Orlando de Lassus] and also wittily 'contin-
ued' the poem for a couple of eight-line stanzas",[37] but she does not further explore
the nature of the wit involved; Jack, while noting verbal substitutions which give
Montgomerie's version "a less courtly context" than Marot's, observes that

> this is imitation of the closest kind. The "invention" lies in Montgomerie
> having composed two additional stanzas, the first explaining the lover's
> motivations and the second converting particular experience into proverbial
> advice for all — "Flie whylome love, and it will follow the".[38]

This is all true enough, but Montgomerie's transpositions are more radical than
either Shire or Jack concedes, and they are most clearly intelligible as part of a
complex shift of cultural reference across both space and time. They convert an
eight-line epigram into a lyric of three stanzas, and in the process Montgomerie
submerges Marot's playfulness in a more serious articulation of the paradoxical
nature of love. The French poet, we should observe, does not mention love at all:

> Ung doulz Nenny avec ung doulx soubzrire
> Est tant honneste; il le vous fault apprendre.
> Quant est d'Ouy, si veniez a le dire,
> D'avoir trop dit je vouldrois vous reprendre;
> Non que je soys ennuye d'entreprendre
> D'avoir le fruict don't le desir me poingt;
> Mais je vouldrois qu'en le me laissant prendre
> Vous me dissiez: non, vous ne l'aurez point![39]

There is, at least at first sight, something slightly queasy about both this and Mont-
gomerie's translation of it: one would not need to push either text very far to find in
it a rapist's charter. But such a reading would miss the playfulness inherent in the
conceit; Marot's speaker seems initially to advocate rejection of his advances, and
it is only in the light of his subsequent argument that we recognise the significance
of the repeated "doulx" in the opening line. The whole epigram is built around
this pretended lesson, but it is also built around the persona himself, whose sexual
preferences — quite strongly signalled by "dont le desir me poingt" — are at least
as much the centre of our attention as the conduct urged upon his *amye*. And that
conduct is, of course, pretended resistance; it is the appearance of opposition that
turns the speaker on.

---

[37] Shire, *Song, Dance and Poetry*, 141.
[38] Jack, *Montgomerie*, 42–43.
[39] Marot, *Œuvres complètes*, ed. Mayer, 5:149.

While Montgomerie takes over this idea and makes it more explicit, urging his female addressee to "let me tak it, fenyeing to refuse" (1. 8), this is by no means the end-point of his lyric. It is not merely the expansion of the original which points the way towards his more serious purposes. The fruit which is unambiguously desired by Marot's speaker becomes for Montgomerie that which "curage ocht to chuse" (1. 6 [my italics]), leaving the speaker's own feelings less certain; this evasion is perhaps linked with the deletion of the lady's own words in the final line of the first stanza, remarked upon by Jack. On the other hand, there is no doubt that Montgomerie's version is once again more physical than his source, especially in the use of "warsill" [wrestle] (1. 9) to describe the lady's desired resistance. It is also more vivid in its application of imagery (Marot's epigram is wholly literal) and in its repeated patterns of idiomatic language and proverbs. This latter element, in particular, reinforced by the alliteration which is characteristic both of proverbial utterance and of Montgomerie's rhetorical practice, indicates the widening of instructive purpose from self-interest to a somewhat perverse kind of moral instruction.

But while the "tutelary" intention behind Montgomerie's extension of Marot's argument is clearly inscribed, its tone is much more elusive. There is a hint of this in the final line of the second stanza ("And quickins curage fra becoming cald"): whereas the "curage" has so far been fairly unconditional, there is a suggestion here that the lover's enthusiasm may diminish if he is too easily gratified. This neatly prepares the way for the shift at the beginning of the third stanza to the lady's point of view: "Wald ye be made of, ye man mak it nyce" [rare and/or haughty]. The focus thus changes from the interests of the lover to those of his addressee(s).[40] There is a strong note of cynicism in the lines which follow, and a piquant ambiguity about where we should locate the "heir" of 1. 18: does the speaker mean in this world, or more specifically in the court environment? Either way, the generalised advice of the final stanza presents the paradox of love, deftly reinforcing a conventional theme, as a problem facing all those who would be loved (a female characteristic, it would seem, according to the poet's assumptions). By a further sleight of hand, the wooer has now become plural: "len thame ay your eir" (21). By means of this final stanza, Marot's brazenly self-interested epigram has become something much more equivocal: still a half-serious wooing poem, no doubt, but one in which there is at least a hint of ironic distance between the view we are given of the posture adopted by the speaker and the underlying social realities of a sophisticated but cynical court.

---

[40] "Ye" can, of course, be either singular or plural; there is no manuscript authority for the title ("An Admonitioun to Young Lassis") assigned to the poem by Cranstoun, and it is unclear whether one woman is being addressed or several.

If the extension of Marot's argument in "De Ouy et Nenny" brings new complexities, Montgomerie's translation of Élégie III presents subtler analytical problems. In the former case, we have argued, the differences are generic and structural, enabling the translator to turn a clever rhetorical ploy to a purpose other than that he found in his source. With "The Elegie", he follows quite closely the form of Marot's argument, remaining firmly within the generic structure of sixteenth-century elegy; both poems are in this respect reflections of the Ovidian tradition which runs so persistently through Renaissance verse.[41] The transformation which Montgomerie achieves in translating the Élégie III comes through an accumulation of relatively minor details rather than through a grand design, but the changes are nevertheless substantial. Underlying all these small modifications is Montgomerie's substitution for Marot's couplets of a more complex interlocking rhyme scheme (closely related to the so-called 'Spenserian' sonnet), which anticipates and echoes each couplet as it occurs: *ababbcbccdcdded*. Many of the little expansions in the Scots version stem from this structural difference; but that does not explain the particular rhetorical motivations which are at work. It is simply inadequate to describes this process, as Jack does, in terms of "seventeen additional lines". Let us take, for example, the openings of the two poems:

> Puis que le jour de mon despart arrive,
> C'est bien raison que ma main vous escrive
> Ce que ne puis vous dire sans tristesse.
> C'est assavoir: or Adieu, ma Maistresse!
> Doncques Adieu, ma Maistresse honnorée.
> Jusque au retour, dont trop la demourée
> Me tardera; toutesfois cependant
> Il vous plaira garder ung cueur ardant
> Que je vous laisse au partir pour hostage,
> Ne demandant pour luy aultre advantage
> For que vueillez contre ceulx le deffendre
> Qui par desir vouldront sa place prendre.
>    (1–12)[42]

---

[41] For discussion of the influence of Ovid in the early modern period, see Caroline Jameson, "Ovid in the Sixteenth Century", in *Ovid*, ed. J.W. Binns (London: Routledge, 1973), 210–42, and Richard F. Hardin, "Ovid in Seventeenth-Century England", *Comparative Literature* 24 (1972): 44–62. Ovid's influence on the development of the elegy, and on the structure of Marot's *Élégies* in particular, is considered by C.M. Scollen, *The Birth of the Elegy in France, 1500–1550* (Geneva: Droz, 1967), 17–48; cf. also Jonathan Bate, *Shakespeare and Ovid* (Oxford: Clarendon Press, 1993), esp. 1–47; and below, 261–67.

[42] Marot, *Œuvres complètes*, ed. Mayer, 3:220.

Now SINCE the day of our depairt appeirs
Guid Resone wald my hand to you suld wryt
That vhilk I can not weill expres but teirs
Videlicet, adeu my Lady vhyt,
Adeu my Love, my lyking and delyt
Till I returne for vhilk I think so lang
That Absence els does all my bouells byt,                    *bowels*
Sik gredie grippis I feell befor I gang.                     *pangs; go*
Resave vhill than A harte lyk for to mang                    *become frantic*
Quhilk freats and fryis in furious flammis of fyre.          *gnaws*
Keep it in gage, bot let it haif no wrang
Of sik as may perhaps his place desyre.
    (52: 1–12)

The two passages are of the same length, but their effects are quite distinct. Marot here exemplifies to the letter Stephen Minta's observation that "love poetry in France tended to be irredeemably abstract in its attitudes until the advent of the Pléiade";[43] while Montgomerie chooses to concretise the images wherever he can. Perhaps the intervening influence of the Pléiade is partly responsible, but some at least of this transformation is surely due to the nature of the Scots lyric tradition, which often prefers concrete imagery, reinforced by such phonaesthetic devices as alliteration.

Where Marot's lover cannot speak "sans tristesse", therefore, Montgomerie's cannot express his grief "but teirs"; and the latter's lady is given a more physical, albeit conventional, presence in the poem through the epithet "vhyt". Where Marot urges his mistress to guard "ung cueur ardant", Montgomerie's heart is "lyk for to mang" — the verb is as vivid as it is colloquial. But these transformations are not unmotivated, nor are they explicable only in terms of a transposition from French rhetorical norms to those of Older Scots: they contribute to a consistent raising of the emotional temperature which is fully manifested in the alliterative bluntness of ll. 7–8, nothing of which is called for by Marot's relatively mild "dont trop la demourée me tardera". Even more remarkable is l. 10, evoked, no doubt, by the literal associations of "ardant", but taking off onto another plane of alliterating misery. Throughout the poem, in fact, Montgomerie seems once again to be at pains to dramatise his speaker's unhappiness to a much greater degree than his original; this is a feature of his aesthetic values which we have repeatedly encountered in his amatory verse, and it is at least partly attributable to the poetic sensibilities which had been developed by the poets of the Pléiade and their successors of the 1570s.

---

[43] Stephen Minta, *Love Poetry in Sixteenth-Century France* (Manchester: Manchester University Press, 1977), 19.

An unobtrusive modification to the opening line leads in a rather different direction, for Marot's "mon despart" has become "our depairt". Even more significantly, "ce despart" in Marot's ll. 21 and 59 will likewise be transformed into "our depairt". The second is clearly more personal; what all three changes do, however, is to emphasise the reciprocity of the separation. There is perhaps a link here with the expansion of the epigram "De Ouy et Nenny", where Montgomerie's attention shifts from the interests of the lover(s) to those of the object(s) of his/their desire: no comparable structural change occurs in "The Elegie" but we have a greater sense than in the original of the effects of the impending separation on both partners, even if the rhetorical expression of this is constantly mediated through the (male) persona. It is as if the lover's pain is seen reflected in the lady's reactions, a corollary of the way in which she is reflected in his heart.

This is perhaps part of the explanation of Montgomerie's expanded version of one of Marot's more elaborate rhetorical flourishes:

> Que pleust a Dieu qu'en ce cueur puissiez lire;
> Vous y pourriez milles choses eslire
> Vous y verriez vostre face au vif paincte;
> Vous y verriez ma loyaulté empraincte;
> Vous y verriez vostre nom engravé
> Avec le dueil qui me tient aggravé
> Pour ce despart; & en voiant ma peine,
> Certes, je croy (& ma foy n'est point vaine)
> Qu'en souffririez pour le moins la moytié,
> Par le moien de la nostre amytié,
> Qui veult aussi que le moitié je sente
> Du dueil qu'aurez d'estre de moy absente.
> (15–26)

> Oh! wold to god ye might behold this harte
> Quharin a thousand things ye suld advert.
> Thair suld ye sie the wound vhilk ye it gaiv,
> Thair suld ye sie the goldin deadly darte,
> Thair suld ye sie hou ye bereft it haiv,
> Thair suld ye sie your Image by the laiv,       *among the rest*
> Thair suld ye sie your hevinly Angels face,
> Thair suld ye soon my permanence persaiv,
> Thair suld ye sie your Name haif only place,
> Thair suld ye sie my languishing alace
> For our depart, bot since ye knou my painis
> I hope if ye considder weill the case
> And spyis the teirs vhilks ouer my visage rains
> If in your breist sik sympathie remanis
> Then sall ye suffer som thing for my saik.

> Quhair constant Love is, aluay it constranis
> In weill or wo coequall pairt to take,
> Lyk as my members all begins to quake
> That of your duill the half I do indure                    *sorrow*
> Quhilk I suppone ye for my Absence mak.
>      (16–35)

Montgomerie has, obviously, doubled the anaphora, but that is only a small part of the rewriting that is going on here. Like the exclamatory "Oh!", some of the additions conform to a standard Petrarchist rhetoric: the lady is portrayed, for example, as having "wounded" the speaker's heart with (Cupid's) "goldin deadly darte". Likewise, the process of concretisation of the lover's suffering is continued in the elaboration of Marot's "en voiant ma peine", which extends from l. 26 over the two following lines, reintroducing the tears with which the Scots version began. All of this reinforces our awareness of the lover's plight; but in suppressing the intricate word-play of Marot's ll. 23–25 Montgomerie returns to his theme of reciprocity, turning the wittiness of the French into a more earnest assertion of the "coequall" sharing of sorrow between true lovers.

In the following passage, we find Montgomerie developing his original in other ways as well. Where Marot assures the lady of her place in his heart (l. 28), the Scots poet, echoing Wyatt, denies the possibility

>              that ony creature
> Can dispossesse you of my hairt, be sure,
> Nor yit remove from you my constant mynd.
>      (36–38)

The emergence of the concept of mind as an affective centre is a striking feature of Wyatt's poetry, reflecting a significant change in sixteenth-century attitudes towards the self. Introduced here in parallel with the more conventionally emotional heart, it perhaps suggests a more comprehensive definition of love than that implied by Marot. That the change of emphasis is not merely fortuitous, or the product of the need to set up a rhyme, is indicated by the fact that Montgomerie does the same thing a few lines later, when Marot's "en mon esprit" (l. 34) becomes "Both in my spreit and in my trublit thoght" (l. 48). Other features of the expansion here — the allusion to Cupid, the characterisation of the lady's "sueet behaviour and your hevinly heu", the subsequent evocation of "these lamps of light, these cristall ees" — belong to the poem's Petrarchist register; though again it is noticeable that these additions tend to be much more physical than the passages in Marot's French to which they correspond.

These developments occur, very largely, within the conceit of a dialogue between the lover and his eye (Marot, ll. 40–54; Montgomerie, ll. 55–69). But this gives way in both versions to the poem's most important tonal shift, from grief at parting to anxiety about the future of the lady's affections while the lover is absent. There is a rhetorical problem here: how is the possibility of the lady's in-fidelity to be broached without giving offence? The answer, of course, is to blame Cupid. The argument is fully developed in Marot, but Montgomerie gives it additional force by again making the language more explicit:

> Et puis j'ay peur (quand de vous je suis loing)
> Que ce pendant Amour ne prenne soing
> De desbander ses deux aveuglez yeux
> Pour contempler les vostres gracieux;
> Si qu'en voyant chose tant singuliere
> Ne prenne en vous amytié familiere;
> Et qu'il ne m'oste, à l'aise et en ung jour,
> Ce que j'ay eu en peine et long sejour.
>   (55–62)

> And than I think vhen I am far auay
> Leist that mein tyme blind Love suld thus assay
> All meins he micht by craft or yit ingyne
> To open vp his blindit ees that they
> Might clerelie see these gratious ees of thyn
> And so beholding sik a sight divyn,
> His mynd to love the shortly suld be mov'd
> And caus me at ane instant for to tyne      *lose*
> The thing quhilk I sa lang and leall haif lov'd.      *loyally*
>   (72–80)

The translation is very close; but even here there are subtle nudgings of the sense. Montgomerie doubles the allusion to Cupid's blindness, and emphasises the danger he represents (softening the imputation against the lady in the process) by alluding to his "craft or yit ingyne". Marot's "amytié familiere", perhaps, implies a certain complicity on the part of the mistress; but in Montgomerie's version all the emphasis is on Cupid's behaviour. Significantly, "mynd" recurs as the seat of love, echoing the earlier engagement of the speaker's mind.

For Montgomerie, even more than for Marot, this brings the persona to the nub of his argument:

> Certainement, si bien ferme vous n'estes,
> Amour vaincra voz responses honnestes,
> Amour est fin, et sa parole farde
> Pour mieulx tromper; donnez vous en doncq garde;
> Car en sa bouche il n'y a rien que Miel,
> Mais en son cueur il n'y a rien que Fiel.

Si vous promect et s'il vous faict le doulx,
Respondez luy: Amour, retirez vous!
   J'en ay choysi ung qui en mainte sorte
Merite bien que dehors moy ne sorte.
   (63–72)

Be ye not constant vhen ye sall be prov'd,
Love sall ou'rcome your onest ansueirs all          *honest*
That ye sall think to yeild it you behov'd.
Love is so slie vhais fairdit language sall         *painted*
Peirce and get entrie throu a stony wall.
I wish you thairfor with him to be war
His mouth is hony, bot his hairt is gall.
On kitlest huiks the sliest baits they are.       *most delicate hooks;*
If he the heght or slielie drau the nar          *most subtle*
Thou ansueir him "Go Love, reteir the hence
For I Love one vho hes my hairt so far
He merits not to tyne him but offence".
   (81–92)

As so often with Montgomerie, proverbial language is invoked to clinch the point, and the notion of "slieness", initially introduced as a translation of "fin" and then developed through the image of the baited hook, is redoubled in the transformation of "s'il vous faict le doulx" into "slielie drau the nar". Montgomerie makes room for this metaphoric play, and for the even more graphic imagery of l. 85, by compressing Marot's one real metaphor, based on the "miel/fiel" rhyme, into a single line. The effect is much more pungent, and the whole tone of Montgomerie's version is more pointed than that of the French. And with good reason, for this is the end of the Scots poem. Montgomerie seems not to have translated Marot's last sixteen lines, in which the speaker declares that he would reject the advances of Helen or Venus themselves were they to appear naked before him. Whether it was the classical rhetoric of these final lines or the reciprocity of fidelity that they assert which led him to reject them can only be a matter for speculation; the latter would be surprising in view of the evidence we have found elsewhere in his translation of a development of the notion of mutual separation. What is clear is that the end of "The Elegie" leaves us very firmly with the lady's imagined rejection of Cupid's advances and her defence of the lover. Where Marot ends with the confident affirmation of "nostre heureuse vie", Montgomerie concentrates on his own anxious injunction to the lady. The result is a greater sense of uncertainty, in which the projected words of dismissal do not quite convince us — or, perhaps, the lover. The threat of betrayal continues to lurk somewhere just beneath the surface of the words. In both these translations from Marot, then, we can see evidence of the multiple ambiguities which are characteristic of Montgomerie's techniques, and, perhaps, of the court poetry of the later sixteenth century.

The emphasis on the legacy of Petrarchism in the work of Montgomerie and his contemporaries has tended to obscure other influences. Little attention has been paid, for example, to the Ovidian strain in Montgomerie's verse, and this is all the more regrettable since not only does the author of the *Metamorphoses* provide his Scottish imitator with material for some of his most effective lyrics, but Montgomerie is arguably among the finest of sixteenth-century adaptors of Ovid's verse. Perhaps it is in part the fact that his rhetoric is only intermittently narrative, and the demands of the musical stanzas which he employs, which enable Montgomerie to capture what C.S. Lewis called Ovid's "neatness, his pert dexterity",[44] but there should be no mistaking the skill with which the Scots poet adapts his source to his own amatory purposes. We cannot be sure, of course, that he was working directly from the Latin: Arthur Golding's influential English version of the *Metamorphoses* was published in 1565–1567, and there were several translations, both in prose and verse, into French and other vernaculars, to which he could in principle have had access.[45] There were, certainly, very many editions of the Latin text, by itself and with allegorical *interpretationes*, and of these vernacular versions: James VI, for example, owned at least three different Latin editions.[46] But the specific form in which Montgomerie read the text is less important than the deftness of the adaptation.

The most thoroughly Ovidian of Montgomerie's lyrics is "Quhen first Apollo Python sleu" [23]. It differs from his other applications of the *Metamorphoses* in largely retaining the narrative structure of the original, although the proportions of the account and some of its details are modified to fit the rhetorical intention. Even the opening line, significantly, takes up the story where Ovid does, echoing the narrative link in 1. 438–451 between the figure of Pyrrha and the story of Apollo and Daphne. Elsewhere, we can clearly see the detail of Ovid's version colouring Montgomerie's Scots:

> . . . eque sagittifera prompsit duo tela pharetra
> diversorum operum: fugat hic, facit illud amorem.
> quod facit, auratum est et cuspide fulget acuta:
> quod fugat, obtusum est et habet sub harundine plumbum.

---

[44] C.S. Lewis, *English Literature in the Sixteenth Century, Excluding Drama* (Oxford: Clarendon Press, 1954), 250.

[45] Notable sixteenth-century translations of the *Metamorphoses* include those into Italian by Nicolo di Agostini (1521) and Lodovico Dolce (1553), into French by Clémont Marot (1534–1536, Books I and II) and Barthélemy Aneau (1556, Book III) and François Habert (1574), and into Spanish by Jorge de Bustamante (before 1550), Antonio Perez (1580) and Felipe Mey (1586).

[46] Warner, "The Library of James VI", xxxvii, lxi, lxii.

hoc deus in nympha Peneide fixit, at illo
laesit Apollineas traiecta per ossa medullas.
    (1. 468–473)[47]

His hurt wes with the goldin heid
Quhilk inward in his hairt did bleid.
No medicin micht him remeid                *cure*
    From Cupids angrie yre.
Hirs with the blunted bolt of leid,
Ane hevy mettall, cauld and deid,
Repelling Love as yee may reid,
    And quencher of desyre.
    (33–40)

Yet as close as Montgomerie's organisation of this passage to his original evidently is, echoing for example Ovid's "obtusum" with "blunted", we nevertheless see him nudging the sense in ways which are rhetorically purposeful, motivated by more than the need to find rhymes to fit his demanding *aaabaaabaaabaaab* stanza-form: in the medicinal metaphor there is a manifest trace of Petrarchist language, which quietly points towards the wooing strategy which only becomes explicit in the poem's final stanza.

    A more remarkable manifestation of Petrarchism, moreover, immediately follows:

His pain wes lyk the Pyralide,
A beist in birning that does breid
And in the fyry flammis feid
    And fosters of the fyre.
    (41–44)

The mythical pyralide, as Cranstoun notes, is ultimately attributable to Pliny's *Historia naturalis* (11.42.36 [**119**]), and it is possible that Montgomerie took his image directly from this widespread and frequently-printed work. But it is even more likely that we have further evidence of the influence of the Pléiade, for the myth had been assimilated by Ronsard to the more familiar image of the lover as moth ineluctably drawn to the candle of the lady's beauty, and was taken up by Jean Passerat, Amadis Jamyn, and others.[48] The figure was evidently unexpected

---

[47] Ovid, *Metamorphoses*, ed. and trans. Frank Justus Miller, revised G.P. Goold, 2 vols., 3rd ed., Loeb Classical Library (Cambridge MA and London: Harvard University Press, 1977), 1:34–35. All quotations are from this edition.

[48] For versions of this topos, see Ronsard, "L'astre ascendant", in idem, *Œuvres complètes*, ed. Laumonier, 4 :73–74, *Élégie VII*, 3 :224, etc.; Jean Passerat, "Epithalamium de M. d'Alincourt", in idem, *Poésies françaises*, ed. Prosper Blanchemin (2 vols, Paris: A. Lemerre,

enough for the Scots poet to feel it necessary to define his terms within the text; but in the context it fits, with a characteristic Mannerist flourish, into the language of passion to which Montgomerie is adapting his Ovidian subject. For the purpose of his poem, we eventually discover, is to hold the unfortunate Daphne up as a negative example, a version of the haughty beloved who (unusually, at least in the tradition of *amour courtois* of which Petrarchism is a variant) is in a sense punished for her treatment of the lover.

There is, certainly, an unresolved contradiction in Mongomerie's handling of this application of his narrative, a shift of position so openly declared that it could scarcely have been missed:

> Sho prayd the Gods hir helpers be
> To saif hir pure Virginitie,
> Quha shup hir in a laurell trie            *shaped*
>    As he did hir embrace.
>
> Nou lovesome Lady let vs leir           *learn*
> Example of these ladyis heir,
> Sen Daphne boght hir love so deir,
>    Hir fortun suld effray you.          *frighten*
>    (77–84)

The metamorphosis which is at first made to seem, following Ovid (1. 545–552), quite literally an answer to a maiden's prayer, is itself abruptly transformed into a cautionary tale. This harsh reversal is reinforced, moreover, by the compression with which Montgomerie treats the detail: the five lines with which Ovid describes Daphne's transformation become a single, terse relative clause, and the direct speech of her prayer is turned into a much more clipped, indirect report. This contrasts very obviously with Montgomerie's retention of direct quotation in the case of Apollo's appeal to Daphne, which dominates the stanza. The signals are unmistakable: it is with the male experience that the poet is concerned, and Daphne — the subject, after all, of Ovid's tale — is in this sense little more than a necessary accessory to the action, and to its ironic "moralisation".

Even where the Scots version retains the spirit of the Latin, it is surely because two very different purposes happen to be temporarily aligned:

---

1880), 1:164 ; and Amadis Jamyn, *Les œuvres poétiques*, ed. Carrington, 2: 205. The figure continued to be popular; cf. Jean Bertaut, "Chante nuptial sur la mariage du Roy et de la Royne" [1600], in idem, *Œuvres Poétiques*, ed. Adolphe Chenièvre (Paris: E. Plot, Nourrit et cie., 1898), 48, and "Pour le Ballet des Dames Couronnees de Myrte" [1602], *Recueil de Quelques Vers Amoureux*, ed. Louis Terreaux, STFM (Paris: Hachette, 1970), 239.

spectat inornatos collo pendere capillos,
et 'Quid, sin comantur?' ait, videt igne micantes
sideribus similes oculos; videt oscula, quae non
est vidisse satis; laudat digitosque manusque
bracchiaque et nudos media plus parte lacertos:
siqua latent, meliora putat, fugit ocior aura
illa levi . . .
    (1. 497–503)

About PENNEUS did repair
This noble Nymph of beuty rare
Quhais comely clothing to declare
    My Author does indyt.
Most from the belt vp scho wes bair.
Behind hir hang hir hevinly heir
Vnkamed, hovering in the air,                                   *uncombed*
    Shed from hir visage vhyt,
With blinkis dulce and debonair                                 *sweet*
Lyk Beuties freshest florish fair
Exem'd clene from Loves lair                                     *exempted*
    To work Apollo spyt.
Hir Countenance did move him mair
Quhen throu hir garments heir and thair
Appeirit hir lustie lims square
    As sho ran by him quyt.
    (49–64)

Montgomerie here develops Ovid's fairly delicate eroticism, changing the bareness of Daphne's arms into a more general nudity and teasing the reader (by echoing lines 527–530 of the Latin text) with a glimpse of her "lustie lims square". But the general purpose of the description remains unaltered, and Montgomerie presumably retains it both as a form of indirect compliment to the physical attractions of the lady, and as a reflection of the male subjectivity which is the dominant dimension of his poem.

The final stanza, as we have seen, transforms the Daphne narrative by making it an object-lesson in the hazards of standoffishness. But Montgomerie further shifts his argument by introducing another Ovidian theme:

Then lyk Penelope appeir
Quha wes so constant tuenty yeir
Quhen your Vlysses is not neir.
    Tentation may assay you,
Yit vary not I you requeir,
And I sall stoppe Vlysses eir.
    (89–94)

The exhortation to be Penelope rather than Daphne is an obvious enough negotiating ploy; what is perhaps more revealing is the poet's allusion to the potential susceptibility of Ulysses to the siren-song of Circe. Like the speaker in "The Elegie", he is willing to offer his lady an exchange of fidelity, provided she dissociates herself from the rejectionist posture of a Daphne. This deployment of Ovidian narrative is, then, a sophisticated wooing-game, a careful selection of material from the *Metamorphoses* which does not seek to disguise the rewriting of its model which is an essential feature of the poet's strategy.

Montgomerie's Ovidianism is no less wittily contrived in "Lyk as Aglauros" [30], where stories from Ovid's *Metamorphoses* and from Apuleius' *Asinus aureus* (also known as *Metamorphoses*) are welded into an elaborate opening conceit:

> Lyk as Aglauros, curious to knau
> Vhat Mercurie inclosit within the creell          *basket*
> (Suppose defendit), ceist not till sho sau
> The serpent chyld that Juno causit to steell,
> Quhilk to hir sisters willing to reveill
> Or sho wes war evin with the word, anone
> Sho wes transformit in a marble stone,
>
> Or as Psyches (by her Mother mov'd
> Hir sleeping Cupid secreitly to sie)
> Resav'd the lamp to look him vhom sho lov'd
> Quhais hevenly beautie blind't hir amorous ee
> That sho foryet to close the Lamp till he          *forgot*
> In wrath auok and fleu scho wist not vhair          *awoke*
> And left his deing Lover in dispair,
>
> Even so am I.
>      (1–15)

The sharp contrast between the extended syntax of the first two rhyme royal stanzas and the four words which clinch the comparison is skilfully achieved: six clauses describe the folly and fate of Aglauros, no fewer than eight that of Psyche. The careful attention to structure is reminiscent of sonnet technique; but whereas the essence of the sonnetteer's skill lies in compression, here Montgomerie is able to extend his argument to fill the larger compass of his stanzas. The key to the contrivance lies in the image of sight, which binds together the two Classical narratives and which runs through the rest of Montgomerie's lyric. The first stanza skilfully compresses two related narratives into a single episode: in Ovid, Aglauros is turned to stone not for her violation of the divine instruction not to open the chest containing the infant Erichthonius (*Met.*, 2. 553–561), but because of her jealous interference in her sister Herse's affair with Mercury (2. 708–832). It is important to Montgomerie's rhetorical purpose that he suppresses this latter part of the story, since its effect in Ovid is to alienate any sympathy we have for Aglauros; she is, after all, an object of identification for the suffering persona here, and this is only explicable if she is seen as a rash but essentially innocent transgressor against divine ordinance. This subtle balance is neatly established by Montgomerie's opening "curious", which reflects comparatively favourably both upon Aglauros' disobedience and upon the "crime" against Cupid for which we shall soon find the speaker to be suffering such misery.

If this is a judicious selection of details from Ovid's account of Aglauros, Montgomerie's handling of Apuleius's story of Cupid and Psyche (4. 28–6. 24) is still more radical. In Apuleius's version it is Psyche's sisters who persuade her to defy her lover's instructions by looking at him by lamplight (5. 20–24), and this episode merely forms part of a much longer romantic narrative which culminates in the marriage of the lovers despite the opposition of Venus. Montgomerie's substitution of the mother for the sisters may simply indicate that he did not know the story at first hand, whether in Latin or in one of the numerous vernacular translations which were published in the course of the sixteenth century.[49] But again the sense of the episode is nuanced to suit the poet's purpose: not only does he emphasise the role of the mother as instigator, but he makes Psyche more passive by having her "receive" the lamp with which she breaks her promise to leave the darkness undisturbed. Nor is there any suggestion in Apuleius's account that Psyche, distraught as she is at Cupid's departure, is in any danger of death. Montgomerie is intent on leading us towards his speaker's own condition, and his reworking of both classical narratives is evidently calculated to emphasise the desperate nature of his plight and the limited degree of his guilt. The 'confession' that he has brought his suffering upon himself by foolishly enslaving himself to a beautiful but unresponsive mistress is, of course, one of the most standard gambits in the tradition of amatory verse, and the rest of the poem fails to live up to the rhetorical sophistication of its opening. The use of Aglauros and Psyche, on the other hand, shows how deft Montgomerie can be when classical narrative provides him with an alternative to the unmediated rhetoric of complaint.

Elsewhere, such material is introduced incidentally, and not necessarily at first hand: in the song "In throu the windoes of myn ees" [28], for example, we have a passing reference to the myth of Theseus and Ariadne:

> Micht I my Ariadne move
> To lend hir Theseus a threed
> Hir leilest lover for to leed

---

[49] The principal translations are those (into French) by Guillaume Michel (1518), Georges de la Bouthière (1553) and Jean Louveau (1553); and (into English) by W. Adlington (1566). See also Julia Haig Gaisser, "Allegorizing Apuleius", in *Acta Conventus Neo-Latini Cantabrigiensis*, ed. R. Schnur, MRTS, forthcoming.

> Out of the Laberinth of love
> Then wer I out of dout of deed,
>     (45–49)

and we have already noted the use of the Icarus legend in the group of sonnets entitled "To The For Me".[50] Such moves are characteristic of the late Petrarchist tradition, and they illustrate the extent to which Ovidian materials permeated sixteenth-century culture, rather than Montgomerie's distinctive rhetorical skills.

We have largely concentrated in this chapter upon Montgomerie's achievement as an adaptor, of Petrarchist materials generally and of the works of Ronsard, Marot, and Ovid in particular. At some points, the evidence we have considered reveals that he was in touch with the most current developments in French courtly verse, with the writing of Desportes, Amadis Jamyn, and their contemporaries in the salons of Paris in the 1570s. In some of his stanzaic lyrics, however, Montgomerie shows himself to be not merely a skilful manipulator of such fashionable conventions, not only a brilliant harmoniser of words and music, but also an innovative artist whose language and imagery are pressing beyond the boundaries of conventional discourse, moving him in the same direction as some of the most radical of his Continental, and English, contemporaries. This is true even of a piece as apparently traditional as "Lyk as the dum solsequium" [**21**], which has been justifiably praised for its graceful use of a French tune,[51] but which is also notable for the wit with which Montgomerie turns the central conceit towards the end. In some ways, we can again see in this stanzaic poem the same architectural principles that we commonly find in the sonnet: the first two stanzas, in particular, fulfil the same structural role that we often encounter in the two quatrains of an octave, the "Lyk as . . . so" pattern signalling the two elements of the conceit. The whole poem, obviously, is built upon the relationship between the sun and the flower which relies upon it for life, with the poet hyperbolically exploiting all the emotional possibilities of the music in his Petrarchist declaration of the consequences of the lady's departure:

> Fra sho depairts
> Ten thousand dairts
> In syndrie airts
> Thirlis throu my hevy hart but rest or rove.     *pierces; relief*
>     My Countenance declairs
>         My inward grief.
>     Good hope almaist dispairs
>         To find relief.
>     (23–30)

---

[50] See above, 238–39.
[51] Shire, *Song, Dance and Poetry*, 142–44.

The comparison between the lady and the sun is among the most conventional of Petrarchist conceits (underlying, for instance, the frequently recurring image of the phoenix), and at this stage of Montgomerie's version it is principally the intricacy of the metrical form which separates his lyric from dozens of Italian and French sonnets on the same theme.

Deftly, however, Montgomerie switches in his third stanza from simile to metaphor, at the same time giving a more positive — and less conventional — emphasis to his emotions:

>           No wo vhen I aualk
>               May me impesh                         *hinder*
>           Bot on my staitly stalk
>               I florish fresh.
>       I spring, I sprout,
>       My leivis ly out,
>   My colour changes in ane hartsum heu.
>           No more I lout
>           Bot stands vp stout
>   As glade of hir for vhom I only greu.
>       (45–54)

There is a certain whimsical quality to the lover's self-representation here, which is not undermined by the fairly clear sexual connotations of "stands vp stout" (which neatly reverse the slighter hint given by the drooping flower at ll. 5–8). This lightening of the tone corresponds to the improvement in the persona's frame of mind as a result of the lady's return, an event which seems to portray, unusually in Montgomerie, a love relationship whose parameters are not merely rejection and despair. The poem becomes a kind of anti-aubade, in which the return of the sun, interpreted metaphorically rather than literally, signifies the celebration of joyful love.

This perception leads the persona, in an apostrophe which connects interestingly with that in Donne's "The Sun Rising", to make a direct appeal to his "Apollo":

>       O happie day
>       Go not auay.
>       Apollo stay
>   Thy Chair from going doun into the West.
>           Of me thou mak
>           Thy Zodiak
>           That I may tak
>   My plesur to behold vhom I love best.
>       (55–62)

The difference between this poem and Donne's, of course, is that the sun here is in no sense literal: whereas for the English poet the literal presence of the sun heralds his separation from his mistress, for Montgomerie it is the metaphorical setting of "his" sun which brings separation. What the poems share is a playful focussing of the cosmological imagery upon the lovers' situation; rhetorically and tonally, Montgomerie is less subversive of amatory convention than Donne, but his reversal of the aubade nevertheless reflects a desire to move beyond the limits of conventional verse. His protagonist's aspirations are also less arrogant than Donne's: the restructuring of the Ptolemaic universe he proposes is, as he immediately recognises, impossible, and the song ends on a note of resignation which is, by Montgomerie's standards, surprisingly low-key:

> I wish in vane
> The to remane
> Sen Primum mobile sayis aluayis nay.
> At leist thy wanewagon
> Turn soon agane.
> Fareweill with patience perforce till day.
> (67–72)

Elegant compliment ultimately prevails, but the wit with which Montgomerie develops the implications of his conceit makes "Lyk as the dum solsequium" one of his most delicately nuanced explorations of amatory convention.

Similar processes can be seen at work in "Melancholie, grit deput of Dispair" [34], which is, on the face of it, a thoroughly conventional, musically elegant song (perhaps, as Shire argues, a dance-song).[52] It reworks the familiar amatory psychomachia with Melancholie and his forces besieging the castle of Plesur in a stately, formal confrontation whose numerous antecedents include not only Dunbar's *Goldyn Targe* but an influential sonnet in Petrarch's *Canzoniere*:

> Amor, che nel penser mio vive e regna
> e 'l suo seggio maggior nel mio cor tene,
> talor armato ne la fronte vene;
> iva si loca et ivi pon sua insegna.[53]

Even here, Montgomerie strikes a boldly vernacular note:

---

[52] Shire, *Song, Dance and Poetry*, 173–78.

[53] Petrarch, *Canzoniere*, 140, ed. Ugo Dotti, 2 vols. (Rome: Donzelli, 1996), 1:432. This is one of the most frequently translated of Petrarch's sonnets, including English versions by both Wyatt and Surrey.

Thoght RIGOUR then be rekles rash
Yit CURAGE bydis the brash                              *attack*
And then the hairt (vhilk never yeild)
Of CONSTANCIE hes maid his sheild
Quharon thair shaftis and sharpest shottis
Lyk hailstanes aff ane studie stottis.                 *anvil; bounce*
    (23–28)

It is, however, in the second stanza that Montgomerie begins to play, and to play subversively, with his own amatory rhetoric. First, he takes up one of the commonplace *sententiae* of medieval and Renaissance moral lyric:

The rendring reid vhilk bouis with euerie blast        *yielding*
In stormis bot stoupis vhen strongest treis
Are to the ground down cast
Bot yit the rok vhilk firmer is and fast
Amidst the rage of roring seas,
He nevir grouis agast.
The busteous blast he byds                             *rough*
With watring wauis and huge                            *weltering*
Quhilk ramping ouer his rigging ryds                   *raging*
Bot can not caus him budge.
Quhat reks then of the reid
Or of the trees vhat reks?
The Rok remanes a Rok indeid
Quhilk nather bouis nor breks.
    So sall my harte
    With patient parte
            Remane
        A rok all rigour to resist,
    And sall not start
    To suffer smart
            For ane
    Quhom to obey I count me blist.
    (36–57)

The traditional part of this conceit is the opposition of flexible reed and uprooted tree, a proverbial figure much used by medieval homilists and other moral writers and taken up by the emblematists, occurring for example in Geoffrey Whitney's *Choice of Emblemes* (1586).[54] But Montgomerie caps this familiar contrast by adding another, developing the motif of resistance from the first stanza and reversing the usual sense of the topos by setting the rock against the normally superior reed.

---

[54] Geoffrey Whitney, *A Choice of Emblemes* (Leiden: Christopher Plantin, 1586), 220.

If there is a hint of playful hyperbole in this ploy, it is as nothing by comparison with the development of the image of the wounded heart with which the poem ends:

> Yea thoght I had a hundreth thousand hairts
> And euiry hairt peirc't with als mony dairts
> And euirie dairt thairof also
> Als mony shafts and mo,
> And eviry shaft thairof must needs
> To haif als mony heeds
> And euirie head als mony huikis
> And evirie huik als mony fluiks                          *barbs*
> And evirie fluik in me war fast,
> So long as breath of lyf micht last
>     I suld not seme for shame to shrink
>     For hir of death to drink,
>     Quhais Angels ees micht ay, I think,
>         Revive me with a wink.
>     (58–71)

Again, the underlying conceit is familiar enough: the piercing of the lover's heart by Cupid's arrows is one of the most persistent images in medieval and Renaissance love lyric, and we have already noted the importance of the archery metaphor in Montgomerie's poetic repertoire. But here he has carried it into new realms of fantasy, making full use of the repetitive patterns of the music to build a cumulative pattern of hyperbolic rhetoric. The key question is about tone: to what degree does the excessiveness of the speaker's hypothetical argument subvert the Petrarchan conceit upon which it is based? It seems to me to do so quite decisively; while the dance-song background may suggest that the piece is not to be taken too seriously, the playfulness of its inflection of familiar images suggests a degree of witty detachment which might be seen to challenge the Petrarchist norms which the lyric apparently claims to endorse.

This witty, and in part subversive, engagement with Petrarchist convention, which we also see in Shakespeare and Donne, is an important indication of the extent to which aesthetic values were changing at the end of the sixteenth century. The suggestion that Montgomerie participates to some degree in this process is not altogether new: Jack, for example, has pointed to a more "metaphysical" dimension in some of his work, citing "As Natur passis nuriture" [24] and "Ressave this harte" [33].[55] But in making out a case for Montgomerie's poetic radicalism, it is important to be clear about the terms we are using. In seeking to identify a

---

[55] Jack, *Montgomerie*, 53–58.

"philosophical, even metaphysical vein" in "As Natur passis nuriture", for example, Jack draws attention to the multiple ironies with which the poet develops his conceit of the gerfalcon who falls in love with a kite, adding that

> the characters are vividly realised and dramatic asides maintain the audience's involvement throughout. Skilful variation of diction and rhythm also underline the bird's fate.

This is all true, and it properly testifies to Montgomerie's rhetorical accomplishments. But in what sense, if at all, does it represent a break with sixteenth-century poetic practice? "As Natur passis nuriture" is, of course, a fable, though its lyrical form means that Montgomerie departs from the normal pattern of the genre, and perhaps reflects the influence of the emblem tradition, by revealing its moralitas in the opening line, and by repeating it as a refrain. By using birds as tokens for human behaviour, however, the poem remains true to its Aesopic roots, while its argument is less revisionist than "Remembers thou in Aesope of a taill?", the fourth sonnet in the Hudson sequence, where a fable more closely related to the Aesopic tradition than that of the love-smitten hawk is radically reinterpreted in terms of the poet's own circumstances. As a symbolic narrative, "As Natur passis nuriture" is closer to Henryson's *Morall Fabillis* than to Donne's "The Flea"; it harks back, moreover, to a lyric tradition as old as Machaut and Froissart.[56]

For the argument of the poem, too, rests in one sense at least upon traditional foundations. It might almost be a reply to Alexander Scott's "Luve preysis bot comparisone", with its insistence that

> love makis nobill ladeis thrall
> To basser men of birth and blud;
> So luve garis sobir wemen small
> Get maistrice owre greit men of gud.[57]                    *mastery*

But Montgomerie's position is actually more conservative than Scott's: so fixed is the hierarchy, his poem asserts, that "Natur ay prevailis at lenth", ensuring that any attempt to escape one's innate character will inevitably backfire. For Scott, moreover, the insistence upon the capacity of love to transcend nature is ultimately part of a sophisticated wooing-game, while Montgomerie seems to be interested

---

[56] Jean Froissart, *Œuvres: Poésies*, ed. A. Scheler, 3 vols. (Brussels: V. Devaux, 1870–1872), 3 :227–28; Guillaume de Machaut, *Œuvres*, ed. Ernest Hoepffner, 3 vols. (Paris: SATF, 1908–1921), 1:98; 2:225. For these and other French examples of the use of the phrase, cf. James Woodrow Hassell Jr., *Middle French Proverbs, Sentences and Proverbial Phrases* (Toronto: University of Toronto Press, 1982), 174, 177.

[57] Scott, *Poems*, ed. Cranstoun, 26.

primarily in the moral principle he is enunciating. Nothing could be further from that preoccupation with the transitoriness of experience which seems so characteristic of the early seventeenth century: the inconstancy of the kite is, it is true, one of the fundamental elements of the fable, but only in order to reinforce the foolishness of the hawk's conduct. Conscious as he is of the ironies of the situation, Montgomerie does not exploit the contradiction that the kite's inconstancy is the only constant part of her nature, a paradox which surely would not have been lost upon a truly "Metaphysical" poet.

We must be careful, then, in locating the innovative dimension in Montgomerie's verse; and in this respect Jack's blurring of the distinction between "metaphysical" preoccupations (in the sense of philosophical themes) and "Metaphysical" poetry (characteristic of, say, Donne and Herbert) is unhelpful. The witty subversion of Petrarchist themes we have noted in "Melancholie grit deput of Despair" and, to a degree, in "Lyk as the dum solsequium" does, on the other hand, suggest an awareness on Montgomerie's part of the exhaustion of the tradition and a need to develop, at least in certain contexts, an alternative mode of discourse. In a handful of other cases, he goes further, pushing Petrarchist language to extremes which we can legitimately call "Baroque", or stepping outside the conventional framework altogether. Sometimes this does not extend beyond a striking use of imagery, as in "Quhy bene ye Musis all so long" (40), where Sarah Dunnigan has recently drawn attention to the "remarkable, almost baroque conceit of visual beauty drawn from the image of the lover's veins":

> Out throu hir snauie skin
> Maist cleirlie kythes within
> Hir saphir veins lyk threids of silk
> Or Violets in vhytest milk.
>   If Natur sheu
>   Hir hevinly heu
>   In vhyt and bleu
>     It wes that ilk.
>     (53–60)

Dunnigan is surely right to see in this a brilliant variation on the conventional description of the lady's beauty in terms of red and white;[58] but what is most notable here is the extraordinary sensuous combination of lapidary imagery, the idea of silken threads, and that of violets in milk. Fully five stanzas are devoted to such elaborate evocation of female loveliness, and this is all the more striking because a passing reference to Hymen at l. 68 indicates that this is again an epithalamial celebration which only purports to present the poet's own passion. In

---

[58] Dunnigan, "Female Gifts", 64.

this light, the metaphorical extremism of the descriptive blason must be seen as pure linguistic display, as conceit pursued not in evocation of the lover's emotional agony but as elegant compliment. This explains the feeling of detachment which the poem conveys: although the lady's beauty both causes and resolves the speaker's pain, he is composed enough to philosophise in his final stanza about the meaning of this "pithie Paradox". As the opening invocation of the Muses suggests, the rhetorical sophistication of the poem's language is intended to do justice to the lady's charms precisely through its witty manipulation of convention. The conceits may point towards the Baroque, but they are ultimately empty of emotional content.

A disconcertingly similar effect is created in "Yong tender plant in spring tym of your yeirs" [37], where the rhetoric certainly suggests a more personal engagement than in "Quhy bene ye Musis". In this case the speaker addresses his beloved directly, and devotes eleven ballade stanzas to persuading her to respond to his advances. The argument is, however, at the opposite extreme from that Montgomerie employs in most of his amatory verse: there is no word of anguish or misery, no hint of grief-stricken death, of a mortal wound from Cupid's arrows, or the poisoning effect of love. Instead, the speaker relies upon proverbial wisdom, seeking to reason the lady into co-operation through the skilful application of logic:

> Tak tym in tyme vhil tyme is to be tane
> Or ye may wish and want it vhen ye wald.
> Ye get no grippe agane if it be gane
> Then vhill ye haif it best is for to hald.
> Thoght ye be yong yit once ye may be ald.
> Tyd will not tarie. Speid or it be spent.
> To prophesie I dar not be so bald
> Bot tyn ye tyme perhaps ye may repent.
> (41–48)

This is an anticipation not of Donne, but of Marvell: Montgomerie's deployment of the carpe diem motif is closer to the cynical ratiocination of Cavalier verse than to the passionate conviction of Donne's wit. The insistence upon the lady's youth in the opening line establishes the poem's tone, and the relentless accumulation of proverbial lore suggests an older lover employing all his wiles to persuade her to comply. He is perfectly prepared to hint at the physical implications of his pursuit ("I haif the moyan lyk ane other man", he observes at l. 76), and he cleverly invokes a children's game to win her over:

> Can ye not play at nevie nevie nak,              [*a children's game*]
> A pretty play whilk Children often wse
> Quhair tentles Bairnis may to their tinsall tak   *heedless; loss*
> The neiv with na thing and the full refuse?       *fist*
>     (65–68)

But this image of innocent play immediately turns into something much more serious:

> I will not skar you sen ye mynd to chuse                    *alarm*
> Bot put your hand by hazard in the creill,                  *basket*
> Yit men hes mater vharvpon to muse
> For they must drau ane adder or ane eill
>     (69–72)

It is clearly the speaker's intention to suggest that he is the eel rather than the adder; yet to choose the latter is scarcely less off-putting than the former, and it is difficult to suppress the idea that he may be more dangerous than he pretends. If we grant the possibility of an ironic distance between Montgomerie and his persona here, then the elaborate persuasiveness of his argument starts to work against itself, and the detachment which marks the poem's tone acquires a much greater ambiguity.

This consciously deliberative style is not, however, necessarily ironic. In "The Secreit Prais of Love" [32], it is employed to present what appears to be, for much of the poem, a genuinely philosophical contemplation of the psychological effects of love:

> As evirie object to the outuard ee
> Dissaivis the sight and semis as it is sene
> Quhen not bot shap and cullour yit we se
> For no thing els is subject to the ene,
> As stains and trees appeiring gray and grene,           *stones*
> Quhais quantities vpon the sight depends,
> Bot qualities the cunning [sense transcends],
>
> Euen sa vha sayis they sie me as I am,
> I men a man, suppose they sie me move,                  *mean*
> Of Ignorance they do tham selfis condam.
> By syllogisme this properly I prove.
> Quha sees by look my loyaltie in love,
> Quhat hurt in hairt, vhat hope or hap I haiv,
> Quhilk ressone movis the senses to consaiv?
>     (1–14)[59]

By the end of the second stanza, the reversion to a much more conventionally affective register signals the poet's ultimate, amatory purpose, and it is this style which eventually takes over the poem, producing a final stanza in which anaphora

---

[59] The final part of l. 7 is missing in the Ker MS.; I have adopted Cranstoun's conjectural reading.

and rhetorical, exclamatory questions combine to assert, with true Petrarchist theatricality, the power of his allegedly concealed passion. But that is not the prevailing manner of the rest of the argument, and Montgomerie's choice of the rhyme royal stanza perhaps reflects his preference here for an emotionally restrained discursiveness:

> Imaginatione is the outuard ee
> To spy the richt Anatomie of mynd
> Quhilk by some secreit sympathie may see
> The force of love vhilk can not be defynd,
> Quharthrou the hairt according to his kynd
> Compassionat, as it appeiris plane
> Participats of plesur or of pane.
> (15–21)

The same effect is apparent in the imagery, as when Montgomerie asks "vho is he can counterfutt the Ape?", or contrasts the limitlessness of love with the capacity of the physical world for definition:

> Suppose the heuins be huge for to behold,
> Contening all within thair compas wyde,
> The starris be tyme (thoght tedious) may be told
> Becaus within a certan bounds they byd.
> The Carde the earth from waters may devyde,          *firmament*
> Bot vho is he can limit Love, I wene,
> Quhom nather carde nor compas can contene?
> (29–35)

This is unquestionably the language of "Metaphysical" conceit, but there is a contest in this poem between two modes of discourse, the Petrarchist assertion of overwhelming passion with which the speaker concludes, and the measured, logical analysis which he attempts throughout the preceding five stanzas. The abandonment of rationalism is perhaps anticipated in the final question of the fifth stanza: "Vho is he can limit Love?". We are back with the insistence on the uncontrollable nature of desire which dominates Montgomerie's more conventional lyrics; but it is striking that he has here attempted to find an alternative view and an alternative language in which to express it.

The poem's final stanza resorts to a more traditional rhetorical device, deploying an anaphoric series of questions the cumulative effect of which is to reinforce the power of love, turning from the more measured tone of the previous couplet to a hyperbolic assertion of love's mysterious omnipotence. Yet this outburst is, in the end, subverted by the diminuendo conclusion of the final couplet, which identifies the all-conquering force as

> A vehemency that words can not reveill
> Quhilk I conclude to suffer and conceill.
> 　(41–42)

This is surprising on a number of counts: it situates the "force" inside the lover rather than making it the external power of Cupid; it reverts to the pointed style of the earlier sections of the poem by punning deftly on "conclude"; and it resorts to the rhetorical figure of occupatio by refusing to define or express the nature of the speaker's feelings. He thus conceals and reveals his love at the same moment, declining to articulate his "vehemency" openly or to identify its object, but nevertheless, despite this reticence, testifying to its inexpressible strength. The effect here is different from that of "Melancholie, grit deput of Dispair", suggesting a quiet, continuing stoicism rather than the overt playfulness we found in that case; by the same token, even the hyperbole of ll. 36–40 is more restrained than the absurdly excessive rhetoric of that poem. The persona of "The Secreit prais of Love" — and "secreit" takes on greater significance once we have read the final couplet — is a metaphysician as well as a Metaphysical, an amatory philosopher rather than an amatory rhetorician. Or so, at any rate, he wishes us to believe.

By way of counter-balance, it is appropriate to conclude this analysis of Montgomerie's rhetorical radicalism with an example which is at the opposite pole to the prevailing ratiocination of that poem. "Ressave this harte" [33] has, as Jack acknowledges, a strongly Petrarchist dimension: the central conceit of the lover bequeathing his heart to the lady is a variant on a familiar line of Petrarchist rhetoric, and the elaborately resigned acceptance of death as the inevitable consequence of the lady's continued "cruelty" is, if anything, even more pervasive. Montgomerie's language, too, observes to a considerable extent the conventions of this tradition, with its allusion to the lover's "secreit smart" and the "prik of jelousie". And yet there are signs that these stylistic limits are too narrow for Montgomerie's purpose. Suddenly, he moves into a much more concrete and immediate mode:

> Remember vhair I said once eftir none
> Or March wer done that thou thy cheeks suld weet　　*wet*
> And for me greet or endit war that Mone,　　*weep*
> 　I sie ouer soon my Prophesie compleit.
> 　(17–20)

There is nothing revolutionary about such a rhetorical ploy, perhaps; it is paralleled by Wyatt in "They fle from me" and by Scott in "Up, helsum hairt", to name just two sixteenth-century examples. What is remarkable, however, is the sense of physical mutability with which Montgomerie infuses his final stanza, going far beyond the rather airy rhetoric of lovesickness so prevalent in the Petrarchist tradition:

> Sen for thy saik Death with his darte me shot
> That I am bot a carioun of clay
> Quha quhylome lay about your snauie throt,
> Nou I must rot vha some tym stoud so stay.                    *strong*
> Quhat sall I say? This warld will auay.
> Anis on a day I seimd a semely sight.
> Thou wants the wight that neuer said the nay.
> Adeu for ay, this is a lang guid nicht.
>     (34–40)

Jack is surely justified in associating these lines both with the medieval tradition of mutability verse and Drummond's "pessimistic reflections".[60] Love is not, as a more traditional Renaissance poet might insist even while threatening to die of grief and frustration, a hedge against mortality; in leaving his beloved his heart "about thy hals to hing" (l. 15), the poet draws a pointed, even macabre, contrast between his living presence "about thy snauie throt" and the physical reality of his death.

The rhetoric of impermanence, however, goes further than this. The assertion that "this warld will auay", echoing the earlier observation that "This is the race that euery man must rin" (l. 30) — and, one might add, every woman — absorbs the lover's fate into a larger awareness of mutability. That is surely the force of the punning phrase "I seimd a semely sight"; even the physical substance of the lover is, he concedes, illusory. Even Dunbar's Deid does not go as far as this; his menacing remark that

> "Albeid that thow wer neuer sa stout,
> Vndir this lyntall sall thow lowt . . ."[61]                    *stoop*

depends for its awfulness upon the real but time-limited corporeality of his victim. For Montgomerie here, by contrast, love itself seems to be part of a world which is, by the end of the poem, insubstantial, and we should not fail to notice the hints, in the speaker's claim to "feill my spreet is summond from above" (l. 22) and in his bequest of his soul to God, of the existence of a higher reality. It is in this dissolution of the temporal world into illusion and decay that the radicalism of "Ressave this harte", tentative as it may be, is eventually to be found, and it points towards the sense of doomed impermanence we see in Jean de Sponde, Quevedo, and their contemporaries.

In these few poems, then, Montgomerie moves radically away from, or beyond, the Petrarchist norms which dominate most of his amatory verse. By turns

---

[60] Jack, *Montgomerie*, 56.
[61] Dunbar, *Poems*, ed. Bawcutt, 1:110.

hyperbolically parodic, wittily or philosophically rational, or moodily preoccupied with the physical reality of death, he abandons in these cases the clichéd rhetoric of helpless emotion which is the staple fare of Petrarchist and Neo-petrarchist poetry. We do not know enough about the chronology of his corpus to be able to say whether there is a connection between these more innovative pieces and the stylistic developments we can see in his autobiographical verse of the early 1590s; what we can say is that the bulk of his amatory poetry, including those pieces which he adapted from Marot and Ronsard, shows the general influence of the fashionable French verse of the 1570s, and that in occasionally breaking the bounds of these conventions he reflects the same aesthetic discontents as many of his contemporaries. He is, perhaps, unlikely to have encountered the revolutionary love poetry of Donne or Shakespeare, still less that of Marino, Jean de Sponde, Quevedo, or Góngora, yet there are a few traces of the same desire to explore new forms of expression. Nor was this impulse confined to amatory verse: we shall see in the following chapter that there are corresponding developments in Montgomerie's religious poetry. He did not live long enough to see the flourishing of Baroque culture, in England or elsewhere; but at his most radical Montgomerie clearly reveals himself to be, however tentatively, a forerunner of that major cultural shift. Nor should this sense of an only partial break with the conventions of contemporary verse blind us to the deftness with which he manipulates and nuances the materials he uses elsewhere: whether he is adapting the Petrarchism of Ronsard or pursuing an Ovidian theme, Montgomerie is never less than the "maister poete", lending his own distinctive coloration to the familiar patterns of sixteenth-century amatory verse.

# Chapter Eight

## "Teich me thy treuth": Montgomerie's Devotional Poetry

The Scottish Reformation must undoubtedly have been one of the defining experiences of Alexander Montgomerie's youth. Brought up, Duff tells us, on "the bitter poison of the Calvinists", he turned to Catholicism in adulthood despite the attendant dangers to his prospects at a Scottish court where religious issues remained a constant source of contention. His friends certainly included his fellow-convert, the English poet Henry Constable, and the Catholic activist Henry Keir; he associated himself with the pro-Catholic faction of the Dukes of Lennox. And yet it is striking that his surviving poetry bears few unambiguous marks of his doctrinal convictions. Not only does he address Patrick Galloway, the king's minister, in broadly supportive terms — a policy which might, after all, be explicable politically — but his devotional and theological verse could for the most part have been produced by a loyal member of the Scottish Kirk. It may be, of course, that this clear impression is in part the result of differential survival: we cannot know to what extent the Ker manuscript was the result of a selective process of compilation, or what other texts may have perished in the seventeenth or subsequent centuries. The possibility of fugitive works of a more strongly anti-Calvinist character is illustrated by the two sonnets attacking the Edinburgh ministers, whether or not those poems were actually written by Montgomerie. But the religious sensibility figured in his authentic extant works is on the whole unmarked by sectarian commitment of any kind, articulating instead a shared language of devotion.

This somewhat ecumenical form of religious verse is by no means confined to Montgomerie: on the contrary, it mirrors a convergence of Catholic and Protestant devotional language which occurred across Europe in the wake of the Council of Trent. Doctrinal differences do, it is true, continue to manifest themselves in much religious writing throughout the later sixteenth century, but there is a world of difference between the rigid hostilities of controversial texts and the much less polarised language of devotional works, whether in prose or verse. As Terence Cave remarks of the situation in France at this period:

> The tendency to identify sin and sickness, which is one of the most important points of departure for penitential poetry, is perfectly valid for both faiths; likewise the themes of death and God's mercy ("grace" need have no

partisan colouring in a poem) and the contrast between God and the sinner. Both can use Biblical material, with only a slight shift of emphasis.[1]

The final phrase is, of course, important; we must be alert for the nuances with which Montgomerie inflects his devotional verse, for while he deals with familiar common religious experience, and as a layman he eschews for the most part serious theological controversy, he is too careful and craftsmanlike a poet to avoid subtle shades of doctrinal meaning.

It is important, too, to recognise that the religious situation in Scotland in the final two decades of the sixteenth century was very different from that in England (or, indeed, in France, where doctrinal differences led to bloody civil war). The presence of Catholics at the court of James VI was, as we have seen, one of the characteristics of his Scottish reign, and there is little sense of government paranoia in Edinburgh of the kind which was endemic in London. The ministers and their English allies, it is true, continued to worry away at the undue influence of the king's Catholic friends, and episodes like the Ruthven Raid indicate that the Protestant faction was capable at times of taking the law into its own hands. But the position of Scottish recusants was, on the whole, much more favourable than that of their English equivalents, and there is nothing of the active persecution of Catholics which was pursued throughout Elizabeth's reign.[2] The extent to which Calvinist theology and the Genevan model of ecclesiastical government would continue to dominate the Scottish Kirk was very far from being a resolved question, and James's own religious convictions were sufficiently uncertain to cause alarm to Protestants and to inspire hope among at least some Catholics. Montgomerie's potential audience was, therefore, theologically heterogeneous, including Calvinists, episcopalians, and Catholics, while his rhetoric of repentance, spiritual hope, and glorification of God's majesty was founded to a large degree upon common ground; we may at times detect signs of a Catholic subtext, but for the most part his religious writing would have been accepted by all sections of his audience, albeit with variously nuanced understandings of its significance.

These differences in the religious context explain in large measure the contrast between Montgomerie's devotional verse and that of the two most notable poets among English Catholics of the period, Robert Southwell S.J. and Henry Constable.[3] For, however true it may be that the language of religious poetry in

---

[1] Terence C. Cave, *Devotional Poetry in France, c. 1570–1613* (Cambridge: Cambridge University Press, 1969), 23.

[2] See Margaret Sanderson, "Catholic Recusancy in Scotland in the Sixteenth Century", *Innes Review* 21 (1970): 87–107.

[3] Joseph D. Scallon SJ, *The Poetry of Robert Southwell S.J.* (Salzburg: Institut für Englische Sprache und Literatur, Universität Salzburg, 1975); for a valuable discussion of Southwell's

general spanned doctrinal divisions, it is clear that Southwell's Jesuit mission is frequently reflected in his verse, while Constable's choice of themes in his *Spirituall Sonnettes* leaves equally little ambiguity about the nature of his theological convictions:

> When thee (O holy sacrificed Lambe)
> in severed sygnes I whyte & liquide see:
> as on thy body slayne I thynke on thee,
> which pale by sheddyng of thy bloode became.
> And when agayne I doe beholde the same
> vayled in whyte to be receav'd of mee:
> thou seemest in thy syndon wrap't to bee
> lyke to a corse, whose monument I am.
> Buryed in me, vnto my sowle appeare
> pryson'd in earth, & bannish't from thy syght,
> lyke our forefathers, who in Limbo were.
> Cleere thow my thoughtes, as thou did'st gyve the light:
> And as thou others freed from purgyng fyre
> quenche in my hart, the flames of badd desyre.[4]

We find nothing in the small corpus of Montgomerie's religious verse to compare with the explicit Catholicism of Constable's devotion to the Sacrament or with his allusion to the doctrine of Purgatory; nor does Montgomerie address himself to the saints in the way that Constable does. Nowhere does he impose Catholic theology on his lyric in such a way as to preclude a Protestant reading, although we shall see that his overall approach to questions of grace and salvation bears unmistakable marks of his personal convictions. While permitting a Catholic interpretation of his devotional verse, then, Montgomerie seems to be at pains to address the widest possible audience, and to remain wherever he can within the bounds of the common idiom of Christian belief.

The importance of the Psalms in the formation of this shared and highly subjective language of devotion is obvious; and it is therefore scarcely surprising that versions of the Psalms themselves should have proliferated throughout sixteenth-century Europe. The Book of Psalms was indeed "the compendium *par excellence* of lyric poetry",[5] and if it provided an especially fruitful model for Protestants, it should not be supposed that its influence was confined to them. In the aftermath

---

prose in the context of English recusancy, see Ronald J. Corthell, "'The secrecy of man': Recusant Discourse and the Elizabethan Subject", *ELR* 19 (1989): 272–90.

[4] Constable, *Poems*, ed. Grundy, 184–85.

[5] Barbara Kiefer Lewalski, *Protestant Poetics and the Seventeenth-Century Religious Lyric* (Princeton: Princeton University Press, 1979), 39.

of the Council of Trent Catholic poets, too, found in the biblical Psalms a key source for a poetic language of devotion, even exhibiting "un interêt plus vivant que les protestants".[6] It was Clément Marot's French versions, however, the first collection of which was printed in 1539 and which became the basis of a translation of the whole Book completed by Theodore Beza after Marot's death, which exercised a dominant influence throughout Protestant northern Europe, inspiring among others the English version of Sternhold, Hopkins, and others (1549), the German of Paulus Melissus Schede (1572), and several Dutch translations, most significantly those of Jan Utenhove (1557), Lucas d'Heere (1565), and Pieter Datheen (1566).[7] There are also, as we shall see below, clear indications that, whatever his theological loyalties may have been, Montgomerie drew upon this 'Huguenot' psalter in making his own Scots versions. Marot's poetic qualities may have weighed more heavily with him than the doctrinal context; or he may have considered that the shared tradition of devotion and praise transcended any theological differences he would need to confront.

Two separate impulses, certainly, are at work in the composition of psalm versions in the sixteenth century, producing two quite different kinds of text. On the one hand, there are the versions included in translations of the Old Testament and those intended for liturgical use, such as the Scots *Gude and Godlie Ballatis* and Sternhold and Hopkins's *Whole Booke of Psalmes*, whose priorities are doctrinal rather than literary. Nothing, indeed, could be *less* poetic than the Stenhold and Hopkins psalter:

> The man is blest that hath not bent
>    to wicked rede his eare:                                   *counsell*
> Nor led his life as sinners do,
>    nor sat in scorners chaire.
> But in the Law of God the Lord
>    doeth set his whole delight,
> And in that Law doth exercise
>    him self both day and night.[8]

---

[6] Michel Jeanneret, *Poésie et Tradition Biblique au XVIe Siècle* (Paris : Corti, 1969), 203.

[7] See Rivkah Zim, *English Metrical Psalms: Poetry as Praise and Prayer* (Cambridge: Cambridge University Press, 1987); *Die Psalmenübersetzung des Paul Schede Melissus* (1572), ed. Max Hermann Jellinek (Halle/Saale: Niemeyer, 1896); on the Dutch psalm versions, see S.J. Lenselink, *De Nederlandse Psalmberijmingen van de Souterliedeken tot Datheen* (Assen: van Gorcum, 1959), and C.A. Höweler and F.H. Matler, *Fontes Hymnodiae Neerlandicae Impressi, 1539–1700* (Nieuwkoop: De Graaf, 1985).

[8] *The Forme of Prayers and Ministration of the Sacraments* (Edinburgh: Robert Lekpreuick, 1565), 1–2.

The versions produced by the poets, by contrast, tend to emphasise the lyrical qualities of the originals. Marot himself neatly balanced these two claims: he employs a wide variety of verse-forms, for example, ranging from decasyllabic couplets and simple quatrains to more elaborate lyric stanzas, but he is careful to retain the sense of his originals, and he uses a "plain" rhetoric acceptable to his Protestant audience. He achieves a judicious compromise between a theologically impeccable Reformed version and a satisfying literary text.

There is no doubt that Montgomerie's psalm versions belong in the latter category, employing more demanding stanzaic forms than Marot and Beza and therefore taking greater liberties with the biblical texts. In most other respects they present fundamental difficulties, even about the number of psalms for which Montgomerie was responsible. All we can say for certain is that he translated at least two and perhaps three: 1 (to the tune of "The Solsequium") and 2 (to the tune of "In throu the windows of myn ees") are found in the Ker manuscript, and both 1 and 23 (again using the "Solsequium" music) occur with a clear attribution to Montgomerie among the late additions to the Bannatyne manuscript.[9] In the case of Psalm 23, however, there is a difficulty, since in 1597 the same text was included in James Melvill's *Ane fruitfull and comfortable exhortation anent death* and apparently claimed by him.[10] The attribution to Montgomerie cannot, therefore, be regarded as certain. There is also a four-line fragment of a version of Psalm 36, appended to early editions of *The Cherrie and the Slae*, which may well be Montgomerie's, although such fillers were not necessarily by the same author as the main text.

It is customary to attribute to Montgomerie the whole of the collection entitled *The Mindes Melodie*, printed by Robert Charteris in 1605 and containing versions of fifteen psalms, the Song of Simeon, and the *Gloria Patri*, without any indication of authorship: two of the items are certainly Montgomerie's translations of Psalms 1 and 23. All seventeen pieces are in the "Solsequium" stanza. Most writers since Laing have accepted the attribution of the whole collection to Montgomerie, largely on the basis of certain observations by the seventeenth-century historian David Calderwood, who was campaigning against the adoption of the new version of the Psalms initiated and partly translated by James VI and I, and published posthumously in 1631. Calderwood evidently supported the continued use of the Sternhold and Hopkins Psalter, impeccably unpoetic and politically correct as it was, and recalled that James's version was not the first attempt to produce an alternative. In one such enterprise, he notes, Montgomerie was involved, a fact he deals with in each of the three documents he apparently wrote against the king's version.

---

[9] *Bannatyne Manuscript*, ed. Fox and Ringler, xx.

[10] *Ane fruitfull and comfortable exhortation anent death* (Edinburgh: Robert Waldegrave, 1597), 110–11. I am grateful to Dr. Sally Mapstone for drawing this version to my attention.

But the terms of these references are not entirely consistent. At one point Calderwood observes:

> If it had bene found expedient to alter these psalmes, Montgomerie and some others, principalls of Inglish poesie in ther tymes, as they gave ther assayes of some psalmes yit extant, so they offered to translate the whole book frielie without ony pryce for ther paines, ather fra the public state or privat mens purses.[11]

The clear implication of this statement is that Montgomerie was involved in some kind of collective effort, and that the 'psalmes yit extant' (which *might* refer to *The Mindes Melodie*) were the fruit of this collaboration. In a subsequent allusion, however, Calderwood seems to suggest that Montgomerie acted alone:

> Alexander Montgomerie had a singulare vaine of poesie, yet he tuik a moir modest cours, for he translated bot a few for a proofe, and offered his travells in that kynde to the kirk. (fol. 249r)

In the third and final reference this latter suggestion is apparently repeated, albeit in a chronological context which could mislead the unwary:

> Howbeit that excellent poet, Mr Mongomerie, gave a proofe of his skill in some, yet the Generall Assemblie holdin at Brunteland, anno 1601, wold not admit a chang, bot ordeaned that metaphrase which was in vse since the Reformation, to be revised be Mr Robert Pont, a man skilfull in the originall toungs, and his travells to be revised at the nixt Generall Assemblie. (fol. 247r)

There certainly was a debate about a revision of the Psalter at the General Assembly held at Burntisland in May 1601, but Montgomerie could not have been involved, having died in 1598. Calderwood indicates elsewhere in his argument, however, that the issue had been discussed at Glasgow in 1581 and at Perth in 1596, and it is possible that it was on one of these occasions that Montgomerie, with or without collaborators, had offered to produce a new version. Why a Catholic should have undertaken such a project is not clear; but his proposed version, or the man himself, was evidently unaccepable to the Kirk authorities.

We cannot, therefore, be certain whether Montgomerie himself translated more than three psalms at most (1, 2, and perhaps 23); it would clearly be unwise

---

[11] NLS, Wodrow Folio Manuscript 42, fol. 246r; this and the following two texts are printed (with some inaccuracies) in "Reasons against the Reception of King James's Metaphrase of the Psalms, 1631", *Bannatyne Miscellany* (Edinburgh: Bannatyne Club, 1827), 1:225–50.

to base any conclusions, either about his use of sources or about the literary or religious character of his versions, on the rest of *The Mindes Melodie*. The situation is, moreover, complicated still further by the presence in that volume, not only of the version of Psalm 23 which is attributed to both Montgomerie and James Melvill, but also of the translation of Psalm 121 which occurs alongside Psalm 23 in Melvill's *Fruitfull and comfortable exhortation*. Despite these problems of attribution, however, a comparison of these less securely canonical pieces with the two we can be sure about and with the disputed Psalm 23 may enable us to reach a slightly firmer view of the origins of the larger collection. This is a point to which we shall return after first considering the psalms which seem quite definitely to be Montgomerie's.

When we turn to the question of the possible influence of Marot we immediately encounter another difficulty: since both poets were translating the same originals, which were, moreover, among the most commented upon of all texts, and were bound, even at their most poetic, by the constraints inherent in the translation of Scripture, the separation of particular influences is virtually impossible. In the details of the respective versions, however, there are certainly striking similarities; none of these is conclusive in itself, but their cumulative effect is to support the possibility, perhaps even the probability, that Montgomerie used the Marot text. Such evidence must remain ambiguous: Marot's own translations were heavily influenced by the prose Psalter of Pierre Robert Olivetan (whose vernacular Bible, revised by Calvin, became the standard Protestant version in France and francophone Switzerland), and in their turn they exerted a powerful influence upon subsequent Protestant paraphrases, so that many of the parallels between Marot and Montgomerie are shared with other sixteenth-century versions. Nevertheless, the sheer frequency of such verbal links, reinforced by a smaller but significant number which are specific to these two versions, leave little doubt that Montgomerie knew and used Marot's work. Thus, when Montgomerie's version of Psalm 1 [1] translates "et in cathedra derisorum non sedit"[12] as "Nor does begin / To sitt with mockers in the scornefull sait" (ll. 7–8) and "sed tanquam gluma [for the more usual *pulvis*], quem proicit ventus a faciae terrae." as "but as the chaffe or sand / Quhilk day by day / Winds dryvis away" (ll. 22–4), there are close verbal echoes of Marot's "Qui des mocqueurs au banc place n'a prise" (l. 3) and "aux festus / Et a la pouldre au gre du vent chassee" (ll. 14–15);[13] but it is equally possible

---

[12] The usual (Gallicanum) Vulgate reading is "pestilentiae" rather than "derisorum", but the substitution was made in some sixteenth-century Latin texts (and their vernacular derivatives) on the basis of the Hebrew version, occurring as early as the 1509 *Quincuplex Psalterium*, published in Paris by Henri Estienne. In general, I have cited the Latin version of the Psalms from the 1528 edition of Robert Estienne.

[13] Marot, *Œuvres complètes*, ed. Mayer, 6:317–18; all references to Marot's psalms are based on this edition.

that "mockers" and "chaffe" are independently derived from the Latin, or from Olivetan's "mocqueurs" (or, for that matter, from the "irrisoribus" which occurs at this point in George Buchanan's paraphrase, published in 1566), and "la paille menue" respectively.

The most convincing body of evidence supporting Montgomerie's use of Marot occurs in his version of Psalm 2 [2]. There are, it is true, significant structural differences between the two texts: whereas Marot allocates a quatrain to each Biblical verse, a principle which leads him into some fairly radical expansions of his original, Montgomerie's approach is much more compressed, fitting the first four verses, for example, into a single eleven-line stanza. There is, moreover, an important difference of tone, for Montgomerie does not follow Marot in emphasising the contemporary relevance of the psalm. The Protestant subtext of the French is clear in Marot's translation of "principes" as "primatz" (l. 6), for example, but there is no such hint in the Scots. But despite these notable differences, there is much in the detail of Montgomerie's version which encourages the suspicion that Marot lies behind it:

> 1. Quare fremuerunt gentes, et populi meditati sunt inania?
> Pourquoy ont este esmeuz les gens, & pourquoy ont pense les peuples chose
> *vaine?*
> > Olivetan's translation (1535)[14]

> Pourquoy se mutinent les gens, & *murmurent* les peuples *en vain?*
> (Olivetan revised by Calvin [1546])[15]

> > Pourquoy font bruyt & s'assemblent les gens?
> > Quelle follie a *murmurer* les maine?
> > Pourquoy sont tant les peuples diligens
> > A mettre sus une enterprise *vaine?*
> > (Marot, 1–4)

---

[14] Quotations from Olivetan's French version are drawn from the second edition (Geneva, 1540). Full accounts of the various editions of rival French versions of the Bible are given by W.J. van Eys, *Bibliographie des Bibles et des Nouveaux Testaments en langue française des XVe et XVIe siècles* (Geneva: Kündig, 1900–1901), and by T.H. Darlow and H.F. Moule, *Historical Catalogue of the Printed Editions of Holy Scripture in the Library of the British and Foreign Bible Society*, 2 vols. (London: Bible House, 1911), 2:376ff.

[15] Calvin's revisions to Olivetan are cited from the edition published by Jean Crespin at Neufchâtel in 1551.

> Why did the Gentiles tumultes raise?
>   what rage was in their braine?
> Why did the Jewish people muse,
>   seeing all is but *vaine*?
>     (Sternhold, 1–4)

> Quhy doth the Heathin rage and rampe
> And peple *murmur* all *in vane*?
>     (Montgomerie, 1–2)

2. Adstiterunt reges terrae . . .
Pourquoy s'aduancent les Rois de la terre
    (Olivetan)

> *Bandez* se sont les grans roys de la terre . . .
>     (Marot, 5)

> The kings and rulers of the earth
>   conspire and ar all bent
> Against the Lord and Christ his Sonne,
>   which he among us sent.
>     (Sternhold, 5–8)

> The kings on earth ar *bandit* plane . . .
>     (Montgomerie, 3)

7. Dominus dixit ad me: Filius meus es . . .
Le Seigneur m'a dict: tu es mon filz . . .
    (Olivetan)

> mon seigneur & pere
> M'a dict: tu es mon *trescher* filz eleu . . .
>     (Marot, 26–27)

> the Lord him self
>   did say to me, I wotte,
> Thou art my *deare and onelie* Sonne:
>     (Sternhold, 25–27)

290 RODERICK J. LYALL

he
Hes said to me,
"Thou art my Sone *beloved* ay . . ."
(Montgomerie, 18–19)

9. . . . et tanquam vas figuli confringes eos.
. . . & les *briseras* comme un vaisseau d'vn potier.
(Olivetan)

Et (s'il te plaist) menu les *briseras*,
Aussi aise comme ung vaisseau de terre.
(Marot, 32–33)

Thou shalt them *bruse* euen with a mace
as men vnder foote trodde:
And as the potters sheards shalt breake
Them with an yron rodde.
(Sternhold, 33–36)

Quhairvth thou sall
Evin *bruis* thame all
In peces lyk a potters shaird.
(Montgomerie, 31–33)

None of the five significant readings here — "murmur", "in vane", "bandit", "beloved", "bruis" — is required by the sixteenth-century Vulgate versions. Three of them, it is true, are shared by all or some of the French editions: "vaine" and "briseras" occur in all the successive editions of Olivetan, while "murmurent" appears (influenced, perhaps, by Marot) in later versions such as those issued by Robert Estienne from the early 1550s. On three occasions, too, there is a notable parallel between Montgomerie's version and Sternhold's: perhaps himself working partly from Marot, the English translator incorporates "vain", "deare", and "bruse" in his text, but there is nothing which reflects Marot's "murmurent" and "bandez". While we may suspect that Montgomerie consulted the Scottish version of the English Psalter (in one of its numerous Edinburgh editions), therefore, there are significant points at which the Scots version is closer to Marot than to Sternhold, or, indeed, to the other French translations. Most significant of all is the fact that Montgomerie echoes Marot's translation of "conuenerunt" as "bandez";[16] the most

---

[16] It should, however, be noted that "se bandent" occurs as a marginal variant in Crespin's 1551 Neufchâtel edition of Olivetan/Calvin.

economical explanation of this detail, combined with other, less conclusive parallels, is surely that the Scots poet used Marot's version, not exclusively, but extensively.[17]

There are further hints of the influence of Marot in the third psalm version which is quite probably by Montgomerie, that of Psalm 23 [**106**]; but here we are much more conscious of the independent artistry of the Scots text than we are of any single model. The cause is clearly the sheer demands placed on the translator's ingenuity by his use of the "Solsequium" stanza, with its tercets and quatrains of short lines rhymed together. There could be no stronger contrast with Marot's measured couplets:

> Mon Dieu me paist soubz sa puissance haulte;
> C'est mon berger, de rien je n'auray faulte.
> En tect bien sur joignant les beaulx herbages
> Coucher me faict . . .[18]

> The Lord most hie
> I know wilbe
> Ane hird to me,
> I can not long haif stress nor stand in neid.
> He makis my lair
> In feildis most fair
> Quhair I bot cair
> Reposing at my plesour saifly feid.
>     (106: 1–8)

The use of "haulte/hie" as an opening rhyme is striking, since "Dominus" is unqualified by any adjective in the Latin, and while metrical requirements might have impelled each poet independently to expand "in loco pascuae" with "beaulx/ so fair", the parallel is also consistent with Montgomerie's use of Marot's psalter. Marot and Montgomerie concur, moreover, in making the pastoral metaphor more explicit by describing Christ as "berger/hird".[19] The most distinctive features of the Scots version, on the other hand, evidently spring from the musical structure Montgomerie has adopted: both the long lines substantially develop the idea in the Latin, and correspond to nothing in Marot or in other sixteenth-century versions.

---

[17] That Marot was not Montgomerie's *sole* source is apparent from, for example, "potters shaird", which is not represented in Marot's version but which is common to virtually all the others.

[18] Marot, *Œuvres complètes*, ed. Mayer, 6:380.

[19] It is worth noting that although the (Gallicanum) Vulgate text has "regit me" in v. 1, it is possible that Marot and/or Montgomerie was influenced by the revised Latin version's "pascit me", which parallels the Septuagint reading "ποιμαίνει με".

For the modern reader, such line-filling is likely to be an irritant rather than a cause for admiration; in a sung version, however, Montgomerie's adaptation of the sense to his elaborate music is both skilful and aesthetically satisfying. Nor is expansion the only technique he employs. Translating verse 5 ("Parasti in conspectu meo mensam, adversus eos qui tribulant me; impinguinasti in oleo caput meum, et calix meus inebrians quam praeclarus est"), Montgomerie goes unerringly for the essentials:

> In dispyt of my foe
> My tabill growis,
> Thow balmes my heid with Ioe                 *joy*
> My cup overflowis . . .
>     (27–30)

This had been translated by Marot into four decasyllabic lines:

> Tu enrichis de vivres necessaires
> Ma table aux yeulx de tous mes adversaires,
> Tu oings mon chef d'huilles & senteurs bonnes,
> Et jusqu'aux bordz pleine tasse me donnes.
>     (11–14)

Here it is Marot who has nudged his original to fill his lines while Montgomerie has compressed wherever he can, making use, for example, of the unusual and effective verbal form "balm" to render in a single word the Vulgate phrase "impinguasti in oleo" and adding the apparently casual "Ioo" [*joy*], thus heightening the emotional effect of the process. A more elaborate development immediately follows, for Montgomerie devotes his next three lines to a judicious expansion of the Latin "misericordia tua subsequetur me omnibus diebus vitae meae":

> Kyndnes and grace
> Marcy and pace
> Sall fallow me for all my wretchit dayis . . . . .

With its partial echo of another Psalm (85 = Vulgate 84:11: "Misericordia et veritas obviaverunt sibi, iustitia et pax osculatae sunt") and the widely-distributed topos of the Four Daughters of God which derives from it, the Scots version lays much greater stress upon divine bounty, while the intruded "wretchit" emphasises the contrast between God's mercies and the misery of the human condition. This is paraphrase at its most sophisticated, and its purpose is evidently to highlight both the awesomeness of Providence and the sorrows which human flesh is prone to.

The skill with which Montgomerie can assimilate the biblical text to the complex structure of his poetic form is also evident in his version of Psalm 1, where he organises six verses into two stanzas of the "Solsequium" tune with minimal disturbance to the original. This is not to say that he is rigidly bound by the text: in one respect in particular he effects a simple adjustment which actually improves his version. The Vulgate (Gallicanum) text reads:

3   Et erit tanquam lignum, quod plantatum est secus decursus aquarum, quod fructum suum dabit in tempore suo, et folium eius non defluet, et omnia quaecumque faciet prosperabuntur.
4   Non sic impii, non sic; sed tanquam pulvis, quem proicit ventus a facie terrae.

Montgomerie, however, manages the division differently, and in the process gives a new slant to the contrast between the virtuous and the sinner:

> For he sall be
> Lyk to the trie
> Quhilk plantit by the running river grouis
>    Quhilk frute does beir
>    In tym of yeir
> Quhais leaf sall never fade nor rute sall louis.          *loosen*
>
>
>    His Actions all
>    Ay prosper sall
>    Quhilk sall not fall
> To godles men bot as the chaffe or sand
>    Quhilk day by day
>    Wind dryvis away.
>    (13–24)

The exigencies of the stanza-form no doubt account for the temporal fillers "in tym of yeir" and "day by day", but the most significant change here is the positioning of the latter part of verse 3 at the beginning of Montgomerie's second stanza. What is in the biblical version merely the last in a list of the attributes of the godly is now much more sharply juxtaposed with the condition of "godles men", and there may even be a hint in "Quhilk sall not fall" that God can be relied upon to protect the virtuous man's actions from the ambitions of the wicked. The contrast between the inevitable rewards of godliness and the punishment of sinners is in any case the structural core of the psalm; but Montgomerie has strengthened this effect by one simple device.

The three psalm versions which can be attributed with reasonable certainty to Montgomerie, then, suggest that Marot was a significant influence upon his translations and that he adapted his source materials with the same mastery we have seen in his secular verse. To what extent, then, can these observations be carried over to the thirteen further psalms and two additional pieces which were printed in *The Mindes Melodie*? All of these, it should be noted, are composed in the "Solsequium" stanza, and it seems probable that the omission of Montgomerie's version of Psalm 2 was a response to the fact that it was based upon a different tune. Of these thirteen psalms, nine were translated by Marot between about 1527 and 1543; the exceptions are 57, 117, 121, and 125. There is little conclusive evidence of dependence on Marot's versions by the Scottish translator: the strongest case can perhaps be made for Psalm 8 (*Domine Dominus noster*), where Marot renders v. 9, "volucres caeli et pisces maris qui perambulant semitas maris', as

> Oyseaulx de l'air qui volent & qui chantent
> Poissons de mer, ceulx qui nagent & hantent
> Par les sentiers de mer grans & petiz,
> Tu les as tous à l'homme assubjectis.
> (29–32)

In *The Mindes Melodie* version this passage is represented by:

> Yea, all such things are preast
>   At his command;
> The fish that swym
> With out-spred fin,
> And fowls, each one, that haunt into the aire.
>   (47–51)

The occurrence in both texts of "hantent/haunt" is not paralleled in other sixteenth-century versions, and, while it might conceivably be a coincidence, the most obvious explanation is that Marot's translation lies behind the Scots. On the other hand, there is little in the quality of the translation to suggest Montgomerie's hand: the expansion of "super caelos" (v. 2) to "Aboue the heauens and christall cleared aire" (l. 8), for example, seems somewhat diffuse and vague, and while the rendering of "gloria et honore coronasti eum et constituisti eum super opera manuum tuarum" (vv. 6–7) as

> And thou his name
> And glorious frame
> Exalts with fame,
> And crownes his head with royall Majestie,
>   And as a King
>   Him sets to raigne
>   Ouer euerie thing,
> That life, breath, forme and shape hath taine of thee
>   (37–44)

does include one significant development in its final line, the overall effect is of an idea being stretched to fit the demands of the stanza-form. This is something we almost never feel about Montgomerie's versions, and it must be acknowledged that if he was responsible for any of the additional psalms in *The Mindes Melodie* then it is a below-par Montgomerie we are reading. It seems safest to concur with Parkinson's judgement and to exclude these poems from the corpus of Montgomerie's authentic works.

The influence of the psalm tradition, however, extends beyond these translations, though elsewhere we find psalmody mingling with other devotional modes. Broadly speaking, Montgomerie's few original religious lyrics can be classified according to their mode of address: those in the first person, where the emphasis is devotional and penitential, and those in the second person, where the poet's concern is more clearly with exhortation and instruction. The latter group includes "A walkning from sin" [5] and "A lesone hou to leirne to die" [6], both of which conform fairly closely to medieval types of didactic lyric, standing in direct line from the religious verse of Henryson, Dunbar, and the anonymous lyrics of the Bannatyne manuscript. This medieval generic inheritance, no doubt, goes a long way toward explaining the emphasis upon repentance, but the repeated call for the addressee to "tak tym in tym" and turn to Christ before it is too late implies the possibility of a redemption in which the repentant Christian is an active participant:

> Seik, knok and ask in Faith with Hope and Love
> And thou sall find and enter and obtene.
> Obey his blissed bidding from above
> So sall thou purchess proffeit to betuene.
> Inclyne thyn eiris and open wp thy ene
> To heir and sie, and comfort all thy kin.
> Do good, repent, in tym to come abstene.
> Think on the end and thou sall seindle sin.          *seldom*
>     (5: 33–40)

The injunction to moral reform is, of course, very general, but the clear suggestion that the individual is responsible for his or her fate is at odds, at least implicitly, with the Calvinist doctrine of Election, while the hint of a belief in the saving power of works in the phrase "do good" is carried a stage further in "A lesone hou to leirne to die":

> Then Prayers, Almesdeids and tearis
> Vhilks yit to skorne yee skantly skar          *you are scarcely frightened*
> Sall mair availl than Jaks and spearis          *quilted coats*
> For to debait thee at that bar
> Quhair nane rebelis bot all obeyis
> Without contineuing of Dayis.
>     (6:61–66)

Here the reference to almsgiving seems to hint strongly at support for the doctrine of good works and thus to imply a Catholic position, but Montgomerie does not press the point beyond the limits of a Protestant reader's tolerance. The contrast is not between works and faith, after all, but between acts of religious devotion and military strength, between the operation of divine justice and the rebelliousness of sin. And it is worth noting that even as convinced a Protestant as Peter Martyr Vermigli is not against works as such, although he makes them conditional upon the operation of predestination:

> Dico igitur, praedestinationem esse sapientissimum propositum Dei, quo ante omnem aeternitatem decrevit constanter, eos, quos dilexit in Christo, vocare ad adoptionem filiorum, ad iustificationem ex fide, *et tandem ad gloriam per opera bona*, quo conformes fiant imagini filij Dei, atque in illis declaretur gloria, et misericordia creatoris.

> [Predestination is the most wise purpose of God by which he has decreed firmly from before all eternity, to call those whom he has loved in Christ to the adoption of sons, to be justified by faith, *and subsequently to glorify through good works*, those who shall be conformed to the image of the Son of God, that in them the glory and mercy of the Creator might be declared.][20] [my italics]

The emphasis here is, of course, very different from that we find in Catholic texts: in the *Schort Catholik Confession* composed in response to the "Negative Confession" of 1581, for example, it is asserted that works are not only "ane secund cause of our iustificatione but also that they merit, and ar worthie of the eternal lyfe".[21] For Montgomerie, too, it is clear that works can "availl", can make a difference, and the implication is that it is not necessary to wait until God creates the prior conditions in which such actions can be performed.

The subtlety with which Montgomerie nuances medieval devotional tradition is even clearer if we compare "A lesone hou to leirne to die" with a sonnet on the same theme by James Melvill:

> Sen sa it is, that quhasoeuer tuik life,
> Man be the death vnto the same put end;                    *must*

---

[20] Peter Martyr Vermigli, *In Epistolam S. Pauli ad Romanos commentarij doctissimi . . .* (Basel: Peter Perna, 1558), 411, quoted in Frank A. James III, *Peter Martyr Vermigli and Predestination: The Augustinian Inheritance of an Italian Reformer* (Oxford: Clarendon Press, 1998), 69.

[21] *Catholic Tractates of the Sixteenth Century, 1573–1600*, ed. T.G. Law (Edinburgh: STS, 1901), 251.

To passe thy course, out through this vale of strife
In holines, O Christian contend.
Stand still in awe, thy God for till offend.
Clieaue to thy Christ, with faith vnfainedly:               *cling*
Repent thy sinnes, thy wicked life amend,
And daylie think on death, that thou man dy.
Set not thy heart on worldlie vanitie,
Whose pleasures are with paine so dearly bought,
Yet presse to play thy part with honestie,
And vse this world, as gif thou vsde it nought.
Let ay this precept be thy Preacher plaine.
Liue heir to die, and die to liue againe.[22]

Like Montgomerie, Melvill urges repentance, but he does so within the context of an apparently fixed definition of "holines", and he gives relatively little attention to the emotional condition of the sinner. Everything hinges upon "unfeigned" faith, while Montgomerie strikingly warns against a "fruitles faith" (6: 10) which leaves the Christian in no position to answer the summons of death. Montgomerie, indeed, employs the well-established medieval device of allegory to dramatize the pitiful condition of the unrepentant sinner, presenting a scene which inevitably recalls the exemplum of the three (or four) friends which forms the basis of *Everyman*. There is also a clear echo of the tropological debate in *The Cherrie and the Slae*, in the prospect of a "bitter battell" in the soul "Betuixt quick hope and dead dispair" (ll. 37–38). It is in such a context, he asserts, that "Prayers, Almesdeids and tearis" will stand the sinner in good stead. The poem's conclusion strikes a very different note from Melvill's, with Montgomerie urging the reader to "hear vhill Chryst knokis at thy hairt / And open it to let him in" (ll. 85–86): if this phrasing places the responsibility upon Christ for the first approach to the unrepentant sinner, it is equally clear that the latter is called upon to respond. Perhaps some such notion as "special help" is implied in the formulation here;[23] what is crucial, however, is the

---

[22] James Melvill, "A Sonnet sounding a warning to die well", in idem, *Fruitfull and Comfortable Exhortation*, 112.

[23] The doctrine of *auxilium speciale*, originating in the work of the fourteenth-century Augustinian Gregory of Rimini, asserted that man could begin the process of spiritual regeneration only after the intervention of the Holy Spirit; its fifteenth-century adherents included the Scot John Ireland, and it contributed significantly to the development of the Reformers' doctrines of grace. See Gordon Leff, *Gregory of Rimini: Tradition and Innovation in Fourteenth Century Thought* (Manchester: Manchester University Press, 1961), 185–96; on the influence of *auxilium speciale* on early Lutheranism, see Heiko A. Oberman, *Masters of the Reformation: The Emergence of a New Intellectual Climate in Europe*, ed. D. Martin (Cambridge: Cambridge University Press, 1981), 64–110.

difference between this interactive relationship between Christ and man and the much more fixed view, implicitly underpinned by the doctrine of election, which emerges from Melvill's sonnet.

Although its rhetorical stance is more complex, "The Poets Dreme" [3] largely belongs to this group of didactic lyrics. From the beginning of the third stanza, at any rate, its argumentative structure is mainly exhortatory, although there is also an extended allusion to Jacob's ladder (ll. 26–36). The traditional typological interpretation which Montgomerie gives this figure, however, equates the ladder with Christ, and the poem's final injunction urges us to "clim by Chryst". Once again, we might see a faint hint of Catholic doctrine, in the claim that grace is available to those "Vhais faith brings furth gude frute": if this last phrase is taken to imply salvation through works, then the poem would appear to be taking a Catholic line. The reference is only incidental, however, and the insistence that such "frute" are derived from faith might equally be seen as offering support for a Protestant view. As is so often the case, Montgomerie is careful not to impose a single doctrinal interpretation, leaving open the possibility of a Catholic reading while employing language which largely emphasizes a shared Christian tradition. It is also notable that he moves to spiritual advice only after a much more personal opening in which it is his own salvation for which the speaker prays, in terms which unequivocally echo the language of the Song of Solomon. This remarkable first stanza brings us close to what is perhaps Montgomerie's finest religious lyric, "Come my childrene dere", and we shall have occasion to pursue the point below. "The Poets Dreme" is a curious hybrid, but its rhetoric finally has more in common with such poems as "A walkning from sin" and "A lesone hou to leirne to die" than with the rest of Montgomerie's devotional poetry.

Such instructional verse, rhetorically sparse and using metaphorical language with the aphoristic terseness of the proverbial, is inevitably somewhat impersonal. It therefore contrasts with much more emotionally engaged lyrics such as "A Godly Prayer" [4] and (if it is indeed Montgomerie's) "Auay vane world",[24] where the keynote is a kind of anguished internality. These poems belong to the tradition of the penitential lyric; and while this is a form the roots of which lie deep in the Middle Ages, the most obvious parallels are again with contemporary French practice. As Terence Cave has shown, there was a powerful vogue for such writing in the last quarter of the sixteenth century, gaining wide currency through anthologies like the Catholic *Muse chrestienne* (1582) and Maisonfleur's more eclectic *Cantiques* (1586).[25] Here the influence of the Psalms, and especially of the Penitential Psalms, is naturally uppermost, and poets from both sides of the doctrinal divide demonstrate their capacity for "controlled improvisation on an

---

[24] For the text, see *Poems*, ed. Cranstoun, 237–38.
[25] Cave, *Devotional Poetry*, 104–35.

established theme". In "A Godly Prayer" Montgomerie places himself firmly within this tradition. Not only is the poem constructed around a refrain (*Peccavi Pater miserere mei*) which echoes both the Psalms and Luke 15:18–21 (the story of the Prodigal Son); further Latin quotations at ll. 14 and 71 also have sources in the Psalms, and the entire argument of unworthiness and self-abnegation is woven together from the elements of biblical paraphrase. As is indicated by his use of Luke, invoked by name at l. 15, Montgomerie does not confine himself to the Psalms. He compares himself in the opening stanza to the Prodigal Son, and in one of the poem's most striking passages he prays for the intervention of Pentecostal inspiration:

> Flie doun on me in forked tongues of fyre
> As thou did on thy oune Apostills vse
> And with thy tyre me fervently infuse
> To laud the, Lord, and longer not delay.
> My former folish fictiouns I refuse.
> Peccavi Pater miserere mei.
>     (51–56)

This echo of Acts 2:3–5 perhaps links back to another allusion to the same book, when the poet takes up Acts 7:49 ("Caelum mihi sedes est, terra autem scabellum pedum meorum"), itself an echo of Isaiah 66:1, with a typically personal inflection (derived from Psalm 139:6–7, with a recollection of Psalm 88:2–4):

> Thoght I suld flie vhair sall I find refuge?
> In hevin o Lord? thair is thy duelling place,
> The erth thy futstule, yea in hel is (alace)
> Doun with the dead, bot all must the obey.
>     (27–30)

One of the most significant features of this poem, indeed, is the balance Montgomerie strikes between universalising biblical allusion and personal reference. There is more to this than the mere use of the first person: immediately before calling down the inspirational power of Pentecostal fire, he "signs" the text with his own identity, asking "Help holy Ghost and be Montgomeries muse" (l. 50). To the degree that this allusion, picked up five lines later in the poet's renunciation of his "former folish fictiouns", attaches the prayer's spiritual anguish to Montgomerie's own biographical circumstances it may be said to lend a specifically personal note to a rhetoric which is already personal in its simulation of interiority; yet it cannot be claimed that the materials with which Montgomerie is working here depart very far from the conventional language of the penitential tradition. The effect of the poem is therefore based upon a paradox: it is precisely Montgomerie's dependence upon biblical quotation which enables him to catch the note of personal engagement. By approximating the spiritual condition of the Psalmist he, like many other sixteenth-century poets, gains access to a rhetoric of penitence which conveys the personal while at the same time transcending it.

"A Godly Prayer" challenges, moreover, another crucial definition of the personal: to what degree does this "signed" lyric reveal Montgomerie's own doctrinal convictions? We have so far found little evidence to support Jack's contention that his religious lyrics "are clearly written from a Catholic viewpoint", but there is at least a hint in this case of the author's confessional position. This is most evident, perhaps, in the liturgical associations of the refrain and of "Sed salvum me fac, dulcis Fili Dei" (l. 14), which, as Jack and Parkinson both note, echoes the ninth Lesson of the Mass for the Dead. Even here, however, there is little in doctrinal terms to indicate the cast of the poet's own beliefs: the rhetoric of penitence is common to both Catholic and Calvinist traditions, and the awareness of the pervasive power of sin which the poem expresses is susceptible to both kinds of theological interpretation. A question like "vho is he vhois Conscience can him clenge / Bot by his birth to Satan he is bund?" (ll. 19–20) is perfectly compatible with the doctrine of Election; but it might also be given a more Catholic reading.[26] It is the emotional experience of repentance, linked with Montgomerie's more personal engagement with his position as a poet, which is central to "A Godly Prayer", and confessional differences seem scarcely relevant to the poem's rhetorical power.

The same applies to "Auay vane world", a spiritualised version of a secular song, which is found in the Ker manuscript (fols. 81r–82r) but which also occurs, without explicit ascription, at the end of Henry Charteris's 1603 edition of Elizabeth Melvill's *Ane Godlie Dreme*. As we noted at the beginning of this study, inclusion by the Ker scribe does not necessarily guarantee Montgomerie's authorship, and Melvill's claim to this poem is at least as strong as his; yet Montgomerie seems clearly to have employed the technique of the *contrafactum* in his psalm translations and on at least one other occasion, in writing "Come, my childrene dere". This poem follows "Auay vane world" in the final folios of the manuscript and has universally been accepted as Montgomerie's: if the fact that "Auay vane world" occurs outside the manuscript's main arrangement be taken as evidence against his authorship, then this argument applies equally to "Come, my childrene dere". There is, however, another problem in the case of "Auay vane world", for the song of which it is evidently a sacred rewriting, Richard Jones's "Farewell, sweet loue", was first printed in 1600.[27] If the Scots *contrafactum* was based upon this edition, then, Montgomerie could not possibly be the author. This argument probably tips the balance in favour of Melvill; yet we cannot be

---

[26] On the issue of sixteenth-century conceptions of conscience, see above, 204–7.

[27] David Greer, "Five Variations on 'Farewell dear loue'", in *The Well Enchanting Skill: Music, Poetry, and Drama in the Culture of the Renaissance*, ed. John Caldwell, Edward Olleson and Susan Wollenberg (Oxford: Oxford University Press, 1990), 213–27; Montgomerie, *Poems*, ed. Parkinson, 2:5–6.

quite certain that Montgomerie did not see, or hear, the song in some earlier form. In analysing the poem, then, we should recognise that it is among the most doubtful items in the Montgomerie corpus, and we should certainly not employ it in defining the character of his religious verse.

The renunciation of the temporal which is the poem's predominant theme is a frequently-explored medieval and Renaissance motif: the *vanitas* tradition runs strongly through sixteenth-century poetry as it had through that of previous centuries. But it is noteworthy here that little attention is given to the nature of this world's distractions, or indeed to their mutability: all the emphasis falls upon the speaker's interior experience. Incidental references characterise the world as the poet's "sueet alluring fo" whose "subtill slychts" hold him as a slave; but we find none of the recurring images of the ship tossed on the Sea of Life, of the flower that must perish, or of the illusoriness of a dream, which conventionally embody the transitoriness of worldly pleasures. All the lyric force of the poem is concentrated instead upon the spiritual necessity of the speaker's escape from the dangers of the corporeal, and his confidence that through divine mercy that escape will indeed be possible. The repeated imperatives which begin each stanza and which reiterate his rejection of the world and of his former life give the emotive effect a kind of stasis, creating the impression of a soul struggling to free itself and yet unable to do so. The speaker admits at the conclusion of the fourth stanza that

> Tho I oft intend, strength fails ay:
> The sair assaults of sin prevailis ay.
>     (31–32)

Such a condition of spiritual stalemate would obviously defeat the devotional purpose of the song, however, and the final stanza triumphantly breaks through to a fulfilment of the promise of the opening lines:

> Quhat sall I say? Ar all my plesurs past?
> Sall worldly lustis nou tak thair leiv at last?
>     Yea, Chryst, these earthly toyes
>     Sall turne in hevinly joyes.
>       Let the world be gone;
>       I'l love Chryst allone.
> Let the world be gone — I cair not:
> Chryst is my love alone — I feir not.
>     (33–40)

The poem finally enacts the process of spiritual liberation which is its true subject, finding the resolution of the protagonist's struggle in the power of his personal relationship with Christ. This, too, is a common sixteenth-century theme, and shared ground between Protestants and Catholics; but the speaker's resolution to "love Chryst allone" might perhaps be seen as more easily reconcilable with Catholic doctrines of spiritual freedom than with a Calvinist emphasis on election. While the authorship of "Auay vane world" must remain unresolved, its devotional rhetoric is incompatible neither with Montgomerie's Catholicism nor with his apparent desire to find a form of religious discourse which would be acceptable to his audience regardless of their own doctrinal commitments.

As with the stanzaic lyrics, the sequence of sonnets in the Ker manuscript begins with a small number of religious poems. This prioritisation of devotional experience may, of course, tell us more about the compiler of the manuscript than it does about Montgomerie's own values — although we have seen that the poet himself makes the (conventional) move of renouncing his secular work in favour of spiritual verse. What is clear is that his command of sonnet structure, his ability to present "sommair reasons, suddenlie applyit", extends to theological as well as to amatory and personal subjects. The first of the sonnets [59] masterfully displays these qualities in praise of the Trinity:

> Svpreme Essence, beginning Vnbegun,
> Ay Trinall ane, ane vndevydit three,
> Eternall Word vha Victorie hes wun
> Ou'r death, ou'r hell Triumphing on the Trie,
>     Forknavlege, Wysdome and All-seing ee,
> Iehovah, Alpha, and Omega all,
> Lyk vnto nane, nor nane like vnto thee,
> Vnmov't vha movis the rounds about the Ball,
> Contener vnconteind, is, was and sall
> Be Sempiternall, Mercifull and Just,
> Creator, vncreatit, nou I call.
> Teich me thy treuth since into thee I trust.
>     Incres, confirme, and kendill from aboue
>     My faith, my hope, bot by the lave my Loue.        *among the rest*

The verbal play is more than a display of rhetorical skill: it is firmly directed towards the expression of God's paradoxical nature and his divine power. This learned evocation of God's essential qualities dominates the poem almost up to the end of the third quatrain, but then the poet turns his argument, using his understanding of the divine nature as a basis for his appeal for God's assistance in reinforcing his faith. What begins as a poem of praise becomes by the end a petition; in a shift for which the Psalms provide many precedents, the speaker brings the argument around to his own spiritual circumstances, employing the well-established Mannerist technique of *vers rapportés* to evoke the Pauline triad of "theological" virtues (derived from 1 Corinthians 13:11–13).[28]

---

[28] Cf. *Poems*, ed. Parkinson, 2:84; and see below, 306.

Once again, however, the nature of the "personal" in this poem is more doubtful than might at first glance appear. Even Montgomerie's authorship of the sonnet cannot be taken wholly for granted, for a very similar piece is found in *A Morning Vision*, published by James Melvill in 1598:

> Supreame essence, beginner, unbegon,
> Distinguished ane, and undevided three:
> Unmoov'd, that moves the roundes abone the Moon,
> Like unto none, nor none like unto Thee;
> Conteiner, uncontein'd, is, was, salbe,
> In gudnes, strength, and wisedome infinite;
> Creator, uncreated, great and hie,
> Eternall Father, Sonne and halie Spreit.
> Incarnat word, o mediator meit!
> Ou'r death and Hell tryumpher on the trie;
> Jehovah, Alpha and Omega sweete:
> Redeemer, from the death and miserie
>> Possesse my [saule] and keepe me in Thy feare,
>> And make me live with Thee, for ever meare.[29]

Even a superficial comparison of the two texts reveals both that they are substantially different versions, and that one is a reworking of the other. But which is the "original", which the revision? And does the presence of one of them at the head of the sonnet section in the Ker manuscript indeed confirm that it was the work of Montgomerie, since there are other instances in which poems by alien hands clearly found their way into the corpus?

One way of approaching these difficulties is through a French sonnet which appears to be the model for both Scots versions. In his *Theanthropogamie*, published by Thomas Vautrollier in London in 1577, the Huguenot poet Marin Le Saulx addresses the Trinity in strikingly similar terms:

> Essence unique et simple, ô Dieu en Trinité!
> Tout bon, tout saint, tout pur, tout grand, tout ineffable,
> Tout puissant eternel à qui nul n'est semblable,
> Pere, parole, esprit, ô triple unité!
> Un en trois, trois en un, unique eternité,
> Createur souverain du grand tout admirable,

---

[29] James Melvill, *A spirituall propine of a pastour to his people* (Edinburgh: Robert Waldegrave 1598), 52. I am, once again, grateful to Dr. Sally Mapstone for pointing out the connection between this text and Montgomerie's sonnet; her work on Melvill's religious verse has paved the way for a major revaluation of his position in later sixteenth-century Scottish poetry.

Qui comprens Ciel et terre, et la mer navigable
D'un point de cercle entier de ton infinité:
Essence en qui le Pere, et le Fils, et l'Esprit,
Distinctement unis, guide, conduit, regit
De ce globe poly, la masse universelle:
Immortel, infiny, Eternel Dieu par soy,
Du monde passager l'inviolable Loy,
Guide moy sur ton char en ta gloire immortelle.[30]

Much of the language which unites the French and Scots texts is, of course, conventional; but the initial use of "Essence", the playing on the nature of the Trinity, the overall movement of the sonnet, and the recurrence of particular words and phrases in broadly corresponding positions all point towards the likelihood that Le Saulx's poem formed the direct inspiration for at least one of the Scots versions. Neither is so close, however, as to be a straightforward translation, and it is not absolutely clear which of the two derives more directly from the French model.

Some internal features, certainly, suggest that Melvill's sonnet is closer to Le Saulx than the version found in the Ker manuscript: "le Pere, et le Fils, et l'Esprit" (l. 9) is reflected in "Eternall Father, Sonne and halie Spreit" (Melvill, l. 8), and the final line of the *Morning Vision* text conveys more of Le Saulx's "Guide moy sur ton char" than Montgomerie's conclusion. Evidence of the sequence of ideas is, however, inconclusive: the line "Like unto none, nor none like unto Thee", apparently adapting Le Saulx's "à qui nul n'est semblable" (l. 3), occurs as l. 4 in Melvill but as l. 7 in Montgomerie; "Creator uncreated" (cf. Le Saulx, "Createur souverain", l. 6) begins l. 5 in Melvill but is delayed until l. 11 in Montgomerie; but "word" and the cosmological reference to "rounds" (representing "D'un point du cercle" in the French sonnet) come closer to their position in Le Saulx in the Montgomerie version than in that published by Melvill. If Melvill preserves features of the French which are absent in Montgomerie's sonnet, therefore, there is also a little evidence that Montgomerie, too, had recourse to the Le Saulx poem. And while Le Saulx and his publisher Vautrollier, as Huguenot exiles in England, were unquestionably closer to the milieu of the Presbyterian Melvill than to that of the Catholic Montgomerie, Vautrollier's presence in Edinburgh from April 1580, first as a bookseller and as a printer from 1584, provided the channel by means of which both men could equally have come to read the *Theanthropogamie*; it was, after all, Vautrollier who printed James's *Essayes of a Prentise* as one of the first products of his Edinburgh press.

Whichever version of "Supreme Essence" should be given priority, both represent, in rhetorical terms, a significant advance on Le Saulx's sonnet. Like most

---

[30] Marin Le Saulx, *Theanthropogamie* (London: Thomas Vautrollier, 1577), sig. K1r.

of the poems in the *Theanthropogamie*, "Essence unique" is formally elegant and well-structured, and thoroughly infused with the encomiastic language of the Psalms; but whichever Scots poet initiated the process of adaptation goes much further, intensifying Le Saulx's conventional phrases by insisting upon the power of paradox. Thus, "un en trois, trois en un" becomes "Distinguished ane, and undevided three" in Melvill and "Ay trinall ane, ane undevydit three" in Montgomerie (l. 2 in each case); and a pattern of negating pairs, established with "beginner / beginning unbegun" in l. 1, runs through both versions as a unifying motif. The contrasting forms of the second line are particularly interesting: Melvill's "distinguished", perhaps suggesting a pun on the senses of "separate" and "celebrated", is the earliest recorded use of the word in either sense, while Montgomerie's "trinal" is strikingly paralleled in the conclusion of Book I of *The Faerie Queene*:

> During the which there was an heauenly noise
> Heard sound through all the Pallace pleasantly,
> Like as it had bene many an Angels voice,
> Singing before th'eternall maiesty,
> In their trinall triplicities on hye . . .[31]

If Spenser's coinage is a probable source for Montgomerie, the latter's version of the sonnet must be later than the publication of the first instalment of *The Faerie Queene* at the beginning of 1590; at any event, its presence in l. 2 has the immediate effect of intensifying the Trinitarian emphasis of the Scots poem.

Just as it is ultimately impossible to determine which of the Scottish sonnets came first, we cannot be sure how far doctrinal considerations explain the differences between the two texts. One of the most remarkable of these is the presence in Melvill's version of the phrase "mediator meit", which is nowhere reflected in Montgomerie; but the notion of Christ's mediating function is so deeply inscribed in Christian tradition, deriving from references in the Pauline epistles (1 Timothy 2:5; Hebrews 12:24), that its presence or absence cannot be said to have any dogmatic significance. There is, perhaps, a greater force in the very different endings of the two versions:

---

[31] Spenser, *The Faerie Queene*, ed. A.C. Hamilton (London/ New York: Longman, 1977), 161. However, Spenser's "trinal triplicities" are the nine choirs of angels, arranged in groups of three, while "trinal ane" is close to patristic Greek Trinitarian usage: both applications, to the Trinity and to the angelic orders, are found in the Pseudo-Dionysius: τριαδικὸν ἑνάδα in the *Divine Names* (593B: *Corpus Dionysiacum*, ed. Beate Regina Suchla, Günther Heil and Adolf Martin Ritter, 2 vols. [Berlin and New York: Walter de Gruyter, 1990–1991], 1:116), τριαδικαὶ διακοσμήσεις in the *Celestial Hierarchy* (200D: *Corpus Dionysiacum*, 2:26). I am grateful to Dr. Leslie MacCoull for these latter references.

Redeemer, from the death and miserie
Possesse my [saule] and keepe me in Thy feare,
And make me live with Thee for ever meare.
    (Melvill)


Teich me thy treuth, since unto thee I trust,
Incres, confirme and strenthen from above
My faith, my hope, and by the lave my love.
    (Montgomerie)

Like Le Saulx, Melvill turns in his final lines to the destiny of his soul, praying that through the redeeming power of Christ and through a proper fear of God's power he may gain admission to eternal heavenly existence. Montgomerie, by contrast, both softens the relationship between himself and God, emphasising "treuth" and "trust", and concentrates, through a neat application of 1 Corinthians 13:11–13 (as we noted above), upon his immediate spiritual condition rather than upon the soterial future. His final line is carefully constructed, following the Pauline doctrine of *caritas* by separating love from the other two members of the triad, marking its greater importance not only by its final position but also by the idiomatic "by the lave' [*in addition to* or *apart from* the rest]. Here is a real difference: Le Saulx and Melvill share a preoccupation with the afterlife, darkened in Melvill's case by a keen awareness of the miseries of the human condition, while Montgomerie seems more concerned with the personal nature of his present relationship with God. This, then, is a significant modulation of his source, a reworking of familiar materials to give a new emphasis which is all the more marked because of the ways in which it contrasts with its recognisable sources.

A similar, and in some ways even more radical, strategy is employed in the second of Montgomerie's theological sonnets [60], where again there is a marked change of direction in the final couplet:

High Architectur, vondrous-vautit-rounds,
Huge-host of Hevin in restles-rolling spheers,
Firme-fixit polis vhilk all the axtrie beirs,
Concordant-discords, suete harmonious sounds,
Boud-Zodiak (circle-belting-Phoebus' bounds),
Celestiall signis, of moneths making yeers,
Bright Titan to the Tropiks that reteirs
Quhais fyrie flammis all chaos face confounds,
Just balanc'd ball amidst the hevins that hings,
All Creaturs that NATUR creat can
To serve the vse of most vnthankfull man,
Admire your maker, only King of Kings.
    Prais him O man his mervels that remarks,
    Quhais mercyis far exceids his wondrous warks.

The rhetorical basis of this poem, too, is derived from the encomiastic tradition of the Psalms: Montgomerie's initial theme, the magnificence of Creation and the light it casts on the beneficence of Providence, is a favourite subject of Catholic and Protestant writers alike throughout the sixteenth century. It seems likely, indeed, that "High Archtitectur" is another conscious rewriting of a previously-existing text, in this case a sonnet by James VI:

> The azured vault, the christall circles bright,
> The gleaming firie torches poudered thair;                    *scattered*
> The changing rounde, the shining beamie light;
> The sadd and bearded fires, the monsters faire;
> The prodiges appearing in the aire;
> The rearding thunders and the blustering windes;             *roaring*
> The foules in hewe, in shape and nature rare;
> The prettie notts that wing'd musicians findes;
> In earthe the sauourie flowres, the metall'd mindes;         *mines*
> The wholesome herbes, the hautie pleasant trees;
> The siluer streames, the beasts of sundrie kinds;
> The bounded roares, and fishes of the seas;
>     All these for teaching man the Lord did frame,
>     To honoure him whose glorie shines in them.[32]

This is, interestingly, a theme which bulks large in Le Saulx's *Theanthropogamie*, where we find, for example, sonnets beginning "Plus tost le ciel vouté priué de sa lumiere" (sig. G3r) and "L'Eternel Dieu regnant sur la voute des cieux" (sig. H2r). In Le Saulx, as in James's poem, the splendours of the visible universe have a straightforward didactic purpose, enabling man to perceive and thus to praise God's "glorie".

The parallels between the structure of the king's sonnet and Montgomerie's are clear enough: the three interlocking quatrains all point towards the summarising couplet, which explains the theological "point"; the first two are concerned with the heavens, descending from the opening "azured vault" to the diversity and harmony of the world of the birds, the third deals with the earth itself. Montgomerie's version, however, goes beyond James's in several respects, and might almost be an answer to it. Both syntactically and doctrinally Montgomerie is more complex than the king, and the power of the design which is carried over from the universe to the structure of the sonnet is even more compressed. The certainty of the poet's devotional *sententia* is, in the first place, disguised by a syntactical ambiguity: only at l. 12, with the imperative and the second-person pronoun, do we discover that the previous eleven lines of appositional phrases are a kind of vocative sequence, all leading to the exhortation, addressed to the

---

[32] James VI and I, *Poems*, ed. Craigie, 1:258 (cf. 2:99).

whole universe, to "admire your maker". What has appeared to be a triumphal description, as in the king's sonnet, turns out at this point to be only secondarily so: the evocation of the splendours of the created world is justified only by the call for those splendours to praise their Creator. Even this, however, is in turn only a secondary purpose, for those very wonders, great as they are, are asserted in the couplet to be less than the wonder of divine forgiveness.

If Montgomerie is in part rewriting and capping James's sonnet, however, there is a further intertext in the form of Ronsard's "Hymne du Ciel".[33] First published in 1555, this poem went through the poet's characteristic processes of revision, and it is the version first included in the 1584 edition which bears the closest resemblance to Montgomerie's sonnet:

> O Ciel rond & vouté, haute maison de Dieu
> Qui prestes en ton sein à toutes choses lieu,
> Et qui roules si tost ta grand' boule esbranlée
> Sur deux essieux fichez . . .
>        (15–18)[34]

There can, surely, be little doubt that Montgomerie found the ideas for the opening lines of his poem in this passage, or that his fourth line was inspired by a somewhat later passage, although here, confusingly, it appears to be the pre-1584 version which more closely resembles his:

> De ton bransle premier, des autres tout divers,
> Tu tires au rebours les corps de l'Univers,
> Bien qu'ilz resistent fort à ta grand' violence,
> Seulz à-part demenans une seconde dance,
> L'un deçà, l'autre là, comme ilz sont agitez
> *Des discordans accordz* de leurs diversitez:
> Ainsi guidant premier si grande compagnie,
> Tu fais une si *douce & plaisante harmonie,*
> Qui nos lucz sont rien aux prix des mopindres sons
> Qui resonnent là haut de diverses façons.
>        (35–44) [my italics][35]

The rhetorical difference between the two texts is clear enough: the sonnet's demand for compression ensures that Montgomerie selects his details carefully, and

---

[33] Ronsard, *Œuvres complètes*, ed. Laumonier, 8:140–49. I am indebted to Dr. Jamie Reid-Baxter for the initial suggestion which led to this analysis.

[34] In the text printed between 1555 and 1583, l. 15 reads "O Ciel net, pur, & beau, haute maison de Dieu".

[35] From 1584, l. 40 reads "Des mouvemens reiglez des leurs diversités".

that he brings together in sharp juxtaposition elements which in Ronsard form part of a more extended discourse. Even here, however, there are interesting similarities, for the rhythmical pattern of Montgomerie's quatrain (the half-lines separated by a caesura in ll. 1 and 4, but not in ll. 2 and 3) manifestly echoes that of ll.15–18 in Ronsard's "Hymne". As in the amatory sonnets discussed in the previous chapter, we can see in Montgomerie's adaptation the most subtle of rhetorical skills.

The double structure of subordination which comprises the sonnet's structure is equally skilfully managed, testimony to a kind of theological wit which confirms the sense that, as a religious poet, Montgomerie is as capable of looking forward as of casting back. But this recognition of the surprises he builds into the final lines should not entirely distract us from the quite remarkable passage that precedes them, with its alliteratively-linked compound adjectives building up to a strongly evocative picture of the Ptolemaic cosmos. The pervasive use of alliteration is, of course, a foregrounding device which is characteristic of Older Scots poetry; here, however, it contributes to a density of reference which goes beyond the rhetoric of praise we find elsewhere in sixteenth-century Scottish devotional verse. The insistence on the syntactic parallelism, reminiscent of the forceful opening of Dunbar's "Done is a battell on the dragon blak", is another key element in the cumulative strategy which leads to the summative, and less heavily end-stopped, ll. 10–11, which in turn prepare for the injunction which completes the third quatrain. "High Architectur", then, illustrates Montgomerie's ability to rework conventional devotional materials in quite surprising ways, confidently pushing traditional methods into new rhetorical territory.

So far we have seen two sides of the relatively restricted corpus of Montgomerie's "original" religious poetry: stanzaic lyrics which deploy familiar penitential material with effective rhetorical control but relatively little innovation, and sonnets which seem to be constructive rewritings of existing works. In the latter cases, we have seen, Montgomerie deploys the full range of his rhetorical skills to create a distinctive message, refocusing the laudatory language of "Supreme Essence" upon the speaker's own spiritual condition and wittily capping the tradition of psalmodic encomium by trumping the visible universe with divine mercy. In all these poems, it is the Psalms which provide the ultimate inspiration, reinforced by Pauline and other New Testament allusions. But Montgomerie's most remarkable religious lyric is drawn from another Biblical source, the Song of Solomon.[36] "Come my Childrene dere" [98] is exceptional in the directness of its language, its hints of a dramatic structure, and its use of amatory imagery to express the relationship of the unspecified speaker with Christ.

---

[36] For the background to this usage, see Max Engammare, *Qu'il me baise des baisiers de sa bouche: La Cantique des Cantiques à la Renaissance* (Geneva: Droz, 1993).

David Parkinson suggests in his edition that this poem is "in the manner of but not necessarily by Montgomerie"; "its language," he remarks, "is fundamentally English, with an overlay of Scots spellings."[37] This latter claim does not seem to be borne out by the evidence of the text. Four rhyme-pairs, in particular, point in the opposite direction: *chuis/refuis* (18/ 19); *glore/befor* (27/30); *chose/lose* (28/29), and *ring/thring* (35/36). In each case, one member of the pair, while not uniquely Scots, is much more likely to turn up in a late sixteenth-century Scottish text than an English one. *Refuis*, in the sense of "rejection", remained current in Scots but was, according to *DOST*, obsolescent in English in the later sixteenth century; *chose* as a noun, likewise, while normal in Scots and rhyming with such words as *suppois*, *formois* and *depois*, seems to have been relatively unusual in English. *Glore*, as a variant of *glory*, is overwhelmingly Scots and so, after about 1500, is *thring* in the sense of "thrust". The rhyme on *loyal/royal* might be thought to indicate an English ear; but *royal* was a perfectly acceptable Older Scots form, alongside *rial(l)* and *real(l)*. On balance, then, the poem seems much more likely to have originated in Scotland than in England. Montgomerie's authorship is, perhaps, not self-evident, especially in view of the poem's slightly odd position in the Ker manuscript, which makes it look like an afterthought.[38] But it shares many features with the more radical parts of the authentic canon, and there does not seem to be any good reason for denying this superb lyric to Montgomerie.

The poem's rhetorical directness is established at the very outset, with an injunction to an imagined audience to witness the song which will follow:

> Come my Childrene dere, drau neir me
> To my Love vhen that I sing.
> Mak your ears and hairts to heir me
> For it is no eirthly thing
> Bot a Love
> Far above
> Other Loves all I say
> Vhich is sure
> To indure
> Vhen as all things sall decay.
> (1–10)

---

[37] *Poems*, ed. Parkinson, 2:5. He does not, however, relegate "Come my Childrene dere" from the canon, as he does "Away vane world".

[38] Written on fols. 82v–83v and (uniquely in this manuscript) provided with music, the poem is the last item in the collection. Like "Away vane world", it would properly belong among the religious lyrics on fols. 2r–8v.

These opening lines also set up the distinction between "eirthly", sexual love and a spiritual love which is, by contrast, eternal. Given this opposition, we can scarcely be in much doubt about the identity of the unnamed "Love" of l. 2, but the "Childrene" of the first line are more problematic: how, we may properly ask, does the term define the relationship between the speaker/singer and the audience, and indeed, the identity of the former is his/her own right? We can scarcely fail to think of Jesus' instruction to "Sinite parvulos/pueros venire ad me" (Mark 10:14; Luke 18:16), and yet this will prove to be a misleading idea: for Jesus is in this case the object of the speaker's love, and not the speaker him/herself.

The second stanza, which is the only part of the song which conforms rhetorically to the expectation of a song to "my Love" established in the opening lines, makes the religious nature of the subject fully explicit:

> O my Lord and Love most loyal,
>     Vhat a prais does thou deserve.
> Thoght thou be a Prince most Royal
>     With thy Angels thee to serve
>         Yit a pure
>         Creature
>     Thou hes lovit al thy lyfe.
>         Thou didst chuis
>         The refuis
>     Of the world to be thy wyfe.
>         (11–20)

The language here is by no means without parallel or precedent in the sixteenth-century tradition of devotional lyric, as we shall see in a moment, but now Montgomerie switches into a more narrative, even dramatic mode:

> Whill I did behold the favor
>     Of his Countenance so fair,
> Whill I smellit the sueet savor
>     Of his garments rich and rair,
>         "Oh" I said,
>         "If I had
>     To my Love yon Prince of glore
>         For my chose
>         Wold I lose
>     Other loves I lov'd befor."
>         (21–30)

It is at this point that the connection with the Song of Solomon is made explicit, through the echo of 4:11, "odor vestimentorum tuorum sicut odor Lebanon"

("and the sauour of thy garment is as the sauour of Lebanon", in the Geneva
Bible), although it should, of course, be observed that in the biblical text it is the
Bride rather than the Bridegroom who is addressed in these terms. Nevertheless,
the sensuous nature of Montgomerie's allusion is clearly intended to evoke the
metaphorical framework of the Song, in which the Bride speaks first in the first
person (as here), and the alignment of sexual and religious love which that text
was traditionally held to achieve.

The implications of this connection are then fully worked out in the final two
stanzas of the version we find in the Ker manuscript:

> Vhill I did these words besyd me
>     With a secreit sigh confes
> Lo my Lord and Love espyd me
>     And dreu neir me vhair I wes
>         Then a ring
>         Did he thring                                          *thrust*
>     On my finger that wes fyne
>         "Tak", quod he,
>         "This to the
>     For a pledge that I am thyne.


> "Nou thou hes that thou desyrit,
>     Me to be thy Lord and Love.
> All the thing that thou requyrit
>     To the heir I do approve
>         Yit agane
>         For my pane
>     Only this I crave of thee,
>         For my pairt
>         Keep thy hairt
>     As a Virgin chast to me."
>     (31–50)

Two rhetorical approaches are brought together here in a way which is most strik-
ing: the application to the relationship with Christ of the language and imagery of
sexual love, implicit from the beginning, is now fully realised; and this relationship
is then further personalised through a dramatically dialogic presentation. This is,
in turn, still further reinforced through the dramatic action of Christ's "thringing"
of a ring on the speaker's finger, echoing the Song of Solomon 8:6.

In "Come my Childrene dere", then, Montgomerie gives full expression to a
theme which he touches on elsewhere in his work; as we saw above, "Auay vane
world" (if it is indeed his) ends with the assertion that "Chryst is my love alone",

while "The Poets Dreme" [3] begins with a much more explicit allusion to the Song of Solomon (5: 2–8):

> God give me grace for to begin
> My spousing garment for to spin
> And to be one till enter in
>    With the brydgrome in blisse
> And sleep na mair in sleuth and sin
> Bot rather ryse and richtly rin
> That hevinly wedfie for to win                  *reward*
>    Vhilk he prepairs for his.
>    (1–8)

As we noted at the outset of this study, it is difficult to read such lines without thinking of George Herbert, but the application of the language of sexual love to devotional lyric is not confined to him and to Montgomerie. It runs through a sixteenth-century lyrical tradition, descending perhaps from the highly affective mysticism of the later Middle Ages, which includes, for example, some of the *Chansons spirituelles* of Marguerite de Navarre:

> Seigneur, quand viendra le jour
>    Tant desiré,
> Que je seray par amour
>    A vous tiré,
> Et que l'union sera
>    Telle entre nous
> Que l'espouse on nommera
>    Comme l'epoux?[39]

[Lord, when will the so greatly desired day come when I shall be drawn to you by love, and when the union between us will be like that between the bride and the bridegroom?]

and — closer to Montgomerie's own milieu — the neglected but equally powerful songs of Katherina Boudewijns, published in Brussels in 1587:

> Jhesus es myn lief en niemant el /
> Waer ick by hem soo waer ick wel /
> Want sonder Godt en can ick niet /
> Heere haelt my uut dit verdriet.

---

[39] Marguerite de Navarre, *Chansons spirituelles*, ed. G. Dottin (Paris: Minard, 1971), 50.

In deser werelt en is geen rust /
Voor dat ghij mijn begeerten blust:
Laet my met u vereenicht zyn /
Soo sal ick wesen uut alle pijn.[40]


[Jesus is my love, and no one else; if I were with Him I would be happy.
Without God I just cannot exist; Lord, take me out of this sorrow. There
is no rest in this world until You quench my desires. Let me be united with
You; so shall I be out of all pain.]

The most influential, ultimately, of these devotional lyrics are those of San Juan
de la Cruz, written in the 1570s but not published until 1618:

Cuan manso y amoroso
Recuerdas en mi seno,
Donde secretamente solo moras:
Y en tu aspirar sabroso
De bien y gloria lleno
Cuan delicadamente me enamoras![41]


[How gently and lovingly you wake in my heart, where in secret you dwell
alone; and by Your sweet breathing, filled with good and glory, how ten-
derly You fill me with love!]

Of Montgomerie's religious lyrics, it is "Come my Childrene dere" which falls
most clearly within this tradition, and it is likely that the music gives a clue to the
song's roots. For if, as seems probable, it is an adaptation of a secular song, then the
poem is a *contrafactum*, one of that large class of sixteenth-century devotional paro-
dies which draw their form, their imagery, even their verbal structure from secular
love poetry.[42] It does not appear that Montgomerie has echoed the language of his
model very directly, in the way that Herbert, for example, retained the argumenta-
tive structure and much of the verbal patterning of the secular song "Soules joy, now

---

[40] Katherina Boudewijns, *Het Prieelken der Gheestelyker Wellusten*, ed. Hermance van
Belle (Antwerp: De Sikkel, 1927), 61. "Wel" is very complex: it contains the ideas of
physical health and of completeness as well as of happiness.

[41] Juan de la Cruz, *Poesías*, ed. Paola Elia (Madrid: Castalia, 1990), 118.

[42] On this tradition see Bruce W. Wardropper, "The Religious Conversion of Pro-
fane Poetry", in *Studies in the Continental Background of Renaissance English Literature*, ed.
Dale B.J. Randall and George Walton Williams (Durham, NC: Duke University Press,
1977), 203–21.

I am gone" in writing "A Parodie"; rather, he seems merely to have allowed the spirit and sensibility of his lost original to infuse his spiritual lyric. In a similar manner, Katherina Boudewijns uses such secular tunes as "Mijn lief is my te nacht ontweken", "Il y avoit une fillette" and "Het was te nacht wel alzoo zoeten nacht" as the basis for her religious songs without, apparently, taking over much of the structure or language of her originals. Montgomerie, of course, also used the *contrafactum* technique elsewhere: his psalm translations are constructed to secular tunes, and the Ker manuscript version of "Auay vane world" notes that the words are set "To the Toon of 'Sall I let hir go'." In addition to the Continental parallels we have already noted, he had a Scottish precedent in the rather crude parodies of the *Gude and Godlie Ballatis*, probably first issued in the 1540s and still, despite their Lutheran background, in current circulation in Montgomerie's lifetime.[43] It is, however, significant that Wardropper observes of the relative scarcity of the *contrafactum* in Britain that

> It is in fact the recusants, may of whom had perforce traveled abroad, who seem to have cultivated *contrafacta* most assiduously.[44]

As a Catholic convert in Reformed Scotland, Montgomerie clearly belongs within this tradition. The relative popularity of the form among the recusants, however, may be due to more than Continental influence: as sacred parody, the *contrafactum* had an essentially coded character, and it may be that this recommended itself to those whose religious experience was in important respects necessarily covert.

This brings us back to the unresolved issue of the meaning of "Come my Childrene dere", and to the identity of the speaker. We have noted that the poem's shifting rhetorical stances enable the poet, however uncertainly, to extend the resonance of the interplay of the secular and the divine. But it remains unclear whose voice we hear inviting his/her "Childrene" to listen to this celebration of love and then recounting a symbolic marriage, although it is clearly cognate with that of the Song's Bride. The lyric abruptness of the song does not require Montgomerie to define his persona at all, and even the gender remains unspecified. Shire suggests, referring back to Montgomerie's Catholic connections, that the poem may have been written for a nun, Gabrielle d'Aubigny, daughter of the late Duke of Lennox, and that the intended speaker may be "mistress of the novices", or alternatively that it "may reflect Montgomerie's own desire in the last years of his life to enter the priestly life", while Jack agrees that the poem "may be specifically related to Montgomerie's priestly aspirations".[45] Either is

---

[43] Three editions were published in the twenty years after the Reformation: (Edinburgh: for Thomas Bassandyne, 1565), [Edinburgh: John Scot, 1567], and (Edinburgh: [John Ros for Henry Charteris], 1578).

[44] Wardropper, "Religious Conversion", 206–7.

[45] Shire, *Song, Dance and Poetry*, 147–48; Jack, *Montgomerie*, 69.

possible, but there is no real evidence to support these suggestions, and it may equally be that there is a more abstract application: the Bride of Christ, addressing her "Childrene", may very well be the Church itself, to which the allegorical interpretation of the Song of Solomon was routinely applied by medieval and Counter-Reformation theologians.[46] This reading of the Song was, naturally, taken over by Protestant exegetes and applied to their Church as well: the Cambridge theologian William Whitaker, for example, interpreted the text in this way in his *Disputatio de Sacra Scriptura* (1588), while the editors of the Geneva version of the Bible assert in a headnote that

> In this Song, Salamon by most sweete and comfortable allegories and parables describeth the perfite loue of Iesus Christ, the true Salamon and King of peace, and the faithfull soule or his Church, which he hath sanctified and appoynted to be his spouse, holy, chaste, and without reprehension . . . Also the earnest affection of the Church which is inflamed with the loue of Christ, desiring to be more and more ioyned to him in loue, and not to be forsaken for any spot or blemish that is in her.[47]

As we find so often in Montgomerie's verse, then, the allusion can be read in at least two opposing ways: both Catholics and Protestants might find in the speaker's love of Christ a reference to their own Church. But still, if an allusion to the Catholic Church is even covertly present in Montgomerie's spiritual love song, that would explain the imprecision of the reference: in late sixteenth-century Scotland, it would be imprudent for a known Catholic to celebrate the relationship of Christ with the Church unambiguously. In one sense, then, the powerful evocation of a personal spiritual experience may be misleading, and the coded nature of the song's ultimate significance might help to explain the uncertainty of the rhetorical point of view.

One more twist must be considered. A second copy of the song, in the late seventeenth-century Taitt manuscript, apparently written for the *sang schuil* at Lauder, adds a further stanza:[48]

> Oh my soul therfor repent the
> Of the love thou hadst before:

---

[46] For patristic and medieval interpretations, see Engammare, *La Cantique des Cantiques*, 25–63; sixteenth-century interpretations are discussed at 251–372.

[47] For Whitaker, see *Disputation on Holy Scripture*, ed. William Fitzgerald (London: Parker Society, 1849), 31–2; the Geneva Bible headnote is cited from the edition by Christopher Barker (London, 1599), 2, fol. 40v.

[48] This addition was pointed out by Walter H. Rubsamen, "Scottish and English Music of the Renaissance in a Newly Discovered Manuscript", in *Festschrift Heinrich Besseler*, ed. Eberhardt Klemm (Leipzig: Deutscher Verlag für Musik, 1961), 259–84.

> Let his countenance content the
>   Since he is the king of glore.
>     So shall he
>     Be to the
>   All the being that thou wouldst have.
>     In his love
>     Shall thou prove
>   Quhat thy heart can voise or crave.
>     (51–60)

We cannot, of course, be sure that this late text represents an authentic conclusion to the song; it may have been added by someone other than Montgomerie in order to give the piece an acceptably Protestant emphasis — an hypothesis which only serves to reinforce the sense that the version in the Ker manuscript supports a Catholic reading. On the other hand, the rhymes *have/crave* and *love/prove* indicate a Scots ear and therefore, perhaps, an earlier rather than a later date, while the shift of rhetorical stance, to an apostrophe to the speaker/singer's soul, merely carries a stage further a process which has characterised the text throughout. There is no strong reason, therefore, apart from its omission from the Ker version, to reject Montgomerie's authorship of this stanza, which does have the merit of enclosing a dramatic passage with otherwise ends very abruptly.

"Come my Childrene dere", it may reasonably be claimed, extends the rhetoric of the *contrafactum* tradition by giving the relationship between Christ and the loving soul a dramatic, dialogic realisation and an allegorical subtext. It is, at least in the former respect, the most innovative of Montgomerie's religious lyrics, and it raises once again important questions about the extent to which he can properly be placed among those European poets who, in the final decades of the sixteenth century, were developing new modes of poetic discourse, especially within the tradition of the lyric. We should be quite clear about the nature and the limits of this claim: Montgomerie's verse, as "Come my Childrene dere" illustrates, reflects the uncertainties of these new rhetorical strategies, and the poems, both secular and religious, in which it is possible to identify such evidence of radical innovation represent a small proportion of his corpus, most of which is highly accomplished, rhetorically sophisticated, but thoroughly conventional. In certain moods, however, he reveals himself to be much more than a skilled court poet of the old school, and poems such as "Come my Childrene dere" can leave us in no doubt that he was capable on occasion of taking the lyric in radically new directions.

If Montgomerie's religious lyrics on the whole display a delicate balance between devotional praise and moral exhortation, the latter clearly predominates in his longest and most ambitious work, *The Cherrie and the Slae* [**100–101**]. The rather odd place which this extended dream-allegory occupies in his corpus is in part the result of its circumstances of composition: begun as we have seen in the early 1580s, during the heyday of Montgomerie's influence at court and the earliest phase of James's court circle, it was apparently only completed in the final year of his life, when he was embittered and in disgrace, the king's literary circle largely dispersed, and his cultural ambitions subordinated to much more concrete political ones. It is difficult to decide, therefore, whether the poem should be seen primarily as a product of soaring "Castalian" confidence or as a testimony to Montgomerie's eventual disillusionment with the court and all its works. In the episode in which the narrator fails in his attempt to fly with Cupid's wings we have, I suggested earlier, a poignant and paradoxical image of the poem's ultimate limitations — and perhaps of the entire "Castalian" project.[49] Yet this could scarcely have been apparent to Montgomerie when he was at work upon *The Cherrie and the Slae* in or before 1584, by which time, it should be noted, the main lines of the argument had probably already been established. The specific conclusion we find in the later published editions *may* only have been worked out after a gap of more than a dozen years, but it is entirely consistent with the direction in which the incomplete first version was evidently heading. In trying to come to terms with Montgomerie's longest, and in a curious way final, work we shall first consider the poem in the form in which he apparently left it in the mid-1580s, then confront the modifications which he made "not long before" his death, and finally attempt to assess the relationship between the two versions and whether there is a significant shift in intention between the first and the second.

*The Cherrie and the Slae* has drawn varied responses from its readers. While it was enormously popular throughout the seventeenth century, going through at least eight editions, its obscurity was evident enough at the beginning of the eighteenth century to cause one reader to remark in general of Montgomerie's capacity to "mask the matter with such skil / As few perceave the drift".[50] By the later nineteenth century, its fortunes were clearly in eclipse. More recently, critics have again come to view the poem positively: for Ian Ross it is Montgomerie's "best poem", while Jack declares it "his finest achievement".[51] As indicated above, my own view is more mixed: while acknowledging the *Cherrie*'s many local strengths and the ultimate force of its argument, I find the combination of the lyric stanza with a long allegorical poem an awkward one, and I do not altogether share Jack's view that Montgomerie succeeds in maintaining the reader's engagement during the long stretches of philosophical debate. This is certainly not to deny the poem's essential seriousness, however, or to claim that the completed version

---

[49] See above, 107–12.

[50] *A Facetious Poem in Imitation of the Cherry and the Slae* (Edinburgh, 1701), quoted by Ian Ross, "The Form and Matter of *The Cherrie and the Slae*", *Texas Studies in English* 37 (1958), 79–91, here 87; and by Jack, *Montgomerie*, 120.

[51] Ross, "Form and Matter", 79; Jack, *Montgomerie*, 132.

fails to present a coherent *philosophical* resolution of the moral problems which are already posed in the sections written in the early 1580s and printed in 1597. To what degree, and in what respects, this ultimate resolution reflects a changed view of the world must form a central theme of the analysis which follows. If, as seems likely, the revision and completion of *The Cherrie and the Slae* was Montgomerie's final poetic statement, then it provides a logical end-point for our consideration of his achievement and a vital insight into the final phase of his spiritual, as well as his creative, journey.

At the point at which Robert Waldegrave's 1597 edition breaks off, the outcome of the debate remains formally in doubt, although the developing influence of Experience, Ressoun, and their companions in balancing the claims of Will, Curage, and Hoip on the one hand and of Dreid, Danger, and Dispair on the other clearly hints at the ultimate resolution of the dreamer's dilemma in a way that will lead him to the desired Cherrie. Structurally, too, the main lines of the allegory had already been established when Montgomerie presumably abandoned the poem in the state in which Waldegrave found it nearly fifteen years later. That is to say, the opening episode in which the protagonist describes his vision of Cupid and his ill-fated attempt to fly, followed by the discovery of the inaccessible Cherrie and the easily-gained Slae, had already been outweighed by a debate nearly twice as long as these preliminary scenes. A central question, the relationship between the Cupid incident and the allegorical disputation, is thus raised by Montgomerie's earliest conception of *The Cherrie and the Slae*; and any attempt to understand this ambitious and difficult poem must seek an answer to it. For the logic of the structure suggests that the encounter with Cupid is integral to the meanings Montgomerie attached to the rival claims of Cherrie and Slae.

In describing his protagonist's doomed attempt to borrow Cupid's wings, Montgomerie takes up, as we have noted above, a contemporary Continental fashion. Over and over again, Desportes and other French poets of the 1570s draw on the myths of Icarus and/or Phaethon as types of (frequently excessive) aspiration. Montgomerie, too, links his flight with Icarus "quha mountit heicher nor he micht" (100: 144–146) and with "fulisch Phaetone" (161–162). In doing so, he links the *Cherrie* with other poems, especially with the sonnet "Love lent me wings of hope and high desyre", where the specific mention of Icarus' waxen wings is particularly suggestive. For Amadis Jamyn and other French poets this conceit, calling up the melting of wax as a figure of desire, "fait surgir, en même temps que l'idée d'une évasion possible, la notion d'un danger précis".[52] For Montgomerie's protagonist, clearly, it is the danger which prevails, as he comically wounds himself in attempting to use Cupid's bow and comes crashing to earth. Although there is no direct suggestion in *The Cherrie and the Slae* that the lover's borrowed wings are made of

---

[52] Mathieu-Castellani, *Thèmes amoureux*, 294.

wax, the presence of the notion behind the text is evidently hinted at by Montgom-
erie's evocation of another Petrarchist commonplace:

> Than furth I drew that deadlie dairt
> Quhilk sumtyme schot his mother
>     Quhairwith I hurt my wanton heart
> In hope to hurt ane vther.
>         It hurt me, it *burned* me
>         The ofter I it handill.
>     Cum se now in me now
>         The butter-flie and candill.
>         (100: 147–154)

The conceit of the lover consumed by the candle of desire unmistakably brings the
wax association into the dominant figure of audacious flight, and we can scarcely
doubt that Montgomerie is here drawing upon a key cluster of images from con-
temporary French verse.

But what is their significance in the context of the allegory of *The Cherrie
and the Slae*, as the poem was originally conceived and as it was subsequently
modified? At a superficial level, Montgomerie is at pains to link the lover's flight
with the subsequent debate over the inaccessible cherries: he invokes the les-
son of experience (100: 173) and blames his adventure on his 'wilfulnes' (100:
189), thus anticipating two of the principal characters in the allegorical dialogue
which follows.[53] The vision of the cherry-tree also seems closely associated with
the protagonist's miserable condition following his disastrous descent, for it is as
the conventionally deranged lover, wandering in a landscape which now seems a
good deal less paradisaical than it had in the opening stanzas, that he first sees
the delightful fruit. His response, moreover, makes a sharp contrast with the up-
ward aspiration with which he began:

> To clime the Craige it was na buit                    *no use*
> Lat be to presse to pull the fruit
> In top of all the trie.
>     I saw na way quhairby to cum
> Be ony craft to get it clum
> Appeirandly to me.
>     The craig was vgly, stay and dreiche,            *high and hazardous*
> The trie heich, lang and smal.
>     I was affrayd to mount sa hich
> For feir to get ane fall.
>     (100: 337–346)

---

[53] On this point see Ross, "Form and Matter", 88.

This sense of repressed desire is enacted in the first stage of the debate, where Danger responds to the promptings of Curage by reminding the protagonist that he owes his present situation to a similar aspiration. One key question posed by the Cherrie/Slae dilemma, therefore, is whether the protagonist will repeat the mistakes of the past, or alternatively whether a quest for the elusive Cherrie can indeed be equated with the earlier encounter with Cupid.

Our response to these issues depends to a large extent upon our understanding of Montgomerie's symbolic language. The Cherrie is, as Jack notes, conventionally associated with sexuality, and it is therefore not unnatural for the reader to accept its attractiveness as linked in some way with the protagonist's initial escapade. This is reinforced by the nature of the Cherrie's advocates, led in this first phase of the debate by Curage: although the latter's name is generally assumed to have its modern sense, *curage* is more commonly associated in Older Scots with sexual inclination than with physical or moral bravery, and his role in the poem is, at least from some points of view, equivalent to Desire. All the more reason, we might think, to conclude that the lure of the Cherrie is morally indefensible, and that Dreid and Danger are justified in their preference for the Slae. As Jack notes, Danger's arguments at this stage are stronger than those of his opponents;[54] and while he and Dispair behave in character by abruptly withdrawing at l. 589, this cannot be said to be a consequence of their moral or logical defeat. Yet Curage and Hoip will in the end be vindicated in their advocacy of boldness, for the fundamental reason that the Cherrie will prove to be, unlike the false ambition of the protagonist's flight with Cupid, a legitimate objective. Like the protagonist, however, we are not yet in a position to see this, and the rhetoric of the poem is carefully structured so as to create in us the mistaken impression that Curage may be as unreliable a mentor as Will. So, no doubt, he may; the difference lies in the intrinsic qualities of the desired object, rather than in the nature of desire itself.

If the dilemma is presented in the opening phase of the debate in terms of the confrontation between Curage and Danger, with Hoip and Dreid playing a secondary part on their respective sides, there is a crucial shift of focus with the arrival at 100: 590 of Experience, accompanied by Ressoun (who is apparently also identified as Wisdome at 100: 690 and 100:718), Wit, and Skill.[55] The new arrivals immediately challenge not Curage but Will, and on the grounds not of his preferred objective but of his competence to lead the assault. He is, according to Experience, "mair talkative nor trowit" (100: 644), and Skill and Ressoun then seek to balance the argument by calling back the discredited Danger. The

---

[54] Jack, *Montgomerie*, 117–18.

[55] Jack (*Montgomerie*, 133) takes Wit and Wisdome to be the same character, but it seems to me that the latter is more naturally a synonym for Ressoun, in early modern moral psychology in general and in the context of the present debate in particular.

debate is not now about the choice between the Cherrie and the Slae, but about
the most appropriate way of approaching the former: are Will, Curage, and Hoip
sufficient guides in themselves, or should their urgency be tempered by the forces
of caution? This is the true centre of the poem's moral argument, and its impor-
tance is emphasised by Wisdome's invocation of the protagonist's previous suf-
fering at the hands of Will:

> "He sayis that man may wyte bot yow
> The first tyme that he fell.
>> He kennis now quhais pennis now          *pinions*
>>> Thou borrowit him to flee.             *lent*
>> His wounds yit quhilk sounds it
>>> He gat them than throw thee."
> (100: 723–728)

Experience takes up the theme, and his reiteration of the disastrous consequences of
the protagonist's attempt, at Will's behest, "to borrow fra the blindit boy /Baith
quiver wingis and bow" (100: 733–734) conclusively binds together the poem's
major elements. Since Will has led him into trouble in the past, we are invited
to conclude, he cannot be relied upon in future. The ultimatum presented to the
protagonist by Experience is now made absolutely clear: he must submit him-
self to Experience and Wisdome, banishing Will and Dispair (100: 771–782), a
proposition which is crisply endorsed by Ressoun (783–784).

The speaker's response in the original version is to vacillate for a further five
stanzas, and then to opt decisively for the "famous foure" whose offices promise
him success. His extended speech here demonstrates that he has indeed learned
his lesson, and he acknowledges that in previously relying on Curage and Will
he "wes not verie wyis" (100: 877): as Dreid justly complains, he was so over-
whelmed by the force of Curage's arguments that he did not bother to listen to the
case made by Dreid and Danger. This reversion to the earlier phase of the debate
is rather puzzling, and it may be linked to the fact that this first version breaks off
at this point, as if Montgomerie were not sure where his rhetorical structure was
leading him. With the protagonist's acceptance of Experience, Ressoun, Wit, and
Skill, the debate seems logically to be at an end, yet Dreid's complaint reopens the
discussion in a way that suggests that Montgomerie was not yet ready to round off
his poem with a successful foray to pick the cherries.

The very last lines of Waldegrave's incomplete text, indeed, develop the de-
bate in a new and tantalising direction. Responding to Dreid's legalistic attempt
to justify his caution, Experience comments with supreme self-confidence:

> "We are na barnis to be begyld",
> Quod he and schuik his heid.

> "For authours quha alledgis vs,
> Thay may not ga about the bus                    *beat about the bush*
> For all thair deidly feid":
>    (100: 926–930)

The precise sense of "alledgis" here is obscure, but it evidently refers back to the previous stanza, where Dreid complains to the speaker that he had been over-reliant on Curage and that "Ye wer determined to trow it / Alledgence past for law" (915–916). Experience's response to this appears to be to the effect that those who invoke his authority cannot escape the full implications of their case, but the remark remains enigmatic, and the fact that the earlier version breaks off at this point may indicate that Montgomerie himself was unable to decide where the argument should go from this point.

If the Waldegrave prints of 1597 are a true reflection of the state of the poem as Montgomerie left it in the 1580s, and the Wreittoun edition of 1636 does indeed record the final rewriting which he carried out in the months before his death, then we can identify three principal areas in which he made substantial alterations: the natural description of the opening; the nine stanzas which he added to the debate after l. 784 of the earlier version; and the thirty-five stanzas which bring the later version to a close. Of these, only the last was strictly necessary, and even in this case a much more concise conclusion was certainly possible: as we have seen, the protagonist's choice of the "famous foure" as his guides towards the end of the earlier version seems to bring the debate to an end. Yet even at this stage Montgomerie seems to have thought that some further elaboration was necessary, and appears to be at pains to defer the resolution. That he did so at such length when he came to complete the poem in 1597–1598 is therefore both a confirmation of his hesitations in the previous decade and an indication of his thinking at the very end of his life; the other modifications can be seen more straightforwardly as a reconsideration of his earlier intentions.

Of these modifications, the revision of the poem's opening is in many ways the most subtle. The first seven stanzas of natural description are thoroughly reworked, while the introduction of Cupid is expanded by the addition of one new stanza. For Shire, these changes reflect the difference in Montgomerie's circumstances, and a much more systematic allegorical meaning in which the "doublenesse" of Cupid points towards the king and the rewritten natural description already contains hints of the poem's Catholic subtext.[56] There is certainly a palpable darkening of tone in the later version, already signalled in the opening stanza, where a passing reference to "the Progne and the Philomene" (100: 5) is expanded into a more explicitly Ovidian allusion:

---

[56] Shire, *Song, Dance and Poetry*, 130–33.

When Philomel had sweetly sung,
To Progne she deplored
    How Tereus cut out her tongue
And falsely her deflorde,
    Which storie so sorie
        To shew, ashamed she seemde.
    To heare her so neare her
        I doubted if I dream'd.
    (101: 7–14)

The harshness of this explicit allusion to rape and mutilation, with its echo of
Montgomerie's sonnet "Sweet Philomene" [84.I], unquestionably lends a sombre
note to the opening which is absent from the earlier version, and the difference is
reinforced by the promotion of the Narcissus story, included in the fourth stanza
of the 1597 prints (100: 48–56), to the second stanza (101: 24–28). One conse-
quence of these moves, certainly, is to put the mark of Ovid much more firmly
upon the poem's opening lines; and we must give due weight to the possibility that
Montgomerie's reasons for tinkering with the text were aesthetic as well as philo-
sophical. Some of the adjustments, such as a strong tendency to insert adjectives
and more expressive verbs, appear to be motivated more by a desire to enhance
the passage rhetorically than by the demands of the allegory, however the latter is
to be understood, and the same is probably true of the most striking of the meta-
phors which Montgomerie now added:

The aire was sober, soft and sweet,
But mistie vapours, wind and weet,
But quyet, calme and cleare
    To foster Floras fragrant flowres
Whereon *Apollos paramours*
Had trinckled many a teare
The which *like silver shakers shynde*
*Imbrodering beauties bed* . . . . .
    (101: 43–50)

Mee thought an heavenly heartsome thing
Where dew like Diamonds did hing
Our twinckling all the trees
    To study on the flourishde twists                    *flower-covered branches*
Admiring *natures alcumists,*
Laborious busie Bees
    Whereof some sweetest hony sought
To stay their lives to sterve
    And some *the waxie vessels* wrought
Their purchase to preserve . . . . .
    (101: 57–66) [my italics]

The comparison of dew with "shakers", metal plates used to decorate clothing (and, apparently, bed-hangings) was not original with Montgomerie,[57] but its effect here is to intensify the assimilation of art to nature which we have previously noted as a characteristic of Mannerist natural description. Something similar, perhaps, is achieved by the brilliant metaphor of the bees as "natures alcumists", turning the base material of pollen into the golden elixir of honey. Such touches seem to be justified more by their sheer poetic quality than by the tone they establish.

At the same time, there is sufficient evidence to substantiate Shire's argument that the emotional contradictions within the landscape are much more fully worked out in the later version than in its predecessor. The introduction of the Corbie (raven), Pye (magpie), Iaye (jay), Crawe, and Kay (jackdaw) into the second stanza, alongside the Cushat (dove), Cuckow and Turtle, creates a cacophonous effect which is phonaesthetically reinforced by the language of the stanza itself, leaving the reader unsurprised that the speaker is "deav'd" by the noise (l. 20). This concentration of scavengers surely connects with the disturbing introduction of the Procne/Philomena story into the first stanza, and may perhaps recall the violence committed by a similar group of birds at the end of Sir David Lindsay's *Testament and Complaynt of the Papyngo*.[58] If this really is part of Montgomerie's intention, however, then it is difficult to reconcile with the supposedly Catholic subtext of *The Cherrie and the Slae*, for the Raven, Magpie, and Kite in Lindsay's poem represent the predatoriness of the pre-Reformation Church. Whatever the truth of this, it is undeniably the case that there is a marked contrast between the conventional birdsong of the *locus amoenus* opening and the harsh noises overheard by Montgomerie's protagonist. Other features of the description also contribute to this effect: whereas in the 1597 prints we are told that

> The Turtle on the vther syde
> Na plesure had to play,
>     So schil in sorrow was her sang
> That throw her voce the roches rang,               *rocks*
>     (100: 44–47)

the equivalent passage in the revised version (now reduced to a single line) states that "The Turtle wailes on withered trees" (101: 23), both the expressiveness of the verb and the descriptiveness of the adjective intensifying the counter-sense of a wasteland which runs against the predominant emphasis upon "the pleasures of that Parke" (101: 71). The dissonant note is unmistakable, and it clearly anticipates

---

[57] It is, certainly, employed in "Quhen Tayis bank wes blumyt brycht" (l. 21), a lyric which is preserved in the Bannatyne MS. and which Montgomerie presumably knew (see *Bannatyne Manuscript*, ed. Tod Ritchie, 3:296–300).

[58] Lindsay, *Works*, ed. Hamer, 1:75–90.

the misery into which the protagonist will soon fall: the problem is to decide what meanings are inherent in the symbolism of the 'grand vol audacieux' and the opposition of Cherrie and Slae, and how, if at all, these had changed between 1585–1586 and 1597–1598.

The second major change which Montgomerie made during this final process of revision was the introduction of a new passage of nine stanzas (101: 799–924), just at the point at which Experience and Reason have demanded the protagonist's acceptance of Experience's authority. To Will's suggestion that the narrator should have picked the cherries during his earlier flight, Reason responds that he had not yet seen them and did not in any case know that he needed them until he was hurt; Shire raises the possibility that there is a coded reference here to Montgomerie's conversion to Catholicism, and that the failure of his earlier flight alludes in some way to the first phase of his career at court.[59] If this were true, it would turn the poem in Montgomerie's final conception interestingly in upon itself, since the abortive flight would somehow have come to symbolise the period in which the first version of the text, including the account of the flight, was composed. Such a self-referential twist is not inconceivable, but there is nothing in the rest of the added passage to reinforce the idea. Rather, Montgomerie develops a spirited debate about human nature and the role of the senses, composed in an idiom which is strikingly closer to that of his later poetry of complaint than to the more courtly language of the earlier sections of the poem:

> "Ye have no feele for to defyne
> Though yee have cunning to declyne
> A man to be a moole.                                    *mule*
>    With little work yet yee may vowde
> To grow a gallant horse and good
> To ride theron at Yoole.
>    But to our ground where wee began
> For all your gustlesse iests.                           *tasteless jokes*
>    I must be master of the man
> But thou to bruital beasts . . ."
>    (101: 869–878)

This is the traditional material of medieval allegory: Reason is a uniquely human attribute, Montgomerie observes, while Will is a lower quality shared with irrational animals. The addition of this exchange, then, simply makes explicit what had earlier been implied, namely the close relationship between the two key figures in the protagonist's eventual success: Reason, an innate quality in man, and Experience, whose emergence depends upon external factors. Without the decisive

---

[59] Shire, *Song, Dance and Poetry*, 134.

influence of moral discrimination, Montgomerie had perhaps come to understand, even Experience cannot guarantee that we learn from our mistakes.

Montgomerie inserted these stanzas just before a crucial turning-point in the action, the first intervention in the debate of the protagonist himself, and ten stanzas before the inconclusive end of the original version. His response to Experience's challenge, as we have seen, is to hesitate for a time before agreeing to be led by the "famous foure": Experience, Reason, Skill, and Wit. Montgomerie made few changes to this passage, but he subtly modified the final lines of his original version as he completed the stanza:

> "For Authors who alledges us
> They *stil would* win about the bus
> *To foster* deadly feede.                                    *enmity*
> For wee are equal for you all.
> No persons wee respect.
> We have been so are yet and shall
> Be found so in effect . . . . ."
>      (101: 1068–74; my italics)

The shift of emphasis from the inevitable failure of the unnamed "authors" to their malicious intentions gives the passage an important new twist, as does the subtle assimilation to the character of Experience of the attributes of God as defined in the *Gloria* and in Revelation 1:8 and 4:8, echoing Montgomerie's own version of "Supreme Essence":

> Contener vnconteind, is, was and sall
> Be . . .
>      (59: 9–10)

This reinforcement of the sovereign power of Experience can be seen as a wry comment on the modulation of Montgomerie's views between the early 1580s and the last year of his life: while the central position of the character in the debate had already been established in the first phase of writing, it is hardly surprising that, after everything that had happened between 1586 and 1597, Montgomerie should now see the implications of maturity in a clearer light than he had been able to do when he left his poem unfinished.

Aesthetically speaking, the extension of the philosophical discussion by a further thirty-five stanzas cannot perhaps be claimed to add very much to the success of a poem which already stretched the static conventions of medieval psychological allegory to their limits. Yet the resolution of the central dilemmas posed by the protagonist's situation is not easily to be achieved, and while the preference for the Cherrie over the Slae is (despite the former's possible sexual implications) predictable from an early stage of the debate, the balancing of the conflicting claims of Hoip and Curage on the one hand and of Dreid and Danger on the other — which remains at issue even after the rejection of Will at the conclusion of the earlier version — presents a subtle psychological and moral problem. That Montgomerie's eventual answer to this should be the familiar Aristotelian principle that

> Sturt followes all extreames.                    *a quarrel*
> Retaine then the meane then,
> The surest way it seemes . . .
> (101: 1426–1428)

does not diminish the significance of the discussion or the figuring of the psychological process by which the allegorical company work through the issue.

The first part of this new material (101: 1085–1316) is built around two oppositions, that between Experience on the one hand and Hoip and Curage on the other, and that between Wit, Experience's ally, and Dreid and Danger. These arguments evidently represent opposite sides of the same question: Montgomerie here reverts to the confrontation between Curage and Danger which had dominated the first phase of the debate and which had culminated in the flight of Danger and Dreid, but with Experience and Wit now able to assume a moderating role it is possible for the choice to be made through reconciliation of the competing forces rather than through the (temporary) victory of one side. The intrusion of Wit into Experience's management of the dispute (ll. 1225–1235) is more significant than its brevity might suggest, not only because Wit's position is forcibly asserted by Experience himself, but because in the poem's final phase Reason will assign a crucial part to Wit in the expedition to pluck the Cherrie. The differentiation of Reason, Wit, and Experience (and, to a lesser degree, Skill) is, indeed, a key to the understanding of the moral psychology which underlies *The Cherrie and the Slae*: while Experience evidently has to do, as we have noted above, with the mind's relation to time and the external world, and Reason primarily denotes considered judgement and moral discrimination, Wit seems closer to a kind of intuitive intelligence. Its ultimate antecedents can perhaps be found in the concept of *intelligentia*, one of the three faculties of the soul according to Augustine's *De Trinitate*.[60] Reason and Experience are, no doubt, most appropriate to preside over Montgomerie's moral discussion in its various stages, but it is Wit whose advice is needed when the final assault on the Cherrie's inaccessible position is to be made. It is he who, at Reason's behest, chooses the *via media* between attempting to scale the steep cliffs and wading through the impossibly deep river, counselling instead

---

[60] Augustine, *De Trinitate*, 10.11.18, ed. W.J. Mountain, 2 vols., CCSL 50–50A (Turnhout: Brepols, 1968), 1:330–31. The other two are *voluntas* and *memoria*; perhaps the latter is equivalent to Montgomerie's Experience.

a course around the waterfall whose presence is first signalled at l. 80; and it is he who is then recognised by reason as the natural partner of Experience in leading the journey itself. Without natural intelligence, Montgomerie suggests, the lessons of life are hardly to be learned; while rational judgement and practical accomplishment logically follow from the combined influence of Wit and Experience.

By l. 1317, the beginning of the final phase of the debate, the leading role of Reason and Experience, assisted by Skill and Wit, is firmly established, and yet it is not until another two hundred lines have passed that Wit is given his opportunity to plot the route to the cherries. First, Reason allocates the function of "medciner" to the protagonist to Skill, in a passage which serves to recall the miserable circumstances in which the narrator found himself at the end of his abortive flight, and to insist upon the healing power of the Cherrie. Even this does not lead immediately to the poem's resolution, however, for Danger, Curage, and their respective allies continue to assert their conflicting natures, and Reason is forced to convene a full council before the questions of whether and how the expedition to the Cherrie is to be taken can be resolved. This repeated deferral of the outcome adds little to the allegorical framework, but it does emphasise the careful balancing of rashness and timidity which has run through the debate from the start. Finally, in Reason's injunction to Dreid and Danger, Hoip and Curage that they should

> . . . come into a band
> Proceeding and leading
>     Each other by the hand,
>     (1566–1568)

we have a reconciliation of this fundamental conflict, an enactment of the Aristotelian mean which Experience has advocated ten stanzas earlier. And the result of the venture, while it may come dangerously close to aesthetic anticlimax, makes good sense doctrinally: as the expedition approaches the tree,

> Which, as yee heard mee tell,
>     Could not be clum, there suddenly
> The fruite for ripnes fell . . .
>     (1576–1578)

As Ross, Shire, and Jack agree, this is surely an emblem of divine grace, confirming our sense that the allegorical meaning of the poem is, finally, theological.

To see *The Cherrie and the Slae* as religious allegory, however, is not necessarily to accept Shire's contention that it enacts, at least in its final form, Montgomerie's conversion to Catholicism. There are, clearly, traditional Eucharistic associations of the cherry, and the poem may allude to these through the narrator's initial

observation that he saw "The fruit betwixt me and the skye / Halfe gaite almaist
to hevin" (100: 324–325; 101: 338–339). But such Christological references would
be meaningful to Protestant and Catholic readers alike, and if the poem's end-
ing permits a Catholic interpretation it certainly does not require it. The "God
my Lord" whom the narrator celebrates in his final stanza, "the everliving Lord"
whom he wishes all nations to "magnifie", is simply the God of all Christians, and
the poem seems to be left carefully open. With the benefit of hindsight, however,
the protagonist's concluding view of the action takes on a poignant significance:
God did, he asserts, "mine health to mee restore / Being so long time pinde".
Within the imaginative space of the allegory this is, of course, true, and the suc-
cessful expedition to obtain the healing cherries manifests the fact. Perhaps we
are also justified in seeing here a declaration of the poet's conviction that he has
come through the worst and now, five years after the crushing legal defeat of
1593, has found a course of action which will grant him the peace he desires. Fate
would, however, have the last word, for soon after completing these lines, the poet
himself was dead. If Duff is to be believed, Montgomerie's personal quest for the
Cherrie would have taken him to Würzburg and into the Benedictine order, in-
stead of which he died in Edinburgh. The dream of being "relievde / Of cares all
and sares all / Which minde and body grievde" remains a dream, framed by the
fabric of allegory.

*The Cherrie and the Slae* is, finally, an impressive achievement, whatever res-
ervations one may have about its formal characteristics. It is often subtle in its
psychological twists and turns, and Montgomerie's musical skill and linguistic
inventiveness frequently come through the intricacy of the stanza. The pithiness
with which he invests the dialogue through the repeated use of proverbs is also a
striking feature of the text: rather than developing a technical theological argu-
ment — which he was in any case not properly qualified to do — he relies upon
the distillation of proverbial wisdom to carry the debate forward:

| | |
|---|---|
| "Friend, huly, haste not halfe so fast | *be careful* |
| Lest," quoth Experience at last, | |
| "Ye buy my doctrine deare. | |
| Hope puts that hast into your head | |
| Which boyles your barmie braine. | *fanciful* |
| Howbeit Fooleshaste comes hulie speede, | *at a cautious pace* |
| Faire heights make fooles be faine. | |
|    Such smyling beguiling | |
|     Bids feare not for no freets | *superstitions* |
|    Yet I now deny now | |
|     That al is gold that gleets. | *shines* |

"Suppose not silver all that shines.
Oft times a tentlesse Merchant tines          *inattentive; loses*
For buying geare be gesse."
          (101: 1278–1291)

Such popular lore gives the poem much of its strongly vernacular feeling, and doubtless contributed to its frequent re-publication in the course of the seventeenth century. If it can fairly be seen, as I have been suggesting, as Montgomerie's final poetic testament, then *The Cherrie and the Slae*'s most powerful claim is as a poem which transcends its courtly origins and ultimately opens out into a comprehensive vision of the individual Christian's central spiritual dilemmas. It adapts the medieval *psychomachia* for the needs and the tastes of a sixteenth-century audience, and if it articulates, in the most subtly modulated form, a Catholic view of Christian action, it does so in terms which manifestly did not alienate a Protestant Scottish readership. Not the least paradoxical aspect of Montgomerie's strange career is the fact that it was this poem from the hand of a Catholic which enjoyed such currency in the century after his death.

# CHAPTER NINE

# THE "LANG GUID NICHT"

Five years after Montgomerie's death, James VI at last inherited the English throne which had been the object of his policies for so long. With the departure of the court to Westminster, an event which at least some of the poets had already anticipated, the principal centre of formal literary activity in Scotland disappeared. William Alexander of Menstrie, Sir Robert Ayton, Alexander Craig of Rosecraig, and the rest evidently hoped that the larger stage of the English court would provide them with a new locus for success, and only William Drummond of Hawthornden was content to address this wider audience from the relative seclusion of his country house near Dalkeith; that this decision did not prevent him from establishing a notable literary reputation is clear from the expedition to Scotland which Ben Jonson made in 1618 in order to visit him.[1] For all these writers, it was English which now had to be the medium of serious literary discourse, and men like Alexander and Ayton quickly abandoned their former poetic practice to accommodate the stylistic expectations of an English readership.[2] There might continue to be a market for Older Scots poetry among a Scottish reading public, but Montgomerie and his fellow-makars would have no imitators until the vernacular revival of the eighteenth century.

As we noted at the very outset of this study, Montgomerie's name was not immediately forgotten in his native land, for *The Cherrie and the Slae* and the *Flyting* seem to have remained among the most widely read Scots works. The former was apparently printed by Andrew Hart in Edinburgh in 1615 (an edition of which no copy now survives), and then went through seven further editions in the course of the seventeenth century, while the *Flyting* was printed seven times between 1629 and 1688. Only Hary's *Wallace* and the works of Sir David Lindsay enjoyed anything like comparable popularity. Between them, it would seem, these texts

---

[1] Another notable exception is Montgomerie's nephew William Mure of Rowallan, who similarly based his career in Scotland. For Mure's verse, see his *Works*, ed. William Tough, 2 vols. (Edinburgh: STS, 1898); and cf. R.D.S. Jack, "Scottish Sonnetteer and Welsh Metaphysical: A Study of the Religious Poetry of Sir William Mure and Henry Vaughan", *SSL* 3 (1965–1966): 240–47.

[2] Alexander, indeed, anticipated James's accession by anglicising his tragedy *Darius*; for his apologia, see William Alexander, Earl of Stirling, *Poetical Works*, ed. L.E. Kastner and H.B. Charlton, 2 vols. (Edinburgh: STS, 1921–1929), 1: cxcvi.

ensured a measure of currency for the Older Scots tradition during an age which could scarcely have been less conducive to the Scottish Muses. But the increasing identification of Montgomerie with these two long works hardly did justice to his considerable poetic gifts. It is possible, as we also noted at the beginning, that more manuscript copies of his lyrics were in circulation than we might now suppose, and the evidence of seventeenth-century song-book manuscripts confirms that a few of his lyrics continued to be sung in the decades after his death; but it was, on the whole, not as an exponent of the sonnet and the stanzaic lyric that he was remembered by his countrymen. The allegorical opacity of *The Cherrie and the Slae*, and its undeniable seriousness, may well have recommended themselves to a society in which the Calvinist sermon was the predominant generic form and religious controversy degenerated at times into civil war; while the sheer formal exuberance of the *Flyting* no doubt ensured its survival when other, more high-minded exemplars of the Older Scots tradition passed into temporary oblivion. The 'suggred stile' of the lyrics, so warmly praised by James at the poet's death, was less to the general taste, and once their natural home, the court, had disappeared from Scotland their currency seems to have been mostly confined to such lairdly households as those of William Mure of Rowallan, Alexander Forbes of Tolquhon, and John Skene of Hallyards. Only with the publication of the second edition of William Forbes's *Cantus, Songs and Fancies* in 1662 did some of these pieces become more widely available in published form.[3]

Among the Catholic exiles, a different view of Montgomerie survived for a time. In distant Würzburg, as we have seen, Thomas Duff apparently knew a good deal about Montgomerie's life and works, and gave *The Cherrie and the Slae* a new readership by publishing his Latin translation there in 1631. His own poetic manuscript contains, moreover, a spiritualised Latin version of "The Solsequium":

> Sic mea stat fortuna quidem: Nisi Jesu
> Te fruari ô animae Lux radiosa meae
> Te mihi se tuleris decies me vulnera mille
> Intereunt varijs cassa quiete malis
> Vultus, et exterior morum gestura dolorem
> Intima qui lacerat pectoris antra notant.
> (15–20)[4]

For Duff, it would seem, Montgomerie was a Catholic hero, a staunch defender of the Faith "with sword and pen", in death a victim of Protestant zealotry. The same

---

[3] Forbes included three of Montgomerie's songs, "Lyk as the dum Solsequium" [21], "Evin dead, behold I breath" [26] and "Before the Greeks durst enterpryse" [43], in his collection.

[4] Würzburg Universitätsbibliothek, MS. M.ch.q.62, fol. 56r.

motivation perhaps inspired Captain Alexander Bruce of Kincavil, who seems to have paid for the Würzburg edition of *Cerasum et Sylvestre Prunum*.[5] Duff was not the only Scottish emigré to preserve Montgomerie's memory. Thomas Dempster, an historian and bibliographer whose work has received a good deal of justified obloquy and neglect which is rather less justified, summed up his achievement with considerable clarity in his *Historia Ecclesiastica Gentis Scotorum*:

> . . . eques Montanus vulgo vocatus, nobilissimo sanguine, Pindarus Scoticus, ingenii elegantia et carminis venustate nulli veterum secundus, regi charissimus Jacobo, qui poeticen mirifice eo aevo amplexebatur, quique poetas claros sodales suos vulgo vocari voluit, multis ingenii sui monumentis patriam Linguam ditavit et exornavit . . .

> [(He was) popularly called 'the Highland knight', and came of the most noble blood; a Scottish Pindar, in no way inferior to the ancients in the elegance of his wit and the beauty of his songs; most dear to King James, who wonderfully esteemed the poetry of his age and who wanted famous vernacular poets among his courtiers; (he) enriched and adorned his native tongue through his wit with his many writings . . .][6]

Like Duff's epitaphs, Dempster's account contains a good deal that is of value: while Montgomerie's right to be seen as a "Scottish Pindar" may be open to question, the association of his work with the national literary ambitions of James VI is accurate enough. It is above all significant that it was among the Catholic exiles that Montgomerie's reputation as a lyric poet remained high in the early seventeenth century; they were unaffected by the identification of literary aspiration with success at an English court, and they were therefore free to give proper weight to his achievement.

Within the mainstream tradition of Scottish literature, however, it was only with the rediscovery of the Ker manuscript that the poet portrayed in these pages began to re-emerge. Eighteenth-century editions of *The Cherrie and the Slae* had included a few of the shorter poems, including "The Solsequium" and sometimes "Supreme Essence", but the first representative collection was that incorporated by James Sibbald in his *Chronicle of Scottish Poetry* (1802): Sibbald saw the Ker manuscript when his third volume was already printed, and added "such of [the poems]

---

[5] The titlepage states that the volume is published "In gratiam illustris et generosi herois D. Alexandri Brussii capitanei cohortis peditum Scotorum, Domini de Kinkawil"; for the Bruce connection, see above, 34–35.

[6] Thomas Dempster, *Historia Ecclesiastica Gentis Scotorum*, 2 vols. (Edinburgh: Bannatyne Club, 1829), 2:496.

as appear worthy of preservation".[7] As with other Older Scots poets, therefore, it is the antiquarian movement which began during the Enlightenment and reached fulfilment in the nineteenth-century publishing societies which is responsible for establishing the basic corpus of Montgomerie's work and a framework within which he can be understood, and James Cranstoun's edition for the Scottish Text Society (1887) became the foundation of all subsequent scholarship.[8] From a textual point of view, Cranstoun's edition, while not without its flaws, is therefore a land-mark, but it accepts and perpetuates the *grand récit* of decline and fall which still persists and which this study has set out to challenge:

> Alexander Montgomerie is, perhaps, the most distinguished name in the poetical literature of Scotland during a period singularly barren of poetic genius. The asceticism born of the religious fervour that had taken deep root in the minds of the people, absorbing lighter interests, warped the fancy, and, for a season, wellnigh silenced the song of the hitherto unfettered Scottish Muse. Sir Robert Aytoun, Sir William Alexander, and William Drummond of Hawthornden are almost the only other noteworthy names in Scottish poetry during what is known as the brilliant Elizabethan period of English literature.[9]

Such faint praise scarcely does justice to the distinctiveness of Montgomerie's poetic voice or to the ambitions of James's court circle, dismissed by Cranstoun with a reference to "the King's literary vanity". Only Helena Shire's *Song, Dance and Poetry* has truly sought to provide an alternative view of Scottish culture in the final quarter of the sixteenth century, and for all its tendentiousness it remains a vital counterbalance to the prevailing narrative of failing Scots culture and a dominant Elizabethan Renaissance.

The estimate of Montgomerie's achievement I have sought to develop dem-onstrates the importance of a bipolar model of British culture before 1603.[10] To see him as a late survival of the *Tottel's Miscellany* poets fails to acknowledge both his debt to the earlier Makars and the subtlety of his skills as a rhetorician. The patterns of literary development in England and Scotland between 1400 and 1600 were fundamentally different: there was much greater linguistic and rhe-torical continuity from the period of Henryson, Dunbar, and Douglas to that

---

[7] James Sibbald (ed.), *Chronicle of Scottish Poetry*, 4 vols. (Edinburgh: J. Sibbald, 1802), 3:493.

[8] On the nineteenth- and early twentieth-century reception of Montgomerie, see Daemen-de Gelder, "Recitations of Nationhood", 189–229.

[9] *Poems*, ed. Cranstoun, xxvi.

[10] See P. Schwyzer, "British History and 'The British history': The Same Old Story?", in *British Identities and English Renaissance Literature*, ed. Baker and Maley, 11–23.

of Montgomerie than we find south of the Border, where phonological change contributed to the archaisisation of Chaucer and the uncertainties of early Tudor poetics. Imposing English critical expectations on Scottish texts simply misses the truth which the eighteen-year-old James VI understood very well: that Scots literature was close to but distinct from English, and demanded its own rhetorical textbook and its own rhetorical norms. That his "Reulis and Cautelis" is a relatively poor specimen of the genre does not detract from that realisation, and neither does the fact that dynastic ambition and the private ambitions of courtier-poets ultimately combined to subvert and defeat the literary renaissance which he set out to create. Montgomerie, of all the "Castalian" poets, transcends the limitations imposed by the quest for royal patronage and the decorum of courtly literature, and he becomes most fully himself as his career at court founders. But in more general terms, the "Jacobean Age" which began with James's accession to the English throne was preceded by another, just as ambiguous in its own ways and coterminous with the "Elizabethan Renaissance". We have caught hints of the relationship between English and Scottish culture in the 1580s and 1590s, but this is a subject deserving of much more careful attention in its own right: English interest in James's *Essayes of a Prentise* is one aspect of the question, but so too are the English connections of the poet and political agent William Fowler and the Scottish associations of Henry Constable and, tantalisingly if less certainly, Christopher Marlowe.[11] As Priscilla Bawcutt has recently observed, it would be "rewarding to explore the existence and implications of cross-Border friendships, particularly those of a literary and humanistic character";[12] in such an enterprise, moreover, it would be vital to remember that such relationships were frequently triangular, involving contacts with the Continent which were reinforced by the presence of both Scots and Englishmen in the Low Countries and which were sometimes capable of transcending religious and political differences.

Awareness of the interaction of two national cultures in sixteenth-century Britain provides a potential antidote to the Anglocentrism of much contemporary scholarship. If Scotland was understandably marginalised by Elizabethan writers, it disappears entirely from otherwise admirable works such as Richard Helgerson's *Forms of Nationhood*; even when discussing William Camden's *Britannia*, Helgerson gives no indication of the complex political resonances of Camden's title, and he alludes to James's *True Law of Free Monarchies* (1598) without any

---

[11] On Marlowe's possible links with Scotland, arising from a claim by Thomas Kyd after the former's death, see Charles Nicholl, *The Reckoning* (London: Cape, 1992; 2nd ed., London: Vintage, 2002), 311–14; Marlowe's friend Matthew Roydon had, according to Kyd, gone to Scotland after the murder.

[12] Priscilla Bawcutt, "Crossing the Border: Scottish Poetry and English Readers in the Sixteenth Century", in *The Rose and the Thistle*, 59–76, here 73.

acknowledgement that it was written by the King of Scotland, albeit one who anticipated his imminent accession to the English throne.[13] The concept of "Britain" did not spring out fully-armed in 1603: as we noted at the outset, it had been current for at least a century, and the "writing of England" must be seen as one — the strongest, perhaps, but still only one — possible view of the relationships which existed on the island. The dynastic alliance between Scotland and England which was achieved in 1503 did not, of course, bear immediate fruit, for not only did James IV die in battle against an English army ten years later, but there was a more extended war in the 1540s which left much of southern Scotland devastated; significantly, the propaganda campaign to which this conflict gave rise involved the revival of English claims to overlordship which had underpinned the thirteenth-century attempt at domination.[14] The etymological connection between "Britain" and the ancestral myth of Brutus and his sons was an important part of this narrative of superiority; against this the prospect of the Scottish monarch wearing the English crown offered an alternative vision of peaceful union. The concept of nationhood in sixteenth-century England cannot properly be understood without a recognition of the complexity created by the Scottish dimension.

By the same token, the perspective derived from a careful study of Montgomerie's career reveals a more complex religious landscape than it is customary to concede. The Protestantism of Sidney and Spenser has reinforced their canonical status within the *grand récit* of the English Renaissance, while such Catholic poets as Southwell and Constable have generally been seen as marginal figures.[15] If recent work has suggested not only that the doctrinal backgrounds of such key figures as Shakespeare and Donne were less unequivocally Protestant than earlier scholars were inclined to assume but that even as impeccable an enthusiast for the English Church as Sir Philip Sidney had some interesting Catholic connections, then the presence of a Catholic poet at the heart of the Scottish court should encourage us to examine more rigorously the interplay of religion, politics and the arts in the early modern period. It is, of course, true that the religious situation was very different in Scotland from that in England: the Calvinist party enjoyed much more influence, even power, than the English Puritans, but on the other hand the king's own position remained equivocal, and for much of his reign in Scotland the Catholic faction was tolerated, and sometimes apparently

---

[13] See Richard Helgerson, *Forms of Nationhood: The Elizabethan Writing of England* (Chicago and London: University of Chicago Press, 1992), 114–17, 77.

[14] On this propaganda campaign, see Marcus Merriman, *The Rough Wooings: Mary, Queen of Scots, 1542–1551* (East Linton: Tuckwell Press, 2001); the Scottish side of the argument is represented by *The Complaint of Scotland*, ed. A.M. Stewart (Edinburgh: STS, 1979), and William Lamb, *Ane Ressonyng betuix ane Scottish merchand and ane Inglis merchand betuix Rowane and Lyonis*, ed. R.J. Lyall (Aberdeen: Aberdeen University Press, 1985).

encouraged, while James evidently had strongly episcopalian sympathies. Edinburgh was therefore the site for a playing-out of alternative doctrinal patterns, anxiously observed by English agents who knew perfectly well that the Scottish model might have profound implications for the future of the Elizabethan settlement. Until 1587, moreover, the complexity of the situation was further increased by the presence in an English prison of the Scottish Catholic heir to the English throne, the focus of Protestant anxiety, Catholic anticipation, and a considerable degree of political intrigue on both sides. Her execution, at which James evidently connived, may have simplified some political relationships, but it did not dispel the ambition of Catholics in both Scotland and England to achieve a restoration of Catholic power and influence.

In literary terms, both the contrastive and the intrinsic value of the Scottish Jacobean court are surely evident from the foregoing discussion. The emergence in Scotland between 1579 and 1585 of a literary circle under royal patronage is a crucial parallel to contemporary developments in England, but the dynamics are sufficiently different to cast new light upon the cultural climate in London. Elizabeth was already in her mid-forties when the new generation of courtier-poets began to emerge towards the end of the 1570s, while James was still only thirty-six when he inherited her throne. The king who presided over the "Castalian" Renaissance was not yet twenty, surrounded by courtier-poets who were a good deal older than he was. Nor can questions of gender and sexuality be left out of account: the English adaptation of Petrarchist language to represent the Queen as "the quintessential, unapproachable yet alluring, Petrarchan mistress"[16] was scarcely an option in Scotland, although we have noted ambiguities in at least one of Montgomerie's poems which might suggest play with the king's potential double role as patron and as love-object.[17] Still more illuminating is the ultimate failure of the Jacobean initiative, of which the increasing marginalisation of Montgomerie after his return to Scotland in 1588 can be seen as a microcosm. Less centralised and yet more deeply integrated into a national project of redefining Englishness, the Elizabethan enterprise flourished, integrating Petrarchist discourse and medieval romance, theatre and pastoral, allegory and madrigal into a common language of cultural identity. That James's "Castalian" circle was unable

---

[15] For an important corrective, see Shell, *Catholicism*, 56–104; see also Christopher Highley, "'The lost British lamb': English catholic Exiles and the Problem of Britain," in *British Identities and English Renaissance Literature*, ed. Baker and Maley, 37–50.

[16] Waller, *Sixteenth-Century Poetry*, 19.

[17] For recent studies of James's homosexuality and its political significance, see David M. Bergeron, *King James and Letters of Homoerotic Desire* (Iowa City: Iowa University Press, 1999); idem, "Writing King James's Sexuality", in *Royal Subjects*, ed. Fischlin and Fortier, 344–68; and Young, *King James and the History of Homosexuality*.

to achieve anything comparable is not due to some large, historically determined pattern of decline or, principally, to a lack of genius. It is the result of quite specific historical contingencies, not the least of which is the powerful magnetic attraction of an English, or arguably British, future. James's own transition from "poetical recreations" to the earnestness of prose is a mirror of his ambitions, and the *Basilicon Doron* sets out a royal agenda which would have disastrous consequences for both England and Scotland in the course of the following century but which leaves no doubt about the king's priorities. Nor were his horizons confined to Britain and Ireland: by the time he became king of England, he was embarked upon a European project which would if successful have made him a central figure in a reunited Christendom.[18]

The initial phase of Montgomerie's poetic career, however, coincided with an earlier stage in the king's development, when his ambitions certainly included (though were not confined to) literary recognition. Perhaps James's active involvement in his literary circle was itself a factor in its disintegration: as his attention turned elsewhere, the momentum seems clearly to have been lost. But other forces were probably also at work: Alexander Hume's defection, for example, sprang from his Calvinist conviction that his secular verse was unworthy and should be destroyed, and the implacable opposition of the Edinburgh ministers to the theatre undoubtedly underlay the absence of any form of indigenous theatrical activity corresponding to the extraordinary efflorescence of dramatic writing in England.[19] It is surely no accident that Montgomerie's prominence also coincided with the political ascendancy first of Lennox and then of Arran, and with the greater openness of the king to pro-Catholic tendencies, or that his return to Scotland coincided with the trauma of the Armada and James's adoption of a more explicitly anti-Spanish policy. It would be dangerous to assume an absolute correspondence between political events and cultural movements, but no less so to read these developments as entirely independent of one another. If literary virtuosity was a key element in Renaissance courtiership, then its exercise depended upon a prince for whom such activity was important, and the apparent displacement of poetic display from the centre of James's attention was only one aspect of a gradual shift in priorities in the later 1580s and the following decade.

Montgomerie's career is interestingly counterpointed by that of William Fowler, whose writing invites the same sort of scrutiny we have accorded Montgomerie in

---

[18] See W.B. Patterson, *King James VI and I and the Reunion of Christendom* (Cambridge: Cambridge University Press, 1997).

[19] For Hume's account of his literary recantation, see *Poems*, ed. Alexander Lawson (Edinburgh: STS, 1902), 6–7; on James's struggle with the Kirk over a visit by an English theatrical company in the later 1590s, see Anna Jean Mill, *Medieval Plays in Scotland* (Edinburgh and London: Blackwood, 1927), 297–305.

these pages. Alone among the "Castalians", Fowler turned to Italian models: his sources included not only Petrarch and Machiavelli, but also Tansillo, Straparola, and other Italian poets drawn from the copious anthologies which were in wide circulation.[20] This interest in Italian literature, we should note, antedated his attested visit to Padua, where he matriculated in 1592; although his major sequence *The Tarantula of Love* and the shorter sequence preserved among his papers (NLS, MS. 2063, fols. 9r–15r) are difficult to date, it seems probable that a good deal of the former, at any rate, was composed before 1592. It may be connected with his other career, as royal servant and political agent: there is evidence of his involvement in political intrigue in the early 1580s, while H.R. Woudhuysen has recently drawn attention to a significant network in Scotland, England, and Italy between 1589 and 1592 which includes Sir Edward Dymoke, Samuel Daniel, Giovanni Battista Guarini and Giacomo Castelvetro as well as Fowler.[21] This trail leads back, moreover, to 1582–1583, when he appears as a pro-French messenger from the Duke of Lennox in the tangled tale of Giordano Bruno's London sojourn.[22] In the complex and treacherous world of sixteenth-century espionage, it is frequently impossible to determine which face lay beneath the ultimate mask: was Fowler (sometime minister of Hawick) a Catholic sympathiser pretending to be a Protestant, or a Protestant agent successfully infiltrated into Catholic circles? The latter seems more likely, but the exact nature of his attachments is not at present clear, and may not be recoverable.[23] What is apparent, however, is that he was a much more successful careerist than Montgomerie: he became secretary to Queen Anne in 1593, and in that role accompanied the royal couple to London in 1603, remaining in the Queen's household until his death in 1612.

Fowler's career prospered as Montgomerie's failed, and no doubt for comparable reasons: his poetry lacks Montgomerie's elegant lyricism and anguished sincerity, but he was evidently a consummate courtier-politician who contrived

---

[20] A detailed study of Fowler's sources is a desideratum; holograph manuscript notes in NLS, MS. 2063 confirm his use of Tansillo, Straparola, and Erasmo Viotto's *Raccolto d'alcune piacevoli rime* (Parma: Heredi di S. Viotto, 1582). For his knowledge of other Italian anthologies, see Janet G. Scott, *Les Sonnets Elizabéthains* (Paris: Champion, 1929), 327–29; cf. R.D.S. Jack, "William Fowler and Italian Literature", *MLR* 65 (1970): 481–92.

[21] Woudhuysen, *Sidney and the Circulation of Manuscripts*, 357–62; the fullest account of Fowler's career remains that in his *Works*, ed. Henry W. Meikle, James Craigie and John Purves, 3 vols. (Edinburgh: STS, 1914–1940), 3:ix–xl.

[22] See John Bossy, *Giordano Bruno and the Embassy Affair* (New Haven and London: Yale University Press, 1991), 15–16, 189–92.

[23] There is no adequate study of the Scottish secret service under James; for important analyses of its English equivalents, see Alison Plowden, *The Elizabethan Secret Service* (Hemel Hempstead: Wheatsheaf, 1991), and Alan Haynes, *Invisible Power: The Elizabethan Secret Services, 1570–1603* (Stroud: Alan Sutton, 1992).

to flourish in the shifting, ambiguous world of Jacobean diplomacy and intrigue. Yet he disappears from the literary canon even more completely than his rival, and his verse is scarcely represented in modern anthologies; his translation of Machiavelli has likewise remained little more than a footnote in literary histories. Other "Castalian" poets have fared little better: John Stewart of Baldynneis, Alexander Hume, and William Alexander of Menstrie remain largely invisible, despite their undoubted cultural importance in Jacobean Scotland.[24] And the strangest case is that of the king himself, who by 1603 had published two collections of verse, two treatises on kingship, an important text on witchcraft, and several shorter prose works. The European appetite for his prose writings in particular was clearly enormous in the immediate aftermath of his accession to the English throne, and his vernacular *Works* (1616–1620) and Latin *Opera* (1619) seem from the large numbers of surviving copies to have enjoyed widespread circulation.[25] Superficial as the king's learning may have been in some respects, he was certainly something of a royal publishing phenomenon. But modern scholarship has given little attention to his literary achievements, which were already the subject of mild derision by the middle of the seventeenth century.[26]

This study has suggested that a proper re-evaluation of the place of Scottish literature in early modern Britain demands a European perspective: that we need a critical practice and vocabulary which acknowledges the parallels between developments in England and Scotland and those taking place in Continental Europe. This is in part a question of intellectual networks: literary scholarship has still not fully recognised the importance of the contacts maintained by scholars like Daniel Rogers in England or John Johnston in Scotland, or by more shadowy figures such as Anthony Bacon or Henry Keir, busy in the world of diplomacy and espionage. The openness of British culture to Continental influence is evidenced, too, by the existence of such libraries as those of Henry Percy, earl of Northumberland, and William Drummond of Hawthornden, where book ownership transcends both

---

[24] Hume's "The Day Estivall" is a notable exception to this general observation, having become a standard piece in Scottish anthologies; it is striking that his "Epistle to Maister Gilbert Mont-creif", a satirical poem reminiscent of and certainly not inferior to Wyatt's satires, is virtually unknown.

[25] For a discussion of the spate of publishing of James's works in a variety of European languages, see R.J. Lyall, "The Marketing of James VI and I: Scotland, England and the Continental Book Trade", *Quaerendo* 32 (2002): 204–17.

[26] Cf. Sir Thomas Urquhart's jibe at Sir William Alexander, later created earl of Stirling: "He was born a poet and aimed to be a king. Therefore would he have his royal title from King James, who was born a king and aimed to be a poet": *The Jewel*, ed. R.D.S. Jack and R.J. Lyall (Edinburgh: Scottish Academic Press, 1983), 168. For an important recent contribution to the reversal of this view, see *Royal Subjects*, ed. Fischlin and Fortier.

national boundaries and doctrinal difference.[27] "New Historicist" scholarship has reaffirmed the permeability of the category of literature; more traditional historical scholarship can provide a framework for a better understanding of the political and social realities within which early modern literature was produced. The religious turmoil of the sixteenth century complicated but in no way diminished the interchange of ideas between Britain and the Continent: Protestant emigré communities in England and English and Scottish Catholic exiles abroad ensured a new base for such communication, and Scottish students in particular continued to study at Continental universities. The flow of information about Montgomerie to Würzburg with which we began our study of his life illustrates the currency of these channels into the seventeenth century, even if the exact route remains uncertain. But a great deal of work remains to be done on almost every aspect of this important area of cultural exchange: the presence of Scottish students and masters in the French Protestant academies; the nature, extent and influence of English and Scottish Catholic communities in France and elsewhere; the intellectual links between Scotland and the Baltic; all these and other topics await thorough, systematic investigation.

A fuller understanding of the European contexts of early modern British literature does not solely depend, however, upon these questions of intellectual infrastructure. I have argued that such concepts as "Mannerism" and "Baroque", widely accepted if still controversial in the discussion of the early modern literatures of Continental Europe, can illuminate our analysis of Scottish and English texts as well. Underlying this contention is the belief that the dynamics of British literatures were not fundamentally different from those at work in France, Spain, Italy, and elsewhere, and that the stresses of courtiership, of doctrinal dissent, and of a growing absolutism were experienced in comparable ways by Montgomerie and Fowler, by Constable and Sidney, by Du Bartas and Desportes. Montgomerie's poetry, as we have seen, reflects these conflicts, even when it seems on a superficial reading to be offering little more than elegant entertainment. In his carefully-modulated encomia, his ventriloquised amatory verse, his coded poems of friendship, and his subtle, politically-correct articulations of his religious views, we can recognise the courtier-poet at his most equivocal, frequently relying upon deeply-inscribed subtexts to convey covert meanings to those who were willing or able to see them. Only in his later career, significantly, alienated from the court and in deep personal trouble, does he find a new and wholly undisguised

---

[27] On the former, see G.R. Batho, "The Library of the 'Wizard' Earl: Henry, Percy, Ninth Earl of Northumberland (1564–1632)", *The Library*, 5th ser. 15 (1960): 246–61, and Hilary Gatti, "Giordano Bruno: The Texts in the Library of the Ninth Earl of Northumberland", *JWCI* 46 (1983): 63–77; on the latter, R.H. MacDonald, ed., *The Library of Drummond of Hawthornden* (Edinburgh: Edinburgh University Press, 1971).

voice, unleashing personal invective at his enemies; even here, it should be ob-
served, his address to the king remains shrouded in casuistical wordplay and
proverbial implication, and we have also found grounds for suspecting that his
denunciatory voice could be turned to a covert purpose, covertly and deniably at-
tacking the ministers of Edinburgh.

The posturing and striking of attitudes, the preoccupation with elegance of
form which frequently encodes deeper anxieties, are characteristic of much Man-
nerist art. In his greatest successes, we might justifiably claim, Montgomerie
was most typical of his age, while in his personal failure he became most fully
himself. By setting our analysis of Montgomerie's verse not only against Marot
and Ronsard but also against the work of his more immediate French contempo-
raries, we have seen how clearly he articulates the perceptions, and employs the
metaphoric language, of European Mannerism. Yet we have also seen that this is
not the whole story. Overwhelmed by his private catastrophe, Montgomerie does
not seem to have pursued the first hints of another kind of language, imagery,
and world-view which we have noted at a few points in his œuvre, that which I
have characterised as Baroque. His friend Henry Constable's return to Scotland
did not come until seven months after Montgomerie's death,[28] and the Scottish
poet probably remained unaware of the Catholic devotional sonnets, part of the
"English Catholic Baroque",[29] which he had begun to write in his Continental
exile. When a comprehensive study of the Baroque literature of Britain comes to
be written, Montgomerie will merit scarcely more than a footnote. Yet he alone
among his Scottish contemporaries strikes a "Metaphysical" note which subverts
the Mannerist language of Petrarchism; his heir in this respect, and the most
successful Scottish courtier-poet of James's English reign, was Sir Robert Ayton,
like Montgomerie consistently marginalised and undervalued in both Scottish
and English criticism.[30] Ayton began his literary career before 1603, and he can
be seen adjusting to his new environment at the London court, and indeed to that
of Charles I. To understand his work we need to appreciate both his "Castalian"
heritage and the world of Cavalier verse into which he moved as he pursued his
career. Nowhere are the cultural anxieties which were triggered in Scotland by
James's departure more powerfully expressed than in Ayton's sonnet "Faire famous
flood", addressed to the River Tweed:

---

[28] Constable, *Poems*, ed. Grundy, 40.

[29] Shell, *Catholicism*, 57.

[30] On Ayton, see Shire, *Song, Dance and Poetry*, 217–34; and M.J.W. Scott, "Robert
Ayton: Scottish Metaphysical", *SLJ* 2 (1975): 5–16. The standard edition of Ayton's works
is that by Charles B. Gullans (Edinburgh: STS, 1963).

And since non's left but thy report alone
To show the world our Captaines last farewell
That courtesye I know when wee are gon
Perhapps your Lord the Sea will it reveale.
And you againe the same will not conceale,
But straight proclaim't through all his bremish bounds,
Till his high tydes these flowing tydeings tell
And soe will send them with his murmering sounds
 To that Religious place whose stately walls
 Does keepe the heart which all out hearts inthralls.[31]

The "Religious place", Ayton's editor suggests, is Melrose, the Tweedside abbey
where the heart of Robert the Bruce was buried; but it seems more likely that the
primary sense refers to Westminster, and the heart is that of James. The echo of
Melrose and Robert I is undoubtedly present, and its effect is to point, in the sub-
tlest way possible, the contrast between Bruce's implacable resistance to English
overlordship of Scotland and the Union which has now taken place. The sonnet's
opening, with its reference to the Tweed "which sometyme did devyde, / But
now conjoynes, two Diadems in one", welcomes the peaceful state which James's
accession portends; the conclusion does not revoke this approval, but there is no
mistaking the sense of loss which the poem as a whole articulates, or the equivocal
nature of the conclusion. Ayton's doubleness here suggests that he is a legitimate
heir to part at least of Montgomerie's achievement as we have encountered it in
these pages.

Ayton, like Fowler, made a career in the royal household at Westminster. But
the most significant Scottish writer of the generation after Montgomerie, and the
man through whose agency most of the latter's works have survived, resisted the
siren call of James's London court. William Drummond of Hawthornden, as we
have seen, was well enough known after the publication of his *Poems* in 1616 to
draw Ben Jonson to Scotland; he may have chosen to remain on his estate near
Edinburgh after returning from France in 1608, but he followed the example of
William Alexander, Ayton, and their contemporaries by writing in English. His
mastery of the language is not the least remarkable aspect of his achievement; but
it is important to recognise also the extent to which Drummond integrated an
extensive range of Continental writing into his work. He is extraordinarily eclectic in
his use of sources: his sonnet-sequence draws on writers as diverse as Sannazaro, Tor-
quato Tasso, and Marino, Ronsard, Pontus de Tyard, and Desportes, Garcilaso de la
Vega and Boscán. If Montgomerie's direct borrowings are from a fairly restricted
range of French writers, Drummond evidently put his impressively extensive li-
brary to frequent and purposeful use. But his sequence is not merely a collage of

---

[31] Ayton, *English and Latin Poems*, ed. Gullans, 167.

sixteenth-century European verse: he understands better than most Petrarchists the full significance of Petrarch's *Canzoniere*, and his two-part structure is similarly balanced on the fulcrum of the Lady's death. Furthermore, he implicitly mocks the exaggerated rhetoric of his protagonist, constantly harping on about his impending demise until the moment that a more literal death exposes the vanity of such emotional excesses. Part Two is full of passionate grief, but it also conveys a more restrained and therefore more affecting sorrow:

> My Lute, bee as thou wast when thou didst grow
> With thy greene Mother in some shadie Grove,
> When immelodious Windes but made thee move,
> And Birds on thee their Ramage did bestow.
> Sith that deare Voyce which did thy Sounds approve,
> Which us'd in such harmonious Straines to flow,
> Is reft from Earth to tune those Spheares above,
> What art thou but a Harbenger of Woe?[32]

The conclusion of the sequence reinforces our sense that Drummond is a perceptive, critical imitator of Petrarch, for the final "Song" skilfully adapts the conventions of dream-allegory in a piece which combines the consolatory rhetoric of the Middle English *Pearl* with seventeenth-century Neoplatonism.

Drummond's Petrarchism, then, restores a sense of unity and a comprehensive spiritual vision to a form the very fragmentariness of which had been an important element in its appeal to sixteenth-century Mannerists. The *Urania* poems which follow the amatory sequence in his 1616 volume and which then form the nucleus of the *Flowres of Sion* (1623) reveal his mastery as a religious poet whose sensibility clearly equals in Baroque intensity that of his better-known contemporaries. It is here that his imagery takes its most powerful form, as in his remarkable sonnet "For the Magdalene":

> These Lockes, of blushing deedes the faire attire,
> Smooth-frizled Waves, sad Shelfes which shadow deepe,
> Soule-stinging Serpents in gilt curles which creepe,
> To touch thy sacred Feete doe now aspire.[33]

In such passages Drummond's creative command of English and sheer metaphorical daring cannot fail to impress; the Baroque developments initiated by Montgomerie achieve full expression in his devotional verse, even if the predom-

---

[32] William Drummond of Hawthornden, *Poetical Works*, ed. L.E. Kastner, 2 vols. (Edinburgh: STS, 1913), 1:60.

[33] *Works*, ed. Kastner, 2:12.

inant influences upon his writing come more obviously from the Continent than from his predecessors who wrote in Scots. The historiography of seventeenth-century Scottish literature needs the concept of the Baroque, and it can scarcely be written without reference to contemporary developments in both England and the rest of Europe. It must also recognise, however, the importance of Montgomerie as a pioneer of this new poetics.

If we set aside the two items which were apparently added as an afterthought, the scribe of the Ker manuscript concludes with a sonnet "Against the God of Love" [97], a bitter denunciation of Cupid, his works, and those who are taken in by him:

| | |
|---|---|
| Blind brutal Boy that with thy bou abuses | |
| Leill leisome Love by Lechery and Lust, | *lawful* |
| Judge, Jakanapis and Jougler maist vnjust, | *upstart, trickster* |
| If in thy rageing RESONE thou refusis, | |
| To be thy Chiftanes changers ay thou chuisis | *captains; turncoats* |
| To beir thy baner, so they be robust. | |
| Fals Tratur, Turk, betrayer vnder trust, | |
| Quhy maks thou Makrels of the Modest Muses? | *bawds* |
| Art thou a God, no, bot a Gok disguysit, | *cuckoo* |
| A bluiter buskit lyk a belly blind | |
| With wings and quaver waving with the Wind,[34] | |
| A plane Playmear for Vanitie devysit. | *hobbyhorse* |
| Thou art a stirk for all thy staitly stylis | *bullock* |
| And these good Geese vhom sik a God begylis. | |

The violent rejection of Cupid is not in itself a revolutionary move: there is a recognisable strand of anti-Cupidianism in sixteenth-century poetry. What is truly remarkable about Montgomerie's sonnet is the way in which the flyting style which he developed during the early 1590s in response to his personal circumstances is here applied to the amatory themes which had dominated so much of his verse. By the final couplet, indeed, he comes to reject the language of Petrarchism itself, the "staitly stylis" which give a false picture of the god's nature. We do not know what basis the scribe had for originally making this the final poem of the collection, the parting shot with which the poet steps into silence. In a certain sense, it takes up and extends some of the thematic concerns of *The Cherrie and the Slae*: the "littil lord of love" who treats the protagonist of that poem so ironically has now become a "blind brutal Boy", whose delusive world any sane person would avoid. It is tempting, therefore, to see the poem, not merely as the expression of a moment of despair and rebellion, but as a conclusive, purposeful

---

[34] Filthy person costumed like the blindfolded player in Blind man's buff.

rejection of "Castalian" poetic values. It certainly makes a stark contrast with the measured tone of a courtly piece like "O lovesome Lady" [41], for all its awareness of the pains of love:

> Somtyme I had gude confidence
>   That plesur suld succeid
> Quhill in the tyme of our Absence
>   Good fortun did me leid
> But nou I find my esperance
>   Almaist ou'rcome with dreid
>   Also
> I feill the fatal Nymphis threid
>   Sen fortun is my fo.
>     (10–18)

The enmity of Fortune is a recurrent motif in Montgomerie's poetry, as we have already seen, but the speaker's dejection here is contained within the parameters of courtly discourse, and by implication within the social world of amatory posturing which is the essence of sixteenth-century Petrarchism. "Blind brutal Boy" may have seemed like a logical end-point to the Ker scribe (and, conceivably, to Montgomerie himself) because of its comprehensive rejection of that discourse and that world, avatars of a larger social context which the poet rejected even as it appears to have rejected him. He had in the process developed other varieties of discourse, not always denunciatory, which point away from the "Castalian" norms of the 1580s towards another Mannerism, the urbanity, disillusionment, and satirical distance which by turns characterise so much seventeenth-century writing.

The reading of Montgomerie's poetry which we have developed here lays down two separate challenges. To those who specialise in the literature of early modern Scotland, it is to recognise that beneath the undoubted historical break effected by the cultural consequences of James's departure for London in 1603 there is a deeper continuity, transcending linguistic practice, which links Montgomerie's Mannerism and incipient development of Baroque style with the writing in English of the following generations, of Drummond, Ayton, Urquhart, and their lesser contemporaries. Although the focus has gradually shifted away from the "Great Tradition" of Henryson, Dunbar, Douglas, and Lindsay towards the achievements of the later sixteenth century, much remains to be done if we are to understand more fully the nature of Scottish Jacobeanism and its links with developments elsewhere in Europe, and to enrich our understanding of the achievement of James VI and his contemporaries with a sharper sense of the contradictions in the culture of Renaissance courts. It is to be hoped that this book has contributed to that process. At the same time, I have argued that there is a palpable need for scholars in English studies to recognise the ways in which the different cultures of Scotland and England before the death of Elizabeth combined to influence post-Union Jacobean Britain, and to begin to give writers within the Scottish tradition the attention that is their due. Montgomerie is not only the finest Scottish poet of his age: he is, I believe, one of the most distinctive and innovative poetic voices in early modern Britain, whose eclipse is testimony to the distorting power of the *grands récits* of nations both small and large. The political forces to which he fell victim in life continued to work upon his reception long after his death: one of the central functions of historicist criticism is surely to redress such historical injustices, and to help us listen more attentively to the voices of the past.

# Bibliography

## Manuscript sources

Arnhem, Gemeentearchief     OA 296
Brussels, Archives Générales du Royaume     Audience, T109/960
Cambridge, University Library     Kk.5.30
————, Magdalen College     Pepys 1408
Dordrecht, Gemeentearchief     11/16
    21/595
    21/596

Dublin, Marsh's Library     Z3.5.21
Edinburgh, National Archives of Scotland     E2/13
    E2/14
    E21/63
    E21/64
    E22/6
    GD3/1/206
    GD3/1/686
    PS1/47
    PS1/58
    PS1/59
    RD1/18
    RD1/21
    RD1/40
    RH6/2130
    RH6/3374
    RH13/38
    RS11/1
    RS11/2
    RS25/15
    RS25/32
    RS36/2

| | |
|---|---|
| ———, National Library of Scotland | Adv. 1.1.6 |
| | Adv. 19.2.10 |
| | Wodrow Folio MS. 42 |
| ———, University Library | De.3.70 |
| | Laing III.447 |
| | Laing Charters, no. 1283 |
| The Hague, Algemeen Rijksarchief | RS6 |
| | RS 1524 |
| | SG533/3120 |
| | SG11094 |
| | SG12536 |
| | Staten van Holland, 344 |
| | Oldenbarnevelt Papers, 2855 |
| London, British Library | Harley 283 |
| ———, Public Record Office | SP9/93 |
| | SP52/49/391 |
| | SP61/12 |
| | SP77/5 |
| | SP78/9 |
| | SP84/8 |
| | SP84/10 |
| | SP84/14 |
| | SP85/5 |
| Oxford, Bodleian Library | Tanner 78 |
| St. Andrews, University Muniments | SL111 L:e2.5–6 |
| Simancas, Archivio General | Casa y Sitios Reales, leg. 85–87 |
| | CMC, 2a época, leg. 44 |
| | leg. 119 |
| | Estado 577 |
| | 827 |
| Würzburg, Universitätsbibliothek | M.ch.q.62 |

# Primary texts

Alexander, William, earl of Stirling. *Poetical Works*, ed. L.E. Kastner and H.B. Charlton. 2 vols. Edinburgh: STS, 1921–1929.

Allen, William, S.J. *The Copie of a Letter Concerning the Yeelding Up of Daventrie.* Antwerp: Joachim Trognesius, 1587.

Augustine of Hippo, St. *De Trinitate*, ed. W.J. Mountain. CCSL 50–50A. 2 vols. Turnhout: Brepols, 1968.

Ayton, Sir Robert. *Latin and English Poems*, ed. Charles B. Gullans. Edinburgh: STS, 1963.

*Ballattis of Luve*, ed. John MacQueen. Edinburgh: Edinburgh University Press, 1971.

Balfour of Pittendreich, Sir James. *Practicks*, ed. Peter G.B. MacNeill. 2 vols. Edinburgh: Stair Society, 1962–1963.

*The Bannatyne Manuscript*, ed. W. Tod Ritchie. 4 vols. Edinburgh: STS, 1928–1934.

*The Bannatyne Manuscript (NLS Adv. MS. 1.1.6)*, ed. Denton Fox and William A. Ringler. London: Scolar Press, 1980.

Barbour, John. *The Brus*, ed. Matthew P. McDiarmid and James A.C. Stevenson. 3 vols. Edinburgh: STS, 1980–1985.

Bawcutt, Priscilla, and Felicity Riddy, eds. *Longer Scottish Poems*. Vol. 1. Edinburgh: Scottish Academic Press, 1987.

Du Bellay, Joachim. *Œuvres poétiques*, ed. Henri Chamard. STFM. 6 vols. Paris: Hachette, 1908–1931.

———. *Les Regrets et autres œuvres poëtiques*, ed. J. Joliffe and M.A. Screech. 2nd ed. Geneva: Droz, 1974.

Belleau, Rémy. *Œuvres poétiques*, ed. Charles Marty-Laveaux. 2 vols. Paris: A. Lemerre, 1878.

Bertaut, Jean. *Œuvres Poétiques*, ed. Adolphe Chenièvre. Paris: E. Plot, Nourrit et cie., 1891.

———. *Recueil de Quelques Vers Amoureux*, ed. Louis Terreaux. STFM. Paris: Hachette, 1970.

Boudewijns, Katherina. *Het Prieelken der Gheestelyker Wellusten*, ed. Hermance van Belle. Antwerp: De Sikkel, 1927.

Buchanan, George. *Rerum Scoticarum Historia*. Edinburgh: Alexander Arbuthnot, 1582.

———. *Vernacular Prose Works*, ed. P. Hume Brown. Edinburgh: STS, 1892.

Burel, John, *Poems*. Edinburgh: Robert Waldegrave, [?1596].

Calderwood, David. *History of the Kirk of Scotland*, ed. Thomas Thomson. 8 vols. Edinburgh: Bannatyne Club, 1839–1845.

*Catholic Tractates of the Sixteenth Century, 1573–1600*, ed. T.G. Law. Edinburgh: STS, 1901.

*Caxton's Aesop*, ed. R.T. Lenaghan. Cambridge, MA: Harvard University Press, 1967.

*Chronicle of Scottish Poetry*, ed. James Sibbald. Edinburgh: J. Sibbald, 1802.

Colonna, Guido della. *Historia Destructionis Troiae*, ed. N.E. Griffin. Cambridge, MA: Harvard University Press, 1936.

———. *Historia Destructionis Troiae*, trans. Mary Elizabeth Meek. Bloomington, IN and London: Indiana University Press, 1974.

*The Complaynt of Scotland*, ed. A.M. Stewart. Edinburgh: STS, 1979.

Constable, Henry. *Poems*, ed. Joan Grundy. Liverpool: Liverpool University Press, 1960.

*Corpus Dionysiacum*, ed. Beate Regina Suchla, Günther Heil, and Adolf Martin Ritter. 2 vols. Berlin and New York: Walter de Gruyter, 1990–1991.

de la Cruz, Juan. *Poesías*, ed. Paola Elia. Madrid: Castalia, 1990.

Damman, Adriaan. *Schediasmata*. Edinburgh: Robert Waldegrave, 1590.

Dempster, Thomas. *Historia Ecclesiastica Gentis Scotorum*. 2 vols, Edinburgh: Bannatyne Club, 1829.

Desportes, Philippe. *Cartels et Masquarades, Épitaphes*, ed. Victor E. Graham. Geneva: Droz, 1958.

———. *Diverse Amours*, ed. Victor E. Graham. Geneva: Droz, 1963.

van der Does, Jan [Janus Dousa]. *Poemata*. Leiden: [Andries Verschout], 1576.

van der Does, Theodor, ed. *Lusus imaginis iocosae, sive Echus*. Utrecht: Aegidius Romanus, 1638.

Douglas, Gavin. *Shorter Poems*, ed. Priscilla Bawcutt. Edinburgh: STS, 1967.

Drummond of Hawthornden, William. *Poetical Works*, ed. L.E. Kastner. 2 vols. Edinburgh: STS, 1913.

Dunbar, William. *Poems*, ed. Priscilla Bawcutt. 2 vols. Glasgow: Association for Scottish Literary Studies, 1998.

*Les Fabulistes latins depuis le siècle d'Auguste jusqu'à la fin du Moyen Age*, ed. Léopold Hervieux. 2nd ed. 5 vols. Paris: Firmin-Didot, 1893–1899.

Fowler, William. *Works*, ed. Henry W. Meikle, James Craigie and John Purves. 3 vols. Edinburgh: STS, 1912–1939.

Froissart, Jean. *Œuvres: Poésies*, ed. A. Scheler. 3 vols. Brussels: V. Devaux, 1870–1872.

Gascoigne, George. *A Hundreth sundrie Flowres*. London: Richard Smith, [1573].

———. *Complete Works*, ed. John W. Cunliffe. 2 vols. Cambridge: Cambridge University Press, 1907-1910.

Grange, John. *Golden Aphroditis*. London: Henry Bynneman, 1577.

d'Heere, Lucas. *Den Hof en Boomgaerd der Poësien*, ed. W. Waterschoot. Zwolle: Tjeenk Willinck, 1969.

Henryson, Robert. *Poems*, ed. Denton Fox. Oxford: Clarendon Press, 1981.

*The Historie and Life of King James the Sext*, ed. Thomas Thomson. Edinburgh: Bannatyne Club, 1825.

Horace. *Odes and Epodes*, ed. and trans. C.E. Bennett. 7th ed. Loeb Classical Library. London and Cambridge, MA: Harvard University Press, 1946.

Hume, Alexander. *Poems*, ed. Alexander Lawson. Edinburgh: STS, 1902.

James VI and I. *New Poems of James I of England*, ed. A.F. Westcott. New York: Columbia University Press, 1911.

———. *Poems*, ed. James Craigie. 2 vols. Edinburgh: Scottish History Society, 1955-1958.

Jamyn, Amadis. *Les œuvres poétiques*, ed. Samuel L. Carrington. 2 vols. Geneva: Droz, 1973-1978.

Knox, John, *Works*, ed. David Laing. 6 vols. London: Wodrow Society, 1846-1864.

Lamb, William. *Ane Ressonyng betuix ane Scottis merchand and ane Inglis merchand betuix Rowane and Lyonis*, ed. R.J. Lyall. Aberdeen: Aberdeen University Press, 1985.

Le Saulx, Marin. *Theanthropogamie*. London: Thomas Vautrollier, 1577.

Leslie, John. *De origine moribus, et rebus gestis Scotorum libri decem*. Rome: Casa del Popolo Romano, 1578.

Lindsay, Sir David. *Warkis*. [Edinburgh]: John Scot for Henry Charteris, 1568.

———. *Works*, ed. Douglas Hamer. 4 vols. Edinburgh: STS, 1931-1936.

Machaut, Guillaume de. *Œuvres*, ed. Ernest Hoepffner. 3 vols. Paris: SATF, 1908-1921.

*The Maitland Folio Manuscript*, ed. W.A. Craigie. 2 vols. Edinburgh: STS, 1919-1927.

*The Maitland Quarto Manuscript*, ed. W.A. Craigie. Edinburgh: STS, 1920.

Marot, Clément. *Œuvres complètes*, ed. C.A. Mayer. 6 vols. London: Athlone Press, 1958-1970; Geneva: Slatkine, 1980.

Melissus, Paul Schede. *Die Psalmenübersetzung des Paul Schede Melissus*, ed. Max Hermann Jellinek. Halle/Saale: Niemeyer, 1896.

Melvill, James. *Ane fruitfull and comfortable exhortation anent death*. Edinburgh: Robert Waldegrave, 1597.

———. *A spirituall propine of a pastour to his people*. Edinburgh: Robert Waldegrave, 1598.

———. *Autobiography and Diary*, ed. Robert Pitcairn. London: Wodrow Society, 1842.

Montgomerie, Alexander. *The Flyting betuixt Montgomery and Polwart*. Edinburgh: Andrew Hart, 1621.

———. *Poems*, ed. James Cranstoun. Edinburgh: STS, 1887.

———. *Poems*, Supplementary Volume, ed. George Stevenson. Edinburgh: STS, 1910.

———. *Poems*, ed. David Parkinson. 2 vols. Edinburgh: STS, 2000.

Moysie, David. *Memoirs of the Affairs of Scotland, 1577-1603*, ed. J. Dennistoun. Glasgow: Maitland Club, 1830.

Mure of Rowallan, Sir William. *Works*, ed. William Tough. 2 vols. Edinburgh: STS, 1898.

*Music of Scotland 1500-1700*, ed. Kenneth Elliott and Helena Mennie Shire. Musica Britannica 15. 3rd ed. London: Stainer and Bell, 1975.

Navarre, Marguerite de. *Chansons spirituelles*, ed. G. Dottin. Paris: Minard, 1971.

Neville, Alexander. *Academiae Cantabrigiensis Lachrymae Tumulo Nobilissimi Equitis, D. Philippi Sidneij Sacratae*. London: John Windet, 1587.

van der Noot, Jan. *Het Bosken en Het Theatre*, ed. W.A.P. Smit and W. Vermeer. Amsterdam and Antwerp: Wereldbibliotheek, 1953.

———. *Poetische Werken*, ed. W. Waterschoot. Ghent: Koninklijke Academie voor Nederlandse Taal- en Letterkunde, 1975.

Nott, G.F., ed. *The Works of Henry Howard, Earl of Surrey and of Sir Thomas Wyatt the Elder*. 2 vols. London: Longman,1815-1816.

Ovid. *Metamorphoses*, ed. and trans. Frank Justus Miller, rev. G.P. Goold. 2 vols. 3rd ed. Loeb Classical Library. Cambridge, MA and London: Harvard University Press, 1977.

Passerat, Jean. *Poésies françaises*, ed. Prosper Blanchemin. 2 vols. Paris: A. Lemerre 1880.

*Paston Letters and Papers of the Fifteenth Century*, ed. Norman Davis. 3 vols. Oxford: Clarendon, 1971- .

Petrarch, Francesco. *Canzoniere*, ed. Ugo Dotti. 2 vols. Rome: Donzelli, 1996.

Poliziano, Angelo. *Rime*, ed. Daniela Delcorno Branca. Florence: Accademia della Crusca, 1986.

Pont, Timothy. *Cuninghame Topographized, 1604-8*, ed. John Shedden Dobie. Glasgow: J. Tweed, 1876.

Ralegh, Sir Walter. *Poems: A Historical Edition*, ed. Michael Rudick. Renaissance English Text Society, 7th ser. 23; Medieval and Renaissance Texts and Studies 209. Tempe, AZ: Arizona Center for Medieval and Renaissance Studies, 1999.

Ramsay, Allan, ed. *The Evergreen*. Edinburgh: Thomas Ruddiman for Allan Ramsay, 1724.

Raymond, Marcel, ed. *La Poésie Française et le Maniérisme 1546-1610(?)*. London: Athlone Press and Geneva: Droz, 1971.

*Rob Stene's Dreme*, ed. David Reid. Stirling: University of Stirling Bibliographical Society,1989.

Ronsard, Pierre de. *Œuvres complètes*, ed. Pierre Laumonier et al. STFM. 20 vols. Paris: Hachette, 1914-1975.

*Satirical Poems of the Time of the Reformation*, ed. James Cranstoun. 2 vols. Edinburgh: STS, 1891-1896.

Scott, Alexander. *Poems*, ed. James Cranstoun. Edinburgh: STS, 1896.

*Select Remains of the Ancient Popular Romance Poetry of Scotland*, ed. David Laing, rev. John Small. Edinburgh and London: Blackwood, 1885.

Shakespeare, William. *Richard II*, ed. Andrew Gurr. Cambridge: Cambridge University Press, 1984.

Sidney, Sir Philip. *Prose Works*, ed. Albert Feuillerat. 4 vols. Cambridge: Cambridge University Press, 1912.

———. *Poems*, ed. William A. Ringler. Oxford: Clarendon Press, 1962.

*A Source-book of Scottish Witchcraft*, ed. Christina Larner et al. Glasgow: 1977.

Southwell, Robert, S.J. *Poems*, ed. James H. McDonald and Nancy Pollard Brown. Oxford: Clarendon Press, 1967.

Spenser, Edmund. *The Faerie Queene*, ed. A.C. Hamilton. London and New York: Longman, 1977.

———. *Shorter Poems*, ed. William A. Oram et al. New Haven and London: Yale University Press, 1989.

Sternhold, Thomas, and John Hopkins, *The Forme of Prayers and Ministration of the Sacraments*. Edinburgh: Robert Lekpreuick, 1565.

Stewart of Baldynneis, John. *Poems*, ed. Thomas Crockett. Vol. 2. Edinburgh: STS, 1913.

Tyrie, James, S.J. *The Refutation of an Ansuer made by Schir Johne Knox to ane letter, send be James Tyrie, to his vmquhile brother*. Paris: Thomas Brumeau, 1573.

Urquhart of Cromarty, Sir Thomas. *The Jewel*, ed. R.D.S. Jack and R.J. Lyall. Edinburgh: Scottish Academic Press, 1983.

Viotto, Erasmo. *Raccolto d'alcune piacevoli rime*. Parma: Heredi di S. Viotto, 1582.

Watson, James. *A Choice Collection of Comic and Serious Scots Poems*. Edinburgh: James Watson, 1706-1711.

Watson, Thomas. *The Hekatompathia, or Passionate Century of Love*, ed. S.K. Heninger Jr. Gainesville, FL: Scholars' Facsimiles and Reprints, 1964.

Whitaker, William. *Disputation on Holy Scripture*, ed. William Fitzgerald. London: Parker Society, 1849.

Whitney, Geoffrey. *A Choice of Emblemes*. Leiden: Christopher Plantin, 1586.

Wyatt, Sir Thomas. *Collected Poems*, ed. Kenneth Muir and Patricia Thomson. Liverpool: Liverpool University Press, 1969.

———. *Collected Poems*, ed. Joost Daalder. Oxford: Oxford University Press, 1975.

## Documentary sources

*Acta Facultatis Artium Universitatis Sanctiandree, 1413-1588*, ed. Annie I. Dunlop. 2 vols. Edinburgh: SHS, 1964.

*The Acts of the Parliaments of Scotland*, ed. T. Thomson and C. Innes. 12 vols. Edinburgh: 1814-1875.

*Booke of the Universall Kirk, Acts and Proceedings of the General Assemblies of the Kirk of Scotland, 1560-1618*. 3 vols and Appendix. Edinburgh: Bannatyne and Maitland Clubs, 1839-1845.

*Calendar of State Papers, Foreign, Elizabeth*, ed. J. Stevenson et al. 23 vols. London: HMSO, 1863-1950.

*Calendar of State Papers relating to Scotland and Mary, Queen of Scots, 1547-1603*, ed. J. Bain *et al.* 12 vols. Edinburgh: 1898-1969.

*Calendar of State Papers, Spanish*, ed. G. Bergenroth et al. 13 vols. London: HMSO, 1862-1954.

*Calendar of the Manuscripts of the Marquis of Salisbury*, ed. S.R. Bird et al. 24 vols. London: Historic Manuscripts Commission, 1883-1976.

*Catalogue of Graduates of the University of Edinburgh*, ed. David Laing. Edinburgh: Bannatyne Club, 1858.

*Correspondence of Robert Dudley Earl of Leicester*, ed. John Bruce. London: Camden Society, 1844.

"Correspondence inedite de Robert Dudley, comte de Leycester et de François et Jean Hotman," ed. P.J. Blok. *Archives du Musée Teyler*, 2ᵉ sér., 12 (1910): 79-296.

*Correspondence de Philippe II sur les affaires des Pays-Bas, 1558-1577*, ed. Prosper Gachard. 5 vols. Brussels: Mucquardt, 1848-1879.

*Correspondence de Philippe II*, Part II, ed. Joseph Lefèvre. 4 vols. Brussels: Palais des académies, 1940-1960.

*Correspondentie van Robert Dudley Graaf van Leycester en andere documenten betreffende zijn gouvernement-generaal in de Nederlanden, 1585-1588*, ed. H. Brugmans. 3 vols. Utrecht: Kemink, 1931.

*De huwelijksintekeningen van Schotse militairen in Nederland, 1574-1655*, ed. J. Maclean. Zutphen: Walburg, 1976.

*Lettres, Instructions et Mémoires de Marie Stuart, reine d'Écosse*, ed. Alexandre Labanoff. 7 vols. London: Dolman, 1844.

*Letters and Papers relating to Patrick, Master of Gray*, ed. Thomas Thomson. Edinburgh: Bannatyne Club, 1835.

Letters of King James VI and I, *ed. G.P.V. Akrigg. Berkeley: University of California Press, 1984.*

Pitcairn, Robert, ed. *Ancient Criminal Trials in Scotland*. 3 vols. Edinburgh: Bannatyne Club, 1833.

*Register of the Privy Council of Scotland*, ed. J.H. Burton et al. 38 vols. Edinburgh: HM General Register House, 1877- .

*Registrum Secreti Sigilli Regum Scotorum*, ed. M. Livingston et al. Edinburgh: HM General Register House, 1948- .

*Registrum Magni Sigilli Regum Scotorum (Register of the Great Seal of Scotland)*, ed. J.M. Thomson et al. 11 vols. Edinburgh: HM General Register House, 1882-1914.

*Relations politiques des Pays-Bas et de l'Angleterre*, ed. Kervyn de Letterhove. 11 vols. Brussels: Hayez, 1882-1900.

*Report of the Manuscripts of the Earl of Ancaster*, ed. S.C. Lomax. Dublin: Historic Manuscripts Commission, 1907.

*Resolutiën der Staten Generaal van 1576 tot 1609*, ed. N. Japikse and H.P. Rijperman. Rijks Geschiedkundige Publicatiën. 14 vols. The Hague: Nijhoff, 1915-1970.

*Resolutiën van der Heeren Staten van Holland en Westvriesland 1524-1795*. 249 vols. The Hague: c. 1750-1798.

## Secondary works

Adams, Michael. "Sir Thomas Wyatt and the Progress of Mannerism in Renaissance English Lyric." Ph.D. diss., University of Michigan, 1988.

Adams, Simon. "A Puritan Crusade? The Composition of the Earl of Leicester's Expedition to the Netherlands, 1585-1586." In *The Dutch in Crisis, 1585-1588: People and Politics in Leicester's Time*, 7-34. Leiden: Sir Thomas Browne Institute, 1988.

Anglo, Sydney. "The Courtier: The Renaissance and Changing Ideals." In *The Courts of Europe: Politics, Patronage and Royalty, 1400-1800*, ed. A.G. Dickens, 33-53. London: Thames and Hudson, 1977.

Archer, John Michael. *Sovereignty and Intelligence: Spying and Court Culture in the English Renaissance*. Stanford, CA: Stanford University Press, 1993.

Atkinson, David. "William Drummond as a Baroque Poet." *SSL* 26 (1991): 394-409.

Baïche, A. *La naissance du baroque français: Poésie et image de la Pléiade à Jean de la Ceppède*. Toulouse: Université de Toulouse-Le-Mirail, 1976.

Baker, David J., and Willy Maley, eds. *British Identities and English Renaissance Literature*. Cambridge: Cambridge University Press, 2002.

Baker-Smith, Dominic. "Sidney's Death and the Poets." In *Sir Philip Sidney: 1586 and the Creation of a Legend*, ed. Jan van Dorsten, idem, and Arthur F. Kinney, 83-103. Leiden: E.J. Brill, 1986.

Baldacci, Luigi. *Il petrarchismo italiano nel Cinquecento*. 2nd ed. Padua: Liviana, 1974.

Bate, Jonathan. *Shakespeare and Ovid*. Oxford: Clarendon Press, 1993.

Batho, G.R. "The Library of the 'Wizard' Earl: Henry Percy, Ninth Earl of Northumberland (1564-1632)." *The Library* 5th ser. 15 (1960): 246-61.

Bawcutt, Priscilla. "The Art of Flyting." *SLJ* 10/2 (December 1983): 5-21.

———. *Dunbar the Makar*. Oxford: Clarendon Press, 1992.

Bell, Sandra. "Poetry and Politics in the Scottish Renaissance." Ph.D. diss., Queen's University, Kingston, Ontario, 1995.

Bellenger, Yvonne. "Du Bellay satirique dans *Les Regrets*?." In *Du Bellay: Actes du Colloque International d'Angers de 26 au 29 mai 1989*, ed. George Cesbron, 1: 45-58. 2 vols. Angers: Presses de l'Université d'Angers, 1990.

Bentley-Crouch, Dana, and Rosalind K. Marshall. "Iconography and Literature in the Service of Diplomacy: The Franco-Scottish Alliance, James V and Scotland's Two French Queens, Madeleine of France and Mary of Guise." In *Stewart Style 1513-1542: Essays on the Court of James V*, ed. Janet Hadley Williams, 273-88. East Linton: Tuckwell Press, 1996.

Bergeron, David M. *King James and Letters of Homoerotic Desire*. Iowa City: Iowa University Press, 1999.

Bernard, John D. *Ceremonies of Innocence: Pastoralism in the Poetry of Edmund Spenser*. Cambridge: Cambridge University Press, 1989.

Bernhart, A. Walter. "Castalian Poetics and the 'Verie Twichestane Musique'." In *Scottish Language and Literature, Medieval and Renaissance*, ed. Dietrich Strauss and Horst W. Drescher, 451-58. Frankfurt/Main, Bern and New York, 1986.

Bor, Pieter Christiaansz. *Oosprongk, begin en vervolgh der Nederlandschen oorlogen, beroerten en borgerlyke oneenigheden*. Amsterdam: widow of Johannes van Someren et al., 1679-84.

Bordonau, Miguel. "La libreria y los libros de Coro del Real Monasterio de San Lorenzo del Escorial." *Bibliotecas y Museos* 71 (1963): 243-73.

Borland, Lois. "Montgomerie and the French Poets of the Early Sixteenth Century." *MP* 11 (1913-1914): 1-8.

Bossy, John. "A Propos of Henry Constable." *Recusant History* 6 (1961-1962): 228-37.

———. *Giordano Bruno and the Embassy Affair*. New Haven and London: Yale University Press, 1991.

Bouwsma, William J. *The Waning of the Renaissance 1550-1640*. New Haven and London: Yale University Press, 2000.

Braden, Gordon. *Petrarchan Love and the Continental Renaissance*. New Haven and London: Yale University Press, 1999.

Brannigan, John. *New Historicism and Cultural Materialism*. Basingstoke: Macmillan, 1998.

Bray, J.S. *Theodore Beza's Doctrine of Predestination*. Nieuwkoop: De Graaf, 1975.

Briquet, C.M. *Les Filigranes*, ed. Allan Stevenson. 4 vols. Amsterdam: Paper Publications Society, 1968.

Brown, Keith. "The Making of a *Politique*: The Counter Reformation and the Regional Politics of John, Eighth Lord Maxwell." *SHR* 66 (1987): 152-75.

Burchmore, David W. "The Image of the Centre in *Colin Clouts Come Home Again.*" *RES* n.s. 28 (1977): 393-406.

Caccia, Ettore, ed. *La Critica Stilistica e il Barocco Letterario.* Florence: Le Monnier, 1958.

Cave, Terence C. *Devotional Poetry in France, c. 1570-1613.* Cambridge: Cambridge University Press, 1969.

Champion, Pierre. *Paris au Temps de Henri III.* Paris: Éditions C.-L.,1942.

Chaney, Richard. "The Problem of Mannerism in Sixteenth-Century French Literature." In *Miscellanea Musicologica: Adelaide Studies in Musicology*, 2: 28-48. Adelaide: Libraries Board of South Australia, 1980.

Colby, Eldridge. *The Echo-Device in Literature.* New York: New York Public Library, 1920.

Corthell, Ronald J. "'The secrecy of man': Recusant Discourse and the Elizabethan Subject." *ELR* 19 (1989): 272-90.

Cowan, Ian. *The Scottish Reformation.* London: Weidenfeld and Nicolson, 1982.

Croce, Benedetto. *Storia dell'età barocca in Italia.* Scritti di storia litteraria e politica 23. Bari: Laterza, 1929.

Cunningham, J.V. "Lyric Style in the 1590s." In idem, *Collected Essays*, 311-24. Chicago: Swallow Press, 1976.

Curtius, E.R. *European Literature and the Latin Middle Ages*, trans. Willard R. Trask. New York: Pantheon Books, 1953; repr. Princeton: Princeton University Press, 1973; repr. 1990.

Cysarz, Herbert. *Deutsche Barockdichtung.* Leipzig: H. Haessel, 1924.

Daemen-de Gelder, K.A.L. "Recitations of Nationhood: The Making of Scottish Literature and the Early Modern Canon." Ph.D. diss., Vrije Universiteit Amsterdam, 2001.

Daniells, Roy. *Milton, Mannerism and Baroque.* Toronto: University of Toronto Press, 1963.

Darlow, T.H., and H.F. Moule. *Historical Catalogue of the Printed Editions of Holy Scripture in the Library of the British and Foreign Bible Society.* 2 vols. London: Bible House, 1903-1911.

Davies, Gareth A. *A Poet at Court: Antonio Hurtado de Mendoza (1586-1644).* Oxford: Dolphin, 1971.

Delumeau, Jean. *Le péché et la peur: la culpibilisation en Occident (XIIIe–XVIIIe siècles)* Paris: Fayard, 1983.

Dilworth, Mark, O.S.B. "New Light on Alexander Montgomerie." *The Bibliotheck* 4 (1965): 230-5.

———. *The Scots in Franconia.* Edinburgh: Scottish Academic Press, 1974.

Donaldson, Ian. *The Rapes of Lucretia: A Myth and its Transformations.* Oxford: Clarendon Press, 1982.

van Dorsten, Jan. "Poets, Patrons and Professors." Ph.D. diss., Rijksuniversiteit Leiden, 1962.

———. *The Anglo-Dutch Renaissance*, ed. J. van den Berg and Alastair Hamilton. Leiden: E.J. Brill, 1988.

Drexler, Marjorie. "Fluid Prejudice: Scottish Origin Myths in the Later Middle Ages." In *People, Politics and Community in the Later Middle Ages*, ed. Joel Rosenthal and Colin Richmond, 60-77. Gloucester and New York: Sutton, 1987.

Dubois, Claude-Gilbert. *Le Maniérisme*. Paris: Presses universitaires de France, 1979.

Dubrow, Heather. *Echoes of Desire: English Petrarchism and its Counterdiscourses*. Ithaca: Cornell University Press, 1995.

Dunlop, G.A. "John Stewart of Baldynneis, the Scottish Desportes." *SHR* 12 (1915): 303-10.

Dunnigan, Sarah M. "Scottish Women Writers, c. 1560-c. 1650." In *A History of Women's Writing in Scotland*, ed. Douglas Gifford and Dorothy McMillan, 15-43. Edinburgh: Edinburgh University Press, 1997.

———. "Female Gifts: Rhetoric, Beauty and the Beloved in the Lyrics of Alexander Montgomerie." *SLJ* 26/2 (Winter 1999): 59-78.

Dunthorne, Hugh. "Scots in the Wars of the Low Countries." In *Scotland and the Low Countries 1194-1994*, ed. Grant G. Simpson, 104-21. East Linton: Tuckwell Press, 1996.

Durkan, John. "Education in the Century of the Reformation." In *Essays on the Scottish Reformation, 1513-1625*, ed. David McRoberts, 145-68. Glasgow: J.S. Burns, 1962.

———. "The Date of Alexander Montgomerie's Death." *Innes Review* 34 (1983): 91-92.

———. "The French Connection in the Sixteenth and Early Seventeenth Centuries." In *Scotland and Europe 1200-1850*, ed. T.C. Smout, 19-44. Edinburgh: John Donald, 1986.

———. "Education: the Laying of Fresh Foundations." In *Humanism in Renaissance Scotland*, ed. John MacQueen, 123-60. Edinburgh: Edinburgh University Press, 1990.

Engammare, Max. *Qu'il me baise des baisiers de sa bouche: La Cantique des Cantiques à la Renaissance*. Geneva: Droz, 1993.

van Eys, W.J. *Bibliographie des Bibles et des Nouveaux Testaments en langue française des XVe et XVIe siècles*. 2 vols. Geneva: Kündig, 1900-1901.

Falls, Cyril. *Elizabeth's Irish Wars*. London: Methuen, 1950.

Fernández Álvarez, Manuel. *Felipe II y su Tiempo*. Madrid: Espasa-Calpe, 1998.

Fischlin, Daniel, and Mark Fortier, eds. *Royal Subjects: Essays on the Writings of James VI and I*. Detroit: Wayne State University Press, 2002.

Fleming, Morna. "The Impact of the Union of the Crowns on Scottish Lyric Poetry 1584-1619." Ph.D. diss., University of Glasgow, 1997.

Fletcher, Jefferson B. "Areopagus and Pléiade." *JEGP* 2 (1898): 429-53.

Fontenrose, Joseph. *The Delphic Oracle: Its Responses and Operations*. Berkeley: University of California Press, 1978.

Forster, Leonard. *The Icy Fire: Five Studies in European Petrarchism*. Cambridge: Cambridge University Press, 1969.

———. "Deutsche und europäische Barockliteratur." *Daphnis* 6 (1977): 31-56.

Fox, Alistair. *The English Renaissance: Identity and Representation in Elizabethan England*. Oxford: Blackwell, 1997.

Fradenburg, Louise Olga. *City, Marriage, Tournament: Arts of Rule in Late Medieval Scotland*. Madison, WI and London: University of Wisconsin Press, 1991.

Fraser, William. *Memorials of the Montgomeries, Earls of Eglinton*. 2 vols, Edinburgh: privately printed,1859.

———. *The Chiefs of Colquhoun and their Country*. 2 vols, Edinburgh: privately printed, 1869.

———. *The Douglas Book*. 4 vols, Edinburgh: privately printed, 1885.

Fucilla, Joseph G. *Estudios sobre el Petrarquismo en España*. Madrid: Consejo Superior de Investigaciones Científicas, 1960.

Getto, G. "Un capitolo di letteratura barocca: G. Chiabrera." *Lettere Italiane* 6 (1954): 55-89.

Geyl, Pieter. *The Revolt of the Netherlands, 1555-1609*. 2nd ed. London: Benn, 1958.

Goldberg, Jonathan. "The Politics of Renaissance Literature: A Review Essay." *ELH* 49 (1982): 514-42.

———. *James I and the Politics of Literature: Jonson, Shakespeare, Donne and their Contemporaries*. Baltimore and London: Johns Hopkins University Press, 1983.

Goldstein, R. James. *The Matter of Scotland: Historical Narrative in Medieval Scotland*. Lincoln, NE and London: University of Nebraska Press, 1993.

Goodare, Julian. *The Scottish Witch-Hunt in Context*. Manchester: Manchester University Press, 2002.

———, and Michael Lynch, eds. *The Reign of James VI*. East Linton: Tuckwell, 2000.

Greenblatt, Stephen. *Renaissance Self-Fashioning: From More to Shakespeare*. Chicago: University of Chicago Press, 1980.

———. *Shakespearean Negotiations: The Circulation of Social Energy in Renaissance England*. Oxford: Clarendon Press, 1988.

———. *Learning to Curse: Essays in Early Modern Culture*. New York and London: Routledge, 1990.

Greene, Thomas M. *The Light in Troy: Imitation and Discovery in Renaissance Poetry*. New Haven and London: Yale University Press, 1982.

Greer, David. 'Five Variations on 'Farewel dear loue'." In *The Well Enchanting Skill: Music, Poetry, and Drama in the Culture of the Renaissance*, ed. John Caldwell, Edward Oleson, and Susan Wollenberg, 213-27. Oxford: Oxford University Press, 1990.

Hallyn, Fernand. *Formes métaphoriques dans la poésie de l'âge baroque en France*. Geneva: Droz, 1975.

Hamilton, Paul. *Historicism*. London and New York: Routledge, 1996.

Hannay, R.K. *The College of Justice: Essays on the Institution and Development of the Court of Session*. Edinburgh: Hodge, 1933; repr. Edinburgh: Stair Society, 1990.

Hardin, Richard F. "Ovid in Sixteenth-Century England." *Comparative Literature* 24 (1972): 44-62.

Harris, William O. "Early Elizabethan Sonnets in Sequence." *SP* 68 (1971): 451-69.

Harvey, Elizabeth D. *Ventriloquized Voices: Feminist Theory and English Renaissance Texts*. London: Routledge, 1992.

Hassell, James Woodrow, Jr. *Middle French Proverbs, Sentences and Proverbial Phrases*. Toronto: University of Toronto Press, 1982.

Hatzfeld, H. *Estudios sobre el Barroco*. Madrid: Gredos, 1964.

Hauser, Arnold. *Mannerism: The Crisis of the Renaissance and the Origin of Modern Art*, trans. Eric Mosbacher. 2 vols. New York: Knopf, 1965.

Haynes, Alan. *Invisible Power: The Elizabethan Secret Services, 1570-1603*. Stroud: Alan Sutton, 1992.

van Heijnsbergen, Theo. "The Love Lyrics of Alexander Scott." *SSL* 26 (1991): 366-79.

Heiple, Daniel L. *Garcilaso de la Vega and the Italian Renaissance* University Park, PA: Pennsylvania State University Press, 1994.

Helgerson, Richard. *Forms of Nationhood: The Elizabethan Writing of England*. Chicago and London: University of Chicago Press, 1992.

Hewitt, George R. *Scotland under Morton, 1572-80*. Edinburgh: John Donald, 1982.

Höweler, C.A. and F.H. Matler. *Fontes Hymnodiae Neerlandicae Impressi, 1539-1700*. Nieuwkoop: De Graaf, 1985.

Hoffmann, Oscar. "Studien zu Montgomerie." *Englische Studien* 20 (1895): 24-69.

Howard, Jean. "The New Historicism in Renaissance Studies." *ELR* 16 (1986): 13-43.

Hunter, G.K. *John Lyly: The Humanist as Courtier*. London: Routledge, 1962.

Israel, Jonathan I. *The Dutch Republic: Its Rise, Greatness, and Fall, 1477-1806*. Oxford: Clarendon Press, 1995.

Jack, R.D.S. "Scottish Sonnetteer and Welsh Metaphysical: A Study of the Religious Poetry of Sir William Mure and Henry Vaughan." *SSL* 3 (1965-1966): 240-47.

―――. "James VI and Renaissance Poetic Theory." *English* 16 (1967): 208-11.

―――. "Montgomerie and the Pirates." *SSL* 5 (1967-1968): 133-36.

————. "The Lyrics of Alexander Montgomerie." *RES* n.s. 20 (1969): 168-81.

————. "William Fowler and Italian Literature." *MLR* 65 (1970): 481-92.

————. "Petrarch in English and Scottish Renaissance Literature." *MLR* 71 (1976): 801-11.

————. "The Theme of Fortune in the Verse of Alexander Montgomerie." *SLJ* 10/2 (December 1983): 25-44.

————. *Alexander Montgomerie.* Edinburgh: Scottish Academic Press, 1985.

————. "Poetry under King James VI." In *The History of Scottish Literature*, ed. idem, 1:125-39. Aberdeen: Aberdeen University Press, 1988.

————. "The French Connection: Scottish and French Literature in the Renaissance." *Scotia* 13 (1989): 1-16.

Jacobs, P. *Prädestination und Verantwortlichkeit bei Calvin.* Neukirchen: Buchhandlung des Erziehungsvereins, 1937.

James, Frank A., III. *Peter Martyr Vermigli and Predestination: The Augustinian Inheritance of an Italian Reformer.* Oxford: Clarendon Press, 1998.

Jameson, Caroline. "Ovid in the Sixteenth Century." In *Ovid*, ed. J.W. Binns, 210-42. London: Routledge, 1973.

Janelle, Pierre. *Robert Southwell the Writer: A Study in Religious Inspiration.* New York: Sheed and Ward, 1935.

Jeanneret, Michel. *Poésie et Tradition Biblique au XVIe Siècle.* Paris: Corti, 1969.

Jed, Stephanie H. *Chaste Thinking: the Rape of Lucretia and the Birth of Humanism.* Bloomington, IN: Indiana University Press, 1989.

Johnson, Paula. *Form and Transformation in Music and Poetry of the English Renaissance.* New Haven and London: Yale University Press, 1972.

Juhala, Amy Lynne. "The household and Court of James VI of Scotland, 1567-1603." Ph.D. diss., University of Edinburgh, 2000.

Kamen, Henry. *Philip II of Spain.* New Haven and London: Yale University Press, 1997.

Keating, L. Clark. *Studies on the Literary Salon in France, 1550-1615.* Cambridge, MA: Harvard University Press, 1941.

Kerrigan, John, ed. *Motives of Woe: Shakespeare and "Female Complaint".* Oxford: Clarendon Press, 1991.

King, John N. *English Reformation Literature: The Tudor Origins of the Protestant Tradition.* Princeton: Princeton University Press, 1982.

Kirkpatrick, Robin. *English and Italian Literature from Dante to Shakespeare: A Study of Sources, Analogy and Difference.* London: Longman, 1995.

Kratzmann, Gregory. *Anglo-Scottish Literary Relations 1430-1550.* Cambridge: Cambridge University Press, 1980.

————. "Political Satire and the Reformation." *SSL* 26 (1991): 423-37.

Larner, Christina, et al. *Witchcraft and Religion: The Politics of Popular Belief.* Oxford: Blackwell, 1984.

Law, T.G. *Collected Essays and Reviews,* ed. P. Hume Brown. Edinburgh: T. and A. Constable, 1904.

Lee, Maurice, Jr. *James Stewart, Earl of Moray: A Political Study of the Reformation in Scotland.* New York: Columbia University Press, 1953.

―――. *John Maitland of Thirlestane and the Foundation of the Stewart Despotism in Scotland.* Princeton: Princeton University Press, 1959.

―――. "Sir Richard Maitland of Lethington: A Christian Laird in the Age of Reformation." In *Action and Conviction in Early Modern Europe,* ed. T.K. Rabb and J.E. Seigel, 117-32. Princeton: Princeton University Press, 1969.

―――. *Government by Pen: Scotland under James VI and I.* Urbana, IL: University of Illinois Press, 1980.

Leff, Gordon. *Gregory of Rimini: Tradition and Innovation in Fourteenth Century Thought.* Manchester: Manchester University Press, 1961.

Lenselink, S.J. *De Nederlandse Psalmberijmingen van de Souterliedeken tot Datheen.* Assen: van Gorcum, 1959.

Lewalski, Barbara Kiefer. *Protestant Poetics and the Seventeenth-Century Religious Lyric.* Princeton: Princeton University Press, 1979.

Lewis, C.S. *English Literature in the Sixteenth Century, Excluding Drama.* Oxford: Clarendon Press, 1954.

Likhachev, N.P. [*La signification paléographique des filigranes.*] St. Petersburg: V.C. Balaschiev, 1899.

Love, Harold. *Scribal Publication in Seventeenth-Century England.* Oxford: Clarendon Press, 1993.

Lyall, R.J. "Politics and Poetry in Fifteenth and Sixteenth Century Scotland." *SLJ* 3/2 (December 1976): 5-29.

―――. "The Medieval Scottish Coronation Service: Some Seventeenth-Century Evidence." *Innes Review* 28 (1977): 3-21.

―――. "'A New-Maid Channoun'? Redefining the Canonical in Older Scots Literature." *SSL* 26 (1991): 1-18.

―――. "Montgomerie and the Netherlands, 1586-88." *Glasgow Review* 1 (1993): 52-66.

―――. "Montgomerie and the Moment of Mannerism." *SLJ* 26/2 (Winter 1999): 41-58.

―――. "The Stylistic Relationship between Dunbar and Douglas." In *William Dunbar: The "Nobill Poyet"*, ed. Sally Mapstone, 69-84. East Linton: Tuckwell Press, 2001.

―――. "Alexander Montgomerie, Anti-Calvinist Propagandist?." *N&Q* n.s. 49 (2002): 210-15.

―――. "'Thrie Truear Hairts': Alexander Montgomerie, Henry Constable, Henry Keir and Cultural Politics in Renaissance Britain." *Innes Review* 54 (2003): 00-000.

———. "The Marketing of James VI and I: Scotland, England and the Continental Book Trade," *Quaerendo* 32 (2002): 204–17.

MacCaffrey, Wallace T. *Elizabeth I: War and Politics, 1588-1603.* Princeton: Princeton University Press, 1992.

McDiarmid, M.P. "John Stewart of Baldynneis." *SHR* 29 (1950): 52-63.

MacDonald, Alasdair A. "The Poetry of Sir Richard Maitland of Lethington." *Transactions of the East Lothian Antiquarian and Field Naturalists' Society* 13 (1972): 7-19.

MacDonald, R.H., ed. *The Library of Drummond of Hawthornden.* Edinburgh: Edinburgh University Press, 1971.

Macdougall, Norman. *James IV.* Edinburgh: John Donald, 1989.

McFarlane, I.D. *A Literary History of France: Renaissance France, 1470-1589.* London and New York: Macmillan, 1974.

———. *Buchanan.* London: Duckworth, 1981.

McGowan, Margaret M. *L'Art du Ballet de Cour (1581-1643).* Paris: Éditions du CNRS, 1963.

Maiorino, Giancarlo. *The Cornucopian Mind and the Baroque Unity of the Arts.* University Park, PA and London: Pennsylvania State University Press, 1990.

Maniates, Maria Rika. *Mannerism in Italian Music and Culture, 1530-1630.* Manchester: Manchester University Press, 1979.

Mapstone, Sally. "The Advice to Princes Tradition in Scottish Literature, 1450-1500." D.Phil. diss., University of Oxford, 1986.

———. "Invective as Poetic: The Cultural Contexts of Polwarth and Montgomerie's *Flyting.*" *SLJ* 26/2 (Winter 1999): 18-40.

———, and Juliette Wood, eds. *The Rose and the Thistle: Essays on the Culture of Late Medieval and Renaissance Scotland.* East Linton: Tuckwell Press, 1998.

Marotti, Arthur F. *Manuscript, Print, and the English Renaissance Lyric.* Ithaca, NY: Cornell University Press, 1995.

Martinez Millán, José, ed. *La corte de Felipe II.* Madrid: Alianza, 1994.

Martz, Louis B. *From Renaissance to Baroque: Essays on Literature and Art.* Columbia, MO and London: University of Missouri Press, 1991.

Mason, Roger A. "Scotching the Brut: Politics, History and National Myth in 16th-Century Britain." In *Scotland and England 1286-1815,* ed. Roger A. Mason, 60-84. Edinburgh: John Donald, 1987.

———. *Kingship and the Commonweal: Political Thought in Renaissance and Reformation Scotland.* East Linton: Tuckwell Press, 1998.

Mathieu-Castellani, Gisèle. *Les Thèmes amoureux dans la poésie française (1570-1600).* Strasbourg: Klincksieck, 1975.

Matthews, William. "The Egyptians in Scotland: The Political History of a Myth." *Viator* 1 (1970): 289-306.

May, Steven W. *The Elizabethan Courtier-Poets: The Poems and their Contexts*. Columbia, MO and London: University of Missouri Press, 1991.

Maynard, Winifred. *Elizabethan Lyric Poetry and its Music*. Oxford: Clarendon Press, 1996.

Merriman, Marcus. *The Rough Wooings: Mary, Queen of Scots, 1542-1551*. East Linton: Tuckwell Press, 2001.

Meynardier, Howard. "The Areopagus of Sidney and Spenser." *MLR* 4 (1908-1909): 289-301.

Mill, Anna Jean. *Medieval Plays in Scotland*. St Andrews University Publications 24. Edinburgh and London: Blackwood, 1927.

Minta, Stephen. *Love Poetry in Sixteenth-Century France*. Manchester: Manchester University Press, 1977.

———. *Petrarch and Petrarchism: the English and French Traditions*. Manchester: Manchester University Press, 1980.

Mirollo, James V. *Mannerism and Renaissance Poetry: Concept, Mode, Inner Design*. New Haven and London: Yale University Press, 1984.

Montrose, Louis A. "Renaissance Literary Studies and the Subject of History." *ELR* 16 (1986): 5-12.

———. "The Elizabethan Subject and the Spenserian Text." In *Literary Theory/Renaissance Texts*, ed. Patricia Parker and David Quint, 303-40. Baltimore and London: Johns Hopkins University Press, 1986.

———. *The Purpose of Playing: Shakespeare and the Cultural Politics of Elizabethan Theatre*. Chicago: University of Chicago Press, 1996.

Neilson, George. "Rob Stene: a Court Satirist under James VI." *SHR* 2 (1905): 253-59.

Nicholl, Charles. *The Reckoning: The Murder of Christopher Marlowe*. London: Cape, 1992; 2nd ed. London: Vintage, 2002.

Nicholson, Ranald. *Scotland: The Later Middle Ages*. Edinburgh: Oliver and Boyd, 1974.

Oberman, Heiko A. *Masters of the Reformation: The Emergence of a New Intellectual Climate in Europe*, ed. D. Martin. Cambridge: Cambridge University Press, 1981.

Oosterhoff, F.G. *Leicester and the Netherlands, 1586-1587*. Utrecht: HES, 1988.

Owst, G.R. *Literature and Pulpit in Medieval England*. 2nd ed. Oxford: Blackwell, 1961.

Parke, H.W., and D.E.W. Wormell. *The Delphic Oracle*. Oxford: Blackwell, 1956.

Parker, Geoffrey. *The Dutch Revolt*. London: Penguin, 1977.

———. *Philip II*. London: Hutchinson, 1979.

———. *The Grand Strategy of Philip II*. New Haven and London: Yale University Press, 1998.

Parkinson, David. "Montgomerie's Language." In *Bryght Lanternis: Essays on the Language and Literature of Medieval and Renaissance Scotland*, ed. J. Derrick McClure and Michael R.G. Spiller, 352-63. Aberdeen: Aberdeen University Press, 1987.

Patterson, Annabel. *Fables of Power: Aesopian Writing and Political History*. Durham, NC: Duke University Press, 1991.

Patterson, Frank Allen. *The Middle English Penitential Lyric*. New York: Columbia University Press, 1911.

Patterson, W.B. *King James VI and I and the Reunion of Christendom*. Cambridge: Cambridge University Press, 1997.

Pellegrini, Giuliano. *Barocco inglese*. Messina: G. d'Anna, 1953.

———. *Dal manierismo al barocco: studi sul teatro inglese del XVII secolo*. Florence: Olschki, 1985

Perry, Curtis. "Royal Authorship and Problems of Manuscript Attribution in the Poems of King James VI and I." *N&Q* n.s. 46 (1999): 243-46.

Peterson, Douglas L. *The English Lyric from Wyatt to Donne*. Princeton: Princeton University Press, 1967, 2nd ed. East Lansing, MI: Colleagues Press, 1990.

Phillips, James E. "Daniel Rogers: A Neo-Latin Link between the Pléiade and Sidney's 'Areopagus'." In *Neo-Latin Poetry of the Sixteenth and Seventeenth Centuries*, ed. James E. Phillips and Don Cameron Allen, 5-28. Los Angeles: William Andrews Clark Memorial Library, 1965.

Plowden, Alison. *The Elizabethan Secret Service*. Hemel Hempstead: Wheatsheaf, 1991.

Pozzi, Giovanni. *Poesia per gioco. Prontuario di figure artificiose*. Bologna: Il Mulino, 1984.

Praz, Mario. *Seicentismo e marinismo in Inghilterra*. Florence: La Voce, 1925

———. *Studies in Seventeenth-Century Imagery*. 2 vols. London: Warburg Institute, 1939.

———. "The Flaming Heart: Richard Crashaw and the Baroque." In idem, *The Flaming Heart*. Garden City, NY: Doubleday Anchor, 1958.

Prouty, C.T. *George Gascoigne, Elizabethan Courtier, Soldier, and Poet*. New York: Columbia University Press, 1942.

Quondam, Amedeo, ed. *Problemi del Manierismo*. Naples: Guida, 1975.

Raimondi, Ezio. *Letteratura barocca*. Florence: Olschki, 1961; repr. 1982.

———. *Rinascimento Inquieto*. Palermo: U. Manfredi, 1965.

Raymond, Marcel. *Baroque et renaissance poétique*. Paris: Corti, 1955.

Reid-Baxter, Jamie. "Politics, Passion and Poetry in the Circle of James VI." In *A Palace in the Wild: Essays on Vernacular Culture and Humanism in Late-Medieval and Renaissance Scotland*, ed. L.A.J.R.Houwen, A.A. Macdonald, and S.L. Mapstone, 199-248. Leuven: Peeters, 2000.

Roberts, John R., and Lorraine Roberts, "'To weave a new webbe in their owne loome': Robert Southwell and Counter-Reformation Poetics." In *Sacred and Profane: Secular and Devotional Interplay in Early Modern British Literature*, ed. Helen Wilcox, Richard Todd and Alasdair Macdonald, 77-83. Amsterdam: VU University Press, 1996.

Roche, Thomas P. *Petrarch and the English Sonnet Sequences*. New York: AMS, 1989.

Rogers, David. "'The Catholic Moderator'." *Recusant History* 5 (1960): 224-35.

Ross, Ian Simpson. "The Form and Matter of *The Cherrie and the Slae*." *University of Texas Studies in English* 37 (1958): 79-91.

————. *William Dunbar.* Leiden: E.J. Brill, 1981.

Roston, Murray. *Milton and the Baroque.* London: Macmillan, 1980.

Rubsamen, Walter H. "Scottish and English Music of the Renaissance in a Newly Discovered Manuscript." In *Festschrift Heinrich Besseler*, 259-84. Leipzig: Deutscher Verlag für Musik, 1961.

Sanderson, Margaret H.B. "Kilwinning at the Time of the Reformation, and its First Minister William Kilpatrick." *Collectanea of the Ayrshire Archaeological and Natural History Society* 10 (1972): 102-26.

————. *Mary Stewart's People: Life in Mary Stewart's Scotland.* Edinburgh: James Thin, 1987.

————. *Ayrshire and the Reformation: People and Change, 1490-1600.* East Linton: Tuckwell Press, 1997.

Santangelo, Giorgio. *Il petrarchismo del Bembo e di altri poeti del '500.* Rome: Istituto Editoriale della Cultura Europea, 1962; repr. 1967.

Scaglione, Aldo. "Cinquecento Mannerism and the Uses of Petrarch." *Medieval and Renaissance Studies* 5 (1971): 122-55.

Scallon, Joseph D., S.J. *The Poetry of Robert Southwell S.J.* Salzburg: Institut für Englische Sprache und Literatur, Universität Salzburg, 1975.

Scollen, C.M. *The Birth of the Elegy in France, 1500-1550.* Geneva: Droz, 1967.

Scott, Janet G. *Les Sonnets Elisabéthains: les sources et l'apport personnel* . Paris: Champion, 1929.

Scott, M.J.W. "Robert Ayton: Scottish Metaphysical." *SLJ* 2 (1975): 5-16.

Scrivano, Riccardo. *Il manierismo nella letteratura del cinquecento.* Padua: Liviana, 1959.

————. *Cultura e Letteratura nel Cinquecento.* Rome: Atenei, 1966.

Segal, Harold B. *The Baroque Poem: A Comparative Survey.* New York: Dutton, 1974.

Semler, L.E. *The English Mannerist Poets and the Visual Arts.* Madison, WI and London: Fairleigh Dickinson University Press / Associated University Presses, 1998.

Shapiro, M. "Tenson et partimen: la tenson fictive." In *Actes du 14ᵉ congrès internationale de linguistique et philologie romanes*, 5: 287-301. Naples and Amsterdam: Macchiaroli / Benjamins, 1981.

Shearman, John. *Mannerism.* London: Penguin, 1967.

Shell, Alison. *Catholicism, Controversy and the English Literary Imagination, 1558-1660.* Cambridge: Cambridge University Press, 1999.

Shire, Helena Mennie. "Musical Servitors to Queen Mary Stuart." *Music and Letters* 40 (1959): 15-18.

————. *Song, Dance and Poetry of the Court of Scotland under King James VI*. Cambridge: Cambridge University Press, 1969.

Slights, Camille Wells. *The Casuistical Tradition in Shakespeare, Donne, Herbert and Milton*. Princeton: Princeton University Press, 1981.

Smith, Pauline M. *The Anti-Courtier Trend in Sixteenth-Century French Literature*. Geneva: Droz, 1966.

Spahr, B.L. "Baroque and Mannerism: Epoch and Style." *Collectanea Germanica* 1 (1967): 78-100.

Speirs, John. *The Scots Literary Tradition*. 2nd ed. London: Faber, 1962.

Spiller, M.R.G. "The 'Copill' in *The Kingis Quair*." *SLJ* 4/1 (May 1977): 61-63.

Steadman, John M. *Redefining a Period Style: "Renaissance", "Mannerist" and "Baroque"*. Pittsburgh: Duquesne University Press, 1990.

Stevens, John. *Music and Poetry in the Early Tudor Court*. London: Methuen, 1961.

Sypher, Wylie. *Four Stages of Renaissance Style: Transformations in Art and Literature 1400-1700*. New York: Doubleday Anchor, 1955.

Ten Raa, F.J.G. and F. de Bas. *Het Staatsche Leger 1568-1795*. 8 vols. Breda: Koninklijke Militaire Academie, 1911-1921; The Hague: Nijhoff, 1940-1964.

Thiolier-Méjean, S. *Les poésies satiriques et morales des troubadours du XIIe à la fin du XIIIe siècle*. Paris: Nizet, 1978.

Valbuena Prat, Angel. *Historia de la Literatura Española*, i. Barcelona: Juventud, 1943; 8th ed. Barcelona: Gustavo Gili, 1974.

Veeser, H. Aram, ed. *The New Historicism*. London: Routledge, 1989.

————. *The New Historicism Reader*. London: Routledge, 1994.

Waller, Gary. *English Poetry of the Sixteenth Century*. London: Arnold, 1986.

Wardropper, Bruce W. "The Religious Conversion of Profane Poetry." In *Studies in the Continental Background of Renaissance English Literature*, ed. Dale B.J. Randall and George Walton Williams, 203-21. Durham, NC: Duke University Press, 1977.

Warkentin, Germaine. "Sidney's *Certain Sonnets*: Speculations on the Evolution of the Text." *The Library* ser. 6, 2 (1980): 430-4.

Warner, George F. "The Library of James VI." *Miscellany of the Scottish History Society*, 1:ix-lxxv. Edinburgh: SHS, 1893.

Warnke, Frank J. *European Metaphysical Poetry*. New Haven: Yale University Press, 1961.

————. *Versions of Baroque*. New Haven and London: Yale University Press, 1972.

Warren, Austin. *Richard Crashaw: A Study in Baroque Sensibility*. London: Faber, 1939.

Waterschoot, W. "Lucas d'Heere en *Den Hof en Boomgaerd der Poësien* (1565)." *Jaarboek "De Fonteine"* 14-15 (1964-1965): 47-119.

Weber, Henri. *La Création Poétique au XVIe Siècle en France*. Paris: Nizet, 1956.

Weisbach, Werner. *Der Barock als Kunst der Gegenreformation*. Berlin: Cassirer, 1921.

Weise, Georg. *Manierismo e Letteratura*. Florence: Olschki, 1976.

Wellek, René. "The Concept of Baroque in Literary Scholarship." In idem, *Concepts of Criticism*, 69-127. New Haven and London: Yale University Press, 1963.

Westcott, Allan F. "Alexander Montgomerie." *MLR* 6 (1911): 1-8.

Wijn, J.W. *Het Beleg van Haarlem*. 2nd ed. The Hague: Nijhoff, 1982.

Wilks, John S. *The Idea of Conscience in Renaissance Tragedy*. London and New York: Routledge, 1990.

Williams, Janet Hadley. "Writing and Publishing in Sixteenth-Century Scotland: Some French Connections." In *Renaissance Reflections: Essays in Memory of C.A. Mayer*, ed. P.M. Smith and T. Peach, 129-44. Paris: Champion, 2002.

Willson, David Harris. *King James VI and I*. London: Jonathan Cape, 1956.

Woudhuysen, H.R. *Sir Philip Sidney and the Circulation of Manuscripts 1558-1640*. Oxford: Clarendon Press, 1993.

Yates, Frances A. *The French Academies of the Sixteenth Century*. London: Warburg Institute, 1947.

Young, Michael B. *James VI and I and the History of Homosexuality*. Basingstoke: Macmillan, 1999.

Zeppegno, L. *Dal Manierismo al Barocco*. Milan: Mondadori, 1975.

Zim, Rivkah. *English Metrical Psalms: Poetry as Praise and Prayer*. Cambridge: Cambridge University Press, 1987.

## Selected Discography

*Notes of Noy, Notes of Joy*. Rowallan Consort. Temple COMD 2058.

*On the Banks of Helicon: Early Music of Scotland*. Baltimore Consort. Dorian DOR 90139.

*Scotland's Music: Selected Works from the History of Scotland's Music*. Linn CKD 008.

*Thus spak Apollo myne: The songs of Alexander Montgomerie*. Paul Rendall (tenor) and Rob MacKillop (lute). Gaudeamus CD GAU 249.

# Index

Adamson, Captain John, 47

Adamson, Patrick, archbishop of St Andrews, 41

Aesopic fable, Montgomerie's use of, 218–19, 272

Alamanni, Luigi, 198, 213

Aldana, Francisco de, 49, 53

Alexander of Menstrie, William (later earl of Stirling), 3, 26, 36, 194, 333, 336, 342, 345

Allen, William, 178, 205, 207

Alva, Duke of, 40

Angus, countess of, see Leslie, Margaret

Angus, earl of, see Douglas, William

Anne of Denmark, queen of Scotland, 150, 154, 179, 341

Apuleius, 265–66

Aquinas, St Thomas, 92, 206

Arbuthnot, Alexander, 5

Areopagus, 6

Ariosto, Lodovico, 12, 108, 213

Arran, earl of, see Stewart, James

Atkinson, David, 26

Aubigné, Agrippe d', 228

Aubigny, Gabrielle d' 315

Augustine, St, 328

Augustus, Emperor, 176

Ayrshire, Protestantism in, 38–39

Ayton, Sir Robert, 26, 333, 336, 344–45, 348

Bacon, Anthony, 342

Baïf, Jean-Antoine de, 74

Balfour, Colonel Bartholemew, 121, 126, 129–30, 133–34

Balfour, Colonel Henry, 46–49, 52, 53–54, 57–58, 121

Balfour, Mr James, 183

"Bankis of Helicon" stanza, 108–9

Barbour, John, 114

Barclay, Alexander, 7, 197–98

Barclay, David, 187, 224

Barclay of Ladyland, Hugh, 141–42, 148, 176, 186, 187, 188, 223–24

Barclay, Peter, 224

Bardesius, Willem, 136

Baroque, 14, 24–28, 60, 230, 273–74, 279, 343–44, 346–47, 348

du Bartas, Guillaume de Salluste, 12, 59, 60, 99, 103, 108, 116, 228, 343

Bawcutt, Priscilla, 6, 79, 81, 337

Beale, Robert, 49

Beaton, James, archbishop of Glasgow, 36, 54–55, 58, 63, 147, 149, 161, 163–64, 168, 177

van der Beke, Jan, 136

du Bellay, Joachim, 18, 59, 61, 102, 105, 180–1, 202

Belleau, Rémy, 74

Bembo, Pietro, 230, 237

Berck, Jan, 132

Bertaut, Jean, 235

Beza, Theodore, 284, 285

Bible, 4

    *See also* Psalms, Song of Solomon

de Bie, Joris, 136, 138

Bingham, Richard, 40

Birague, Flaminio de, 239

Blackhall, Andrew, 108

Blair of Adamstoun, David, 41

Blair of that Ilk, John, 41
"Bludy Sark" rebellion (1489), 153–54
Boccaccio, Giovanni, 210
Boethius, 167
Boscán, Juan, 17, 345
Bothwell, earl of, see Stewart, Francis
Boudewijns, Katherina, 313–14, 315
Bowes, Sir Robert, 97, 181, 184, 188
Boyd, Captain David, 121
Boyd, James, archbishop of Glasgow, 149, 163–64
Boyd, Robert, lord, 157, 158
Boyd, Thomas, 42, 44
Braunsberg (Braniewo), University of, 34
Breughel, Pieter, the Elder, 211
Bruce of Kincavill, Alexander, 34, 335
Bruce, Robert, 35–36
Bruce of Binning, Robert, 36
Bruce, Mr Robert, 183
Bruce, William, 35, 51
Bruno, Giordano, 341
Brunol, Thomas, 126
Buchanan, George, 12, 153, 200, 288
Burel, John, 150
Burghley, Lord, see, Cecil, William

Caesar, Julius, 210
Cairns, Mr John, 181–3
Calderwood, David, 63–64, 285–86
Calvin, Jean, 43, 92, 287–88
Calvinism 204, 295
Camden, William, 337
Campbell, Captain Alexander, 47
Campion, Edward, 85
Casa, Giovanni della 17
"Castalian Band", 5–6, 223
"Castalian" movement, 11, 79, 99–101, 193–94, 215, 219–20, 223, 243, 318, 337, 339–40, 342, 344, 348
Castelvetro, Giacomo, 341
Castiglione, Baldassare, 197, 201
Catherine of Navarre, 150
Cato, 201
Cavalier verse, 274
Cavalieri, Tommaso de', 16

Cave, Terence, 281–82, 298
Caxton, William, 208, 218–19
Cecil, Sir Thomas, 119, 123, 128,
Cecil, William, lord Burghley, 49, 55–56, 148, 181, 188
Ceppède, Jean, de la, 24–25
Chapman, George, 49
Charles I, king of England and Scotland, 344
Charles IX, king of France, 68–69
Charteris, Henry, 70, 300
Charteris, Robert, 285
Chartier, Alain, 196
Chaucer, Geoffrey, 4, 337
Chilmor (Chalmer), Thomas, 126
Churchyard, Thomas, 49
Cicero, 43
Claudian, 213
Clerk, David, 57
Cockburn, Robert, 46–47
Coligny, Admiral Gaspar de, 56
Coligny, Louise de, princess of Orange, 128
Colonna, Guido della, 113–14
Colquhoun of Luss, Sir Humphrey, 115–16
Commissary Court, Edinburgh, 162–65, 171
Complaynt of Scotland, 74
The Consail and Teiching at the Vys Man gaif his Sone, 201
Conscience, alternative definitions of, 204–6
Constable, Henry, 27–28, 29, 30, 59, 128, 151, 174, 178–79, 251, 281, 282–83, 337, 338, 343, 344
Contrafactum, 300–1, 314–15, 317
Copran, Thomas, 122
Counter-Reformation, 27, 316
Court of Session, see Session, Lords of
Cowan, Ian, 39
Craig of Rosecraig, Alexander, 4, 333
Craig, Mr John, 183
Craig, Thomas, 171
Cranstoun, James, 87, 171, 262, 336
Cressede, 91

Cruz, Juan de la, 53, 314
Cunninghame, Jean, 116
Curtius, E.R., 14

Damman, Adriaan, 12, 284
Daniel, Samuel, 341
Darnley, Lord, *see*, Stewart, Henry
Datheen, Pieter, 284
Davison, William, 52–53, 56–58
Davy du Perron, Jacques, 235
Delphic oracle, 114–15
Dempster, Thomas, 3335
"De regimine principum", 152
Desportes, Philippe, 12, 18, 59, 90, 108, 213, 228, 235, 236, 238–89, 267, 319, 343, 345
Devereux, Penelope, lady Rich, 128, 178
Devereux, Robert, earl of Essex, 178–79, 185
Dilworth, Mark, 33, 191
van der Does (Dousa), Theodor, 106
Donne, John, 2, 7, 14, 24–5, 268–69, 271–74, 279, 338
van Dorsten, Jan, 50, 128
Doublet, Philips, 138–39
Douglas, Archibald, 121, 122
Douglas, Gavin, 4, 18, 83, 336, 348
Douglas, George, 58
Douglas, William, earl of Angus, 88–89
Douglas, James, earl of Morton, 39–41, 44, 55, 88
Douglas, Margaret, 159–60
Douglas, Robert, 148
Drummond, Margaret, countess of Eglinton, 95
Drummond of Carnock, Sir Robert, 157, 158–59
Drummond of Hawthornden, William, 26, 28, 228–29, 278, 333, 336, 342, 345–47, 348
Dudley, Robert, earl of Leicester, 57, 93, 119–20, 123–27, 129, 134–36, 140
Duff, Thomas, 24, 31, 33–36, 38, 44, 51, 61, 142, 191–93, 330, 334–35
Dunbar, William, 4, 7, 17, 18–19, 45, 68–69, 71, 79, 110–11, 115, 152,

159, 195, 198–99, 201, 232, 269, 278, 295, 309, 336, 348
Duncan-Jones, Katherine, 105
Dunnigan, Sarah, 160–61, 273
Durkan, John, 42–43
Dyer, Sir Edward, 6, 10, 11, 228
Dymoke, Sir Edward, 341

Edinburgh, entry of James VI into, 63–65
Edmonstoun, Captain, 47
Eglinton, countess of, *see*, Drummond, Margaret
Eglinton, earl of, *see*, Montgomerie, Hugh
Eglinton, earls of, 38
Elizabeth I, queen of England, 4, 57, 105, 120, 123, 181, 194, 195, 282, 339, 349
Errington, Nicholas, 59
Erroll, earl of, *see*, Hay, Francis
Erskine, Alexander, master of Mar, 58
Erskine, John, earl of Mar, 39, 44, 158
Erskine, William, 143, 146–47, 149, 161–65, 167, 171, 175, 177, 181, 184, 196
Escorial, 52–53, 60
Escovedo, Juan, 56
Essex, earl of, *see*, Devereux, Robert
Estienne, Robert, 290
Evans, Temperance, 85
*Everyman*, 297

Famars, Charles de Liévin, lord of, 53–54
Fielding, Henry, 219
Figueroa, Francisco de, 49
First Book of Discipline, 42–43
Flyting, 79
Fontenay, Guy de, 141
Forbes of Tolquhon, Alexander, 334
Forbes, William, 334
Forster, Leonard, 94
Fowler, Thomas, 146, 148, 178
Fowler, William, 7, 12–13, 100, 108, 194, 337, 340–41, 343, 345

Fox, Denton, 36
Francis II, king of France, 11–12
Fraser, Margaret (mother of Mont-
　gomerie), 44
Frederick II, king of Denmark, 141
Froissart, Jean, 272

Galloway, Patrick, 151, 157, 281
Garcilaso de la Vega, 17, 345
Gascoigne, George, 10, 49–50, 102, 105
Gathelos, 72
Gembloux, battle of, 52, 57–58
Gibb, John, 97
Giles, Henry, 84–86
Giles, Pamela, 115
Glasgow, archbishop of, see, Beaton,
　James; Boyd, James; Montgomerie,
　Robert
Glasgow, deanery of, 41–42, 99
Goldberg, Jonathan, 8
Golding, Arthur, 261
Góngora, Luis de, 24–25, 279
Gordon, George, earl of Huntly, 145–
　48, 154, 162, 181, 185
Gower, John, 4
Gowrie, earl of, see Ruthven, William
Graham, Agnes, 78
Graham of Fintry, David, 146
Graham, John, earl of Montrose, 88
Grange, John, 105
Grands Rhétoriqueurs, 17
Gray, Patrick, master of Gray, 111–17,
　119–23, 124, 128–29, 226
Gray, William, 43
Greenblatt, Stephen, 8–9
Greene, Robert, 10
Greville, Fulke, 6, 227–29
Grey of Wilton, Lord, 49
van Groeneveld, Arent, 136
Guaras, Antonio de, 40
Guarini, Giovanni Battista, 17, 341
Gude and Godlie Ballatis, 284, 315
Guevara, Antonio de, 197, 213
Guise, Duke of, 35, 55, 60, 63, 141
Gyre-Carling, The, 81

Halkerstoun, James, 50, 129, 188
Hamilton, Lord Claude, 162
Hamilton, David, 56
Hamilton of Bothwellhaugh, James,
　56–58
Hamilton, Jean, 115
Hamilton, John, 56
Hamilton, Thomas, 1, 98
Hart, Andrew, 34, 75–78, 190, 333
Harvey, Gabriel, 6
Hary, Blind, 333
Hatzfeld, H., 15
Hawes, Stephen, 7
Hay, Francis, earl of Erroll, 145–48, 154
Hay, Jean, 240
Hay, Captain William, 133
d'Heere, Lucas, 24, 50, 284
Helgerson, Richard, 337
Henry III, king of France, 59, 126,
　178, 202, 228
Henry IV, king of France, 126, 150
Henryson, Robert, 4, 7, 91–2, 111, 151,
　153, 208, 272, 295, 336, 348
Hepburn of Wauchton, Patrick, 58
Herbert, George, 273, 313, 314–15
Herrera, Fernando de, 53, 227
Hoccleve, Thomas, 197
Hohenlohe, Philips, Count, 130–31,
　134–35, 139
Hohensachsen, Johan, lord of, 136
Hoffmann, Oscar, 241
Holt, William, 85
Homer, 176, 220
Hopkins, John, 284
Horace, 43, 196, 213–14
Horsey, Edward, 56
Hotman, Jean, 178
Howell, Thomas, 108–9
Hudson, Robert, 7, 66, 100, 101, 212–
　20, 224, 227
Hudson, Thomas, 12, 66, 100, 103,
　108
Hume, Alexander, 100, 110, 194, 205–
　6, 228, 340, 342

Hume of Polwarth, Patrick, 2–3, 18, 44–45, 61, 66, 73, 75, 101, 167
  *Flyting with Montgomerie, 44–45,* **75–83**, *87,* 101–2
  *Promine, 18,* **66–70**, *71, 110, 211*
  "Hunters Nomenclatura", 43
Hutten, Ulrich von, 196–97

Icarus, 222, 239, 267, 319–20

Jack, R.D.S. 17, 29, 33, 79, 84, 87, 91,115, 212, 231, 233, 241, 243, 245, 253–54, 255, 272–73, 278, 300, 315, 318, 321, 329, 337
"Jacobean" period, 26, 194, 337, 339–40, 348–49
James I, king of Scotland, 4
  *Kingis Quair,* 4, 166, 215
James III, king of Scotland, 153
James IV, king of Scotland, 7, 153, 198, 338
James V, king of Scotland, 4, 11, 70, 79, 82
James VI and I, king of Scotland and England, 3, 11–12, 18, 38, 41, 59, 63–66, 79, 97, 103–5, 112–15, 116, 123, 124, 129, 146, 149–51, 151–57, 161, 174–80, 186, 200, 210, 211, 216–19, 221, 243, 261, 282, 285, 333, 336, 337–38, 340, 344, 348
  *Works:*
  "Admonitioun to the Maister Poete," 83, 101–2, 116, 212–13, 223
  "The azured vault", 307–8
  *Basilicon Doron,* 340
  *Daemonologie,* 152
  "Ane epitaphe on John Shaw", 157
  *Essayes of a Prentise* 12,, 93, 102–3, 115, 304
  *Lepanto,* 12
  *Ane Meditatioun on 1 Chronicles 15:25–29,* 145
  *Opera,* 342
  *Phoenix,* 99, 104, 222
  *Poeticall Exercises,* 143
  "Reulis and Cautelis", 7, 9, 78, 102–3, 107–8, 107–8, 174, 193, 337
  "Sen thocht is frie", 97–98, 99
  "Sonnet to Chanceller Maitlane", 154–55
  *Trew Law of Free Monarchies,* 337–38
  "What drousie sleepe" 193–94
  *Works,* 342
Jamyn, Amadis, 59, 68–69, 228, 235, 238, 262, 267, 319
Jannequin, Clément, 95–96, 243
Jansdochter, Marieken, 132
Jodelle, Étienne, 60, 227, 235
Jones, Richard, 300
John of Austria , Don, 52–56, 119
John of Salisbury, 196
Johnston, John, 342
Jonson, Ben, 333, 345
Juvenal, 198

Keir, Henry, 35, 55n, 58–9, 61, 97, 178–79, 202, 281, 342
Keir, Walter, 97
Kennedy, Vanavius (?Gavin), 131
Kennedy, Walter, 45, 79
Ker, Margaret, 28–29
Ker of Ferniehurst, Thomas, 58
Kerrigan , John, 90
Kesson (Kesone), Henry, 53
Killigrew, Henry, 39, 47, 138
King, Mr Alexander, 163, 169, 171
King, Mr James, 1, 163–64, 171
*King Hart,* 232
Kirkpatrick, Mr William, 42–43
Knox, Mr Andrew, 188
Knox, John, 38, 204

Lane, Ralph, 40
Langland, William, 224
Lassus, Orlando de, 252–53
Lauder, *sang schuil* at, 316
Lauder, James, 239–41

Lawson, James, 64–65
Leicester, earl of, *see* Dudley, Robert
Lennox, duchess of, *see*, Ruthven, Lilias
Lennox, duke of, *see* Stuart, Esmé;
    Stuart, Ludovick
Lennox, earl of, *see* Stewart, John; Stuart,
    Esmé
León, Luis de, 53, 213
Le Saulx, Marin, 303–6, 307
Leslie, John, bishop of Ross, 58, 153
Leslie, Andrew, earl of Rothes, 84
Leslie, Margaret, countess of Angus,
    88–90
Lewis, C.S., 7, 9, 261
Lily, William, 43
Linacre, Thomas, 43
Lindsay, Christian, 212–13, 215, 220
Lindsay, Sir David, 4, 68, 70, 79, 81–82,
    195, 201, 203, 209, 210, 325, 333,
    348
Lope de Vega, 105
Lucrece, 91
Luther, Martin, 92, 206
Lyly, John, 10

Machaut, Guillaume de, 272
Machiavelli, Niccolo, 12, 92, 197, 341
MacQueen, John, 212
Maisonfleur, Étienne de, 298
Maitland of Thirlestane, John, 117,
    145, 148, 154–56, 200
Maitland of Lethington, Sir Richard,
    67, 108, 200–1, 206
Maitland, William, 200
Malherbe, François de, 228
Manderscheidt, Erika, Grafin von, 141
Maniates, Maria Rika, 16
Mannerism, 14–24, 70, 103, 238, 248,
    263, 302, 343–44, 346
Manuscripts:
    *BL MS. Additional 24,195,* 97
    *BL MS. Harley 7578,* 76
    *EUL, MS. De.3.7 (Ker MS.),* 2, 28–
        29, 31, 103, 115, 129, 174, 204,
        208, 230, 239, 244, 251, 281,

    285, 300, 302, 303–4, 310, 312,
    315, 317, 335–36, 347–48
    *EUL, Laing MS. III.447,* 30
    *Huntington Library MS. HM 105,*
        (Tullibardine MS.), 76–79
    *Magdalene Coll. Cambridge MS.,*
        (Maitland Quarto MS.), 29
    *NAS, RH13/38,* 98
    *NLS, MS. Adv. 1.1.6 (Bannatyne*
        *MS.),* 29, 36–37, 285, 295
    *William Andrews Clark Memorial*
        *Library,* MS. T135Z B724 (Taitt
        MS.), 316–17
Mapstone, Sally, 76–78
March, countess of, *see* Stewart, Eliza-
    beth
Mar, earl of, *see* Erskine, John
Mar, master of, *see*, Erskine, Alexander
March, earl of, *see*, Stewart, Robert,
Margaret Tudor, queen of Scotland, 159
Marguerite de Navarre, 313
Marino, Giambattista, 24–25, 279, 337
Marlowe, Christopher, 10, 337
Marot, Clément, 13, 59, 61, 90 229,
    235, **252–60**, 267, 279, 284, **287–
    94**, 344
Martin, Andrew, 84–86
Marvell, Andrew, 274
Mary Magdalene, 91–92
Mary of Lorraine (or Guise), 11–12, 199
Mary, queen of Scots, 4, 11, 38, 42,
    54–55, 58, 60–61, 67, 71, 73, 87–88,
    135, 141, 178, 199–200, 239–40,
    243, 244, 339
Mathieu-Castellani, Gisèle, 235, 236,
    239
Maxwell, John, lord, 155
May, Steven W., 228
Mayhew, Henry, 250
Melvill, Elizabeth, 300
Melvill, James, 39, 41, 43, 285, 287,
    296–98, 303–6
Mendoza, Bernardino de, 85, 121, 122
"Metaphysical" poetry, 26, 230, 244,
    273, 276–77, 344

Michault, Pierre, 196

Michelangelo, 16–17

*Mindes Melodie, The*, 285–87, 294–95

Minta, Stephen, 256

Montaigne, Michel de, 92

Montgomerie of Braidstane, Captain Adam, 122

Montgomerie, Agnes, 37

Montgomerie, Alexander : date of birth 9, 37–38, 42; education of, 42–44; in Argyll, 44–46; early service in the Netherlands, 46–50, 51–58 possible visit to Spain, 51–53; at Scottish court, 63–117, 151–59; "maister poete" 7; conversion to Catholicism, 31, 38, 51–53; part owner of "James Bonaventor" 84–86; pension of, 98–99, 146–48, 161–81, 186; captain in the Netherlands, 23–24, 117, 119–43, 165; return to Scotland, 139, 145; involved in seizure of Ailsa Craig 29, 188; outlawed 29, 188; plans to leave for Würzburg 27–29, 191–92; dies, 192; dispute over burial, 192–3; French models for poetry, 13, 18, 59; Mannerism in 18, 22–23, 157–60, 343–44; "anti-aulic" satire, 204–21; attitude to Calvinism 31, 142–43, 151, 182–84, 190–91, 281, influence of Ovid upon, 261–67; adaptations from Marot, 252–60, 287–95; translations from Ronsard, 94–96, 237–52;, possible authorship of *The Mindes Melodie*, 285–87, 294–95

    *Works*:

      "The First Psalme", [1], 36, 285, **287–88, 292–93**

      "The 2 Psalm" [2], 285, **288–90**

      "The Poets Dreme" [3], **298**, 313

      "A godly Prayer" [4], 34, 36, **298–300**

      "A walkning from sin" [5], 295, 298

"A lesone hou to leirne to die" [6], **295–88**

"The Oppositione of the Court to Conscience" [8], **204–8**

"An Invectione against Fortune" [9], **208–10**

"The Poets Complante", [11], 129, **165–67**, 177, 179

"A late regrate of Leirning to Love" [12], 236, 237

"To the Echo" [14], **105–7**

"Lyk as the dum Solsequium" [21], 34, 36, 244, **267–69**, 334, 335

"Quhen first Apollo Python slew" [23] **261–65**

"As Natur passis nuriture" [24], **271–72**

"Evin dead, behold I breath" [26], 237

"In throu the windoes of myn ees" [28], **234–35**, 237, 266–67

"Lyk as Aglauros" [30], **265–66**

"The Secreit prais of Love" [32], 27, **275–77**

"Rassave this harte" [33] 27, 271, **277–78**

"Melancholie, grit deput of Dispair" [34], 244, **269–71**, 277

"The cruell pane and grevous smarte" [35], 238

"On Love and fortune I complene" [36], **232–33**

"Yong tender plant" [37], 274–75

"Quhen folish Phaeton" [38], 234

"Quhy bene ye Musis all so long" [40], 27

"O lovesome Lady" [41], 348

"O pleasand plant" [42], 22–23

"Before the Greeks durst enterpryse" [43], **112–15**, 158

"Hay nou the day dauis" [46], **210–12**

"A bony No" [47], **252–54**, 257

"Awalk Montgomeries Muse",
[**48**], **185–87**, 211, 223

"Remember rightly vhen ye reid"
[**49**], 231

"The Elegie" [**52**], 252, **255–60**,
265

*The Navigatioun* [**53**], 30, 65–66,
**70–75**, 82, 103, 202, 226

*A Cartell of the Thre Ventrous
Knichts* [**54**], 30, 65, 75

"Epitaphe of the Maister of work
Drummond of Carnok" [**56**],
158–59

"Epitaphe of Jhone and Patrik
Shaues" [**57**], 157–58, 159

"Supreme Essence" [**59**], 34,
**302–6**, 309, 327

"High Architectur" [**60**], **306–9**

"To Maister Patrick Galloway"
[**63**], **151**, 157, 202

"To his Majestie" [**64**], **151–54**

"In Praise of Maister John Mait-
land chanceller" [**66**], **154–56**,
202

"In Prais of the Kings Vranie"
[**67**], **103–5**, 202

"To his Majestie for his Pensioun"
[**68**], 165, **167–70**, 184

"To the Lords of Session" [**69**],
**174–80**, 175, 210

"To his Aduersars Lauyers" [**70**],
**170–72**

"Of Maister John Sharpe" [**71**],
1–3, **172–74**

"To Robert Hudson" [**72**],
**212–20**, 223, 224, 226, 227,
250, 272

"To Master J. Murray" [**73**],
**222–23**

"To Maistres Lily Duches of
Lennox" [**74**], 159

"A Ladyis Lamentatioun" [**75**],
**87–93**

"Fane wald I speir", [**76**], 230

"Bright amorous ee" [**77**], 30, **251**

"James Lauder I wald se mare"
[**78**], **239–41**

"I trou your Love by loving so
vnsene" [**79**], **239–41**

"His Maistres Name" [**82**], 115

"Ha! Lytill dog" [**83**], 242, **250–1**

"To M.D., for Skelmurley" [**84**],
**159–61**, 232

"O happy star" [**85**], 93, **94–96**,
159, 161, 241, 243

"To The For Me" [**86**], 160,
**237–39**, 267

"Vhat subject, sacred sisters"
[**87**], **242–48**

"Had I a foe that hated me to
dead" [**89**], **248–49**

"The Poets Apologie to the
Kirk of Edinburgh" [**91**], 31,
**184–85**

"To his Majestie that he wrote
not against, vmquhill Jane
Cuninghame" [**93**], 116

"From London to William Mur-
ray" [**94**], **221**

"Ayrshire" sonnets [**95**], **223–26**

"Against the God of Love" [**97**],
**347–48**

"Come, my childrene dere" [**98**],
27, 298, 300, **309–17**

*Flyting* [**99**], 2–3, **75–83**, 167,
196, 217, 333–34

*The Cherrie and the Slae* [**100–1**],
2, 29, 34, 37, **107–12**, **188–
91**, 211, 229, 239, 240–1, 285,
**317–31**, 333–34, 347

"Ye hevinis abone" [**102**], 93–94

"Luiffaris leif of" [**103**], 93–94

"Irkit I am with langsum luvis
lair" [**105**], 37

"The xxiij sphalme" [**106**], 36,
285, **291–92**

"Ane ansuer to ane Ingliss railar
praysing his awin genealogy" 37

"Away vane world", 298, **300–2**,
315

Sonnets against the Edinburgh ministers, 31, **181–84**
Montgomerie, Elizabeth (daughter of John M. of Hessilheid, 37
Montgomerie, Elizabeth (daughter of Hugh M. of Hessilheid), 41
Montgomerie, Captain Ezechiel, 223–24
Montgomerie, George, 37
Montgomerie, Grissell, 187, 224
Montgomerie, Hugh, earl of Eglinton, 44
Montgomerie of Hessilheid, Hugh, 37, 38–39, 42, 98, 187
Montgomerie of Hessilheid, John, 37, 41
Montgomerie, Margaret, 93–96, 159, 161, 241
Montgomerie of Giffen, Patrick, 187
Montgomerie, Robert, 'poete' 37
Montgomerie, Robert, bishop of Argyll, 45–46
Montgomerie, Robert, archbishop of Glasgow, 45–46, 99, 149, 164
Montgomerie, Captain Robert, 39–42, 99
Montgomerie of Skelmorlie, Robert (6th laird), 187
Montgomerie of Skelmorlie, Robert (7th laird), 86, 159–60
Montrose, Louis, 8
Moray, earl of, *see*, Stewart, James
Morgan, Thomas, 40, 48
Morton, earl of, *see* Douglas, James
Moysie, David, 88
Mudie of Brekness, Francis, 1–3
Mure of Rowallan, John, 41
Mure of Rowallan, William, 3334
Murray, Mr J., 222–23
Murray, John, 222, 225
Murray of Tullibardine, William, 76–78
Murray, William, 221
*Muse Chrestienne*, 298

Nassau, Count Maurice van, 133, 135
Navarre, queen of, 55
"Negative Confession" 296

Neville, Alexander, 129
New Historicism, 8–9, 13, 25, 343
Nieuwenaar, Adolf, Count, 136
van der Noot, Jan, 24, 50
Norris, Sir John, 130, 133
Northumberland, earl of, *see*, Percy, Henry

*Odyssey*, 114
Ogilvie, Captain, 47
Ogilvie, lord, 58
Oliphant, Captain David, 123–27, 131, 133
Olivetan, Pierre Robert, 287–90
Orange, princess of, *see*, Coligny, Louise de
Orange, William ('the Silent'), Prince of, 39–40, 47, 49, 52, 56
Ovid, 59, 90, 93, 105, 160, 176, 229, 238, 255, **261–67**, 267, 279, 323–24
Oxford, earl of, *see* de Vere, Edward

Paris, Scottish Catholic community in, 58–59
Parkinson, David, 29, 31, 77, 115, 240, 295, 300, 310
Parma, Duke of, 119, 132, 140, 142, 145, 181
Parsons, Robert, 85
Passerat, Jean, 262
Paton, Colonel Archibald, 131, 133–34, 140
Paton, Captain William, 134
*Pearl*, 346
Pentland, Captain John, 49
Percy, Henry, earl of Northumberland, 342
Petrarch, Francisco, 12, 16, 108, 160, 220, 227, 230, 232, 237–38, 269, 341, 346
Petrarchism, 16, 23, 26, 160–61, 169, 216, 227–28, 230–5, 258, 262, 267–68, 271, 276, 279, 320, 346, 348
Philip II, king of Spain, 24, 48, 51, 53, 85, 141, 186

Piccolomini, Aeneas Silvius, 196
Pléiade, 6, 59, 74, 103, 228, 250, 256, 262
Pliny, 262
Poliziano, Angelo, 105
Pont, Mr Robert, 286
Pont, Timothy, 42
Pont-à-Mousson, Catholic academy at, 35
Poyntz, John, 197
Praz, Mario, 26
Prestoun, Mr John, 162, 171
Pringle, Thomas, 146
Privy Council, Scottish, 1–2, 84, 122, 142,
Psalms, Book of, 282–95, 298–99, 309
Puttenham, George, 102, 202

Quevedo, Francisco de, 278–79

Ralegh, Sir Walter, 180–81
Ramsay, Allan, 34, 190
Ramsay, Cuthbert, 86
Ramsay, Richard, 84–86
Randolph, Thomas, 88, 122
Rapin, Nicolas, 59
*Ratis Raving*, 201
Reformation in Scotland, 4–5, 282
Reid, David, 156
Reid-Baxter, Jamie, 159
Requesens, Don Luis de, 48
Retz, Claude-Catherine de Clermont-Dampierre, maréchale de, 59, 228
Ringler, William A., 10, 36
del Rio, Dr Luis, 56
*Rob Stene's Dreme*, 156–57
Robert I, king of Scotland, 345
Roberton, Mr William, 98
Robinson, Captain Thomas, 46
Rogers, Daniel, 342
Rolland, John, 67
"Romulus" fable collections, 218–19
Ronsard, Pierre de, 13, 18, 30, 60–61, 74, 90, 93–96, 202, 213, 228–29,

235–36, 237, **241–52**, 262, 267, 279, 308–9, 344, 345
Ross, bishop of, *see*, Leslie, John
Ross, Ian, 318, 329
Russell, Sir William, 140
Rutherford, John, 76
Ruthven, Lilias, duchess of Lennox, 159
Ruthven, William, earl of Gowrie, 79, 97, 159, 221
Ruthven Raid, 79, 97, 158, 212–13, 282

St Andrews, archbishop of, *see*, Adamson, Patrick
Sannazaro, Jacopo, 239, 345
Scève, Maurice, 17
Schede, Paulus Melissus, 284
*Schort Catholik Confession*, 296
Scota, 72
Scott, Alexander, 4–5, 18, 20–22, 68, 71, 99, 107, 195, 213, 226, 229, 233–34, 243, 272, 277
Scott, Robert, 157–58
Secundus, Johannes, 105
Segal, Harold B., 15, 26
Sempill, Dorothy, 187
Sempill, Janet, 187
Sempill, Marion, 41
Sempill, Robert, 5, 67, 200, 226
Sempill, Robert, lord, 185–87, 211, 223, 225
Sempill, Colonel William, 146
Session, Lords of, 162–63, 165, 167–70, 171, 174
Seton of Parbroath, David, 148
Seton, Robert lord, 57, 58, 93, 96, 159, 162
Shakespeare, William 7, 10, 14, 70, 245, 271, 279, 338
Sharp, John, 1, 64, 163, 169, 172–74
Shaw, Captain James, 56–57
Shaw, John, 157–58
Shaw, Robert, 157–58
Shearman, John, 15
Shell, Alison, 27

Shire, Helena Mennie, 5, 75, 85, 95–96, 100, 108, 115, 156, 187, 191, 212, 221, 225, 237, 239, 240, 243, 252–53, 269, 315, 325, 329, 336
Sibbald, James, 335
Sidney, Sir Philip, 2, 6, 7, 9–10, 24, 105, 120, 123, 127–29, 143, 211, 227–29, 230, 338, 343
    *Certain Sonnets,* 10–11, 160, 237
Sinclair, Thomas, 132
Skelton, John, 7, 197–98
Skene of Hallyards, John, 334
Slights, Camille Wells, 205
*Song of Solomon,* 298, 309, 311–13, 315–16
Southwell, Robert, 27, 282, 338
Spahr, B.L., 15
Spain, Scottish relations with, 145, 340
Spanish Armada, 145, 161, 340
Speirs, John, 19
Spenser, Edmund, 6, 7, 9–10, 11, 93, 112, 202–3, 211, 229, 305, 338
"Spenserian" sonnet, 93, 255
Sponde, Jean de, 278–79
Stanley, Sir William, 140
Steinhöwel, Heinrich, 218
Sternhold, Thomas, 284–85, 289–90
Stevenson, George, 30, 33, 78, 84, 142, 189–90
Stevin, Robert, 101, 156–57
Stewart, Elizabeth, countess of March, 89–90
Stewart, Esmé, *see* Stuart
Stewart, Francis, earl of Bothwell, 146, 148, 154, 185
Stewart, Henry, lord Darnley, 38
Stewart, James, earl of Moray, 44, 56
Stewart, Captain James (later earl of Arran), 89–90, 116–17, 169, 226, 340
Stewart, John, earl of Lennox, 38, 44
Stewart of Baldynneis, John, 7, 12, 18, 59, 100, 108, 194, 228, 342
Stewart, Ludovick, *see,* Stuart
Stewart, Patrick, earl of Orkney 1

Stewart, Robert, earl of March, 89
Stewart, William, 39
Stewart of Houston, Colonel William, 121, 140–2, 148, 150, 176
Stirling, James, 171
Straparola, Giovanni Francesco, 341
Stuart, Arabella, 178
Stuart, Esmé, sieur d'Aubigny, earl (later duke) of Lennox, 38, 59–60, 63, 85, 87, 97–8, 99, 116, 154, 159, 169, 173, 178, 202, 210, 221, 222, 281, 315, 340, 341
Stuart, Ludovick, duke of Lennox, 38, 59, 116, 159, 161–62, 178–79, 281
Sypher, Wylie, 14

Tansillo, Luigi, 13, 17, 18, 341
Tasso, Bernardo, 16, 17
Tasso, Torquato 18, 105, 345
Tebaldeo, Antonio, 105
Teelincx, Joos Ewoutsz., 136
Thomson, William, 126
*The Thre Prestis of Peblis,* 152
Tornes, William, 132
*Tottel's Miscellany,* 9, 336
Traill, Captain David, 133
Tremellius, Johann Immanuel, 103
Trent, Council of, 27, 281, 284
Turberville, George, 9
Tyard, Pontus de, 90, 345
Tyrie, James, 204
Tyrone rebellion, 188

Urquhart of Cromarty, Sir Thomas, 26, 348
Utenhove, Jan, 284

Valcke, Jakob, 136
Vautrollier, Thomas, 102, 303–4
de Vere, Edward, earl of Oxford, 11, 228
Verhagen, Jaeneke, 126
Villeroy, Madeleine de l'Aubépine, marquise de, 59, 208
Vilnius, University of, 34

Virgil, 43, 101, 176

Waddell, Captain William, 133
Waldegrave, Robert, 29, 112, 189–90,
    319, 322–23
Waller, Gary, 67, 202
Walsingham, Thomas, 55, 57, 120,
    122, 124–26, 140, 178, 181
Wardropper, Bruce W., 315
Warner, George F., 41
Warnke, Frank J., 26
Watts, William, 85
Wellek, René, 26
Wemyss of Wemyss, Sir David, 89
Whitaker, William, 316
Whitney, Geoffrey, 270
Wijaert, Captain, 54
Wilkes, Thomas, 131
Wilks, John S., 204
Wilson, Thomas, 53–55
Wishart, Alexander, 54
Wishart, George, 39
Witchcraft in Scotland, 152
Wood, Thomas, 108
Woodshaw, Edward, 57
Woudhuysen, H.R., 2, 341
Wreittoun, John, 34, 323
Würzburg, Scottish Benedictine mon-
    astery at, 27–28, 191–92, 330, 343
Wyatt, Sir Thomas, 7, 17, 21, 180,
    197–98, 203, 229, 258, 277
Wyer, Captain, 53–54, 57

Young, Isobel, 239–41

Zutphen, siege of, 127, 129